CORPORATE LAW

ICSA STUDY TEXT

CORPORATE LAW

2ND EDITION

SUSAN McLAUGHLIN

The Governance Institute

ICSA Study Text in Corporate Law 2nd edition is published by ICSA Publishing Ltd.
Saffron House
6–10 Kirby Street
London EC1N 8TS

First published as *Unlocking Company Law* in 2009 by Hodder Education and now published by Taylor & Francis Books Ltd, a member of the Informa Group of 2, 3 & 4 Park Square, Milton Park, Abingdon, Oxon OX14 4RN.
© Susan McLaughlin, 2009.

All additional material for this and the first edition (especially chapters 3, 7-9, 11, 14, 16-18)
© ICSA Publishing Ltd, 2010, 2013.
Reprinted 2015, 2016.

All rights reserved. No part of this publication may be reproduced, stored in a retrieval system, or transmitted, in any form, or by any means, electronic, mechanical, photocopying, recording or otherwise, without prior permission, in writing, from the publisher.

Designed and typeset by Paul Barrett Book Production, Cambridge
Printed by Hobbs the Printers Ltd, Totton, Hampshire

British Cataloguing in Publication Data
A catalogue record for this book is available from the British Library.

ISBN 978 1 86072 577 7

Contents

How to use this study text ix
The Corporate Law syllabus xii
Acronyms and abbreviations xv
List of figures xvi
List of cases xvii
Acknowledgements xxiii

PART ONE The Nature and Structure of a Company 1

Chapter 1 Introduction to corporate law 3
1 'Corporate law' and 'company law' 3
2 What we mean by company law 3
3 Sources of company law 8
4 Historical development of company law 10
5 Influence of the EU on UK company law 12
6 The Financial Conduct Authority and the Listing Regime 14

Chapter 2 Legal structures of business organisations 16
1 Unincorporated business organisation legal structures 16
2 Incorporated business organisation legal structures 19
3 Social enterprise private legal structures 28
4 European organisation legal structures 32

Chapter 3 Promoters and company formation 36
1 Promoters 36
2 Pre-incorporation contracts 38
3 Registering a UK company 41
4 Certificate of incorporation 44
5 Trading certificate 46
6 Company numbers and names 46
7 Re-registration of a UK company 52
8 Company registers and records: the statutory books and registers 54
9 Annual returns and reports and accounts 55

Chapter 4 The company as a distinct legal person 59
1 The registered company as a corporation 59
2 What is a corporation? 59
3 The consequences of incorporation/separate legal personality 61
4 *Salomon v A. Salomon & Co. Ltd* 62
5 Limited liability 64
6 Corporate groups and separate legal personality 66
7 Limits on the implication of incorporation/separate legal personality 68

Chapter 5 The constitution of the company 80
1 What is the constitution of a company? 80
2 Pre-Companies Act 2006 constitutions 81

	3 The objects and capacity of a company 81
	4 What are the Articles of Association? 84
	5 The Articles as a statutory contract and enforcement 87
	6 Amending the Articles of Association 92
	7 Contracts with terms derived from the Articles 98
	8 Shareholders' agreements 98
Chapter 6	**Legally binding the company** 102
	1 Company deeds 102
	2 Company seals 104
	3 . Contracts that bind the company 104
	4 Authority of the board of directors to bind the company 106
	5 Authority of individuals to bind the company 111

PART TWO Capital and Membership 119

Chapter 7	**Companies, capital markets and market abuse** 120
	1 The prospectus 120
	2 Listing particulars 128
	3 Underwriting and commission 128
	4 Market abuse and regulation 129
	5 Criminal liability for market abuse 130
	6 The civil regime for market abuse 135
Chapter 8	**Membership, shares and share capital** 137
	1 Becoming a shareholder 137
	2 Becoming a member and the register of members 138
	3 The legal nature of a share 139
	4 Different types of shares 139
	5 Class rights 140
	6 Share capital 146
	7 Alteration of share capital 149
	8 Allotment and issue of shares 149
	9 Payment for shares, discounts and premiums 151
	10 Statutory pre-emption rights of existing shareholders and rights issues 153
	11 Transfer and transmission of shares 157
	12 Share certificates and warrants 160
	13 Partly paid shares: calls, liens, surrender and forfeiture 161
Chapter 9	**Capital maintenance** 164
	1 Share capital and creditors 164
	2 The doctrine of capital maintenance 168
	3 Minimum share capital requirements 169
	4 Statutory prohibition on reduction of share capital 169
	5 Purchase and redemption of a company's own shares 171
	6 Regulation of distributions 173
	7 Shareholder last principle on a winding up 180
	8 A broader concept of capital maintenance? 180
	9 Financial assistance for the purchase of its own shares 181
Chapter 10	**Loan capital** 186
	1 Debentures 186
	2 Secured creditors: fixed and floating charges 188

PART THREE Company Management and Shareholder Remedies 201

Chapter 11 Directors, shareholders and the division of powers 203
1. Shareholders as a governing organ of the company 203
2. The board of directors as a governing organ of the company 207
3. Directors 208
4. The company secretary 219
5. The auditor 222

Chapter 12 Directors' duties 228
1. Legal duties of directors 228
2. Legislative reform of directors' duties 230
3. To whom do directors owe their duties? 230
4. Corporate governance duties of directors 232
5. Conflict of interest duties 239
6. Directors contracting with their companies 245
7. Remedies 250
8. Relief from liability, indemnification, exclusion of liability and insurance 252

Chapter 13 Minority shareholder protection 255
1. The rule in *Foss v Harbottle* 255
2. Statutory derivative claims 258
3. Personal and representative actions by shareholders 262
4. Unfairly prejudicial conduct petitions 265
5. Just and equitable winding up petitions 272
6. Company investigations 275

PART FOUR Meetings and Resolutions 279

Chapter 14 Members' meetings and decision-making 281
1. Company meetings 281
2. Records of meetings and resolutions 285
3. Company resolutions and decisions 285
4. Corporate representatives 290
5. Proxies 290
6. Shareholder engagement 290

Chapter 15 Directors' meetings and decision-making 292
1. Sole director companies 292
2. Board meetings 292
3. Board decisions 293
4. UK Corporate Governance Code (September 2012) 294

PART FIVE Company Restructuring and Winding Up 297

Chapter 16 Company restructuring 299
1. Insolvency Act 1986, s. 110 schemes of reconstruction 299
2. Part 26 schemes of arrangement 301
3. Part 26, Part 27 and the Cross-Border Merger Regulations: plc mergers and divisions 305

Chapter 17 Takeovers 307
1. The City Code and the EU Takeover Directive 307
2. Methods of restructuring and takeovers 308
3. Takeovers, mergers, acquisitions and disposals 308

	4	Scope of application of the City Code 309
	5	Part 26 scheme of arrangement takeovers 309
	6	The nature and purpose of the City Code 310
	7	The City Code General Principles 310
	8	Outline of the basic takeover bid process 311
	9	Minority shareholder treatment 312
	10	Key additional legal rules and problem areas in takeovers 313
	11	The system for regulating takeovers 315

Chapter 18 Corporate rescue 320
- 1 Company voluntary arrangements 320
- 2 The small company moratorium 322
- 3 Administration 323

Chapter 19 Winding up and company dissolution 332
- 1 Sources of insolvency law 333
- 2 Types of winding up 333
- 3 Property not available to a liquidator 336
- 4 Order of distribution of assets 337
- 5 Company dissolution 338
- 6 Prohibition on the re-use of insolvent company names 339
- 7 Disclaiming onerous property 341
- 8 Challenging pre-liquidation transactions 341
- 9 Swelling the company's assets: personal contributions 348

Appendices
- 1 Model Articles for private companies limited by shares 353
- 2 Model Articles for public companies 368
- 3 UK Corporate Governance Code September 2012 395

Glossary 413
Directory 422
Index 424

How to use this study text

ICSA study texts developed to support ICSA's Chartered Secretaries Qualifying Scheme (CSQS) follow a standard format and include a range of navigational, self-testing and illustrative features to help you get the most out of the support materials.

Each text is divided into three main sections:

- introductory material
- the text itself, divided into Parts and Chapters
- additional reference information

The sections below show you how to find your way around the text and make the most of its features.

Introductory material

The introductory section of each text includes a full contents list and the module syllabus which re-iterates the module aims, learning outcomes and syllabus content for the module in question.

Where relevant, the introductory section will also include a list of acronyms and abbreviations or a list of legal cases for reference.

The text itself

Each **part** opens with a list of the chapters to follow, an overview of what will be covered and learning outcomes for the part. Part openings also include a case study, which introduces a real-world scenario related to the topics covered in that part. Questions based on this case and designed to test the application of theory into practice appear in the chapters and at part endings (see below).

Every **chapter** opens with a list of the topics covered and an introduction specific to that chapter. Chapters are structured to allow students to break the content down into manageable sections for study. Each chapter ends with a summary of key content to reinforce understanding.

Part opening

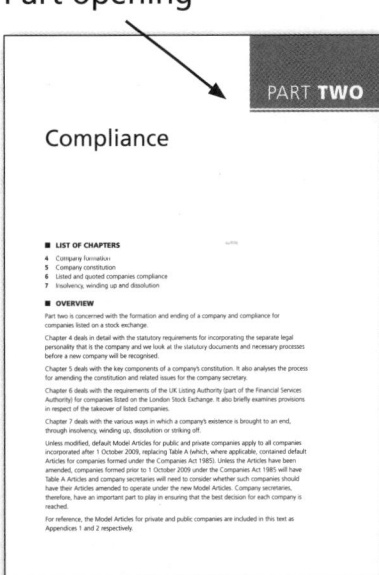

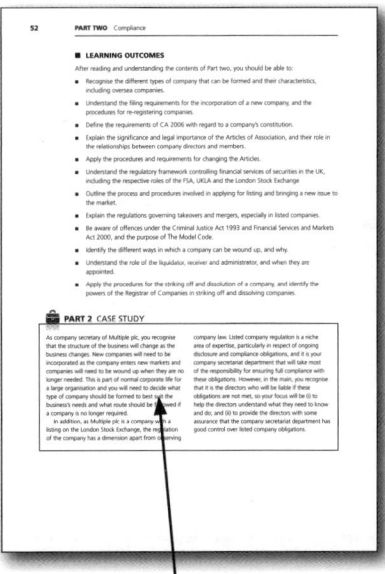

Part case study

Chapter opening

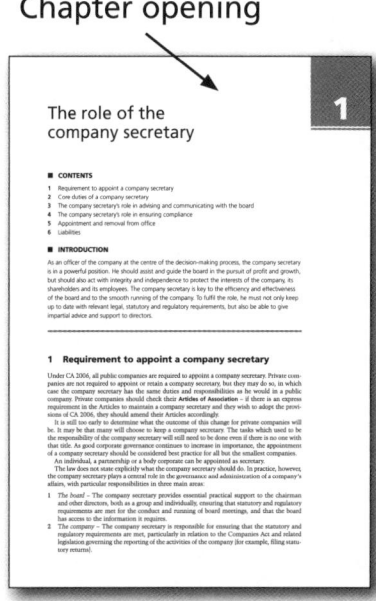

Features

The text is enhanced by a range of illustrative and self-testing features to assist understanding and to help you prepare for the examination. Each feature is presented in a standard format, so that you will become familiar with how to use them in your study.

The texts also include tables, figures and checklists and, where relevant, sample documents and forms.

Case Examples

Case examples present short, illustrative case studies which look at how concepts are applied in practice.

Checklist

Sample wording

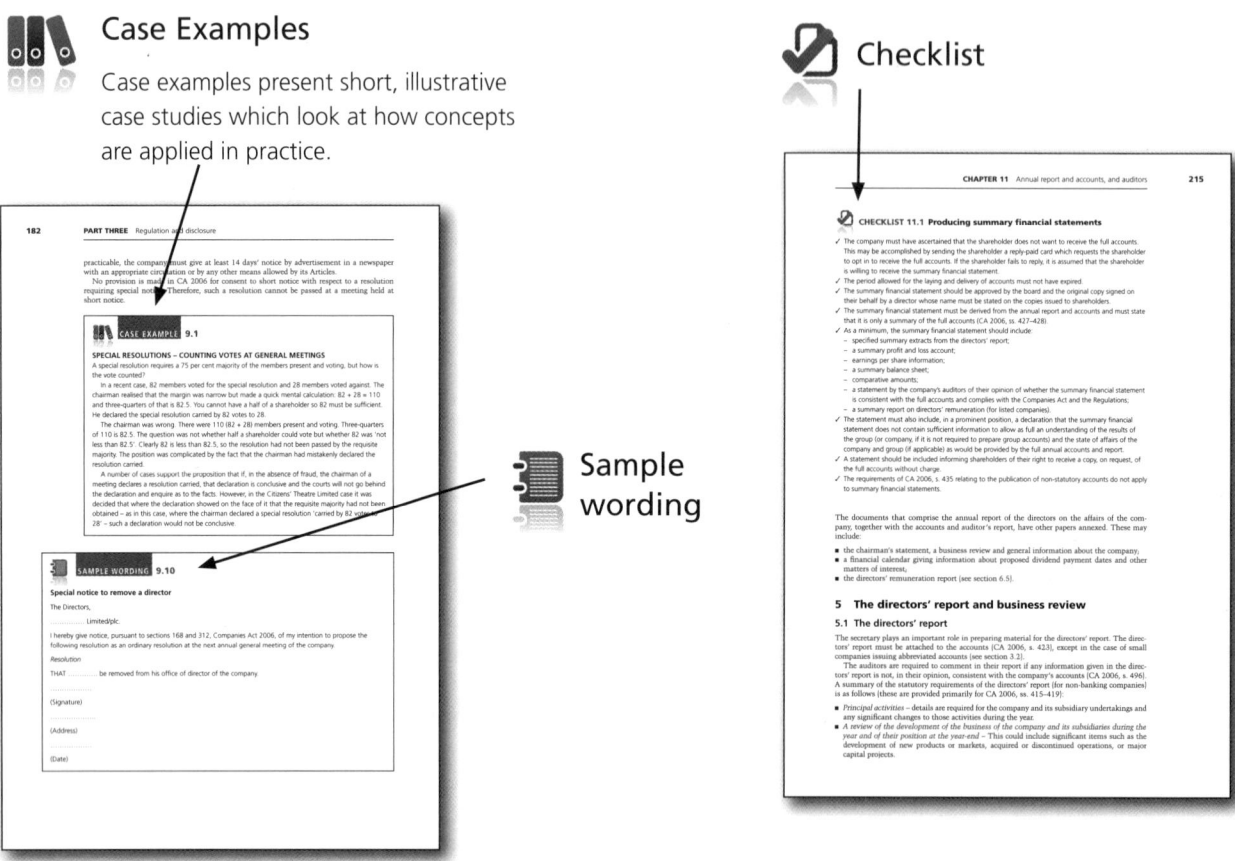

Case Law

Case law summaries provide overviews of significant legal cases.

Case Questions

Case questions relate to the part opening case study, encouraging you to apply the theory you're learning to a real-world business scenario.

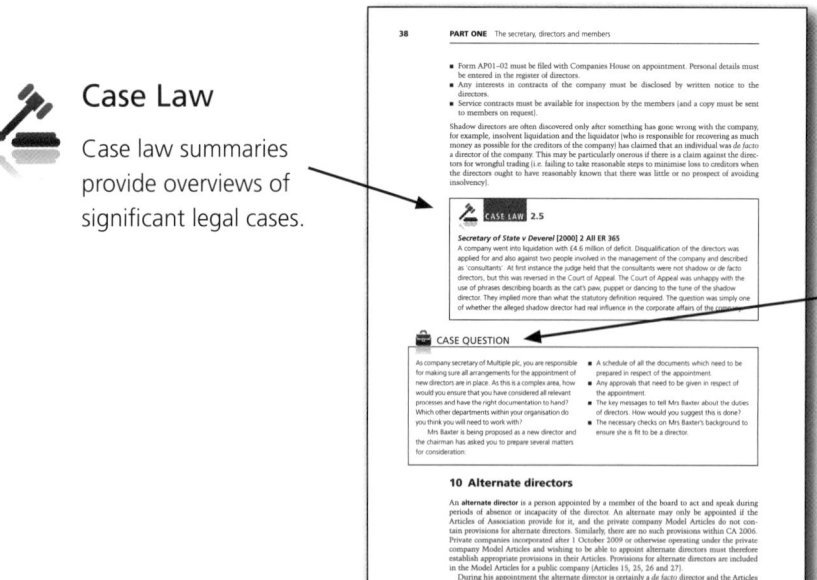

How to use this study text

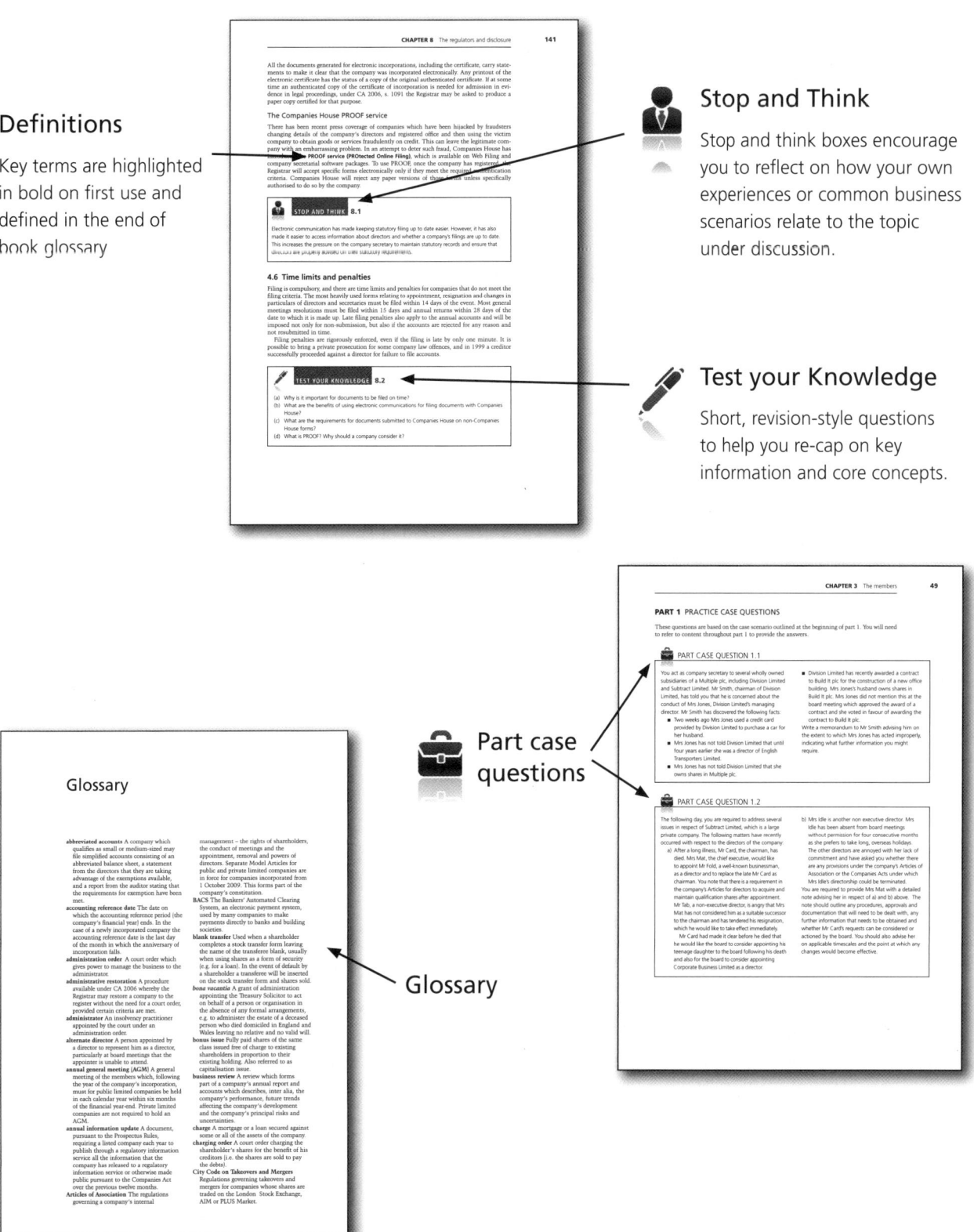

Definitions
Key terms are highlighted in bold on first use and defined in the end of book glossary

Stop and Think
Stop and think boxes encourage you to reflect on how your own experiences or common business scenarios relate to the topic under discussion.

Test your Knowledge
Short, revision-style questions to help you re-cap on key information and core concepts.

Part case questions

Glossary

Reference material

The text ends with a range of additional guidance and reference material.
Most texts will include Appendices which comprise additional reference material specific to that module.

Other reference material includes a glossary of key terms, a directory of further reading and web resources and a comprehensive index.

Corporate Law syllabus

Module outline and aims

This module provides an understanding of the legal framework governing organisations, with particular focus on the registered company. Its themes relate closely to those of the Corporate Governance module and draw heavily upon the Companies Act 2006 (CA 2006) and related legislation.

Chartered Secretaries work in a range of organisations and are involved with issues of regulatory compliance. The aim of the module is to provide an understanding of the legal framework governing organisations, dealing with legal principles and their practical application.

Learning outcomes

On successful completion of this module, you will be able to:

- Demonstrate knowledge of the theories, concepts and principles related to the structure and regulation of commercial organisations.
- Give a reasoned opinion on the legal structures available to organisations and their appropriateness.
- Identify the legal and other issues arising in complex scenarios and apply relevant law such as the Companies Act 2006.
- Understand the impact of the external regulatory environment on the structure of commercial organisations.
- Present advice on structural and legal issues in a relevant form.

Syllabus content

The nature and structure of a company – weighting 20%

Sources of company law: statutes and secondary legislation, case law, the impact of EU law, self-regulation.

Types of companies: registered (unlimited, limited by shares, limited by guarantee, overseas, community interest), chartered and statutory (in outline only), charitable incorporated organisations (in outline only), limited liability partnerships (LLPs).

Unincorporated business structures: sole traders, general partnerships, limited partnerships, associations (in outline only).

Promotion and pre-incorporation contracts: role of a promoter, duties and liability for breach of duty, liability for pre-incorporation contracts.

Formation and registration of companies: formation procedures and documents, the role of the registrar, the certificate of incorporation, the trading certificate, choice and use of the company name.

Consequences of incorporation: separate legal personality, the veil of incorporation, lifting the veil of incorporation, the criminal and civil liability of a company, shareholder liability and company liability, corporate groups.

The constitution of a company: the memorandum and the articles of association, content, model articles, the statutory contract, alteration of the constitution, shareholder agreements, class rights in the articles.

Company contracts: executing company contracts, company capacity and abolition of the doctrine of *ultra vires*, s.40, the rule in *Turqand's* case, the authority of agents to bind the company.

Capital and membership – weighting 25%

Raising capital from the public: the role of the prospectus and listing particulars, content and the general duty of disclosure, statutory compensation for misleading statements, common law remedies, underwriting and commission.

Shares and class rights: types of shares, class rights, variation of class rights, alteration of share capital, the issue of shares, payment for shares, premiums and discounts, statutory pre-emption rights.

Capital maintenance: the doctrine of capital maintenance, share capital reductions, purchase and redemption of a company's own shares, dividends and liability for improperly paid dividends, the prohibition on financial assistance.

Membership: becoming a member, share certificates and warrants, the members' register, transfer and transmission of shares, calls, liens, forfeiture and surrender of shares.

Loan capital: debentures (types, use of a trust deed, secured and unsecured), fixed and floating charges, charges over book debts, crystallisation of floating charges, priority of charges, registration and avoidance of charges.

The regulation of market abuse: insider dealing and market manipulation, criminal offences, inside information, insiders, defences and criminal penalties, the civil regulatory regime and civil penalties.

Company management and shareholder remedies – weighting 25%

Directors: types, appointment, remuneration, retirement and removal, disqualification orders and undertakings, the division of power between the board of directors and the general meeting.

Directors' duties: the codification process, scope and nature of the general duties, duty to act within powers, duty to promote the success of the company, duty to exercise independent judgment, duty to exercise reasonable skill, care and diligence, duty to avoid a conflict of interest, duty not to accept benefits from third parties, duty to declare interest in proposed and existing transactions or arrangements, civil consequences for breach of duty, release and ratification of breach of duty.

Transactions with directors requiring members' approval: long-term service contracts, substantial property transactions, loans to directors, compensation for loss of office.

The company secretary: appointment and qualifications, role, authority to bind the company.

The auditor: the audit requirement, appointment and removal, rights and duties, liability for negligence and criminal liability.

Enforcement of directors' duties under the common law: the rule in *Foss v Harbottle*.

Enforcement of directors' duties under statute: the derivative action under s. 260 CA 2006, costs.

Enforcement of shareholder rights: personal and representative actions, recovery of reflective loss, petitions under s. 994 CA 2006, petitions under s. 122 IA 1986, grounds, claimants, remedies and costs.

Public enforcement: company investigations (in outline only).

Meetings and resolutions – weighting 10%

Company meetings: the annual general meeting, general meetings, class meetings, court-ordered meetings, notice periods, content of notices, adjournments and the minutes.

Company resolutions: ordinary resolutions, special resolutions, written resolutions, the *Duomatic* principle and informal unanimous consent, voting and the use of proxies, electronic communications and corporate representatives.

Board meetings and board decisions.

Company restructuring and winding up – weighting 20%

Methods of restructuring: the procedure in s. 110 IA 1986, schemes of arrangement, amalgamations and reconstructions under Part 26 CA 2006.

Takeovers: the City Code, the work of the Takeover Panel, the EU Takeover Directive and relevant provisions of CA 2006.

Alternatives to winding up: the company voluntary arrangement, the nominee, proposal and approval of the arrangement, the small company moratorium, implementing and terminating the arrangement.

Alternatives to winding up: administration orders, the purpose of administration, appointment of administrator, interim moratorium, effects of administration on directors, contracts and employees, role and power of administrators, ending the administration.

Winding up: voluntary and compulsory winding up orders, commencement of winding up, grounds, appointment of the liquidator, function and powers of a liquidator, effect of a winding up order, order of distribution of assets, property not available to a liquidator, trust property and retention of title (ROT) clauses, completion of the winding up and company dissolution.

Challenging pre-liquidation transactions and personal contributions: misfeasance proceedings under s. 212 IA 1986, transactions at an undervalue, preferences, extortionate credit transactions, avoidance of floating charges, disclaiming onerous property, fraudulent and wrongful trading

Prohibition in the re-use of company names.

Acronyms and abbreviations

AGM	annual general meeting
AIM	Alternative Investment Market
art.	article
BIS	Department for Business, Innovation and Skills
CA	Court of Appeal
CDDA	Company Directors Disqualification Act 1986
CIB	Companies Investigations Branch
CIC	community interest company
CIO	charitable incorporated organisation
City Code	City Code on Takeovers and Mergers
Code	UK Corporate Governance Code
CPR	Civil Procedure Rules
CVA	company voluntary arrangement
DMSCs	different Member State companies
DTI	Department of Trade and Industry
DTR	Disclosure and Transparency Rules
EC	European Community
ECHR	European Convention on Human Rights
EEIG	European Economic Interest Grouping
EU	European Union
FCA	Financial Conduct Authority
FRC	Financial Reporting Council
FRS	Financial Reporting Standards
FSA	Financial Services Act 2012
FSAP	Financial Services Action Plan
FSMA	Financial Services and Markets Act 2000
GAAP	Generally Accepted Accounting Practice
HL	House of Lords
HMRC	Her Majesty's Revenue and Customs
IAS	International Accounting Standards
IPO	initial public offering
ISC	Institutional Shareholders Committee
LLP	limited liability partnership
LR	Listing Rules
LSE	London Stock Exchange
Ltd	limited
MAD	Market Abuse Directive
NED	non-executive director
PAYE	Pay As You Earn
PLC	public limited company
PR	Prospectus Rules
reg.	regulation
SC	UK Supreme Court
SCE	pan-European Co-operative Society
sch.	Schedule
SE	Societas Europaea
SMEs	small, medium and micro-sized businesses
SPE	Societas Privata Europaea
TFEU	Treaty on the Functioning of the European Union
TUV	transfer at an undervalue
VAT	Value Added Tax
UK	United Kingdom
UKLA	United Kingdom Listing Authority
USA	United States of America

List of figures

Figure 1.1	Company law includes parts of securities regulation and insolvency law	
Figure 1.2	Corporate governance	4
Figure 2.1	Types of registered companies	20
Figure 2.2	Quoted companies (Companies Act 2006, s. 385)	23
Figure 2.3	Listed securities	24
Figure 2.4	Small and medium-sized companies for Companies Act 2006 purposes	25
Figure 4.1	Types of legal persons	60
Figure 4.2	Typical scenario 1	69
Figure 4.3	Typical scenario 2	70
Figure 4.4	Typical scenario 3	70
Figure 4.5	Using a company to avoid existing obligations	71
Figure 4.6	*The Rialto No. 2*	72
Figure 4.7	Statutory provisions supplementing the rights of a creditor against the company	77
Figure 5.1	Contractual relationships created by the s. 33 statutory contract	87
Figure 6.1	Board of directors purporting to act outside its powers	107
Figure 6.2	Board of directors purporting to delegate a power it does not have	109
Figure 6.3	Individual director acts outside the express actual authority granted to him by the board of directors	112
Figure 10.1	Fixed charge against real property: stages of enforcement	189
Figure 10.2	Fixed charge against personal property: stages of enforcement	190
Figure 10.3	Floating charge against single class of assets	192
Figure 10.4	Floating charge against different classes of assets	192
Figure 10.5	Priority of charges: fixed and floating charges	198
Figure 10.6	Priority of charges: two floating charges	198
Figure 10.7	Priority of charges: two general floating charges	198
Figure 12.1	Categorisation of directors' duties	229
Figure 12.2	Enlightened shareholder value and s. 172	231
Figure 12.3	Directors' corporate governance duties	233
Figure 12.4	Directors' conflict of interest duties	240
Figure 19.1	The effect of grant of a late security on unsecured creditors and distribution of a company's assets in a winding up	346
Figure 19.2	Connected persons for the purposes of the fair dealing provisions of the Insolvency Act 1986	347

List of cases

A Company (No. 001126 of 1992) [1993], *Re* BCC 325	272
A Company (No. 001363 of 1988) ex parte S-P [1989], *Re* BCLC 579	274
A Company (No. 002567 of 1982) [1983], *Re* 1 WLR 927	274
A Company (No. 00330 of 1991) [1991] *Re* BCLC 597	265
A Company (No. 00477 of 1986) [1986], *Re* BCLC 376	267
A Company (No. 005134 of 1986), ex parte Harries [1989], *Re* BCLC 383	269
A Company (No. 005287 of 1985) [1986], *Re* BCLC 68	265
A Company (No. 005685) ex parte Schwartz (No. 2) [1989], *Re* BCLC 427	265
Ad Valorem Factors Ltd v Ricketts [2004] 1 All ER 894 (CA)	339, 340
Adams v Cape Industries plc [1990] Ch 433	67, 68, 71, 73, 74, 76
Affleck v Newcastle Mind [1999] ICR 852 (EAT)	29
AG of Hong Kong v Reid [1994] 1 AC 324 (PC)	244, 250
Agnew v Commissioner of Inland Revenue (Re Brumark Investments Ltd) [2001] 2 AC 710 (PC)	191, 195
Airbase (UK) Limited [2008], *Re* EWHC 124 (Ch)	85, 338
Allen v Gold Reefs of West Africa Ltd [1900] 1 Ch 656 (CA)	94–5, 100, 289, 290
Al-Nakib Investments Jersey Ltd v Longcroft) [1990] 3 All ER 321	127
Aluminium Industrie Vaassen BV v Romalpa Aluminium [1976] 2 All ER 552	336
Amalgamated Pest Control v McCarron [1995] 1 QdR 583	85, 100, 289
Anglo-Continental Supply Co Ltd [1922], *Re* 2 Ch 723	303
Antonio Gramsci Shipping Corp v Stepanovs [2011] EWHC 333	68, 73
Armagas Ltd v Mundogas SA [1986] AC 717	114
Ashbury Carriage and Iron Company Ltd v Riche (1875) LR 7 HL 653	81–2
Astec (BSR) plc [1998], *Re* 2 BCLC 556	289
Atlas Maritime Company SA v Avalon Maritime Limited (No 1) [1991] 4 All ER 769	73
Automatic Bottle Makers Ltd [1926], *Re* Ch 412	197, 199
Automatic Self Cleansing v Cuninghame [1906] 2 Ch 34	205
Aveling Barford Ltd v Perion Ltd [1989] BCLC 626	174, 177
Ayerst (Inspector of Taxes) v C & K (Construction) Ltd [1976] AC 167	169
Bairstow v Queen's Moat Houses [2001] 2 BCLC 531	179
Baltic Real Estate Ltd (No. 2) [1993], *Re* BCLC 503	266
Bank of Tokyo Ltd v Karoon (1987) AC 45 (CA)	73
Barclays Bank v British and Commonwealth Holdings plc [1996] BCLC 1	180
Barings plc (No. 5) [1999], *Re* 1 BCLC 433	238–9
Barrett v Duckett [1995] 1 BCLC 243	260, 261
Barron v Potter [1914] 1 Ch 895	206
Beattie v E & F Beattie Ltd [1938] Ch 708 (CA)	89–90
Bellerby v Rowland & Marwood's SS Co Ltd [1902] 2 Ch 14	162
Benjamin Cope & Sons Ltd [1914], *Re* 1 Ch 800	197, 199
Bhullar v Bhullar [2003] 2 BCLC 241(CA)	244
Biosource Technologies Inc v Axis Genetics plc [2000] 1 BCLC 286	326
Birch v Cropper (1899) 14 App Cas 525 HL	139, 141
Bird Precision Bellow Ltd [1984], *Re* 3 All ER 44	271
Bluebrook Ltd, In the matter of [2009] EWHC 2114 (Ch)	301
Boardman v Phipps [1967] 2 AC 46 (HL)	244
Borden (UK) Ltd v Scottish Timber Products Ltd [1979] 3 All ER 961	336
Borland's Trustee v Steel [1901] 1 Ch 279	134
Boulting v ACTT [1963] 2 QB 606	235
Bovey Hotel Ventures Ltd (1981), *Re* (unreported)	266

Bradford Investments Plc (No. 1) [1991], *Re* BCLC 224	141, 285
Brady v Brady [1989] AC 755 (HL)	183
Bratton Seymour Service Co Ltd v Oxborough [1992] BCLC 693 (CA)	87
Braymist v Wise Finance Co Ltd (2002) Ch 273 (CA)	40
Breckland Group Holdings Ltd v London & Suffolk Properties Ltd [1989] BCLC 100	205
Brian D Pierson (Contractors) Ltd [2001], *Re* 1 BCLC 275	238
Brightlife Ltd [1987], *Re* Ch 200	188, 191
Bristol Airport plc v Powdrill [1990] BCLC 585	326
British & Commonwealth Holdings Ltd v Barclays Bank [1996] 1 WLR 1	304
British Bank of the Middle East v Sun Life Assurance Company of Canada (UK) Ltd [1983] 2 Lloyd's Rep 9 (HL)	115
Brown v British Abrasive Wheel Co Ltd [1919] 1 Ch 290	94, 95
Browne v La Trinidad (1887) 37 Ch D 1	89
BTR plc [1987], *Re* 4 BCC 45	151
Bushell v Faith [1969] 2 Ch 438 (HL)	85–6, 100
Canadian Aero Service Ltd v O'Mally (1973) 40 DLR (3d) 371	242–3
Cane v Jones [1980] 1 WLR 1451	288
Caparo Industries Ltd v Dickman [1990] 2 AC 605 (HL)	68, 226
Cardiff Saving Bank, Marquis of Bute [1892], *Re* 2 Ch 100	237
Carlen v Drury (1812) 1 Ves & B 149	256
Carlton Lodge Club v C&E Commissioners [1975] 1 WLR 66 (CA)	29
Carruth v ICI [1937] AC 707	304
Cartmell's Case (1874) LR 9	236
Castell & Brown Ltd [1898], *Re* 1 Ch 315	197, 199
Celtic Extraction Ltd [1999], *Re* 2 BCLC 555	341
Chandler v Cape [2012] EWCA Civ 525	68, 69
Charterbridge Corporation Ltd v Lloyds Bank Ltd [1970] Ch 62	235
Cinematic Finance Ltd v Ryder [2010] EWHC 3387	259
Citco Banking Corporation v Pusser's Ltd (2007) Bus LR 960 (PC)	96
City Branch Group Ltd [2005], *Re* 1 WLR 3505	266
City Equitable Fire Insurance Co Ltd [1925], *Re* Ch 407	237, 238
Clark v Urquhart [1930] AC 28	126
Cobden Investments Ltd v RWM Langport Ltd [2008] EWHC 2810	235
Cohen v Selby [2001] 1 BCLC 176	250
Colonial Bank v Whinney (1886) 11 App Cas 426	139
Conservative & Unionist Central Office v Burrell [1982] 1 WLR 522 (CA) 32	28
Cook v Deeks [1916] 1 AC 554 (PC)	257, 260
Courage Group's Pension Schemes [1987], *In re* 1 WLR 495	304, 305
Cotronic (UK) Ltd v Dezonie [1991] BCC 200	39
Criterion Properties plc v Stratford UK Properties LLC [2006] 1 BCLC 729 (HL)	315
Cumana Ltd [1986], *Re* BCLC 430 (CA)	269
Cumbrian Newspapers Group Ltd v Cumberland and Westmoreland Newspaper and Printing Co Ltd [1987] Ch 1	141–2
D'Jan (of London) Ltd [1994], *Re* 1 BCLC 561	237, 253
Dafen Tinplate Co Ltd v Llanelly Steel Company (1907) Ltd [1920] 2 Ch 124	94
Davies v Barnes Webster & Sons Ltd (unreported) (2011)	29
Day v Cook [2002] 1 BCLC 1	263
Derry v Peek (1889) 14 App Cas 337	127
DHN Food Distributors Ltd v Tower Hamlets LBC (1976) 1 WLR 852 (CA)	63, 73, 74
Dimbleby & Sons Ltd v National Union of Journalists [1984] 1 WLR 427 (HL)	76
Diplock [1948], *Re* Ch 465 (CA)	180
Discoverers Finance Corporation Ltd, Lindlar's Case [1910], *Re* 1 Ch 312	25
Dorman Long & Co Ltd [1934], *Re* 1 Ch 635	304
Duomatic Ltd [1969], *Re* 2 Ch 365	253, 288
Ebrahimi v Westbourne Galleries Ltd [1973] AC 360 (HL) 273	268, 272
Edwards v Halliwell [1950] 2 All ER 1064	256
Eley v Positive Government Security Life Assurance Co (1876) 1 ExD 88 (CA)	89
Elgindata Ltd [1991], *Re* BCLC	268
Erlanger v New Sombrero (1878) 3 App Cas 1218 (HL)	37

Erwen Warnick B V v J Townend & Sons (Hull) Ltd [1979] AC 731	50
Eurocruit Europe Ltd (In Liquidation) [2007], *Re* EWHC 1433 (Ch)	349
Euro Brokers Holdings Ltd v Monecor (London) Ltd [2003] BCLC 506 (CA)	288
Evans v Chapman (1902) 86 LT 381	87
Exchange Banking Co, Flitcroft's Case [1882] *Re* 21 Ch D 519 (CA)	173, 175, 178
Exchange Travel Ltd (No. 3) [1996], *Re* 2 BCLC 524	343
Express Engineering Works Ltd [1920], *Re* 1 Ch 466 (CA)	288
Expro International Group plc [2008], *Re* EWHC 154	317
Facia Footwear Ltd v Hinchcliffe [1998] 1 BCLC 218	232
Fairway Magazines Ltd [1993], *Re* BCLC 643	243
Fallon v Fellows [2001] STC 1409	305
First Energy (UK) Ltd v Hungarian International Bank Ltd [1993] 2 Lloyd's Rep 194	114, 115
First Independent Factors and Finance Ltd v Mountford [2008] 2 BCLC 297	340
Foss v Harbottle (1843) 2 Hare 461	230, 255–6, 262
Foster Bryant Surveying Ltd v Bryant & Savernake Property Consultants Ltd [2007] 2 BCLC 239 (CA)	243, 244
Franbar Holdings Ltd v Patel [2008] BCC 885 (Ch D)	260
Freeman Lockyer v Buckhurst Park Properties (Mangal) Ltd [1964] 2 QB 480 (CA)	112, 114
Fulham Football Club Ltd v Cabra Estates plc [1994] 1 BCLC 363	236
Full Cup International Trading Ltd [1995], *Re* BCC 682	273
Gamlestaden Fastigheter AB v Baltic Partner Ltd [2008] 1 BCLC 4681 (BC)	265, 268
Gardner v Parker [2004] 2 BCLC 554	264
General Accident v Midland Bank Ltd [1940] 2 KB 388	64
Giles v Rhind [2003] 1 BCLC 1 (CA)	264
Gilford Motor Company Ltd v Horne [1933] Ch 935	74
Grace v Biagioli [2006] 2 BCLC 70	270
Grant v UK Switchback Railway Co (1888) 40 Ch D 135 (CA)	91, 110
Greenhalgh v Arderne Cinemas Ltd [1951] Ch 286 (CA)	95–6, 139, 148
GT Whyte & Co Ltd [1983], *Re* BCLC 311	345
Guidezone Ltd [2000], *Re* 2 BCLC 321	267
Guinness plc v Saunders [1990] 2 AC 663	98, 100, 216
Halt Garage (1964) Ltd [1982], *Re* 3 All ER 1016	174, 289
Harrison (JJ) (Properties) Ltd v Harrison [2001] 1 BCLC 162	250
Hawk Insurance Company Ltd [1922], *Re* 2 Ch 723	302
Hawkes Hill Publishing Co Ltd [2007], *Re* BCC 937	349
Heald v O'Connor [1971] WLR 497	184
Hedley Byrne & Co. Ltd v Heller and Partners Ltd [1964] AC 465	127, 226
Hely Hutchinson v Brayhead Ltd [1968] 1 QB 549 (CA)	112, 113, 114, 116
Herring [1908], *Re* 2 Ch 493	187
Hickman v Kent or Romney Sheep Breeders Association [1915] 1 Ch 881	88, 89
Hill v Permanent Trustee Company of New South Wales [1930] AC 720 (PC)	168
Hogg v Cramphorn Ltd [1967] Ch 254	150, 233, 234
House of Fraser v AGCE Investments Ltd [1987] AC 387 (HL)	145, 146
Howard Smith v Ampol Petroleum Ltd [1974] AC 821 (PC)	150, 233, 234
Howard v Patent Ivory Manufacturing Co (1888) 38 Ch D 156	41
Hughes v Weiss [2012] EWHC 2363	259
Hunting Plc [2005], *Re* 2 BCLC 211	145
Hutton v West Cork Railway Co (1883) Ch D 654 (CA)	180, 289
Iesini Westrip Holdings Ltd [2010] BCC 420	260
Independent Automatic Sales Ltd v Knowles & Foster [1962] 1 WLR 974	193
ING Re (UK) Ltd v R&V Versicherung AG [2007]1 BCLC 108	114
Item Software (UK) Ltd v Fassihi [2005] 2 BCLC 91 (CA)	235
James v Buena Ventura Nitrate Grounds Syndicate Limited [1896] 1 Ch 456	94
Jessel Trust Ltd [1985], *Re* BCLC 119	304
John Shaw & Sons (Salford) Ltd v Shaw [1935] 2 KB 113 (CA)	205
Johnson v Gore Wood & Co [2001] 2 AC 1 (HL)	263
Jones v Lipman [1962] 1 WLR 832 (Ch Div)	75
Joplin Brewery Co Ltd [1902], *Re* 1 Ch 79	196
Keay & Loughrey [2010] JBL 151	261

Kelner v Baxter [1866–67] LR 2 CP 174	39
Kiani v Cooper [2010] BCC 463	259, 261
Knowles v Scott [1891] 1 Ch 717	334
Koenigsblatt v Sweet [1923] 2 Ch 314	110
Lady Forrest (Murchison) Gold Mine Ltd [1901], Re 1 Ch 582	38
Lagunas Nitrate v Lagunas Syndicate (1899) 2 Ch 392	38
Lee Panavision v Lee Lighting Ltd [1992] BCLC 22 (CA)	233, 234
Lee v Showmen's Guild [1952] 2 QB 329	29
Leeds United Holdings plc [1996], Re 2 BCLC 545	266
Lennard's Carrying Company Ltd v Asiatic Petroleum Co Ltd [1915] AC 705 (HL)	61
Levinger v Licences etc., Insurance Co (1936) 54 LL L Rep 68	64
Levy v Abercorris Slate and Slab Co (1887) 37 ChD 260	185
Lexi Holdings plc v Luqman [2009] EWCA Civ 117	239
Link Agricultural Property Ltd v Shanahan (1998) 28 ACSR 498	211
Logicrose Ltd v Southend UFC Ltd [1988] 1 WLR 1256	251
Lomax Leisure Ltd [1999], Re 2 BCLC 126	326
London and Mashonaland Exploration Co Ltd v New Mashonaland Exploration Co Ltd [1891] WN 165	243
London School of Electronics [1986], Re Ch 211	270
Lovett v Carson Country Homes Ltd [2009] EWHC 1143	103, 116
Macaura v Northern Assurance Co [1925] AC 619 (HL)	64
MacDougall v Gardiner (1875) 1 Ch D 13 (CA)	94, 256
Mackenzie & Co Ltd [1916], Re 2 Ch 450	144
Macro (Ipswich) Ltd [1994], Re 2 BCLC 354	269
Maidstone Buildings Provisions Ltd [1971], Re 1 WLR 1085	220
Marleasing SA v La Comercial Internacional de Alimentacion Case C-106/89 [1990] ECR 1-4135	108
Marseilles Extension Railway Company, ex parte Credit Foncier and	207
Meridian Global Funds Management Asia Ltd v Securities Commission [1995] 2 AC 500 (Privy Council)	61
MC Bacon Ltd [1990], Re BCLC 324	342, 343
Milgate Developments Ltd [1993], Re BCLC 291	272
Monolithic Building Co [1915], Re Ch 643	196
Morphitis v Bernasconi and Others [2003] Ch 552 (CA)	350
Mytravel Group Plc [2004], Re EWHC 2741	304
National Telephone Company [1914], Re 1 Ch 755	141
National Westminster Bank v IRC [1995] 1 AC 111 (HL)	149
New British Iron Co, ex parte Beckwith [1898], Re 1 Ch 324	98, 100
New Bullas Trading Ltd [1994], Re 1 BCLC 485 (PC)	191
Newborne v Sensolid [1954] 1 QB 45	39
NFU Development Trust Ltd [1973], Re 1 All ER 135	301
Northern Counties Securities Ltd v Jackson & Steeple Ltd [1974] 1 WLR 1133	289
Northern Engineering Industries plc [1994], Re 2 BCLC 704 (CA)	145–6
Northumberland Avenue Hotel Co [1866], Re 33 Ch D 16 (CA)	40
Nurcombe v Nurcombe [1985] 1 WLR 370	260
O'Neill v Phillips [1999] 1 WLR 1092	267, 268, 271
Ord v Belhaven Pubs Ltd [1998] 2 BCC 607 (CA)	74
Oshkosh B'Gosh Inc v Dan Marbel Inc Ltd [1989] BCLC 507	40
PAL SC Realisations 2007 Ltd v Inflexion Fund 2 Limited Partnership [2010] EWHC 2850	338
Panorama Developments (Guildford) Ltd v Fidelis Furnishing Fabrics Ltd [1971] 2 QB 711	219, 220
Parry v Bartlett & Another [2011] EWHC 3146	259, 261
Patrick and Lyon Ltd [1933], Re Ch 786	350
Payne v The Cork Company Ltd [1900] 1 Ch 308	300
Peachdart Ltd [1984], Re Ch 131	336
Pender v Lushington (1877) 6 Ch D 70	92, 289
Percival v Wright [1902] 2 Ch 421	230
Permacell Finesse Limited (in liquidation) [2008], Re BCC 208	338

Perry v Day [2005] 2 BCLC 405	264
Peters' American Delicacy Co. Ltd v Heatg [1939] 61 CLR 457	94
Peveril Gold Mines Ltd [1898], *Re* 1 Ch 122 (CA)	85
Philips v Brewin Dolphin Bell Lawrie Ltd [2001] 1 WLR 143	342
Phillips v Manufacturers' Securities Limited (1917) 116 LT 290 (CA)	94
Phonogram Ltd v Lane (1982)	39
Plus Group Ltd v Pyke [2002] 2 BCLC 201 (CA)	243
Precision Dippings Ltd v Precision Dippings Marketing Ltd [1986] Ch 447 (CA)	178
Preston v Grand Collier Dock Co (1840) 11 Sim 327	65
Profinance Trust SA v Gladstone [2002] 1 BCLC 141	271
Prudential Assurance Co Ltd v Newman Industries Ltd (No. 2) [1982] Ch 204	263
Punt v Symons & Co Ltd [1903] 2 Ch 506	148
Qayoumi v Oakhouse Property Holdings plc [2003] 1 BCLC 352	261
Quintex Ltd (No. 2) [1990], *Re* 2 ACSR 479	110, 115
R (Alconbury Developments Ltd) v Secretary of State for the Environment, Transport and Regions [2003] 2 AC 295	61
R (Northern Cyprus Tourist Centre Limited) v Transport for London [2005] UKHRR 1231	61
R v A Noble & Sons (Clothing) Ltd [1983] BCLC 273	266
R v Bailey and Rigby [2006] 2 Cr App R (S) 36	134
R v GM Holdings Ltd [1942] Ch 235	182
R v Page [1996] CrimLR 821	133
R v Panel on Takeovers and Mergers, ex parte Datafin plc [1987] 1 All ER 564 (CA)	317, 318
R v Registrar of Companies ex parte Attorney General Ltd [1991] BCLC 476	43
R v Registrar of Companies, ex parte Central Bank of India [1986] QB 1114	196
R v William James Hipwell [2006] EWCA Crim 736	134
Rayfield v Hands [1960] Ch 1	87, 88
Regal (Hastings) Ltd v Gulliver [1967] 2 AC 134	243, 244, 251
Regentcrest plc v Cohen [2001] BCC 494 (Ch)	235
Rhondda Waste Disposal Ltd [2000], *Re* BCC 653	326
Rica Gold Washing Co Ltd [1879], *Re* 11 Ch D 36	272
Richards v Lundy [2000] 1 BCLC 376	269
Roberts & Cooper Ltd [1929], *Re* 2 Ch 383	141
Royal British Bank v Turquand (1856) 6 E&B 327	110
Ruben v Great Fingall Consolidated [1906] AC 43	103
Russell v Northern Bank Development Corporation [1992] 1 WLR 588 (HL)	85, 93, 99–100
Salmon v Quin & Axtens Ltd [1909] AC 442 (HL)	87, 90–91
Salomon v A. Salomon & Co Ltd [1897] AC 22 (HL)	11, 62–3, 74, 76, 77, 149, 288
Saltdean Estate Co Ltd [1968], *Re* 1 WLR 1844	145
Sam Weller & Sons Ltd [1990], *Re* BCLC 80	269
Saul D Harrison & Sons plc (1995), *Re*	266
Savoy Hotel Ltd [1981], *Re* 3 All ER 346	301, 302
Scott v Frank F. Scott (London) Ltd [1940] Ch 749 (CA)	87
Scottish Co-operative Wholesale Society Ltd v Meyer [1959] AC 324 (HL)	211, 236
Scottish Insurance Corporation Ltd v Wilsons & Clyde Coal Co Ltd [1949] AC 462 (HL)	141, 144, 146, 171
Severn and Wye and Severn Bridge Railway Co [1896], *Re* 1 Ch 559	174
Sherborne Park Residents Co Ltd [1986], *Re* 2 BCC 99, 528	261, 262, 263, 272
Shipley v Marshall [(1863) 14 CBNS	193
Sidebottom v Kershaw, Leese & Co Ltd [1920] 1 Ch 154	94, 96
Siebe Gorman & Co Ltd v Barclays Bank Ltd [1979] 2 Lloyds Rep 142	191, 197
Sinclair Investments (UK) Ltd v Versailles Trade Finance Ltd [2011] EWCA Civ 347	244, 251
Southern Counties Fresh Foods Ltd [2011], *Re* EWHC 1370	235
SMC Electronics Ltd v Akhter Computers Ltd [2001] 1 BCLC 433 (CA)	116
Smith & Fawcett [1942], *Re* Ch 304	233, 234
Smith (Administrator of Coslett (Contractors) Ltd) v Bridgend County Borough Council [2001] 1 All ER 292	196
Smith v Croft (No. 2) [1988] Ch 114	260, 261

Smith v Henniker-Major & Co (A firm) [2002] 1 WLR 616 (CA)	107, 108
Snook v London and West Riding Investments Ltd [1967] 2 QB 786, 803	74
Sound City (Films) Ltd [1947], *Re* Ch 169	143
South African Supply and Cold Storage Co [1904], *Re* 2 Ch 268	304
South Western Mineral Water Co Ltd v Ashmore [1967] 1 WLR 1110	184
Southern Foundries (1926) Ltd v Shirlaw [1940] AC 701 (HL)	93
Sovereign Life Assurance Co v Dodd [1892] 2QB 573	303
Spectrum Plus Ltd [2005], *Re* 2 AC 680 (HL)	185, 190, 191, 194, 195, 199, 344
SSSL Realisations (2002) Ltd [2007], *Re* 1 BCLC 29	341
Stainer v Lee & Others [2010] EWHC 1539	259, 261
Steele v Gourley (1886) 3 TLR 118	29
Stevens v Mysore Reefs (Kangundi) Mining Co Ltd [1902] 1 Ch 745	83
Stimpson v Southern Private Landlords Association [2010] BCC 387 (Ch D)	259
Sycotex Pty Ltd v Balser (1993) 13 ACSR 766	232
T & N Ltd (No. 3) [2007], *Re* 1 BCLC 563	301
Target Holdings Limited v Redferns [1996] 1 AC 421 (HL)	251
Tesco Supermarkets Ltd v Nattrass [1972] AC 153 (HL)	61
Thorby v Goldberg (1964) 112 CLR 597	236
Trevor v Whitworth (1887) 12 App Cas 409 (HL)	167
Trustor v Smallbone (No. 2) [2001] WLR 1177 (Ch Div) 81	75–6
Twycross v Grant [1877]	36
Re Uniq plc [2011] EWHC 749 (Ch)	301
Unisoft Group Ltd (No. 3) [1994], *Re* 1 BCLC 609	286, 289
United Pan-Europe Communications NV v Deutsche Bank AG [2000] 2 BCLC 461 251	
VTB Capital plc v Nutritek International Corp [2013] EWSC 5	68, 69, 73
Wallersteiner v Moir (No. 2) [1975] QB 373	261
Warner International and Overseas Engineering Co Ltd v Kilburn, Brown & Co [1914] 84 LJ KB 365	128
Waugh v HB Clifford & Sons Ltd [1982] Ch 374 (CA)	115
Webb v Earle (1875) LR 20 Eq 566	141
Webb, Hale & Co v Alexandria Water Co (1905) 93 LT 339	161
Webster v Sandersons Solicitors (A Firm) [2009] EWCA Civ 830	264
Westburn Sugar Refineries Ltd, ex parte [1951] AC 625	171
West Coast Capital (Lios) Ltd [2008], *Re* CSOH 72	235
Whaley Bridge Calico Printing v Green [1879] 5 QBD 109	36
White v Bristol Aeroplane Co [1953] Ch 65 (CA)	144
Will v United Lankat Plantations Co [1914] AC 11 (HL)	141
Wills v Corfe Joinery Ltd [1998] 2 BCLC 75	343
Wood v Odessa Waterworks Co [1889] LR 42 Ch D 636 95,	88, 173, 262
Woolfson v Strathclyde RC (1978) SC 90 (HL)	73, 74
Wrexham Association Football Club Ltd (in admin) v Crucialmove Ltd [2007] BCC 139 (CA)	109, 111
Xenos v Wickham (1867) LR 2 HL 296	103
Yeovil Glove Co Ltd [1965], *Re* Ch 148	345
York Building Co v MacKenzie (1795) 3 Pat 378	228
Yorkshire Railway Wagon Co v Maclure (1882) 21 Ch D 309, 318	75
Yorkshire Woolcombers Association Ltd (1903), *Re* 2 ch 284	191, 193
Yukong Lines Ltd of Korea v Rendsburg Investments Corporation of Liberia, The Rialto No. 2 [1998] 1 WLR 294 (QBD)	72, 73

Acknowledgements

The publisher would like to thank the following for permission to reproduce the following material in this study text:

Appendix 3: The UK Corporate Governance Code (2012)
© Financial Reporting Council (FRC). Reproduced with the kind permission of the Financial Reporting Council. All rights reserved. For further information, please visit www.frc.org.uk or call +44 (0)20 7492 2300

PART **ONE**

The nature and structure of a company

■ LIST OF CHAPTERS

1 Introduction to corporate law
2 Legal structures of business organisations
3 Promoters and company formation
4 The company as a distinct legal person
5 The constitution of the company
6 Legally binding the company

■ OVERVIEW

The first part of this study text addresses the different aspects of the nature and structure of companies.

Chapter 1 is introductory. It explains the terms corporate law and company law, before moving on to explore the relationship between company law and specialised areas of law, such as insolvency law and securities regulation. We also take a brief historical look at the development of the statutory framework governing companies and the role played by the European Union in the development of UK company law.

Chapter 2 places the registered company into the context of different legal structures through which businesses may be conducted in the UK. Both unincorporated and incorporated business forms are explained and the chapter looks at some of the more popular legal structures used in the third sector.

Chapter 3 examines the role of the promoter of a company and the legal difficulties presented by contracts entered into on behalf of a company before it comes into existence. The process for registering a company is explained, as is the legal requirement to keep basic registers and records (the statutory books and registers) and register reports and accounts.

Chapter 4 focuses on a registered company as a legal person separate and distinct from the individuals who bring it into existence. The implications of this artificial legal personality status are examined with focus on the steps that can be taken by those who deal with a company to protect themselves, and situations in which legal protections, both statutory and case-based, have been put in place.

Chapter 5 focuses on the constitution of a registered company. It is important to understand the structure of pre-Companies Act 2006 constitutions and the effect the 2006 Act has had on them, particularly the objects clauses in their Memorandum of Association. The chapter also covers the status of the Articles of Association, and how to amend it, followed by the important role played by shareholders' agreements that sit alongside the formal constitutional documents required by the Companies Acts.

Finally, in Chapter 6 the main focus is on how a company acquires or becomes subject to contractual rights and liabilities.

■ LEARNING OUTCOMES

After reading this part you should understand:

- The scope of 'corporate law' and 'company law'.
- The relationship between core company law, insolvency law, securities regulation and corporate governance.
- The role of the Financial Conduct Authority (FCA) in relation to securities and the structure of the Listing Regime.
- Legal structures available, including unincorporated and incorporated business organisation legal structures and European Union organisation legal structures.
- The role and duties of promoters.
- Pre-incorporation contracts.
- How a UK company is registered, the requirement for the statutory books and registers and annual returns and reports and accounts.
- The consequences and limits of incorporation/separate legal personality.
- Limited liability and how it is legally effected.
- The constitution of a company, how to alter it and the limits on alteration.
- The role of shareholder agreements.
- How companies enter into deeds and contracts.
- The authority of agents to bind the company.

PART 1 CASE STUDY

Cherie, Tony and Harriet are karate experts. They have a dream to run a karate school for children and identify premises they believe would be a perfect location, near to three schools. They make enquiries and the premises are available to let on a three-year lease at £12,000 per annum with a deposit of £10,000 payable. The premises are in need of decoration and they believe this would cost £10,000. Equipment is expected to cost a further £10,000. They draw up a business plan and visit the Blair Bank which indicates a willingness to lend them £40,000 provided they set up their business with an acceptable legal structure and can offer Blair Bank 'the usual protections'. Cherie and Harriet own a house together. Tony is their tenant.

A local gym is being refurbished and is selling off its gym equipment cheaply. Cherie signs a contract to purchase £5,000 of gym equipment 'for and on behalf of *Karate Kids* Ltd' before any such company has been incorporated.

Cherie, Tony and Harriet wish to ensure that none of them can sell their interest in the business to a third party without the consent of the others and want to be able to buy out the interest of any of them, should they set up in competition with the karate school.

The day after a company is registered, Tony contracts to buy kick bags for the company for £50,000. Cherie and Harriet are not happy about this purchase and Harriet telephones the supplier, KB plc, to explain that they wish to cancel the contract. KB plc states that the contract is binding and if they do not want the kick bags they must pay KB plc £5,000, which is KB's lost profit on the sale.

Introduction to corporate law

■ CONTENTS

1. 'Corporate law' and 'company law'
2. What we mean by company law
3. Sources of company law
4. Historical development of company law
5. Influence of the EU on UK company law
6. The Financial Conduct Authority and the Listing Regime

■ INTRODUCTION

The material in this chapter is introductory in nature. The chapter begins with an explanation of the terms 'corporate' and 'company law' before moving on to explore what we mean by company law and its relationship to specialised areas of law. The key sources of company law are then identified and the role of self-regulation considered.

A brief historical look at the development of the statutory framework governing companies and the role played by the European Union in the development of UK company law follows, helping us to understand what has shaped the law we see today. Finally, a brief examination of the rationale behind the most recent major overhaul of company law, the Companies Act 2006, is followed by an introduction to the Financial Conduct Authority (the renamed and refocused Financial Services Authority following the passing of the Financial Services Act 2012) and the Listing Regime.

1 'Corporate law' and 'company law'

Corporate law is the term used in a number of countries (such as the USA) and has grown to become the preferred international term for what UK lawyers refer to as company law. The use of the term company law persists in the UK because the core statute governing corporations run for profit is, and for over 150 years has been, named the Companies Act and companies registered under those Acts form by far the most numerous class of corporations in the UK. The different types of corporations that exist in the UK are examined briefly in chapter 2 and the corporate concept at the heart of company law is explored in chapter 4.

2 What we mean by company law

2.1 Core company law

The focus of this text is what is sometimes referred to as 'core company law', which is essentially the law governing the creation and operation of registered limited companies. It is very easy to identify core company law today as it is almost all contained in the 1,300 sections and 16 schedules of the Companies Act 2006, Regulations made pursuant to that Act and cases clarifying the application of the statutory rules and principles.

That said, the Companies Act 2006 is not a comprehensive code of core company law in the sense of a body of rules that has replaced all common law rules and equitable principles previously found in cases. Certain aspects of core company law, such as remedies available for breach of directors' duties, remain case-stated law distinct from statute law and many cases interpreting provisions of past Companies Acts remain relevant today. The Companies Act 2006 is also not the only current statute containing core company law. Key relevant statutes and the role of case law in core company law are considered in section 4 below.

Limits of core company law

A comprehensive review of law relevant to companies would include insolvency law and securities regulation (also known as capital markets law or financial services law) to the extent that they apply to companies. In the last 25 years, each of these areas of law has become a highly developed and voluminous legal subject in its own right. Realistically, neither can be covered in any depth in a company law text of moderate length.

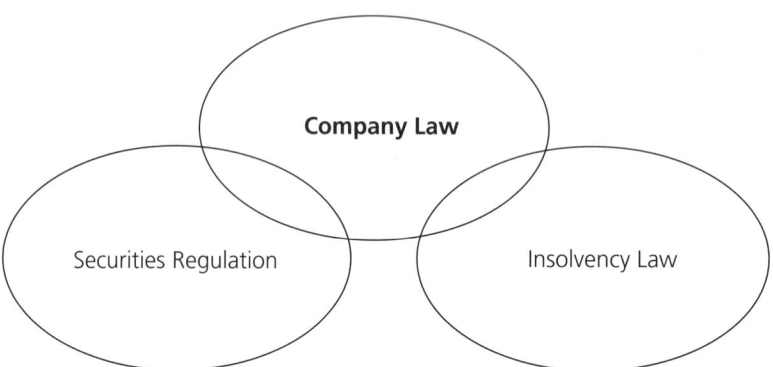

FIGURE 1.1 Company law includes parts of securities regulation and insolvency law

Corporate governance has attracted a great deal of attention as an important aspect of company law and it is appropriate to say a few words about it in the context of setting out what we mean by company law. Corporate governance is not a legal term; rather, it is a label, or heading, under which to analyse the questions how, by whom and to what end corporate decisions must or should be taken. Within that debate, the issue of how far the law can and should be used to achieve good corporate governance arises.

Those who support extensive use of law and regulation to improve corporate governance are said to support the juridification of corporate governance, those against are said to prefer private ordering. Company law and corporate governance overlap to the extent that a large part of company law is about how and by whom corporate decisions can or must be made. Textbooks on company law differ in the extent to which they deal with insolvency law, securities regulation and corporate governance. The approach taken in this text to each is set out in the following three sections.

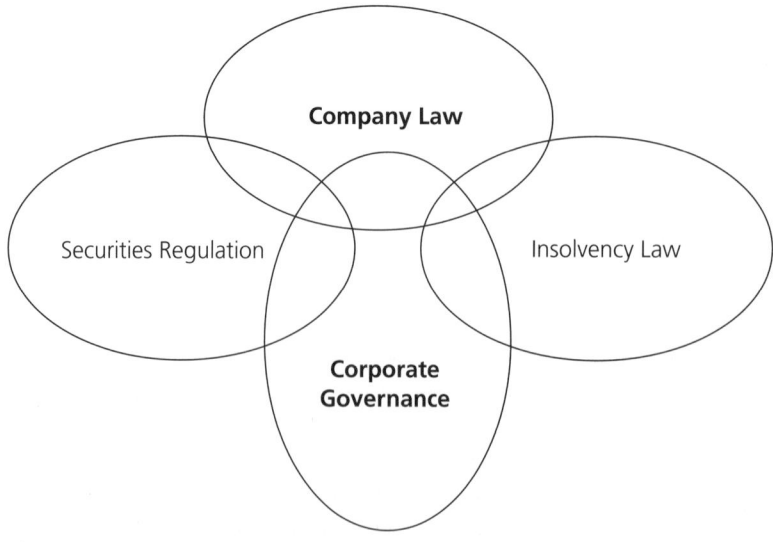

FIGURE 1.2 Corporate governance

2.2 Insolvency law

Even though it is theoretically possible, companies do not continue in existence forever. They either outlive their usefulness or become financially unviable. Before a company ceases to exist, or is 'dissolved', its ongoing operations are brought to an end, its assets are sold and the proceeds of sale used to pay those to whom it owes money. This process is called winding up or liquidating the company.

Some companies that are **wound up** or **liquidated** are able to pay all their debts in full, that is, they are 'solvent', yet the law governing winding up of solvent companies is set out in the Insolvency Act 1986 (and rules made pursuant to that Act, the most important of which are the Insolvency Rules 1986). The explanation for this is that most winding ups involve insolvent companies and when, in the mid-1980s, the law governing insolvent company winding ups was moved out of company law legislation into specific insolvency legislation, it made sense to deal with solvent winding ups in the same statute. This avoided the need for duplication of those winding up provisions relevant to both solvent and insolvent companies in both the Companies Act 1985 (now replaced by the Companies Act 2006) and the Insolvency Act 1986.

Note that, while insolvency is a term relevant to both companies and individuals, in the UK the term bankruptcy is used only to refer to the insolvency of individuals. Thus it is incorrect to refer to a company going bankrupt. Although insolvency law is a highly detailed and specialised area of the law, it is important to have some knowledge of the key formal processes set out in the Insolvency Act 1986 which assist the rescue, or effect the liquidation, of a company: voluntary arrangements, administration and liquidation. These are examined in part 5 of this study text.

During the liquidation process, the person appointed to conduct the winding up of a company, the **liquidator**, has the power (among others), to apply to court for orders that certain individuals, often directors or people closely connected with directors, contribute sums to the company to swell the assets available for distribution to creditors. It is important for anyone seeking to understand the law governing directors to be acquainted with the full range of potential liabilities and exposures of directors, so the relevant provisions of the Insolvency Act 1986 are covered in part 5 of this study text.

Liquidators have powers to review and challenge the validity of certain transactions entered into by the company in the period of up to two years (three years for extortionate credit transactions) leading up to the commencement of winding up proceedings. Again, it is important for anybody seeking to understand the rights of those who deal with companies to know the potential for such transactions to be challenged by a liquidator. The relevant provisions are also covered in part 5.

Finally, once the assets of a company have been turned into money and any contributions secured, a liquidator is required to follow a statutory order of distribution, which determines the priority of payment of different types of creditors. Given the significance of this statutory ordering to the decision whether or not to deal with a company and the terms on which to do so, the statutory order of distribution on liquidation is also covered in part 5.

2.3 Securities regulation

The object of securities law is essentially to provide protection to those who decide to invest their money in **securities** (basically, shares and corporate bonds), and the large number of complex investment products financial service providers have built around securities.

Through the lens of securities law, a **public company** (distinct from a **private company**, which is prohibited from offering its securities to the public) can be viewed as a legal structure available to businesses to facilitate the raising of capital in the capital markets. From this perspective, securities law is of critical relevance to public companies. The law in this area is, however, detailed and specialised and can only be touched on in a basic company law text. The key UK governing statute, the Financial Services and Markets Act 2000, has been amended, most recently by the Financial Services Act 2012. The key regulatory body, now known as the Financial Conduct Authority (FCA), is considered briefly in the final section of this chapter.

The areas of law regarded as securities regulation covered (though not in depth) in this text are:

- The law governing prospectuses to support an offer of securities to the public (chapter 7).
- Public disclosure rules imposed on companies with listed securities (periodic reporting and disclosure of price-sensitive information) (chapter 3).

- Market protection laws: insider dealing and market abuse regulations (chapter 7).
- The EU Takeover Directive and the City Code on Takeovers and Mergers (chapter 17).

2.4 Corporate governance

Corporate governance means different things to different people in different contexts. Whenever the term is used, the first question to ask is, in what sense is it being used? If this is not clear, it is usually helpful to examine the context in which the term is being used.

Corporate governance and small companies

The vast majority of independent companies (i.e. companies that are not part of a larger corporate group of companies) are managed by individuals who own or control the company, or a large part of it. Additional shareholders are typically related to the majority owner or participate in managing the company alongside the majority owner, and it is not uncommon for them to be both relatives and co-managers. Most of these companies are not large and are registered as private rather than public companies. Questions about how such a company is governed usually arise out of one of two types of dispute.

The first type of dispute raises the question whether the board of directors or the majority shareholder can behave, or cause the company to behave (i.e. can the company be governed), in a manner objectionable to, and alleged to be inconsistent with, the interests of its minority shareholders. The second type of dispute raises the question of whether or not the board of directors or the shareholders can behave, or cause the company to behave (i.e. can the company be governed), in a manner that undermines the ability of the company to pay its creditors.

Whilst other groups, such as employees, suppliers and customers, may be affected by the manner in which a small company is governed, such impacts are typically either relatively minor or can be worked around simply because of the size of operation. Self-interested action by managers or directors of small companies is not generally an issue because the managers/directors own the company. To the extent that the managers/directors do not own all the shares, their pursuit of self-interest raises issues of not only, or even mainly, how to prevent abuse of management power, but rather what legal constraints exist, or should exist, on majority shareholders.

Company laws important to regulating small company governance include not only the obvious, such as directors' duties and disclosure obligations, but also constraints on majority shareholders and the remedies available to minority shareholders, particularly in the context of unfairly prejudicial conduct petitions (see chapter 13). Principally found in the Companies Act 2006, relevant laws can also be found in insolvency law.

For the above reasons, a legalistic approach to the concept of corporate governance is often taken and can be justified in relation to small companies. This is unlikely to remain the case. Driven by political focus on small and medium-sized businesses (SMEs) as important drivers of economic growth, there is increasing interest in improving SME corporate governance, particularly at the EU level. Developments can be followed on the European Commission's Small Business Portal on its website, Europa.

Corporate governance and large companies

In relation to large companies, corporate governance is typically addressed as a much more complex and broad-ranging concept because of the clear impact the quality of corporate governance of large companies with extensive business operations has on the economy and society. The study of how existing company law influences corporate governance is more complex in relation to public companies than it is to typical private companies. This complexity arises in part out of the model of ownership of many large companies.

The scope of impact of business operations

The larger the business of a company, the greater the impact its operations has on a larger number of individuals and, consequently, the economy. Consider the potential for the environment to be very significantly adversely affected by a company that owns and is actively expanding its network of oil pipelines. Similarly, a large company may run nuclear power stations producing by-products, best practice waste management of which involves the storage into the long-term future of active nuclear material. A large company may employ a significant proportion of workers in a locality. It may be the largest purchaser of a particular product or products in the country so that producers depend on it continuing to buy a large share of their output. (Companies owning large supermarket chains as purchasers of milk exemplify this.) A large company may be one of only a handful of suppliers of a particular product or service, such as mobile telephony, with millions of consumer (distinct from business) customers.

The point to note is that the effect of decision-making by large companies can significantly affect the environment, the local community, the livelihood of large numbers of people who work for the company, consumer choice and the viability of suppliers. The various groups affected by, or interested in, a company are sometimes referred to as **stakeholders**.

The extent to which the interests of different stakeholders as a matter of law must be, as a matter of fact are and as a matter of policy should be taken into account in company decision-making are important issues that fall within the corporate governance rubric. Closely related questions are who must be, who is and who should be involved in company decision-making.

The questions to what extent are the interests of different stakeholders taken into account as a matter of practice and who actually takes part in (or perhaps the question should be who actually influences) company decision-making, are questions of fact. The focus here needs to be on empirical studies yet, as it appears that little empirical research has taken place in the UK on decision-making in companies, these questions are often answered, somewhat unsatisfactorily, by making assumptions.

The separation of ownership and control of companies

The second factor adding to the complexity of corporate governance of large companies is the model of ownership of large publicly-traded companies. Separation of those who own a company (the shareholders) from those who manage the company (the directors) has long been a feature of large companies in the UK. This raises the problem of ensuring that those who manage companies do not run them for their own personal benefit rather than for the benefit of those on whose behalf the law requires companies to be managed.

The management self-interest problem is exacerbated where a company's shares are owned by a large number of shareholders with no single person owning a significant shareholding. This pattern of shareholding is called 'atomistic' or 'dispersed'. The interest of shareholders in publicly traded companies is first and foremost (if not exclusively) financial in nature. Shareholders seek dividends, increased share value (that is, they want the price at which they can sell their shares to increase) and, ideally, both.

In this type of company, legal protection based on a balance of power between the board of directors and shareholders would have little, if any, meaningful effect if shareholders had little inclination to exercise the powers reserved to the shareholding body: the divorce of ownership and control would be virtually complete. Yet it is precisely here that the most stringent laws promoting good practice in corporate governance are believed to be necessary. This explains why corporate governance law and practice is most developed for companies with listed securities. It also explains why relevant laws are found not in core company law, but in securities law.

The approach to corporate governance taken in this text

The Companies Act 2006 corporate governance provisions are supplemented by securities regulation and an array of codes and guidance. The most important code is the UK Corporate Governance Code which sets out to establish good practice by boards of directors of companies with a Premium Listing (the new term for Primary Listing) of equity shares. The most recent version of the UK Corporate Governance Code, published in September 2012, is set out in Appendix 3 and is referenced at appropriate places in the text. It sets out standards of good practice in relation to board:

- leadership and effectiveness;
- accountability;
- remuneration; and
- relations with shareholders.

It is an example of a self-regulatory measure which has become underpinned by statute (the Listing Rules promulgated pursuant to the Financial Services and Markets Act 2000). A relatively new and wholly self-regulatory code that supplements the UK Corporate Governance

Code is the Stewardship Code, now in its second, revised edition (September 2012) (both codes are considered in section 3.3 below).

3 Sources of company law

3.1 Legislation

Statute law takes the lead in the sources of company law. The main statute containing company law is currently the Companies Act 2006. The most important statutes containing provisions regarded as part of core company law are:

- Companies Act 2006;
- Insolvency Act 1986;
- Company Directors Disqualification Act 1986;
- Financial Services and Markets Act 2000;
- Criminal Justice Act 1993 (insider dealing);
- Companies Act 1985 (company investigations); and
- Companies (Audit, Investigations and Community Enterprise) Act 2004 (company investigations and community interest companies (CICs)).

These Acts have all been amended since being enacted and are supplemented by detailed rules contained in statutory regulations.

The Companies Act 2006 is the most recent statute pursuant to which a company can be registered. Each successive Act setting out the process for registration since 1862 has been called the Companies Act. In practice, it is often important to know under which Companies Act a company has been registered and to consult that Act because the content of the Articles of Association scheduled to each Act is different.

The term Companies Acts is defined in s. 2 of the Companies Act 2006. It essentially means the company law provisions (Parts 1–39) of the Companies Act 2006 and the community interest provisions (Part 2) of the Companies (Audit, Investigations and Community Enterprise) Act 2004. The term is sometimes used in a different sense, however, to refer to the Companies Acts over time, in aggregate.

3.2 Case law

The study of cases is an important part of understanding company law. Principles that remain case-stated distinct from principles set out in the relevant statutes make up only a small part of company law, but even though many common law and equitable principles are now set out in the Companies Act 2006 or another current statute, the cases in which they were developed remain relevant to demonstrate how they apply in practice.

Provided that the Act is intended simply to state the existing law rather than change it, old cases help us to understand how a statutory rule will be applied in the future. A good example is the first of the general duties owed by a director to the company set out in s. 171 of the Companies Act 2006. The general duties owed by a director to the company have been developed by judges in case law over more than 150 years before becoming statutory duties set out in the Companies Act 2006. Case law provides a rich source of examples of application of the principles in practice, or 'declaratory precedent'.

Clearly, before old case law can be relied on, it is essential to know in relation to any given section of the Act, whether the Act is intended to change the law or not. Change may render some but not all past cases irrelevant. It may also render a part but not all of a case irrelevant. The key learning is that in this situation, great care needs to be taken when seeking to rely on past cases.

Many core company law cases are concerned with the meaning and application of repealed statutes, particularly sections from previous Companies Acts. Here again, if the earlier statutory rule appears to have been re-enacted in the Companies Act 2006, care must be taken to determine whether or not there has been a change in the statutory language and, if it has changed, whether or not the change is intended:

- to make no change to the law, that is, no substantive change. The language may have been changed to clean up the drafting, perhaps to make the section easier to understand or to reconcile the language with related sections of the Act;

- to incorporate case law development of the meaning of a section of the Act. An example of this is s. 33 which, unlike s. 14 of the Companies Act 1985 (the predecessor provision), makes it clear that the contract in a company's Articles can be enforced against the company, a point established in *Hickman v Kent or Romney Sheep Breeders' Association* [1915] 1 Ch 881; or
- to change the law.

The intention of the legislature, particularly where it is to change the law, may be clear from the face of the new section. An example is s. 188 of the Companies Act 2006, which requires shareholder approval by general resolution of a director's service contract that runs for more than two years. In comparison, s. 319 of the Companies Act 1985 (the predecessor section) required shareholder approval for a director's service contract that runs for more than five years. In places, however, the legislative intention is not clear. An example is s. 168 of the Companies Act 2006, which provides for a director to be removed from office by the shareholders by general resolution, but omits reference to provision to the contrary in the company's Articles. The predecessor section (s. 303 of the Companies Act 1985) referred to the company's Articles. The effect of the omission from the new section is not clear.

Company law and law generally

Company law should not be approached as a self-contained body of legal learning. As you develop your career as a company secretary, you will need to be aware that company law involves the application of more generic areas of law in the context of companies. These areas include public law, criminal law, contract and tort law, property law, EU law and equity and trust law. The importance of these general legal subjects to the study of company law should not be underestimated.

3.3 Self-regulation

The term self-regulation is used to contrast rules, principles or norms, which may be expressed in a code or guidance, compliance with which is expected by those involved in a profession or industry (or who provide a particular facility such as a trading market) with legal regulations which carry the sanction of legal penalties if contravened. Often perceived as a dichotomy, self-regulation and legal regulation may be better viewed as two ends of a spectrum. The relationship between the two can be complex. Self-regulation can be a very effective way to maintain high standards of behaviour. Historically, self-regulation has been relied on in the UK to provide protection for shareholders, creditors and investors.

Traditionally, regulation of the City of London was largely left to the professionals practising in the City. For example, the London Stock Exchange existed for many years as a self-regulating stock exchange. The **City Code on Takeovers and Mergers** operated for almost 40 years without government regulatory backing, enforced by the Panel on Takeovers and Mergers (see part 5). This tradition was continued when the first version of the UK Code on Corporate Governance was produced in 1992. Written and recommended by the Cadbury Committee, set up by the Financial Reporting Council, the London Stock Exchange and the accounting profession, it was a voluntary code. Its self-regulatory nature was not wholly endorsed as the following quotation from the *Financial Times* indicates:

> The committees' recommendations are steps in the right direction. But, if the government is to address the problems which led to the Maxwell, Polly Peck, BCCI and other recent scandals, then new rules in a legal framework are required ... Shareholders, investors and creditors will have been disappointed that just when the corporate failures of recent years cried out for bold and imaginative legal reform, the body from which so much had been expected came up with a little tinkering and a voluntary code.
>
> (Cadbury Committee Draft Orders Mixed News for Shareholders, *Financial Times*, 2 June 1992)

As already stated, the current version of the Code is underpinned by statute. In contrast, the most important new code established in recent years, the Stewardship Code (September 2012), has no statutory backing.

Debate about the strengths and shortcomings of self-regulation and its relationship with legal regulation to protect investors was refuelled by the stark failures in the regulation of financial markets culminating in the 2007 credit crunch and ensuing financial turmoil. Many legal and self-regulatory initiatives have ensued, principally focused on the regulation of banks and the financial services industry.

> (a) Explain how securities regulation and insolvency law are relevant to company law.
> (b) What does the term corporate governance mean?
> (c) What are the two primary sources of company law?
> (d) Name seven statutes relevant to company law and identify the most important of them.

4 Historical development of company law

4.1 The first registered companies

The opportunity to create a company by an inexpensive process (registration of documents) and as a matter of right (rather than discretion or favour) has existed in England for over 160 years, since the passing of the Joint Stock Companies Act 1844. The Act followed the influential report earlier that year on joint stock companies chaired by William Gladstone. Another significant feature of modern company law that can be traced back to Gladstone's report and the 1844 Act is public disclosure of information about registered companies. These days, information about a company, its directors and members and annual reports and accounts must be filed at Companies House with the **Registrar of Companies** where it is available for inspection by members of the public (see chapter 3).

When a company is registered, we speak about it being **incorporated**. The term is used in s. 15(1) of the Companies Act 2006: 'On the registration of a company, the Registrar of Companies shall give a certificate that the company is incorporated.' The term comes from the Latin *corporare*, which means 'to furnish with a body'. The process of registering a company brings into existence, or 'embodies', a new legal person. All legal persons, registered companies included, enjoy legal rights and are subject to enforceable legal liabilities.

Significant legal benefits arise when a company owns and conducts a business rather than that business being owned and conducted mutually by a group of individuals. Complexity is swept away regarding such questions as: Who are the parties to a contract entered into in the course of the business? Who can be sued to recover money lent to the business? Who owns the property used in the business? Instead of multiple individuals (everyone who owns a part of the business or participates in management) being named as parties to a contract or litigation, a single legal person is substituted: the company. This benefits both those owning and running the business and those with whom business is conducted. In this respect companies, unlike unincorporated business structures, simplify and, therefore, facilitate the efficient conduct of business.

The use of a company to conduct a business brings the efficiency benefits outlined above but also brings with it the potential for the company to have insufficient funds to pay those to whom it owes money, its **creditors**. Owners, or **members**, of companies registered under the 1844 Act were required to contribute funds to an unlimited amount to the company to enable the company to pay its creditors. These first registered companies were what are now call 'unlimited companies', a term used in s. 3(4) of the Companies Act 2006 to describe a company in which 'there is no limit on the liability of its members'. It is still possible to register an unlimited company but as this text is focused on companies formed for profit and unlimited companies are rarely used for this purpose, little will be found about unlimited companies in this text.

4.2 Arguments for and against limited liability for company members

The question whether or not to allow companies to be registered with members, or shareholders, who are not required to contribute any sum to the company beyond the price agreed to be paid to buy shares in the company was debated throughout the first half of the nineteenth century. The main argument against allowing members limited liability was that it would encourage and facilitate even more recklessness and fraudulent activity than was increasingly rife in the growing financial and corporate services markets. Supporters argued limited liability would:

- encourage investment in companies;
- facilitate transferability of shares; and
- provide clarity and certainty as to the assets available to creditors of the company.

All of which, it was said, were essential to access the capital needed to fund the growth of capital-intensive industries such as the railways and mining. Demands for limited liability finally succeeded. This was due in no small part to the fact that shortly after incorporation was made easily available, various attempts to enforce the unlimited liability system provided for in the 1844 Act proved it to be unworkable.

The Limited Liability Act 1855 was enacted and was quickly replaced, along with the 1844 Act, by the Joint Stock Companies Act 1856. The 1856 Act is regarded as the first modern Companies Act although it was the next consolidating Act, adopted in 1862, that bore the name 'Companies Act'.

Limited liability was introduced to provide protection and encouragement to investors in companies and as a direct result of the difficulty of operating a system of unlimited liability of members of companies with freely transferable shares. When company shares are traded on a public stock exchange the list of members is typically long and rapidly changing which makes it difficult to track members down and enforce contributions.

4.3 The model company for which company law was designed

The introduction of limited liability is an example of how, in its early stages, company law developed to cater for companies with a relatively large number of shareholders and publicly-traded shares. This model of ownership assumes that the owners of the company (the members or shareholders) are different individuals from the managers of the company (the directors). This separation of ownership and control gives rise to one of the key problems regulated by company law, namely the inclination of managers/directors to act in their self-interest rather than in the interests of the company and its owners/shareholders. In economics it is termed the agency problem. It is this problem that underlies the imposition of strict **fiduciary** duties on directors and extensive public disclosure obligations on companies.

In fact, today the shares of only a tiny proportion (significantly less than 1%) of registered companies are traded on a public stock exchange. Less than 2,000 of more than two million registered companies are quoted companies.

4.4 Closely-held companies

By far the most common type of company is a small company with a handful, if not (as is increasingly the case) a single shareholder. The directors of these companies are significant shareholders if not the sole shareholder. Separation of ownership and control is either not present or insignificant. These companies are sometimes referred to as closely-held companies, referring to the small number of shareholders. The key problem company law wrestles with in closely-held companies is not how to control management/the directors, but how to protect minority shareholders (who may or may not be involved in management) from the self-interested behaviour of majority shareholders.

Use of the registered limited company as a corporate structure by sole trader businessmen gathered pace in the 1890s. This development was legally contentious. Whereas the Companies Act 1862 required a company to have a minimum of seven shareholders, businessmen were satisfying this requirement by issuing one share each to members of their families, or to other individuals to hold the share on trust for the benefit of the businessman. They thereby created, in fact if not in law, a company owned and controlled by a sole member.

In the seminal case of *Salomon v A. Salomon and Co. Ltd* [1897] AC 22 (HL), creditors of just such a company challenged this practice as an abuse of the Companies Act 1862 registration process. They were successful both at first instance and in the Court of Appeal. It took an appeal to the House of Lords for the judges to clarify that the Companies Act 1862 permitted the registration of a company owned and controlled, in effect, by a single shareholder who could not be sued to recover the debts of the company and whose liability to contribute funds to the company was limited. It is interesting to reflect on how different company law might be today if the strident judgments of the members of the Court of Appeal, firmly set against endorsing limited liability for sole traders 'hiding' behind registered companies, had not been appealed and overturned by the House of Lords.

Introduction in the Companies Act 1907 of the distinction between **private** and **public** companies (for the current distinction see Table 2.1, p. 22) was evidence of acceptance by the legislature that:

- the registered company was not the sole preserve of companies with publicly traded shares; and
- not all laws developed with companies with publicly traded shares in mind were appropriate for closely-held companies.

The 1907 Act requirement for public companies to disclose their annual balance sheets, for example, was not considered appropriate for private companies. Private companies were not required to disclose annual accounts until 1967.

By 1911, two out of every three of the 50,000 companies registered were private companies. The preponderance of private companies is even more emphasised today with more than 99 out of every 100 new companies being registered as private companies.

4.5 Twentieth-century developments

Until the UK joined the European Union in 1973, company law was periodically reformed and consolidated following a review and report by a committee established for the purpose by the government department responsible for trade, now the **Department for Business, Innovation and Skills (BIS)**. Following UK membership of the EU, company law continued to be subject to in-depth national reviews. Significant reforms were made in the 1980s in the specialised areas of securities regulation (financial service law) and insolvency law. These areas of law were restructured, with relevant parts of company law being carved out, reformed and relocated in the Financial Services Act 1986 (since replaced by the Financial Services and Markets Act 2000 (FSMA)), the Insolvency Act 1986 and the Company Directors Disqualification Act 1986 (CDDA), an Act that provides for the Secretary of State to apply to the court for orders disqualifying unfit directors of companies from participating in the management of companies. In contrast, notwithstanding the consolidation and partial rewriting of disparate statutes resulting in the Companies Act 1985, reform of core company law was neither fundamental nor structured.

After 1973, changes to core company law occurred piecemeal, mainly in response to EU initiatives, until a root-and-branch review of company law was announced, in 1998, with a clear commitment from the government to enact a Companies Act fit for purpose in the twenty-first century. A seven-year review ensued, resulting in the enactment of the Companies Act 2006.

TEST YOUR KNOWLEDGE 1.2

(a) Since when has it been possible to register a company using a relatively straightforward, inexpensive process?
(b) What are the principal arguments for and against allowing company members to have limited liability to contribute to the assets of a company?
(c) When was a legal distinction first drawn between a private and a public company?

5 Influence of the EU on UK company law

Membership of the EU continues to have a significant influence on the development of UK company law. As with developments at the UK level, EU core company law initiatives need to be seen alongside EU financial services, securities or capital markets law. The two directorates of the European Commission responsible for developments in these areas are DG MARKT and DG Enterprise and Industry, and a wealth of information about their work can be found on the European Commission's Europa website. The key developments are outlined in the following paragraphs.

Initially, EU company law concentrated on harmonisation of core company law to facilitate the single market (pursuant to what is now Article 50 of the Treaty on the Functioning of the European Union (TFEU)). Traditionally, the aims of the European company law harmonisation programme have been stated by the European Commission to include:

- providing equivalent protection through the EU for shareholders and other parties concerned with companies;
- ensuring freedom of establishment for companies throughout the EU;
- fostering efficiency and competitiveness of business;
- promoting cross-border cooperation between companies in the Member States; and
- stimulating discussions between Member States on the modernisation of company law and corporate governance.

Member States have been required to make significant, often technical, changes to their national company law in the pursuit of equivalent protection for members and others dealing with companies across the European Union. At the end of 2012, a welcome initiative was announced to codify the numerous harmonisation directives in effect.

An important body of European Court case law also exists, fleshing out the meaning of freedom of establishment (now set out in Article 49 TFEU), as it applies to companies. Unfortunately, this topic is beyond the scope of this text as it is a subject the European Commission has announced an intention to focus on in coming years.

Efforts have been made over the years, and are continuing, to put supra-national European company structures in place and the European public limited liability company, 'European Company' or **Societas Europaea (SE), the European Economic Interest Grouping (EEIG)** and the European Private Company or **Societas Privata Europaea (SPE)**, are all briefly described, together with the rationale for its development, alongside other business organisation structures in chapter 2.

Important landmarks in the development of European company law have included the Financial Services Action Plan (FSAP) in 2000 and the Action Plan on Company Law and Corporate Governance (the Action Plan) in 2003, each of which have been in large part implemented. Recent work of the European Commission on banking and financial market regulation is both extensive and beyond the scope of this book.

The latest significant core company law development at EU level has been the wide-ranging 2012 consultation on the future of European Company Law culminating in the European Commission's Action Plan, published in December 2012, entitled *European Company Law and Corporate Governance – a Modern Legal Framework for More Engaged Shareholders and Sustainable Companies*. Initiatives outlined in that plan to modernise and enhance European company law will follow three main lines: enhancing transparency between companies and investors; encouraging long-term shareholder engagement; and improving the framework for cross-border operation of companies.

STOP AND THINK 1.1

Core company law is essentially facilitative in nature. It enables the efficient establishment of companies and in large part respects the right of those who establish and work in companies to agree the terms governing the rights between them. Contract law and property law are at its core. In contrast, securities regulation is part of the EU effort to integrate financial markets. It has investor protection at its centre and consequently is focused on imposing requirements on financial market operators and the companies the securities of which are traded. In contrast to contract and property laws, at the core of securities regulation, or financial markets law, we find public law (government regulation) and criminal law.

TEST YOUR KNOWLEDGE 1.3

(a) What steps have been taken at EU level in relation to company law?
(b) Name two EU company structures currently available.
(c) What aim was the EU Financial Services Action Plan drawn up to pursue?
(d) What are the objectives of the Companies Act 2006?

6 The Financial Conduct Authority and the Listing Regime

6.1 The Financial Conduct Authority

The Financial Conduct Authority (FCA) is the new name for the Financial Services Authority (FSA) following amendment of the Financial Services and Markets Act 2000 (FSMA) by the Financial Services Act 2012 (FSA 2012). The FSMA gives the FCA a wide range of rule-making, investigatory and enforcement powers in order to achieve its strategic and operational objectives as set out in the Act. Its strategic objective is ensuring that financial markets function well. Its three operational objectives are:

- the consumer protection objective: securing an appropriate degree of protection for consumers;
- the integrity objective: protecting and enhancing the integrity of the UK financial system; and
- the competition objective: promoting effective competition in the interests of consumers in the markets for regulated financial services, or services provided by a recognised investment exchange in carrying on regulated activities.

The principal role of the FCA for our purposes is its role as the UK Listing Authority (UKLA), i.e. the UK's securities regulator under Part VI of the FSMA (see FSA 2012, s. 16). As such it is the keeper of the Official List, a list of securities issued by companies for the purpose of being traded on a UK regulated market (the most important of which markets, for equity shares, is the Main Market of the London Stock Exchange, the only other being the ICAP Securities & Derivatives Exchange Main Board).

6.2 The Listing Regime

The Listing Regime is a set of rules, called the Listing Rules, made by the FCA, as the UK Listing Authority, setting out the obligations that must be complied with to obtain admission of securities to the Official List, and the continuing obligations of companies with listed securities. In fact, different parts of the Listing Rules apply to different types of organisations and different types of securities. The Listing Rules can be found, together with the Prospectus Rules and the Disclosure and Transparency Rules (DTRs), in the *FCA Handbook*, which is available on the FCA website.

The Listing Regime is structured into two segments, Premium and Standard. Across these two segments, eight distinct groups of listing obligations exist, known as 'listing categories'. The Premium Listing segment covers three categories of obligations, or 'listing categories', for three different types of issuers of equity shares. All three Premium Listing categories contain what are referred to as 'super-equivalent UK obligations', indicating the imposition of more stringent obligations than the obligations that must be satisfied as a matter of EU law for securities to be admitted to the Official List, known as the EU minimum standards. The Standard Listing segment contains five listing categories, for five different types of securities. The obligations contained in the chapters of the Listing Rules governing the five Standard Listing categories are based on the EU minimum standards. Since 2010, both UK and overseas companies have been able to seek either a Premium or Standard Listing.

The structure of the Listing Rules (LR) is as follows:

- Premium Listing Segment (equity shares)
  - commercial company
  - closed-ended investment fund
  - open-ended investment company
- Standard Listing Segment
  - shares
  - debt and debt-like instruments
  - certificates representing certain securities
  - securitised derivatives
  - miscellaneous securities

A company can seek a Premium or Standard Listing of its shares on either of the two regulated markets for shares in the UK (the London Stock Exchange Main Market or the ICAP Securities & Derivatives Exchange Main Board). As part of the super-equivalent obligations, companies with Premium Listings of equity shares are required by Listing Rules 9.8.6 R (companies incorporated in the UK) and 9.8.7 R (overseas companies) to state in their annual report and accounts whether or not they have complied with the UK Corporate Governance Code and give reasons for any non-compliance.

CHAPTER SUMMARY

- Corporate law is the international term for what is called in the UK company law. It is essentially the law governing the establishment, structure and operation of corporate bodies used to run businesses for profit.
- Although primarily found in the Companies Act 2006, core company law contains parts of insolvency law and securities regulation.
- The key sources of company law are case law, statutes, statutory instruments or government regulations and self-regulatory rules and codes such as the UK Stewardship Code (September 2012). The principal statutes are:
  - Companies Act 2006
  - Insolvency Act 1986
  - Company Directors Disqualification Act 1986
  - Financial Services and Markets Act 2000
  - Criminal Justice Act 1993 (insider dealing)
  - Companies Act 1985 (company investigations)
  - Companies (Audit, Investigations and Community Enterprise) Act 2004
- Registered companies have existed in the UK since 1844 and limited liability was first available for registered companies in 1855. Private and public companies were first distinguished in 1907.
- Since 1973, UK membership of the EU has influenced the development of UK company law as harmonisation of company law in all Member States has been pursued.
- The FCA is the UK's official regulator of securities, the organisations that issue them and the markets on which they are traded.
- The Listing Regime is a set of rules made by the FCA made up of the Listing Rules, Disclosure and Transparency Rules and Prospectus Rules which regulate admission to the official list and the continuing obligations of companies with listed securities.
- Companies with Premium Listings are subject to super-equivalent requirements, including the obligation to comply with the UK Corporate Governance Code (September 2012) or explain why not.

2 Legal structures of business organisations

■ **CONTENTS**

1 Unincorporated business organisation legal structures
2 Incorporated business organisation legal structures
3 Social enterprise private legal structures
4 European organisation legal structures

■ **INTRODUCTION**

The aim of this chapter is to put the registered company into context by examining the different legal structures through which businesses may be conducted in the UK. The available structures are categorised into unincorporated structures and incorporated structures. The registered limited company is the most popular incorporated structure.

This chapter also looks at some of the more popular legal structures used in not-for-profit organisations, or 'social enterprises', the so-called third sector or 'civil society', including the new structure for charities, the charitable incorporated organisation. EU initiatives in relation to business organisations and civil society entities are gathered together and briefly reviewed in the final section.

1 Unincorporated business organisation legal structures

The term 'unincorporated organisation' describes any organisation which is not a legal person, separate and distinct in law from its members. It is an organisation which is not a 'corporation', 'corporate entity' or 'artificial legal entity'. Businesses run purely to make profits which do not involve a corporate entity usually take the legal form of a **sole trader** (who may employ others to work in the business) or a partnership. Unincorporated organisations which are neither sole traders nor partnerships are often referred to as **unincorporated associations**. More often than not, they are not run purely for profit and many are 'not-for-profit' organisations. For this reason unincorporated associations are examined below under 'social enterprise private legal structures'.

1.1 Sole traders

No 'core' business organisation law exists relevant to sole traders or 'sole practitioners' (the term preferred by professionals) because there is no organisation to regulate. A sole trader is an individual who offers goods or services to others in return for payment. In the context of distinguishing a sole trader from an employee, a sole trader is referred to as an 'independent contractor'.

The individual who is the sole trader is the party to contracts, owns all the property used in the course of trade or business and receives all the income and profits from the business. A sole trader can contract with individuals to help in the business, whether by entering into a contract for services with an independent contractor or a contract of employment (a contract of service) with an employee. In the latter case, the individual sole trader is the employer.

The individual who is the sole trader is also the person sued if anything goes wrong in the course of the business. If a judgment is obtained against the individual, all of his assets (personal or used in the business) are available to settle or pay that judgment debt.

No legal person, separate from the individual, is created, therefore the sole trader carries on an unincorporated business. The individual cannot be an employee of the business because he cannot contract with himself. Both of these points mean that, in contrast to establishing a company through which to conduct a business, there is little opportunity for a sole trader to minimise his tax liability. A sole trader is taxed as a self-employed person and the profit from carrying on the business is subject to income tax. If the individual has taxable income from outside the business (e.g. interest on savings in a building society), the business profits are added to that income and the rates of tax (45%, 40% and 20%) are applied to the total income.

Setting up in business as a sole trader is easy. The sole trader registers as self-employed with Her Majesty's Revenue & Customs (HMRC). Any laws applicable to the particular type of business or practice in which the sole trader is involved also need to be complied with. If earnings are expected to exceed the relevant threshold, a sole trader will need to register for value added tax (VAT) purposes, and a sole trader who employs anybody must register with HMRC for Pay As You Earn (PAYE) purposes. No information about a sole trader's business needs to be made available to the public: a sole trader has financial and business privacy.

Individuals who wish to own and manage a business on their own can choose to conduct their business as a sole trader or through a company. The decision whether to establish a company may, however, be customer-led and, therefore, less a choice of the individual but more of a trading necessity. Potential customers may prefer to contract with a company to provide the services of an individual rather than contracting directly with that individual. In doing so, they avoid the consequences of an individual being found to be an employee, who would otherwise have more rights than would arise out of a contract for services with a service-delivering company.

1.2 Partnerships

General partnerships

Partnership is a legal relationship defined in the Partnership Act 1890 (the Act). The Act has set out the basic structure of partnership law with no significant substantive change for over a century. There are no necessary formalities required to create a partnership.

> 'Partnership is the relation which subsists between persons carrying on a business in common with a view of profit.' (s. 1(1))

Whether or not a partnership exists is decided by applying the statutory test to the facts. Whether an express (written or oral) or implied agreement is entered into or not, if two or more persons carry on a business together ('in common'), with the intention of making a profit, a partnership will exist because the arrangement falls within s. 1(1) of the Act. The relationship between the members of a company is not a partnership, a point put beyond doubt by s. 1(2).

Section 2 contains rules to help to decide whether or not a partnership exists. These rules deal with sharing profits (*prima facie* evidence of partnership, s. 2(3)), and sharing income and ownership of property (neither in themselves enough to evidence a partnership, ss. 2(2) and 2(1), respectively). The Act defines partners collectively as a firm (s. 4).

The Act continues, setting out internal rules governing relations between the partners themselves, and external rules governing relations between the partnership and those dealing with the partnership. Most internal rules in the Act are not mandatory rules but default or 'opt-out' rules, that is, rules that apply unless the partners agree otherwise. Agreement otherwise can be oral or evidenced by behaviour, but is most commonly evidenced by a written contract between the partners setting out the main terms on which the partnership is to operate. Written partnership agreements range from very simple, to very detailed, documents. Law firm partnership agreements are typically very long and involved.

Two important examples of simple default rules regularly opted out of and in many cases replaced by long and complex provisions are the capital and profit and loss sharing rule, and the management rule, both found in s. 24 of the Act:

'(1) All the partners are entitled to share equally in the capital and profits of the business, and must contribute equally towards the losses whether of capital or otherwise sustained by the firm ...
(5) Every partner may take part in the management of the partnership business'.

In law, partnerships are not legal persons or entities distinct from the partners. A partnership is an unincorporated association. A partnership cannot own legal property; the property is owned by the partners (using a trust in many cases to vest the legal title in a limited number of partners to be held for all partners). Nor can a partnership enter into a contract. Contracts, even those that appear on the face of the contractual document to be with a firm (the partnership) because the firm is named as the party to the agreement, are in fact contracts with the individuals who are the partners in the firm. The Law Commission has described the unincorporated legal status of partnerships as 'a throwback to the nineteenth century' and an anomaly, whose end it considers is long overdue. As discussed below, however, the government has chosen not to implement the Law Commission's proposals for partnerships to be incorporated organisations.

The unincorporated status of partnerships makes the external rules that apply between partners and third parties critically important. In default of agreement to the contrary, partners have authority to bind the other partners in the firm to contracts: partners are **agents** of one another. Moreover, s. 9 confirms that every partner in a firm is liable, jointly with the other partners, for all debts and obligations of the firm incurred while he is a partner. Section 10 extends this liability to cover wrongful acts or omissions of any partner acting in the ordinary course of the partnership business. Critically, a partner's liability is unlimited (although see limited partnerships below for the special case where a non-managing partner can limit his contribution to the sum invested in the partnership).

Unlike companies and LLPs, partnerships are not subject to public disclosure obligations. This is important for those who choose to operate their business as a partnership. With the abolition of the restriction on the size of partnerships, it is arguable that, for large partnerships, absence of public disclosure should be revisited.

A partnership is automatically dissolved every time there is a change of partner. One of the main aims of this chapter is to draw attention to distinguishing features between partnerships and registered companies. Transferability of shares is a key characteristic of registered companies. Shareholders are able to sell their shares, that is, they can, in effect, withdraw their investment in the company, without affecting the company's financial position. The shareholder exits the company by receiving his investment from the new owner of the shares. Transferability exists for shareholders of companies with publicly traded shares but is not always a reality for the owner of private company shares for which it can be very difficult to find a buyer.

The ability of the company to continue unaffected by changes in ownership is in stark contrast to partnerships – or at least it is in theory. In practice, tax rules combined with appropriate provisions in partnership agreements mean that whilst, in theory, a change in partners operates to terminate a partnership, in fact, the partnership business is not wound up and the business continues largely as before, with one less partner.

Limited partnerships

Limited partnerships are unincorporated firms provided for by the Limited Partnership Act 1907. They should not be confused with limited liability partnerships. LLPs are incorporated entities provided for by the Limited Liability Partnership Act 2000 and are considered below.

Limited partnerships are partnerships with at least one general partner and one or more limited partners who contribute an agreed sum to the partnership and are not liable for the debts and obligations of the firm beyond that amount. Limited partners may not participate in management of the partnership and have no power to bind the firm.

Limited partnerships must be registered at Companies House and the Registrar of Companies issues a certificate of registration, which is conclusive evidence that a limited partnership has been formed on the date shown on the certificate. The names of all of the partners (general and limited) and the sums contributed by limited partners are available for public inspection but there is no requirement for a limited partnership to file accounts. Since 2009, new limited partnerships (only) must include the words Limited Partnership or the letters LP at the end of their name (see the Legislative Reform (Limited Partnerships) Order 2009 (SI 2009/1940).

>
> **TEST YOUR KNOWLEDGE 2.1**
>
> (a) What are the two principal legal structures of unincorporated business entities?
> (b) Is it possible for a sole trader to conduct his business through a registered company?
> (c) What is the definition of a partnership and where can it be found?
> (d) What happens automatically as a matter of law when a partner retires from a partnership?
> (e) What is a limited partnership?

2 Incorporated business organisation legal structures

2.1 Chartered and statutory companies

Formation of a business corporation by obtaining a charter of incorporation from the Crown (the grants of which are overseen by the Privy Council), or securing a private Act of Parliament is improbable today. It is much easier and less expensive to register a company, and the grant or Act would be unlikely to be forthcoming for a purely profit-making venture.

Although once used to run private businesses, most surviving chartered and statutory corporations are not-for-profit organisations. Examples include the Law Society, the Institute of Chartered Secretaries and Administrators and the Institute of Chartered Accountants.

2.2 Registered companies

The registered company is the most popular legal structure for business organisations in the UK. The types of companies that can be registered in the UK are displayed in Figure 2.1. The first key distinction to make is between limited and unlimited companies. As unlimited companies are not attractive for running a business for profit, the most important type of registered company is the limited company. Focusing on limited companies, the next key distinction to be made is between companies limited by shares and companies limited by guarantee. Companies limited by shares rather than by guarantee are used by businesses as they are more flexible. Companies limited by shares can be private (denoted by Limited, or 'Ltd' at the end of their name) or public (denoted by public limited company, or 'plc' at the end of their name).

Only public companies may offer their shares to the public and the price paid for this opportunity is a more stringent company law regime. Many public companies do not offer shares to the public. If a public company wants its shares to be traded on a regulated market (e.g. the Main Market of the London Stock Exchange), it must seek admission of those shares both to the Official List maintained by the UK Listing Authority (the FCA), and to trading on the regulated market.

A number of sections of the Companies Act 2006 are applicable to some public companies but not others. The terms 'quoted company' and 'traded company' are defined in the Act for the purpose of indicating those public companies to which particular sections of the Companies Act 2006 apply. The term 'listed company' is not used in the Companies Act 2006. It is used in the Listing Rules (promulgated pursuant to the FSMA) and, for these purposes, it is defined in the FCA Handbook Glossary.

The Companies Act 2006 also categorises registered companies as small, medium sized and others for various audit, accounts and reporting purposes. More onerous requirements are imposed on larger companies.

Each of these types and categories of registered company is considered in turn in the following paragraphs. Community Interest Companies are considered in section 3 below, along with other legal structures for social enterprises.

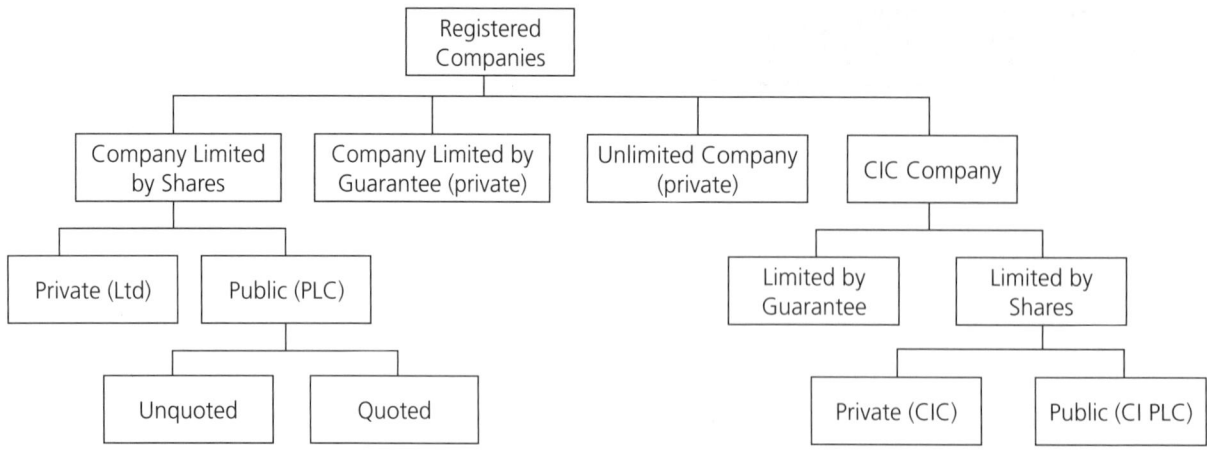

FIGURE 2.1 Types of registered companies

Unlimited companies

Unlimited companies, which must be private companies, are uncommon in business. When they are found in business contexts it is often as part of a tax planning structure due to some overseas tax authorities (including the US revenue service) regarding them as tax-transparent, or 'flow-through' entities (i.e. ignoring them for tax purposes). In the event of a winding up, the members of an unlimited company are required to contribute sums to the company sufficient for payment of its debts and liabilities (Insolvency Act 1986, s. 74(1)).

Limited companies

Companies limited by guarantee
Companies limited by guarantee are all private companies and traditionally have been the registered company of choice for charitable companies (meaning companies registered under the Companies Acts with exclusively charitable objects). A new form of company designed specifically for charities, the Charitable Incorporated Organisation, is now available and time will tell whether it proves more popular than the company limited by guarantee (see below, under social enterprise private legal structures). Interestingly, Network Rail Ltd is a private company limited by guarantee. Formed in 2002 to take over Railtrack and responsibility for the UK's rail network, it is a not-for-profit organisation that receives significant funds from the government. Nonetheless, it asserts on its website that it 'operates as a commercial business' and that the board runs the company 'to the standards required of a publicly listed company'.

Companies limited by shares
Companies limited by shares have members, or shareholders, who own shares in the company. The concept of 'limited' is explored in chapter 4. Essentially, the shareholders of a **limited company** are not required to contribute sums to the company sufficient for payment of its debts and liabilities but are simply required to pay to the company the price they have agreed to pay for their shares.

Overseas companies

An **overseas company** is a company incorporated outside the United Kingdom (s. 1044).

The Companies Act 2006 (ss. 1044–1059) and the Overseas Companies Regulations 2009 made pursuant to the 2006 Act have merged the two old regimes by which overseas companies where required to register their place of business and branches in the UK. The new regime requires all overseas companies to register particulars with the Registrar of Companies within one month of 'opening a UK establishment', whether it is a place of business in the UK or a branch in the UK (s. 1046).

Registration requires delivery to the Registrar of Companies of:

- a completed 'Registration of an overseas company opening a UK establishment' application (Form OS IN01);
- the current registration fee;
- a certified copy of the company's constitutional documents; and

- a copy of the company's latest set of accounts if required to be filed under the law of the place of incorporation or, if an EEA state, are not required to be audited and filed in the Member State of incorporation.

An overseas company that has registered particulars under s. 1046 is not a UK registered company for the purposes of the Companies Act 2006.

Groups, holding and subsidiary companies

Corporate groups are a familiar feature in the UK. Basically, a corporate group exists where a parent company owns or controls, directly or indirectly, subsidiary companies. Company law focuses primarily on individual companies, and some of the difficulties this can present are explored in chapter 4. The concept of the group is relevant to the Companies Act 2006 primarily because group accounts have to be filed by the parent company (in addition to individual accounts for each company within the group). A company may be a parent company even though it is not a holding company: the concept of parent company for these purposes is broader than the concept of holding company.

Holding company status for the purposes of the 2006 Act is based on holding a majority of voting rights or the right to appoint or remove a majority of directors of another company (s. 1159). In contrast, parent status may result merely from having the right to exercise dominant influence over another undertaking (s. 1162, see s. 1162(4)).

The definitions of a **subsidiary**, wholly-owned subsidiary and holding company are found in the Companies Act, s. 1159 as supplemented by schedule 6 to the Act.

'(1) A company is a "subsidiary" of another company, its "holding company", if that other company—
   (a) holds a majority of the voting rights in it, or
   (b) is a member of it and has the right to appoint or remove a majority of its board of directors, or
   (c) is a member of it and controls alone, pursuant to an agreement with other members, a majority of the voting rights in it, or if it is a subsidiary of a company that is itself a subsidiary of that other company.
(2) A company is a "wholly-owned subsidiary" of another company if it has no members except that other and that other's wholly-owned subsidiaries or persons acting on behalf of that other or its wholly-owned subsidiaries.' (s. 1159)

The definition of parent and subsidiary undertaking are found in s. 1162 as supplemented by schedule 7. A parent company is a parent undertaking that is a company.

'(1) This section (together with Schedule 7) defines 'parent undertaking' and "subsidiary undertaking" for the purposes of the Companies Acts.
(2) An undertaking is a parent undertaking in relation to another undertaking, a subsidiary undertaking, if—
   (a) it holds a majority of the voting rights in the undertaking, or
   (b) it is a member of the undertaking and has the right to appoint or remove a majority of its board of directors, or
   (c) it has the right to exercise a dominant influence over the undertaking—
      (i) by virtue of provisions contained in the undertaking's articles, or
      (ii) by virtue of a control contract, or
   (d) it is a member of the undertaking and controls alone, pursuant to an agreement with other shareholders or members, a majority of the voting rights in the undertaking.
(3) For the purposes of subsection (2) an undertaking shall be treated as a member of another undertaking—
   (a) if any of its subsidiary undertakings is a member of that undertaking, or
   (b) if any shares in that other undertaking are held by a person acting on behalf of the undertaking or any of its subsidiary undertakings.
(4) An undertaking is also a parent undertaking in relation to another undertaking, a subsidiary undertaking, if—
   (a) it has the power to exercise, or actually exercises, dominant influence or control over it, or
   (b) it and the subsidiary undertaking are managed on a unified basis.

(5) A parent undertaking shall be treated as the parent undertaking of undertakings in relation to which any of its subsidiary undertakings are, or are to be treated as, parent undertakings; and references to its subsidiary undertakings shall be construed accordingly.
(6) Schedule 7 contains provisions explaining expressions used in this section and otherwise supplementing this section.
(7) In this section and that Schedule references to shares, in relation to an undertaking, are to allotted shares.' (s. 1162)

TEST YOUR KNOWLEDGE 2.2

(a) What is the essential difference between a limited and unlimited company?
(b) In what circumstances are overseas companies required to register in the UK?
(c) What is a corporate group?
(d) Is a parent company the same as a holding company?
(e) Is it necessary for all the shares of Company A to be owned by Company B for Company A to be a subsidiary of Company B? If not, what is the test for subsidiary status?

Public and private companies

As stated above, companies limited by shares may be public or private companies. The principal legal difference between public (plc) and private companies (Ltd or Limited) is that public companies may offer their shares to the public. A private company may not offer its shares to the public (Companies Act 2006, s. 755). The main differences between public and private limited companies are set out in Table 2.1.

TABLE 2.1 Key legal differences between private (Ltd) and public (plc) limited companies

Difference	Companies Act 2006
Ltd cannot offer shares to the public	s. 755
Ltd can have one director, plc needs a minimum of two	s. 154
No authorised minimum nominal value of allotted share capital for Ltds, £50,000 for plcs of which a minimum of 25% must be paid up	ss. 761 and 763
Plc needs a trading certificate before it can do business or exercise any borrowing powers	s. 761
A different set of model articles exists for private companies limited by shares and public companies	s. 19(2) and regulations made thereunder
Ltd need not hold AGMs; only needs meetings to remove directors pursuant to s. 168 or remove auditors pursuant to s. 510	N/A
Ltds need not have a company secretary	s. 270
Ltd can pass written resolutions of shareholders	ss. 288–300
Ltds can give financial assistance for the purchase of their own shares	N/A
Ltds can purchase and redeem shares out of capital	s. 710
Ltds can reduce their share capital without court approval by special resolution and a solvency certificate	ss. 641–43
Ltds can, if they meet the criteria, qualify for the small companies regime for accounts and reports and/or for the small company exemption from audit; plcs do not qualify for either (ss. 384 and 478)	s. 381 (accounts) s. 477 (audit)

Quoted companies

Quoted company is the term used in the Companies Act 2006 to identify registered companies with (in simple terms) equity shares traded on a UK or other European regulated market or one of the two most well-known US stock markets, the New York Stock Exchange and NASDAQ (see Companies Act 2006, s. 385 for the precise definition of quoted company). Quoted companies are illustrated in Figure 2.2. They are subject to enhanced disclosure requirements under the 2006 Act, such as in the business review in its directors' report (see s. 417(5)).

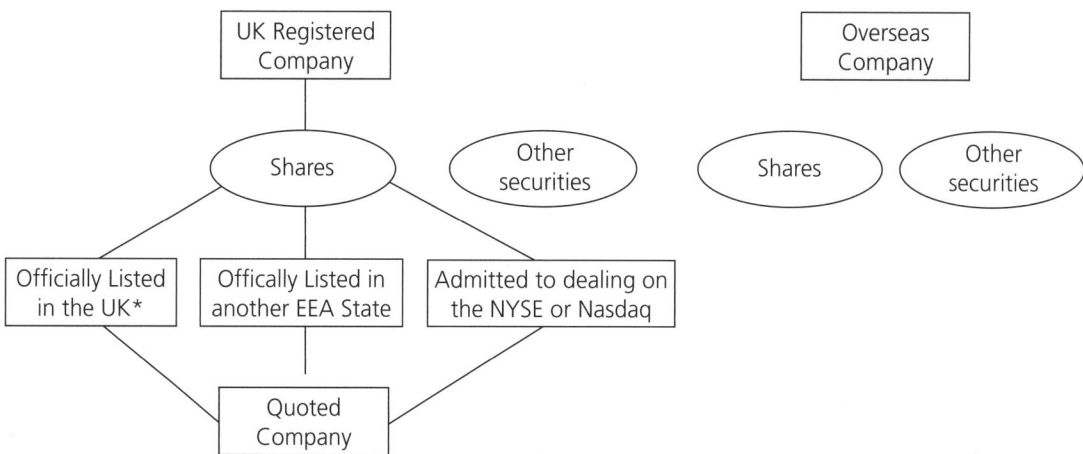

* Note that the two UK markets for officially listed shares are the London Stock Exchange Main Market and the ISDX Main Board Market

FIGURE 2.2 Quoted companies (Companies Act 2006 s.385)

Traded companies

The concept of the **traded company** was introduced into the Companies Act 2006 with effect from August 2009 as part of implementation in the UK of the Shareholder Rights Directive (2007/36/EC) (by The Companies (Shareholders' Rights) Regulations 2009 (S.I. 2009/1632)). It is a company with shares that carry the right to vote at a general meeting admitted to trading on a UK or other European regulated market (s. 360C). It is relevant to laws governing shareholder resolutions and meetings.

Listed companies

The term **listed company** is not defined in statute. If you use it, it is essential to state the meaning you have given to the term and the purpose for which you are using it. In the Glossary to the FSA Handbook, for example, listed company is defined as a company that has any class of its securities listed (i.e. included on an official list). Whilst this definition applies to the use of the term in the Listing Rules it does not apply to the use of the term in the Disclosure or Prospectus Rules. When read, the meaning should always be checked.

Listed securities

In European Union securities law, the term 'listed' attaches to a particular security, such as a class of shares or a class of debt securities issued by a company. In the UK, 'listed securities' are defined in the FSMA as securities admitted to the UK Official List (see s. 103). The UK Official List is a list of securities maintained by the FCA, acting as the UK competent authority (also referred to a 'listing authority'), pursuant to the FSMA, s. 74. A security is only admitted to the Official List following a successful application to the FCA (s. 75).

The FCA will not admit a security to the Official List unless it has been accepted for trading on a regulated market for listed securities. The most important of those markets is the London Stock Exchange Main Market but it is not the only one. The only other regulated market for equities in the UK at the time of writing is the ICAP Securities & Derivatives Exchange Main Board (the ISDX Main Board). A company seeking to have its securities admitted to the Official List must:

- comply with the Listing Rules published by the FCA; and
- obtain the security's admission to trading on a regulated market for listed securities (the London Stock Exchange Main Market or the ICAP Securities & Derivatives Exchange Main Board).

To summarise, all companies with securities officially listed in the UK need to comply with the Listing Rules promulgated by the FCA pursuant to the FSMA and with the rules imposed by the regulated market on which the securities are admitted to trading. The relevant rules of the LSE Main Market are the LSE Admission and Disclosure Standards.

STOP AND THINK 2.1

Historically, the UK competent authority, or listing authority, was the London Stock Exchange (LSE). Now, the FCA is the UK competent authority for EU purposes. It is the FCA that maintains the official list rather than the LSE. In a discussion paper in 2008 the FSA described two principal consequences arising from this change following which the concept of 'listed security' is no longer the exclusive preserve of the LSE.

'First, there is considerable scope for confusion about what the term "Listing" means in the UK. In most jurisdictions, it is synonymous with admission to trading on an exchange, whereas in the UK, admission to the Official List and admission to trading are different (although linked) concepts. Second, although historically long-associated with the London Stock Exchange's (LSE) Main Market, the Official List is not in fact ... linked to any single trading platform or venue.'

A Review of the Structure of the Listing Regime
(Discussion Paper 08/01: January 2008)

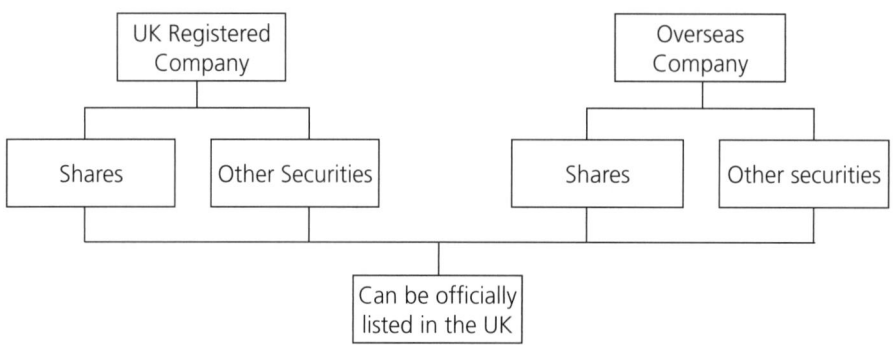

FIGURE 2.3 Listed securities

TEST YOUR KNOWLEDGE 2.3

(a) Identify 12 key differences between private and public companies.
(b) Which of the differences identified in (a) do you consider to be the most important difference?
(c) What is a quoted company?
(d) What does the term 'listed security' mean and where is it defined?
(e) What types of listing can equity shares have on a regulated market such as the London Stock Exchange?

Small and medium-sized companies

The Companies Act categorised registered companies into small companies, medium-sized companies and other companies for the purposes of determining a company's audit, accounts and reporting obligations under the Act. The definitions of small and medium-sized company are summarised in Figure 2.4. The requirement that a small company satisfy both the balance sheet and annual turnover thresholds to qualify for audit exemption has been removed by the Companies and Limited Liability Partnerships (Accounts and Audit Exemptions and Change of Accounting Framework) Regulations 2012 (SI 2012/ 2301).

Medium-sized company:

Must satisfy two out of three of the following (s. 465):

- ≤ £25.9m annual turnover;
- ≤ £12.9m balance sheet;
- ≤ 250 employees.

To take advantage of the accounts & reports rules for medium-sized companies, a company must also be a private company (s. 467).

Small company:

Must satisfy two out of three of the following (s. 382):

- ≤ £6.5m annual turnover;
- ≤ £3.26 balance sheet;
- ≤ 50 employees.

To take advantage of the accounts & reports small companies regime, must also be a private company (s. 384).

To be exempt from filing a directors report with the registrar, must also be a private company (s. 415A)

To be exempt from audit, must satisfy both turnover and balance sheet tests, and be a private company.

FIGURE 2.4 Small and medium-sized companies for Companies Act 2006 purposes

Key legal characteristics of registered companies

The registered company is believed to have become popular because, since 1862, it has offered businesses the following five attractive characteristics:

- separate legal personality;
- limited liability;
- transferable shares;
- a legal framework designed to pre-empt and provide remedies for problems arising out of the separation of ownership (by shareholders) and control (by the board of directors); and
- asset shielding.

Separate legal personality and limited liability
Separate legal personality and limited liability are considered in chapter 4. However, it should be noted that in relation to private companies, significant limits to the enjoyment of these characteristics exist in practice. The fundamental rule that a shareholder is not liable for the debts and liabilities of a company, for example, is regularly contractually undermined by the creditors of a private company requiring the shareholders to guarantee the company's liabilities.

This practice does not undermine the principles of separate personality or limited liability in legal theory but it does go a long way to removing their beneficial consequences.

Transferable shares
The transferability of shares, famously confirmed by Buckley LJ in *Re Discoverers Finance Corporation Ltd, Lindlar's Case* [1910] 1 Ch 312, is now stated in the Companies Act 2006, s. 544(1). Provisions in a private company's constitution often carefully limit a shareholder's right to transfer shares. Even in the absence of such constitutional or contractual limits on the right of a member to sell his or her shares, it is often very difficult to sell shares in a private company because they cannot be offered to the public, they are difficult to value, they are usually regarded as a speculative investment carrying significant risk and anybody buying them will face the same problems finding a buyer when they come to sell the shares.

Internal dispute resolution
Essentially, company law was originally designed (and to this day in large part remains designed) to deal with companies controlled by one group of individuals, the directors, and owned by a different, larger group of individuals, the shareholders. Management of a registered company is invariably vested not in the shareholders (the owners) but in the board of directors. Shareholders have limited powers to direct the board on specific points and can remove one or more of the directors, or the entire board, so it is sometimes said that shareholders retain 'residual' control. In reality, this separation of ownership and control is largely irrelevant to most small companies because the directors are the shareholders.

For large companies, the legal framework of company law and, increasingly, securities law, facilitates exploitation of the benefits of having professional managers running a business funded by 'investor' shareholders. The main interest of a shareholder with a small shareholding in a large company is to receive a dividend each year and to benefit from an increase in value of his or her shares which value can be realised by selling the shares to a third party, ideally on a stock market.

Asset shielding
The fact that the assets of a company are shielded from the claims of the personal creditors of shareholders is a characteristic of the registered company that has received increasing attention in recent years. The benefit this brings is not enjoyed by the shareholder directly, but by the company and its creditors. If a personal creditor of a shareholder wishes to realise the value of the shareholders' interest in a company, the company cannot be made to pay out any money to the shareholder. In this way, the finances of the company are protected from the insolvency of the owners, something which reduces the risk of doing business with a company, and therefore, it is argued, promotes efficient commerce.

Small private companies
In light of the discussion above, it may be asked: what are the principal benefits of incorporation to private or small companies? Ease of contracting and the protection from unlimited liability to trade creditors that separate legal personality offers should not be overlooked. Two further benefits that are often influential in an individual choosing to establish a company rather than using another legal structure of business organisation are:

- customer protection from employer obligations; and
- tax planning opportunities.

The first of these is touched upon at the end of section 1.1. The second is illustrated by contrasting a business run by a sole trader and the same business being run by a company established by an otherwise would-be sole trader. The profits of the business run by the sole trader are income of the sole trader in the year in which they arise. They are added to other taxable income of the sole trader and the aggregate sum is subject to income tax. There is little, if any, scope for tax planning to minimise taxes.

In contrast, the profits of the company can be dealt with in a variety of ways. The value that the profits represent can be transferred to the owner of the company and/or people close to him who have been issued with shares in the company as dividends, capital gains, or above-market rate remuneration for services or interest on loans made to the company.

TEST YOUR KNOWLEDGE 2.4

(a) Describe five key characteristics of a registered limited company.
(b) What does the term 'asset shielding' mean and why is it important to company shareholders and creditors?

2.3 Limited liability partnerships

The limited liability partnership (LLP) combines the organisational flexibility and tax status of a partnership with limited liability for its members and entity shielding for creditors. It exists due to intense lobbying by the accountancy profession. Accountants sought, and in the LLP have secured, protection from unlimited liability, particularly in relation to auditing service shortcomings. Companies that have not been audited properly may sue the company's auditors (see chapter 11).

LLPs are incorporated organisations governed by the Limited Liability Partnerships Act 2000 and detailed regulations which in large part adapt and apply provisions of the Companies Acts 2006 and the Insolvency Act 1986 to LLPs. An amended version of the Limited Liability Partnerships Regulations 2001 (SI 2001/1090) remains in force but the main regulations are now the Limited Liability Partnerships (Application of Companies Act 2006) Regulations 2009 (SI 2009/1804) which apply to LLPs the Companies Act 2006 provisions relating to:

- the formalities of doing business;
- names and trading disclosures;
- registered offices;
- the register of directors and protection from disclosure of residential addresses;
- debentures;
- annual returns;
- the registration of charges;
- arrangements and reconstructions;
- fraudulent trading;
- protection of members against unfair prejudice;
- dissolution and restoration to the register; and
- the registrar of companies.

Specific regulations apply the accounts and audit provisions of the 2006 Act to LLPs, with modification (see The Limited Liability Partnerships (Accounts and Audit) (Application of Companies Act 2006) Regulations 2008 (SI 2008/1911) as amended). The special reports and accounts regimes for small companies (on the one hand) and medium and large companies have also been adapted and applied to LLPs.

LLPs are separate legal entities from their members yet they are 'tax-transparent'. This means that HMRC looks through the LLP, ignoring its existence for tax purposes, and treats the profits of the LLP business as if they have been earned by the members of the LLP, just as in an ordinary partnership. The limited liability of members of an LLP mirrors the liability of a shareholder in a limited company. This is achieved by the version of s. 74 of the Insolvency Act 1986 applicable to LLPs (as substituted by reg. 4(2)(f) and sch. 3 of the Limited Liability Partnership Regulations 2001 (SI 2001/1090)):

> 'When a limited liability partnership is wound up every present and past member of the limited liability partnership who has agreed with the other members or with the limited liability partnership that he will, in circumstances which have arisen, be liable to contribute to the assets of the limited liability partnership in the event that the limited liability partnership

goes into liquidation is liable, to the extent that he has so agreed, to contribute to its assets to any amount sufficient for payment of its debts and liabilities, and the expenses of the winding up, and for the adjustment of the rights of the contributories among themselves.

However, a past member shall only be liable if the obligation arising from such agreement survived his ceasing to be a member of the limited liability partnership.'

LLPs offer the benefits of asset shielding and continue in existence notwithstanding the death or resignation of a member. For a number of reasons a member is unlikely to be able to exit with the ease with which shareholders can exit a company with publicly traded shares. Even were the LLP agreement to permit transfer, a member is likely to find difficulty finding a buyer for his interest. Provisions in the LLP agreement are likely to preclude transfer and contain provisions governing the rights of an exiting member to withdraw his or her investments.

TEST YOUR KNOWLEDGE 2.5

(a) What is the difference between a limited partnership and a limited liability partnership?
(b) What is meant by the term 'tax-transparent'?
(c) Name two key attractions of an LLP to a professional practice.
(d) In what circumstance is an LLP not available for use to run a business or professional practice but a registered company is available?
(e) Why would an entrepreneur choose to structure a business as an LLP rather than a registered private company?

3 Social enterprise private legal structures

A great deal of definitional uncertainty exists in the world of 'social enterprise' or the 'third sector'. The terms are generally used to describe organisations that are neither run purely for profit nor are government organisations. A wide range of legal structures are used by social enterprise organisations and the aim of this section is simply to introduce the more common legal structures that are not used in the private for-profit sector.

3.1 Unincorporated associations

The term 'unincorporated association' is often used to refer to unincorporated organisations which are neither sole traders nor partnerships.

In *Conservative & Unionist Central Office v Burrell* [1982] 1 WLR 522 (CA), Lawton LJ described an unincorporated association as:

'... two or more persons bound together for one or more common purposes, not being business purposes, by mutual undertakings, each having mutual duties and obligations, in an organisation which has rules which identify in whom control of it and its funds rests and upon what terms and which can be joined or left at will.'

Although useful in that it identifies key characteristics required before a contractual arrangement between individuals will be regarded as establishing an 'association', this definition was stated for the purposes of tax legislation and is probably a narrower definition than that usually assumed when the term unincorporated associations is used. In fact, many unincorporated associations do engage in business. The point to note is that unincorporated associations rarely engage in business purely to make profits; they tend to be 'not-for-profit' organisations.

Typical examples of unincorporated associations are sports or other social clubs and cooperatives. They are usually run to further social, environmental or cultural objectives for the benefit of their members, the local community or the public generally. Many of them are charities. Those which can be said to be engaged in business fall into what the government refers to as the 'third sector': non-governmental organisations which exist to reinvest the surpluses they make (or at least a part of those surpluses) to further their objectives (rather than to distribute profits to members or investors).

A number of legal problems stem from an unincorporated association not having a separate legal personality. The basic legal points to note relate to property ownership, criminal liability, tort liability and the ability to benefit from and be bound by contracts.

Property ownership

An unincorporated association cannot own property. The legal title to property will usually vest in one, several or all of the members on trust for the benefit of the members.

Criminal liability

The exposure of unincorporated associations to criminal liability depends on whether the crime is a common law or statutory offence. An unincorporated association is incapable of being liable for a common law offence because of its lack of separate personality. A number of statutes, however, treat unincorporated associations as persons that can commit statutory offences.

Tort liability

Where a third party has a tortious claim against an unincorporated association, they can name the unincorporated association and its office bearers as the defendants to the legal claim. In the reported English law cases in which action has been brought, the funds of the unincorporated association (including, crucially, access to insurance payments) have been sufficient to pay the claim in full. If the funds were to be inadequate, it remains unclear whether the members would be held to be jointly and severally liable. A member of an unincorporated association may be surprised to know that they may be sued for a sum that may be substantially in excess of the amount of any subscriptions they have agreed to pay. Again, this lack of clarity renders the law unsatisfactory.

Where a member of an unincorporated association seeks to bring an action in tort, for example, for damages suffered either due to the state of the association's premises or the negligence of another association member (who may or may not be a member of the committee), the courts have found that neither general members nor the management committee members are vicariously liable for the negligently caused injury.

Contracts

An unincorporated association is not a separate entity in law and therefore cannot enter into a contract. The law relating to unincorporated association contracts is very unclear and consequently unsatisfactory.

Depending upon the facts, a person seeking to supply an unincorporated association with goods or services will contract with all, a number of, or one of the members. That member is/those members are usually a member/s of the management committee of the unincorporated association. They will be bound by the contract based on having expressly or impliedly authorised the person who signs or otherwise performs the act of agreeing to the contract to bind them (see *Steele v Gourley* (1886) 3 TLR 118). The personal liability of the treasurer and member of the management committee of a rugby club under a contract entered into for building work at the club was confirmed in *Davies v Barnes Webster & Sons Ltd* (unreported) (2011).

Turning to employees, in *Affleck v Newcastle Mind* [1999] ICR 852 (EAT), the employment contract of an employee of an unincorporated association was held to have been made with 'the management committee and its members for the time being'. The rights of an employee of an unincorporated association remain to this day surprisingly unexplored.

Turning finally to contracts between a member and an unincorporated association, the membership contract appears to exist between all the members *inter se*, even though they are very often unlikely to know who the other members are (see *Lee v Showmen's Guild* [1952] 2 QB 329 at 341). Where a member purports to contract with the unincorporated assoaniation, for example, by purchasing a drink at his social club's bar, the legal analysis is not always as straightforward as one might think. The member who buys a drink at the bar, for example, is not buying the drink from the club. Rather, the other members of the club are relinquishing their interest in the drink in consideration of the payment (see *Carlton Lodge Club v C&E Commissioners* [1975] 1 WLR 66 (CA)).

3.2 Charitable incorporated organisations

Charities are established using a number of different legal structures, both unincorporated and incorporated. While it is possible to establish a charity as a company limited by shares, this is extremely unusual and most incorporated charities are companies limited by guarantee. Note, however, that charities often own companies limited by shares through which they run businesses for the benefit of the parent charity. Profits of the registered company are paid out to the charity, as the shareholder dividends.

A new form of company specifically designed for charities, the **charitable incorporated organisation (CIO)** is now available under the Charities Act 2011 and implementing regulations (see, in particular, The Charitable Incorporated Organisations (General) Regulations 2012 (SI 2012/3012)). The principal benefit is that charities wishing to benefit from a corporate (rather than unincorporated) structure will be able to register a CIO with the Charity Commission, allowing them to deal with only one regulator rather than two, as has previously been the case, with charities adopting a corporate structure in the past having to register as a charity with the Charity Commission and also a registered company with the Registrar of Companies. The single regulator module is expected to lead to more small and medium-sized charities adopting a corporate form than would otherwise be the case.

3.3 Community interest companies

The **community interest company (CIC)** is a corporate vehicle introduced in October 2004 as a unique legal structure to assist social enterprise, that is, organisations that combine social purpose with commercial activities. They are governed by a combination of the Companies Act 2006 and Part 2 of the Companies (Audit, Investigations and Community Enterprise) Act 2004. CICs are formed by registering (with the Registrar of Companies at Companies House) a public or private company limited by shares or guarantee which satisfies additional regulations, compliance with which is supervised by the Regulator of Community Interest Companies. CICs cannot be registered as charities.

In comparison to a non-CIC registered company, a CIC has three main additional characteristics:

1 It must be carried on for the benefit of the community.
2 It is subject to an 'asset lock', a general term to describe various restrictions on profits and assets designed to ensure that it is being run for the benefit of the community.
3 It must file community interest annual reports which are available to the public.

3.4 UK mutual organisations

'Mutual organisation' is not a specifically defined term. It is used most often to refer to an organisation, whether incorporated or not, run for the benefit of its members, who are its customers, rather than an organisation run to provide services for one group, its customers, from which to make profits for another group, its shareholders. Organisations run for the benefit of both members and the public, and even organisations run for the benefit of persons other than its members are also sometimes included under the 'mutual organisations' rubric.

Mutual organisations can be established using different legal structures, including the registered company. In the UK a number of insurers, such as the NFU Mutual and the Police Mutual Assurance, are mutual organisations, as are a number of financial organisations such as building societies, credit unions and friendly societies, each of which is considered briefly below.

As part of its role as registrar of mutual societies, the FCA maintains a 'mutuals register'. This is a public record of industrial and provident societies, building societies, credit unions and the various kinds of society registered under the Friendly Societies Acts.

In the Coalition Agreement, the Government stated its desire to promote mutuals and the Treasury was tasked to develop policy to help to achieve this aim. Two pieces of legislation have followed, the Co-operative and Community Benefit Societies and Credit Unions Act 2010 and the Legislative Reform (Industrial and Provident Societies and Credit Unions) Order 2011 (2011 No 2687). The 2010 Act, providing (among other things) for industrial and provident societies to be renamed, being known in the future as either cooperatives or community benefit societies, is yet to be commenced. The 2011 Order, which is in force in part, introduces changes designed to give more flexibility and broaden the scope of activity available to industrial and provident societies and credit unions, allowing them to grow larger and operate with fewer legal constraints.

Industrial and provident societies

A society qualifies for registration as an industrial and provident society under the Industrial and Provident Society Act 1965 if it has at least three members, runs a business and either is a *bona fide* cooperative or that business is run for the benefit of the community. The society also has to demonstrate that there are special reasons why it should not be registered as a company under the Companies Acts before it will be registered under the 1965 Act. 'Community' in this context means persons other than its own members, which distinguishes industrial and provident societies from mutual organisations run for the benefit of members only. The principal benefits of registration are that the society obtains incorporated status and its members have limited liability.

The registering authority for organisations registered under the Industrial and Provident Societies Act 1965 is the FCA, but note that this role is separate and distinct from the FCA's role under the FSMA. If an industrial and provident society has charitable objects, it is an exempt charity and is not required to register with the Charity Commission. Working men's clubs, benevolent societies and specially-authorised societies registered under the Friendly Societies Act 1974 are permitted to re-register as industrial and provident societies.

Friendly societies

The FCA defines a friendly society as: 'a voluntary mutual organisation whose main purpose is to assist members (usually financially) during sickness, unemployment or retirement, and to provide life assurance'.

This definition excludes working men's clubs, benevolent societies and specially authorised societies that were also permitted to register under the Friendly Societies Act 1974. Since 1993, no new friendly societies have been permitted to register (Friendly Societies Act 1992) and working men's clubs, benevolent societies and specially authorised societies previously permitted to register under the Friendly Societies legislation may now register as industrial and provident societies and thereby achieve corporate status and limited liability. Having grown in number prior to the establishment of the welfare state to provide financial assistance to people in ill health or old age, there are now only about 200 friendly societies in existence, typically offering small-scale financial services, including insurance and savings plans. Friendly societies are not incorporated.

Credit unions

Credit unions are incorporated entities with limited liability registered under the Industrial and Provident Societies Act 1965 as credit unions in accordance with the Credit Unions Act 1979. As their name suggests, credit unions lend money to their members. Consequently, they are subject to FCA regulation under the FSMA.

Building societies

Building societies are regulated by the FCA, which took over the functions of the Building Societies Commissioner following enactment of the FSMA. Building societies become incorporated on being registered and issued with a certificate of incorporation pursuant to the Building Societies Act 1986 (as extensively amended). The 1986 Act governs building societies in much the same way as the Companies Act 2006 governs registered companies. It regulates, for example, the constitution, governance, purpose and public disclosures required of building societies.

Section 5(1) of the 1986 Act states that an organisation may register as a building society if and only if 'Its purpose or principal purpose is that of making loans which are secured on residential property and are funded substantially by its members'. Following deregulation in 1994 and 1997 many building societies expanded into a wider range of financial products making them very similar in their product offerings to banks. Like banks, they fund loans by borrowing on the wholesale money markets, although they are limited by s. 7 of the 1986 Act which requires 50% of lending to be funded by member deposits.

Building societies are owned by their members, hence they are mutual organisations. Members who are indebted to the building society are called 'borrowing members' and those with savings deposited are called 'shareholding members'. The liability of building society members is limited (Building Societies Act 1986, para. 6 of sch. 2 and para. 7(4) of sch. 15).

TEST YOUR KNOWLEDGE 2.6

(a) What is an unincorporated association and in what circumstances does it usually exist?
(b) What type of registered company is typically used by charities?
(c) What are the three key additional regulatory requirements for a registered company to be a community interest company?
(d) Name four different types of organisations that fall into the category of UK mutual organisations.

4 European organisation legal structures

The European Commission has proposed a number of pan-European forms of organisation. Forms of business organisation have been proposed (and two adopted) as part of its programme of company law reform (which is part of the European Commission's efforts to make a single market a reality in the European Union). Forms of 'social enterprise' enterprises, on the other hand, have been proposed under the European Commission's social economy programme (one of the principal concerns of which is the level of employment within the European Community).

4.1 European business organisation structures

The European Union has established two pan-European corporate forms and the European Commission has issued a draft Regulation for a third.

European Economic Interest Group (EEIG)

A European Economic Interest Group (EEIG) is a legal entity separate from its members that has been available since 1989. Members may be individuals or other business organisations, the condition for membership being that each member carries on business within the EU with its principal administration within the EU and, if it is not an individual, is an entity formed in accordance with the laws of a Member State with its registered offices in the EU. At least two members must be from different Member States.

The EEIG is available to those carrying on businesses (in its widest sense) in different Member States who wish to work more closely together but do not wish to merge or have one business organisation take over the other, or, perhaps a merger is too expensive or difficult. It can be seen as a type of joint venture although it is different from the typical joint ventures in the UK, which are:

- corporate vehicle joint ventures (in which two or more business organisations establish a jointly owned company to pursue a shared venture); or
- contractual joint ventures (in which two or more business organisations enter into a contract governing their respective rights and obligations in relation to a joint business venture).

EEIGs are not established to make profit themselves, but to facilitate their members' profit-making by facilitating cross-border cooperation. Like LLPs, even though they are separate legal entities and can enter into contracts and own property, they are tax-transparent. Unlike LLPs and most registered companies, however, the members of an EEIG do not benefit from limited liability. Members are jointly and severally liable for the debts and other liabilities of the EEIG. EEIGs are registered with the company's registrar in a Member State. Very few have been registered at Companies House. The governing primary legislation is EC Regulation 2137/85. The original governing UK regulations, the European Economic Interest Grouping Regulations 1989 (SI 1989/638), have been extensively updated and amended by the European Economic Interest Grouping (Amendment) Regulations 2009 (SI 2009/2399). Examples of where an EEIG might be used are where research companies in different Member States cooperate in a large research project, or where producers of complementary products in different Member States launch a joint marketing operation.

European public limited liability company or societas europaea

European Union plans in the 1970s to create a European supra-national company registration system allowing for incorporation of supra-national European companies not registered in any particular Member State proved to be premature. The organisational entity ultimately made available as a result of this initiative is the European public limited liability company, or societas europaea (SE). It has been possible to register an SE with a Member State company registrar since 8 October 2004.

SEs have not proved popular to date, with only a handful registered with the Registrar of Companies after more than a decade. In 2011, a European Commission report on the future of EU company law recognised the need for simplification if the SE is to become a viable alternative to national companies.

This limited use of the SE form of organisation is due in part to the limited circumstances in which an SE can be formed. SEs may be formed:

- by merging two or more companies registered in at least two different Member States (different Member State companies (DMSCs));
- as a holding company of two or more DMSCs;
- as a subsidiary of two or more DMSCs; or
- by transforming into an SE a company that has had a subsidiary in a different Member State for at least two years.

The SE is a separate legal person, treated as if formed under the laws of the Member State in which it is registered. The SE allows the parent company of a corporate group operating in more than one Member State to be governed by a single applicable law. That law is found in part in EC Regulation 2157/2001 (supplemented by Directive 2001/86/EC), but the applicable law is in large part the law of the Member State in which the SE is registered. In the UK that is the European Public Limited Liability Company Regulations 2004 (SI 2004/2326), as extensively updated and amended by the European Public Limited-Liability Company (Amendment) Regulations 2009 (SI 2009/2400).

European private limited liability company or societas privata europaea

The European Commission 2003 Action Plan announced that a feasibility study should be undertaken to determine the need for a European Private Company (SPE). Such a form could assist both large corporate groups wishing to reduce the costs of administering their groups of subsidiaries in Europe and SMEs seeking to operate in more than one Member State.

The feasibility study apparently showed that stakeholders are divided as to whether there is such a need as well as on the scope and content of an SPE proposal. Nonetheless, the European Parliament adopted a resolution in 2007 requesting the EU Commission to draw up an SPE Regulation which, following two consultations (part of the EU Commission's impact assessment) it did in June 2008: the EU Commission Proposal for a Council Regulation on the Statute for a European private company (COM 2008 396/3). The progress of this proposal can be followed on the Europa Internal Market Company Law and Corporate Governance website.

4.2 European social economy entity structures

As at January 2013, the only pan-European social economy entity structure proposed by the European Commission to have been adopted is the European Co-operative Society (SCE). It is stated on Europa that the EU Commission is in continuous dialogue with the cooperatives, mutuals, associations and foundations in Europe (CMAF or social economy) through dialogue with 'Social Economy Europe' (SEE) which is the EU-level representative institution for the social economy. SEE considers its role as including strengthening the legal recognition of social economy structures. Proposals put forward by the European Commission are outlined below.

European Co-operative Society

European Co-operative Societies are provided for by Council Regulation (EC) No 1435/2003 of 22 July 2003 on the Statute for a European Cooperative Society (SCE), together with a supplementing Council Directive 2003/72/EC regarding the involvement of employees.

Based on the SE model, the regulation provides for SCEs to be separate legal entities registered with the companies' registrar in one Member State with members from more than one Member State. The essential difference between an SCE and an SE is that the main object of an SCE must be the satisfaction of its members' needs (or the development of their economic and social activities), rather than pursuit of profit to pay for capital investment.

European Association and European Mutual Society

Proposals for a pan-European form for associations and mutual societies originated in the European Commission's social economy programme rather than part of the European Commission's internal market/company law programme. Nonetheless, in its 2003 Action Plan on company law, the European Commission expressed its intention to actively support development of new European legal forms for these entities. Support was withdrawn, however, when the European Commission reviewed the Action Plan in 2004/5 and proposed regulations were withdrawn.

European Foundation

European Foundations are organisations the activities of which focus on the public benefit. Examples of typical areas of activity are social and health services, fostering research and promoting culture, including by awarding grants and running projects. The European Commission's Proposal for a Council Regulation on the Statute for a European Foundation (FE) (COM(2012) 35 final) received backing from the European Economic and Social Committee in September 2012 and is under consideration by the European Parliament and the Council of Ministers of the EU. The European Foundation entity proposed is an incorporated entity with a public benefit purpose. Details can be found in the documents accessible from the Europa European Foundations website.

TEST YOUR KNOWLEDGE 2.7

(a) What is an EEIG?
(b) Briefly describe a European Public Limited Liability Company.
(c) What is the current status of proposals for a European Private Limited Liability Company?
(d) How does an SCE differ from an SE?

CHAPTER SUMMARY

- Key unincorporated business organisations legal structures are: sole traders (no governing act; no limited liability; can employ others); partnerships (governed by the Partnership Act 1890; participation of non-managing limited partners possible: Limited Partnership Act 1907).
- Unincorporated associations are used for non-profit enterprises.
- Key incorporated business organisation legal structures are chartered and statutory companies, registered companies and limited liability partnerships:
  - chartered and statutory companies are largely long-standing organisations; new corporations are virtually exclusively formed as registered companies;
  - limited rather than unlimited companies are used for business enterprises;
  - public companies can offer shares to the public. Private companies cannot (s. 755) and are subject to a less stringent regulatory regime;
  - public companies are not all companies with listed securities;
  - super-equivalent listing standards apply to all companies (whether UK or overseas) with a premium listing on the London Stock Exchange.
- Limited Liability Partnerships are governed by the Limited Liability Partnerships Act 2000; are tax-transparent but otherwise separate legal entities from the members.
- Overseas companies with a UK establishment must register with the Registrar of Companies (s. 1046).

- Key social enterprise private legal structures are: unincorporated associations (the governing law is very underdeveloped); charitable incorporated organisations (provided for in the Charities Act 2011); community interest companies (CICs) (governed by Companies Act 2006 and Part 2 of the Companies (Audit, Investigations and Community Enterprise) Act 2004) and mutual organisations (which includes industrial and provident societies, friendly societies, credit unions and building societies).
- European Economic Interest Groups (EEIGs) and the Societas Europaea (SEs) (a pan-European Public Limited Company vehicle) have not proved popular.
- A proposal exists to establish a pan-European Private Limited Company vehicle, the Societas Privata Europaea (SPE).

3 Promoters and company formation

■ **CONTENTS**

1. Promoters
2. Pre-incorporation contracts
3. Registering a UK company
4. Certificate of incorporation
5. Trading certificate
6. Company numbers and names
7. Re-registration of a UK company
8. Company registers and records: the statutory books and registers
9. Annual returns and reports and accounts

■ **INTRODUCTION**

In this chapter the role of the promoter of a company is examined, as are the legal difficulties presented by contracts entered into on behalf of a company before it comes into existence. The process for registering a company is examined and the legal requirement to keep basic registers and records (the statutory books and registers) is outlined as are the annual and periodic requirements to register reports and accounts.

1 Promoters

The term **promoter** is used to describe a person involved in setting up a company who is not purely providing professional or administrative services (such as a solicitor or an accountant) to those who are setting up the company (the incorporators). As Bowen LJ stated in *Whaley Bridge Calico Printing v Green* (1879) 5 QBD 109, 'promoter' is not a term of law but one of business. He stated that a promoter is a term 'usefully summing up in a single word a number of business operations familiar to the commercial world by which a company is generally brought into existence'.

A promoter is not necessarily involved in all stages of, or in all the tasks performed in, setting up a company and a promoter's role will vary with each individual project. Typical acts of a promoter are:

- raising the idea of forming a company for the purpose in question;
- soliciting the interest of others;
- finding directors, shareholders and other investors;
- acquiring business assets for use by the new company;
- negotiating business contracts on behalf of the new company.

The words of Cockburn CJ, in *Twycross v Grant* [1877], are often quoted to describe a promoter.

> 'one who undertakes to form a company with reference to a given project and to set it going and who takes the necessary steps to accomplish that purpose ... and so long as the work of formation continues, those who carry on that work must, I think, retain the character of promoters.'

In law, it is important to know whether or not a person is a promoter, and the points in time at which he first became and ceased to be a promoter, because the law regards a promoter as a fiduciary who owes duties of loyalty and good faith to the promoted company.

Older cases often involved one or more promoters personally acquiring property with a view to, and subsequently, selling that property at a substantial profit to the company they had promoted. Any profit made by promoters in this way is made as a result of their position as fiduciaries and, paralleling the position of trustees, is a breach of **fiduciary duty** unless the arrangements have been fully disclosed to, and consent has been obtained from, the 'beneficiary'. The difficulties the courts faced applying this basic fiduciary principle to promoters were in deciding what constituted full disclosure and whose consent was needed in the context of a newly-formed company with a board of directors, initial shareholders (the subscribers to the Memorandum who were often the promoters themselves) and additional shareholders who had joined the company as the result of shares being offered to the public by the issuing of a prospectus.

The courts found that if there was a board of directors independent from the promoters, the promoters could disclose their interest to the board and the board could decide on behalf of the company whether or not to purchase the promoters' property. Provided this happened, there was no breach of fiduciary duty by the promoters.

CASE LAW 3.1

***Erlanger v New Sombrero Phosphate Company* (1878) 3 App Cas 1218 (HL)**

The lease of a West Indies island was acquired for £55,000 by a syndicate of bankers headed by Erlanger. The lease was sold for £110,000, through a nominee company, to a company promoted by Erlanger. The purchase of the lease was 'ratified' without enquiry at a board meeting of the newly-formed company at which not all directors were present and only one director was independent of Erlanger. The public subscribed for shares without the real circumstances of the sale being disclosed to them. The sale of the lease was approved (without proper disclosure) at the first shareholders' meeting. The company's business went badly, the true facts were discovered, the original directors were removed and the new directors brought legal proceedings to have the sale of the lease to the company rescinded. Held: the contract should be set aside with an order for members of the syndicate to repay the purchase monies.

Lord Cairns stated:

'... it is ... incumbent upon the promoters to take care that in forming the company they provide it with an executive, that is, to say, with a board of directors, who shall both be aware that the property which they are asked to buy is the property of the promoters, and who shall be competent and impartial judges as to whether the purchase ought or ought not to be made. I do not say that the owner of the property may not promote and form a ... company, and then sell his property to it, but I do say that if he does he is bound that he sells it to the company through the medium of a board of directors who can and do exercise an independent judgment on the transaction and who are not left under the belief that the property belongs not to the promoter but to some other person.'

Where, as was often the case, there was no board of directors independent of the promoters, the promoters needed to make disclosure to the shareholders and secure their consent but this worked only if the shareholders were independent of the promoters. Full disclosure of the arrangements in a prospectus, so that any shareholder who decided to invest in the company did so with knowledge of the arrangements, was found to be enough to prevent a breach of fiduciary duty.

CASE LAW 3.2

***Lagunas Nitrate Co v Lagunas Syndicate* [1899] 2 Ch 392**
Two promoters were the only directors of a company and the first two shareholders (subscribers to the Memorandum). The company therefore did not have an independent board. A prospectus was published inviting members of the public to take shares in the company in which the interest of the promoters in the property they had sold to the company was made clear. The Court of Appeal held that there was no breach of fiduciary duty because there had been adequate disclosure.

The point in time at which a promoter acquires property that he subsequently sells to the company is relevant. If he acquires property before becoming a promoter and subsequently sells the property to a company he has promoted, the rights of the company are not wholly clear from the cases. If the promoter has not disclosed his interest, the company can rescind the contract. Where rescission is not possible, however (perhaps because the property cannot be returned to the promoter), the promoter is apparently not liable to account to the company for any profit he has made on the sale (*Re Lady Forrest (Murchison) Gold Mine Ltd* [1901] 1 Ch 582). Whether or not the company can claim equitable compensation to recoup its losses from the promoter is not clear. Conaglen (2003) argues that the promoter will be liable to pay equitable compensation.

STOP AND THINK 3.1

There are few if any modern cases about the fiduciary duties of promoters. The reason for this is that detailed securities regulations, including the Prospectus Rules, have resulted in the fiduciary duties of promoters no longer playing an important role in protecting prospective investors in companies. A parallel can be drawn with the importance of fiduciary duties in the prevention of insider dealing. Insider dealing regulation is now part of securities regulation and is driven, at least at EU level, by the desire for fair markets.

TEST YOUR KNOWLEDGE 3.1

(a) Identify five acts typically performed by a promoter.
(b) What have displaced fiduciary duties as the key protection for investors seeking to invest in companies?
(c) What, if any, remedies are available and to whom if a promoter sells property he owns personally to a newly-formed company he has promoted?

2 Pre-incorporation contracts

2.1 What is a pre-incorporation contract?

A pre-incorporation contract is a contract to which a company appears to be a party that has been entered into before the company has been registered. It is a contract made before the company exists.

Agency law, a combination of common law and equity, governed the rights of those involved in a pre-incorporation contract situation before EU law required the UK to legislate to change the law. Agency law stated that:

1 An agent cannot bind a non-existent principal.
2 If the company did not exist at the time a contract is entered into, the contract is not binding on the subsequently formed company.
3 A person who purports to contract on behalf of a non-existent company may or may not:
   (a) be personally liable pursuant to the contract;
   (b) have rights to sue the other party to the contract.
4 Whether or not a person is liable or has rights depends upon the real intent as revealed by the contract, that is, the correct construction of the contract. In the words of Oliver LJ, 'what we have to look at is whether the agent intended himself to be a party to the contract?' (*Phonogram Ltd v Lane* [1982] QB 938 (CA) at 945, approved in *Cotronic (UK) Ltd v Dezonie* [1991] BCC 200.)
5 The court finding in relation to intent often turned on the way in which the contract had been signed so that if the contract was signed 'on behalf of' a company, the person signing would usually be personally liable (see *Kelner v Baxter* (1866–67) LR 2 CP 174). If, however, the contract was signed as if the signatory was the company, such as a signature appearing above the printed company name, the signatory would not usually be liable (see *Newborne v Sensolid* [1954] 1 QB 45).
6 If the person is not personally liable under the contract, the third party may be able to sue him for breach of warranty of authority.

These rules involved fine distinctions being drawn and did not provide much protection to a third party who believed that he was contracting with the company. The law has been amended by what is now s. 51 of the Companies Act 2006, the predecessor provision of which was introduced to implement art. 7 of the First Company Law Directive (68/151/EEC). That Directive and s. 51 focus on protection of the third party.

'A contract that purports to be made by or on behalf of a company at a time when the company has not been formed has effect, *subject to any agreement to the contrary*, as one made with the person purporting to act for the company or as agent for it, and *he is personally liable on the contract* accordingly.' (s. 51(1); emphasis added)

2.2 What is meant by 'subject to any agreement to the contrary'?

Section 51 states that the person purporting to act for, or as agent of, the company is personally liable on the contract unless there is any agreement to the contrary. The meaning of these words was considered in a case involving the pop group Cheap, Mean and Nasty.

 **CASE LAW 3.3**

***Phonogram Ltd v Lane* [1982] QB 938 (CA)**
Lane negotiated with a record company, Phonogram Limited, to obtain a recording deal for the pop group Cheap, Mean and Nasty. He signed a contract with Phonogram Limited which provided for an advance of £6,000. He signed the contract 'for and on behalf of Fragile Management Limited'. The sum advanced became repayable and Phonogram Limited discovered that Fragile Management Limited had never existed. It sued Lane to recover the money, relying on the predecessor section to what is now s. 51 of the Companies Act 2006.

Held: Lane was ordered to repay the money. In the course of his judgment Lord Denning MR gave the words 'subject to any agreement to the contrary' a very narrow meaning:

> 'If there was an express agreement that the man who was signing was not to be liable, the section would not apply. But unless there is a clear exclusion of personal liability [s. 51(1)] should be given its full effect. It means that … where a person purports to contract on behalf of a company not yet formed, then however he expresses his signature he himself is personally liable on the contract.'

2.3 Can the person made liable by s. 51 enforce the contract?

Section 51(1) states that the person who purports to enter into the contract 'is personally liable on the contract' which, it has been argued, implies that the person cannot enforce the agreement. This interpretation of the statutory provision was rejected by Arden LJ in *Braymist Ltd v Wise Finance Co Ltd* [2002] Ch 273 (CA) in a judgment that examined the correct approach to the interpretation of 'domestic directive-based legislation'.

CASE LAW 3.4

Braymist Ltd v Wise Finance Co Ltd [2002] Ch 273 (CA)

A firm of solicitors, Sturges, signed a contract as agents on behalf of an as yet unregistered company, Braymist Ltd. The contract was an agreement for Braymist to sell land to Wise, a property developer. Wise changed its mind and did not want to perform the contract. Sturges sued to enforce the contract.

Held: Sturges was entitled to enforce the contract against Wise. Parliament did not intend to determine the rules and it is the common law rules that apply to determine whether a person who is made liable on a contract by (what is now) s. 51 is entitled to enforce the contract.

'As I see it, the purpose of [s. 51] was limited to: (i) complying with the UK treaty obligations to implement art. 7 of the Directive, (ii) removing the possibility that the agent would be held not liable on the ground that he merely confirmed the company's signature, and (iii) putting such persons or agents in the same position as regards the enforcement of the contract as they would be at common law and in particular (in the case of agents) this is the same position as agents who contracted as agents.'

2.4 Can a company ratify or adopt a pre-incorporation contract?

A company cannot unilaterally, by adoption or ratification, obtain the benefit of a contract purporting to have been made on its behalf before the company came into existence.

CASE LAW 3.5

Re Northumberland Avenue Hotel Co (1866) 33 Ch D 16 (CA)

Doyle, acting as agent for a hotel company, entered into an agreement with Wallis to lease certain property and build on it. The company was not incorporated until after the contract had been entered into. The articles of the company purported to adopt the contract, the company took possession of the land, and the company assumed that the contract was an existing and binding contract. The building was not completed, the company went into liquidation and Wallis claimed in the liquidation.

Held: The contract did not bind the company. Lopes LJ stated:

'It is ... clear that the company, after it came into existence, could not ratify that contract, because the company was not in existence at the time the contract was made. No doubt the company, after it came into existence, might have entered into a new contract upon the same terms as the agreement ... and we are asked to infer such a contract from the conduct and transactions of the company after it came into existence.'

This inability to ratify a pre-incorporation contract has been reversed in a number of common law jurisdictions but remains law in England, notwithstanding recommendations by the Jenkins Committee (Cmnd 1749, 1962) that it be reversed.

Note that if an off-the-shelf company is in existence at the time a contract was entered into, that company can ratify the contract and the signatory will not be liable pursuant to s. 51, provided, however, there is evidence that the off-the-shelf company was the company that was intended to be a party to the contract (see *Oshkosh B'Gosh Inc v Dan Marbel Inc Ltd* [1989] BCLC 507).

2.5 How can a company become a party to a pre-incorporation contract?

The answer to how a company can become a party to a pre-incorporation contract is found in *Braymist*.

> 'The United Kingdom's implementation of article 7 makes no reference to the possibility of the company enforcing the contract when it has been formed. Since so far as it was concerned the contract was a nullity it could only do this by entering into a contract of novation with the agent.'

Novation is a tripartite transaction in which the parties to the original agreement, together with the company, enter into a new agreement. Novation is usually achieved by all three parties signing a formal document. It is possible, however, for a new agreement to be found to exist based on evidence of changes to the contract having been agreed to by the company and the third party, such that the court is able to say that a new contract has come into existence, as was found in *Howard v Patent Ivory Manufacturing Co* (1888) 38 Ch D 156.

TEST YOUR KNOWLEDGE 3.2

(a) What is a pre-incorporation contract?
(b) What is the basic common law agency principle that applies to a contract purportedly entered into by a non-existent principal?
(c) What is the principle of law that came out of the litigation involving the pop group Cheap, Mean and Nasty?
(d) What was the practical issue at stake in *Braymist v Wise Finance Co Ltd* and how was it resolved?
(e) Is it possible for a company to adopt a pre-incorporation contract by the board of directors deciding to adopt it?

3 Registering a UK company

This section describes how to register a UK company under the Companies Act 2006.

3.1 Specialist company formation companies

Rather than dealing with Companies House directly, specialist company registration businesses can be found online offering to register companies on behalf of those seeking to set up a registered company (the incorporators). The key benefits of obtaining a company from a company registration business are simplicity and the saving of the time that would otherwise be taken familiarising oneself with the process and gathering together and completing the relevant information and forms.

The main shortcoming of companies obtained from a company registration business, and of self-registered companies, is that the constitution of the company, the articles of association will not be fully made to order or 'bespoked' to the needs of the incorporators. In many cases no attempt is made at all to reflect the wishes of the incorporators in the articles of association. Nonetheless, in 2000, the Company Law Review Steering Committee Group estimated that 60% of companies being registered were registered by specialist company formation companies.

3.2 Where to register

A 'UK company' is a company registered under the Companies Act 2006, s. 1183. Although reference is made throughout the Act, and in this text, to the Registrar of Companies, there are in fact three registrars (s. 1060):

APPLICATION TO REGISTER A COMPANY

In accordance with Section 9 of the Companies Act 2006.

IN01
Application to register a company

A fee is payable with this form.
Please see 'How to pay' on the last page.

✓ **What this form is for**
You may use this form to register a private or public company.

✗ **What this form is NOT for**
You cannot use this form to register a limited liability partnership. To do this, please use form LL IN01.

For further information, please refer to our guidance at www.companieshouse.gov.uk

Part 1 — Company details

→ **Filling in this form**
Please complete in typescript or in bold black capitals.

All fields are mandatory unless specified or indicated by *

A1 Company details

Please show the proposed company name below.

Proposed company name in full ❶

For official use

❶ **Duplicate names**
Duplicate names are not permitted. A list of registered names can be found on our website. There are various rules that may affect your choice of name. More information is available at: www.companieshouse.gov.uk

A2 Company name restrictions ❷

Please tick the box only if the proposed company name contains sensitive or restricted words or expressions that require you to seek comments of a government department or other specified body.

☐ I confirm that the proposed company name contains sensitive or restricted words or expressions and that approval, where appropriate, has been sought of a government department or other specified body and I attach a copy of their response.

❷ **Company name restrictions**
A list of sensitive or restricted words or expressions that require consent can be found in guidance available on our website: www.companieshouse.gov.uk

A3 Exemption from name ending with 'Limited' or 'Cyfyngedig' ❸

Please tick the box if you wish to apply for exemption from the requirement to have the name ending with 'Limited', Cyfyngedig' or permitted alternative.

☐ I confirm that the above proposed company meets the conditions for exemption from the requirement to have a name ending with 'Limited', 'Cyfyngedig' or permitted alternative.

❸ **Name ending exemption**
Only private companies that are limited by guarantee and meet other specific requirements are eligible to apply for this.
For more details, please go to our website: www.companieshouse.gov.uk

A4 Company type ❹

Please tick the box that describes the proposed company type and members' liability (only one box must be ticked):

☐ Public limited by shares
☐ Private limited by shares
☐ Private limited by guarantee
☐ Private unlimited with share capital
☐ Private unlimited without share capital

❹ **Company type**
If you are unsure of your company's type, please go to our website: www.companieshouse.gov.uk

BIS | Department for Business Innovation & Skills

CHFP000
05/10 Version 4.0

- the registrar for England and Wales (Cardiff);
- the registrar for Scotland (Edinburgh); and
- the registrar for Northern Ireland (Belfast).

The intended location of the **registered office** of a UK company determines to which registrar the registration documents must be delivered (s. 9(6)). England and Wales, Scotland and Northern Ireland are three different legal systems with separate court systems. The law of the jurisdiction in which the company is registered will govern the internal affairs of the company. The Registrar of Companies for England & Wales is based at Companies House, an Executive Agency of the Department for Business, Innovation and Skills.

3.3 Registration requirements: general

A UK company is formed by one or more persons (which may be companies) subscribing their names to a Memorandum of Association and complying with the registration requirements contained in ss. 9–13 of the Companies Act 2006. If the Registrar of Companies is satisfied that the registration requirements of the Act have been complied with, he must register the documents delivered to him and must issue a certificate that the company is incorporated (ss. 14 and 15). A refusal by the Registrar of Companies to register a company is subject to judicial review.

A company may not be formed for an unlawful purpose (s. 7(2)), but as there is no longer a requirement to state the purpose or purposes for which a company is being incorporated (known as the company's 'objects' (s. 31(1)), in any of the documents delivered to the Registrar of Companies, it is unlikely that the Registrar will have information to be in a position to enforce this provision by refusing to register a company.

A notorious case involving a company registered to run a brothel (*R v Registrar of Companies ex parte Attorney General Ltd* [1991] BCLC 476) established that even though s. 15(4) states that a certificate of incorporation is conclusive evidence 'that the requirements of this Act as to registration have been complied with', a certificate of incorporation is not conclusive evidence that a company has been formed for a lawful purpose.

3.4 Registration requirements: submitting an application to register

The registration procedure is very simple and inexpensive. An application can be made in hard copy or electronically with the requisite forms and documents being 'delivered' to the Registrar of Companies online or by post and a certificate received within hours. An application to register a company must include the following (s. 9):

1 IN01 (see specimen first page), which states:
   - the proposed company name;
   - whether the proposed registered office is to be in England and Wales, Scotland or Northern Ireland;
   - whether or not the liability of the members is to be limited and if so by shares or guarantee; and
   - whether the company is to be private (Limited/Ltd) or public (plc).
2 **Memorandum of Association** in prescribed form (ss. 7 and 8)
   - only one subscriber is required and there is no maximum;
   - subscribers agree to take at least one share (each); and
   - subscribers express the wish to form a company and agree to become members.
3 Articles of Association
   - Articles are the internal rules of the company;
   - if none are submitted, relevant **Model Articles** will apply;
   - may (not must) contain a statement of objects (s. 31);
   - if the Articles contain an entrenched provision, notice of this must be given by the company to the Registrar of Companies (s. 23(1)).
   - The Model Articles for Private Companies Limited by Shares and Model Article for Public Companies can be found in Appendices 1 and 2 respectively.
4 Statement of capital and initial shareholdings (s. 10) (unless the company is to be limited by guarantee, in which case a statement of guarantee is required, see s. 11), which states:
   - number of shares to be taken on registration;

- total nominal value of those shares;
- for each class:
  - prescribed particulars of rights attached to those shares;
  - number of shares of that class;
  - total nominal value of shares of that class;
- amount to be paid up and amount unpaid on each share;
- prescribed particulars to identify subscribers;
- in relation to each subscriber:
  - number, nominal value and class of shares he is to take;
  - amount to be paid up and amount unpaid on each share;
- this must be updated each time the capital is altered, for example, if additional shares are allotted.

5   Statement of proposed registered address.
6   Statement of proposed officers (s. 12):
- proposed directors' particulars including residential address; and
- proposed secretary's particulars (if company is to have one).

7   Statement of compliance that the registration requirements have been complied with (s. 13).
8   Fee (£13–£100 depending upon mode of registration of documents and timing).

The statement of capital and initial shareholdings (4), statement of proposed registered address (5), statement of proposed officers (6), and statement of compliance (7) form part of the IN01 Application to Register a Company form.

TEST YOUR KNOWLEDGE 3.3

(a) Which law (English, Scottish or Northern Irish) will govern the internal affairs of a UK-registered company?
(b) List what must be included in an application to register a company.
(c) Is it necessary to send hard copy documents to the Registrar of Companies to register a company?
(d) What happens if no articles of association are included in an application to register a company?

4   Certificate of incorporation

Section 15(1) of the Companies Act 2006 makes it clear that registered companies become incorporated and separate legal persons on registration, when the Registrar of Companies issues a certificate of registration.

> 'On the registration of a company, the Registrar of Companies shall give a certificate that the company is incorporated.'

Section 16(2) of the Companies Act 2006 makes it clear who the members of a registered company are and that the members may vary over time.

> 'The subscribers to the memorandum, together with such other persons as may from time to time become members of the company, are a body corporate by the name stated in the certificate of incorporation.'

A sample certificate of incorporation is shown opposite. If a company is re-registered, a new certificate of incorporation is issued.

CHAPTER 3 Promoters and company formation · **45**

CERTIFICATE OF INCORPORATION

CERTIFICATE OF INCORPORATION
OF A PRIVATE LIMITED COMPANY

Company No. 1234567

SPECIMEN

The Registrar of Companies for England and Wales hereby certifies that:

[Company name]

is this day incorporated under the Companies Act 2006 as a private company limited by shares and the situation of the registered office is in England and Wales.

Given at Companies House, on the [date]

THE OFFICIAL SEAL OF THE REGISTRAR OF COMPANIES

Companies House
—— for the record ——

The above information was communicated by electronic means and authenticated by the Registrar of Companies under section 1115 of the Companies Act 2006

5 Trading certificate

A public company must not do business or exercise any borrowing powers without having a **trading certificate** (s. 761) (a certificate application form is shown on p.47). The Companies Act 2006 imposes a minimum share capital requirement on public companies which must have allotted shares of no less than the authorised minimum as a condition of the Registrar of Companies issuing a trading certificate (s. 761(2)).

The authorised minimum nominal value of the issued shares of a public company is £50,000 or the prescribed Euro equivalent (s. 763). Public companies may not issue shares unless they are paid up as to at least one quarter nominal value and the whole of any premium (s. 586) and shares issued at the time of incorporation must be paid for in cash (s. 584). The result is that a company registered as a public company must have at least £12,500 in cash when it commences business and the right to call for at least a further £37,500 from shareholders. Laws governing payment for shares are important to ensure that the company is entitled to receive from a shareholder at least the nominal value of his shares: shares may not be issued at a discount (s. 580).

A public company that does business or exercises any borrowing powers without having a trading certificate contravenes s. 761. If the company fails to comply with any obligation under a transaction entered into whilst in contravention of s. 761 within 21 days of being called upon to do so, s. 767(3) operates to make the directors of the company jointly and severally liable to indemnify any other party to the transaction in respect of any loss or damage it suffers by reason of the company's failure to comply with its obligations. This is an example of a statutory provision supplementing the rights of a person with rights against a company by rendering the directors of the company liable for the obligations of the company. Contravention of s. 761 is also a criminal offence (s. 767(1))

TEST YOUR KNOWLEDGE 3.4

(a) When is a certificate of incorporation issued and by whom?
(b) Which registered companies are required to have a trading certificate?
(c) What condition must be satisfied before the Registrar of Companies will issue a trading certificate?
(d) What are the consequences of a public company doing business without having a trading certificate?

6 Company numbers and names

When a company is registered it is given a registered number, often called the company number (s. 1066). This number appears on the certificate of incorporation and the register of companies. During its existence a company may change its name but its company number never changes. When a company is registered, or a change of name is sought, the proposed name must comply with the Companies Act 2006.

6.1 Company numbers

It can be very difficult to know which company entered into an agreement if, after entering into the agreement, the company has changed its name. It is particularly confusing where a company's name is changed and its old name is given to a new company. An old agreement may appear to have been entered into by the new company when in fact it was entered into by the company that previously had that name. This is not an academic issue; it occurs frequently in practice and causes problems.

Identification difficulty can be avoided by including the company number as part of the identification of a company in a written contract rather than relying on referring to a company by its name. In the example given, if the old agreement stated the company number of the company

APPLICATION FOR TRADING CERTIFICATE FOR A PUBLIC COMPANY

In accordance with Sections 761 & 762 of the Companies Act 2006.

SH50
Application for trading certificate for a public company

✓ **What this form is for**
You may use this form to make an application by a public company for a trading certificate.

✗ **What this form is NOT for**
You cannot use this form to make an application for a trading certificate following a re-registration from a private company to public company.

For further information, please refer to our guidance at www.companieshouse.gov.uk

1 Company details

Company number [   ]
Company name in full [   ]

→ **Filling in this form**
Please complete in typescript or in bold black capitals.

All fields are mandatory unless specified or indicated by *

2 The application

The above company applies for a certificate entitling them to do business and exercise borrowing powers and confirms that:

1. the aggregate nominal value of the company's allotted share capital is not less than the authorised minimum.
2. the company is designating its authorised minimum capital in ❶
   ☐ Sterling
   ☐ Euros
3. the ❷
   ☐ amount of preliminary expenses
   ☐ estimated amount of the preliminary expenses of the company is
   _____

❶ One of the boxes needs to be ticked only where the company satisfies the authorised minimum in both Sterling and Euros.

❷ Please tick one box only.

3 Amount paid or benefit given

Has any amount or benefit been paid or given or is intended to be paid or given to any promoter of the company?

→ **Yes** Complete **Section 4**.
→ **No** Go to **Section 5** Statement of compliance.

4 Promoters

Promoter number 1

Amount paid or intend to be paid [   ]
Any benefit given or intended to be given [   ]
Consideration for such payment or benefit [   ]

BIS | Department for Business Innovation & Skills

CHFP000
05/10 Version 4.0

that had entered into it, it would be clear that the new company, albeit having the same company name, is a different company because it has a different company number. Unfortunately, not all jurisdictions have this benefit. Companies registered in Delaware, the most popular state in which to incorporate in the USA, for example, do not have unique company numbers.

6.2 Company names

The law governing company names is contained in Part 5 of the Companies Act 2006. A company sometimes trades using a business name different from its company name. A company with the company name Gas Appliances Limited, for example, may trade under the name 'Flames For You' which is its business name. Rules governing business names are contained in Part 41 of the Companies Act 2006. The rules, which replace the Business Names Act 1985, apply not only to companies but to any person carrying on business in the UK.

The legal issues in relation to company names and company business names fall into four categories:

- limits on company names;
- procedure for changing a company name;
- trading disclosures; and
- regulation of business names (Part 41).

Choosing a company name: limits on company names

The Companies Act 2006 provisions allow:

- the Registrar of Companies to refuse to register certain company names;
- the Secretary of State to direct that a company name be changed in certain circumstances;
- a company names adjudicator to order that a company name be changed, on the successful application by a person with goodwill.

These provisions need to be taken into account when choosing a company name when both registering a company and changing the name of an existing company. The detailed rights of the Registrar of Companies and the Secretary of State are contained in The Company and Business Names (Miscellaneous Provisions) Regulations 2009 (SI 2009/1085), referred to as the CBN (MP) Regulations 2009. The main points are summarised in Tables 3.1 and 3.2. The rights of a person with goodwill are considered in the paragraphs following the tables.

TABLE 3.1 Registrar of Companies' rights to refuse to register a name

Registrar of Companies' rights to refuse to register a name
Prohibited names (s. 53) A company must not be registered by a name if, in the opinion of the Secretary of State, its use would constitute an offence or it is offensive.
Approval of names by the Secretary of State (SS) (ss. 54 and 55) A company will not be registered with a name that: (i) would be likely to give the impression that the company is connected with Her Majesty's Government, a local authority or any public authority specified in the Company, Limited Liability Partnership and Business names (Sensitive Words and Expressions) Regulations 2009 (SI 2009/2615); or (ii) includes a sensitive word or expression listed in those regulations, unless evidence is produced that the name has been approved by the SS. Example: 'NHS Pottery Services Limited' will not be registered without the approval of the SS who will not consider the request for approval unless provided with the reply from the Department of Health to a request in writing seeking its views.

Prohibited characters (s. 57)
A company may not be registered by a name that includes any characters, signs, symbol or punctuation, or the placing or number thereof, that is not permitted by the CBN (MP) Regulations 2009 (see reg. 2 and Sch. 1).
Example:
'*Burst Limited' will not be registered because '*' cannot be used as one of the first three characters.
Indications of company type or legal form by limited companies (ss. 58–64)
A company name must indicate the type of company it is, in a manner provided for in the Act.
Examples:
The name of a private limited company that is not a CIC, Welsh or exempt must end with 'limited' or 'ltd'.
The name of a public limited company that is not a CIC or Welsh must end with 'public limited company' or 'plc.'
Inappropriate use of indications of company type or form (s. 65)
A company must not be registered by a name that includes specified words, expressions or other indications associated with a particular type of company or form of organisation or words similar thereto prohibited by the SS in the CBN (MP) Regulations 2009 (see regs. 4–6).
Example:
An unlimited company must not have a name that ends with the word 'limited'.
Names the same as the name of an existing company (s. 66)
The Registrar of Companies will not register a company with a name that is the same as a name on the company register. The Companies Act 2006 and CBN (MP) Regulations 2009 contain guidance as to how the Registrar of Companies will approach deciding whether or not one name is the same as another for these purposes and provisions to ensure that trivial difference between names will be ignored by the Registrar of Companies when deciding whether or not a name is 'the same as' a name on the company register (see reg. 7 and sch. 3).
Example:
The proposed name 'Sands Co Public Limited Company' will not be registered if there is an existing company named 'S and S plc'. This is because gaps are ignored for the purposes of comparison, so 'S and S' is regarded as the same as 'sands', 'Co' is ignored, and 'plc' is equivalent to 'Public Limited Company'.
Note that reg. 8 of the CBN (MP) Regulations 2009 allows for a company to be registered with a name that would otherwise be prohibited by s.66 if the existing company consents and is part of the same corporate group as the company whose name is being registered or changed.

TABLE 3.2 Secretary of State's rights to direct that a name be changed

Secretary of State's rights to direct that a name be changed
Company ceasing to be entitled to an exemption from the requirement to end its name with 'limited' (s. 64)
If it appears to the Secretary of State that a company whose name does not include 'limited' or any of the permitted alternatives has ceased to be entitled to an exemption, he may direct the company to change its name so that it ends with 'limited' or one of the permitted alternatives.
Names the same as or similar to the name of an existing company (ss. 67 and 68)
The Secretary of State may direct a company to change its name if it has been registered in a name that is the same as or, in the opinion of the Secretary of State, too like an existing company name. Such direction must be given within 12 months of registration by the name in question.

> **Misleading information given for the purposes of a company's registration with a particular name (s. 75)**
> If it appears to the Secretary of State that misleading information has been given for the purposes of a company's registration by a particular name, or that an undertaking or assurance has been given for that purpose and has not been fulfilled, the Secretary of State may direct the company to change its name. Such a direction must be given within five years of the company's registration by the name in question.

> **Misleading indication of activities (s. 76)**
> If in the opinion of the Secretary of State the name by which a company is registered gives so misleading an indication of the nature of its activities as to be likely to cause harm to the public, the Secretary of State may direct the company to change its name.

In addition to company law considerations, it is important to choose a company name that will not leave the company open to challenge based on the argument that the conduct of business under that name infringes the intellectual property rights of another person. These rights include, though they may not be limited to, the right to bring an action for infringement of a registered trade mark and the right of a trader to bring a tort action for passing-off.

Passing-off

A **passing-off** action may be brought against any person who misrepresents to the public that the goods or services it, the misrepresenting person, is providing, are associated with the claimant trader, thereby causing damage to the claimant trader. The claimant trader must demonstrate that it has goodwill that has been damaged by the misrepresentation (see *Erwen Warnick B V v J Townend & Sons (Hull) Ltd* [1979] AC 731, *per* Lord Fraser at 742 (HL)). Goodwill refers to all those attributes of a business that attract and retain customers not accounted for elsewhere. Goodwill is an intangible asset of a business that can be bought and sold. Merely calling a company a name can never amount to passing-off.

Objection to a name, based on goodwill

The legal protection given to the owner of goodwill has been enhanced, on the recommendation of the Company Law Review, by the introduction of ss. 69–74 of the Companies Act 2006. The Companies Act provisions are in addition to, and complement, the tort of passing-off. They provide for a person with goodwill (s. 69) to apply to a company names adjudicator for an order that a company name be changed (s. 73). The details are contained in the Company Names Adjudicator Rules 2008 (SI 2008/1738).

The applicant must establish that the respondent company's name is the same as a name associated with the applicant in which it has goodwill, or is so sufficiently similar to such a name that its use would be likely to mislead by suggesting a connection between the respondent company and the applicant. The concept of 'goodwill' is extended for the purposes of such an application, being defined in s. 69(7) to include 'reputation of any description'. There is no time limit on the making of an application which could but, as the following comments suggest, is unlikely to be made years after a company has been registered with a particular name.

The provisions are intended to catch only those cases in which the company name has been chosen to exploit another's reputation or goodwill, in other words, to provide a remedy where there has been opportunistic registration. Consequently, the provisions have been drawn very narrowly and an objection cannot be upheld, and no order that a company name be changed can be made, if the respondent company establishes any one of the following five defences:

1. that the name was registered before the commencement of the activities on which the applicant relies to show goodwill;
2. that the respondent company:
   - is operating under the name, or
   - is proposing to do so and has incurred substantial start-up costs in preparation, or
   - was formerly operating under the name and is now dormant;
3. that the name was registered in the ordinary course of a company formation business and the company is available for sale to the applicant on the standard terms of that business;

4 that the name was adopted in good faith;
5 that the interests of the applicant are not adversely affected to any significant extent.

Any decision of a company names adjudicator may be appealed to the court (s. 74).

Procedure to change a company name

A company may change its name by the following process (ss. 77–81):

1 The company:
   - passes a special resolution;
   - forwards a copy of the resolution to the Registrar of Companies;
   - gives notice of change of name to the Registrar of Companies.
2 The Registrar of Companies:
   - satisfies himself that:
     - the new name complies with the requirements of the Act; and
     - the other requirements of the Act have been complied with;
   - enters the new name on the register of companies in place of the old name;
   - issues a new certificate of incorporation.

The change of name has effect from the date on which the new certificate is issued (s. 81). If the Articles provide another means by which the company's name can be changed, that means is substituted for the special resolution in the process above. There are special provisions to accommodate a change of name directed or ordered by the Secretary of State, a company names adjudicator or the court (s. 77).

Trading disclosures

The trading disclosures required by regulations made pursuant to ss. 82 and 84 of the Companies Act 2006 extend beyond the obligation to disclose the company name in specified locations. All information mandated by The Companies (Trading Disclosures) Regulations 2008 (SI 2008/495) (which is amended by the Companies (Trading Disclosures) (Amendment) Regulations 2009 (SI 2009/218)) must be readable by the naked eye (reg. 2).

Subject to exceptions set out in the regulations, a company is required to:

1 Display its company name, so that the name may be easily seen by any visitor (regs. 3–5), at:
   - its registered office;
   - any place where it keeps company records;
   - any place at which it carries on business.
2 Disclose its company name on its (reg. 6):
   - websites;
   - business letters, notices and other official publications;
   - bills of exchange, promissory notes, endorsements and order forms;
   - cheques purporting to be signed by or on behalf of the company;
   - orders for money, goods or services purporting to be signed by or on behalf of the company;
   - bills of parcels, invoices and other demands for payment, receipts and letters of credit;
   - applications for licences to carry on a trade or activity;
   - all other forms of its business correspondence and documentation.
3 Disclose the part of the UK in which the company is registered, the company's registered number and the address of the company's registered office and ensure that any share capital referred to (which is optional) is paid-up share capital (reg. 7) on its:
   - websites;
   - business letters;
   - order forms.

Additionally, where a company's business letter includes the name of any director of that company, other than in the text or as a signatory, the letter must disclose the name of every director of that company (reg. 8). Finally, a company must reply within five working days of a request from any person it deals with in the course of business, disclosing the address of its registered office and the place at which its records can be inspected (reg. 9).

If a company fails, without reasonable excuse, to comply with any of the above requirements, an offence is committed by both the company and every officer of the company in default. Any person guilty of an offence is liable on summary conviction to a fine and, for continued contravention, a daily default fine (reg. 10).

Business names used by companies

A business name is a name used in the course of carrying on a business. Just as a sole trader may carry on business under his own name or a name different from his personal name and a partnership may trade under the names of the partners or a name different from the names of the partners, so a company may trade under its company name or a different name. Although business names are not registered with any government department, business name laws must be adhered to.

The law governing business names, including the law applicable to registered companies, which used to be found in the Business Names Act 1985 and regulations made thereunder, is now contained in the Companies Act 2006 (Part 41, ss. 1192/1208) and regulations made pursuant to that Act. For non-company businesses (only) these rules extend beyond regulating the choice of name to requiring certain trading disclosures.

Chapter 1 of Part 41 of the 2006 Act (ss. 1192–1198) applies to registered companies. Basically, a company may not, without the approval of the Secretary of State, use a business name:

- suggesting connection with the government or a public authority (s. 1193);
- that includes a sensitive word as listed from time to time in regulations (s. 1194);
- inappropriately suggesting that the company is a particular type of company or has a particular legal form (s. 1197); or
- giving a misleading indication of the nature of the activities conducted so as to be likely to cause harm to the public (s. 1198).

The first two bullet points mirror the requirement to obtain approval before a company could be registered with the name in question (see ss. 54 and 55) and the third and fourth bullet points complement ss. 58, 59 and 76 regulating registrable names. Sections 54, 55, 58, 59 and 76 are covered in Tables 3.1 and 3.2.

TEST YOUR KNOWLEDGE 3.5

(a) Can a company ever change its name or number?
(b) Which provisions of the Companies Act 2006 need to be taken into account when choosing a company name?
(c) What is the procedure for changing the name of a company?
(d) Where are the rules governing business names used by companies to be found?

7 Re-registration of a UK company

The status of a registered company as a public or private company and as a limited or unlimited company can be altered by re-registration under Part 7 (ss. 89–111) of the Companies Act 2006. Alteration from private to public and vice versa are commented on in this section. The Companies Act 2006 provisions differ very little from the predecessor provisions under the Companies Act 1985.

7.1 From private to public

Few companies are registered as public companies from the start. Most public companies begin life as a private company and are re-registered as a public company at a later date, usually to enable the company to offer shares to the public, something a private company is prohibited from doing by s. 755. The first time a company offers shares to the public is called an IPO, an initial public offering (see chapter 7).

Re-registration as a public company is a relatively straightforward process (ss. 90–96) but does require the company to involve its auditors. This is to ensure that the balance sheet gives a true and fair view of the company's financial position. Where, as is very common, a private company has received non-cash assets in return for issuing shares, the auditor's report will confirm that the assets have been accounted for in accordance with the requirements of the Companies Act 2006.

A re-registration application is made by delivering to the Registrar of Companies:

- a statement of the company's proposed name on re-registration;
- a statement of the proposed secretary (if the company does not already have one);
- a copy of the special resolution that has been passed that the company should be re-registered;
- a copy of the Articles as proposed to be amended;
- a copy of the company's balance sheet, together with an unqualified report by the company's auditors on the balance sheet, and a statement by the auditor that in his opinion at the balance sheet date the amount of the company's net assets was not less than the sum of its called-up share capital and undistributable reserves; and
- a statement of compliance that the requirements as to re-registration have been complied with.

The requirements as to re-registration not reflected in the documents above, compliance with which are confirmed by the statement of compliance, are that:

1. At the time the special resolution is passed:
   - the nominal value of the allotted share capital must not be less than the authorised minimum (£50,000); and
   - each allotted share must be paid up at least as to one-quarter of the nominal value of the share and the whole of any premium.
2. Between the balance sheet date and the date on which the application for re-registration is delivered there must have been no change in the company's financial position that results in the amount of the company's net assets being less than the aggregate of its called-up share capital and undistributable reserves.

If the Registrar of Companies is satisfied that the company is entitled to be re-registered, he must issue a certificate of incorporation reflecting the alteration (s. 96(2)). Unlike companies registered in the first instance as public companies, the re-registered company does not need a trading certificate (s. 761(1)). This is because the conditions for issuance of a trading certificate (that the nominal value of the allotted share capital is not less than the authorised minimum (£50,000) and each allotted share is paid up at least as to one quarter of the nominal value of the share and the whole of any premium) are covered by the re-registration process (s. 91).

7.2 From public to private

It is also common for a public company to be re-registered as a private company. One situation in which this may occur is in a reconstruction following a takeover in which a public company has been acquired and the new owner re-registers it as a private company. Re-registration may also be required because the share capital of a public company falls below the mandatory authorised minimum.

A less common but not unknown scenario for such a re-registration is where an entrepreneur has grown his company, taken it public, offered shares to the public, listed those shares on the stock exchange but retained a substantial shareholding himself. He may then decide that he/the company (for he may not distinguish between the two in his mind quite to the extent required by law) is too constrained by the rigours of securities regulations and market forces and take the company private again.

Richard Branson is an example. Virgin Group Limited is a private company owned by Richard Branson's Virgin Group (51%) and Singapore Airlines (49%). The company was a plc, its shares were listed in 1986, then it was taken private two years later and re-registered as a private company. The term 'take private' is not always used to mean that a public company has been re-registered as a private company; it is sometimes used to mean that the company no longer has shares listed on a stock exchange.

Re-registration of a public company as a private company is governed by ss. 97–101. The process is straightforward unless one or more minority shareholders object. As for re-registration from private to public, a special resolution that the company should be re-registered is needed. Most companies with their registered office and place of central management and control in the UK are subject to the protections of the City Code on Takeovers and Mergers. When such a company is being taken private, shareholders need to be informed, before voting on the resolution, of the protections they will be giving up by agreeing to the company's re-registration and the Code Executive should be consulted on this. The Articles need to be amended and copies of the proposed Articles and the special resolution, together with a statement of compliance as to the requirements of re-registration, need to be sent to the Registrar of Companies who, provided he is satisfied that the company is entitled to be re-registered, must re-register the company and issue an altered certificate of incorporation (s. 96).

Shares of a private company are usually far more difficult to sell than shares in a public company, and this is certainly the case if the public company is a quoted company. For this reason, shareholders may object to a company being taken private. Shareholders who together hold at least 5% of the nominal value of the company's shares or 50 or more shareholders, provided they have not voted in favour of the re-registration, may, within 28 days of it being passed, apply to court to cancel a re-registration resolution. The court may confirm or cancel the resolution and may do so 'on such terms as it thinks fit'. Section 98 provides no indication of the factors a court is to take into consideration when exercising its discretionary powers. Section 98(5) does, however, expressly provide that the court may provide that the company purchase the shares of the opposing minority shareholders, and this will resolve the problem going private presents for most minority shareholders.

TEST YOUR KNOWLEDGE 3.6

(a) What is the most common reason for a private company seeking to re-register as a public company?
(b) Describe the process by which a company may re-register from private to public.
(c) Is a trading certificate required before a re-registered company can conduct business? If not, why not?
(d) Why might a public company be re-registered as a private company?

8 Company registers and records: the statutory books and registers

From the point of registration forward, a company is required to maintain at its registered office (unless the Registrar of Companies has been notified of another location) company registers and records, often referred to as the statutory books and registers of the company. The basic documents required are:

- certificate of incorporation (current and any past certificates);
- trading certificate (public companies only);
- Memorandum of Association;
- current statement of capital;
- Articles of Association;
- copies of resolutions of members (s. 355);
- minutes of meetings of the members (s. 355) and classes of members (s. 359);
- minutes of meetings of the board of directors (s. 248).
- **register of members** (ss. 113–121);
- register of directors (s. 162);
- register of secretaries (s. 275) (if the company has a secretary);
- register of interests disclosed to it in the context of a company investigation pursuant to s. 793 (ss. 808 and 809) (public companies only); and

- register of debenture holders (if one is kept, which it is not required, even if the company has issued debentures) (s. 743).

Accounting records also need to be kept (s. 386) (see below). Documents and records may be kept in electronic form (s. 1135).

9 Annual returns and reports and accounts

9.1 Annual returns

A company must make an **annual return** on a prescribed form (AR01) to the Registrar of Companies (s. 854) and pay a nominal fee. The information to be contained in the return is (ss. 855 and 856):

- registered office address;
- type of company it is and its principal business activities;
- the names of directors at any time in the preceding year;
- the name of the company secretary at any time in the preceding year;
- any address different from the registered office at which the register of members or debenture holders are kept;
- a statement of capital;
- a list of shareholders, their shareholdings and changes thereto (a full list is only required every three years and special rules apply to traded companies); and
- a statement as to whether any of the company's shares are admitted to trading on a relevant market.

The Secretary of State has power to make regulations changing the information to be contained in annual returns (s. 857) and has used this power to make the obligation to supply details of shareholders less onerous for traded companies (see s. 856B and the Companies Act (Annual Returns) Regulations 2011 (SI2011/1487).

9.2 Reports and accounts

The directors of companies must prepare annual accounts and reports (ss. 394, 415 and 420), and send them to shareholders (s. 423) and the Registrar of Companies (s. 441). A small company is exempt from sending its directors' report to the Registrar of Companies (s. 415A and 444) and small and medium-sized companies may send **abbreviated accounts**. If a shareholder does not elect to receive full accounts and reports (which includes failing to respond within 28 days to an opportunity to elect to receive them), a company may, subject to certain conditions being met, send a shareholder a summary financial statement instead of the company's full accounts and reports (s.426 and the Companies (Summary Financial Statement) Regulations 2008 (SI 2008/374)). The shareholder retains the right to request a copy of the full accounts and reports (s. 426(2)).

To enable it to perform this obligation, companies must keep accounting records sufficient to (s. 386):

- Show and explain the company's transactions.
- Disclose the company's financial position with reasonable accuracy.
- Enable annual accounts to be drawn up in accordance with the Act.

Public companies (including all quoted companies) are required to lay accounts and reports before a general meeting (s. 437), and quoted companies must additionally make them available on their website (s. 430).

A very helpful table summarising the accounts and reports filing requirements for difference categories of companies under the Companies Act 2006 is contained in BIS Guidance for UK Companies on Accounting and Reporting (June 2008) which can be accessed via the BIS Companies Act 2006 website.

Individual company accounts

The annual accounts and reports of an individual company are made up of:

- a profit and loss account;
- a balance sheet;
- notes to the accounts (i.e. to the above two);
- a directors' report;
- a directors' remuneration report (quoted companies only); and
- an auditors' report (unless the company is exempt from audit, see below).

Group accounts

If a company is a parent company it must prepare group accounts covering all the companies in the corporate group (s; 399), unless:

- all its subsidiaries are excluded from consolidation (s; 402); or
- it is a member of a larger group (in which case the obligation to prepare group accounts rests with the ultimate parent company (ss. 399(2)–401)).

When required, group accounts are prepared *in addition to* individual company accounts. They consist of a consolidated profit and loss account, balance sheet and notes thereto.

Historically, the emphasis has been on disclosure of financial information in annual accounts and reports. Recently, however, the information required to be disclosed has been extended beyond financial information to include business information. Reporting of non-financial business information is referred to as 'narrative reporting'.

Narrative reporting

Narrative reporting has proved to be a controversial issue. Following a lengthy process of consideration and public consultation, the Government has produced draft regulations on which it is consulting (the draft Companies Act 2006 (Strategic Report and Directors' Report) Regulations 2013: 1 October 2013), which, if enacted, would put a new framework for narrative reporting in place. The regulations would replace the directors' report with two documents, a strategic report (required of all companies except small companies) and an annual directors' statement (required of all companies). The following text focuses on the business review, the principal existing narrative reporting requirement, which is included in the directors' report. Two further existing narrative reporting requirements are the directors' remuneration report, required of quoted companies (s. 420), and the corporate governance statement, required of listed companies (DTR 7.1).

All companies except small companies are required to include a business review within their annual directors' report (s. 417). The business review must contain:

- a fair review of the company's business and a description of the principal risks and uncertainties facing the company; and
- a balanced and comprehensive analysis of the development and performance of the company's business during the financial year and the position of the business at year end.

Quoted companies are required to include the following additional information in their business reviews:

- the main trends and developments likely to affect the future development, performance and position of the company's business;
- information about environmental matters, company employees and social and community issues and company policies and their effectiveness in relation to these matters; and
- information about 'persons with whom the company has contractual or other arrangements which are essential to the business of the company'.

Certain information may be carved out and not reported:

- disclosure of information about impending developments or matters in the course of negotiations if the disclosure would, in the opinion of the directors, be seriously prejudicial to the interest of the company (s. 417(10));
- disclosure of information about a person if the disclosure would, in the opinion of the directors, be seriously prejudicial to that person and contrary to the public interest (s. 417(11)).

Periodic disclosure under the Financial Services and Markets Act 2000

In addition to Companies Act annual disclosure requirements, the basic regime for periodic disclosure imposed by the Disclosure and Transparency Rules (DTR) promulgated by the FCA pursuant to the FSMA, on companies with listed securities (essentially, companies with shares listed for trading on the London Stock Exchange Main Market) is as follows.

Annual Financial Report (DTR 4)

Within four months of the end of the financial year the company must make public an annual financial report including:

- audited financial statements;
- a management report; and
- responsibility statements.

Half-yearly financial reports (DTR 4)

A company must make public half-yearly financial reports including:

- condensed set of financial statements;
- an interim management report; and
- responsibility statements.

Interim management statements (DTR 4)

A company must make public quarterly interim management statements, covering the first and third quarters of the company's financial year, providing:

- an explanation of material events and transactions that have taken place during the relevant period and their impact on the financial position of the issuer; and
- a general description of the financial position and performance of the issuer during the relevant period.

Inside information disclosure (DTR 2)

In addition to periodic reports and statements, companies subject to the DTRs are required to disclose inside information to the market as soon as possible. Inside information is information of a precise nature which:

- is not generally available;
- relates, directly or indirectly, to the company or the shares; and
- would, if generally available, be likely to have a significant effect on the price of the shares.

The question to ask to determine whether or not information should be disclosed as inside information is: would the information in question be likely to be used by a reasonable investor as part of the basis of his investment decisions and therefore be likely to have a significant effect on the price of the shares? If the answer is yes, the information must be disclosed. Information likely to be relevant to a reasonable investor's decision includes information which affects the assets and liabilities of the company, the performance or expectation of performance of the company's business or businesses, the company's financial condition and any major new developments in the company's business.

TEST YOUR KNOWLEDGE 3.7

(a) Identify eight basic documentary records a company is required to keep apart from its statutory registers.
(b) Which registers is a company required to keep?
(c) What makes up an individual company annual accounts and reports?
(d) Which registered companies are required to file a business review?
(e) How does the content of the business review of a quoted company differ from that of a non-quoted company?

CHAPTER SUMMARY

- A promoter is a person involved in setting up a business who is not purely providing professional or administrative services.
- The promoter owes fiduciary duties to the company (*Erlanger v New Sombrero* (1878)) and must disclose his interest in a company contract to the company (*Lagunas Nitrate v Lagunas Syndicate* (1899)).
- Failure to disclose renders the agreement voidable. Whether or not the promoter must account for profits if the contract cannot be rescinded is moot (*Re Lady Forrest (Murchison) Gold Mine Ltd* (1901) suggests not).
- Common law and equitable duties of a promoter have largely been superseded by securities regulation (see FSMA and the Prospectus Rules).
- A pre-incorporation contract is a contract entered into before the company is registered/in existence. The company cannot be bound and the signatory purporting to act for the company is bound by the contract (s. 51) unless there is a clear exclusion of personal liability (*Phonogram Ltd v Lane* (1982)).
- The person made liable by s. 51 may also enforce the contract (*Braymist Ltd v Wise Finance Co Ltd* (2002)). A company may not become a party to a pre-incorporation contract by ratification (*Re Northumberland Avenue Hotel Co Ltd* (1866)).
- A company may become a party to a pre-incorporation contract by novation (*Howard v Patent Ivory* (1888)).
- Companies are registered with the Registrar of Companies in Cardiff, Edinburgh or Belfast by submitting Form INO1, a Memorandum of Association and the relevant fee.
- On registration and issue of a certificate of incorporation by the Registrar of Companies an artificial person comes into existence.
- A company number is issued on registration and never changes.
- Company names are subject to detailed regulation.
- Companies may re-register from private to public (and must do so before issuing shares to the public) and from public to private.
- Companies are required to keep extensive registers and records: the statutory books and registers.
- Returns and reports and accounts must be filed annually with the Registrar of Companies.

The company as a distinct legal person

■ CONTENTS

1. The registered company as a corporation
2. What is a corporation?
3. The consequences of incorporation/separate legal personality
4. *Salomon v A. Salomon & Co. Ltd*
5. Limited liability
6. Corporate groups and separate legal personality
7. Limits on the implication of incorporation/separate legal personality

■ INTRODUCTION

When a registered company is created a new legal person comes into existence. The new legal person is an artificial legal person or a 'corporation'. In this chapter we look at the implications of this artificial legal personality status and focus on the steps that can be taken by those who deal with a company to protect themselves. We also look at the situations in which legal protections, both statutory and case-based, have been put in place to ameliorate the difficulties that can arise as a result of the law insisting on the separate personality of a company from either its members or those who manage it.

1 The registered company as a corporation

The Companies Act 2006 makes it clear that registered companies become incorporated and separate legal persons on registration:

'On the registration of a company, the Registrar of Companies shall give a certificate that the company is incorporated.' (s. 15(1))

The Companies Act 2006 also makes it clear that a registered company is a 'body corporate' made up of members which members may vary over time:

'The subscribers to the memorandum, together with such other persons as may from time to time become members of the company, are a body corporate by the name stated in the certificate of incorporation.' (s. 16(2))

2 What is a corporation?

To understand the meaning of corporation, it is important to understand the concept of a legal person. A legal person is a being or entity with the capacity to:

- enjoy (by virtue of its existence), or acquire, enforceable legal rights or property; and
- be (by virtue of its existence), or become subject to, enforceable legal obligations and liabilities.

Legal persons fall into two categories:

- natural persons (individuals, including you yourself); and
- artificial or juristic persons.

The word 'individual' is used in this text to refer to a natural person. The term 'person' is used to cover both natural and artificial persons. All artificial or juristic persons are corporations. As we saw in chapter 3, the process of registration creates a new legal person with the ability to have legal rights and incur legal liabilities.

Corporations fall into two categories:

- corporations sole; and
- corporations aggregate.

Corporations sole are limited by law to one member at any given time. Corporations sole are often attached as an incident of an office. Examples are the Crown and the Archbishop of Canterbury. Mayors are also generally corporations sole. The corporation sole is distinct in law from the individual who occupies the post at any point in time. The individual office-holder changes over time, but the corporation sole continues with no need to transfer any property or rights to the new incumbent. The individual's acts in the capacity of the corporation are separate from the individual's personal acts.

In the study of business organisations, we are not concerned with corporations sole but with corporations aggregate. Corporations aggregate may (but need not) have more than one member at any given time. Statutory corporations, chartered corporations, registered companies, building societies, industrial and provident societies and limited liability partnerships are all examples of corporations aggregate. Figure 4.1 illustrates the classification of legal persons.

In general terms, a company, because it is a corporation, is a person in law separate from any and all of the individuals involved in the company whether those individuals are its owners/shareholders, its managers/directors or are involved in some other way.

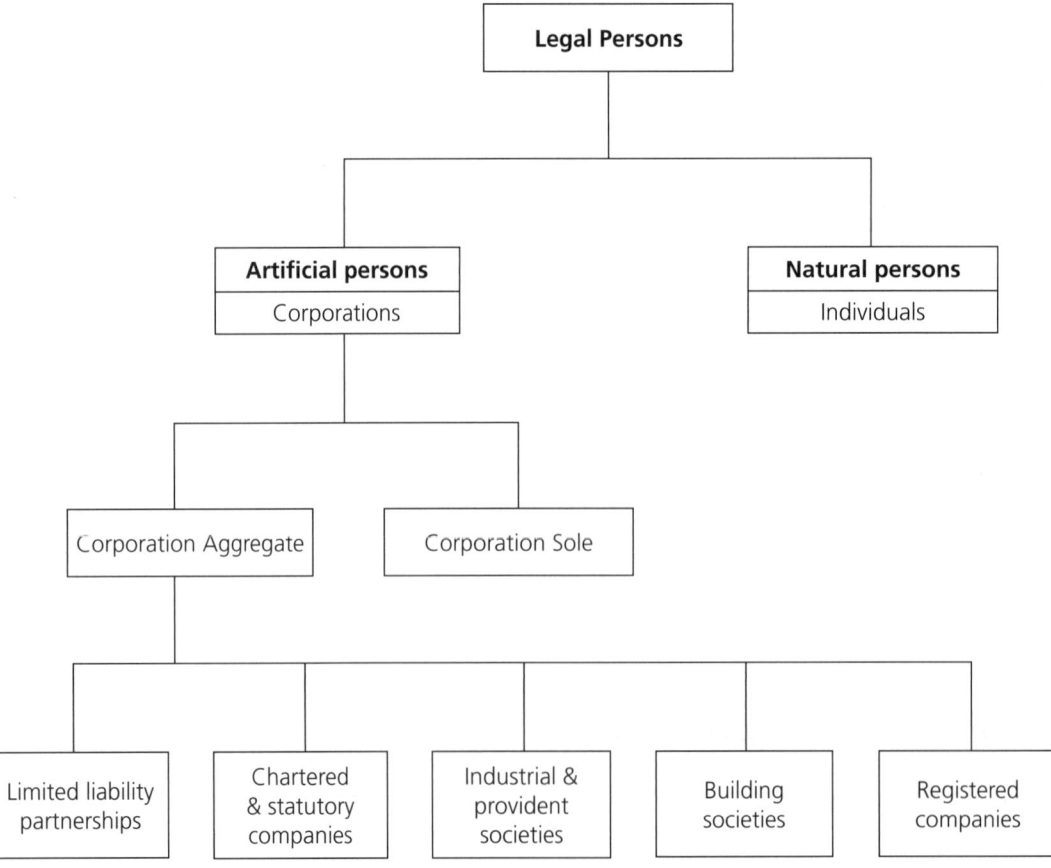

FIGURE 4.1 Types of legal persons

3 The consequences of incorporation/separate legal personality

In general terms a company has the capacity to:

- enjoy (by virtue of its existence), or acquire, enforceable legal rights or property; and
- be (by virtue of its existence), or become subject to, enforceable legal obligations and liabilities.

In specific terms, a company can:

- own property;
- be a party to a contract;
- act tortiously;
- be a victim of tortious behaviour;
- commit a crime;
- be the victim of a crime;
- sue and be sued;

And has:

- a nationality;
- a domicile; and
- human rights.

All of the above rights and liabilities parallel the capacity of an individual, but the scope and content of some of those rights and liabilities are not exactly the same as those of an individual. For example, although some human rights make sense in the context of an artificial person, others do not. Examples of human rights set out in the European Convention on Human Rights (ECHR) exercisable by companies are:

- the right to require a fair trial in the determination of its civil rights and obligations or any criminal charge against it (ECHR, Art. 6) (see *R (Alconbury Developments Ltd) v Secretary of State for the Environment, Transport and Regions* [2003] 2 AC 295);
- freedom of expression (ECHR, Art. 10) (see *R (Northern Cyprus Tourist Centre Limited) v Transport for London* [2005] UKHRR 1231);
- prohibition of discrimination (ECHR Article 14); and
- the right to protection of company property (ECHR, Art. 1 of Protocol 1).

In relation to criminal liability, a number of criminal offences are specifically aimed at companies, particularly under the Companies Act 2006. Other offences have been drafted with companies as one class of accused in mind (e.g. offences under the Health and Safety at Work Act 1974). In relation to crime generally, many crimes were established with individuals in mind and the courts have wrestled to establish principles governing both when an offence will be one of which a company may be found guilty, and, if the crime can be committed by a company, whose acts, knowledge and thoughts will be treated as those of the company for the purposes of establishing the criminal state of mind (*mens rea*) and the criminal act (*actus reus*).

Having established that a company is capable of being found guilty of a criminal offence requiring a criminal state of mind, the leading principle developed by the courts to attribute the acts, knowledge and thoughts of an individual to a company is referred to as the 'identification theory' (*Lennard's Carrying Company Ltd v Asiatic Petroleum Co Ltd* [1915] AC 705 (HL)). This theory was confirmed and applied in the leading case of *Tesco Supermarkets Ltd v Nattrass* [1972] AC 153 (HL) which involved Tesco advertising goods for sale at a price less than that at which it was actually offering them for sale. At the time, this was an offence under the Trade Descriptions Act 1968 (since repealed and replaced by a different offence under the Consumer Protection Act 1987). The test derived from *Lennard's Carrying Company* and applied in *Tesco v Natrass* to determine whether an individual was to be identified with the company was the 'directing mind and will' of the company. However, in *Meridian Global Funds Management Asia Ltd v Securities Commission* [1995] 2 AC 500 (Privy Council) Lord Hoffman both clarified the operation of the test and cautioned that although in some cases the directing mind and will of the company was the correct test, it was not appropriate in all cases.

The narrowness of the identification theory inhibited successful prosecution of companies following such national tragedies as the capsizing of the *Herald of Free Enterprise* (which caused

192 deaths), the *Piper Alpha* North Sea oil platform explosion (which caused 167 deaths) and the Paddington rail crash (which caused 31 deaths). Public outcry at the failure of the courts to deliver 'justice' resulted in the passage of the Corporate Manslaughter and Corporate Homicide Act 2007, which reflects a systems-based principle of organisational behaviour rather than the individualistic principle developed by the courts. An overview of the Act can be found on the Ministry of Justice website.

Imputing wrongful acts to a company for the purposes of establishing criminal liability is one part of the overarching issue of attribution of acts to a company to determine its rights and liabilities. In addition to attribution rules in a company's constitution, and in the Companies Act and other statutes, the principles of vicarious liability and agency law are used to ascertain the rights and liabilities of a company, particularly in **tort** and contract respectively.

A company differs from a natural person in that it:

- has perpetual existence until dissolved; and
- has owners.

TEST YOUR KNOWLEDGE 4.1

(a) What are the two categories of legal person?
(b) What types of corporation are there?
(c) What are the key legal consequences of a registered company being a corporation?
(d) Identify two key characteristics that distinguish an artificial person from a natural person.

4 *Salomon v A. Salomon & Co Ltd*

The most famous case illustrating the operation of the concept of the separate legal personality of a company is *Salomon v A. Salomon & Co Ltd* [1897] AC 22 (HL). The case is important because it confirmed the ability of a sole trader to transfer his business into a registered company and thereby insulate himself from the liabilities of the business.

Before this case, the full significance of the ability to incorporate a limited liability company by registration was not appreciated. As the judgments at first instance and in the Court of Appeal indicate, it was not widely understood at the time that sole trader owners of small businesses could use the Act to secure limited liability and insulate their personal property from business risks.

CASE LAW 4.1

Salomon v A. Salomon & Co Ltd [1897] AC 22 (HL)

Mr Salomon owned and ran a profitable boot and shoe manufacturing business as a sole trader. He wished to run his business through a limited company, which he achieved by registering a company and selling his business to that company.

The statute governing company registrations at that time required seven subscribers to the Memorandum of Association, i.e. seven original members or shareholders. Mr Salomon satisfied this requirement by himself, his wife and his five grown-up children becoming subscribers (under the Companies Act 2006 only one subscriber or member is required). The initial nominal share capital of the company was £40,000. This was divided into 40,000 shares with a nominal value of £1 each. Seven £1 shares were issued, one being issued to each shareholder/member/subscriber which made the initial issued share capital of the company £7. The first directors were appointed by the shareholders and were Mr Salomon and his two eldest sons.

 **CASE LAW** 4.1 *continued*

The sale price of the business to the company was 'the sanguine expectations of a fond owner' rather than the market value of the business. In short, the business was sold to the company at an overvalue. In return for the business being transferred to the company, the £39,000 purchase price for the business was 'paid' by the company to Mr Salomon in the following way:

- £9,000 was paid in cash (£8,000 of which, with no legal obligation to do so, Mr Salomon used to pay off debts of the business).
- 20,000 shares of £1 each were issued to Mr Salomon, credited as fully paid-up shares (i.e. the shares were regarded as having been paid for by Mr Salomon, not in cash but 'in kind', by the transfer to the company of £20,000 worth of the business).
- A £10,000 secured loan note, or 'debenture', was issued to Mr Salomon recording that the company owed Mr Salomon £10,000 pounds secured by a charge over the company's assets.

Virtually immediately after the transfer the profitability of the business began to decline. The company found itself in debt and unable to pay its debts as they fell due. Mr Salomon cancelled his loan note, the debenture, and the company entered into loan arrangements/debentures with Mr Broderip who became a secured creditor of the company. The company failed to pay interest on the loan when it fell due and Mr Broderip exercised his right, as a secured creditor, to have a receiver appointed. Shortly thereafter the company went into liquidation. The company's assets were sold by the liquidator to realise cash to pay both the secured and the unsecured creditors of the company.

Secured creditors are entitled to be paid before the unsecured creditors of a company. The proceeds of sale of the company's assets were insufficient even to pay the secured creditor, Mr Broderip, in full. In these unhappy circumstances, the liquidator brought an action against Mr Broderip and Mr Salomon alleging the loan notes issued by the company were fraudulent and invalid. The liquidator was successful at first instance and in the Court of Appeal, but was appealed to the House of Lords. Held: Mr Salomon had done nothing wrong, was not liable for the debts of the company, and the loans between him and the company and Broderip and the company were valid.

The first instance and Court of Appeal decisions

The first instance judge in *Salomon* decided that fraud was not established on the facts of the case. He did, however, use agency principles to decide that the company was Mr Salomon's agent and on that basis he ordered Mr Salomon, the principal, to indemnify the company, the agent, for the debts the company had incurred as his agent. The Court of Appeal rejected the first instance agency argument. Lindley LJ preferred to hold that the company was the trustee of Mr Salomon who was the beneficiary. Lindley LJ described the company as, 'A trustee improperly brought into existence by him to enable him to do what the statute prohibits', therefore, he held, the beneficiary (Mr Salomon) must indemnify the trustee, the company.

Lopes LJ regarded the family member/shareholders as 'dummies'. What the Act required, he stated, were, 'seven independent *bona fide* members, who had a mind and a will of their own'. According to Lopes LJ, 'The transaction is a device to apply the machinery of the [1862 Act] to a state of things never contemplated by that Act – an ingenious device to obtain the protections of the Act, and in my judgment in a way inconsistent with and opposed to its policy and provisions.' He ordered that the sale of the business to the company be set aside as a sale by Salomon to himself with none of the incidents of a sale, but being a fiction.

The House of Lords decision

In dismissing the claims of the liquidator, members of the House of Lords disagreed with the decisions at first instance and in the Court of Appeal which, they said, had misconceived the scope and effect of the 1862 Act. Lord MacNaghten's judgment was particularly lucid.

> 'though it may be that after incorporation the business is precisely the same as it was before, and the same persons are managers and the same hands receive the profits, the company is

not in law the agent of the subscribers or trustee of them. Nor are the members liable, in any shape or form, except to the extent and in the manner provided by the Act.'

4.1 Separate legal personality and insurance

One area in particular in which difficulty arose as a result of the failure of businessmen to appreciate the 'tyrannical sway' the corporate entity metaphor holds over the courts (as Kahn-Freund has described it) is insurance of company property. In three cases – *Macaura* (see Case Law 4.2), *General Accident v Midland Bank Ltd* [1940] 2 KB 388 and *Levinger v Licences etc., Insurance Co* (1936) 54 LL L Rep 68 – insurance companies have avoided paying out under insurance contracts for which they have received premiums, based on the insured property being owned not by the party insuring it (the shareholder of the company), but rather by the company itself.

CASE LAW 4.2

Macaura v Northern Assurance Co [1925] AC 619 (HL)

After selling his property (timber) to a company in return for shares, Macaura, the sole shareholder of Irish Canadian Sawmills Ltd, insured the timber against fire in his own name. The timber was destroyed by fire and Macaura claimed on the insurance policy. Held: The property belonged to the company, not to the shareholder. Even though the timber had been destroyed by an insured event, Macaura had no insurable interest in the timber as 'he stood in no "legal or equitable relation" to it' and so could not recover under the insurance policy.

TEST YOUR KNOWLEDGE 4.2

(a) Summarise the material facts of *Salomon v A. Salomon & Co. Ltd*.
(b) What was the decision of the first instance court in Salomon and how were agency principles applied to the company?
(c) What was the decision of the Court of Appeal in Salomon and how were trust principles applied by Lindley LJ in his judgment?
(d) What did the House of Lords decide about the liability of Mr Salomon for the debts of the company and the validity of the debentures?

5 Limited liability

It follows from the separate identity of the company from its owners/shareholders and managers/directors that if a company incurs debts, those debts are the debts of the company, owed by the company to the lender/creditor. Without more, the debts of the company are not the debts of any other person. This means that not even the owners/shareholders of the company are liable to pay any sum owed by the company to the lender/creditor. Any legal action to recover the debt must be brought by the creditor naming the company as the defendant in the legal action. The owners/shareholders of the company are not parties to the contract pursuant to which the sum owed (the debt) is due to the creditor therefore action against them will fail.

One important question that cannot be answered simply by referring to the separate legal personality of the company is this:

- What, if any, liability does an owner/shareholder of a company have to contribute money to the company to enable the company to pay its lenders/creditors?

The answer depends on whether the company in question is a limited or unlimited company.

5.1 Limited and unlimited companies

Owners of registered companies do not necessarily or always limit their liability to contribute sums to the company so that the company can pay the sums it, the company, owes to third parties: limited liability is an option available to incorporators of a registered company. As Figure 2.2 shows, it is possible to register a private company under the Companies Act 2006 with unlimited liability. Section 3(4) makes this clear.

'If there is no limit on the liability of its members, the company is an "unlimited company".'

Unlimited companies are not popular vehicles for business organisations, but it is useful to focus on them here as they throw into sharp relief the difference between the concepts of separate legal personality and limited liability, concepts which are often treated as a single concept by students, resulting in misunderstanding. The liability of a shareholder to pay money into a company needs to be considered both when the company is trading, and when the company has ceased trading and is being wound up.

5.2 Shareholder payments to a company that is trading

A person can become a shareholder by acquiring shares in a company either from the company itself or from an existing shareholder. Most shares obtained from existing shareholders involve a stock exchange transaction. Most stock exchanges forbid trading in shares in relation to which any sum remains payable to the company by the shareholder. For this reason, this section will concentrate on shares acquired from the company. Acquisition of shares from an existing shareholder will not be considered further.

Shares may be allotted and issued by a company and acquired by a shareholder on a fully paid-up, partly paid-up or nil-paid basis. Shares are fully paid-up when the shareholder pays to the company the whole of the share price (the amount due to the company) on allotment. As long as the company continues to trade, the company has no legal right to require a shareholder with fully paid-up shares to pay any further sum of money into the company. This is true whether the company is a limited or unlimited company.

Where shares are obtained from a company on a partly paid-up, or nil-paid, basis the shareholder, at the time of allotment, does not pay to the company a part, or any part (as the case may be), of the price payable for the shares. In such a case the company is entitled to call on the shareholder to pay to the company any part, or the whole, of the amount of the share price as yet unpaid, at any time.

The power to make such calls on shareholders, to determine when and how much, is ordinarily given to the directors who must exercise the power in accordance with their duties to the company. The common law rule that all shareholders must be treated equally when calls are made (see *Preston v Grand Collier Dock Co* (1840) 11 Sim 327), can now be contracted out of by including a provision in the Articles of Association permitting shares to be allotted on the basis that different calls can be made on different shareholders at different times (see s. 581(a) of the Companies Act 2006).

While a company continues to trade, the most a shareholder can be required to pay into the company is the price he has agreed to pay, but has not yet paid, for his or her shares.

5.3 Shareholder payments to a company that is being wound up

The law governing the obligation of a shareholder to contribute money to a company that has ceased trading and is being wound up is found in s. 74 of the Insolvency Act 1986. When a company is being wound up, it is essential to distinguish limited and unlimited companies.

The starting point for both limited and unlimited companies is s. 74(1) which provided that:

'When a company is wound up, every past and present member is liable to contribute to its assets to any amount sufficient for payment of its debts and liabilities.'

In the event of a company being wound up, a shareholder, without more, is required to contribute to the assets of a company sufficient to enable the company to pay its creditors and meet its other liabilities. Note, however, that even in relation to an unlimited company, a member is not liable to contribute to debts or liabilities incurred by the company after he or she has ceased to be a member and also is not liable to contribute anything at all if he or she has not been a member for a year or more at the time of the commencement of the winding up (see s. 74(2)(a) and (b)).

Section 74 goes on to make specific provision for a company limited by shares. Section 74(2)(d) provides:

> 'in the case of a company limited by shares, no contribution is required from any member exceeding the amount (if any) unpaid on the shares in respect of which he is liable as a present or past member.'

In relation to a company limited by shares, whether a public or a private company, s. 74(2)(d) of the Insolvency Act 1986 is the statutory basis on which the liability of shareholders to contribute to the company to enable it to pay its debts and other liabilities is limited. The limit is the amount (if any) unpaid on the shares. If that amount has been paid to the company, a shareholder is under no further obligation to contribute.

5.4 Justifications for limited liability

Shareholders of the first registered companies did not have limited liability. As outlined in chapter 1, the debate as to the costs and benefits limited liability would bring were still being debated when the first incorporation statute was enacted, in 1844. Although the debate was soon won by those advocating the beneficial consequences of limiting the liability of shareholders, limited liability was initially introduced for large companies only, that is, companies with a minimum of 25 shareholders that met certain minimum share value and issued share capital requirements (see s. 1 of the Limited Liability Act 1855). This restricted availability was relaxed the very next year by the Joint Stock Companies Act 1856.

The key benefits of limited liability are:

- encouragement of investment by members of the public in companies;
- facilitation of the transferability of shares; and
- clarity and certainty as to the assets available to creditors of the company.

TEST YOUR KNOWLEDGE 4.3

(a) What is the liability of a member of an unlimited company to contribute to the assets of the company whilst the company is continuing to trade?
(b) What is the liability of a member of an unlimited company to contribute to the assets of the company in the event of a winding up?
(c) What is the liability of a member of a company limited by shares to contribute to the assets of the company in the event of a winding up?
(d) Name three key benefits believed to be delivered by limited liability.

6 Corporate groups and separate legal personality

It follows from the separate legal personality of companies and the ability of a company to own property that one company can own shares in another company. This is the basis for the existence of corporate groups that can be, and are not uncommonly, made up of hundreds of companies, all owned, ultimately, by one parent company.

A corporate group is a single economic entity. Public disclosure laws recognise this to the extent that accounts made available to the public must be compiled on a group basis. Fundamentally, however, company law sees a corporate group as a series of individual companies. Each company within the group owns its own property and is liable for its own debts and other liabilities. It is preservation of the reputation of the parent of a corporate group that in many cases will cause a parent company to ensure that claims made against its subsidiaries are paid, rather than any legal obligation to pay such claims, for, as we have seen, a shareholder (and therefore a parent company) is not liable for the debts or other liabilities of the company. If the liability of a subsidiary is large enough, a parent company will incur the public opprobrium suffered from leaving it to 'sink' (i.e. become insolvent) and leave creditors wholly or only partly paid. There is no law that prevents a parent company from doing this.

The right of one company to establish a wholly-owned subsidiary company to perform risky operations and thereby protect the assets of other companies in the corporate group from the claims of persons damaged by the risky activity is clear in English law. However, it is not universally accepted as a satisfactory state of affairs and is not the case throughout Europe. Attempts to change the law to introduce parent liability for its subsidiaries have been made as part of the EU company law harmonisation programme, but the draft 9th Company Law Directive containing proposals on this issue has been withdrawn.

Attempts have also been made in a number of cases to argue that one company in a corporate group is required as a matter of law to pay liabilities incurred by another company in the corporate group based on a 'single economic entity' theory. Notwithstanding one or two cases in which this theory seemed to have been accepted, the most famous of which was *DHN Food Distributors Ltd v Tower Hamlets LBC* [1976] 1 WLR 852 (CA), this basis for imposing liability has since been firmly rejected by the English courts.

The most difficult scenario to accept is the organisation of a corporate group deliberately so as to minimise exposure of the group's wealth to tort victims. The Court of Appeal confirmed that English law endorses this behaviour in *Adams v Cape Industries plc* [1990] Ch 433.

 **CASE LAW 4.3**

***Adams v Cape Industries plc* [1990] Ch 433 (CA)**

A number of class actions were brought in Texan courts by US workers injured by exposure to asbestos mined in South Africa by subsidiary companies within the Cape corporate group. The asbestos had been marketed in the USA by NAAC, a wholly-owned subsidiary company within the Cape corporate group, incorporated in Illinois. NAAC ceased to trade and was put into liquidation and two new subsidiaries, CPC (incorporated in Illinois) and AMC (a Liechtenstein entity), were incorporated by the Cape corporate group to market asbestos in the USA. Judgments were awarded by the Texan court against, among others, Cape (the group parent company) and Capasco (another wholly-owned subsidiary within the Cape corporate group, incorporated in England).

The case is concerned with the circumstances in which a judgment awarded by a foreign court will be enforced by the English courts. Essentially, Jimmy Adams, the applicant in England, had to show that at the relevant time the judgment debtors (Cape and Capasco) were present in the USA. Adams' counsel, Mr Morison, argued:

- NAAC was part of the same corporate group as Cape and Capasco and the presence of NAAC in the US should constitute presence of Cape and Capasco.
- AMC and CPC, through which asbestos was marketed in the USA after NAAC ceased to trade, were sham companies established to mask the real situation and the veil should be lifted and their presence treated as the presence of Cape and Capasco.
- Cape and Capasco were present through marketing and selling asbestos through their agents, NAAC, AMC and CPC.

Held: the Texan judgments would not be enforced by the English courts.

In refusing to allow enforcement of the Texan judgments and finding in favour of Cape, the court rejected each of the arguments to overcome the separate legal personality of each company within a corporate group. In the course of rejecting them, the Court of Appeal reviewed the circumstances in which English courts are willing to avoid the consequences of the separate legal personality of a company in order to allow a creditor of a company a remedy against the company's shareholder. These circumstances are considered in the following section.

The claimant in *Adams v Cape* [1990] represented the victims of tortious behaviour of a company and the victims were denied a remedy against the shareholder (the parent company) which had valuable assets to meet the judgments. The vulnerability of tort victims was not emphasised in the nineteenth-century debate over allowing shareholders limited liability which had focused on trade and financial creditors who, it is argued, providing they have access to accurate information, can look after themselves in that they can negotiate protections or reflect the risk of doing business with a particular company in their terms of business and pricing. If this is accepted, there is no reason for the law to require shareholders to contribute to a company to enable it to pay its debts. Rather, the focus of the law should be adequate public disclosure of information.

In the context of parent company liability to the tort victims of subsidiary companies, the Court of Appeal in the recent case of *Chandler v Cape* [2012] EWCA Civ 525 confirmed the strict separate legal entity approach taken to parent company liability in *Adams v Cape*. It also confirmed that a parent company may be liable in tort for personal injury caused to employees of a subsidiary based on application of the test in *Caparo Industries Plc v Dickman* [1990] 2 A.C. 605 to ascertain whether or not, in all the circumstances, the parent company owed a duty of care to the employee.

STOP AND THINK 4.1

Employer liability insurance is compulsory and liability insurance is available to companies to insure against tort liability to consumers and the public. Is the availability of insurance an adequate answer to the argument that limited liability should not apply to the extent that a company incurs tort liability?

TEST YOUR KNOWLEDGE 4.4

(a) Is a parent company liable for the debts of its subsidiary companies?
(b) Is the concept of the single economic entity recognised in company law?
(c) Summarise the facts of *Adams v Cape Industries* plc.
(d) What was the decision of the court in *Adams v Cape*?
(e) What type of creditor was the claimant in *Adams v Cape*?

7 Limits on the implication of incorporation/separate legal personality

We have identified the main consequences of the separate legal personality of a company (sections 3 and 4 above). It is important to understand the ways in which these consequences may be supplemented or curtailed so as to provide a person with a remedy different from that dictated by a strict application of the separate legal personality doctrine. There are three routes by which to supplement or curtail the doctrine to achieve such a remedy: self-help action, piercing the corporate veil and relying on a statutory provision to found a remedy.

The most common outcome is for a claimant against a company to be awarded a remedy against the company's shareholder, although in some cases a remedy is sought against a company owned or controlled by a person against whom a claimant has its principal remedy. The question whether a court is permitted to impose contractual liability on a shareholder in circumstances in which the company he controls is party to the contract, but the circumstances are such that the corporate veil should be pierced has arisen in several recent cases. The Supreme Court in *VTB Capital plc v Nutritek International Corp* [2013] EWSC 5 went further than the Court of Appeal, over-ruled *Antonio Gramsci Shipping Corp v Stepanovs* [2011] EWHC 333 on the point, holding that the imposition of contractual liability on a shareholder was not an available remedy based on piercing the corporate veil, and subjecting the 'doctrine' of piercing the corporate veil to sceptical scrutiny (see below).

Self-help action

First, a person dealing with a company can often work around the main consequence of the company being a person separate from its shareholders, that its shareholders are not liable for the debts and obligations of the company, by putting appropriate contractual or agency arrangements in place. This behaviour is often called 'self-help' action.

Piercing the corporate veil

Second, the courts sometimes refuse to apply the doctrine of separate legal personality. The terms 'lifting the corporate veil' and 'piercing the corporate veil' are used in this context. Such imagery can hinder rather than help to explain what the court is doing and why, particularly as these terms have not been used consistently. It is easy to overestimate the importance of this topic because there was a time when the courts were very receptive to arguments urging them to ignore the separate legal personality of a company. However, in recent years courts have adopted a much stricter approach to suggested departures from the separate personality doctrine, an approach confirmed by the Court of Appeal in *Chandler v Cape* and the Supreme Court in *VTB* (in which the court reviewed the authorities on piercing the corporate veil).

Statutory provisions

Finally, statutory provisions may, in certain circumstances, supplement or otherwise affect rights. If a person has a right against a company, a statutory provision may supplement that person's rights by providing a statutory right in addition to the existing rights. This right may be against the shareholders or the directors, for example. Alternatively, a statutory provision may state that the acts of one company are to be regarded as the acts of its parent company (the shareholder), perhaps for the purpose of determining whether or not compensation is payable pursuant to the statute. Statutory provisions that operate when a company is being wound up are especially important and need to be addressed separately from those applicable when a company is still trading, or, as it is said, is still 'a going concern'.

Each of these routes is explored below. First, it is helpful to consider typical scenarios in which there is a wish to provide a claimant with a different remedy from that dictated by a strict application of the separate personality doctrine.

7.1 Typical scenarios

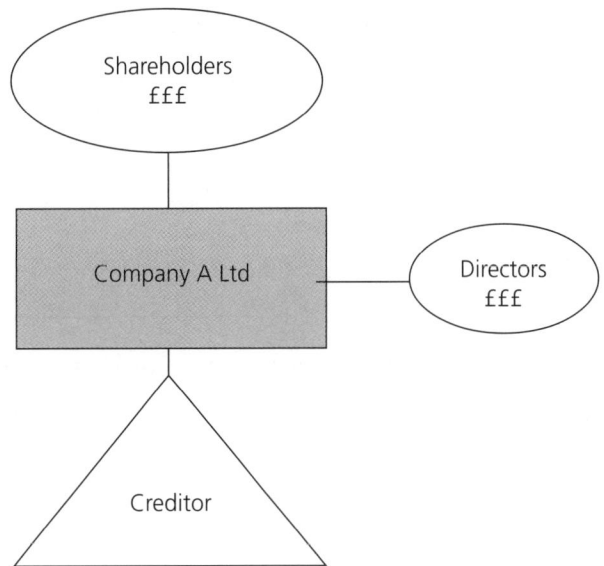

FIGURE 4.2 Typical scenario 1

70 **PART ONE** The nature and structure of a company

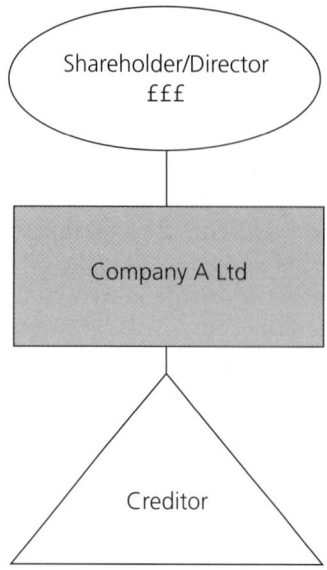

Can the creditor sue the sole shareholder/director to recover the sum owed to it by Company A Ltd?

FIGURE 4.3 Typical scenario 2

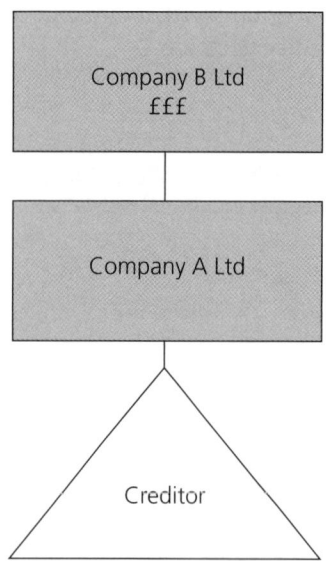

Can the creditor sue Company B Ltd to recover the sum owed to it by Company A Ltd?

FIGURE 4.4 Typical scenario 3

E is employed by O as a salesman.
E's contract of employment contains restrictive covenants.
One covenant prohibits E from selling products to any of the customers of his employer for 12 months after his employment terminates.
E decides to resign his employment with O.
E forms Company Ex Ltd which sells products to a customer of O.

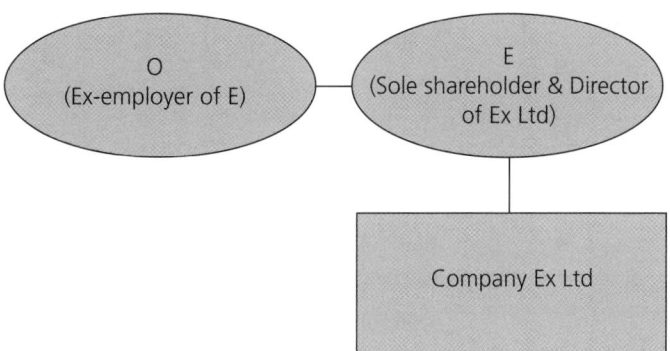

Can O obtain an injunction restraining Company Ex Ltd from selling to O's customers?

FIGURE 4.5 Using a company to avoid existing obligations

7.2 Self-help action to mitigate the consequences of incorporation

Contractual arrangements

In Figures 4.2–4.4, the creditor could have insisted that the shareholder (or one or more of the shareholders) guarantee the obligations of Company A Ltd under any loan between the creditor and Company A Ltd. Such guarantees are very common in the context of corporate groups, when they are called 'parent guarantees'. They are also very common in the context of sole member or closely-held companies.

In Figure 4.5, O, the ex-employer, could protect itself by appropriate language in E's contract of employment. The contractual clause containing the restrictive covenant could be drafted so that the restriction covered sales to O's customers by E or any company owned or controlled by E. It would also be sensible to define control for the purposes of the covenant.

These are two illustrations of how contracts can be used to work around the consequences of incorporation. Agency is a particular type of contractual relationship. An agency relationship may be put in place between a company and its shareholder. A claimant often seeks to establish that a company is the agent of its shareholder so that the claimant has a claim against the principal (the shareholder) rather than the (insolvent) agent/company.

Agency and the consequences of incorporation

There is no presumption of agency between a company and its shareholder(s). If the facts support the argument, however, it may be possible to argue in the context of Figures 4.3 and 4.4 (ignoring Figure 4.2 because this argument is less likely to succeed where there is more than one shareholder) that when it entered into the loan agreement (or whichever contract has given rise to the sum of money being owed to the creditor), Company A Ltd acted as the agent of the shareholder/parent company. If this argument succeeds, the shareholder/parent company, as the principal, is the party to the loan/contract, not Company A Ltd, and the creditor can sue the shareholder/parent company to recover the sum owed because it is owed by the shareholder/parent company.

In such a case, agency does not override or undermine the separate personality of Company A Ltd. Company A Ltd must be a separate legal entity from its shareholder/parent company to play the role of agent. Its separate legal personality is a precondition to the agency argument succeeding.

In *Adams v Cape* (1990), it was argued that certain subsidiaries of Cape which were present in the USA acted as Cape's agent. Although it was clear that the subsidiaries in question acted as the agent of Cape for certain specific purposes, it was found as a matter of fact that there was no agency between the subsidiaries and Cape such as to make the presence of the subsidiaries in the USA the presence of Cape. This case highlights the difficulty in establishing an agency relationship between a parent and a subsidiary company in the absence of clear written evidence that such a relationship has been agreed by both parties. In this light, agency can be seen as a contractual self-help remedy.

Agency was used in a different way as a step in an argument (which failed) to impose liability on the indirect owner of a company in *Yukong Lines Ltd of Korea v Rendsburg Investments Corporation of Liberia, The Rialto No. 2* [1998] 1 WLR 294 (QBD).

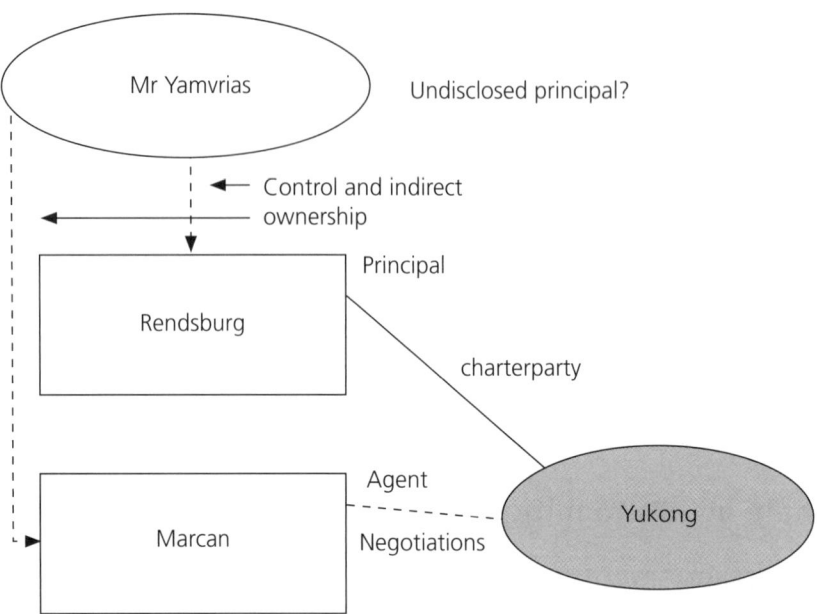

FIGURE 4.6 *The Rialto No. 2*

 **CASE LAW 4.4**

Yukong Lines Ltd of Korea v Rendsburg Investments Corporation of Liberia, The Rialto No. 2 [1998] 1 WLR 294 (QBD)

Yukong was a Korean shipping company. It negotiated with Marcan to enter into a charterparty (a lease of a ship). Marcan was the agent of Rendsburg, a Liberian company, and the parties to the charterparty were Yukong and Rendsburg. Before the ship was delivered by Yukong, assets were moved out of Rendsburg and Rendsburg repudiated the charterparty. Yukong found itself with a right to sue a company, Rendsburg, which had no money to pay the damages suffered by Yukong as a result of the repudiatory breach. Yukong argued that Mr Yamvrias, a director of Marcam and the indirect owner (along with his family) of both Marcan and Rendsburg, was the undisclosed principal of Rendsburg. If this could be proved, Mr Yamvrias (a wealthy man) would be the correct party to the charterparty and Yukong could sue Mr Yamvrias for damages for breach of contract. Held:

- Mr Yamvrias controlled Rendsburg and the ultimate beneficial interest in both Rendsburg and Marcam companies rested with him and other members of his family.
- Mr Yamvrias had caused assets of Rendsburg to be moved out of the company to put those assets beyond the reach of Yukong.
- Mr Yamvrias had signed the charterparty expressly as agent for Rendsburg.
- The parties to the charterparty were Rendsburg and Yukong.
- Yamvrias did not enter into the charterparty as undisclosed principal of Rendsburg: there was no evidence of this.
- Movement of the funds out of Rendsburg was not enough to treat Yamvrias as a party to the charterparty.
- Yukong must look to the insolvency laws to protect itself in a case such as this where it finds itself to be a contingent judgment creditor of an insolvent company (Rendsburg).

Although the claimant, Yukong, was unsuccessful in *The Rialto No. 2*, the case illustrates how agency may provide a claimant with a remedy against a shareholder of a company.

To summarise, claimants dissatisfied with their rights against a company have often put forward agency arguments to support a remedy against the shareholder. This will succeed or fail depending on whether or not the facts support the assertion that an agency relationship exists making the company the agent of the shareholder.

7.3 Piercing the corporate veil: court-developed limits on the consequences of incorporation

Over the years, claimants have put forward three further arguments to support requests for remedies against one or more shareholders of the company. These arguments are based on the single economic entity theory, the façade theory and the justice theory.

Each of these theories was exhaustively examined by the Court of Appeal in *Adams v Cape* (1990) and, more recently, the Supreme Court in *VTB Capital plc (Appellant) v Nutritek International Corp and others (Respondents)* [2013] UKSC 5 examined whether a doctrine of 'piercing the corporate veil' exists at all. As a result, it may be stated with confidence that of the three theories, it is only the façade theory, if any, that provides a basis for 'piercing the corporate veil', that is, treating a company and the shareholder standing behind the company, as a single entity in law so that some of the rights, liabilities or activities of the company are the rights, liabilities or activities of the shareholder (see *Atlas Maritime Company SA v Avalon Maritime Limited (No 1)* [1991] 4 All ER 769), and vice versa.

In *VTB*, whilst not going so far as to accept the submission of counsel for the Respondents that, 'whatever has been said about it in previous cases, the court cannot in fact pierce the corporate veil', Lord Neuberger stated:

> 'The notion that there is no principled basis upon which it can be said that one can pierce the veil of incorporation receives some support from the fact that the precise nature, basis and meaning of the principle are all somewhat obscure, as are the precise nature of circumstances in which the principle can apply.'

It was not necessary for the court to decide whether the doctrine actually exists as a doctrine rather than a rubric beneath which a range of cases are collected together, all of which can be justified on other legal grounds, as, to decide the case, it was sufficient to find that there no reliable authority exists to support the proposition that a person who controls a company may be declared to be subject to the obligations under a contract between a third party and the company where neither the third party nor the company intended the controller to be a party. Accordingly, doubt was also cast on the correctness of Burton J's decision in *Antonio Gramsci Shipping Corp v Stepanovs* [2011] EWHC 333.

Single economic entity theory

The proposition that a court can treat a group of companies as a single entity in law because they are/it is a single economic entity is false. In *Adams v Cape* (1990), Slade LJ quoted with approval the following words of Goff LJ (as he then was) in *Bank of Tokyo Ltd v Karoon* (1987) AC 45 (CA):

> 'Counsel suggested beguilingly that it would be technical for us to distinguish between parent and subsidiary company in this context; economically, he said, they were one. But we are concerned not with economics but the law. The distinction between the two is, in law, fundamental and cannot here be bridged.'

The apparent acceptance of the single economic entity theory by Lord Denning in *DHN Ltd v Tower Hamlets LBC* (1976) (CA) can no longer be regarded as good law. The correctness of the reasoning in the case has been doubted by the House of Lords in *Woolfson v Strathclyde RC* (1978) SC 90 (HL) in which, referencing the *DHN* decision, Lord Keith of Kinkel said:

> 'I have some doubts whether in this respect the Court of Appeal properly applied the principle that it is appropriate to pierce the corporate veil only where special circumstances exist indicating that it is a mere façade concealing the true facts.'

DHN involved compensation under the Land Compensation Act 1961. It is now regarded as an example of a case involving interpretation of a statutory provision pursuant to which a parent and two subsidiary companies were to be treated as one unit for the purposes of entitlement to statutory compensation for disturbance, a point made by Slade LJ in *Adams v Cape Industries plc* (1990).

Ord v Belhaven Pubs Ltd [1998] 2 BCC 607 (CA) provides a clear illustration of the single entity theory being rejected because it offends against the separate legal personality doctrine.

 **CASE LAW 4.4**

Ord v Belhaven Pubs Ltd [1998] 2 BCC 607 (CA)

The plaintiff sued the defendant company in contract and tort arising out of the entry into a lease of a pub from the defendant in 1989. During proceedings the defendant company ceased trading, had no assets and the plaintiff sought to replace its parent, Ascot Holdings Ltd, or a sister company in the group, Ascot Estates Ltd, as the defendant. In an attempt to rationalise the group's operating structure, the group had been reorganised to consolidate the hotels business and assets in the defendant and the pubs in Ascot Estates Ltd. Properties had been transferred at book value. In 1992 assets were transferred from the defendant company to its parent company, Ascot Holdings Ltd, at above book value. At first instance the judge decided to treat the group as a single entity and permitted the substitution of the parent company as the defendant in the action. She spoke of the parent company being the 'controlling mind' of the subsidiaries and of the 'concept of corporate benefit' or 'concept of the economic unit'.

Held on appeal: Reversing the first instance decision, neither the parent nor the sister company was liable for the liabilities of the defendant. To disregard the distinction between the legal entities involved in order to render the holding company potentially liable was at odds with the whole concept of corporate personality, limited liability and the decision in *Salomon v Salomon*.

As we have seen, the court in *Adams v Cape* Industries plc (1990) rejected the single legal entity theory in a case involving tort victims of a subsidiary company who had suffered physical injury, unlike the Ords who had suffered purely economic loss. The court in *Adams v Cape* denied the tort victims access to parent company funds to pay unpaid judgments obtained against subsidiary companies.

Façade theory

If the company is a 'mere façade concealing the true facts', the corporate veil will be pierced. Authority for this proposition is the House of Lords decision in *Woolfson v Strathclyde Regional Council* (above), although Lord Kinkel cited no authority for this proposition and gave no indication of the meaning of 'façade'. Ten years later, Slade LJ commented on the authorities on façade in the Court of Appeal in *Adams v Cape* (1990) (at 543).

> 'From the authorities cited to us we are left with rather sparse guidance as to the principles which should guide the court in determining whether or not the arrangements of a corporate group involve a façade within the meaning of that word as used by the House of Lords in Woolfson.'

In the cases in which the courts have treated the company and the shareholder as one, the terms used to describe the company (apart from 'façade') are 'device', 'stratagem', 'mask', 'cloak' and 'sham', all of which terms were used in *Gilford Motor Company Ltd v Horne* [1933] Ch 935. This basis for ignoring the separate legal personality of the company may be seen as an application of a legal principle or doctrine of general application, the 'sham doctrine'. The sham doctrine was acknowledged by Diplock LJ in *Snook v London and West Riding Investments Ltd* [1967] 2 QB 786, 803 in the following terms:

> 'it means acts done or documents executed by the parties to the "sham" which are intended by them to give to third parties or to the court the appearance of creating between the parties

legal rights and obligations different from the actual legal rights and obligations (if any) which the parties intend to create.'

The consequence of the finding that acts or documents are a sham is illustrated by the words of Lindley LJ in *Yorkshire Railway Wagon Co v Maclure* (1882) 21 Ch D 309, 318. Speaking in the context of a transaction entered into by a company he stated: 'If it were a mere cloak or screen for another transaction one could see through it.' If a company is a sham, it is ignored and this act of ignoring it is a piercing of the corporate veil.

We have seen how, because of the apparently unlimited range of circumstances in which it is possible to create a separate legal personality, two or more legal persons may exist where there is only one economic entity or economic interest in existence. This is the case where an individual forms a sole member company (or a company in which a number of shareholders hold their shares on trust for one individual), or where a company forms and owns all the shares in another company (a 'wholly-owned subsidiary company'). The sham-based cases are situations in which in fact, or in substance (if not in legal form), there is no difference between one person's economic interest and the company's economic interest.

Where a company is formed with the intention of using it to avoid an existing legal liability, the court will pierce the veil based on a finding of sham.

Gilford Motor Company Ltd v Horne [1933] Ch 935

An ex-employee was unable to escape a restrictive covenant in favour of his ex-employer by carrying out the restricted activity through a company he had formed for that purpose (see Figure 4.5).

Jones v Lipman [1962] 1 WLR 832 (Ch Div)

A person who had contracted to sell a piece of land was not permitted to avoid an order for specific performance by transferring the land to a company created solely for the purpose of avoiding the transfer to the buyer. The company was subject to the specific decree order.

It is not necessary to establish that the company was formed with the intention to avoid an existing legal obligation. *Trustor v Smallbone (No. 2)* [2001] WLR 1177 (Ch Div) demonstrates that a company may have been formed for a perfectly proper purpose, but if it is later used as a vehicle to facilitate a breach of duty, its separate legal personality will not be allowed to inhibit a court ordering a remedy reflecting the reality of the situation.

Trustor v Smallbone (No. 2) [2001] WLR 1177 (Ch Div)

Dishonestly, without authority and in breach of duty to Trustor AB, its managing director, Smallbone, transferred c. £20 million to a Gibraltan company, Introcom Ltd. Introcom Ltd was owned indirectly, via a Lichtenstein trust, by Smallbone, who also controlled the company. Introcom Ltd had been set up earlier in connection with another matter, as a vehicle for remuneration for Smallbone. The court ordered Introcom Ltd to repay the sum received to Trustor AB on the ground that it had knowingly received the money, i.e. had received the money with knowledge of Smallbone's breach of fiduciary duty. Trustor AB then sought to make Smallbone liable to repay the money received by Introcom Ltd.

 **CASE LAW 4.8** *continued*

Held: The court was entitled to pierce the corporate veil and recognise the receipt of the company (Introcom Ltd) as that of the individual in control of the company (Smallbone). The company was used as a device or façade in that it was used as the vehicle for the receipt of the money and its use was improper as it was the means by which Smallbone committed inexcusable breaches of his duty as a director of Trustor AB.

Justice theory

It has been argued that if justice requires it, a remedy should be available against the shareholder for a wrong done by the company. Presented in these general terms, the argument offends against the doctrine of legal certainty and may be rejected for this reason alone. Delivering the judgment of the Court of Appeal in *Adams v Cape* (1990), Slade LJ rejected the argument as unfounded:

> 'Mr. Morison ... submitted that the court will, in appropriate circumstances, ignore the distinction in law between members of a group of companies treating them as one, and that broadly speaking, it will do so whenever it considers that justice so demands. In support of this submission, he referred us to a number of authorities ... Mr. Morison described the theme of all these cases as being that where legal technicalities would produce injustice in cases involving members of a group of companies, such technicalities should not be allowed to prevail. We do not think that the cases relied on go nearly so far as this. As Sir Godfray submitted, save in cases which turn on the wording of particular statutes or contracts, the court is not free to disregard the principle of *Salomon v. A. Salomon & Co. Ltd.* [1897] A.C. 22 merely because it considers that justice so requires.'

There are, however, many situations when courts will look through a company and ignore its existence. The façade theory provides examples of this. Other examples exist that do not fit together neatly into a theory. Rather than attempting to create a general theory for when courts will pierce the corporate veil, the approach suggested by Davies and others to explain these cases is to examine the purpose of the legal rule or principle in issue in each case.

Approached in this way, the existence of a company becomes simply a fact in the context of the application of the rule or principle. In each case, the court is refining the rule or principle in issue by explaining how that rule operates in the context involving a company, rather than the court developing a general rule or principle of company law that must be applied regardless of the rule or principle in issue.

7.4 Statutory provisions supplementing available remedies

Statutory provisions regularly supplement or otherwise affect the rights of individuals and companies. A statute may, for example, create a statutory cause of action or provide a defence to a claim. Ordinarily, these provisions do not impinge on the separate legal personalities of companies. Occasionally, however, the operation of a statute may result in the separate legal personality of a company being ignored, or, put another way, the corporate veil being pierced. This was the case in *DHN*.

The approach to statutory interpretation to be adopted when the interpretation of a statute will result in the piercing of the corporate veil is found in *Dimbleby & Sons Ltd v National Union of Journalists* [1984] 1 WLR 427 (HL).

In *Dimbleby*, the House of Lords has expressed the view that while, if it is the intention of Parliament that the separate personality of one or more companies be ignored, one would expect this to be expressly stated in the statute, even in the absence of clear words, such an intention may be the inexorable result of a purposive construction of the statute. Such result was not inexorable in the *Dimbleby* case in which the National Union of Journalists (NUJ) argued, unsuccessfully, that a sister company of the employer company with which the NUJ was in dispute, was itself 'an employer who is party to the dispute'.

'The "corporate veil" in the case of companies incorporated under the Companies Act is drawn by statute and it can be pierced by some other statute if such other statute so provides; but in view of its raison d'etre and its consistent recognition by the courts since *Salomon v. Salomon and Co. Ltd.* [1897] A.C. 22, one would expect that any parliamentary intention to pierce the corporate veil would be expressed in clear and unequivocal language. I do not wholly exclude the possibility that even in the absence of express words stating that in specified circumstances one company, although separately incorporated, is to be treated as sharing the same legal personality of another, a purposive construction of the statute may nevertheless lead inexorably to the conclusion that such must have been the intention of Parliament.'

Examples of statutory provisions that supplement or otherwise affect the rights of a claimant in relation to a company are set out below. The examples are taken from company law and insolvency law. They are not an exhaustive list. A number of tax statute provisions are designed to preclude the use of the corporate form to avoid liabilities. To achieve this, the statutory provisions sometimes require the separate legal personality of companies to be ignored.

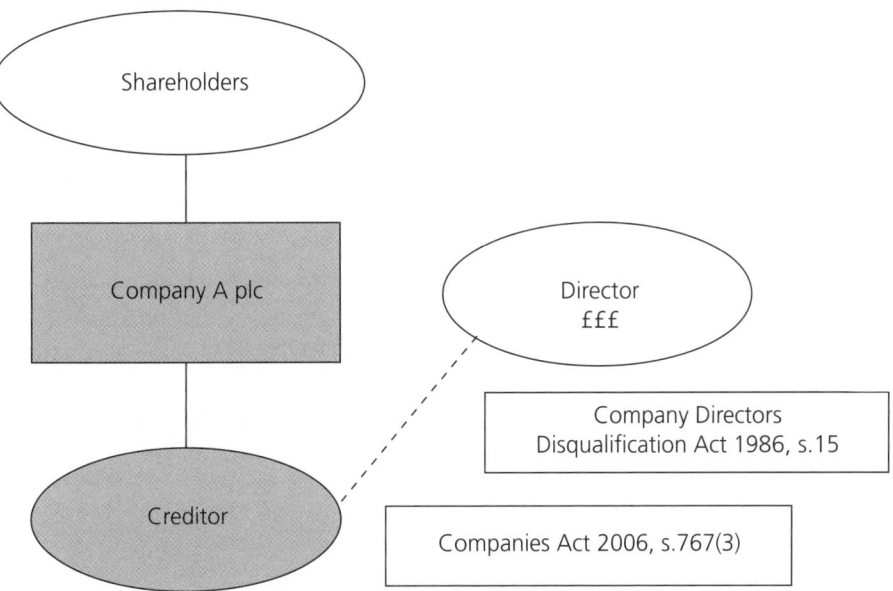

FIGURE 4.7 Statutory provisions supplementing the rights of a creditor against the company

Companies Act 2006, s. 767(3)

The Companies Act 2006 imposes a minimum share capital requirement on public companies which must be complied with before the Registrar of Companies will issue a trading certificate under s. 761. Where a public company does business or exercises any borrowing powers without having a trading certificate it contravenes s. 761. If the company defaults on any obligation under a transaction entered into whilst in contravention of s. 761, s. 767(3) operates to make the directors of the company jointly and severally liable to indemnify any other party to the transaction in respect of any loss or damage suffered by him by reason of the company's failure to comply with its obligations. This is an example of a statutory provision supplementing the rights of a person with rights against a company by rendering the directors of the company liable for the obligations of the company.

Company Directors Disqualification Act 1986, s. 15

Section 15 of the Company Directors Disqualification Act 1986 (CDDA) operates to make a person who is involved in the management of a company while disqualified pursuant to the Act jointly and severally liable with the company for debts incurred by the company during the time he was so involved. This is another example of a statutory provision supplementing the rights of a person who has rights against the company. The operation of s. 15 (CDDA) and s. 767(3) of the Companies Act 2006 are illustrated in Figure 4.7.

Fraudulent or wrongful trading, Insolvency Act 1986, ss. 213 and 214

When a company has ceased trading and is being wound up, statutory provisions enable the liquidator to apply to the court for orders against any persons who were knowingly a party to fraudulent trading by the company (s. 213) or any director who allowed the company to continue to trade when he knew or should have known there was no reasonable prospect of avoiding insolvent liquidation (s. 214). The orders require those persons to contribute to the assets of the company.

These statutory provisions do not give rights directly to creditors of a company, but they are important examples of how the strict consequence of the separate legal personality of the company, that creditors have access only to the assets of the company, is ameliorated by entitling the liquidator to bring actions that will benefit creditors against directors and (in some cases) shareholders. These and similar statutory provisions are examined in part 5.

TEST YOUR KNOWLEDGE 4.5

(a) Identify three routes by which to supplement the separate corporate personality doctrine so that a creditor has a remedy against someone apart from the company.
(b) Is a subsidiary company presumed to be the agent of its parent company?
(c) Identify three theories on the basis of which courts have in the past been willing to 'pierce the corporate veil'.
(d) Which of these theories remain available today to justify piercing the corporate veil?
(e) What is the approach to statutory interpretation adopted when the interpretation of a statute may result in effect in piercing the corporate veil?
(f) Do the Companies Act 2006, s. 767 and the Company Directors Disqualification Act 1986, s. 15 impose liability on shareholders?

CHAPTER SUMMARY

- On registration a company becomes a separate legal person (s. 15(1)).
- Without more, the shareholders of a company cannot be sued to enforce contracts to which the company is a party (*Salomon v A Salomon & Co Ltd* (1897); *Ord v Belhaven* (1998)).
- Property owned by the company is not owned by its shareholders and shareholders have no insurable interest in it (*Macaura v Northern Assurance Co* (1925)). Companies may own shares in other companies. Corporate groups may be organised so as to minimise the legal liabilities of individual companies in the group (*Adams v Cape* (1990)).
- Limited liability is a concept distinct from separate legal personality. A shareholder of an unlimited company must contribute sums to the company in a winding up to enable the company to pay its creditors in full, (Insolvency Act 1986, s. 74(1)). A shareholder of a limited company is not required to contribute more than the amount unpaid for the shares he owns, (Insolvency Act 1986, s. 74(2)(d)).
- A company can make calls on nil-paid or partly paid-up shares until all shares are fully paid-up (*Preston v Grand Collier Dock Co* (1840)).
- Persons dealing with a company can take self-help action to mitigate the consequences of each company having a separate legal personality.
- Statutes sometimes provide a person dealing with a company with an alternative remedy to the remedy they have against the company.
- A disqualified director who takes part in management will be liable for the debts and other liabilities of the company, (Company Directors Disqualification Act 1986, s. 15).
- It is a matter of statutory interpretation whether or not a statute permits or requires the separate legal personality of a company to be ignored, (*Dimbleby v National Union of Journalists* (1984)).
- The liquidator of a company has a range of statutory powers to bring actions against directors and others to swell the assets available for distribution to creditors, Insolvency Act 1986, ss. 212–214).

- The court will pierce the corporate veil and disregard the separate legal personality of a company in some, very limited, circumstances.
- The single economic entity theory of a corporate group is not relevant in law to determining the liability of a parent company; each company in a corporate group is a separate legal entity (*Adams v Cape* (1990); *Chandler v Cape* (2011); *VTB v Nutriek* (2013)).
- If the company is a sham its separate legal personality will be ignored (*Jones v Lipman* (1962); *Gilford v Horne* (1933); *Trustor v Smallbone* (No. 2) (2001)).

5 The constitution of the company

■ CONTENTS

1. What is the constitution of a company?
2. Pre-Companies Act 2006 constitutions
3. The objects and capacity of a company
4. What are the Articles of Association?
5. The Articles as a statutory contract and enforcement
6. Amending the Articles of Association
7. Contracts with terms derived from the Articles
8. Shareholders' agreements

■ INTRODUCTION

The most important constitutional document of a company is the Articles of Association. This was not the case before the Companies Act 2006 and in this chapter we look at the effect the 2006 Act has had on the constitutions of companies registered under previous companies acts, particularly on the objects clauses of those companies. We then examine the Articles of Association, principally its legal status and how to amend it, followed by consideration of the important role played by shareholders' agreements that exist alongside the formal constitutional documents required by the Companies Act.

1 What is the constitution of a company?

The constitution is the company's governance system, the rules and principles prescribing how it is to function. There is no comprehensive legal definition and this governance system is a combination of:

1. legal rules and principles found in statutes and case law (general company law); and
2. rules and principles adopted by members of the company contained in:
   - the Articles of Association;
   - special resolutions;
   - 'any resolution or agreement agreed to by all the members ... that, if not so agreed, would not have been effective for its purpose unless passed by a special resolution' (s. 29).

Unfortunately, which shareholder decisions and agreements fall into the final bullet point is not clear. This is an important issue because all constitutional documents, decisions and agreements must be registered with the Registrar of Companies and are available for public scrutiny (s. 30). They must be sent to a member on request (s. 32), with criminal liability for the company and every officer in default arising in the event of non-compliance. Some shareholders' agreements fall within s. 29 and therefore must be registered, but some do not. Shareholders' agreements are discussed at section 8 below.

For the purposes of supplying members with copies, the meaning of 'constitutional documents' is extended to include a current statement of capital (or, in the case of a company limited by guarantee, the statement of guarantee), and the current (as well as any past) certificate of incorporation (s. 32).

2 Pre-Companies Act 2006 constitutions

It is important to understand some of the key principles of company law relevant to company constitutions prior to the 2006 Act because:

- many company law cases, of continued relevance under the 2006 Act, are difficult to understand without a basic understanding of the concepts of the objects and capacity of a company and the doctrine of *ultra vires*; and
- companies already in existence when the relevant provisions of the 2006 Act came into effect continue to have 'old-style Memoranda of Associations' and so it is important to know about these, their original role, and the effect the 2006 Act has had on the role they play.

3 The objects and capacity of a company

3.1 Pre-Companies Act 2006 companies

Old-style Memoranda of Association

The objects and capacity of a pre-Companies Act 2006 company are rooted in its Memorandum of Association, the mandatory provisions of which, for a company limited by shares, were:

- the company name;
- if the company was to be registered as a public company, this fact had to be stated;
- whether the registered office was to be in England, Wales or Scotland;
- the company's objects;
- that the liability of the members was limited;
- the share capital and how it was divided into shares of fixed amount; and
- the name and address of each of the subscribers (the first members of the company) and the number of shares each agreed to acquire on registration.

Objects, capacity and the *ultra vires* doctrine

Companies registered before the Companies Act 2006 had to be registered to pursue one or more 'objects' or types of business which were set out in the **objects clause** of the company's old-style Memorandum of Association. Traditionally, the object of a company would be specific, such as 'to operate a railway'.

The rationale for requiring a registered company to state its object/s was to ensure that members and creditors of the company were clearly informed of the line of business the company had been formed to pursue. In *Ashbury Carriage and Iron Company Ltd v Riche* (1875) LR 7 HL 653 the House of Lords confirmed that the *ultra vires* doctrine applied to registered companies. This meant that the legal capacity of a registered company was limited to pursuit of the objects for which it was formed, as specified in its Memorandum of Association.

 **CASE LAW 5.1**

***Ashbury Carriage and Iron Company Ltd v Riche* (1875) LR 7 HL 653**

Ashbury Carriage and Iron Company Ltd was registered under the Joint Stock Companies Act 1862 with the objects, specified in its Memorandum of Association, of dealing in railway carriages and other railway plant and related lines of business which did not include the funding or construction of railway lines. The company entered into a contract to provide finance for the construction of a railway line in Belgium. When the company was sued to enforce the contract it argued that entry into the contract was *ultra vires* the company, the contract was void, and that this remained the legal position even if the shareholders had authorised the contract or subsequently approved entry into it.

CASE LAW 5.1 continued

Held: In favour of the company, *per* Lord Cairns: 'In my opinion, beyond all doubt, on the true construction of the statute of 1862, creating this corporation, it appears that it was the intention of the Legislature, not implied, but actually expressed, that the corporation should not enter, having regard to its Memorandum of Association, into a contract of this description ... every Court ... is bound to treat that contract, entered into contrary to the enactment, I will not say as illegal, but as extra vires, and wholly null and void ... I am clearly of opinion that this contract was entirely, as I have said, beyond the objects in the Memorandum of Association. If so, it was thereby placed beyond the powers of the company to make the contract. If so, my Lords, it is not a question whether the contract ever was ratified or was not ratified. It was a contract void from its beginning, it was void because the company could not make the contract.'

Unfortunately, the term *ultra vires* is not always used in this strict sense and a great deal of confusion has arisen, particularly as a result of it being used to describe a situation where, although the company has the legal capacity to act in a certain way, the particular individual within the company who performs the act (often, although not necessarily, a director), or the board of directors collectively, does not have the authority to do so. This is not a case of *ultra vires* but rather of 'excess of powers' in that an agent of the company acts outside the scope of his or their authority, rather than the company acting outside its legal capacity.

The practice of drafting the objects of a company very broadly quickly rendered the strict *ultra vires* doctrine of little practical relevance to most companies, as almost any conceivable act would fall within the broadly stated objects. Even where *ultra vires* remained relevant to a given company, the effect of a company acting outside its capacity was altered when the 1st European Company Law Directive was implemented in the UK (by s. 9(1) of the European Communities Act 1972). Rather than protecting company members, this Directive focused on protecting those who traded with companies. At common law, if a third party contracted with a company and entry into the contract turned out to be outside the capacity of the company and therefore *ultra vires*, the legal right of the company to walk away (because the contract was null and void) protected the shareholders from the board of directors using company assets to pursue goals outside the line of business shareholders understood to be the object of the company when they invested in the company. This preserved the expectations of shareholders, but left the third party's expectations defeated as he was unable to enforce the contract.

UK implementation of the Directive was initially half-hearted but, incrementally, application of the *ultra vires* doctrine to companies has been eroded until it remains relevant to charitable companies only (s. 42). The unlimited legal capacity of a non-charitable registered company is confirmed by what is now s. 39(1) of the Companies Act 2006:

'The validity of an act done by a company shall not be called into question on the ground of lack of capacity by reason of anything in the company's constitution.'

Impact of the 2006 Act on the constitution of existing companies

Every company already in existence before the Companies Act 2006 took effect will have an old-style Memorandum and will probably continue beyond that date to have an old-style Memorandum registered with the Registrar of Companies as there is no obligation to take any action to change this situation. However, from that date, s. 28 provides for an objects clause in a company's Memorandum of Association to be treated as a provision of the company's Articles of Association. Objects clauses in the Articles of a company do not limit the capacity of the company. However, because they are deemed to be provisions of the Articles, objects clauses of pre-2006 companies, just like the objects clauses of those companies registered under the 2006 Act that choose to have objects clauses, remain relevant, but for different legal reasons which are outlined below.

3.2 Companies registered under the Companies Act 2006

Any company registered under the Companies Act 2006 has a new-style Memorandum of Association.

New-style Memoranda of Association

A new-style Memorandum of Association is simply a prescribed form document to be completed and filed with the Registrar of Companies at the time the company is registered. It is never updated. It simply states (s. 8), as a matter of record, that the subscribers:

- wish to form a company under the Act;
- agree to become a member and, if the company is to have a share capital, to take at least one share each.

Only one member is required for a company registered under the 2006 Act, whether it is a public or private company (s. 7(1)). Single member private companies were permitted under the 1985 Act, but public companies were required to have a minimum of two members. This technical requirement was regularly satisfied by simply allotting one share to a person to hold the legal title as bare trustee for the other, main shareholder as beneficiary.

As a result of s. 39(1), together with the change in the role of the Memorandum of Association, the *ultra vires* doctrine is no longer relevant to non-charitable registered companies and all non-charitable companies have the capacity of a natural person.

A company registered under the 2006 Act need not state the objects it is registered to pursue and, unless the Articles specifically restrict them, the objects of the company are unrestricted (s. 31(1)). Companies are not expected to choose to state objects in their Articles, although some may do so. The legal implications of an objects clause in the Articles (which are the same as the legal implications of an objects clause of a pre-2006 Act company deemed to be a provision of its Articles) are as follows:

1. An objects clause operates as a limitation on the authority of the board of directors to bind the company (although the common law position on this is significantly altered by ss. 40 and 41 in order to protect third parties).
2. An objects clause operates as a provision of the company's constitution and:
   - a director owes the company a duty to act in accordance with the company's constitution (s. 171);
   - a shareholder can apply for an injunction to prevent a company from acting outside its constitution, that is, beyond its restricted objects (*Stevens v Mysore Reefs (Kangundi) Mining Co Ltd* [1902] 1 Ch 745);
3. Should the object no longer be pursuable or capable of achievement, the 'substratum' of the company may be regarded as gone, which has been held to be a good ground for the court to order that the company be wound up under the Insolvency Act 1986, s. 122(1)(g), on the basis that 'the court is of the opinion that it is just and equitable that the company should be wound up'.

TEST YOUR KNOWLEDGE 5.1

(a) What is meant by a company's 'objects'?
(b) Explain what is meant by the phrase '*ultra vires* the capacity of the company'.
(c) What is the capacity of a non-charitable registered company?
(d) Are all companies required to have objects?
(e) What is the impact of the Companies Act 2006 on the objects clause of a pre-2006 Act company?
(f) What are the consequences of a company acting outside its objects clause today?
(g) What is the content of a new-style Memorandum of Association?

4 What are the Articles of Association?

The most important constitutional document of a company registered under the Companies Act 2006 is the Articles of Association. The Articles of Association contain the internal rules of the company. They state the organisational structure of the company, allocate powers to and between the organs of the company (the board of directors and the shareholders) and prescribe procedures for decision-making.

4.1 Drafting Articles and the Model Articles

Although Articles can be drafted from scratch, they rarely are. Company legislation has always contained Model or default Articles and different sets of Model Articles exist for different types of companies. The Model Articles for companies limited by share capital registered under the Companies Act 1985 is known as **Table A** and is relevant to both public and private companies. The default Articles under the Companies Act 2006 are called the Model Articles and there are different Model Articles for private companies limited by shares and public companies. The Model Articles for Private Companies Limited by Shares is a shorter and less formal set of rules (53 Articles) than the Model Articles for Public Companies (86 Articles). Both sets of Model Articles appear in Appendices 1 and 2.

The Model Articles apply in the absence of alternative Articles being filed on registration of the company (s. 20(1)(a)). The Model Articles also apply in so far as proposed alternative Articles 'do not exclude or modify the relevant Model Articles' (s. 20(1)(b)). The normal practice is for part only of the relevant Model Articles to be adopted, supplemented by particular Articles appropriate to the circumstances in which the company is being formed and the wishes of the prospective members. Form IN01 clearly offers these three options. Option 1 provides for adoption of the Model Articles for the type of company being registered without amendment or supplement, Option 3 provides for a bespoke set of articles to be attached to Form IN01, and Option 2 provides for the Model Articles for the type of company being registered to be adopted 'with additional or amended provisions' as set out in a document to be attached to Form IN01.

4.2 Ascertaining the Articles of Association

On registration of the company, the initial Articles (whether the Model Articles, wholly bespoke articles or somewhere in between) become a document of public record. Articles can be amended, usually by special resolution, so it is always important to check that you have the most up to date version of the Articles of a company. If you are reviewing a company's documents to ascertain its Articles, always check whether, since inception, there have been any amendments to the original Articles and whether a new set of Articles has been adopted.

For older companies, always check which Table A forms the basis of the Articles, as there have been different versions over time. Where a copy has not been attached, but simply referred to, it is sometimes necessary to refer to Table A from the companies act current at the time the company was incorporated.

4.3 Content of the Articles of Association

Range of issues typically covered by the Articles

The following list is not comprehensive but gives a general indication of the principal matters covered by the Articles of a company limited by share capital:

1 Directors
    - Directors' powers and responsibilities
    - Decision-making by directors
    - Appointment of directors
    - Directors' indemnity and insurance
2 Decision-making by members
    - Organisation of general meetings
    - Voting at general meetings
    - Restrictions on members' rights
    - Application of rules to class meetings

3   Shares and distributions
   - Issue of shares
   - Interests in shares
   - Share certificates and uncertificated shares
   - Liability of members
   - Partly-paid shares
   - Transfer of shares
   - Distributions (dividends)
   - Capitalisation of profits

This list is based on the Model Articles for Public Companies, but most of the matters covered are also relevant to private companies limited by share capital (see Appendices 1 and 2).

Limits on the content of the Articles

The content of the Articles is a matter to be agreed by the original members of the company and may be changed from time to time as the company develops (see amendment of Articles below). Basically, any matter may be included in the Articles subject to the general principle that Articles inconsistent with the law are void and unenforceable. Articles that purport to override certain statutory rights or powers have been held to be void and unenforceable.

An example of an article being void because it purported to exclude a statutory right is *Re Peveril Gold Mines Ltd* [1898] 1 Ch 122 (CA). The statutory right in question was the right of a shareholder to petition the court to wind up the company.

CASE LAW 5.2

Re Peveril Gold Mines Ltd [1898] 1 Ch 122 (CA)
A provision in the Articles of the company purported to limit the statutory right of a shareholder to petition the court to wind up the company under s. 82 of the Companies Act 1862 (now s. 124(1) of the Insolvency Act 1986).
   Held: The article was void. *Per* Chitty, LJ: 'In my opinion, this condition is annexed to the incorporation of a company with limited liability – that the company may be wound up under the circumstances, and at the instance of the persons, prescribed by the Act, and the Articles of Association cannot validly provide that the shareholders, who are entitled under s. 82 to petition for a winding up, shall not do so except on certain conditions'.

A second example of a statutory power that cannot be overridden by an article is the power of a company to amend its Articles by special resolution, currently found in s. 21 of the Companies Act 2006. This was confirmed by Lindley MR in the Court of Appeal in the leading case on amendment of the Articles, *Allen v Gold Reefs of West Africa Ltd* [1900] 1 Ch 656 (CA).

> 'the company is empowered by the statute to alter the regulations contained in its Articles from time to time by special resolution ... and any regulation or article purporting to deprive the company of this power is invalid on the ground that it is contrary to the statute ...'

Note that specific provisions of a company's Articles can be entrenched pursuant to s. 22 of the 2006 Act, and this section is considered below, under amendment of the Articles.

The principle that Articles inconsistent with the law are void is simple to state but can be difficult to apply. It presupposes clarity as to which laws are mandatory and which may be opted out of, something not always clear in company law. Even if a particular statutory provision is asserted to be mandatory, on a number of occasions the courts have endorsed arrangements that in effect, if not in form, permit the statutory provision to be opted-out of. Three cases exemplify this: *Bushell v Faith* [1969] 2 Ch 438 (HL) and *Amalgamated Pest Control v McCarron* [1995] 1 QdR 583 (Queensland Supreme Court, Australia) which both involve weighted voting rights, and *Russell v Northern Bank Development Corporation* [1992] 1 WLR 588 (HL), which, as it involved the impact of a voting agreement in a shareholders' agreement, is discussed under shareholders' agreements in section 8 below.

 **CASE LAW 5.3**

Bushell v Faith [1969] 2 Ch 438 (HL)
A company had a share capital of 300 £1 shares with 100 shares owned by Mr Faith, Mrs Bushell and Dr Bayne each. An Article provided: 'In the event of a resolution being proposed at any general meeting of the company for the removal from office of any director, any shares held by that director shall on a pole in respect of such resolution carry the right to three votes per share'. An attempt was made to remove Mr Faith by ordinary resolution of the shareholders, relying on what is now s. 168 Companies Act 2006.

Held: Mr Faith could insist on three votes per share in any resolution to remove him from office, the result being that he could always outvote the other two shareholders, even though they owned two-thirds of the shares and could carry any other ordinary resolution. *Per* Lord Donavon: 'Any case where the Articles prescribed that a director should be removable during his period of office only by a special resolution or an extraordinary resolution ... is overridden by [the Companies Act s. 168]. A simple majority of the votes will now suffice ... It is now contended, however, that [s. 168] does something more; namely that it provides in effect that when the ordinary resolution proposing the removal of the director is put to the meeting each member present shall have one vote per share ... Why should this be? The section does not say so as it easily could ... Parliament followed its practice of leaving to companies and their shareholders liberty to allocate voting rights as they please.'

Is s. 168 a mandatory rule or not? It can be circumvented by the use of weighted voting rights which suggests that it is not. Note, however, that the Listing Rules forbid the circumventing of s. 168 by provisions such as this in the Articles. The rule for companies with listed shares is therefore different from the rule for other companies (whether private or public). For companies with listed shares, it is a mandatory rule.

The reasoning in *Bushell v Faith* was followed in the case of *Amalgamated Pest Control* [1995] 1QdR 583 (Queensland Supreme Court, Australia). There, the Articles of Association gave one member 26% of the votes on any special resolution, with the result that he could defeat any special resolution. The Queensland Supreme Court upheld this allocation of voting rights.

Finally, in relation to the content of the Articles, although Articles are a type of agreement between all the shareholders of a company, they are a document of public record and subject to unique rules, including rules as to amendment and enforcement, which makes them a *sui generis* arrangement. Because of this, shareholders often prefer to capture the agreement between them in a separate agreement, a 'shareholders' agreement' (see section 8 below). Shareholders' agreements often contain important arrangements that impact on the way a company is managed and may render the Articles misleading if not read in conjunction with the shareholders' agreement.

 TEST YOUR KNOWLEDGE 5.2

(a) What role is played by the Articles of Association of a registered company?
(b) How many sets of Model Articles exist?
(c) Outline the key matters addressed by the Model Articles for Public Companies.
(d) Identify two statutory rights that cannot be over-ridden by provision to the contrary in the Articles of Association of a registered company.

5 The Articles as a statutory contract and enforcement

Section 33(1) of the Companies Act 2006 makes it clear that a contract is created by the Articles of Association.

> 'The provisions of a company's constitution bind the company and its members to the same extent as if there were covenants on the part of the company and of each member to observe those provisions.'

Although not made clear by the language used in the predecessor section, s. 33 has been redrafted to make it clear that the company is a party to the statutory contract. Each member is a party to the statutory contract which is not just a contract between each member and the company, but also between each member and each other member (*Salmon v Quin & Axtens Ltd* [1909] AC 442 (HL) and *Rayfield v Hands* [1960] Ch 1, each considered below).

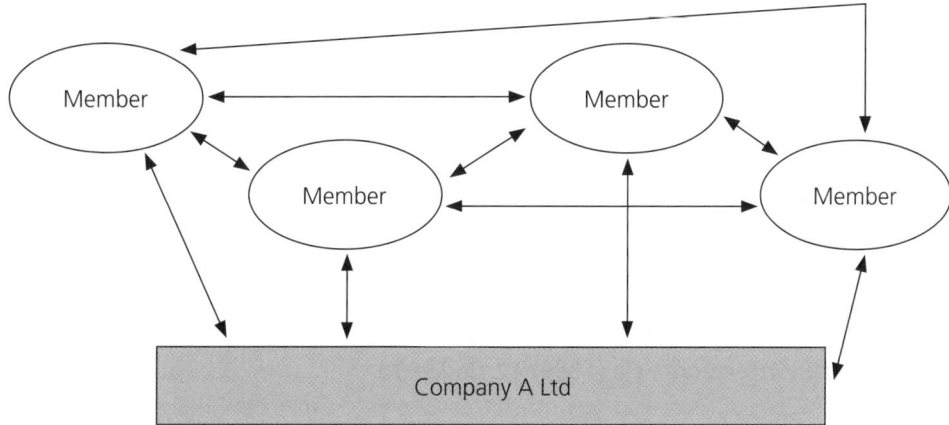

FIGURE 5.1 Contractual relationships created by the s. 33 statutory contract

The statutory contract has noteworthy characteristics that distinguish it from a typical contract as follows:

- Amendment of a contract usually requires the agreement of all parties, yet the Articles can be amended (subject to entrenchment) by a special resolution, which requires the support of only 75% of the members (s. 21(1)).
- A contract usually binds only those parties who agree to it, yet all members at any time are bound by the Articles so that a new member who has played no part in the drafting of the Articles, upon being registered as a member, is bound by the Articles.
- The Articles cannot be challenged based on the doctrines of misrepresentation, mistake (common law or equitable) or undue influence (*Bratton Seymour Service Co Ltd v Oxborough* [1992] BCLC 693 (CA)).
- The court may not rectify the Articles even if they do not represent the intentions of the members on incorporation (*Evans v Chapman* (1902) 86 LT 381; *Scott v Frank F. Scott (London) Ltd* [1940] Ch 749 (CA)).
- The Articles are exempt from the Contract (Rights of Third Parties) Act 1999 (see s. 6(2) of that Act), so that a third party cannot enforce a provision in the Articles.
- The Articles are not subject to ss. 2–4 of the Unfair Contract Terms Act 1977 (see sch. 1, para. 1(d) to that Act).

If the Articles were an ordinary contract, enforcement of its provisions would be straightforward; parties to the contract could both enforce the contract and have the contract enforced against them. Unfortunately, in relation to the statutory contract, the answer is not that straightforward.

5.1 Enforcement by the company

The company can enforce the Articles against individual members, as illustrated by *Hickman v Kent or Romney Sheep Breeders Association* [1915] 1 Ch 881.

 **CASE LAW 5.4**

Hickman v Kent or Romney Sheep Breeders Association [1915] 1 Ch 881

Articles provided for disputes between a member and the company to be referred to arbitration. A member sued in court to enforce his rights as a member, including his right to have his sheep registered by the company in its published flock book.

Held: The court stayed the court proceedings brought by the member as the member was bound by the Articles to arbitrate the dispute and the company was entitled to enforce the arbitration clause in the Articles against the member.

5.2 Enforcement by members

Some of the provisions in the Articles can be enforced by a member, whether against the company (as in *Wood v Odessa Waterworks Co* (1889) 42 Ch D 636) or against other members (as in *Rayfield v Hands* [1960] Ch 1).

 **CASE LAW 5.5**

Wood v Odessa Waterworks Co (1889) 42 Ch D 636

Provisions in the Articles of Association governed the rights of the members in respect of the division of the profits of the company. A member, on behalf of himself and all other members, brought an action for an injunction to restrain the company from acting on an ordinary resolution supporting a board proposal that profits be used to give debenture bonds to members instead of dividends, on the ground that to do so contravened the Articles of Association of the company.

Held *per* Stirling J: 'What I have to determine is, whether that which is proposed to be done is in accordance with the Articles of Association as they stand, and, in my judgment, it is not, and therefore the Plaintiff is entitled to an injunction so far as relates to the payment of dividends.'

 **CASE LAW 5.6**

Rayfield v Hands [1960] Ch 1

Articles provided that a shareholder wishing to sell his shares must offer them to those members who were directors and those member/directors were required to buy the shares at a fair price. The member/directors refused to buy the shares and Mr Rayfield sued them to enforce the provision in the Articles.

Held: Mr Rayfield could enforce the article against the member/directors who were ordered to take the shares. Note that Vaisey J sounded a note of caution as to the range of application of this principle of direct enforcement by one member against another: 'The conclusion to which I have come may not be of so general application as to extend to Articles of Association of every company, for it is, I think, material to remember that this private company is one of that class of companies which bears a close analogy to a partnership.'

It appears that some types of provisions in the Articles may not be enforceable by members. The cases in which the courts have imposed restrictions on enforcement fall into two categories, cases concerning enforcement of outsider rights and cases concerning internal irregularities.

Can a member sue to enforce outsider rights in the Articles?

The widely-held view appears to be that a member cannot sue to enforce outsider rights. An outsider right attaches to a person in a capacity other than as a member (such as the right to be a director or the company solicitor) rather than in his capacity as member (such as the right to attend and vote at meetings). The cases of *Eley v Positive Government Security Life Assurance Co* (1876) 1 ExD 88 (CA), *Browne v La Trinidad* (1887) 37 Ch D 1, *Hickman v Kent or Romney Sheep Breeders Association* [1915] 1 Ch 881 and *Beattie v E & F Beattie Ltd* [1938] Ch 708 (CA), are commonly cited in support of this restriction on enforcement. However, the case law is inconsistent and the position remains unclear.

 **CASE LAW 5.7**

Eley v Positive Government Security Life Assurance Co (1876) 1 ExD 88 (CA)
Articles required the company to employ Eley as its solicitor unless he had been guilty of misconduct. The company used a different solicitor and Eley sued the company for breach of contract arguing that the Articles formed a contract between himself and the company. Eley was treated as suing in his capacity as an 'outsider', not as a member.
   Held: Eley could not rely on or enforce the Articles which were 'a matter between the directors and shareholders, and not between them and the plaintiff.' The court also rejected the argument that the relevant article was evidence of an agreement between the company and Eley separate from the Articles.

Eley clearly supports the proposition that the Articles can only confer rights on a member, not on a third party or 'outsider'. However, this is merely an illustration of the doctrine of privity: the outsider is not a party to the contract and therefore cannot enforce the contract. In fact, although he was not a member at the time the Articles were adopted (on incorporation of the company), Eley was a member of the company at the time of the court case, but this fact does not seem to have been brought to the attention of the court as it was not addressed in the judgment. It is not clear that this case would have been decided the same way if Eley had sued as a member (*qua* member), rather than as an outsider. On its face, the case is not authority for the proposition that a member cannot enforce outsider rights, but for the more limited and obvious common law proposition that a non-party to a contract cannot sue to enforce the contract.

 **CASE LAW 5.8**

Browne v La Trinidad (1887) 37 Ch D 1 (CA)
Articles entitled Mr Browne to be a director for a fixed period. Browne was a member of the company, but could not enforce the right to be a director, even in his capacity as a member, as it was a matter 'not connected with the holding of shares'.

The third case cited in support of the unenforceability of outsider rights by a member is *Hickman* (above), yet, on its facts, *Hickman* involved membership rights, not outsider rights and anything said in the case about enforcement of outsider rights is strictly obiter dictum, not being necessary to support the decision in the case. It is unfortunate, therefore, that the Court of Appeal in *Beattie* placed such importance on the following two oft-quoted passages from the judgment of Astbury J in *Hickman*:

'An outsider to whom rights purport to be given by the articles in his capacity as such outsider, whether he is or subsequently becomes a member, cannot sue on those articles treating them as contracts between himself and the company to enforce those rights. Those are not part of the general regulations of the company applicable alike to all shareholders and can only exist by virtue of some contact between such person and the company.

... no right merely purporting to be given by an article to a person, whether as a member or not, in a capacity other than that of member, as, for instance, as solicitor, promoter, director, can be enforced against the company'.

The most important case supporting the unenforceability of outsider rights is *Beattie v E & F Beattie Ltd* [1938] Ch 708 (CA).

Beattie v E & F Beattie Ltd [1938] Ch 708 (CA)

A derivative action was brought on behalf of the company by a member seeking an injunction stopping a director, Ernest Beattie (EB), from denying the member access to the books and accounts of the company. In effect, the company was suing a director for breach of duty in his capacity as director. EB was both a director and a member of the company. He applied to have the action stayed on the ground that the Articles contained a provision requiring all disputes between members of the company or between members and the company to be referred to arbitration. (If a valid arbitration clause exists the courts will normally 'stay' or pause court proceedings to enable the dispute to be resolved by arbitration.)

Held: EB could not invoke the article and insist on arbitration as this was not a dispute between the company and himself as a member. It was an action against him in his capacity as a director (an outsider) and the Articles were not relevant. *Per* Wilfred Greene MR: 'the contractual force given to the Articles of Association by [s. 33] is limited to such provisions of the Articles as apply to the relationship of the members in their capacity as members.'

Note that Ernest Beattie was not seeking to enforce the Articles '*qua* member'. Rather, in proceedings already underway in which he was being sued in his capacity as a director, he sought to assert his contractual rights as a member of the company. Focusing on this aspect of the case, it could be said that this case, like *Eley*, is simply an illustration of privity: Ernest Beattie, the director, was not, in that capacity, a party to the contract in the Articles; nor was the dispute between him and the company a dispute between the company and a member as member. As Greene MR commented, by seeking to have the dispute referred to arbitration, 'he is not, in my judgment, seeking to enforce a right which is common to himself and all other members'. The question was left open in this case whether the court would have stayed the derivative action if an action had been brought by a member (even Mr Beattie himself), as member, to enforce the arbitration clause in the Articles, thereby requiring what was a dispute between members and the company (about access to company records) to be arbitrated.

Turning to consider authority for the counter-proposition, i.e. the proposition that outsider rights in the Articles are enforceable, the leading case is *Salmon v Quinn & Axtens Ltd* [1909] 1 Ch 311 (HL). The House of Lords permitted a shareholder to enforce a veto given to him in the Articles in his capacity of managing director (not shareholder/member).

Salmon v Quinn & Axtens Ltd [1909] 1 Ch 311 (HL)

Messrs Axtens and Salmon held a large majority of shares in the company. By the Articles:
- General management of the company was given to the board of directors subject to the right of members, by ordinary resolution 'being not inconsistent with the Articles', to decide matters.

CASE LAW 5.10 continued

- Each of two managing directors (Messrs Axtens and Salmon) was given power to veto decisions of the board relating to acquiring and letting premises.

In accordance with the Articles, as managing director, Mr Salmon (S) vetoed a decision, but his veto was ignored and the other directors secured an ordinary resolution of the members to support their decision. S, in his capacity as a member of the company enforcing the Articles, sought an injunction to restrain the decision being carried out.

Held: The House of Lords granted the injunction reasoning that this was an attempt to bypass rules on decision-making contained within the Articles. It was an attempt to amend the Articles by an ordinary resolution rather than by a special resolution (see the next section on amendment of Articles). The court would prevent the company acting on a decision taken unconstitutionally.

Mr Salmon, a director and member of the company, in effect enforced the rights in the Articles given to a managing director. The managing director's veto right was not common to all shareholders, thus Mr Salmon enforced an 'outsider' right. He enforced this 'outsider' right by bringing an action as a member to enforce the Articles. Lord Wedderburn has argued that this case establishes that members can indirectly enforce outsider rights in the Articles by suing as members to require the company not to depart from the contract in the Articles (Wedderburn, 1957).

Can a member sue to enforce the Articles where there has been an internal irregularity?

Courts will not provide a remedy to an individual shareholder seeking to enforce a limitation or procedure set out in the Articles if a majority of the members could, consistently with the statute and the Articles, bring about the outcome being complained of. This is based on the principle of majority rule: an individual member of a company cannot usurp the power of the majority of the members. The concept of internal irregularity limits the personal rights of an individual member. Internal irregularities are breaches of those limits or procedures imposed on the company that can be complained of only by a majority of the members. If a majority of the members condones or 'ratifies' the irregularity, an individual shareholder is powerless to enforce the stipulated limit or procedure.

In the case of *Grant v UK Switchback Railways Company* (1888) 40 Ch D 135 (CA), directors acted in breach of restrictions imposed by the Articles but an individual shareholder could not bring an action because the matter in issue was a mere internal irregularity that could be and had been ratified by an ordinary resolution (i.e. by a simple majority vote) of shareholders.

CASE LAW 5.11

Grant v UK Switchback Railways Company (1888) 40 Ch D 135 (CA)
The Articles disqualified a director from voting to approve entry into any contract in which he was personally interested. The board of directors entered into a contract to sell the business of the company. All but one of the directors were personally interested in the sale contract. A member applied for an injunction restraining the company from carrying out the contract as it was entered into in breach of the Articles. Before the application was heard a general meeting of the company was held at which an ordinary resolution was passed approving and adopting the contract and authorising the directors to carry it into effect.

Held: The Court of Appeal refused to grant an injunction. The directors had no authority to enter into the contract but the shareholders could ratify the unauthorised act by ordinary resolution and had done so.

In the earlier case of *MacDougall v Gardiner* (1875) 1 Ch D 13 (CA), the Court of Appeal had strongly asserted the importance of not engaging the courts in matters internal to a company at the suit of an individual shareholder. Mellish LJ stressed the importance of respecting majority rule. He did not require the majority to have expressed its will to defeat the action of an individual shareholder, it was enough that a meeting could be called at which the majority could correct the irregularity.

This unwillingness of the courts to interfere in the internal management of companies, contrasts with cases such as *Pender v Lushington* (1877) 6 Ch D 70 that focus on the rights of shareholders.

CASE LAW 5.12

Pender v Lushington (1877) 6 Ch D 70

The Articles provided for one vote for every ten shares with no member entitled to more than 100 votes in total. Pender transferred some of his shares to nominees to hold on trust and those nominees sought to vote along with Pender on a resolution.

The chairman of the company refused to count the nominee's votes and the resolution was defeated. Pender and the nominee shareholders brought an action seeking an injunction.

Held: They were entitled to an injunction preventing the company from acting contrary to the resolution. *Per* Jessel MR, 'This is an action by Mr. Pender for himself. He is a member of the company, and … he is entitled to have his vote recorded – an individual right in respect of which he has a right to sue. That has nothing to do with the question like that raised in *Foss v Harbottle* and that line of cases. He has a right to say, "you shall record my vote, as that is a right of property belonging to my interest in this company, and if you refuse to record my vote I will institute legal proceedings against you to compel you".'

It is very difficult to reconcile these very different approaches taken by the courts. A great deal of uncertainty remains as to which rights stated in the Articles can be enforced by members and, consequently, it is impossible to provide a comprehensive definition of the personal rights of a shareholder.

TEST YOUR KNOWLEDGE 5.3

(a) Between which parties does the s. 33 statutory contract operate?
(b) Identify six characteristics of the s. 33 statutory contract that distinguish it from a typical contract.
(c) What is an 'outsider right' for the purposes of enforcing a provision of a company's Articles of Association?
(d) Can a member sue to enforce outsider rights set out in the Articles of Association?
(e) Can you reconcile *Salmon v Quinn & Axtens Ltd* with *Beattie v E & F Beattie Ltd*?

6 Amending the Articles of Association

6.1 Statutory provisions governing amendment

Section 21 states that a company may amend its Articles by special resolution. The relevant special resolution (s. 30) and a copy of the new Articles (s. 26) must be sent to the Registrar of Companies. A shareholder is not bound by an amendment that requires him to take more shares or increases his liability to pay money to the company (s. 25).

By way of exceptions to the need for a special resolution to amend the Articles, s. 551(8) states that a resolution to give, vary, revoke or renew authorisation of the directors to exercise the power of the company to allot shares in the company may be an ordinary resolution 'even though it amends the company's Articles'. Section 551(9) brings any such resolution within the s. 30 obligation to forward a copy to the Registrar of Companies. Section 685(2) also acknowledges that changes to the Articles can be brought about by ordinary resolutions in cases in which the directors are authorised by ordinary resolution, pursuant to s. 685(1), to determine the terms and conditions of redemption of shares.

6.2 Contractual provisions affecting amendment

Provisions in the Articles

The common law principle that a company cannot, by putting a provision to that effect in its Articles, deprive itself of the statutory power to amend its Articles by special resolution is subject to the s. 22 right to entrench provisions in the Articles.

> '(1) A company's Articles may contain provision ('provision for entrenchment') to the effect that specified provisions of the Articles may be amended or repealed only if conditions are met, or procedures are complied with, that are more restrictive than those applicable in the case of a special resolution.
> (2) Provision for entrenchment may only be made –
>   (a) in the company's Articles on formation, or
>   (b) by an amendment of the company's Articles agreed to by all the members of the company.
> (3) Provision for entrenchment does not prevent amendment of the company's Articles –
>   (a) by agreement of all the members of the company,
>   (b) by order of a court.' (s. 22)

Article provisions can only be entrenched on incorporation or, if at a later date, only by unanimous consent of the shareholders, and the existence of a provision for entrenchment must be drawn to the attention of the Registrar of Companies (s. 23).

Provisions in company contracts

A company cannot enter into a specifically enforceable agreement not to exercise its statutory power to amend its Articles (see *Russell v Northern Bank Development Corporation* [1992] 1 WLR 588 (HL), considered at section 8 below). A company may amend its Articles and act on the amended Articles even if this means that the company is in breach of a contract previously entered into. The remedy for the other party to the contract is damages, not an injunction, if the effect of an injunction would be to stop the company relying on its amended Articles, thereby, in effect, restricting its power to amend its Articles.

 **CASE LAW 5.13**

Southern Foundries (1926) Ltd v Shirlaw [1940] AC 701 (HL)

The company contracted with Shirlaw that he was to be managing director of the company for ten years. The Articles provided that if a managing director ceased to be a director his appointment as managing director would also end. The company was taken over and the new owners amended the Articles to provide that they could remove any director by written instrument. Shirlaw was removed as a director and the company treated his managing directorship as also at an end, relying on the relevant article, even though this contradicted the agreement between Shirlaw and the company as Shirlaw had only been the managing director for just over two years. Shirlaw sued the company and the new owner for damages.

Held: Shirlaw was entitled to damages. The company was entitled to rely on the amended Articles. No injunction could be granted to prevent the adoption of new Articles. *Per* L Porter: 'A company cannot be precluded from altering its Articles thereby giving itself power to act upon the provisions of the altered Articles – but so to act may nevertheless be a breach of the contract if it is contrary to a stipulation in a contract validly made before variation.'

Provisions in shareholders' agreements

Unlike a company agreement, a shareholders' agreement can have a significant effect on the statutory power of a company to amend its Articles. This is considered in section 8 below.

6.3 Court-developed restrictions on amendment

In addition to statutory provisions expressly addressing amendment of the Articles and contractual provisions affecting the statutory power of a company to amend its Articles, the courts have developed restrictions governing exercise of the statutory power to amend the Articles.

No amendment to remove accrued rights

An amendment that deprives a shareholder of rights retrospectively, that is, rights that have already accrued, will not be effective unless the shareholder agrees to it (*James v Buena Ventura Nitrate Grounds Syndicate Limited* [1896] 1 Ch 456).

No amendment to introduce an article that could not have been included on incorporation

Articles inconsistent with mandatory company law rules are void and unenforceable (see section 4.3 above). It follows that any amended article purporting to override such a company law rule, equally, is void and unenforceable. Note, however, that even if it is permissible to include a particular provision in the Articles at the outset, when a company is originally incorporated, it does not necessarily follow that such a provision may be added to the Articles by amendment by special resolution.

There seems to be at least one type of provision courts permit on incorporation but will not allow to be introduced into the Articles by amendment, at least not without the consent of the affected shareholder(s). This is a bare **squeeze-out** provision (also known as a bare compulsory transfer provision) which allows a shareholder to be bought out and excluded from continued participation in a company without that right to exclude being conditional on behaviour of the shareholder that would in some way justify exclusion, such as competing with the company. Bare squeeze-out clauses may be included in Articles on incorporation (*Phillips v Manufacturers' Securities Limited* (1917) 116 LT 290 (CA)).

The cases on bare squeeze-outs are consistent with a rule that a shareholder's right to continue to own shares in a company cannot be taken away by amendment of the Articles by special resolution except where:

- the amendment provides for the shareholder 'to receive fair value for his shares', and
- the shareholders' continued membership in the company is detrimental to the conduct of the company's affairs so that the exclusion is for a proper purpose.

The key cases on squeeze-out rights, *Sidebottom v Kershaw, Leese & Co Ltd* [1920] 1 Ch 154, *Brown v British Abrasive Wheel Co Ltd* [1919] 1 Ch 290 and *Dafen Tinplate Co Ltd v Llanelly Steel Company* (1907) Ltd [1920] 2 Ch 124, are discussed after an examination of the cases setting out the general approach of the courts.

Amendment must be *bona fide* for the benefit of the company as a whole

We now turn to the most important judicial restriction on the power of amendment of the Articles. In *Allen v Gold Reefs of West Africa Ltd* [1900] 1 Ch 656 (CA), referring to what is now s. 22 of the 2006 Act, Lindley MR stated what has come to be regarded as the definitive, if not always helpful, statement of the common law restriction on the exercise of the power to amend the Articles, that the statutory power to amend must be exercised '*bona fide* for the benefit of the company as a whole'. The burden of proof is on the person who challenges the validity of the amendment (see *Peters' American Delicacy Co Ltd v Heath* (1939) 61 CLR 457).

CASE LAW 5.14

***Allen v Gold Reefs of West Africa Ltd* [1900] 1 Ch 656 (CA)**
Emilio Zuccani owned partly paid shares and was the only owner of fully-paid shares in the company. He died owing the company over £6,000, the aggregate of sums called-up but still unpaid on his partly paid-up shares. Articles provided for a **lien** in favour of the company 'upon all shares (not being fully paid) held by such member in respect of debts owed by a shareholder to the company'. After Mr Zuccani's death the company amended the Articles to omit the language in brackets thereby extending the company's lien to cover fully paid-up shares. Mr Zuccani's executors sought a declaration that the company had no lien upon the fully paid-up shares. They argued, among other points, that the resolution creating a lien upon Mr Zuccani's fully paid-up shares was an oppressive act as against him, he being the only holder of fully paid-up shares in the company.

Held: The amendment was valid. Any suspicions excited by the fact that the amendment only affected Zucanni's executor were dispelled once it was realised that this was because Zuccani was the only holder of paid-up shares who at the time was in arrear of calls. The altered Articles applied to all holders of fully paid shares, made no distinction between them, and therefore the directors could not be charged with bad faith. Lindley, MR stated the following now famous words: 'The power ... conferred on companies to alter ... their Articles ... must, like all other powers, be exercised subject to those general principles of law and equity which are applicable to all powers conferred on majorities and enabling them to bind minorities. *It must be exercised not only in the manner required by law, but also, bona fide for the benefit of the company as a whole and it must not be exceeded.* These conditions are always implied, and are seldom, if ever, expressed. But if they are complied with, I can discover no ground for judicially putting any other restrictions on the power conferred by the section than those contained in it.' (emphasis added)

Application of the *Allen* principle where the company's interests are not affected by the amendment

In *Allen* the amendment directly affected the interests of the company. As Romer LJ stated:

> 'It appears to me the shareholders were acting in the truest and best interests of the company in exercising the legal right to alter the Articles so that the company might as one result obtain payment of the debt due from Mr Zuccani. The shareholders were only bound to look to the interests of the company. They were not bound to consult or consider Mr Zuccani's separate or private interests.'

The *Allen* principle is more difficult to apply where the amendment in question does not particularly affect the interests of the company as a separate entity, but rather solely impacts on shareholders and has different effects on the minority and majority shareholders. Examples are amendments affecting the distribution of dividends or capital and amendments affecting the power of shareholders to retain and dispose of their shares. The Court of Appeal in *Greenhalgh v Arderne Cinemas Ltd* [1951] Ch 286 (CA) tried to deal with this by developing what has subsequently come to be known as the 'discrimination test'.

CASE LAW 5.15

***Greenhalgh v Arderne Cinemas Ltd* [1951] Ch 286 (CA)**
Pre-emption rights in the Articles gave existing shareholders the right to buy shares of any shareholder who wished to sell. The Articles were amended to add a provision that any member could transfer shares to anyone if the transfer was approved by ordinary resolution. The effect of this amendment was to take away from the minority the right to acquire other members' shares

CASE LAW 5.15 continued

(provided an ordinary resolution could be secured). Held: The amendment was valid. The court applied the principle in *Allen v Gold Reefs of West Africa* but Evershed MR sought to explain the application of the principle. He stated: 'a special resolution ... would be liable to be impeached if the effect of it were to discriminate between the majority shareholders and the minority shareholders, so as to give the former an advantage of which the latter were deprived.'

The fact that the amendment in *Greenhalgh* was held not to bring about the type of discrimination that fell within the scope of the principle immediately created uncertainty as to exactly which type of discrimination was such as to cause a court to restrain the majority. In *Citco Banking Corporation v Pusser's Ltd* (2007) Bus LR 960 (PC) Lord Hoffmann reviewed the cases, including *Greenhalgh*, and expressed the view that the *Allen* test was not helpful in cases in which the interests of the company are not affected. Although he stated that another test of validity is required for such cases, it was not necessary to decide the case to expound an alternative, which he declined to do.

'It must however be acknowledged that the test of "*bona fide* for the benefit of the company as a whole" will not enable one to decide all cases in which amendments of the Articles operate to the disadvantage of some shareholder or group of shareholders. Such amendments are sometimes only for the purpose of regulating the rights of shareholders in matters in which the company as a corporate entity has no interest, such as the distribution of dividends or capital or the power to dispose of shares ... Some other test of validity is required.'

Application of the *Allen* principle in squeeze-out cases

As discussed above, the *Allen* principle has been applied to amendments introducing squeeze-out provisions in three leading cases.

CASE LAW 5.16

Sidebottom v Kershaw, Leese & Co Ltd [1920] 1 Ch 154 (CA)
The Articles were amended to provide that any shareholder who competed with the company could be compelled to sell his shares to nominees of the directors at full value, i.e. a compulsory transfer/expulsion provision but conditioned on the shareholder behaving contrary to the interests of the company.

Held: An expulsion clause can be included in Articles on the registration of a company. Articles can be amended to include such a provision provided the exercise of the power of alteration is bona fide for the benefit of the company as a whole. An alteration applicable to all shareholders is not open to challenge solely on the basis of its impact on a particular shareholder. Here, the amendment was passed bona fide for the benefit of the company as a whole therefore was allowed to stand.

CASE LAW 5.17

Brown v British Abrasive Wheel Co Ltd [1919] 1 Ch 290
Holders of 98% of the shares in the company were willing to provide capital to fund development of the company only if they could acquire the other 2%. They sought to amend the Articles to permit them to acquire the shares at fair value. Held: The minority shareholder was entitled to an injunction preventing the shareholders from altering the Articles. The court found as a matter of fact that the majority had acted for their own benefit, not the benefit of the company.

CASE LAW 5.18

Dafen Tinplate v Llanelly Steel Company (1907) Ltd [1920] 2 Ch 124

The company had been founded on the expectation that shareholders would purchase their supplies from the company. A shareholder began sourcing supplies from a competing company in which he had an interest. The Articles were amended to provide a right of the majority shareholders to decide that the shares of any member (other than one principal shareholder) be offered for sale by the directors to anyone the directors chose, at fair value as decided by the directors.

Held: The court did not allow the amendment to stand on the basis that to say that such an unrestricted power of expropriation was for the benefit of the company was to confuse the interests of the majority with the benefit of the company as a whole.

Reform of the *Allen* principle

In relation to the right of majorities to bind minorities, calls for the governing legal principles to be clarified or changed and, in either case, placed on a statutory footing in the 2006 Act, have not been acted upon. In part this has been explained by the difficulty of coming up with more appropriate legal principles to govern than those found in the case law (and the belief that this is not a particularly important area of law to clarify because a shareholder who is not satisfied with an amendment can obtain an appropriate remedy by bringing an unfair prejudice petition under s. 994 of the 2006 Act).

STOP AND THINK 5.1

Unfair prejudice petitions, the existence of which, it has been argued, reduces the importance of the law limiting the right of majority shareholders to amend the constitution of a company, are considered in part 3. Is it clear that amendment of the Articles in accordance with the statutory power (s. 21) could found a successful unfair prejudice petition? In the absence of clear rules as to the rights of a minority shareholder to protection in the context of amendment of the Articles, such a petition would need to be based on unfair prejudice to the interests of the shareholder, interests being interpreted to extend beyond strict legal rights. This extended concept of 'interest' is problematic and, as part 3 demonstrates, appears to be confined to 'quasi-partnership' companies.

TEST YOUR KNOWLEDGE 5.4

(a) How may a registered company amend its Articles of Association?
(b) Is a shareholder bound by an amendment to the Articles that requires him to take more shares or increases his liability to pay money to the company?
(c) How may a registered company entrench provisions of its Articles of Association?
(d) What restriction on the power of amendment of the Articles was laid down in the case of *Allen v Gold Reefs of West Africa*?
(e) Summarise the decisions in the three leading cases on squeeze-out provisions in Articles of Association.
(f) Is it possible to amend the Articles of Association of a registered company to introduce an unrestricted power of expropriation?

7 Contracts with terms derived from the Articles

Individual Articles (often confusingly referred to in old cases as 'regulations') are often found to have been embodied in, and form part of, a separate contract between a company and a third person. This approach has been taken in cases involving directors suing for remuneration stated in the Articles. These cases are examples of the courts applying principles of contract law to identify the express terms of an agreement, implying terms into that agreement (where appropriate), and construing (give meaning to) those terms. It is important not to confuse this use of one or more individual articles (as evidence of the terms of a separate agreement between the company and the relevant third party), with enforcement of the statutory contract. The argument was rejected in *Eley* (see section 6.2) but was accepted in *Re New British Iron Co, ex parte Beckwith* [1898] 1 Ch 324.

 CASE LAW 5.19

Re New British Iron Co, ex parte Beckwith [1898] 1 Ch 324

Article 62 fixed the sum of £1,000 as payable as remuneration to the board of directors, to be divided among them as they saw fit. When the company went into liquidation, without having paid any remuneration, it became important to determine whether or not the remuneration was due to the directors as members (the directors were also shareholders in the company) or otherwise.

Held *per* Wright, J: 'That article is not in itself a contract between the company and the directors ... But where on the footing of that article the directors are employed by the company and accept office the terms of art. 62 are embodied in and form part of the contract between the company and the directors'. The remuneration was due to the directors, 'under a distinct contract with the company.'

Guinness plc v Saunders [1990] 2 AC 663 is a more recent case in which the court treated the relevant Articles as terms embodied in a separate contract between a director and the company. This is not an express part of the decision in the case but must be a step in the reasoning.

 CASE LAW 5.20

Guinness plc v Saunders [1990] 2 AC 663

Articles provided that remuneration for work outside the scope of the ordinary duties of a director had to be fixed by the board of directors as a whole. Mr Ward was a director of Guinness plc who performed work outside the normal scope and was given special remuneration of £5.2 million by a committee of the board. The sum should have been fixed by the board of directors as the committee had no authority to make the payment. Mr Ward was ordered to repay the money to the company. Mr Ward argued that a *quantum meruit* sum was owed to him.

Held: Where parties to a contract have agreed how remuneration is to be determined, the court will not award a *quantum meruit* even if the agreement has not been implemented.

8 Shareholders' agreements

Shareholders' agreements are often entered into when the company is first registered but may be entered into at any time. They may or may not be part of the 'official' constitution of the company subject to the relevant registration requirements. Whether or not they are registrable, they can fundamentally affect the way a company is managed and controlled. Shareholders' agreements are often entered into rather than putting the relevant provisions in the Articles, to provide clarity in relation to enforceability compared to the lack of clarity surrounding enforceability of the Articles of Association, discussed above.

Another reason why shareholders' agreements are used is to preserve confidentiality, yet it is incorrect to assume that all shareholders' agreements can lawfully be kept confidential. Great care must be taken when drafting a shareholders' agreement to ensure that, if confidentiality is required, it does not fall within s. 29 of the Companies Act 2006 and therefore become registrable with the Registrar of Companies pursuant to s. 30 and available for public scrutiny. Failure to register a registrable shareholders' agreement is a criminal offence committed by the company and every officer in default.

Shareholders' agreements are used by the shareholders of closely-held companies, meaning companies with a small number of shareholders. They are impractical for companies with a large number of shareholders and are rarely of interest to those who buy company shares purely as a financial investment. Shareholders' agreements are used as a matter of course in a number of common business transactions, such as joint ventures. The document usually referred to as the 'joint venture agreement' is a particular type of shareholders' agreement.

Many provisions in shareholders' agreements could appear in the Articles but are deliberately put into a shareholders' agreement, usually in pursuit of confidentiality and enforceability. The matters dealt with in shareholders' agreements vary depending upon the context in which the agreement is put in place and range from appointment of directors for fixed term, protection from removal of particular individuals from the board of directors using weighted voting rights, rights regarding withdrawal from the company, pre-emption rights providing that if one shareholder wishes to sell his shares he must first offer them to the others, payment of dividends and restrictive covenants.

Shareholders' agreements are contracts entered into by two or more shareholders. Ordinary rules of contract apply which means that shareholders' agreements bind only those shareholders who enter into the agreement and can only be amended with the agreement of all parties to the agreement.

8.1 Parties to shareholders' agreements

The company can be, and often is, made a party to a shareholders' agreement. The contractual undertakings of the company are subject to special considerations, which often make the contractual obligations of the company unenforceable. Unenforceability of one or more of the company's obligations may or may not affect the operation of the agreement between the shareholders; whether or not it does will depend upon the correct construction of the agreement. It is important to draft the agreement so that, as far as possible, the obligations of the shareholders are stated separately from the obligations of the company. This provides the best likelihood that the problematic obligations can be deleted, or 'blue-lined' out of the agreement, leaving the obligations of the shareholders intact.

8.2 Enforcing shareholders' agreements

If a shareholder who is a party to a shareholders' agreement breaches the agreement, any other shareholder who is a party to the agreement who has suffered loss caused by the breach that is not too remote may sue for damages for breach of contract. The availability of other remedies, such as mandatory injunctions, depends upon the application of contract law principles. The leading case on enforcement of shareholders agreements is *Russell v Northern Bank Development Corporation* [1992] 1 WLR 588 (HL).

CASE LAW 5.21

Russell v Northern Bank Development Corporation [1992] 1 WLR 588 (HL)

A shareholders' agreement was entered into between the five shareholders of Tyrone Brick Limited. The company was also a party to the agreement. Clause 3 provided, among other things, that no further share capital was to be created without the written consent of all parties to the agreement. The board of directors proposed a resolution to increase the share capital. One shareholder, Russell,

 **CASE LAW 5.21** *continued*

sought an injunction restraining the other shareholders who were party to the agreement from voting in support of the resolution and a declaration that clause 3 was valid and binding on both the shareholders and the company.

Held: In relation to the shareholders, the agreement was not a restriction on the statutory powers of the company to alter its share capital, its Memorandum or Articles of Association. Clause 3 was valid and enforceable between the shareholders and Russell was entitled to a declaration that the shareholders were bound by clause 3 as to how to exercise their votes and in an appropriate case would be entitled to an injunction. The agreement was held to be unenforceable against the company.

8.3 The effect of the enforceability of shareholders' agreements

In *Russell* the House of Lords confirmed that shareholders' agreements can be enforced against shareholders. Enforcing a shareholders' agreement can and often does have the effect of circumventing a statutory provision that appears to be mandatory and which the courts will not permit the company to contract out of directly.

By way of illustration, s. 21 of the Companies Act 2006 states that a company may amend its Articles by special resolution, a power that has appeared in previous Companies Acts. It is a long-established principle that a company cannot deprive itself of this statutory power by putting a provision to that effect in its Articles (see *Allen v Gold Reefs of West Africa Ltd* [1900] 1 Ch 656, discussed above). *Russell v Northern Bank Development Corporation* (1992) decided that a company also cannot contract out of this statutory power by entering into an agreement the performance of which has the effect of denying the company the power to exercise its statutory power to amend its Articles.

Such an undertaking by the company was described as, 'as obnoxious as if it had been contained in the Articles of Association and therefore … unenforceable as being contrary to the [Act]'. In reality, however, the company does not need to contract out of this statutory power. The same result, that the power to amend its Articles cannot be exercised, can be achieved by the shareholders entering into a voting arrangement in a shareholders' agreement. Farrar describes this state of the law as a 'triumph of form over substance', for although we can state categorically that a company cannot contract out of the mandatory power in the Companies Act 2006 (the form), that mandatory power can effectively be excluded (the substance). This is a further example of the courts upholding arrangements that circumvent supposedly mandatory statutory provisions (see *Bushell v Faith* [1969] 2 Ch 438 (HL) and *Amalgamated Pest Control v McCarron* [1995] 1QdR 583 (Queensland Supreme Court, Australia), both considered earlier in this chapter).

 TEST YOUR KNOWLEDGE 5.5

(a) What argument can a director make to secure the right to payment of a level of remuneration provided for in the Articles of Association? (consider *Re New British Iron Co, ex parte Beckwith*).

(b) What limit on the availability of quantum meruit payments was confirmed in *Guinness plc v Saunders*?

(c) Why are shareholders' agreements entered into rather than their provisions appearing in the Articles of Association?

(d) Can a company contract out of the statutory power to amend its Articles by entering into an agreement the performance of which would have the effect of denying the company that power?

CHAPTER SUMMARY

- Constitutional documents of a company formed under the Companies Act 2006 are (ss. 29 and 32): Articles, special resolutions, resolutions/agreements of all members that would otherwise have to have been made by special resolution, current statement of capital and certificate of incorporation.
- Historically, a registered company had to have an object clause in its Memorandum of Association. Today, all clauses in Memoranda of Association are treated as Article provisions (s. 28)
- The *ultra vires* doctrine has been wholly abolished for non-charitable companies and a company has the capacity of a natural person (s. 39).
- A 2006 Act registered company may choose to but need not restrict its objects in its Articles (s. 31).
- The impact of restricted objects on third parties is as a limitation on the powers of the board/authority of a company agent which is relevant only to persons dealing with the company in bad faith (s. 40).
- If Articles are not registered, relevant default Model Articles will apply (s. 20(1)(a)).
- Model Articles apply insofar as registered Articles do not exclude or modify them, (s. 20(1)(b)).
- Articles may not override mandatory laws such as the right of a shareholder to petition the court to wind up the company, (*Re Peveril Gold Mines* (1898)).
- Weighted voting rights may operate to undermine the mandatory nature of statutory provisions, (*Bushell v Faith* (1969)) but note Listing Rules prohibit weighted voting rights undermining the right of shareholders to remove directors by ordinary resolution.
- The Articles form a statutory contract (s. 33) enforcement of the provisions of which raises a number of moot issues including:
  - Can a shareholder enforce non-membership rights? (*Beattie v Beattie* (1938) says no (*obiter*); *Salmon v Quinn & Axtens* (1909) suggests yes.)
  - Can a shareholder require the company to act in accordance with the Articles if an ordinary resolution could authorise or ratify the challenged behaviour? (*Grant v UK Switchback Railways* (1888) says no but it is unclear what amounts to an internal management matter and what amounts to a personal right).
  - Can one shareholder enforce the Articles against another shareholder? (*Rayfield v Hands* (1960) says yes, but cautions that the decision may be confined to quasi-partnership cases).
- Article provisions may be found to be embodied in a separate contract between a company and a third person, typically a director's service contract (*Re New British Iron Co, ex parte Beckwith* (1898); *Guinness plc v Saunders* (1990)).
- Articles may be amended by special resolution (s. 21), unless they are entrenched (s. 22).
- A contract clause not to amend its Articles will not be specifically enforced against a company, but the company may be liable in damages if it alters its Articles in breach of the contract (*Russell v Northern Bank Development Corporation* (1992); *Southern Foundries (1926) Ltd v Shirlaw* (1940)).
- Accrued rights may not be removed by amendment of the Articles (*James v Buena Ventura Nitrate Grounds Syndicate Limited* (1896)).
- Amendments must be bona fide for the benefit of the company as a whole, (*Allen v Gold Reefs of West Africa Ltd* (1900)).
- Where the company as an entity is not impacted by the amendment, such as squeeze-out cases, the test is difficult to apply, (*Greenhalgh v Arderne Cinemas Ltd* (1951); *Sidebottom v Kershaw* (1920); *Brown v British Abrasive Wheel* (1919) and *Dafen Tinplate v Llanelly Steel Company* (1907)).
- Shareholders' agreements may undermine the rule preventing Articles overriding mandatory statutory rights of the company such as the right to alter the Articles by special resolution (*Russell v Northern Bank Development Corporation* (1992)).

6 Legally binding the company

■ **CONTENTS**

1 Company deeds
2 Company seals
3 Contracts that bind the company
4 Authority of the board of directors to bind the company
5 Authority of individuals to bind the company

■ **INTRODUCTION**

The legal position of a company can be changed by deed or as a result of less formal documents and/or behaviour. The most frequently changed rights and liabilities are its contractual rights and liabilities, and the main focus of this chapter is how a company acquires or becomes subject to contractual rights and liabilities. Contractual rights and liabilities can arise from contracts by way of deed but most arise as a result of simple contracts.

The key issue in relation to simple contracts is whether or not an individual purporting to act on behalf of the company is authorised to change the legal position of the company in the way in which he has purported to change it. While the requirement of 'authority' of the individual is not confined to simple contracts, it presents itself as a live issue in relation to simple contracts more often than in relation to deeds.

This chapter begins with an examination of how a company becomes bound by a deed. Historically, seals were required to bind a company to a deed. Although this is no longer the case, seals are still in use today and it is appropriate, therefore, to examine the relevance and role of company seals before turning to focus on contracts.

1 Company deeds

1.1 Use of deeds

Deeds are formal documents (sometimes called instruments) affecting the legal rights and obligations of one or more legal persons. A deed may convey (effect the legal transfer of) property from one person to another. This type of deed is usually executed, or 'made', as a deed by the transferor (the person transferring the property) only. A deed may also contain the terms of an agreement entered into between two or more legal persons, in which case it is called a formal contract and is executed as a deed by all parties to the contract.

1.2 Requirements for a company to be bound by a deed

A company can be a party to a deed. The requirements for a company to be bound by a deed, as a deed, are set out in a combination of the Law of Property (Miscellaneous Provisions) Act 1989 (c. 34) (referenced as the LP(MP)A 1989) and the Companies Act 2006 (ss. 44 and 46). LP(MP)A 1989, s. 1(2) states:

'(2) An instrument shall not be a deed unless—
(a) it makes it clear on its face that it is intended to be a deed by the person making it or, as the case may be, by the parties to it (whether by describing itself as a deed or expressing itself to be executed or signed as a deed or otherwise); and
(b) it is validly executed as a deed by that person or, as the case may be, one or more of those parties.'

The rules for how a company validly executes a deed to comply with s. 1(2)(b) are found in ss. 44 and 46 of the Companies Act 2006. Even if ss. 44 and 46 are complied with, the document must also comply with LP(MP)A 1989, s. 1(2)(a): it must be clear on its face that it is intended to be a deed.

Section 44 deals with execution of any document by a company and s. 46 focuses on execution of a document as a deed. Section 44 provides that a document is executed by a company if either:

1 the company's **common seal** (see below) is affixed to it; or
2 it is expressed to be executed by the company and is signed by:
   - two authorised signatories (two directors or one director and the company secretary), or
   - a director in the presence of a witness who attests to his signature.

Section 46 then adds that for a document to be validly executed as a deed for the purposes of LP(MP)A 1989, s. 1(2)(b), the validly executed document must be 'delivered as a deed'.

To deliver a deed is to evince an intention to be bound (*Xenos v Wickham* (1867) LR 2 HL 296). The act of executing a document indicates just such an intention unless the facts indicate otherwise. This is now captured in s. 46(2), which states that a document is presumed to be delivered upon its being executed, unless a contrary intention is proved. Accordingly, although it is common in practice to state on the document the words 'delivered as a deed', these words are not strictly necessary as no reference to delivery needs to be made.

The presumption is that the deed is delivered upon being executed. This is very often not the intention, and it is common therefore to expressly address delivery on the face of the deed to pinpoint the date on which the deed is to become effective. Typical language used in a contract by way of deed would be, 'This deed is delivered on the date written at the start of this agreement'.

1.3 Looking behind a deed

Since 1989, the company law statute has provided that if a document purports to be validly executed (which today would mean purports to be executed in accordance with s. 44 above), it is deemed to have been duly executed. This deeming provision, however, only operates in favour of a purchaser in good faith for valuable consideration (s. 44(5)). It cannot be relied upon by a volunteer or a person who lacks good faith. Although s. 44(5) also cannot be relied upon by the company, this is not usually a problem as the defect in the document can usually be overcome by a unilateral act of the company, such as ratification.

The question that has caused difficulty is whether s. 44(5) protects a third party relying on a 'forged' document. In *Ruben v Great Fingall Consolidated* [1906] AC 439, a case concerning the company seal being attached to share certificates, the House of Lords found that if signatures on a document are forged, the company is not bound because the document is a nullity. The scope of this 'forgery' carve out from s. 44(5) has been questioned in recent years. In *Lovett v Carson Country Homes Ltd* [2009] EWHC 1143 (Ch), Justice Davis pointed out that even in *Ruben* the House of Lords acknowledged that there may be circumstances in which a company is estopped from disputing the validity of a forged deed. Although the Law Commission looked at this issue in 1996–98 and concluded that no reform was needed, Justice Davis has described their conclusion as 'unfortunate'. The scope of s. 44(5) remains unclear.

> **TEST YOUR KNOWLEDGE 6.1**
>
> (a) What are the requirements for a company to be bound by a deed and where are the rules to be found?
> (b) How may a company execute a document?
> (c) What does the Companies Act 2006 state about a document that purports to be validly executed?
> (d) Who can rely on s. 44(5)?
> (e) Can s. 44(5) be relied on if the document is a forgery?

2 Company seals

Company seals are anachronisms. They are literally metal presses that emboss the name and (in most cases) also the number of a registered company into the document to which they are affixed, usually where a red circle or 'wafer' has been stuck onto the document. No company is required to have a seal (s. 45) and even if a company has a seal, it is not necessary to use it unless the Articles of the company require its use in particular circumstances. Deeds and other documents can be validly executed without a seal and share certificates can be issued without being sealed (to mention the prime examples of documents that have historically been sealed).

The Model Articles (art. 49 (for private companies) and art. 81 (for public companies)) do not assume a company has a seal. They simply provide that any seal that a company has may only be used by authority of the directors. Once the seal has been affixed to a document, the Model Articles state that, unless the directors direct otherwise, a document must be signed by at least one authorised person in the presence of a witness who attests the signature. An authorised person for this purpose is a director, the company secretary or any person authorised by the directors for the purpose of signing documents to which the common seal is applied.

3 Contracts that bind the company

Contracts can be classified into:

- formal agreements (deeds); and
- simple contracts (parol agreements).

A company can be a party to either type of agreement. The difficulty a company has, like any other artificial legal person, is how can it enter into such contracts.

3.1 Formal agreements (deeds)

If the terms of a contract are set out in a document that makes it clear on its face that it is intended to be a deed, and is executed and delivered as a deed by the company in accordance with the rules set out earlier in this chapter, the company will be legally bound by that formal contract. The benefits of entering into a contract by way of deed are that, unlike in relation to simple contracts, it can be enforced without evidence of consideration and the limitation period for actions brought under it is 12 years, not six as it is for simple contracts (Limitation Act 1980, s. 5).

3.2 Simple contracts

Simple contracts range from oral agreements to detailed agreements between the parties captured in lengthy documents. Even if it is evidenced by a very formal-looking document, a contract remains a simple contract for legal purposes unless the document satisfies the rules regarding deeds.

The statutory provisions governing companies entering into simple contracts discussed in this chapter apply in addition to, and must be read subject to, any legal formalities required in the case of a similar contract made by an individual (s. 43(2)). A contract for the sale of land, for example, must be in writing signed by or on behalf of each of the parties to the contract (Law of Property (Miscellaneous Provisions) Act 1989, s. 2). Whether the parties are individuals, companies or a mixture of the two, an agreement for the sale of land will not be valid unless it complies with this formality. The Companies Act 2006 simply deals with the issues arising as a result of the company being an artificial rather than a natural person.

A distinction is drawn in the Act between contracts that are *made by a company* and contracts that are *made on behalf of the company* by a person acting under the company's authority, express or implied.

Contracts made by a company

Sections 43(1)(a) and 44(4) together provide that a contract may be 'made by a company' by:

1 writing under its common seal; or
2 writing expressed to be executed by the company and signed by:
   - two authorised persons, or
   - a director in the presence of a witness who attests his signature.

If a contract is set out in writing and that document is either sealed or executed in accordance with s. 44, the company will be bound by the contract. Contracts 'made by a company' for the purposes of s. 43 may be deeds, but if the document does not make it clear on its face that it is intended to be a deed, it can still be a contract 'made by the company'.

Good reason to separate out subsections s. 43(1)(a) from (b) would exist if s. 43(1)(a) were to establish an absolute rule such that, provided the conditions for a contract being 'made by the company' appeared on the face of the document to have been complied with, there would be no room to argue an absence of authority on the part of the individual attaching the seal, the individual signing adjacent to the seal as required by the Articles (of most companies), or the authorised signatories signing the document. No such absolute rule exists and how far it is permissible to look behind the face of a document is not wholly clear. As we have seen when we examined looking behind a deed (section 6.1.3 above), in the circumstances most likely to arise, s. 44(5) bans such examination.

CASE EXAMPLE 6.1

The seal of Company A Limited is affixed to a written contract between Company A Limited and B which is also signed by a director of Company A Limited whose signature is attested by a witness, as required by Company A Limited's Articles for use of the company seal. Is Company A Limited bound by the terms of the agreement?

The basic rule is that the agreement can be enforced against the company by a third party, B in this example (s. 43(1)(a)).

CASE EXAMPLE 6.2

A written contract is expressed to be between Company A Limited and B. At the end of the document it states, 'signed on behalf of Company A Limited by'. A director and the company secretary have signed the agreement in the space that follows. Is Company A Limited bound by the terms of the agreement?

The basic rule is that the agreement can be enforced against the company by a third party, B, in this example (ss. 43(1)(a) and 44(4)).

Contracts made on behalf of companies

Companies can only perform acts through individuals and those individuals act on behalf of the company. Whether or not a contract has been made on behalf of a company usually involves consideration of agency law, as applied by the courts in the context of companies, and the Companies Act 2006.

The principal legal question arising in relation to whether or not a contract has been 'made on behalf of a company' is: did the individual or the organ of governance of the company (usually the board of directors) that purported to agree the terms on behalf of the company have legal authority to do so? A company will only be bound by a contract if, at the time the contract was allegedly entered into, the board of directors or the individual, on whose acts the third party is relying to allege that a contract has been entered into, was acting within the scope of its or his authority as an agent of the company.

The individual, or agent, may be a director of the company but this is not necessary. A non-director employee may be an agent of the company and an independent contractor may be appointed by the company to act as its agent for one or more particular purposes. The starting point for analysis of the existence of authority to bind the company is the authority of the board of directors.

4 Authority of the board of directors to bind the company

When we look at the board of directors in chapter 11 we will see that the Articles of a company invariably state that the directors are responsible for the management of the company and they are empowered *collectively* to exercise all the powers of the company for this purpose (Model Articles, art. 3). It is by the exercise of powers of the company that the legal rights and liabilities of the company are changed. If there are no other provisions in the Articles relevant to the exercise of powers of the company, the board of directors has authority to bind the company to any contracts. Remember, the board of directors must act collectively in exercising the powers vested in it. The power to bind the company to a contract is exercised by the board of directors making a valid decision of the board, usually by board resolution (see chapter 15 for how boards take valid decisions).

What if there are provisions in the Articles, in addition to art. 3, relevant to the exercise of powers by the company? Notwithstanding the art. 3 default position in the Model Articles, it is not uncommon for the general authority of the board to be limited by Articles that reserve certain powers to the shareholders. A typical example is an article requiring loans by the company for over a specified amount to be approved in advance by the shareholders.

What, then, are the consequences of the board of directors purporting to exercise a power of the company outside the board's actual authority? For example, what are the consequences of the board purporting to commit the company to borrow a sum beyond the level the board is authorised by the Articles to commit the company to borrow?

- If they discover the board's plans in advance, the shareholders may be able to obtain an injunction to prevent the board acting outside its powers. This common law right is expressly preserved by s. 40(4).
- Each director who participates in the board decision to exercise the company power outside the powers of the board, may be liable for breach of duty (see chapter 12, directors' duties, particularly s. 171). Again, this potential liability is expressly preserved by s. 40(5).
- The loan contract may or may not be enforceable.

It is the enforceability of the loan contract that is examined here. Two sub-questions arise:

- Can the third party enforce the contract against the company?
- Can the company enforce the contract against the third party?

4.1 The Companies Act 2006, s. 40 and board authority

The answer to whether or not a third party can enforce against a company a contract purportedly entered into by the board of directors when the board does not have the power to enter into the contract is now almost always determined by the application of s. 40 of the Companies Act 2006 which provides:

'(1) In favour of a person dealing with a company in good faith, the power of the directors to bind the company, or authorise others to do so, is deemed to be free of any limitation under the company's constitution.
(2) For this purpose–
   (a) a person 'deals with' a company if he is a party to any transaction or other act to which the company is a party.
   (b) a person dealing with a company–
       (i) is not bound to enquire as to any limitation on the powers of the directors to bind the company or authorise others to do so,
       (ii) is presumed to have acted in good faith unless the contrary is proved, and
       (iii) is not to be regarded as acting in bad faith by reason only of his knowing that an act is beyond the powers of the directors under the company's constitution'.

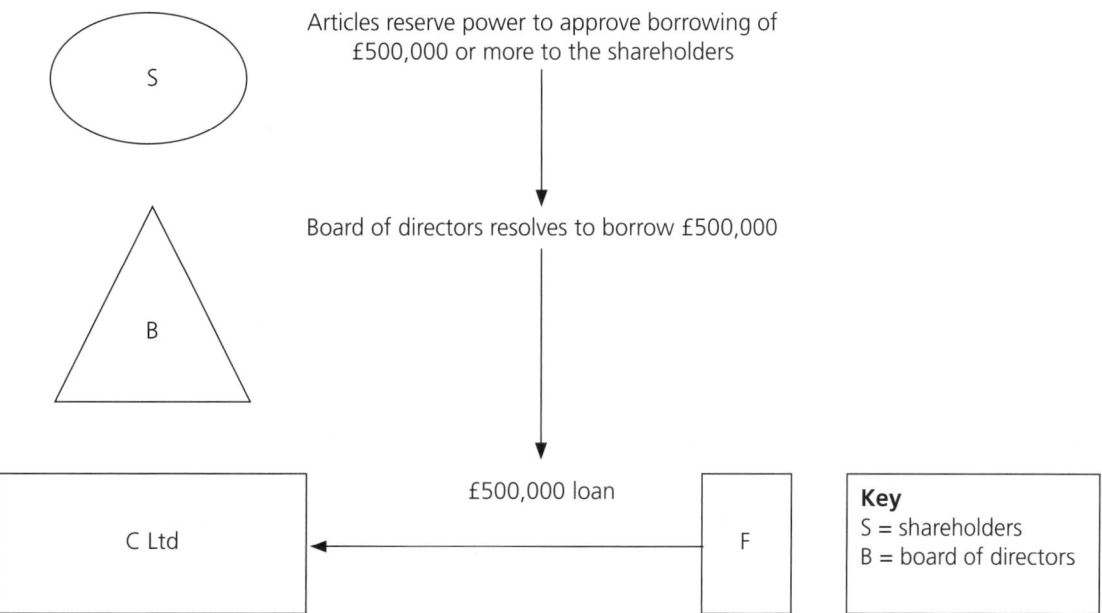

FIGURE 6.1 Board of directors purporting to act outside its powers

Consider the hypothetical scenario in Figure 6.1. Is C Ltd bound by the loan from F? To work out the answer, apply the following analysis:

- Is the power to approve borrowings of £500,000 or more reserved to shareholders a 'limitation under the constitution' on the power of the board of directors for the purposes of s. 40 (see s. 40(1))?
- Is F a 'person' entitled to rely on s. 40 (see s. 40(1))?
- Was F 'dealing with [the] company' (see s. 40(2)(a))?
- Was F dealing 'in good faith' (see s. 40(2)(b))?

If the answer to each question is yes, the power of the board to bind the company is deemed free of the requirement to obtain the approval in advance of the shareholders and C Ltd is bound by the loan agreement.

'Persons' entitled to rely on s. 40

The question whether or not a company insider is a 'person' for the purposes of s. 40(1), and therefore potentially able to rely on s. 40, arose in *Smith v Henniker-Major & Co (A firm)* [2002] 1 WLR 616 (CA).

Smith v Henniker-Major & Co (A firm) [2002] 1 WLR 616 (CA)

Smith, a director who was also the chairman and 30% shareholder of a company, held a meeting at which he alone was present and purported to pass a board resolution by which the company decided to assign to him the right to sue a firm of solicitors. The firm of solicitors argued that the assignment was invalid as the resolution was taken at a meeting without a quorum of two directors as required by the Articles of the company. The director argued that he was a person dealing with the company in good faith and as such could rely on what is now s. 40 to ignore the procedural shortcoming in the decision of the company which made the subsequent assignment unenforceable. At first instance the judge found that the director had been dealing with the company, could rely on the statutory provision, and therefore the assignment was valid.

Held on appeal: Smith could not rely on the section and the assignment was invalid. The words of the section were wide enough to include a director, but it was up to the courts to interpret the section and as there was no possible policy reason for interpreting it so as to enable a director in Smith's position to 'rely on his own mistake', the court would look to the common law. The case of *Morris v Kanssen* [1946] AC 459 (HL) clearly applied, which decided that the law would not permit directors to rely on a presumption, 'that that is rightly done which they have themselves wrongly done' for to do so, 'is to encourage ignorance and condone dereliction from duty'.

The case does not decide that a director will never be able to rely on s. 40: indeed Carnwarth LJ emphasised this and considered the facts in the case to be 'quite exceptional'. It is possible for a director to seek to rely on s. 40. The potential for s. 40 to operate to bind the company to a contract with a director is confirmed by s. 41. Section 41 provides that where, because of s. 40, a company is bound by a contract with a director or a person connected to a director, the agreement will be voidable by the company (subject to protecting independent third party rights (s. 41(6)), and the director and any other director who authorised the transaction will be liable to account to, or indemnify, the company (s. 41(3)).

Persons 'dealing with the company'

In the words of the sub-section, a person deals with a company for the purposes of s. 40(2)(a), 'if he is a party to any transaction or other act to which the company is a party'. As the sub-section lays down a precondition to a decision whether the person in question is or is not a party to a transaction with the company, the language of the sub-section is not at all helpful: it presumes that which it is there to help to determine. Consequently, to avoid s. 40 having no application at all, a purposive rather than a literal interpretation of s. 40(2)(a) is required. Also, because the section is an implementation of the 1st European Company Law Directive, the *Marleasing* principle of conforming interpretation is relevant (*Marleasing SA v La Comercial Internacional de Alimentacion* Case C-106/89 [1990] ECR 1-4135).

For the sub-section to make any sense, in every case in which s. 40 is relevant to a contract 'dealing with the company' must mean being a party to a transaction *to which the company merely purports to be a party* (but to which, without s. 40, it is not a party). This calls for the courts to decide whether there are any circumstances in which a person, dealing with another who purports to be acting on behalf of the company, should not be entitled to argue that he has the protection afforded to third parties by art. 9(2) of the 1st Company Law Directive, as implemented (very poorly) by s. 40. Put another way, the sub-section requires the courts to determine whether or not there are any circumstances in which the contract in issue is so defective that regardless of the good faith of the third party a court will not ignore the want of authority or other legal defect in the formation of the contract. In *Smith v Henniker-Major & Co (A firm)* [2002] 1 WLR 616 (CA), Carnwath LJ commented that a purposive approach to the section 'suggests a low threshold'. On the underlying approach of the courts, however, he went on to comment:

> 'where, as here, the language of a statute, even one based on a Directive, has to be stretched in a purposive way to achieve its object, I see no reason why, in setting the limits, we should not be guided by what the common law would deem appropriate in a similar context.'

Unfortunately, the case does not give a clearer answer than this to the question when will a third party seeking to rely on s. 40 not be able to because he is not dealing with the company.

Dealing in good faith

As a reading of s. 40(2)(b), set out above, indicates, a person dealing with the company is almost always going to be found to be acting in good faith for the purposes of s. 40. The burden of proving that he was not in good faith is on the party asserting the lack of good faith (i.e. the company). *Wrexham Association Football Club Ltd (in admin) v Crucialmove Ltd* [2007] BCC 139 (CA) is authority for the proposition that where the circumstances are such as to put a third party on notice to make further enquiries as to whether the person purporting to bind the company has authority to do so, and the third party fails to make such enquiries, they will not be regarded as acting in good faith for the purposes of s. 40.

Consider the hypothetical scenario in Figure 6.2. Is C Ltd bound by the loan from F? The analysis to work out the answer is almost exactly the same as it was for the hypothetical scenario in Figure 6.1. The only difference in the legal analysis is that the language of s. 40(1) relied on to override the limitation in the Articles is the second power of the directors mentioned in that subsection, 'the power of the directors to bind the company, *or authorise others to do so*' (emphasis added). The power of the board of directors of C Ltd to authorise D to negotiate and sign a loan agreement with F is deemed to be free of the £500,000 loan limitation on the power of the board set out in the Articles. D therefore has actual authority to bind the company to the loan with F.

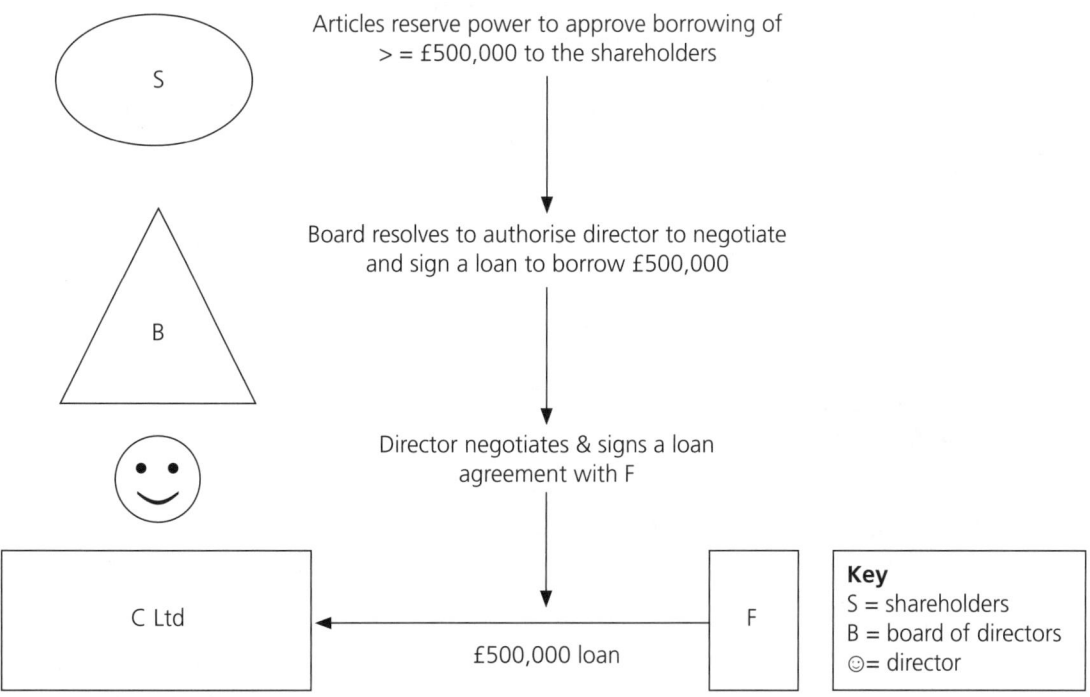

FIGURE 6.2 Board of directors purporting to delegate a power it does not have

Situations outside s. 40

Section 40 will not be relevant in a number of situations including the following:

- If the company is seeking to rely on a contract and the third party is arguing an absence of authority, s. 40 cannot be used by the company because it only operates in favour of the contractor.
- If the third party is not acting in good faith, s. 40 will not assist him.
- If the third party is not a 'person' dealing with the company for the purposes of the section, s. 40 will not assist him.

- If the third party is not 'dealing with the company'.
- Potentially, if the individual purporting to act as agent of the company has not been granted express authority by the directors (a moot issue).

In all these situations (though only potentially in the last mentioned circumstance) the enforceability of the contract will be determined by the common law.

4.2 The common law position and board authority

Where s. 40 does not apply, the starting point at common law is that if the board enters into a contract on behalf of the company without authority to do so, the contract cannot be enforced by the third party contractor against the company. Nor may the company enforce the contract against the third party contractor (*Re Quintex Ltd (No. 2)* (1990) 2 ACSR 479). The inability of the company to enforce the contract can usually be overcome quite easily by the company adopting or ratifying the contract.

Ratification will be brought about in most cases by the shareholders passing an ordinary resolution (*Grant v UK Switchback Railway Co* (1888) 40 Ch D 135 (CA)), although it is possible for a company to ratify a contract by conduct. Ratification validates the acts of the board (or any other purported agent previously lacking authority) from the point in time when the acts took place and is, therefore, 'equivalent to an antecedent authority' (*Koenigsblatt v Sweet* [1923] 2 Ch 314). Remember from our consideration of pre-incorporation contracts that the company must have been in existence at the time the agent purported to act on its behalf. It is not possible to ratify an act performed when the principal (the company) did not exist (see chapter 3).

Where a restriction on the power of the board exists, the board has no actual authority to bind the company (the principal), but what of **ostensible authority**? Historically, arguments that the board had ostensible authority were met and defeated by the constructive notice rule which deemed a person dealing with a company to have notice of the contents of the company's public documents. The most important public documents of a company are its Memorandum and Articles of Association (although, as we saw in chapter 5, the Memorandum is much less important today than it used to be). Consequently, a third party would be deemed to have notice of any limitation on the power of the board contained in the Articles. For a third party to argue he had relied on a representation that the board had authority would contradict this imputed knowledge and the contract would be unenforceable for lack of authority.

The harshness of the constructive notice rule on third parties is mitigated by the rule in *Royal British Bank v Turquand* (1856) 6 E&B 327.

CASE LAW 6.2

Royal British Bank v Turquand (1856) 6 E&B 327

A bond was sealed and signed by two directors and the company secretary of a railway and coal mining joint stock company acknowledging the indebtedness of the company in the sum of £2,000 to the Royal British Bank. The company argued that the company was not bound by the bond because (i) the company's deed of settlement (the equivalent to the Articles of a company registered under the 2006 Act) 'allowed the directors to borrow on bond such sum or sums of money as shall from time to time, by a resolution passed at a general meeting of the company, be authorised to be borrowed'; and (ii) no sufficiently specific resolution had been passed. The court fell just short of finding that a resolution that had been passed was enough to satisfy the deed of settlement and empower the directors to borrow the money on bond.

Held: Although no ordinary resolution had been passed, the Royal British Bank 'had the right to infer the fact of a resolution authorising that which on the face of the document appeared to be legitimately done'. In answer to the argument that the bank had constructive notice of the deed of settlement (i.e. the Articles), the court held that this was correct, but in the absence of circumstances putting it on enquiry, the bank was entitled to assume that the matters of indoor management required by the documents of which it had constructive notice had been complied with. Here, the bank was entitled to assume that an adequate ordinary resolution had been put in place as required by the deed of settlement.

Turquand's case established what is sometimes referred to as the 'indoor management rule' This means that a third party may assume that the internal procedures which provide the board with the authority to act (and specified in a company's public documents) have been gone through, even though this may not be the case. A third party who has been put on notice that those procedures have *not* been gone through (by something more than constructive or actual notice of the public documents) may not rely on the internal management rule. *Wrexham Association Football Club Ltd (in admin) v Crucialmove Ltd* [2007] BCC 139 (CA) is an example of circumstances in which a third party will be considered to have been put on notice that internal procedures have not been complied with and denied the right to rely on the rule in *Turquand's* case.

A third party who can rely on *Turquand's* case to mitigate the constructive notice rule may argue that the board has authority (based on the statement in the Articles which sets out the board's authority), to enter into the type of contract in question, and that any limitation on that power simply amounts to an internal procedure that he can assume has been gone through. Be sure to distinguish this situation from one in which the board is not authorised to enter into the type of contract in issue, for example, where the Articles contain an absolute prohibition on directors entering into a certain type of contract, in which case no basis on which to argue the existence of ostensible authority will exist. As was the case in *Turquand's* case itself, the ostensible authority argument applies where the third party finds 'not a prohibition ... but a permission to do so on certain conditions' (*per* Jervis CJ).

TEST YOUR KNOWLEDGE 6.2

(a) Is a registered company required to have a company seal?
(b) Is a company that has a company seal required to use it?
(c) What is the extent of the authority of the directors *collectively* to enter into contracts on behalf of the company under the Model Articles?
(d) In what circumstances is s. 40 relevant?
(e) What, precisely, is the consequence of a person being able to rely on s. 40?
(f) Who may rely on s. 40?
(g) Is *Turquand's* case still relevant today? If so, in what circumstances?

5 Authority of individuals to bind the company

The Articles of a company typically empower the board of directors to delegate any of its powers (Model Articles, art. 5), and authorise further delegation of its powers by any person to whom it has delegated powers. A board of directors typically delegates powers not by expressly using the terms 'delegation' and 'powers' but by allocating management responsibilities to individuals and approving the appointment of individuals to named roles within the company. In the absence of limitations on the powers of the board, if the allocated management responsibilities or the performance of the role involves the individual acting so as to legally bind the company, the individual will be an agent of the company with actual authority to bind the company.

If, and to what extent, the board's allocation or appointment of an individual actually delegates powers to that individual is a matter of construction of the terms of the allocation or appointment. The authority of the agent is a question of fact. Exactly the same analysis applies to further delegations of power by those to whom the board has delegated powers. And so the powers of the company cascade down, to be exercised at different levels within the company, yet the authority of every agent of a company can be traced back to the board of directors.

The authority described in the previous paragraphs is actual authority. Concern to protect third parties dealing with companies resulted in the development of the concept of ostensible authority and the authority of an agent nowadays may be either actual authority (express or implied) or ostensible authority. Ostensible authority is also called apparent authority: the terms are interchangeable. Although based on very different legal reasoning, both actual and ostensible authority can be traced back to the board of directors and, ultimately, to the Articles of the company. The company is, in agency terminology, the principal.

5.1 Actual authority

Actual authority is based on a consensual agreement between the principal (the company) and the agent. The principal consents to the agent exercising the legal power of the company to enter into contracts. The basis of actual authority was described by Diplock LJ in *Freeman Lockyer v Buckhurst Park Properties (Mangal) Ltd* [1964] 2 QB 480.

> 'An "actual" authority is a legal relationship between principal and agent created by a consensual agreement to which they alone are parties. Its scope is to be ascertained by applying ordinary principles of construction of contracts, including any proper implications from the express words used, the usages of the trade, or the course of business between the parties. To this agreement the contractor is a stranger.'

In contrast, as Lord Pearson emphasised in *Hely Hutchinson v Brayhead Ltd* [1968] 1 QB 549 (CA), ostensible authority does not operate between the company and the agent. It operates between the company and the third party contractor.

> 'If the question arises between the principal and the agent – either of them claiming against the other – actual authority must be proved. There is no question of ostensible authority as between those two parties.'

Actual authority may be express actual authority or implied actual authority.

Express actual authority

The board of directors of Company A Limited passed a board resolution authorising the finance director, on behalf of the company, to negotiate and enter into a 10-year lease of a pasteurising machine from Extra PLC, Full PLC or Glow PLC. The finance director has express authority to bind the company to a lease falling within the description in the board resolution. He may contract with any of Extra PLC, Full PLC or Glow PLC.

Express actual authority

Consider the hypothetical scenario in Figure 6.3. Is C Ltd bound by the loan agreement with F?

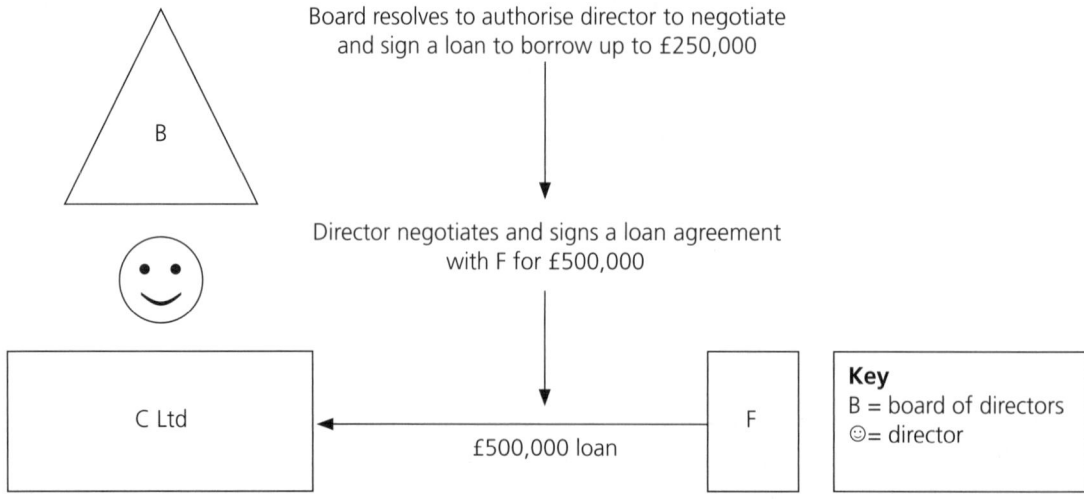

FIGURE 6.3 Individual director acts outside the express actual authority granted to him by the board of directors

Turning now to focus on implied actual authority, the leading case on implied actual authority in the context of a company as the principal is *Hely Hutchinson v Brayhead Ltd* [1968] 1 QB 549 (CA). It confirms that a person appointed by the board to a position within a company will have usual authority, that is, implied actual authority, to do all such things as fall within the usual scope of that office. The case actually demonstrates another point, that is, the importance of taking into account the conduct of the company and the individual and all the circumstances of the case.

CASE LAW 6.3

Hely Hutchinson v Brayhead Ltd [1968] 1 QB 549 (CA)

Richards was chairman of the board of an industrial holding company (Brayhead) and its chief executive or '*de facto* managing director'. Richards regularly entered into contracts on behalf of Brayhead which he disclosed to the board afterwards, sometimes seeking formal ratification after he had committed the company. The board acquiesced in Richards' entry into contracts. Brayhead was planning to merge with another company, Perdio. In these circumstances, Richards signed contracts purportedly binding Brayhead to guarantee Perdio's borrowings from a third party and indemnifying the third party against certain losses. The question arose, did Richards have authority to bind Brayhead to such contracts? At first instance, Roskill J found that Richards had ostensible authority.

Held on appeal: Richards had actual implied authority. Lord Denning MR found that Mr Richards had no express authority to enter into the contracts in issue on behalf of the company, nor was such authority implied from the nature of his office. Although Richards had been duly appointed chairman of the company, in itself, that office did not carry with it authority to enter into the contracts in issue without the sanction of the board. '*But I think he had authority implied from the conduct of the parties and the circumstances of the case* ... such authority being implied from the circumstance that the board by their conduct over many months had acquiesced in his acting as their chief executive and committing Brayhead Ltd to contracts without the necessity of sanction from the board' (emphasis added).

CASE EXAMPLE 6.4

Implied actual authority

The board of directors of Company B Ltd resolved to approve the appointment of Paul Bailey to the position of Head of Marketing with responsibility for running the marketing department. Past Heads of Marketing have signed a range of contracts on behalf of the company such as contracts for the purchase of marketing services including television advertising time and billboard space. Paul Bailey has implied actual authority to enter into agreements on behalf of Company B Ltd but the exact scope of his implied actual authority to enter into contracts is not clear. The scope of authority is ascertained from the conduct of the board and the circumstances of the case of which the appointment to the role is an important part but it is not the only fact relevant to the existence and scope of Paul Bailey's authority.

Now consider Case Example 6.4 with slightly amended facts. Consider that the resolution appointing Paul Bailey expressly stated that the Head of Marketing had authority to commit the company to marketing contracts to a value of no more than £500,000 and Paul Bailey signs a contract purporting to commit the company to purchase £600,000 of marketing services. An agent who is subject to an express limit on his authority cannot have implied actual authority that exceeds that limit. It is in just such a case that a third party must turn to ostensible authority.

5.2 Ostensible authority

As the words of Lord Pearson in *Hely-Hutchinson v Brayhead Ltd* quoted above make clear, unlike actual authority, ostensible authority does not operate between the company and the agent; it operates between the company and a third party. It is based on **estoppel** arising out of reliance by the party dealing with the company on a representation made by the company or an agent of the company.

Diplock LJ set out the conditions that need to be satisfied to establish ostensible authority in *Freeman Lockyer v Buckhurst Park Properties (Mangal) Ltd* [1964] 2 QB 480 (CA).

> 'to entitle a contractor to enforce against a company a contract entered into on behalf of the company by an agent who had no actual authority to do so ... [i]t must be shown:
> (1) that a representation that an agent had authority to enter on behalf of the company into a contract of the kind sought to be enforced was made to the contractor;
> (2) that such representation was made by a person or persons who had "actual" authority to manage the business of the company either generally or in respect of those matters to which the contract relates;
> (3) that he (the contractor) was induced by such representation to enter into the contract, i.e., that he in fact relied upon it; and ...' [the fourth requirement is no longer relevant].

The most difficult condition for a third party contractor to satisfy is often the second one, to show that the representation on which they relied was made by a person who had authority to bind the company to the contract in issue. Although Diplock LJ stated that the person making the representation needs to have *actual* authority, subsequent case law suggests that ostensible authority may suffice, (see *ING Re (UK) Ltd v R&V Versicherung AG* [2007] 1 BCLC 108).

In the modern world, the third party often communicates only with the individual who lacks authority. Consequently, it is representations made by that individual that the third party is often forced to rely on. Two different situations need to be considered which can be distinguished in theory. The distinction is difficult to sustain in the real world as it can come down to nothing more than a difference in the form of words used by a putative agent, rather than a difference in the substance of the situation.

The first situation is where an agent purports to confer authority on himself. In *Armagas Ltd v Mundogas SA* [1986] AC 717, the court emphasised that where the third party knows, or should know, of a general limit on the agent's actual authority, *an agent cannot usually pull himself up by his own bootstraps*, so to speak, and confer ostensible authority on himself by his own representations that he has more extensive authority than he actually has. Even in *Armagas*, however, Lord Keith acknowledged that there may be circumstances in which an agent who is known to have no general authority to enter into transactions of the type in issue, can be reasonably believed to have specific authority to enter into the particular transaction in issue 'by reason of circumstances created by the principal'.

The 'circumstances created by the principal' (the company) may amount to giving the agent authority to communicate to the third party notice that a contract has been approved by the company (i.e., approved by the board or a person within the company authorised approve it), and this is the second situation. In other words, it is possible for the second condition of *Freeman Lockyer* to be satisfied by a 'representation' to the third party which is nothing more than giving a person a role in a company, the usual authority attached to which is to communicate to third parties that the company has approved a contract. The agent whose authority is in question then has express or implied actual authority to communicate the message that the contract in question has been authorised by the company. This second situation occurred in *First Energy (UK) Ltd v Hungarian International Bank Ltd* [1993] 2 Lloyd's Rep 194.

CASE EXAMPLE 6.4

***First Energy (UK) Ltd v Hungarian International Bank Ltd* [1993] 2 Lloyd's Rep 194 (CA)**

Jamison, the senior manager in charge of the Manchester office of HIB, negotiated with Croft the terms of a credit facility for First Energy. Jamison expressly told Croft that he, Jamison, had no authority to sanction a facility. Subsequently, Jamison wrote to Croft offering to finance three projects and this offer was accepted by Croft. Held *per* Steyn LJ: 'In context the letter was calculated to convey to First Energy that Mr. Jamison had obtained the approval of the transaction at the appropriate level at head office.' Jamison, whilst not having authority to enter into a credit facility on behalf of the bank, did have ostensible authority to communicate head office approval to Croft which is what he had done. The fact that Croft knew that Jamison's actual authority to enter into transactions on behalf of HIB was limited did not necessarily mean that his authority to communicate decisions on their behalf was limited also.

Where a more senior employee confirms the authority of a more junior employee to a third party, it is the authority of the senior employee that needs the closest scrutiny: did the senior employee have authority to confirm the authority of the junior employee? *British Bank of the Middle East v Sun Life Assurance Company of Canada (UK) Ltd* [1983] 2 Lloyd's Rep 9 (HL) was such a case.

CASE LAW 6.5

***British Bank of the Middle East v Sun Life Assurance Company of Canada (UK) Ltd* [1983] 2 Lloyd's Rep 9 (HL)**

A branch manager of Sun Life wrote to the claimant to confirm that a junior employee in the Sun Life branch office had authority to sign undertakings to release loan monies to the claimant.

Held: The branch manager had no usual or ostensible authority to represent to the claimant that the junior employee had actual authority to sign such documents as all such undertakings were, as a matter of usual practice, signed at the insurance company's head office and this fact was known in the market generally and was also known by the claimant, who had addressed a letter to the head office seeking confirmation that the junior employee had authority to sign the undertaking. (The branch manager had replied to a letter addressed to his superior.)

STOP AND THINK 6.1

What is a representation for the purposes of ostensible authority? The behaviour by the company that can amount to a representation to satisfy the test is not confined to a statement of authority. The most common 'statement' is in fact the act of appointing a person to a particular role, or executive or management position, within the company. The issue then becomes, would this appointment lead a reasonable man to believe that the 'agent' had actual authority to enter into the contract in issue? What factors do you believe should be important in determining this?

5.3 Implied actual authority and ostensible authority contrasted

Although implied actual authority and ostensible authority often exist at the same time, there are a number of important differences between them. The parties between whom implied actual authority and ostensible authority operate are different. Implied actual authority operates between the principal (the company) and the individual and ostensible authority operates between the principal (the company) and the third party contractor.

The legal theory on which each type of authority is based are very different. Implied actual authority is based on consensual agreement whereas ostensible authority is based on reliance and estoppel.

Whilst both implied actual authority and ostensible authority may be present at the same time, Lord Denning MR, in his judgment in *Hely Hutchinson v Brayhead Ltd* [1968] 1 QB 549 (CA), offered the following example of how the scope of implied actual and ostensible authority may not be coterminous.

> '... sometimes ostensible authority exceeds actual authority. For instance, when the board appoint the managing director, they may expressly limit his authority by saying he is not to order goods worth more than £500 without the sanction of the board. In that case his actual authority is subject to the £500 limitation, but his ostensible authority includes all the usual authority of a managing director. The company is bound by his ostensible authority in his dealings with those who do not know of the limitation.'

Finally, implied actual authority allows a company to insist on enforcing the contract against a third party whereas a company cannot rely on the ostensible authority of its agent to enforce a contract against a third party (*Re Quintex Ltd (No. 2)* (1990) 2 ACSR 479). The company can usually overcome this issue by ratifying the entry into the contract in question, although this course was not open to the company in *Re Quintex Ltd (No. 2)*.

For further illustration of the interplay between different types of authority see *Waugh v HB Clifford & Sons Ltd* [1982] Ch 374 (CA) (the relationship between implied actual and apparent authority), and *SMC Electronics Ltd v Akhter Computers Ltd* [2001] 1 BCLC 433 (CA) in which the court indicated that had it not been able to find that express authority existed, it could have found the existence of both implied actual and ostensible authority.

TEST YOUR KNOWLEDGE 6.3

(a) When will an individual have power to bind a company to a contract?
(b) Compare and contrast actual authority and ostensible or apparent authority.
(c) What are the conditions that need to be satisfied to establish the existence of ostensible authority?
(d) Can a company rely on the existence of ostensible authority to enforce a contract against a third party?

CHAPTER SUMMARY

- A company will only be bound by a deed if the document is clear on its face that it is intended to be a deed and is validly executed as a deed.
  A document is validly executed as a deed by a company if:
  - *either* (i) the common seal is affixed; or (ii) the document is expressed to be executed by the company and is signed by two authorised signatories, or by a director in the presence of a witness who attests the signature (Companies Act 2006, s. 44);
  - *and* it is delivered as a deed (Companies Act 2006, s. 46).
- If a deed purports to be validly executed, it is deemed validly executed in relation to a purchaser in good faith for valuable consideration, (s. 44(5)) but it is not clear that this will protect a third party if signatures have been forged (*Ruben v Great Fingall Consolidated* (1906) and *Lovett v Carson Country Homes Ltd* (2009)).
- There is no obligation for a registered company to have a company seal (s. 45) or to use one, unless use is mandated by the Articles and the Model Articles do not mandate use.
- If a contract is set out in writing and that document is either sealed or executed in accordance with s. 44, the company will be bound by the contract.

- Contracts can also be entered into by agents acting on behalf of the company.
- In favour of a person dealing in good faith with the company, s. 40 overrides limitations set out in the constitution on the powers of the board to bind the company. Dealing with the company is given a purposive interpretation, (*Smith v Henniker-Major* (2002)). Good faith is rebuttably presumed, knowledge of lack of authority is not automatically bad faith and a person is not bound to enquire about authority, (s 40(2)(b)).
- Section 40(2)(b) does not absolve a person from any duty to enquire as to authority when the circumstances put him on inquiry (*Wrexham AFC v Crucialmove Ltd* (2008)).
- The scope of s. 40 is moot: it is unclear whether s. 40(1) should be interpreted to deem the power of any individual to be free of any limitation under the constitution or only the power of the directors collectively and any person to whom they purport to expressly grant authority.
- The common law position and the rule in *Turquand's* case provided that if the board has no authority to act, a contract does not bind the company or the third party (*Quintex Ltd (No. 2)* (1990)). Board authority may be actual or ostensible and the constructive notice of public documents doctrine is mitigated by the indoor management rule (*Royal British Bank v Turquand* (1856)).
- If a third party has actual notice that the required procedure has not been gone through or has been put on inquiry, they cannot rely on the indoor management rule (*Wrexham AFC v Crucialmove Ltd* (2008)).
- Actual authority may be express or implied and is based on a consensual agreement between the company and the agent, (*Hely Hutchinson v Brayhead* (1968)).
- Ostensible authority operates between the company and the third party relying on the authority of the purported agent and is based on estoppel (*Freeman Lockyer v Buckhurst Park* (1964)).
- Both implied and ostensible authority is common in company employees.

PART 1 CASE QUESTIONS

Return to the opening case at the start of this Part and re-read it. Think generally about the issues it raises, the law in relation to which has been covered in the chapters in this Part, before attempting to answer the following questions.

1. Advise Cherie, Tony and Harriet on the legal structures available to them and the benefits and shortcomings of each. Assuming that they decide to set up a company, what type of company should they set up and why?
2. What is the nature of the 'usual protections' to which Blair Bank has referred?
3. Outline the steps Cherie, Tony and Harriet need to take to register a company. Is the name used by Cherie an acceptable name for a company?
4. What is the liability situation under the contract to buy the gym equipment?
5. How can Cherie, Tony and Harriet ensure that none of them can sell out their interest in the business to a third party without the consent of the others?
6. How can Cherie, Tony and Harriet ensure that they have the option to buy out the interest of any of them who sets up in competition with the karate school.
7. Is the contract with KB plc to buy kick bags for £50,000 binding on the company?
8. If the karate school is so successful that they wish to expand rapidly and need £200,000 to do so, what step do they need to take before they can contemplate selling shares in the company to the public?

PART TWO

Capital and membership

■ LIST OF CHAPTERS

7 Companies, capital markets and market abuse
8 Membership, shares and share capital
9 Capital maintenance
10 Loan capital

■ OVERVIEW

In part 2 we look at two related but very different topics: raising capital to fund a company's operations; and the concept of membership of a company.

A company wishing to expand its operations, by opening up a new factory for example, is unlikely to have money to fund the expansion in its bank account. A company may borrow money from a bank or other lending institution or go direct to the public to access funds, by issuing debt or equity securities to the public, by making a public offering. Public offerings and laws designed to protect the integrity of capital markets are covered in chapter 7.

Member is a generic term relevant to all types of registered companies. In this text we focus on registered companies with share capital. This includes private companies limited by shares (rather than private companies limited by guarantee or unlimited private companies) and public companies (plcs), all of which have share capital and hence shareholders. The shareholders are the members of the company, so that for most of our purposes the term member is synonymous with shareholder. The concepts of membership, shares, share capital and capital maintenance are examined in chapters 8 and 9.

The legal relationship between a company and the bank or other institution lending it money is governed by contract law. The rights and liabilities of the company and the lender are set out in the loan documentation which establishes a contract between the company and the lender. If the loan is secured, property law is also important. Although general law governing lending is not covered, debentures and secured lending are covered in chapter 10.

■ LEARNING OUTCOMES

After reading part 2 you should be able to:

- Understand and explain the basic process for raising capital from the public, particularly the role of the prospectus and listing particulars and the regulatory framework that governs the issue of shares to the public.

- Understand the law governing market abuse and the criminal and civil offences which may be committed.
- Explain the legal nature of a share, the different types of shares and the rights attached to them.
- Apply the law governing the allotment and issue of shares, pre-emption rights and payments.
- Explain the doctrine of capital maintenance, understand the minimum share capital requirements and explain the processes required for altering share capital, capital reductions and the purchase and redemption of a company's own shares.
- Explain the restrictions on the payment of distributions/dividends and rights to recover improperly paid dividends.
- Understand the significance of share certificates, warrants and the members' register and explain in outline the processes involved in and the difference between the transfer and transmission of shares.
- Understand the law and rights and liabilities of a company when it borrows money.

PART 2 CASE STUDY

Growing Well Ltd was incorporated in 2004 to operate an organic farm business. Two years later, in response to securing a supply contract with a major national retailer, it needed capital to expand its operation.

Frederick, Charles' father-in-law and one of the company's founders, expressed an interest in investing up to £250,000 in the company and this investment went ahead. Ambitious beyond this scale, the founders wished to raise a further £1.25 million in capital. This was obtained by taking out a private loan secured by a fixed charge on the company's book debts.

Between 2006 and 2009, Growing Well Ltd went from strength to strength and its leading herb brand became a household name. A successful initial public offering in 2009 meant that its equity shares were admitted to trading on the London Stock Exchange Main Market and, although Frederick was not happy, it paid off the expensive preference shares it had issued to him. Growing consumer scepticism about organic products began to hit its sales figures in 2009 and its share price began to fall.

The positive side of the share price fall was that Mr Green, an Australian entrepreneur, approached the finance director seeking talks about potentially acquiring the company. Mr Green was known to have made a number of acquisitions of organic businesses over the previous five years and to be looking for a UK business. At a board meeting in December 2009 the finance director sought approval from the directors to release information to Mr Green and indicated that Mr Green appeared to be 'very hungry'. Charles mentioned this to Frederick over dinner. Frederick immediately purchased 100,000 shares at £1.50. Six months later, the company was sold to Mr Green at an agreed price of £2.50 a share. Frederick was very happy with his £100,000 profit.

Companies, capital markets and market abuse

■ CONTENTS

1 The prospectus
2 Listing particulars
3 Underwriting and commission
4 Market abuse and regulation
5 Criminal liability for market abuse
6 The civil regime for market abuse

■ INTRODUCTION

A private company is prohibited from offering its shares or other **securities** of the company to the public (Companies Act 2006, s. 755(1)). Consequently, a private company contemplating raising capital from the public must first re-register as a public company (see part 1). As this chapter is concerned with capital markets, it is relevant to public companies only.

A registered public company may be regarded as a legal structure for raising capital to conduct one or more businesses in pursuit of profits. Capital can be raised from the capital markets by issuing shares, bonds or debenture stock (company securities) to investors who become shareholders or bondholders/debenture holders.

In this chapter we consider the law regulating public offers of securities by companies. As we have noted, this takes us into the world of securities regulation, which has investor protection at its heart. This chapter also examines the law governing **insider dealing** and market manipulation, which together are referred to as **market abuse**. The criminal offences that may be committed by a person who engages in market abuse behaviour are examined, as well as the civil law regime that governs market abuse.

1 The prospectus

1.1 Statutory requirement

The detailed rules requiring extensive accurate information to be available when a company's securities are offered to the public are not found in core company law but in the Financial Services and Markets Act 2000 (FSMA) (as amended, particularly by the Financial Services Act 2012), and the Prospectus Rules (PR) issued by the FCA pursuant to that Act (FSMA, s. 84). EU Regulations are law in the UK without the need for implementation, however, the relevant EU prospectus regulations are reflected in the Prospectus Rules; the annexes from the EU regulations have been copied into Appendix 3 to the Prospectus Rules, for ease of reference.

The relevant statutory provisions and Prospectus Rules implement and reflect the EU Prospectus Directive (2003/71/EC) and the detailed provisions of the EU Prospectus Regulation (809/2004) (both as amended, particularly by EU Directive 2010/73/EU and EU Regulations 486/2012 and 862/2012 respectively). The EU Prospectus Directive is a maximum protection directive in relation to the format and content of prospectuses, the aim being to harmonise the content of prospectuses throughout the European Economic Area (EEA) and provide for the issue of a single prospectus valid for use across the EEA (i.e. a 'passport' for issuers in relation to particular securities). Following a review by the EU Commission of the working of the EU Prospectus Directive, the UK rules governing prospectuses were amended in 2011 and 2012 to implement and reflect the changes made at EU level resulting from the review.

Essentially, subject to exemptions (see FSMA, ss. 85(6) and 86), by s. 85, a company must publish a prospectus, electronically (whether it is published in hard copy or not), before it:

- makes an offer of securities to the public; or
- applies for the admission of securities to trading on a regulated market.

These two situations are said to 'trigger' the prospectus requirement. The definition of 'offer to the public' for the purposes of determining whether or not a prospectus is needed is found in the FSMA, s. 102B. Note that the FSMA and Prospectus Rules are not confined in their application to securities on the Official List or admitted to trading on a regulated market. They also apply to public offers of unlisted securities such as an offer to the public of securities to be traded on **AIM**.

A prospectus must be submitted to, and approved in advance by, the FCA (FSMA, s. 85). Advertisements published by the company in the context of offering shares to the public are also regulated (see PR 3.3).

1.2 Exemptions

Different exemptions from the obligation to make a prospectus available to the public exist depending upon whether the prospectus is made available in relation to (i) offering shares to the public (for which exemptions, see s. 86) or (ii) seeking an admission to trading on a regulated market (for which exemptions, see s. 85(6)). Focusing on offering shares to the public, the key exempt offers are:

- offers to qualified investors only;
- offers to fewer than 150 investors other than qualified investors;
- offers where the total consideration is less than €5 million (s. 85(5)(a) and schedule 11A);
- offers where the minimum nominal value of a share or payable by one investor is €100,000 (c. £85,000) or more;
- offers in connection with takeovers; and
- offers to employees and/or directors.

Notwithstanding these exemptions, a company making an Initial Public Offering (IPO) of shares to be traded on the London Stock Exchange (LSE) Main Market will almost always need to make a prospectus available because, whilst it may be entitled to an exemption listed above in relation to the offer to the public, it is also seeking an admission to trading, therefore must make a prospectus available unless an admission to trading exemption also applies. The admission to trading exemptions are basically available only when the shares are already admitted to trading on another regulated market or are of a class already admitted to trading.

1.3 Admission of securities to AIM

In 2004, the London Stock Exchange responded to the fact that the new law on prospectuses would apply to companies seeking admission of securities to AIM by pre-emptively turning AIM into an *exchange-regulated* market, rather than a regulated market. This change means that making an application for the *admission of securities to trading on AIM* in itself does *not* trigger the need for a prospectus. A prospectus is needed if there is an *offer of securities to the public* to which no exemption applies. A rights issue by an AIM company will trigger the need for a prospectus unless an exemption applies, as it is a public offer. The same is true of an open offer. A placing will not trigger a prospectus because it will involve the offer of shares only to a qualified investor.

1.4 Initial public offerings and admission of securities to LSE Main Market

The typical situation in which a prospectus is issued is an IPO where a company offers shares to the public for the first time and seeks admission of those shares to trading on the Main Market of the London Stock Exchange (LSE). Before the shares are admitted to trading on the LSE Main Market, the company will need to have them admitted to the official list by the FCA, acting as the UK Listing Authority (UKLA).

In this typical scenario the prospectus plays two roles. First, it is the document by which information is supplied to the FCA (the regulator) for the purposes of admitting the shares to the official list; and, second, it is the document published to investors inviting them to invest in the company's shares.

TEST YOUR KNOWLEDGE 7.1

(a) In which two key situations must a company publish a prospectus?
(b) Does the requirement to publish a prospectus apply if a company seeks to have its shares admitted to trading on AIM?
(c) What are the six main exemptions from the requirement to publish a prospectus triggered by an offer of securities to the public?
(d) Can a company making an IPO rely on the offer exemptions to avoid the obligation to make a prospectus available?

1.5 Prospectus content

General duty of disclosure

The FSMA, s. 87A sets out the criteria for approval of prospectuses by the FCA. The FCA cannot approve a prospectus unless it contains the necessary information. Essentially, a prospectus must contain all information 'necessary to enable investors to make an informed assessment of the assets and liabilities, financial position, profits and losses, and prospects' of the company and any guarantor and the rights attaching to the shares (s. 87A(2)). The information must be presented in an easily analysable and comprehensible form and a prospectus must include a summary in non-technical language conveying the essential characteristics of and risks associated with the company and any guarantor (s. 87A(3)–(6)).

The UK Prospectus Regulations (SI2012/1538) amend s. 87A, introducing a new concept of 'the key information' which means the information which is essential to enable investors to understand the transferable securities to which the prospectus relates and to decide whether to consider the offer further. Section 87A(10) provides that the key information must include:

(a) the essential characteristics of, and risks associated with, the issuer and any guarantor, including their assets, liabilities and financial positions;
(b) the essential characteristics of, and risks associated with, investment in the transferable securities, including any rights attaching to the securities;
(c) the general terms of the offer, including an estimate of the expenses charged to an investor by the issuer and the person offering the securities to the public, if not the issuer;
(d) details of the admission to trading; and
(e) the reasons for the offer and proposed use of the proceeds.

Liability for shortcomings in the content of a prospectus have been enlarged to cover key information.

Specific content

A long list of matters which may be dealt with by prospectus rules is set out in the FSMA s. 84, the first being 'the required form and content of a prospectus (including a summary)' (s. 84(1)(a)). The Prospectus Rules provide in PR 2.2 that a prospectus has to consist of three components, whether they are in three separate documents or all three components are contained within one document (a single document is normal for IPOs of equity securities). The three components are:

- a summary in the prescribed format (PR Appendix 3 Annex XXII);
- a registration document (information about the company/issuer) (PR Appendix 3 Annex 1 & 2); and
- a securities note (information about the shares) (PR Appendix 3 Annex 3).

Summary

The rules governing the format and content of the summary have been significantly altered as a result of the EU review into the working of the law governing prospectuses. The changes emphasise the importance of the summary and are aimed at facilitating comparison between one share offer and another. The summary must contain the key information in the format and order set out in Annex XXII to the EU Prospectus Regulation 809/2004 (as introduced by the Amendment Regulation 486/2012). Annex XXII has been copied into Appendix 3 to the Prospectus Rules. The summary must consist of five tables in the following order, each table setting out elements in the order in which they appear in Annex XXII:

A – introduction and warnings;
B – information on the issuer and guarantor;
C – information on the securities;
D – information on risks; and
E – information on the offer.

Prospectus company information requirements

The information that must appear in the registration document is set out in Prospectus Rules Appendix 3 Annex I (copied from the Prospectus Regulation), which lists:

1. those responsible for the information given in the prospectus and a responsibility statement;
2. statutory auditor details;
3. selected historic financial information;
4. risk factors: prominent disclosure of risk factors specific to the company or its industry;
5. history and development of the company and its investments;
6. business overview;
7. organisational structure;
8. property, plants and equipment;
9. operating and financial review;
10. capital resources;
11. research and development, patents and licences;
12. trend information;
13. profit forecasts or estimates;
14. administrative, management and supervisory bodies and senior management;
15. remuneration and benefits;
16. board practices;
17. employees;
18. major shareholders;
19. related party transactions;
20. financial information concerning the issuer's assets and liabilities:
    (a) audited accounts for at least three years and other financial information
    (b) dividend policy
    (c) legal or arbitration proceedings
    (d) significant changes in the issuer's financial or trading position;
21. additional information:
    (a) Share capital
    (b) Memorandum and Articles of Association;
22. material contracts;

23 third party information and statements by experts and declarations of interest;
24 documents on display; and
25 information on holdings.

Prospectus securities information requirements

The information that makes up the securities note component of a prospectus is set out in PR Appendix 3 Annex III. Basically, it is:

1 the persons responsible for the information given in the prospectus and a responsibility statement;
2 risk factors: prominent disclosure of risk factors that are material to the securities being offered and/or admitted to trading;
3 essential information:
   (a) working capital statement;
   (b) capitalisation and indebtedness;
   (c) interest of natural and legal persons involved in the issue/offer;
   (d) reasons for the offer and use of proceeds.
4 information concerning the securities to be offered/admitted to trading;
5 terms and conditions of the offer;
6 admission to trading and dealing arrangements;
7 selling shareholders;
8 expenses of the offer;
9 dilutions; and
10 additional information.

1.6 Process

In the typical scenario of raising capital from the public by an IPO of securities to be traded on the LSE Main Market, the process is three-fold:

1 A prospectus must first be submitted for approval by the FCA, and, when approved, filed with the FCA and made available to the public (PR 3.2.1).
2 An application must be made to the FCA for admission of the securities to the Official List.
3 An application must be made for admission to trading on the LSE Main Market.

The process is complex and specialist advice will be required from a range of professionals, including lawyers, investment bankers and accountants.

Prospectus approval

The key documents to be submitted with the relevant fee to the FCA when seeking approval of a prospectus are:

- Form A;
- the prospectus;
- copies of any document incorporated into the prospectus by reference; and
- contact details for FCA queries.

Following FCA approval, a prospectus must be made available to the public. A prospectus is treated as having been made available to the public for these purposes when it has been published in a newspaper widely circulated in the UK or free copies have been made available to the public at the LSE offices or the company's registered office, or it has been displayed on the company's or LSE's website (PR 3.2.4). It is now compulsory to display a prospectus either on the company's website or, where appropriate, on the website of a financial intermediary who has placed or sold the share issue (PR 3.2.4).

Admission to the Official List

The following documents must be submitted to the FCA in the course of securing the admission of securities to the Official List:

- an application for admission of securities to the Official List;
- the approved prospectus;
- written confirmation of the number of shares to be allotted pursuant to a board resolution allotting the shares; and
- the completed shareholder statement.

The hearing of the application will be on the same day as the stock exchange hearing for admission to trading. The FCA may refuse to list the shares if, for a reason related to the company, it considers that admission would be detrimental to the interests of investors (FSMS s. 75(5)). Admission to the official list is announced by the FCA using the Regulatory News Service. This will be at the same time as the London Stock Exchange announces the admission to trading (which is announced on the LSE's website).

Admission to trading on the LSE Main Market

To obtain admission to trading on the LSE Main Market, the company must follow the LSE Admission and Disclosure Standards. This includes submission to the LSE of the following documents:

- Form 1;
- an electronic copy of the approved prospectus; and
- an electronic copy of the board resolution allotting the shares.

TEST YOUR KNOWLEDGE 7.2

(a) What must the information in a prospectus enable an investor to do?
(b) What are the three component parts of a prospectus?
(c) What are the three stages of the process for an IPO of securities to be traded on the LSE Main Market?

1.7 Liability for prospectuses

Criminal liability

A person who makes an offer of securities to the public or applies for the admission of securities to trading on a regulated market without making an approved prospectus available to the public is guilty of an offence and is liable on indictment to imprisonment for up to two years or an unlimited fine or both (s. 85(3)).

In addition to potentially falling within the scope of a generic crime such as obtaining by deception under the Theft Act 1968, the issue of a defective prospectus may amount to market abuse under the FSMA, s. 397. This provision is considered under market abuse later in this chapter.

Civil liability

For non-issue
Non-issue of a prospectus in contravention of s. 85 is actionable at the suit of a person who suffers loss as a result of the contravention (s. 85(4)).

For untrue or misleading statements or failure to provide key information
An investor who applies for shares and suffers a loss as a result of untrue or misleading information or the omissions of required information from a prospectus can seek compensation from those who are responsible for the prospectus (s. 90(10) and (11)). A 2012 amendment to s. 90(12) opens up the possibility for a person to be liable for compensation based solely on a prospectus summary, if, when read with the rest of the prospectus, the summary does not include the key information (see section 1.5 above). The court has held (in relation to the predecessor section to s. 90) that damages should be measured as for the tort of deceit so that there is no need for loss to be foreseeable for it to be recoverable (*Clark v Urquhart* [1930] AC 28).

Pursuant to the FSMA s. 84(1)(d), the persons responsible for a prospectus are defined in PR 5.5. The rule is complex but essentially, in relation to equity shares, those responsible are:

- the company;
- the directors of the company;
- any person who accepts responsibility for all or part of the prospectus and is named in the prospectus as having accepted responsibility; or
- any person, not being in one of the categories above, who has authorised the contents of the prospectus.

Those responsible for a particular prospectus must be named in the prospectus (see prospectus content above) and, as the list immediately above suggests, different persons may be responsible for different parts of a prospectus.

The liability imposed by s. 90 is subject to exemptions set out in Schedule 10 to the FSMA. The most important exemption is where a person responsible for a statement in a prospectus can satisfy the court that, at the time the prospectus was submitted to the FCA, he reasonably believed (having made such enquiries, if any, as were reasonable) that the statement was true and not misleading, or the matter whose omission caused the loss was properly omitted, and that he continued in that belief until such time as the securities were acquired or, before they were acquired, he had taken all such steps as it was reasonable for him to have taken to secure that a correction was brought to the attention of the subsequent acquirers.

Another important defence is the expert statement defence. Essentially, it is a defence to a s. 90 claim if the responsible person reasonably believed that an expert, who had made the statement in a prospectus that has proved to be untrue or misleading, was competent and had consented to the statement appearing in the prospectus.

The standard based upon which s. 90 imposes personal liability is negligence. This is unusual in securities regulation. Section 90 is also considered to be stringent because there is no need for the claimant to establish reliance or the materiality of the statement or omission.

Liability under general law
The statutory liability under s. 90 is in addition to any other liability for statements in a prospectus that may exist, which liability is expressly preserved by s. 90(6). In relation to the company, the purchaser of shares may be able to claim successfully for breach of contract or a claim based on misrepresentation may be available under the Misrepresentation Act 1967. These claims can only be made against the company as it is the company that is the party to the contract to acquire the shares. A contract or 1967 Act-based claim will not be available in relation to the directors.

In relation to the directors or any other relevant defendant, such as the company's auditors, in the absence of a contractual relationship between that person and the investor, any claim would need to be based on the tort of deceit (*Derry v Peek* (1889) 14 App Cas 337) or negligent misstatement (*Hedley Byrne & Co Ltd v Heller and Partners Ltd* [1964] AC 465).

A duty of care must be found to exist before liability for negligent misstatement can be established. Directors have been found to owe a duty of care to subscribers for shares, but not to owe a duty of care to investors who purchased shares not from the company, but in the 'after market' (*Al-Nakib Investments Jersey Ltd v Longcroft*) [1990] 3 All ER 321. The benefit of such a claim to the claimant could be that a claim could succeed where a claim under s. 90 would not, possibly due to the availability of a schedule 10 exemption.

TEST YOUR KNOWLEDGE 7.3

(a) Which criminal offences may be committed by a person who fails to make a prospectus available to the public in contravention of the FSMA, s. 85?
(b) Does civil liability attach to a failure to make a prospectus available to the public in contravention of the FSMA, s. 85 and what is the basis of any such liability?
(c) In what circumstances does s. 90 impose liability?

2 Listing particulars

Since the new Prospectus Rules came into operation in 2005 as a result of the implementation of the EU Prospectus Directive, listing particulars are relevant in only relatively limited circumstances. First, they are not relevant if the FSMA requires a prospectus to be issued. Second, they are only required where the Listing Rules make the issue of listing particulars and approval by the FCA of those listing particulars a prerequisite to securities of the type in question being admitted to the official list (s. 79).

The Listing Rules require listing particulars in relation to: specialist securities for which a prospectus is not required under the Listing Rules; and securities listed in Schedule 11A of the FSMA (Listing Rules 4.1). 'Specialist securities' for these purposes means securities which, because of their nature, are normally bought and traded by a limited number of investors who are particularly knowledgeable in investment matters (see *FCA Handbook* glossary). Schedule 11A includes securities such as units in an open-ended investment scheme and non-equity securities issued by or linked with EEA state governments or shares in an EEA state central banks.

3 Underwriting and commission

3.1 Underwriting

Before a company makes a public offering of securities it is common practice for the issue to be underwritten, in whole or in part, by an investment bank. This means that a legally-binding agreement is entered into between the company and the bank by which the bank undertakes, in relation to specified shares to be offered to the public, to apply for those specified shares not subscribed for by the public. The contractual obligation to acquire the shares is usually reinforced by the bank authorising an agent controlled by the company to apply, on behalf of the bank, for the otherwise unsubscribed for shares. This, in effect, upgrades the rights of the company as it will have a legal claim against the bank for the price of the shares, rather than simply a damages claim for breach of the bank's obligation to apply for the shares.

The shares to which the underwriting agreement relates are ordinarily specified in a draft prospectus and if the final prospectus differs from the draft prospectus on which the underwriting agreement is based, the bank may be released from the underwriting obligation (*Warner International and Overseas Engineering Co Ltd v Kilburn, Brown & Co* [1914] 84 LJ KB 365.

3.2 Underwriting commission

The consideration for the bank's promise, or the price of the underwriting, is the underwriting commission which is usually expressed as a percentage of the nominal value of the share issue.

Shares may not be issued at a discount to their nominal value (Companies Act 2006, s. 580(1); and see chapter 8). Yet looked at from one perspective, underwriting commission can be characterised as a discount for s. 580(1) purposes. Furthermore, s. 552 prohibits the payment of underwriting commission. The s. 552 prohibition is, however, subject to underwriting commission permitted by s. 533. Section 533 also protects underwriting commission that meets the conditions of that section from a challenge under s. 580.

Section 553 of the Companies Act 2006 essentially provides that a company may pay a commission to a person in consideration of his subscribing (or agreeing to subscribe), whether absolutely or conditionally, for shares in the company, or procuring (or agreeing to procure) subscriptions for shares in the company, (again, either absolutely or unconditionally), if the following conditions are satisfied:

- the payment of the commission is authorised by the company's Articles; and
- the commission does not exceed the lesser of:
  - 10% of the price at which the shares are issued; or
  - the amount authorised by the Articles.

Section 553 further provides that a promoter or any other person who receives payment of a sum from the company may apply any part of that sum in payment of any commission, if the payment of the commission directly by the company would be permitted by s. 553.

Finally, note that payment of the expenses of issue, which includes underwriting commission, is expressly recognised as a proper use of sums transferred to a share premium account as the result of a share issue (s. 610).

TEST YOUR KNOWLEDGE 7.4

(a) When are listing particulars, rather than a prospectus, needed?
(b) What principal obligation is undertaken by an underwriter of a share issue?
(c) What restrictions are placed on underwriting commission by the Companies Act 2006?
(d) Can underwriting commission be paid out of a share premium account?

4 Market abuse and regulation

The law on market abuse will almost certainly change in the not-too-distant future because the EU has proposed reforms, collectively referred to as 'MAD 2'. MAD 2 is made up of a proposed EU Market Abuse Regulation (MAR) (which will become law in the UK without the need for the UK to take any steps to implement it) and an EU Directive on criminal sanctions for insider dealing and market manipulation (CSMAD) which EU Member States will need to implement into their national law. One reason why a directive rather than a regulation is being used to address the criminal law dimensions of the reforms is because the EU has no legislative authority to create crimes that automatically become law in Member States. MAR will come into effect two years after it is adopted by the EU, and the deadline for transposition of CSMAD will be aligned with MAR coming into force. As MAD 2 will not be adopted until summer 2013 at the very earliest, the earliest the new rules will apply is mid-2015. Accordingly, whilst you may need to keep an eye on the reforms as they move through the EU legislative process, the text that follows is based on the law as at February 2013.

Market abuse is an umbrella term that currently covers two categories of unlawful behaviour: insider dealing and market manipulation. Insider dealing describes various uses of information which is not publicly available (insider information) and market manipulation describes both distortion of the price-setting mechanism of financial instruments and dissemination of false or misleading information; in short, market manipulation is creating a false market in securities.

The law in the UK in this area initially focused on insider dealing before it was expanded to cover the broader range of behaviours amounting to market manipulation. UK law also initially focused exclusively on criminalising market abuse behaviour. At European level, the Market Abuse Directive (2003/6/EC) required Member States to implement a civil regulatory regime (which the UK has done), the sanctions for contravention of which include unlimited civil financial penalties.

The result of the foregoing piecemeal evolution of the law is that the UK law on market abuse is found in the following places:

Insider dealing

Criminal offences: Criminal Justice Act 1993 s. 52
Regulatory regime including civil penalties: Financial Services and Markets Act 2000, Part VIII (ss 118-131) (as amended) (FSMA).

Market manipulation

Criminal offences: Financial Services Act 2012 ss. 89–91
Regulatory regime including civil penalties: FSMA, Part VIII (ss 118–131) (as amended)

5 Criminal liability for market abuse

5.1 Insider dealing

The City Code on Takeovers and Mergers (see chapter 17) had been relied on to regulate insider dealing before the behaviour was criminalised in 1980. Currently, the Criminal Justice Act 1993, s. 52 establishes three insider dealing offences which only individuals may commit. Conspiracy to commit an insider dealing offence is also an offence under the Criminal Law Act 1977, s. 1. The FSMA gives the FCA the power to prosecute the 1993 and 1977 Act offences, although it does not have exclusive prosecutorial power.

Insider dealing is also regulated by the FCA under Part VIII of the FSMA 2000 (as amended) because it is a form of market abuse. The FCA may impose a range of civil penalties on both individuals and companies found to have transgressed the relevant sections of the FSMA.

Criminal offences

The three insider dealing offences established by the Criminal Justice Act 1993, s. 52 are the dealing, encouraging dealing and disclosure offences, as follows:

- whilst having information as an insider:
  - dealing in securities that are price affected securities;
  - encouraging another person to deal in securities that are (whether or not that other person knows it) price affected securities in relation to the information, knowing or having reasonable cause to believe that the dealing would take place; and
  - disclosing the information otherwise than in the proper performance of the functions of his employment, office or profession, to another person.

In relation to the dealing and encouraging to deal offences (the latter is also known as 'tipping'), the acquisition or disposal must occur on a regulated market as defined for the purposes of the offences. The definition is found in s. 60 of the 1993 Act which contains a broad definition extending the term to include, for example, AIM.

The definitions of the key terms used in the criminal offences are critical to determine whether or not a crime has been committed. They are also very technical. Three concepts, 'having information as an insider', **inside information** and 'made public' are considered in the following paragraphs.

Insider

The concept of having information as an insider set out in s. 57 contains the mental element of the insider dealing offences. Basically, a person has information as an insider if, and only if, it is, and he knows that it is, inside information and he has it, and he knows that he has it, from an inside source.

For these purposes a person has information from an inside source if, and only if, he has it through being a director, employee or shareholder of the company or through having access to the information by virtue of his employment, office or profession or, the direct or indirect source of his information is one of those persons.

Note that the knowledge required of the accused for a successful prosecution is two-fold: knowledge that the information is inside information and knowledge that the person he receives it from is an inside source.

Inside information

Four aspects of inside information are identified in the definition in s. 56 of the 1993 Act. To qualify as inside information, the information has to:

1. relate to particular securities or to a particular issuer or issuers of securities and not to securities generally or to issuers of securities generally;
2. be specific or precise;
3. not have been made public; and
4. be such that if it were made public it would be likely to have a significant effect on the price of any securities.

The concept of 'made public' appears twice and is critical to a determination of whether or not information is 'inside' information or not.

Made public

The Act contains guidance on the meaning of the term 'made public' including the non-exhaustive lists in s. 58, of circumstances in which information will be taken to have been made public, or may be treated as having been made public:

'58 (2) Information is made public if—
    (a) it is published in accordance with the rules of a regulated market for the purpose of informing investors and their professional advisers;
    (b) it is contained in records which by virtue of any enactment are open to inspection by the public;
    (c) it can be readily acquired by those likely to deal in any securities—
        (i) to which the information relates, or
        (ii) of an issuer to which the information relates; or
    (d) it is derived from information which has been made public.
(3) Information may be treated as made public even though—
    (a) it can be acquired only by persons exercising diligence or expertise;
    (b) it is communicated to a section of the public and not to the public at large;
    (c) it can be acquired only by observation;
    (d) it is communicated only on payment of a fee; or
    (e) it is published only outside the United Kingdom.'

As these lists indicate, information may be regarded as made public even if nobody is in fact cognisant of it. The breadth of the concept is appropriate given that it operates as a carve-out from potential criminal liability. If the information is available to the public, even if not accessed, it must be right that a person who accesses it and uses it cannot be convicted of a crime based on misuse of inside information.

Defences

Section 53 and Schedule 1 to the 1993 Act contain defences to the insider dealing criminal offences. The three general defences to each of the three offences are dealt with separately as follows:

Defences to dealing
53 (1) An individual is not guilty of insider dealing by virtue of dealing in securities if he shows—
    (a) that he did not at the time expect the dealing to result in a profit attributable to the fact that the information in question was price-sensitive information in relation to the securities, or
    (b) that at the time he believed on reasonable grounds that the information had been disclosed widely enough to ensure that none of those taking part in the dealing would be prejudiced by not having the information, or
    (c) that he would have done what he did even if he had not had the information.

Defences to encouraging dealing
53 (2) An individual is not guilty of insider dealing by virtue of encouraging another person to deal in securities if he shows—
    (a) that he did not at the time expect the dealing to result in a profit attributable to the fact that the information in question was price-sensitive information in relation to the securities, or
    (b) that at the time he believed on reasonable grounds that the information had been or would be disclosed widely enough to ensure that none of those taking part in the dealing would be prejudiced by not having the information, or
    (c) that he would have done what he did even if he had not had the information.

Defence to disclosure of inside information:
53 (3) An individual is not guilty of insider dealing by virtue of a disclosure of information if he shows—

(a) that he did not at the time expect any person, because of the disclosure, to deal in securities in the circumstances mentioned in subsection (3) of section 52; or

(b) that, although he had such an expectation at the time, he did not expect the dealing to result in a profit attributable to the fact that the information was price-sensitive information in relation to the securities.

Price-sensitive information is relevant to the defences to all three offences and means information which would, if made public, be likely to have a significant effect on the price of the securities (s. 56(2)). The Act provides no guidance on what amounts to 'significant', which must be determined on a case-by-case basis. It is probably satisfied by something less than an 'untoward movement' in share price for the purposes of the City Code on Takeovers and Mergers, rule 2.2 being more closely aligned with the concept of price-sensitive information for the purposes of the Disclosure Rules, which require immediate disclosure of information likely to have a significant effect on the price of a security.

Criminal penalties

Section 61 sets out the penalties for insider dealing. On summary conviction, the punishment is a fine not exceeding the statutory maximum or imprisonment for a term not exceeding six months, or both; and on conviction on indictment, the punishment is a fine or imprisonment for a term not exceeding seven years, or both. As at June 2010 the FCA had secured the imposition of five prison sentences for insider dealing.

CASE EXAMPLE 7.1

Consider what, if any, insider dealing offences may have taken place in the following circumstances:

Charles, the company secretary of Company A plc learned at a board meeting of Company A plc that Company B plc had made an approach to the finance director of Company A plc to discuss a takeover of the company. Before the takeover was made public, Charles called his daughter, Deborah, and advised her to buy shares in Company A plc. He told her she should buy them in her married name. Also, Charles mentioned to his friend Jed that it looked as if his days at Company A plc were numbered as a big US company was sniffing around. Deborah and Jed subsequently each bought 50,000 shares in Company A plc at 20 pence a share. Neither had ever bought shares before. One month later a takeover of Company A plc was announced at 50 pence per share. Deborah and Jed each made a profit of £15,000.

STOP AND THINK 7.1

Beginning with its first criminal prosecution of insider dealing behaviour in March 2009, a case involving a solicitor and in-house counsel, the FCA stepped up its activity in relation to insider dealing as part of its general crackdown on market abuse. The *Guardian* reported on 23 March 2010 that the FCA (then called the FSA), ' ... has warned the City to "be afraid" of its crackdown on dirty dealing', and had raided 16 premises with the help of 143 of its own employees and officers from the Serious Organised Crime Agency (SOCA), the first time it had worked with SOCA. The move was seen by the City, the *Guardian* reported, '... as an attempt by the FSA to show determination in eradicating insider dealing, which has been traditionally difficult to prosecute'. The FSA reported the investigation to be its 'largest ever operation against insider dealing'. The results of recent trials, and trials pending for insider dealing since the crackdown can be tracked on the FCA website. At the end of 2012 the FCA had secured 21 convictions in relation to insider dealing.

> **TEST YOUR KNOWLEDGE 7.4**
>
> (a) What are the three insider dealing offences found in the Criminal Justice Act 1993?
> (b) What is 'price-sensitive information'?
> (c) What is 'inside information'?
> (d) What must a person know to 'have information as an insider'?

5.2 Market manipulation

Market manipulation (not being insider dealing) was first criminalised in the UK by the Financial Services Act 1986, six years after insider dealing had been criminalised. The relevant provisions of the 1986 Act were subsequently repealed and re-enacted in the FSMA 2000, s. 397. The criminal offences created by s. 397 existed alongside the civil regime in Part VIII of the FSMA which regulates market manipulation as well as insider dealing, i.e., market abuse generally. The UK Government has pressed ahead with reform of s. 397 (ahead of MAD 2) and has extended criminal liability to market manipulation of benchmarks, such as manipulation of LIBOR, in the wake of the recent LIBOR scandal. The new offences are set out in the FSA 2012, ss. 89–91.

Criminal offences

The statutory provisions governing the market manipulation criminal offences are now ss. 89–95 of the Financial Services Act 2012. The two offences set out in s. 89 (the misleading statement offence) and s. 90 (the misleading impression offence) replace the two offences in s. 397 of the FSMA which no longer exist as that section has been repealed (by FSA 2012 s. 95). A third offence, found in s. 91, is new. It has been created to deal with manipulation of benchmark rates, the most famous and widely used benchmark being LIBOR.

The misleading statements offence
In the explanatory notes to the FSA 2012, the s. 89 misleading statement offence is described as largely restating the effect of s. 397(2). However, in one sense it appears to be narrower than its predecessor offence in that it is limited to the making of statements or the concealing of material facts, whereas s. 397(2) extended to making statements, *promises or forecasts*.

Basically, a person who:

(a) makes a statement which he knows to be false or misleading in a material respect;
(b) makes a statement which is false or misleading in a material respect, being reckless as to whether it is; or
(c) dishonestly conceals any material facts whether in connection with a statement made by P or otherwise,

commits an offence if he makes the statement or conceals the facts with the intention of inducing or is reckless as to whether making it or concealing them may induce, another person (whether or not the person to whom the statement is made):

(a) to enter into or offer to enter into, or to refrain from entering or offering to enter into, a relevant agreement; or
(b) to exercise, or refrain from exercising, any rights conferred by a relevant investment.

Subsection 89(3) provides for the same defences as those that existed in relation to the predecessor offence in s. 397. It is a defence to show that the statements were made in conformity with price stabilising or control of information rules.

The misleading impression offence
The offence of creating a misleading impression in s. 90 appears to be broader than its predecessor. Not only is it an offence under s. 90 to create a misleading impression to induce another to deal or refrain from dealing, it is also an offence to create a misleading impression *intending to profit or cause loss to another*. Also, it is not necessary to establish that the defendant knew the impression to be false, it is sufficient that the defendant was reckless as to whether the

impression was false or not. Finally, the defendant must simply be aware that the impression is *likely* to result in personal gain or loss to another person.

Basically, a person ('P') who does any act or engages in any course of conduct which creates a false or misleading impression as to the market in or the price or value of any relevant investments commits an offence if he intends to create the impression and the case falls within subsection 90(2) or (3) (or both). The relevant subsections are very carefully worded and are therefore here set out in full:

'(2) The case falls within this subsection if P intends, by creating the impression, to induce another person to acquire, dispose of, subscribe for or underwrite the investments or to refrain from doing so or to exercise or refrain from exercising any rights conferred by the investments.

(3) The case falls within this subsection if—
   (a) P knows that the impression is false or misleading or is reckless as to whether it is, and
   (b) P intends by creating the impression to produce any of the results in subsection (4) or is aware that creating the impression is likely to produce any of the results in that subsection.

(4) Those results are—
   (a) the making of a gain for P or another, or
   (b) the causing of loss to another person or the exposing of another person to the risk of loss.'

Again, the defences are the same as for the predecessor offence. In addition to proving that the statements were made in conformity with price stabilising or control of information rules, it is a defence that the person concerned reasonably believed that his conduct would not create an impression that was false or misleading (s. 90(9)).

The misleading statements etc in relation to benchmarks offence
The new offence in s. 91 relating to the making of a false or misleading statement, or the creation of a false or misleading impression, in connection with the setting of a relevant benchmark, is outside the remit of this text. Basically, the explanatory note to the FSA 2012 states that a person making the statement or creating the impression must know or be reckless as to whether the statement or impression is false or misleading, and the motive of the person is immaterial.

Criminal penalties

The criminal penalties for committing ss. 89–91 offences are similar to those for the insider dealing offences under the 1993 Act: on summary conviction, imprisonment for a term not exceeding 12 months or a fine not exceeding the statutory maximum, or both, and on conviction on indictment, imprisonment for a term not exceeding seven years or a fine, or both (s. 92).

In *R v Bailey and Rigby* [2006] 2 Cr App R (S) 36 the court stated the factors to take into account when sentencing an offender under the predecessor provision s. 397(8):

- the offender's degree of recklessness;
- the financial context of the making of the statement;
- the financial consequences of the statement;
- whether deliberately deceptive steps had been taken by the offender in making the statement;
- the importance of protecting investors by reinforcing financial market openness and integrity.

 **CASE EXAMPLE 7.2**

Consider whether the following facts disclose any market manipulation offences:

A financial journalist, Gerald, bought shares in Company X plc. The following week he wrote a newspaper column tipping them for growth. The week after that the price of the shares increased by 20%. In the same period the relevant market index fell by 1%. Gerald had no information to support the statements made in his column (see *R v William James Hipwell* [2006] EWCA Crim 736).

> **TEST YOUR KNOWLEDGE 7.5**
>
> (a) When was market manipulation (not being insider dealing) first criminalised in the UK?
> (b) Which two types of behaviour are criminalised as market manipulation?
> (c) What are the criminal penalties for market manipulation?

6 The civil regime for market abuse

The Market Abuse Directive, which requires Member States to implement a civil regulatory regime, came into force in July 2005 and has been implemented in the UK by amendments to Part VIII of the FSMA and revisions to the FCA Disclosure and Transparency Rules. Also, the FCA is required by the FSMA s. 119 to issue a code, to 'give appropriate guidance to those determining whether or not behaviour amounts to market abuse'. The Code of Market Conduct, first issued by the FCA in 2001, was revised in 2008 to reflect the MAD and has been subsequently amended. It can be found as MAR 1 in the Business Standards segment of the FCA Handbook.

The civil offence of market abuse is found in s. 118 of the FSMA. The offence applies to behaviour relating to a 'qualifying investment' traded on a 'prescribed market' as those terms are defined in the Financial Services and Markets Act 2000 (Prescribed Markets and Qualifying Investments) Order 2001 (SI 2001/996) as amended. Shares and bonds are qualifying investments and 'prescribed market' is a broader term than 'regulated market' as it includes all markets established under the rules of a regulated investment exchange – consequently, AIM is included.

The civil market abuse offence in s. 118 covers a broader range of behaviour than the criminal offences considered above. Civil market abuse consists of one or more of the following seven types of behaviour:

- insider dealing;
- improper disclosure;
- misuse of information;
- manipulating transactions;
- manipulating devices;
- dissemination; and
- distortion and misleading behaviour.

6.1 Safe harbours, defences and penalties

Behaviour that falls into either of two 'safe harbours' is not market abuse. The first safe harbour arises from the FSMA, s. 122, which sets out the effect of the Code of Market Conduct and specifies that 'if a person behaves in a way which is described (in the code in force under s. 119 at the time of the behaviour) as behaviour that, in the [FCA's] opinion, does not amount to market abuse, that behaviour of his is to be taken, for the purposes of this Act, as not amounting to market abuse'. Note that the Code simply provides guidance and creates a safe harbour, it does not impose additional requirements that need to be evidenced before a finding of abuse can be made. The second safe harbour is s. 118A(5) which, among other types, excludes from market abuse behaviour that ' … conforms with a rule which includes a provision to the effect that behaviour conforming with the rule does not amount to market abuse'. The rules referred to are, essentially, FCA-promulgated rules (including the Listing Rules and the Disclosure Rules), and the City Code.

Section 123, which authorises the FCA to impose unlimited financial penalties of such amounts as it considers appropriate, states that the FCA may not impose a penalty on a person for market abuse if there are reasonable grounds for it to be satisfied that he believed, on reasonable grounds, that his behaviour did not amount to market abuse, or he took all reasonable precautions and exercised all due diligence to avoid engaging in market abuse.

Other sanctions that may be applied in the case of market abuse include compensation payments to victims, an account of profits, injunctions and public statements of censure (see Part XXV of the FSMA).

The UK market abuse civil regime is rooted in the UK's more stringent regime that existed before the MAD. The enhanced stringency is referred to as 'super-equivalency' and consists of the regulation of misuse of information (s. 118(4)) and misleading behaviour and market distortion (s. 118(8)). Continuation of these super-equivalent rules is now provided for until 31 December 2014 as initial plans to remove them have been suspended pending MAD 2.

>
>
> **TEST YOUR KNOWLEDGE 7.6**
>
> (a) What is the function of the Code of Market Conduct?
> (b) Which seven types of behaviour constitute market abuse for the purposes of the FSMA, s. 118?
> (c) Describe two 'safe harbours' in relation to market abuse.
> (d) What sanctions can be applied in the case of behaviour described in s. 118?

CHAPTER SUMMARY

- The Financial Services and Markets Act 2000 and Prospectus Rules require a company to publish a prospectus before it makes an offer of securities to the public or applies for the admission of securities to trading on a regulated market.
- Key exemptions are: offers to qualified investors only; offers to fewer than 150 investors other than qualified investors; offers where the total consideration is less than €5 million, offers where the minimum nominal value of a share or payable by one investor is €100,000 or more, offers in connection with takeovers, and offers to employees and/or directors.
- Prospectuses are not required solely for *admission of securities to trading* on AIM.
- The FCA cannot approve a prospectus unless it contains all information necessary to enable investors to make an informed assessment of the assets and liabilities, financial position, profits and losses, and prospects of the company and any guarantor and the rights attaching to the shares, (FSMA, s. 87A).
- Specific content requirements are found in the Prospectus Rules.
- Failure to publish an approved prospectus where one is required is a criminal offence (s. 85(3)).
- Statutory compensation may be payable by 'the persons responsible' for a prospectus for non-issue of a prospectus (s. 85(4)), publication of untrue or misleading statements in a prospectus, and omission of key information (s. 90). Common law remedies may also be available.
- Listing particulars, distinct from a prospectus, are required in a number of specialist circumstances (s. 79).
- In a public offering of shares, it is common for an investment bank to underwrite the share offer.
- Underwriting commission is usually expressed as a percentage of the nominal value of the share issue and the Companies Act 2006, s. 533 permits such payments.
- The Criminal Justice Act 1993, s. 52 establishes three insider dealing offences which only individuals may commit.
- The FSA 2012 ss. 89–91 create several market manipulation criminal offences.
- The FSMA 2000 as amended implements the Market Abuse Directive (MAD) in the UK.
- FSMA 2000, s. 118 establishes a civil market abuse offence covering a broader range of behaviour than the criminal offences. It extends to seven types of behaviour: insider dealing, improper disclosure, misuse of information, manipulating transactions, manipulating devices, dissemination of false or misleading information and distortion and misleading behaviour.
- As required by FSMA 2000, s. 119, the FCA has issued a Code of Market Conduct giving guidance as to what does and what does not amount to market abuse.
- By FSMA 2000, s. 123 the FCA is authorised to impose unlimited financial penalties of such amounts as it considers appropriate.
- Two 'safe harbours' are behaviour described in the code or in the rules as not market abuse.
- The FCA may not impose a penalty if there are reasonable grounds for it to be satisfied that a person believed, on reasonable grounds, that his behaviour did not amount to market abuse, or took all reasonable precautions and exercised all due diligence to avoid engaging in market abuse.

Membership, shares and share capital

■ CONTENTS

1. Becoming a shareholder
2. Becoming a member and the register of members
3. The legal nature of a share
4. Different types of shares
5. Class rights
6. Share capital
7. Alteration of share capital
8. Allotment and issue of shares
9. Payment for shares, discounts and premiums
10. Statutory pre-emption rights of existing shareholders and rights issues
11. Transfer and transmission of shares
12. Share certificates and warrants
13. Partly paid shares: calls, liens, surrender and forfeiture

■ INTRODUCTION

This chapter opens with an explanation of how a person becomes a shareholder or member of a company and the significance of the register of members. The legal nature of a share is then examined. The chapter continues by explaining the concept of different classes of shares and the law governing variation of class rights. The chapter then explains the concept of share capital and the power of a company to increase its share capital by issuing new shares. (Reduction of share capital is considered in chapter 9.) The chapter continues with a look at pre-emption rights. The following sections explain how shares are transferred or transmitted, and examines share certificates and share warrants. Finally, the consequences of failure to pay instalments and calls on partly paid shares are considered.

1 Becoming a shareholder

A number of routes lead to a person having a right to shares in a registered company. Those persons with a right to shares include:

- subscribers to the Memorandum of Association;
- subscribers to a new issue of shares who have been allotted shares;
- acquirers/transferees of existing shares transferred by an existing shareholder; and
- persons who acquires the right to shares by operation of law on a member's:
  - death;
  - insolvency/bankruptcy; or
  - declaration of mental unfitness.

Having the right to shares does not make a person a member of a company. Membership is determined by the appearance of a person's name on a company's register of members.

2 Becoming a member and the register of members

The Companies Act, s. 112 defines member in relation to a company's register of members:

'(1) The subscribers of a company's memorandum are deemed to have agreed to become members of the company, and on its registration become members and must be entered as such in its register of members.
(2) Every other person who agrees to become a member of a company, and whose name is entered in its register of members, is a member of the company.'

This makes it essential to maintain an up-to-date and accurate register of members, which is the responsibility of the company secretary. Section 113 states that each company must keep a register of its members including the following information:

- the names and addresses of the members;
- the date on which each person was registered as a member;
- the date at which any person ceased to be a member;
- the shares held by each member, distinguishing each share (where appropriate) by its number and class; and
- the amount paid on each share.

If a company has more than 50 members, it must also maintain an index of members containing sufficient indication to permit the entry on the register of members to be found (s. 115). Both the register and index must be made available for inspection (ss. 114 and 115) and, if a company fails to maintain a register or index or to make them available for inspection in accordance with the Act, an offence is committed by the company and every officer of the company who is in default.

If a company is incorporated as or subsequently becomes a sole member company, a statement that the company has only one member and the date from which it became a company with only one member must be entered on the register of members (s. 123). The entries required to be made on the register of members in the event that the company issues share warrants is considered in section 5 below.

Before making entries or changes to the register of members, the company secretary must ensure that he has the correct evidence to support the entry. From the date of registration, subscribers to the Memorandum become members (s. 112) and s. 16 states that from registration they become the holders of the shares specified in the statement of capital and initial shareholdings. Sections 16 and 112, the Memorandum and the statement of capital and initial shareholdings provide the basis and information for the first entries on the register of members.

Turning to subsequent entries, s. 558 provides:

'For the purposes of the Companies Acts shares in a company are taken to be allotted when a person acquires the unconditional right to be included in the company's register of members in respect of the shares.'

Accordingly, the names of subscribers for a new issue of shares may only be added to the register, or the shares held by existing members who subscribe for further shares may only be altered, if the shares subscribed for have been allotted. Ordinarily, this will occur when the board resolves to allot the shares to the subscribers.

Changes to the register of members following a transfer of shares and transmission of legal title by operation of law, are addressed in section 11.

TEST YOUR KNOWLEDGE 8.1

(a) Identify four routes to gaining the right to shares.
(b) Who is a member of a company with a share capital?
(c) What information is required in the register of members?
(d) When are shares taken to have been allotted?

3 The legal nature of a share

A share in a company is a legally complex concept. The limited statutory definition of share in s. 540 is far from illuminating: 'In the Companies Acts "share", in relation to a company, means share in the company.'

The Act confirms that a share is a piece of personal property (s. 541), and the House of Lords in *Colonial Bank v Whinney* (1886) 11 App Cas 426 confirmed that a share is a 'chose in action'. Classification as a chose in action is usually relevant to determine the rules governing legal transfer: assignment of a chose in action is governed by the Law of Property Act 1925, s. 136. As special rules govern the transfer of legal title to most shares, the status of a share as a chose in action is of limited practical relevance.

Both the entitlement (interest) and liability aspects of a share and the contractual nature of the relationship between a shareholder and the company are identified in Farwell J's classic judicial statement of the nature of a share in *Borland's Trustee v Steel* [1901] 1 Ch 279:

> 'A share is the interest of a shareholder in the company measured by a sum of money for the purposes of liability in the first place, and of interest in the second, but also consisting of a series of mutual covenants entered into by all the shareholders inter se in accordance with section [33] of the Companies Act [2006]. The contract contained in the Articles of association is one of the original incidents of the share. A share ... is an interest measured by a sum of money and made up of various rights contained in the contract.'

This statement does not stress the rights of a shareholder to vote and thereby participate in decision-making, or the exercise of powers, by the company. This decision-making, or voting participation, aspect of share ownership is focused on in part 4.

4 Different types of shares

There is a legal presumption that each share in a company provides the owner with the same rights and liabilities as every other share. This is called the 'presumption of equality' (see *Birch v Cropper* (1899) 14 App Cas 525 HL).

This presumption can be displaced by the company issuing shares with different rights attaching to them. Shares with the same rights and liabilities are called a 'class of shares'. A new class of shares is created by a company issuing shares with rights or liabilities that differ in some respect from all existing shares in the company. There is no legal limit to the number of classes of shares a company may have.

4.1 Residual ordinary shares

Most companies have only one class of shares, called here residual **ordinary shares**. The rights of a residual ordinary shareholder are found in company law (common law principles and statutory provisions) and in the constitution of the company (principally the Articles). As has been noted, shareholders are entitled to share the wealth generated by a company. Residual ordinary shares carry the same right to share in the profits of the company as every other residual ordinary share. Should the company be wound up, each residual ordinary share will carry the right to share in the residual wealth of the company as every other residual ordinary share. The third right attached to a residual ordinary share is the right to vote on shareholder resolutions. Without more, every residual ordinary shareholder has one vote in respect of each share on a resolution on a poll (s. 284) (see chapter 14 for the meaning of poll).

4.2 Other classes of shares

Different classes of shares usually arise from the creation of shares differing from residual ordinary shares (and any other already existing classes) in one or more of the following key respects:

- nominal value (*Greenhalgh v Arderne Cinema's Ltd* [1946] 1 All ER 512 (CA));
- rights to participate in declared dividends;
- rights to participate in residual wealth on a winding up; or
- voting rights.

That said, a new class of shares may be created when a share is issued with rights differing in virtually any way from the residual ordinary shares and any other classes of shares the company already has. This is examined further in section 5.2.

4.3 Class names

The names given to certain types of shares with certain key characteristics are not always legally significant. They may be merely descriptive, whether of one or more characteristic of the shares, such as **preference shares** or of those to whom the shares are typically issued, such as employees' shares or **founders' shares**. The name preference shares simply indicates that the shares have some degree of preference versus other shareholders in relation to either, or both, **dividends** and capital participation.

Redeemable shares, on the other hand, is not only a name but also a legal description (s. 684(1)) of shares that are liable to be redeemed at the option of the company or the shareholder and must be so redeemed in accordance with the Companies Act 2006 (ss. 684–689). Difficulties can arise when shares that are not redeemable shares for the purposes of the 2006 Act are none the less given the name 'redeemable shares'.

4.4 Equity and non-equity shares

Where a company has a class of shares that 'neither as respects dividends nor as respects capital, carries any right to participate beyond a specified amount in a distribution', those shares are part of the share capital of the company but they are not equity shares and do not form part of the equity share capital of the company (s. 548) (see below). The distinction between equity and non-equity shares reflects the fact that some shares are in many ways fulfilling the role of debt. One typical type of preference shareholder, in return for the first bite of the company's wealth after the creditors in the form of preferential rights to a fixed rate dividend and receipt of the sum they paid to the company back in priority to other (equity) shareholders receiving any capital back, forgoes the right to participate to any greater extent in the wealth generated by the company and is a non-equity shareholder.

Equity share capital connotes:

- an unlimited opportunity to share in the financial success of the company, which opportunity becomes a right in the event of a solvent winding up; and
- the first layer of capital at risk and to be lost in the event of insolvency.

TEST YOUR KNOWLEDGE 8.2

(a) Explain what a share is in your own words.
(b) What is the 'presumption of equality'?
(c) What are the four key respects in which one class of shares may differ from another class of shares.
(d) Distinguish equity and non-equity shares.

5 Class rights

5.1 Ascertaining the rights attached to shares

The specific rights of second and subsequent classes of shares are found in the Articles or the shareholders' resolution authorising their issue. These rights may override or be supplemented by common law principles and statutory provisions. Following the issue of new shares, the rights and liabilities attaching to them must be stated in the amended statement of capital that must be sent, along with the return of allotment, to the Registrar of Companies (s. 555).

The specific rights of new classes of shares should be stated clearly in the Articles or authorising resolution. This avoids the need to depend on presumptions or implied terms in determining those rights. Current practice is for the rights to be set out very clearly in the Articles, but this has not always been the case. The courts have regularly been called on to determine the rights and liabilities attached to a class of shares that have been issued without the precise rights intended to attach having been captured in the Articles or authorising resolution.

In the course of deciding these cases the courts have developed a number of rules or 'canons' of construction for the purposes of working out the rights of shares issues with inadequately stated rights and liabilities. The main canons of construction are:

- All shares have the same rights and liabilities unless the company and the shareholder have agreed otherwise (*Birch v Cropper* (1899)).
- If new shares are issued, they will carry the same rights and liabilities as the residual ordinary shares except to the extent provided otherwise.
- If voting rights have been specified, those rights are presumed to be exhaustive: the shares carry no right to vote on a resolution on any matter beyond those matters (*Re Bradford Investment Ltd* [1991] BCLC 224).
- If dividend rights have been specified, those rights are presumed to be exhaustive: the shares carry no rights to participate in dividends beyond the expressly stated rights (*Will v United Lankat Plantations Co* [1914] AC 11 (HL)).
- If capital participation rights have been specified, those rights are presumed to be exhaustive: the shares carry no rights to participate in capital beyond the expressly stated rights (*Scottish Insurance Corporation Ltd v Wilsons & Clyde Coal Co Ltd* [1949] AC 462 (HL)).
- If shares carry a right to receive a dividend of a specified amount before other shares (known as a 'preferential dividend'), such as 10% of the nominal price per year, the dividend rights are presumed to be cumulative: if 10% is not paid in one year, 20% will be payable in the second year and, if not paid, 30% will be payable in the third year, etc.) (*Webb v Earle* (1875) LR 20 Eq 566).
- A preferential dividend is presumed to be not payable unless it has been declared by the company. Whilst this presumption will be rebutted by language suggesting otherwise, such as provision in the Articles or authorising resolution that, subject to distributable profits being available, dividends are automatically payable on 1 May of each year, it would be courting negligence on the part of a solicitor to allow the terms of issue not to deal clearly with this matter as the legal presumption does not reflect commercial reality (*Re Roberts & Cooper Ltd* [1929] 2 Ch 383 and *Re Bradford Investments Plc (No. 1)* [1991] BCLC 224).

The presumption that stated class rights are deemed to be exhaustive was set out in *Re National Telephone Company* [1914] 1 Ch 755:

'either with regard to dividends or with regard to the rights in a winding up, the express gift or attachment of preferential rights to preference shares, on their creation, is **prima facie**, a definition of the whole of their rights in that respect and negatives any further or other right to which, but for the specified rights, they would have been entitled.'

5.2 The concept of class rights

The precise range of rights that are in law 'class rights' becomes important when a company seeks to vary the rights of one class of shareholders. Unless provision is made otherwise in the Articles, class rights may be varied only with the consent of holders of 75% of the class. To understand when consent of the class is needed, it is necessary to know what is and what is not a class right. This issue is explored further under class rights and variation.

There is no comprehensive definition of 'class rights' but it has been explored in the context of what is now s. 630, the protection given to shareholders when there is an attempt to change or vary the rights attached to the type of shares they hold.

The concept was explored in *Cumbrian Newspapers Group Ltd v Cumberland and Westmoreland Newspaper and Printing Co Ltd* [1987] Ch 1 which recognised as class rights for the purposes of s. 630 rights not attaching to any particular shares but exercisable only for so long as the shareholder was owner of shares in the company.

CASE LAW 8.1

***Cumbrian Newspapers Group Ltd v Cumberland and Westmoreland Newspaper and Printing Co Ltd* [1987] Ch 1**

Pursuant to an agreement by which Cumberland acquired one of Cumbrian's newspapers, Cumbrian acquired just over 10% of the shares in Cumberland and the Articles of Cumberland were amended to allow Cumbrian to prevent a take-over of Cumberland by giving Cumbrian (only) the following rights: rights of pre-emption over other ordinary shares; rights in respect of unissued shares; and so long as Cumbrian held no less than 10% of the shares in Cumberland, the right to appoint a director. Cumberland sought to remove these rights by special resolution of the ordinary shareholders. Cumbrian argued removal of the rights was a variation of class rights for the purposes of the statute (now s. 630) therefore its (the class holder's) approval was needed. Removal of the rights would be a variation, being an 'abrogation', but the question was, were they 'class rights'?

Held: Even though they were not attached to particular shares, the rights were conferred on Cumbrian in the capacity of shareholder of the company and therefore were class rights and could not be varied without the approval of holders of 75% of the class.

The decision in the case has attracted criticism and may no longer be good law as a result of s. 629(1) which states:

> 'For the purposes of the Companies Acts shares are of one class if the right attached to them are in all respects uniform.'

By expressly referring to rights attached to shares, this section may have excluded from class rights the type of rights in *Cumberland*. The effect of s. 629 remains to be determined.

The concept of class rights, then, remains unclear in English law. Three ways of interpreting the concept are discussed by Ferran (1999):

- Class rights are those rights which are exclusive to the class and distinct from right attaching to any other class (the narrow concept).
- Class rights are all the rights which, under the constitution, attach to shares in the company, irrespective of whether those rights are exclusive to a particular class or also enjoyed by other classes (the broad concept).
- Class rights are rights which are exclusive to the class and dividend and capital rights, rights to vote and rights relating to protection of class rights (the middle concept).

The case of *Greenhalgh v Arderne Cinemas Ltd* [1946] 1 All ER 512 (CA) is cited as supporting the middle concept by implication, but in the absence of more compelling authority, the issue of what are and are not class rights remains moot.

This uncertainty surrounding the concept of class rights can have acute practical significance. It makes it extremely important to spell out clearly, in the Articles or authorising resolution, the situations in which the holders of a particular type of share are protected from the company attempting to change the rights that attach to that type of shares. Express provision of a protective mechanism should be made in the Articles or the authorising resolution, such as stipulating that the rights cannot be varied or changed in any way without the prior approval of the holders of 75% of the shares of the type in question.

TEST YOUR KNOWLEDGE 8.3

(a) Where are the rights that attach to a share set out?
(b) What is the presumption of exhaustion as set out in *Re National Telephone Company* [1914] 1 Ch 755.
(c) What is a preferential dividend and what does it mean to say that a dividend is cumulative?
(d) What are the three concepts of class rights identified by Ferran and which is believed to apply in UK company law?

5.3 Variation of class rights

A company may seek to vary the rights attaching to a class of shares. Shares entitled to a 10% preferential dividend, for example, may be considered a very expensive way to access capital. The company may wish to either reduce the rate of preferred dividend payable or get rid of the preference shares altogether by buying them back and cancelling them, thereby reducing the share capital of the company.

The statutory procedure to be complied with before class rights may be varied is set out in the Companies Act 2006 (ss. 630–640). The Articles may provide less protection than is provided by the statute (s. 630(2)(a)). Alternatively, more onerous restrictions on the variation of rights than those in the statute may be imposed and these may be in the Articles or in the authorising resolution of the class of shares.

Essentially, under the statute, holders of 75% by nominal value of the shares in the affected class must approve a variation in advance (s. 630). Even if 75% of the holders approve the variation, the holders of 15% may, within 21 days of approval, apply to the court to have the variation cancelled (s. 633(1)). The court may disallow the variation if it is satisfied that, having regard to all the circumstances of the case, the variation would unfairly prejudice the shareholders of the class represented by the applicant (s. 633(5)). The minority shareholders believing themselves to be unfairly prejudiced by a variation supported by a majority of the class may, as an alternative course of action, petition the court under s. 994 (considered below). In view of the broad-ranging remedies available to a court under s. 994, it is likely to be a preferable route for disaffected minority shareholders, which may explain why there appears to be only one reported case on what is now s. 633 (*Re Sound City (Films) Ltd* [1947] Ch 169).

The strength or weakness of the protection given to holders of classes of shares by the statutory provision (s. 630) and provisions in the Articles depends upon the breadth or narrowness of interpretation of the terms 'variation' and 'class right'.

As already noted, there is no comprehensive definition of variation for the purposes of s. 630. A variation of rights can be a variation to improve or enhance the rights of the class as well as a variation adversely affecting those rights. Also, the Act makes it clear that an abrogation of rights is a variation for the purposes of the Act (s. 630(6)). Consequently, a reduction of capital by way of repayment of capital and cancellation of shares of a particular class may be a variation.

The courts have confined the concept of variation by drawing a distinction between class rights and the enjoyment of class rights. This has resulted in it being possible to adversely affect the financial position of holders of a class of shares in a number of ways without the company having to go through the variation procedure because the change is merely a change in the enjoyment of class rights.

CASE EXAMPLE 8.1

The dilution of voting control by the issue of more shares of the same class (in the case in hand, preference shares) to ordinary shareholders has been held not to be a variation of rights necessarily.

CASE LAW 8.2

White v Bristol Aeroplane Co [1953] Ch 65 (CA)
The company proposed to issue further preference shares to ordinary shareholders, to be paid for out of company reserves. This would dilute the voting control of existing preference shareholders. The Articles contained a provision governing when the consent of a class was required. The Articles stated that all or any rights and privileges attached to any class of shares forming part of the capital from time to time of the company might be affected, modified, varied, dealt with or abrogated in any manner with the sanction of an extraordinary resolution passed at a separate meeting of the members of that class. The preference shareholders objected to the proposed issue, arguing that the issue of the new preference shares would 'affect' the rights attached to their shares.

Held: The issue of further preference shares would not be a variation of, or affect the rights attached to, the shares and therefore preference shareholder consent was not needed. The proposed issue would affect the enjoyment of existing rights not the rights themselves.

CASE LAW 8.3

Re Mackenzie & Co Ltd [1916] 2 Ch 450
Preference shareholders were entitled to a dividend of 4% of the amount paid up on their £20 shares and no priority as to capital on a winding up. The ordinary shareholders in general meeting agreed a reduction in the company's share capital, reducing the nominal value of all shares, both ordinary and preference shares, rateably, that is, by the same proportion. Each preference share was reduced in nominal value to £12. Even though the preferential dividend expressed in percentage terms was not changed but remained at 4%, the change in nominal value reduced the dividend provided for on a fully paid-up preference share from 80 pence (4% of £20) to 48 pence (4% of £12).

Held: The reduction in share capital was not a variation of the preference shareholders' rights. The right to a 4% dividend remained the same even if the enjoyment of the right was changed.

A company may reduce its share capital by returning nominal capital to preference shareholders with priority rights to return of capital on a winding up and no further capital participation without approval of the holders of the class. The preference shareholders cannot complain about the loss of the right to share in the future wealth of the company by continuing to receive their preferential dividends.

CASE LAW 8.4

Scottish Insurance v Wilsons & Clyde Coal Co [1949] AC 462 (HL)
The company sought court approval for a reduction in its share capital by paying nominal share capital back to its 7% preference shareholders and extinguishing their shares. Preference shareholders argued that the reduction should not be approved as it was unfair to them.

Held: As a matter of interpretation of the rights attached to the preference shares, they entitled the holder to priority return of capital but no further participation in capital on a winding up. The capital reduction was fair.

CASE LAW 8.5

***House of Fraser v AGCE Investments Ltd* [1987] AC 387 (HL)**
Preference shareholders were entitled to prior repayment of nominal capital 'on a winding up or otherwise' but no further participation in the capital. Preference share capital was not needed by the company which reduced its share capital by a special resolution of ordinary shareholders in general meeting, returning the preference share capital to the class of preference shareholders and extinguishing the shares. The Articles provided for class approval if the special rights attaching to a class were 'modified, commuted, affected or dealt with'. No class meeting was held to approve the reduction. When the company sought court approval for the reduction in capital, as required by the Act, the preference shareholders argued the court could not approve the reduction of capital in the absence of consent of the holders of the class.

Held: The reduction was not a modification, etc, of the preference shareholders' rights but an extinction of the shares in strict accordance with the contract in the Articles. Applying *Re Saltdean Estate Co Ltd* [1968] 1 WLR 1844, the right to prior return of nominal capital on a winding up meant that the preference shares could be cancelled on a reduction of share capital.

CASE LAW 8.6

***Re Hunting Plc* [2005] 2 BCLC 211**
On an application by the company for confirmation by the court of a resolution to reduce its issued share capital by the cancellation of convertible preference shares, preference shareholders argued that the scheme of reduction was unfair to them. Held: the reduction was approved. A company is entitled to reduce its capital by cancelling preference shares to replace the preference share capital with cheaper capital. The reduction was not unfair to the preference shareholders because they knew when they acquired shares they were assuming the risk of being paid off in full.

In *Re Saltdean Estate Co Ltd* [1968] 1 WLR 1844, Buckley J confirmed that prior payment of preference shares on a reduction of capital is part of the bargain a preference shareholder enters into.

> 'The liability to prior repayment on a reduction of capital, corresponding to their right to prior return of capital in a winding up ... is part of the bargain between the shareholders and forms an integral part of the definition or delimitation of the bundle of rights which make up a preference share. Giving effect to it does not involve the variation or abrogation of any right attached to such a share.'

The rights of the preference shareholders may be enhanced by provisions in the Articles which specify that particular action by the company does amount to a variation of rights for which approval of the class is required.

CASE LAW 8.7

***Re Northern Engineering Industries plc* [1994] 2 BCLC 704 (CA)**
The company proposed to reduce its capital by way of paying off its preference shares and cancelling them. The Articles provided that the rights attached to any class of shares shall be deemed to be varied by 'the reduction of the capital paid up on those shares' (7(b)) and for the consent of 75% of the holders of a class of shares to be obtained before the rights could be varied or abrogated

CASE LAW 8.7 *continued*

(6). The judge refused to confirm the reduction of capital on the grounds that it was a variation of the rights of the preference shares to which the consent of the holders had not been obtained. The company appealed.

Held: Dismissing the appeal, the reduction proposed by the company was caught by article 7(b) which was inserted to protect the rights of preference shareholders and the protection required the class holders to give their consent by an appropriate class vote not only where the reduction was piecemeal but also where it involved a complete repayment of their investment.

In view of the narrow protection afforded by the statutory provisions and the often narrow interpretation of provisions in Articles, those intending to become holders of class rights will need to ensure that there are sufficiently protective provisions in the authorising resolution or in the Articles, requiring their consent to changes that affect the enjoyment of the rights as well as to changes to the rights themselves, or for adequate compensation to be paid when the enjoyment of rights are taken away.

A specific example of the latter has become the norm as a result of the decisions that demonstrated that it is not, without more, unfair and is consistent with the statutory protection, for a company, without securing approval of the class, to repay and remove from the company at any time the holders of shares with limited capital participation rights simply by paying them the nominal value of their shares (*Scottish Insurance v Wilsons & Clyde Coal Co* [1949] AC 462 (HL), *House of Fraser v AGCE Investments Ltd* [1987] AC 387 (HL)). These decisions confirmed that limited capital participation shares are, in effect, shares redeemable at the will of the company. This led to the introduction of the 'Spens formula', language inserted into the rights of listed shares with limited capital participation rights but full dividend participation rights, providing for payment to shareholders of the market price rather than the nominal price of their shares should the shares be cancelled before the company is wound up.

To the extent that, at the point of cancellation, a company has retained profits (rather than having paid them out as dividends), those profits are reflected in the market price of the shares. The Spens formula protects the class shareholders against losing those valuable dividend rights. The Spens formula does not, however, offer protection from loss of the expected future profits.

TEST YOUR KNOWLEDGE 8.4

(a) Why is it important to know whether a feature of a share is a class right or not?
(b) Give an example of a change that is not a variation of class rights but is regarded merely as a change in the enjoyment of class rights.
(c) What is the significance of a court ruling that a change is merely a change in the enjoyment of class rights?
(d) To which type of shares is the Spens formula relevant and what does it provide for?

6 Share capital

The share capital rules for companies registered under the Companies Act 2006 focus on issued shares. Issued share capital includes shares taken on the formation of the company by the subscribers and shares that have been subsequently issued (s. 546). The old concept of authorised share capital has been abandoned.

6.1 Share capital statements

The first shareholders of a company are those who sign the Memorandum of Association at the time of registration and thereby agree to become a member of the company and take at least one share (s. 8). The shares taken by, or issued to, those who sign the Memorandum make up the initial share capital of the company.

A statement of initial share capital must be included in the application to register a company (s. 9(4)), and an updated statement of capital must be sent or 'returned' to the Registrar of Companies each time the company's share capital is altered. The statement of share capital of a company therefore contains details of the issued share capital. A statement of share capital must state:

1. the total number of issued shares of the company;
2. the total nominal value of those issued shares; and
3. for each class:
   - the prescribed particulars of rights attached to those shares;
   - the number of issued shares of that class;
   - the total nominal value of shares of that class; and
4. the amount paid up and the amount unpaid on each issued share (whether on account of the nominal value or by way of premium).

CASE EXAMPLE 8.2

Company B Ltd

1. C and D both subscribe to the (new-style) memorandum of association of Company B Ltd in which they each agree to take 1 × £1 share.
2. The company issues 1 × £1 share to C and 1 × £1 to D.
3. Neither C nor D pay for their shares which are issued on a nil-paid basis.
4. The statement of initial share capital states:
- Total number of shares issued: 2
- Total nominal value of those shares: £2
- The amount paid-up on each share: Nil
- The amount payable   £1 per share
- All shares are ordinary shares.

6.2 The language of share capital

The share capital of Company B Ltd in the example above is £2. This is the **issued share capital**. Issued share capital is the total nominal value of the issued shares. **Nominal value** is the fixed monetary value attached to the share, also referred to as the 'par' value. It is also the minimum amount for which the share can be issued, that is, a holder must be required to contribute at least the nominal value. A share issued at less than nominal value is issued at a discount, which is prohibited (s. 580(1)). The nominal value of all shares in Company A Ltd and Company B Ltd in the examples above is £1.

Nominal value and premium

All shares must have a fixed nominal value (s. 542). Like authorised share capital, the nominal value of a share can be misleading and is regarded by some to be unnecessary. The nominal value bears no necessary relationship to the issue price of the share or the market or underlying value of the share. Shares are often issued at a price higher than nominal value. The difference between the issue price and the nominal value of a share is called the **share premium**. If a share with a nominal value of £1 is issued at £1.20, the share premium is 20 pence. Share premiums do not technically form part of the company's share capital. That said, the limits on what a company can do with share premium amounts are very similar to the limits on the share capital.

Nominal value is important to work out the proportion, or rateable share, of the residual wealth of the company to which each shareholder is entitled. If a company has share capital of £100 made up of 100 × £1 ordinary shares, each share entitles its owner to one hundredth of the residual wealth of the company.

If a company issues 100 × £1 shares and 100 × £2 shares, it has 200 issued shares and £300 share capital. Even if the only difference in the shares is their nominal value, the shares are different classes of shares (*Greenhalgh* (1946)). They will not be treated as having equal entitlement to share in the residual assets of the company and this difference in rights is brought about by the nominal value. Without more being stated in the Articles or other authorising resolution, each will be entitled to receive back the nominal share value before any remaining surplus is distributed.

How the surplus is to be distributed is a question of interpretation of the rights attaching to the shares and great care should be taken to ensure that this issue is dealt with clearly. The nominal value, fixed at the time of issue and, unlike the issue price, the same for all shares in the class, is therefore important. If nominal values are abolished, a fixed value that does not vary over time will still need to be attached to each share for the purpose of ascertaining the capital to be returned to each shareholder. At the moment we call that fixed value the nominal value.

The issue price of a share does not have to be paid when the share is issued. All or part of the price can be deferred: the issued share capital of a company is not necessarily the same as the **paid-up share capital**. The paid-up share capital is the sum of those parts of the nominal value of issued shares already contributed to the company. Company B Ltd's issued share capital is £2 but its paid-up share capital is £0. The fact that the unpaid part of the purchase price can be called up distinguishes a partly-paid share (which is permitted) from a share issued at a discount (which is prohibited).

Called-up share capital (s. 547)

The issued share capital figure is important because it reflects the minimum sum shareholders are required to pay to the company. The company can issue calls on shareholders to pay the amount outstanding on their shares. Company B Ltd can call on C and D to pay £1 each. If C and D had paid 40 pence on each share when the shares were issued, the paid-up share capital of the company would be 80 pence (2 × 40 pence). Company B Ltd could call on C and D to pay up to 60 pence each, either in one call or in a series of calls of parts of the outstanding 60 pence. The 'called-up share capital' is the sum of the amounts paid for shares when issued, sums subsequently called up (even if the called amounts have not been paid), and sums due on a specified date without further call (s. 547). If C and D had each paid 40 pence on their shares on issue and Company B Ltd subsequently called up 20 pence per share, Company B Ltd's called-up share capital would be £1.20 calculate as follows:

Paid-up share capital (80 pence) + called-up amount (2 × 20 pence = 40 pence).

If a part of the share capital has not been called up or paid up and the company enters into insolvent liquidation, or is wound up, the liquidator can require the shareholders to pay the unpaid amount if this is needed to pay the creditors of the company. Where shares are fully paid, as virtually all listed shares are, a shareholder is under no obligation to contribute further to the company. Where shares are issued at nominal value, the nominal share value (£1) and the issued share capital (£2) establishes the limit on the liability of a shareholder.

TEST YOUR KNOWLEDGE 8.5

(a) What is the initial share capital of a company?
(b) What is the nominal value of a share?
(c) Identify two reasons why the nominal value of a share is important.
(d) What is a share premium?

7 Alteration of share capital

The initial share capital of a company is determined by the shares taken by those who sign the Memorandum of Association. A company may not alter its share capital except in a way provided for in s. 617 of the Companies Act 2006. The 2006 Act contained extensive rules regulating alterations of capital most of which are focused on share capital reduction (see chapter 9 below).

7.1 Increasing the share capital

After registration the company may decide to increase its share capital. By s. 617(2)(a), a company may increase its share capital but must do so in accordance with Part 17 of the Act. Unlike a reduction, an increase in share capital is not considered by the courts and legislature to be a particularly problematic issue. As value is being added to the company, the issue of new shares is not regarded as threatening the position of the company's creditors. Core company law rules regulating the issue of new shares are designed to protect the rights of existing shareholders.

If the capital of a company is to be increased by the offering of shares to the public, detailed securities regulation must be complied with. A private company may not offer shares to the public, but if it wishes to raise money from the public, it may re-register as a public company and then make an initial public offering. Regulation of public offers of shares is touched upon in chapter 7 where the prospectus requirements are examined. This section is concerned with the core company law rules on share issues.

7.2 Reasons for increasing the share capital

There are many reasons why a company may wish to increase its share capital. Some of the more common, acceptable, reasons are:

- to raise money for the running of the company (*Punt v Symons & Co Ltd* [1903] 2 Ch 506);
- to issue shares in return for assets transferred to the business (such as in return for the boot business in *Salomon*).

A couple of unacceptable reasons for increasing share capital are:

- to forestall a takeover bid (*Hogg v Cramphorn Ltd* [1967] Ch 254);
- to change the seat of control of a company (*Howard Smith v Ampol Petroleum Ltd* [1974] AC 821 (PC)).

8 Allotment and issue of shares

8.1 Note on terminology

The terms 'allotment' and 'issue' are often used interchangeably and in most contexts this is unobjectionable. However, he distinction between the terms becomes important when focusing on the process for becoming a shareholder. First, there is an **allotment of shares**, which occurs when a contract for the issue of shares is put in place. As the 2006 Act states:

> 's. 558 When shares are allotted
> For the purposes of the Companies Acts shares in a company are taken to be allotted when a person acquires the unconditional right to be included in the company's register of members in respect of the shares'.

Allotment is followed by the actual issue of the shares, which occurs when the name of the owner is registered in the company's register of members (*National Westminster Bank v IRC* [1995] 1 AC 111 (HL)). A person obtains legal title to the shares and becomes a member of the company when his name is registered.

The terms 'member' and 'shareholder' are also often used interchangeably and, again, this is unobjectionable in most contexts. Member is a generic term covering shareholders, guarantors (of companies limited by guarantee) and members of unlimited companies. All shareholders are members of a company, but not all members are shareholders.

TABLE 8.1 Authority to allot and issue shares

Type of company	Source of authority of directors to issue shares	Provisions in the Articles
Private company with one class of shares only	The Act authorises the directors to issue shares of the same class (s. 550)	None are needed but Articles may restrict the power of the directors to issue shares (s. 550(b))
Private company with one class of shares seeking to issue a different class of shares	Either the Articles can authorise the directors to issue shares, or an ordinary resolution is needed to authorise the directors to issue shares (s. 551(1)) The grant of authority to issue must state the maximum amount of shares that may be allotted under it (s. 551(3)) The authority must be for no longer than five years (s. 551(3)) The authority can be varied or revoked at any time by ordinary resolution (s. 551(4))	Art 22 of the Model Articles for Private Company Limited by Shares and art 43 of the Model Articles for Public companies provide that the company may issues shares with such rights or restrictions as are determined by ordinary resolution and that the company may issue redeemable shares and the directors may determine the terms, condition and manner of redemption of such redeemable shares
Private company with more than one class of shares		
Public company		

8.2 The authority of the directors to allot new shares

Whether or not the board of directors has authority to allot shares is determined by ss. 550 and 551 of the Act, the company's Articles and relevant shareholder resolutions authorising the board of directors to allot shares. The rules are summarised in Table 8.1. Note that a company cannot issue a new class of shares unless its articles state that it can. The Model Articles for both private companies limited by shares and public companies allow the company to issue new shares.

8.3 Exercise of the authority to allot and issue shares

If the board is authorised to allot and issue shares, the power will be exercised by the board deciding to exercise that authority, or power, usually by passing a board resolution. A director who knowingly makes an unauthorised allotment or permits or authorises an unauthorised allotment of shares is guilty of an offence (s. 549(4)) and liable to a fine. If shares are allotted without authority the allotment will not, however, be invalid for that reason (s. 549(6)).

Directors who participate in the board decision to allot must act in accordance with their duties to the company. One of those duties is set out in s. 171.

> 's. 171 Duty to act within powers
> A director of a company must –
> (a) act in accordance with the company's constitution, and
> (b) only exercise powers for the purposes for which they are conferred.'

An allotment for the purpose of manipulating voting power of one group of shareholder at the expense of another is an allotment for an improper purpose and will be set aside (subject to protection of third party rights) *(Howard Smith v Ampol Petroleum Limited* [1974] AC 821). Also, an allotment with the dominant purpose of preserving the directors' control of the management of the company is an allotment for an improper purpose and will be set aside (subject to protection of third party rights) *(Hogg v Cramphorn Ltd* [1967] Ch 254). Section 171 is considered further in Chapter 12.

8.4 Completing the issue of shares

A shareholder does not have legal title to shares and those shares have not been issued unless and until his name appears in relation to those shares in the register of members. An allotment of shares must be registered, that is, the register of members must reflect the new shareholdings, as soon as possible and in any event within two months of the date of the allotment (s. 554).

If a company fails to register shares, it fails to carry out the contract of allotment and the person to whom the shares should be issued may sue the company for breach of contract and recover damages, or, if damages are not adequate, the court may order specific performance of the contract of allotment. Damages are likely to be adequate if the shares are available on the secondary market, that is, if the person can obtain shares from another shareholder (*Re BTR plc* (1987) 4 BCC 45).

A company must complete share certificates in relation to allotted shares within two months of the allotment (s. 769), although this obligation can be expressly overridden and does not apply to uncertificated, that is, dematerialised, shares.

8.5 Public disclosure of an increase of share capital

A return of allotment and (updated) statement of capital must be sent to the Registrar of Companies within one month of making an allotment (s. 555). In the case of a public company, the Registrar of Companies must publish receipt of the return and statement of capital, which is satisfied by notice of receipt appearing in a supplement to the *London Gazette* (ss. 1077 and 1078).

TEST YOUR KNOWLEDGE 8.6

(a) Identify four reasons why a company may wish to increase its share capital.
(b) At what point is a share allotted?
(c) How do you determine whether or not the directors of a private company have the power to issue shares of a new class?
(d) What must be sent to the Registrar of Companies when shares have been allotted?

9 Payment for shares, discounts and premiums

9.1 Issue price and discounts

All shares must have a fixed nominal value (s. 542). Shares may not be issued at a discount (s. 580) which means that the issue price may not be less than the nominal share value. If shares are issued at a discount the owner is liable to pay the company the discount amount and interest on the discount amount (s. 580(2)).

One way round the prohibition on discounts would be for the company to agree to pay a commission to a person who agrees to buy shares. Consider a £1 ordinary share issued for £1. It is not issued at a discount. If, however, the company has agreed with the shareholder to pay a commission of 20% for agreeing to purchase the share, the net effect is that the company ends up with 80 pence, which is less than the nominal value. The Act regulates this loophole by prohibiting such commission payments both to the shareholder and to any person in return for them finding a purchaser (s. 552) unless the Articles authorise the payment of such commissions and the commission is no more than 10% of the issue price (s. 553).

The prohibition on issuing shares at below nominal value is intended to protect creditors and existing shareholders. Creditors are assured that the company has had (or has rights to call up) the full amount of the stated share capital and share capital has traditionally been regarded as considered important by creditors as a financial cushion (see capital maintenance in chapter 9). Shareholders are protected from new shareholders obtaining, at a reduced price, equivalent rights to participate in the voting and wealth of the company as they, the existing shareholders, have (remember, the company's wealth is shared between shareholders based on the number of shares owned and their nominal value).

9.2 Payment for shares

The protections outlined in the previous section are lost if shares can be paid for with non-cash consideration which is over-valued. Shares may be paid for in money or money's worth (s. 582) and the form that payment, or the consideration for the shares, will be agreed as part of the terms of issue.

 **CASE EXAMPLE 8.3**

> Company D Ltd wishes to issue 1 million × £1 ordinary shares. The shares cannot be issued for less than £1 each, a total £1 million consideration. The company agrees to issue the shares to J in return for J transferring a plot of land to the company. The company and the new shareholder agree that the land is worth £1 million so the shares are issued fully-paid. If the land is in fact worth less than £1 million, the shares have been issued in return for less real value than their nominal value.

What, if any, law governs the valuation of asset or services provided as payment (in whole or in part) of the issue price? The answer is that a private company and a new shareholder are essentially free to agree the value to be assigned. The 2006 Act provisions addressing the form that non-cash consideration may take and the potential for over-valuation apply only to public companies.

A public company may not accept as payment for shares:

- an undertaking by any person that he or another will do work or perform services for the company or any other person (s. 585);
- an undertaking to be performed more than five years after the date of allotment (s. 587);
- non-cash consideration, unless the consideration has been independently valued in accordance with the Act (s. 593) (but note that cash consideration is given a broad definition in the Act (s. 583)).

Shares may be issued nil-paid, partly-paid or fully-paid. The company may call up, or require the shareholder to pay, the whole or any unpaid part of the issue price (not just the nominal value) from time to time. All shareholders within the relevant class must be treated equally unless the Articles authorise the company to agree otherwise, in which case shares can be issued with different paid-up amounts and different times for payment of calls for different shareholders (s. 581).

Although a company has the right to call up any outstanding part of the issue price, which must be at least the nominal value, a bird in the hand is worth two in the bush and the value of the right to call is only as good as the ability of the shareholder to pay. The amount of a call is owed by the shareholder to the company as a debt and the debtor/shareholder may be unable to pay the debt. Public companies are therefore required to issue shares on which at least 25% of the nominal value and the full amount of any premium is paid-up at the time of issue (s. 586).

9.3 Shares issued at a premium

The issue price may be more than the nominal value and the extent to which the issue price exceeds the nominal value is called the premium. If existing shareholders are to be protected, the issue price of a new share of the same class should be the 'real value' of an existing share. There are a number of different ways of arriving at the real value of a share. For listed shares, the real value is often taken to be the price at which the shares are trading in the market: the quoted share price. The market price of a share can be volatile, and may be very different from the value of the share based on the net assets of the company (very crudely, the residual wealth of the company divided by the number of shares) or the earnings potential of the company. Consequently, there is enormous scope for judgement in arriving at the appropriate issue price of a share. If shares are issued at a price higher than the nominal value the sum in excess, the premium, must be transferred to a share premium account (s. 610).

Directors who exercise the power or authority to allot shares must exercise that power in accordance with the duties that as directors they owe to the company. In particular, when involved in deciding the issue price, a director will need to act in accordance with s. 172 of the Act and 'act in the way he considers, in good faith, would be most likely to promote the success of the company for the benefit of its members as a whole'. This duty is examined in chapter 13.

9.4 Capitalisation: issue of bonus shares

A company may issue shares to its existing members credited as fully-paid. This is called a bonus share issue. Bonus shares are paid for, and may only be paid for, by the company out of the sums previously received as premium, or undistributed profits. The effect is that sums reflected in the accounts of the company as premium or undistributed profits of the company are turned into share capital. This is called 'capitalisation'. If the shares are paid for out of undistributed profits, the company will reduce its ability to pay dividends to the extent of the capitalisation.

CASE EXAMPLE 8.4

Company E Ltd has a share capital of £1,000 made up of 1,000 × £1 shares. 500 of those shares were issued at nominal value (£1) on registration of the company to K and 500 were issued two years later at an issue price of £1.10 to L. The company has been trading for five years and has not distributed any of the £500 profits it has made. It has an undistributed profit reserve of £500. The relevant accounts of the company will show:

	£
Share capital	1,000
Premium Account	50
Distributable reserves	500

The company decides to issue 550 × £1 bonus shares. K and L each receive 275 fully paid-up £1 shares. The relevant accounts now show:

	£
Share capital	1,550
Premium Account	0
Distributable reserves	0

Company E Ltd has a larger share capital than before. It has no distributable profits and will be unable to declare any dividends until it has generated more profits.

TEST YOUR KNOWLEDGE 8.7

(a) Why is the issue of shares at a discount prohibited?
(b) What may a public company not accept as payment for shares?
(c) What laws apply, in addition to the prohibition on issue at a discount, when the directors decide the price at which to issue shares?
(d) How may a company fund the issue of bonus shares?

10 Statutory pre-emption rights of existing shareholders and rights issues

10.1 The rationale for pre-emption rights

The purpose of **pre-emption rights** is to protect existing equity shareholders from their rights in the equity or residual wealth of the company, and their share of the voting rights, being diluted by the issue of new shares. Statutory pre-emption rights, in ss. 560–577 of the Act, give equity shareholders the right of first refusal to take up any new equity shares. Each equity shareholder is entitled to be offered that proportion of the new shares as would preserve his proportionate interest in the equitable share capital of the company. This is his **pro rata** share of the new issue. The operation of pre-emption rights is best illustrated by an example.

CASE EXAMPLE 8.5

Company C Ltd (a private company) has a share capital of 100 × £1 ordinary shares. E, F, G and H own 25 of those shares each. The directors of Company C Ltd decide the company needs to raise £100. They decide to exercise their authority to issue new shares to issue £100 × £1 ordinary shares. An investor (I) approaches the directors and offers to pay £1.20 per share for the shares.

Are the directors permitted to issue the shares to I?

Before the directors can issue the shares to the investor they must determine whether or not any of E, F, G or H, the existing equity shareholders, is entitled to exercise statutory pre-emption rights in relation to the new shares.

If no pre-emption rights exist, the directors can issue the shares to I and the interests in the share capital of the company would be as set out in Table 8.2.

TABLE 8.2 Interests in the share capital of Company C Ltd

Shareholder	Number of shares owned	Share of equity share capital owned and share of voting rights	
		Before	After
E	25	25%	12.5%
F	25	25%	12.5%
G	25	25%	12.5%
H	25	25%	12.5%
I	100	0%	50%
Total	200	100%	100%

There has been significant dilution of the proportionate interests of the original shareholders in the equity share capital.

If the statutory rights apply to all the existing shareholders, E, F, G and H, the new shares must be offered to them in proportion to their existing shares of the equity share capital. The equity share capital is £100 of which each of E, F, G and H own £25, 25 per cent or one quarter. They must each be offered 25 per cent or one quarter of the new shares, which is 25 shares each and the offer must be open for acceptance for at least 21 days (s. 562(5)). If they all accept the offer, after the new shares are issued, they will each own 50 shares equal to £50 or 25 per cent or one quarter of the £200 equity share capital of the company. The interests in the share capital of the company would be as set out in Table 8.3.

TABLE 8.3 Interests in the share capital of Company C Ltd (2)

Shareholder	Number of shares owned	Share of equity share capital owned and share of voting rights	
		Before	After
E	50	25%	25%
F	50	25%	25%
G	50	25%	25%
H	50	25%	25%
Total	200	100%	100%

There has been no dilution of their proportionate interests in the equity share capital. Note that it is the nominal share value of the shares (£1) that determines the share capital, not the issue price of the shares (£1.20). The shares must be offered to the existing shareholders at the same price (£1.20) or a more favourable price than they would be offered to I. It is common practice for listed companies to offer new shares to existing ordinary shareholders at below market value (see rights issues below).

Each of the shareholders is free to refuse the offer, in which event, if the shares they are offered are subsequently taken-up by somebody else, perhaps I, the shareholder will have a reduced proportion of the equity share capital. Let's assume that E and F take up their share of the new shares but G and H decline to take up the shares offered to them. The 50 shares offered to G and H are taken up by I. The interests in the share capital of the company would be as set out in Table 8.4.

TABLE 8.4 Interests in the shares of Company C Ltd (3)

Shareholder	Number of shares owned	Share of equity share capital owned and share of voting rights	
		Before	After
E	50	25%	25%
F	50	25%	25%
G	25	25%	12.5%
H	25	25%	12.5%
I	50	0	25%
Total	200	100%	100%

This demonstrates how the share interests of G and H have been diluted, by them not exercising their pre-emption rights, from 25 per cent to 12.5 per cent. Pre-emption offers can be made on an open or renounceable basis. Each can only be accepted by the shareholder to whom it is made but a renounceable offer, once accepted, may be assigned to another person (see rights issues below).

10.2 Limits on the application of statutory pre-emption rights

Statutory pre-emption rights apply only to the issue of equity securities (s. 560) and only in favour of the holders of equity shares which are referred to in s. 560 as ordinary shares. A share is not an ordinary share or an equity security which 'neither as respects dividends nor as respects capital, carries any right to participate beyond a specified amount in a distribution'.

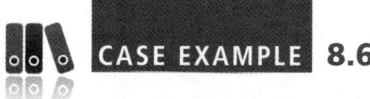

CASE EXAMPLE 8.6

A £1, 6 per cent dividend preference share with priority as to return of nominal capital is not an ordinary share or equity security for the purposes of pre-emption rights because:
- the right to participate in dividends is limited to 6 per cent of the nominal share value per annum, which is a specified amount: 6 pence per annum;
- the right to participate in capital is limited to return of nominal capital, which is a specified amount: £1.

Statutory pre-emption rights also do not apply to the issue of:
- bonus shares (s. 564);
- shares for non-cash consideration (whether wholly or only in part (s. 565)); or
- shares to be held under an employee share scheme (s. 566).

The removal from the scope of pre-emption rights of shares issued for partly or wholly non-cash consideration makes it relatively easy to avoid statutory pre-emption rights.

Statutory pre-emption rights may not apply in a variety of circumstances as follows:

- A private company may exclude the statutory pre-emption rights by provision in its Articles (s. 567).
- A private company with only one class of shares may authorise its directors, by provision in the Articles or by special resolution, to allot shares of that class without pre-emption rights or with modified pre-emption rights (s. 569).
- If a company's Articles contain intra-class pre-emption rights, that is, provision for new shares of a particular class of ordinary shares to be offered pro-rata to existing members of that class of ordinary shares, the statutory pre-emption rights will not apply if the pre-emption rights in the Articles have been complied with (s. 568).
- A company may authorise its directors, by provision in the Articles or by special resolution, to allot shares without pre-emption rights or with modified pre-emption rights (s. 570).
- A company may disapply or modify the statutory pre-emption rights in relation to a specified allotment by passing a special resolution (s. 571) recommended by the directors and supported by a written statement of the directors setting out the reasons for the dis-application, the price and justification for the price of the shares to be allotted.

10.3 Companies with listed shares: rights issues and open offers

In addition to the statutory pre-emption right provisions described above, companies with listed shares must comply with the Listing Rules issued by the FCA. The relevant rules are found in Listing Rules 9.3.11 and 9.3.12.

An existing shareholder who has pre-emption rights may not be in a financial position to exercise them and therefore faces dilution of his voting and interest in the company. Where shares are traded on a stock exchange, shareholders face the additional prospect of an immediate reduction in the market price of their existing shares when, as is often the case, shares are offered to existing shareholders at a discount to the market price. To avoid this immediate adverse financial impact, most new issues of equity shares by listed companies take the form of a 'rights issue'. This is in contrast to an 'open offer'. The details of how rights issues are structured are beyond the scope of this book. They can be found in books on securities regulation or corporate finance.

Basically, rights issues involve the provisional allotment of a pro-rata proportion of new equity shares to existing equity shareholders, by way of a provisional allotment letter (PAL). The provisionally allotted shares are nil-paid, that is, the price of the shares remains wholly unpaid. A shareholder may take up the offer, by subscribing and paying the company for the provisionally allotted shares, or he can renounce the offer. If the shareholder renounces the offer, that is not the end of the story. The shareholder can trade, or sell, the right to subscribe for the pre-emption shares by signing the PAL and passing it to a purchaser of the rights. The shareholder receives consideration for the transfer of the rights to the third party and the third party subscribes and pays for the shares. The benefit of an open offer cannot be transferred in this way. For this reason, listing rules restrict the discount from market price that can be applied to shares offered on an open offer pre-emptive basis. The normal maximum discount for an open offer is 10 per cent of market value (though this is subject to exceptions (Listing Rule 9.5.10)).

10.4 Consequences of contravention of pre-emption rights

If shares are allotted in contravention of the statutory pre-emption rights of existing shareholders, the allotment is not, for that reason, invalid. Section 563 provides a statutory right to compensation to any person to whom an offer should have been made for any loss, damage, costs or expenses sustained or incurred by reason of the contravention. The company and every officer who knowingly authorised or permitted the contravention are jointly and severally liable to compensate the shareholders. A two-year limitation period runs from delivery of the return of allotment to the Registrar of Companies.

No criminal penalties apply to contravention of the statutory pre-emption rights but there is criminal liability for false statements in directors' written statements supporting a recommendation for a special resolution to disapply pre-emption rights (s. 572).

> **TEST YOUR KNOWLEDGE 8.8**
>
> (a) What is the rationale for pre-emption rights?
> (b) What are renounceable pre-emption rights?
> (c) In what two ways is the concept of 'equity' share important in relation to pre-emption rights?
> (d) Identify three types of share issues to which pre-emption rights do not apply.
> (e) Identify five further situations in which pre-emption rights may not apply.
> (f) What are the consequences of shares being allotted in contravention of statutory pre-emption rights?

11 Transfer and transmission of shares

Transfer of shares must be distinguished from the transmission of shares. Where issued shares have been **transferred** by the registered member to a third party, chapter 1 of Part 22 to the Companies Act 2006, and ss. 770 and 771 in particular, governs the conditions and procedure to be followed to amend the register of members. These sections apply unless the shares are dematerialised, in which case the process will be governed by chapter 2 of Part 21 to the Companies Act and regulations made pursuant to that chapter.

11.1 Transfer of certificated shares

Articles 26 and 63, of the Model Articles for Private Companies Limited by Shares and the Model Articles for Public Companies respectively, state that the transferor remains the holder of a **certificated** share until the transferee's name is entered in the register of members as holder of it. Section 770 prohibits the register of a transfer of shares unless a 'proper instrument of transfer' has been delivered to the company. A proper instrument of transfer is ordinarily a **stock transfer form** in prescribed form as set out in a schedule to the Stock Transfer Act 1963. A copy of the basic stock transfer form is shown on pp. 164–5. The form is not a deed but must be executed by the transferor. It must be sent to the Stamp Office and, unless the transaction is certified to be exempt from *ad valorem* stamp duty because it is below the threshold, stamped or adjudicated as not subject to **stamp duty** before being presented to the company. The share certificates for the shares being transferred should accompany the stock transfer form.

On receipt of a stamped stock transfer form and the share certificates, the company secretary must amend the register of members (s. 771) unless the board of directors exercises any power it may have to refuse to register the transfer. Power to refuse to register a transfer of certificated shares is given to directors by art. 26(5) (private companies) and art. 63(5) (public companies), although the power in relation to a public company is very narrow, basically addressing technical shortcomings in the transfer documentation or process.

The ability to restrict transferability by inserting provisions in the Articles is regularly exercised by private companies. Although the Model Articles for Private Companies Limited by Shares do not contain any such restrictions, this is because there are a number of ways in which transfer may be restricted and it was not considered appropriate to select one particular restriction formula for inclusion in the Model Articles as a default rule.

If the directors exercise the power to refuse to register a transfer, the company secretary must give the transferee notice of refusal to register the transfer, together with its reason for the refusal, as soon as practicable and in any event within two months after the date on which the transfer is lodged with the company (s. 771(2)).

11.2 Transfer of dematerialised or uncertificated shares

Shares traded on stock exchanges, listed shares, are uncertificated, also known as 'dematerialised' shares. The legal title to a dematerialised share is recorded in, and transfers are made by, **CREST**, the national computerised securities depository and electronic transfer system first established in 1996. Buyers and sellers of uncertificated shares must have access to the CREST system. They may be a member of CREST or access CREST through a broker. Many share

STOCK TRANSFER FORM

STOCK TRANSFER FORM   (Above this line for Registrars only)

	Certificate lodged with the Registrar
	(For completion by the Registrar/Stock Exchange)

Full name of Undertaking	
Full description of Security	

Number or amount of Shares, Stock or other security and, in figures column only, number and denomination of units, if any.	Words	Figures (units of)

Name(s) of registered holder(s) should be given in full: the address should be given where there is only one holder. If the transfer is not made by the registered holder(s) insert also the name(s) and capacity (e.g., Executor(s)), of the person(s) making the transfer.	in the name(s) of

I/We hereby transfer the above security out of the name(s) aforesaid to the person(s) named below Signature of transferor(s) 1. .... 3. .... 2. .... 4. .... A body corporate should execute this transfer under its common seal or otherwise in accordance with applicable statutory requirements	Stamp of Selling Broker(s), for transactions which are not stock exchange transactions, of Agent(s), if any, acting for the Transferor(s). Date ....

Full name(s), postal address(es) (including County or, if applicable, Postal District number) of the person(s) to whom the security is transferred. Please state title, if any, or whether Mr, Mrs, or Miss. Please complete in type or Block Capitals	

I/We request that such entries be made in the register as are necessary to give effect to this transfer.	
Stamp of Buying Broker(s) (if any).	Stamp or name and address of person lodging this form (if other than the Buying Broker(s)).

| Reference to the Registrar in this form means the registrar or registration agent of the undertaking, not the Registrar of Companies at Companies House ||

FORM OF CERTIFICATE REQUIRED WHERE TRANSFER IS EXEMPT FROM *AD VALOREM* STAMP DUTY AS BELOW THRESHOLD

I/we[1] certify that the transaction effected by this instrument does not form part of a larger transaction or series of transactions in respect of which the amount or value, or aggregate amount or value, of the consideration exceeds £1,000.

I/we[1] confirm that I/we[1] have been duly authorised by the transferor to sign this certificate and that the facts of the transaction are within my/our[1] knowledge.[2]

1. Delete as appropriate.

2. Delete second sentence if certificate is given by transferor or his solicitor.

Signature(s)   *Description ('Transferor, 'Solicitor', etc.)*

....
....
....

Date

....

Notes

1. If the above certificate has been completed, this transfer does not need to be submitted to the Stamp Office but should be sent directly to the Company or its Registrars.
2. If the above certificate is not completed, this transfer must be submitted to the Stamp Office and duly stamped.

transfers take place in the name of nominee brokers who hold legal title to the shares on trust for the beneficiary seller/buyer.

If all shares of a company are uncertificated, the company's register of members will be maintained by CREST. If some shares are uncertificated and some certificated, the company's register of members will be kept in two parts; the uncertificated share part will be maintained by CREST and the certificated share part will be maintained by the company. A buyer (or his nominee) normally becomes the legal owner of shares when those shares are credited to his (or his nominee's) CREST account and his name is entered in the register of members maintained by CREST. The Companies Act 2006 contains provisions enabling the Treasury and the Secretary of State to make regulations governing the transfer of title to uncertificated shares (see ss. 783–790). The current governing regulations are The Uncertificated Securities Regulations 2001 (SI 2001/3755) as amended by the Companies Act 2006 (Commencement No. 2, Consequential Amendments, Transitional Provisions and Savings) Order 2007 (SI 2007/1093) and the Companies Act 2006 (Consequential Amendments) (Uncertificated Securities) Order 2009 (SI 2009/1889).

11.3 Transmission of shares

Shares are transmitted when a person acquires the right to them by operation of law (see section 1 above). The company secretary must take care to ensure that the documents received by the company evidence the **transmission** and form the basis for altering the register of members. In the case of death of a member, for example, s. 774 deals with evidence of the **grant of probate** and s. 773 provides that an instrument of transfer of shares made by a personal representative of a deceased member is as effective as if the personal representative had been a member of the company at the time of the execution of the instrument.

TEST YOUR KNOWLEDGE 8.9

(a) What is a proper instrument of transfer for the purposes of s. 770?
(b) On what grounds may a public company refuse to register a share transfer of certificated shares?
(c) What is a dematerialised share?
(d) Identify three situations in which a person obtains title to shares by operation of law.

12 Share certificates and warrants

A **share certificate** sealed or executed by the company is *prima facie* evidence of the title to the shares of the member named on the certificate (s. 768).

The issue of share certificates is governed by both the Articles (see arts. 24 and 25 of the Model Articles for Private Companies Limited by Shares and arts. 46–49 of the Model Articles for Public Companies) and provisions in the Companies Act 2006. Unless shares are uncertificated, the company must issue share certificates within two months of the date of allotment (s. 769) or on which a transfer of its shares is lodged with the company unless the company is entitled not to register the transfer and does not register the transfer (s. 776). If s. 769 or s. 776 is not complied with, an offence is committed by every officer of the company who is in default (ss. 769(3) and 776(5)).

If the company, having been served with a notice requiring it to make good any default in issuing a share certificate, fails to make good the default within ten days of service, an application may be made to the court and the court may make an order directing the company to make good the default within such time as is specified in the court order.

Share warrants (also known as 'bearer shares') may be issued by a company if its Articles permit it to do so. Article 51 of the Model Articles for Public Companies permits the issue of share warrants. The Model Articles for Private Companies Limited by Shares do not. Issue of share warrants is also governed by the Companies Act 2006 which limits share warrants to fully-paid shares (s. 779).

On issue of a share warrant, the register of members must be changed to remove the name of the member entitled to the shares in respect of which the warrant is issued (see above). The register must also reflect the fact that the warrant has been issued, state the shares included in the warrant (distinguishing each share by its number if it has a number) and the date the warrant was issued (s. 122).

Share warrants are negotiable instruments. This means that the rights that attach to a share warrant can be transferred to a new holder, or 'bearer' of the warrant by transfer of possession of the share warrant (*Webb, Hale & Co v Alexandria Water Co* (1905) 93 LT 339).

Holders of share warrants are not members of a company, though they may have similar rights to members: the rights will be determined by consideration of the Articles of the company and the board resolution determining the conditions of issue, which will cover such issues as the right to attend meetings and vote and the right to dividends. Share warrant holders are often informed of the payment of a dividend by an advertisement. Numbered coupons are often attached to share warrants which are exchanged for dividend payments.

If share warrants are surrendered for cancellation, the date of surrender of the warrant must be indicated in the register of members (s. 122(6)) and the holder of the warrant is entitled to have his name entered as a member on the register of members. Within two months of surrender the company must issue share certificates for the shares specified in the warrant (s. 780). Failure to comply with s. 780 is an offence by every officer of the company who is in default (s. 780(3)).

TEST YOUR KNOWLEDGE 8.10

(a) What is the time limit for the issue of shares to an allottee or the transferee of shares?
(b) What steps should an allotee or transferee of shares take if the company fails to issue share certificate in the time permitted?
(c) What is a share warrant?
(d) Is the holder of a share warrant a member of a company?

13 Partly-paid shares: calls, liens, surrender and forfeiture

Article 21 of the Model Articles for Private Companies Limited by Shares states that with the exception of shares taken on the formation of the company, all shares must be fully paid up. Calls, mortgages, liens, surrender and forfeiture of shares are therefore not important for companies that adopt the Model Articles for Private Companies Limited by Shares. In relation to public companies, arts. 52–62 of the Model Articles for Public Companies contain provisions governing these matters.

13.1 Calls and liens

If shares are issued partly paid, the company may, from time to time, call up, or require the shareholder to pay, the whole or any unpaid part of the issue price (not just the nominal value). This right is set out in art. 54 of the Model Articles for Public Companies. All shareholders within the relevant class must be treated equally unless the Articles authorise the company to agree otherwise, in which case, shares can be issued with different paid-up amounts and different times for payment of calls for different shareholders (s. 581).

Although a company has the right to call up any outstanding part of the issue price, which must be at least the nominal value, a bird in the hand is worth two in the bush and the value of the right to call is only as good as the ability of the shareholder to pay. The amount of a call is owed by the shareholder to the company as a debt and the debtor/shareholder may be unable to pay the debt. Public companies are therefore required to issue shares on which at least 25 per cent of the nominal value and the full amount of any premium is paid-up at the time of issue (s. 586). In fact, shares are generally issued fully paid or subject to a timetable of instalments resulting in them being fully paid so calls are not that common today nor as important as when shares were typically of high nominal value and issued partly paid.

The company has a lien over all partly-paid shares for any part of the nominal value or premium at which the share was issued which has not been paid, whether payable immediately or at some time in the future (art. 52 of the Model Articles for Public Companies). A company's lien takes priority over any third party's interest in the shares.

If the date for any payment has passed, the company may issue a lien enforcement notice requiring payment within 14 days of the notice. On failure of the person to pay the sum due, the company can sell the shares, for which purposes the directors may authorise any person to execute an instrument of transfer. The proceeds of sale are then applied to pay the sum outstanding, and any remaining sum is repaid to the shareholder.

13.2 Forfeiture and surrender

A notice of intended **forfeiture** may be sent in relation to any shares in respect of which a call has been made (art. 58 of the Model Articles for Public Companies). The notice will require payment of the call and accrued interest by a specified date and if the notice is not complied with on or before the specified date the directors may decide that the shares are forfeited. The effects of forfeiture are set out in Model Article 60. The person whose shares are forfeited ceases to be a member but remains liable to the company for all sums payable under the Articles at the date of forfeiture. The shares are deemed to be property of the company and may be sold, re-allotted or otherwise disposed of.

Any shares subject to forfeiture or that have been forfeited, may be surrendered by the member and surrendered shares may be dealt with in the same way as forfeited shares (Model Articles for Public Companies, art. 62). Note that the surrender of shares process cannot be used in place of the reduction of capital processes set out in the Act (*Bellerby v Rowland & Marwood's SS Co Ltd* [1902] 2 Ch 14).

TEST YOUR KNOWLEDGE 8.11

(a) Is a private company entitled to issue partly-paid shares?
(b) Is a public company permitted to issue nil-paid shares?
(c) Describe the operation of the lien provided for in the Model Article for Public Companies.
(d) What is the effect of forfeiture of shares on the liability of the person whose shares are forfeited?

CHAPTER SUMMARY

- Those with a right to shares are: subscribers to the Memorandum, subscribers to a new issue of shares who have been allotted shares; those who have acquired shares from an existing shareholder and those who have acquired the right to shares by operation of law on a member's death, insolvency/bankruptcy or declaration of mental unfitness.
- The members of a company are, by s. 112:
  - the subscribers of a company's Memorandum; and
  - those whose name is entered in its register of members.
- A share is a bundle of rights and responsibilities and is classically defined in *Borland's Trustee v Steel* (1901).
- Subject to the Articles, a company may have any number of classes of shares. The main rights that differ from class to class are voting rights, dividend rights and capital participation rights. What are and what are not class rights is unclear in English law, so it is extremely important to spell out clearly, in the Articles or authorising resolution, rights and restrictions attached to the shares in question.
- Shares with rights restricted to a specified amount in respect of dividends and capital are not equity shares for the purposes of the Companies Act 2006 (s. 548).

- Class rights may be varied with the consent of 75 per cent of the class holders or as otherwise provided in the Articles (ss. 630–640).
- Holders of 15 per cent may apply to the court to have a variation cancelled (s. 633(1)) or may wish to petition the court under s. 994.
- Courts interpret variation of class rights narrowly. A mere change in the enjoyment of rights is not a variation, (*White v Bristol Aeroplane Co* (1953)).
- The share capital of a company is the number of shares issued multiplied by the nominal value. A company is no longer required to have an authorised share capital.
- All shares must have a fixed nominal value (s. 542) which determines both the capital repayable before the surplus is distributed and the share of the surplus to which a shareholder is entitled in the event of a solvent winding up.
- Share capital can be increased by the issue of shares or decreased by following a number of processes, in either case, the process followed must be strictly in accordance with the Companies Act 2006.
- Directors must issues shares in accordance with the company's constitution and for the purpose for which the power to issue shares is conferred on them, i.e., not for an improper purpose such as to thwart a takeover bid (*Howard Smith v Ampol Petroleum Ltd* (1974)).
- Shares may not be issued at a discount to the nominal value (s. 580).
- Shares may be paid for in money or money's worth (s. 582).
- If shares are issued at a price higher than the nominal value, the excess is called the premium and must be transferred to a share premium account (s. 610).
- Directors must exercise the power to decide the issue price of shares in accordance with their directors' duties.
- To preserve their share of the company, existing equity shareholders are entitled to statutory pre-emption rights when equity shares are allotted (s. 561).
- Pre-emption rights do not apply in certain situations (ss. 564–566) and can be excluded and disapplied in a variety of ways including by special resolution, (ss. 567–571).
- Certificated shares are transferred by execution of a stock transfer form in prescribed form which must be certified as exempt or stamped and sent to the company and the name of the transferee entered in the register of members (Stamp Transfer Act 1963 and Companies Act 2006).
- Dematerialised shares are transferred through the operation of the CREST system
- A share certificate sealed or executed by the company is *prima facie* evidence of the title to the shares of the member named on the certificate (s. 768).
- Share warrants may be issued by a company if its Articles permit it to do so. Article 51 of the Model Articles for public companies provides for the issue of share warrants.
- Article 21 of the Model Articles for private companies states that with the exception of shares taken on the formation of the company, all shares must be fully paid up, making calls, liens, surrender and forfeiture irrelevant where the Model Articles are adopted.
- Articles 52–62 of the Model Articles for public companies contain provisions governing calls and liens, surrender and forfeiture for non-payment of calls.

9 Capital maintenance

■ **CONTENTS**

1 Share capital and creditors
2 The doctrine of capital maintenance
3 Minimum share capital requirements
4 Statutory prohibition on reduction of share capital
5 Purchase and redemption of a company's own shares
6 Regulation of distributions
7 Shareholder last principle on a winding up
8 A broader concept of capital maintenance?
9 Financial assistance for the purchase of its own shares

■ **INTRODUCTION**

In chapter 8 we learned about a company's share capital. We know that the share capital of a company is the number of issued shares x nominal value of those shares (e.g. 100 × £1 = £100). On registration, a company begins life with its initial share capital, which it can increase from time to time by issuing more shares. The company uses its share capital to fund its trading operations with the aim of making profits. The company may supplement its share capital by incurring debt, i.e. by borrowing money from creditors to fund its trading operations.

In this chapter we look briefly at the importance of share capital to creditors before reviewing the laws regulating reduction of share capital. We also examine the laws regulating other actions by which companies return money to shareholders, principally by distributions. Together, these laws are often referred to as 'capital maintenance'.

We then look at the broader issue of how the law regulates gratuitous payments by a company to non-shareholders, including political donations. Finally, we turn to the prohibition on a company giving financial assistance for the purchase of its own shares, which is an extension to the prohibition on a company buying its own shares but is aimed at a different mischief from capital maintenance laws.

1 Share capital and creditors

At the start of a company's life, a financial creditor will be interested to know how much share capital the company has before the creditor will be prepared to lend money to the company. The creditor wishes to be paid interest on any sum it lends to the company and to be paid back that sum at the point, or various points, in the future at which it becomes due and repayable.

If a company has a negligible share capital, virtually the entire risk of the company making trading losses lies with the creditor. Every £1 the company loses in trading is £1 it cannot pay back to the lender. The creditor may have a legal right to sue the company to recover the sum contractually due and payable to it, but that right is only valuable if the company has the money to pay the sum due (see Case Example 9.1 below).

If, however, a company has substantial share capital, the risk of the company making trading losses lies with the shareholders up to the amount of the share capital. Every £1 the company loses, up to the amount of the share capital, is a loss borne by the shareholders. This is because the shareholders cannot insist on taking their capital back from the company while it is a going concern and, if the company is wound up, its shareholders are only entitled to receive money back from the company after all the creditors have been paid in full (the shareholder last principle) (see Case Example 9.2 below).

The company may not reduce its share capital and return money to its shareholders except as authorised by, and subject to compliance with procedures in, the 2006 Act, and the company cannot pay money to shareholders, whether in the form of dividends or otherwise, unless the company has profits out of which to make the payment.

The following examples illustrate the importance of share capital in the early stages of a company's operation. They also introduce the concepts of assets, liabilities and capital in the balance sheet of a company. Understanding the basics of how share capital and profits and losses affect a company's balance sheet is essential to understanding capital maintenance. The following examples are simplified to demonstrate the basic principles.

CASE EXAMPLE 9.1

A company with virtually no share capital

Company A Ltd is registered with a share capital of £1 made up of 1 × £1 ordinary share, fully paid up. Company A Ltd borrows £1,000 from B, repayable in 12 months. Company A Ltd has assets of £1,001. This is stated in its balance sheet as follows:

Balance Sheet of Company A Ltd as at 1 January 2008

	£	
Assets		
Cash at bank	1,001	
Liabilities		
Sum owed to B	1,000	
Net assets	1	
Capital		
Share capital	1	(Number of issued shares × nominal value)

The basic balance sheet equation, or accounting equation, is:

Assets = Liabilities + Capital

'Capital' is made up of a number of components, the main ones are:

Capital = share capital + share premium + reserves (accumulated profits and losses)

The only component of capital in the above balance sheet is share capital.

'Net assets' is also an important concept:

Assets − Liabilities = net assets

£1,001 − £1,000 = £1

Net assets is also equal to capital. In this balance sheet, net assets is equal to the share capital because share capital is equal to the capital, but net assets will not always equal the share capital. Indeed, the moment the company has profits or losses its net assets will diverge from its share capital, as the 1 January 2009 balance sheet of Company A Ltd shows.

Company A Ltd trades for 12 months and incurs trading losses of £500. It then has £501. B demands repayment of the £1,000 owed and due to it from Company A Ltd. Even if B sues Company A Ltd, the most it can receive is £501 because that is all the money Company A Ltd has. The balance sheet now looks as follows:

Balance Sheet of Company A Ltd as at 1 January 2009

	£	
Assets		
Cash at bank	501	
Liabilities		
Sum owed to B	1,000	
Net assets	(499)	
Capital		
Share capital	1	(Number of issued shares × nominal value)
Profit & loss	(500)	(Accumulated profits and losses)

CASE EXAMPLE 9.1 continued

Parentheses round a number indicate that it is a negative number. Note that the share capital amount remains the same. It reflects the number of shares in issue and their nominal value. It does not change unless more shares are issued (a share capital increase) or issued shares are cancelled (a share capital reduction). In this balance sheet, net assets is:

Assets – Liabilities
£501 – £1,000 = (£499)

This is not equal to the share capital of £1 because there are two components to
Capital: share capital and accumulated profits and losses. The accumulated profits and loss here is a loss of £500, so Capital is:

share capital + profit and loss (accumulated profits and losses)
£1 + (500) = (£499)

The shareholders cannot receive their share capital back from Company A Ltd while the company is a going concern. The company cannot pay a dividend to shareholders because it has no profits available for the purpose (it has made a loss). B is entitled to all the assets of the company. Even if he receives them he remains only partly repaid. He has borne all but £1 of the trading risk of the company; he has absorbed all but £1 of the trading losses.

CASE EXAMPLE 9.2

A company with substantial share capital

Company C Ltd is registered with a share capital of £1,000 made up of 1,000 × £1 ordinary shares, fully paid up. Company C Ltd borrows £1,000 from B, repayable in 12 months. Company C Ltd has assets of £2,000. This is stated in its balance sheet as follows:

Balance Sheet of Company C Ltd as at 1 January 2008

	£	
Assets		
Cash at bank	2,000	
Liabilities		
Sum owed to B	1,000	
Net assets	1,000	
Capital		
Share capital	1,000	(number of issued shares × nominal value)

Company C Ltd trades for 12 months and incurs trading losses of £500. It then has £1,500. B demands repayment of the £1,000 owed and due from Company C Ltd. Even though Company C Ltd has lost £500, it is still able to repay B.

Balance Sheet of Company C Ltd as at 1 January 2009

	£	
Assets		
Cash at bank	1,500	
Liabilities		
Sum owed to B	1,000	
Net assets	500	
Capital		
Share capital	1,000	(Number of issued shares × nominal value)
Profit & loss	(500)	(Accumulated profits and losses)

CASE EXAMPLE 9.2 *continued*

The shareholders cannot receive their share capital back while Company C Ltd is a going concern. The company cannot pay a dividend to shareholders because it has no profits available for the purpose (it has made a loss). The trading loss is borne by the shareholders as, after B has been paid £1,000, only £500 remains of their £1,000 share capital. Their shares are worth only £500, or 50 pence each. Unlike in Case Example 9.1, the creditor has been protected from the trading losses of the company by the share capital and will be protected until the net assets of the company are zero.

CASE EXAMPLE 9.3

Shares issued at a premium

If a company issues shares at an issue price above the nominal value of the shares, the amount by which the issue price exceeds the nominal value is the premium. The issue of £1 ordinary shares at an issue price of £2 is an example. The amount of the premium is not reflected in the share capital but in the share premium account, and the premium account balance appears in the balance sheet. With two exceptions, the premium account amount is subject to the same maintenance rules as the share capital. It is an 'undistributable reserve'. It cannot be returned to shareholders (except as authorised by, and subject to compliance with procedures in, the 2006 Act) and it does not count as profits for the purposes of distribution.

If the £1 ordinary shares of Company C Ltd in Case example 9.2 had been issued at the issue price of £2, the balance sheet of Company C Ltd would have looked like this:

Balance Sheet of Company C Ltd as at 1 January 2008

	£	
Assets		
Cash at bank	3,000	
Liabilities		
Sum owed to B	1,000	
Net assets	2,000	
Capital		
Share capital	1,000	(number of issued shares × nominal value)
Share premium	1,000	(premium paid on issue of shares)

Neither the share capital nor the share premium account balance may be distributed to shareholders: the creditors will be protected by the amount of the share premium as well as the share capital.

In *Trevor v Whitworth* (1887) 12 App Cas 409 (HL), Lord Watson explained the creditor protection rationale for the existence of capital maintenance rules.

> 'Persons who deal with, and give credit to a limited company, naturally rely upon the fact that the company is trading with a certain amount of capital already paid, as well as upon the responsibility of its members for the capital remaining at call; and they are entitled to assume that no part of the capital which has been paid into the coffers of the company has been subsequently paid out, except in the legitimate course of its business.'

The relevance of share capital over the life of a company

Case Examples 9.1–9.3 demonstrate how share capital can protect a creditor from losing money as a result of a company experiencing trading losses. They are based on a single financial creditor lending money to a company at the outset of its operations and cover only the first year of the company's life. In such a simple, somewhat unrealistic, scenario share capital is observed to represent a cushion for creditors against the risk of the company defaulting. In practice, a financial creditor will seek to secure any sum lent to the company. Taking security offers far greater protection to a creditor than the initial share capital contributed to a company.

The ability of the share capital to protect creditors and the importance of share capital to creditors reduces over the life of a company. First, the initial share capital becomes an increasingly historic figure, eroded in real terms by inflation. Second, creditors who extend credit to a company with a trading record will have more information about the company available to them than the limited information available on formation.

Is capital maintenance important to creditors?

Focusing on issued capital, private companies must have a share capital but it may be wholly minimal, such as, in theory, one share of one penny. Although public companies are required to have a minimum share capital of £50,000, this is not a substantial sum of money for a company in business in today's world.

Of the companies formed and registered in 2007–8, 90 per cent had issued capital of £100 or less. Of all companies on the register as at March 2007, 79 per cent had issued capital of £100 or less and 90 per cent had issued capital of £5,000 or less.

The rules and facts above indicate that for most companies share capital offers little comfort to creditors that the company will be able to pay its debts. This raises the question of why the Companies Act 2006 contains such detailed rules relating to reductions in share capital, redemption of shares and a company acquiring its own shares.

In relation to private companies, the law has been simplified in relation to reduction of share capital, but the procedure for a private company to redeem or acquire its own shares out of capital remains unnecessarily complex. In relation to public companies, notwithstanding the stated aims of the reform of company law culminating in the 2006 Act, the law has not been simplified. This is explained in part by UK law having to reflect EU law, specifically, the 2nd Company Law Directive (77/91/EEC), which mandates capital maintenance rules for public companies.

2 The doctrine of capital maintenance

Capital maintenance is referred to as a 'principle', 'doctrine' or 'core concept' of company law. It is not a straightforward concept and its precise scope is unclear. Lord Russell identified the two key components of capital maintenance (when a company is not being wound up) in *Hill v Permanent Trustee Company of New South Wales* [1930] AC 720 (PC).

> 'A limited company not in liquidation can make no payment by way of return of capital to its shareholders except as a step in an authorised reduction of capital. Any other payment made by it by means of which it parts with moneys to its shareholders must and can only be made by way of dividing profits. Whether the payment is called "dividend" or "bonus", or any other name, it still must remain a payment on division of profits.'

The two fundamental legal principles identified in Lord Russell's judgment can now be found in the Companies Act 2006:

1   A limited company having a share capital may not reduce its share capital except as authorised by statute (s. 617).
2   Distributions of a company's assets to its members, whether in cash or otherwise, may only be made out of profits available for the purpose (s. 830 and see also s. 831 in relation to public companies). To appreciate the operation and role played by capital maintenance in company law, it is important also to be aware of legal rules supporting and refining these key principles. Accordingly, the capital maintenance concept can be regarded as short-hand for:
    - minimum share capital rules (ss. 763–767);
    - the basic prohibition on a company reducing its share capital (s. 617);
    - detailed exceptions to the prohibition on a company reducing its share capital (Parts 17 and 18 of the 2006 Act);
    - the requirement that distributions to shareholders may only be paid out of profits available for the purpose (ss. 829–853); and

- the shareholder last principle on winding-up (Insolvency Act 1986, ss. 107 and 143(1); *Ayerst (Inspector of Taxes) v C & K (Construction) Ltd* [1976] AC 167).

TEST YOUR KNOWLEDGE 9.1

(a) What was the creditor protection rationale for the existence of the rule against returning share capital to shareholders identified in *Trevor v Whitworth*?
(b) Does this rationale continue to be relevant today?
(c) What are the two key components of the capital maintenance doctrine?
(d) Identify five sets of legal rules that support the doctrine of capital maintenance.

3 Minimum share capital requirements

Public companies and private companies limited by shares must have a share capital. Incorporators are required to register a statement of capital and initial shareholdings on registration indicating the number of shares issued and their nominal value (s. 10).

3.1 Private companies

The share capital of a private company can be as small as the incorporators choose (e.g. one share of 1 penny).

3.2 Public companies

Public companies must have allotted shares of no less than the authorised minimum as a condition of the Registrar of Companies issuing a trading certificate. As we have seen, a public company must not do business without having a trading certificate (s. 761) and the authorised minimum nominal value of the issued shares of a public company is £50,000 or the prescribed Euro equivalent (ss. 761(2) and 763).

Public companies may not issue shares unless they are paid up as to at least one quarter nominal value (s. 586). Shares issued at the time of incorporation must be paid for in cash (s. 584). The result is that a company registered as a public company must have at least £12,500 in cash when it commences business and the right to call for at least a further £37,500 from shareholders. Laws governing payment for shares are important to ensure that the company is entitled to receive from a shareholder at least the nominal value of his shares: shares may not be issued at a discount.

4 Statutory prohibition on reduction of share capital

Once a company s been registered with its initial share capital, the company may not alter its share capital except in the ways set out in s. 617. There is no need for specific authorisation in a company's Articles to reduce its share capital in accordance with the Act. If, however, the Articles contain any restriction or prohibition on reduction of share capital, the provisions in the Articles must be complied with (s. 641(6)).

4.1 Private company reduction of share capital

A private company may reduce its share capital by either of two procedures. It may use the old procedure (still the only procedure available to a public company to reduce its share capital and requires confirmation by court order) or it can use a new, simplified procedure, introduced by the Companies Act 2006 and contained in ss. 641–644. The fact that the new procedure has been introduced acknowledges that maintaining share capital is not important to the creditors of private companies. The critical basis for a reduction is the opinion of the directors that the company is solvent and will remain solvent for the following year.

The solvency statement process

A private company may reduce its share capital by the following process (ss. 641(1)(a) and 642–644):

1. Directors conduct a review of the company's solvency.
2. Every director signs a **solvency statement**.
3. Directors send a proposed special resolution to members (with a copy of the solvency statement if the resolution is to be a written resolution).
4. Shareholders pass a special resolution (which can be passed at a meeting or a written resolution) within 15 days of the date of the solvency statement.
5. The following must be registered with the Registrar of Companies (s. 644):
    - copy of solvency statement;
    - special resolution;
    - statement of capital as reduced; and
    - confirmatory statement regarding compliance with the reduction of capital process.

The reduction does not take effect until the required documents and statements have been registered.

The solvency statement (s. 643)

The solvency statement needed to support a share capital reduction is a prescribed form statement (s. 643(3)). It must be signed by all directors. Each director must confirm that he has formed the opinion that:

- on the date of the statement there is no ground on which the company could be found to be unable to pay (or otherwise discharge) its debts; and
- the company will be able to pay (or otherwise discharge) its debts as they fall due during the year immediately following the date of the statement.

If the directors make a solvency statement without having reasonable grounds for the opinion expressed in it, and which is then delivered to the Registrar of Companies, every director who is in default commits a criminal offence and is liable for imprisonment of up to 12 months or a fine or both (s. 643(4) and (5)).

Right of shareholders and creditors to object

In contrast to a reduction of capital by confirmation of the court (ss. 645 and 646), neither creditors nor those shareholders who do not support the reduction of share capital have an opportunity during the process to object to a reduction of capital effected by the solvency statement route. Note, however, the need to ensure that if there is a variation of class rights, the variation of class rights procedure is gone through. Minority shareholders who object may be able to bring a derivative claim if the directors have breached their duties in the course of the reduction, or the circumstances may found a successful unfair prejudice petition. Both of these procedures are examined in part 3.

4.2 Public company reduction of share capital

A public company (and a private company, although it seems unlikely that a private company will use this more cumbersome procedure in future) may reduce its share capital by special resolution but must secure a confirmation order from the court (ss. 641(1)(b) and 645–651).

The process is as follows:

1. A special resolution must be passed.
2. The company must settle a list of creditors for the court and either:
    - obtain the consent of all creditors; or
    - pay off, or set aside a sum to pay off, any creditor who does not consent.
3. The company must present a petition to the court to confirm the reduction.

4 The court may make an order confirming the reduction 'on such terms and conditions as it thinks fit' (s. 648(1)).
5 The following must be registered with the Registrar of Companies (s. 649):
- special resolution;
- copy of the court order; and
- statement of capital as reduced, approved by the court.

The reduction does not take effect until the required documents and statements have been registered.

Court confirmation

When the court is considering a petition to reduce share capital it must consider the interests of the creditors, the shareholders and members of the public who may invest or become creditors of the company (*Ex parte Westburn Sugar Refineries Ltd* [1951] AC 625). In relation to creditors, the court must not confirm the reduction unless it is satisfied in relation to every creditor who has not consented to the reduction that either his debt has been paid-off or a sum has been set aside by the company to pay him off (s. 648(2)). An offence is committed, punishable by a fine, by every officer of the company who intentionally or recklessly conceals the name of a creditor or misrepresents the nature or amount of a creditor's debt or claim (s. 647). The right of a creditor to object to a reduction of share capital has been restricted to require a creditor to show that there is a real likelihood that the reduction would result in the company being unable to discharge his debt or claim when it fell due (s. 646(1) as amended).

In relation to shareholders, the court must consider whether or not the reduction is fair and equitable as between shareholders, whether of the same or different classes (see *Scottish Insurance Corporation Ltd v Wilsons & Clyde Coal Co Ltd* [1949] AC 462 (HL)). Note that where the reduction involves a particular class of shareholders, the variation of rights procedure may have to be gone through (see chapter 8, section 5.3 and the cases considered there).

5 Purchase and redemption of a company's own shares

Section 617 expressly states that the statutory prohibition on a company reducing its share capital does not affect the power of a company to acquire its own shares in accordance with Part 18 of the Act. This is supported in Part 18 by s. 658, which prohibits the acquisition by a company of its own shares, 'except in accordance with the provisions of this Part'. The company may acquire its shares either by purchasing shares or redeeming redeemable shares.

5.1 Public companies

The statutory power of a public company to acquire its own shares is basically restricted to acquisition using **distributable profits** or the proceeds of a new issue of shares made for the purpose (ss. 687(2) and 692(2)).

Acquisition of own shares out of the proceeds of a new issue of shares

Where shares are bought by a company out of the proceeds of a new issue of shares, the acquired shares are cancelled and the share capital is reduced (ss. 688 and 706), but new shares have been issued which increase the share capital by at least the amount of the reduction. The overall effect is that there is no reduction in share capital, and is not considered further in this chapter.

Acquisition of own shares using distributable profits

No effective reduction of share capital is also the result achieved by the operation of s. 733 in relation to the acquisition by a company of its own shares using distributable profits. Where shares are bought by a company using distributable profits, the acquired shares are cancelled and the share capital is reduced (ss. 688 and 706), but s. 733 requires a sum equal to the nominal value of the shares acquired (the reduction in capital), to be transferred to an account called the 'capital redemption reserve'. Section 733(6) provides that, with one exception, the provisions of the Act relating to the reduction of share capital apply to the capital redemption reserve. Consequently, the capital redemption reserve is treated like share capital and is undistributable. If the share capital account and the capital redemption reserve account are added together, they equal the share capital amount before the acquisition of the shares. This means that the company's share capital is technically reduced but in practical terms the company must be operated as if its share capital remained the same as before the reduction.

The exception to treating the capital redemption reserve in the same way as share capital is that the capital redemption reserve can be used to pay up new shares issued to existing shareholders as fully-paid bonus shares. The result of such an issue is to turn the amount used from the capital redemption reserve to fund the bonus share issue into share capital. That being the case, the exception is consistent with the acquisition of shares using distributable profits being in practical effect not a reduction of share capital at all. For this reason, such an acquisition is not considered further in this chapter.

A public company seeking to acquire shares out of capital must use the reduction of capital procedure for which court confirmation is required (see above).

5.2 Private companies

In addition to being able to acquire its own shares using distributable profits or the proceeds of a new issue of shares made for the purpose, just as a public company can, a private company is also permitted to acquire its own shares out of capital (ss. 687(1) and 692(1)) provided it does so in accordance with Chapter 5 of Part 18 of the 2006 Act (ss. 709–723). When a company acquires its own shares out of capital, the shares are cancelled and there is a real reduction in share capital.

Acquisition of shares out of capital

If a private company intends to redeem (s. 687) or purchase (s. 690) its own shares out of capital, the shares must be fully paid up and paid for on acquisition (although on a **redemption** of shares, payment may be deferred if the terms of redemption so provide) (ss. 686 and 691). In addition to ss. 709–723 (the provisions specifically relevant to the use of capital to pay for a share acquisition), redeemable shares will be redeemed in accordance with their terms of redemption, and the **off-market purchase** procedure set out in the Act will need to be complied with for other purchases of shares (ss. 693–700 and 702–708).

Briefly:

1 The purchase contract must be available for inspection (s. 702).
2 The terms of the purchase contract must be made available to shareholders (s. 696).
3 A special resolution must be passed authorising the terms of the purchase contract (s. 694).
4 All profits available for distribution and the proceeds of any fresh issue of shares must be applied to pay for acquisition before any capital may be used (s. 710).
5 Directors must enquire into the affairs and prospects of the company (s. 714).
6 A directors' statement is required including:
  - the amount of the capital payment permissible;
  - a solvency statement as in s. 643 (see above) (s. 714).
7 An auditor's report is required (s. 714(6)) stating that:
  - the amount of the permissible capital payment is in his view properly determined; and
  - he is not aware of anything to indicate that the opinion expressed by the directors in their statement is unreasonable in the circumstances.
8 The directors' statement and auditor's report must be available for inspection (s. 720).
9 The directors' and auditor's report must be made available to shareholders (s. 718).
10 A special resolution must be passed authorising payment out of capital (s. 716).
11 Public notice (in the *Gazette*) of any proposed payment out of capital is required (s. 719).
12 The shares must be cancelled (ss. 688 and 706).

13 The following must be sent to the Registrar of Companies:
- notice of redemption (s. 689) or purchase of shares (s. 707) as the case may be;
- statement of capital (ss. 689 and 708); and
- both special resolutions.

The directors' statement must be in prescribed form containing the prescribed information and paragraph 5 of the Companies (Shares And Share Capital) Order 2009 (SI No 2009/388) states that it must be signed by *all* directors. Creditors and any shareholder who has not consented have five weeks from the date of the special resolution authorising the payment of capital within which to object to the use of the capital to redeem or acquire the company's shares. The objection is made by application to the court to cancel the special resolution (s. 721).

TEST YOUR KNOWLEDGE 9.2

(a) What is the minimum share capital requirement for a public company?
(b) Outline the process by which a public company may reduce its share capital.
(c) Of what must the court be satisfied before it confirms a reduction of capital?
(d) Is a public company permitted to acquire its own shares out of capital? (Do not overlook ss. 645–651.)

6 Regulation of distributions

Restrictions on the ability of a company to reduce its share capital or acquire its own shares using capital do not prevent a company from paying sums of money to shareholders that do not cause a reduction in the company's formal share capital. The payment of value to shareholders is further controlled by restrictions on distributions to shareholders. These restrictions are found in both case law (*Re Exchange Banking Co, Flitcroft's Case* (1882) 21 Ch D 519 (CA)), and the Companies Act 2006 (ss. 829–853).

The common law and statutory restrictions are cumulative (s. 851). The statutory restrictions are stricter for public companies than they are for private companies as a result of s. 831.

6.1 Dividends and distributions

Definition of distribution

Distribution for the purposes of the statutory restrictions is very widely defined in s. 829 as 'every distribution of a company's assets to shareholders, whether in cash or otherwise'. The following four activities are expressly excluded from the statutory definition either because they are subject to control by other provisions of the Act or do not give rise to any problem:

- a reduction of share capital (considered at section 5 above);
- acquisition of shares in accordance with the Act (considered at section 6 above);
- the issue of bonus shares (this increases the share capital of the company);
- a distribution of assets to shareholders on its winding up (this will only occur after all creditors have been paid in full; see the shareholder last principle considered at section 7 below).

Dividends

The most common type of distribution is a dividend. Dividends are the amounts companies pay shareholders in return for share capital. Although an individual shareholder may not insist on receiving a dividend, large companies generally need to meet shareholders' expectations by paying dividends or risk facing a fall in their share price.

Authority to declare and pay dividends is not dealt with in the Act but in a company's Articles. Companies typically pay an annual dividend, also referred to as a 'final dividend', and may pay **interim dividends**. The Model Articles for private companies and those for public companies provide for annual or final dividends to be recommended by directors and declared by general resolution of the shareholders. Shareholders cannot declare a dividend of an amount greater than that recommended by the directors, although they may substitute a smaller amount.

Directors are usually authorised by the Articles to pay interim dividends without recourse to the shareholders, in which event they may do so from time to time during the course of the financial year of the company. Quoted companies often pay dividends twice a year. Directors are also usually authorised to pay at intervals any dividend payable at a fixed rate if it appears to them that the profits available for distribution justify the payment. This allows dividends to be paid on preference shares without recourse to shareholders. Model Articles 30 (private companies) and 70 (public companies) provide for all of the above.

At common law a dividend is paid based on the nominal value of shares held by shareholders. Although the Model Articles for Private Companies Limited by Shares are silent on this point, it is common for Articles to provide that dividends should be paid based on the amounts paid up on the shares (see Model Articles for Public Companies, art. 71). This means that if a dividend of 8 pence is declared on £1 ordinary shares, the holder of a fully paid up £1 ordinary share will receive 8 pence whereas the holder of a £1 ordinary share on which only 50 pence is paid up will receive only 4 pence.

Dividends must be paid in cash unless the Articles permit payment otherwise (*Wood v Odessa Waterworks Co* (1889) 42 Ch D 636). Once a dividend has been declared, it becomes a debt payable by the company to the shareholder and a shareholder may sue to enforce that debt (*Re Severn and Wye and Severn Bridge Railway Co* [1896] 1 Ch 559).

Disguised distributions

Transactions with shareholders in a different capacity than that of shareholder may need to be assessed to determine whether or not they are 'disguised' distributions or payments out of capital. Typical transactions that need to be considered are:

1. sale of company property at an undervalue to a buyer who is a shareholder (*Aveling Barford Ltd v Perion Ltd* [1989] BCLC 626);
2. purchase of property at an over-value by the company from a seller who is a shareholder;
3. payment of excessive director's fees to directors who are shareholders (*Re Halt Garage (1964) Ltd* [1982] 3 All ER 1016);
4. payment of excessive employees' wages to employees who are shareholders;
5. excessive group service payments: excessive sums paid by subsidiaries to parent companies in return for a bundle of corporate services.

Corporate gifts to shareholders

Gifts to shareholders will not be permitted to the extent that the net gain by the shareholder is a payment out of capital or the company does not have distributable profits equal to or greater than that net gain. Net gain means the amount by which the value obtained by the shareholder exceeds the value obtained by the company from the transaction. In other words, the company is not permitted to make disguised gifts to shareholders.

CASE EXAMPLE 9.4

Shareholder A has property valued at £100,000. He sells the property to the company for £150,000. This is a disguised distribution of £50,000. The company has, in effect, given the shareholder £50,000 of company money.

The question the court asks is whether or not the payment is a genuine exercise of the power of the company resulting in a genuine payment rather than a disguised gift out of capital. This is not a wholly subjective test based on the honesty of the directors approving the payment. Nor is it for the court to substitute its own commercial judgement. Patent excess or unreasonableness will cast doubt on the genuineness of the transaction (*Re Halt Garage* (1964) Ltd [1982] 3 All ER 1016).

TEST YOUR KNOWLEDGE 9.3

(a) What is a distribution?
(b) What is the process for the declaration of a dividend set out in the Model Articles for Private Companies Limited by Shares and the Model Articles for Public Companies?
(c) Do dividends have to be paid in cash?
(d) What is the test applied by the court to determine whether or not a payment is a disguised return of capital to a shareholder?

6.2 Restrictions applicable to both private and public companies

Common law restriction

At common law, a company may not pay a dividend out of capital. This principle was stated and demonstrated clearly in *Re Exchange Banking Co, Flitcroft's Case* (1882) 21 Ch D 519 (CA).

 **CASE LAW 9.1**

***Re Exchange Banking Co, Flitcroft's Case* (1882) 21 Ch D 519 (CA)**
Between 1873 and 1875 the directors of a banking company had presented reports and balance sheets to shareholders in which debts known by the directors to be bad were entered as assets. As a result, apparent profits were shown when the directors knew the company had no distributable profits. In reliance on those accounts, the shareholders passed resolutions declaring dividends and those dividends were paid. The liquidator of the insolvent company sought an order that five of its former directors were jointly and severally liable to repay the amount of dividends paid to shareholders out of capital.

Held *per* Cotton LJ: 'The assets of a company are to be dealt with only for purposes of its business. The application of the capital in paying dividends was therefore a misapplication.' As regards each dividend the court held that persons who were directors when it was paid were jointly and severally liable for the whole amount paid. The shareholders could not ratify such payments even if they knew the facts because a payment of dividends out of capital is incapable of ratification.

Statutory restriction: s. 830

Section 830 of the Companies Act 2006 states that 'a company may only make a distribution out of profits available for the purpose'.

Profits available for the purpose

Profits available for the purpose are defined in s. 830(2):

> 'A company's profits available for distribution are its accumulated, realised profits, so far as not previously utilised by distribution or capitalisation, less its accumulated, realised losses, so far as not previously written off in a reduction or reorganisation of capital duly made.'

Setting aside for a moment the difficult question of whether or not a profit or loss has been 'realised', if a company is to be sure that it complies with s. 830 it must keep a running total of its realised profits, less its realised losses and distributions already made, from the day it commences business. Only if the figure is positive at the time the company wishes to make a distribution does the company have profits available to distribute.

CASE EXAMPLE 9.5

Company A Ltd is registered on 1 January 2000. It has the following realised profits and realised losses, makes no distributions and has the following profits available for the purpose of distribution at the end of each of its first five years of operation:

	2000	2001	2002	2003	2004
Realised Profits (RP)	10	15	10	5	0
Realised Losses (RL)	5	10	5	10	5
RP–RL	5	5	5	(5)	(5)
PROFITS AVAILABLE FOR THE PURPOSE: Cumulative RP–RL	5	10	15	10	5

Note: All figures are in 000s; figures in brackets are negative.

Company A Ltd could have paid a dividend of £15,000 at the end of 2002. It did not and because it made a loss in 2003 it could only have paid a dividend of £10,000 at the end of 2003. Due to a further loss in 2004, it could only pay a dividend of £5,000 at the end of 2004.

If Company A Ltd pays the dividends indicated in the following table in the year indicated, the 'profits available for the purpose' figure is adjusted accordingly:

	2000	2001	2002	2003	2004
Cumulative RP–RL (year end)	5	10	15	10	5
Dividends paid (D)	0	5	0	5	0
Cumulative Ds (CD)	0	5	5	10	10
PROFITS AVAILABLE FOR THE PURPOSE: Cumulative (RP–RL) – CD (or zero)	5	5	10	0	0

Relevant accounts

Whether or not a distribution may be made without contravening the Act is determined by reference to a company's accounts and the Act uses the concept of 'relevant accounts' (s. 836). These will usually be the last annual individual accounts of the company compiled in accordance with the Act accompanied (unless the company is exempt) by an auditor's report (s. 837(3)). If the auditor's report is qualified, s. 837(4) requires a written statement to be made by the auditor as to whether or not the matters in respect of which his report is qualified are material to determining whether a distribution complies with the statutory distribution provisions and either a copy of that statement must be sent to each member of a private company or it must be laid before a meeting of a public company.

As a result of the EU Regulation on the Application of International Accounting Standards (EC No 1606/2002), publicly traded companies must prepare their group accounts in accordance with EU International Financial Reporting Standards (EU-IFRS), referred to in the Act as International Accounting Standards (IAS). Dividends are not, however, justified by reference to group accounts but individual company accounts. In relation to individual company accounts, all companies have the choice of preparing their individual accounts in accordance with EU IFRS (referred to as 'IAS individual accounts') or UK Generally Accepted Accounting Practice (UK GAAP) (referred to as 'Companies Act individual accounts') (s. 395).

If a company wishes to make a distribution before the end of its first year, initial accounts need to be compiled that satisfy s. 839. These will be the relevant accounts for the purposes of the distribution. If a company wishes to make an interim dividend based on trading after the date of the last annual accounts, it will need to justify that distribution by reference to interim accounts that satisfy s. 838.

'Realised profits' and 'realised losses'

Notwithstanding the fundamental importance of the concept of 'realised' to the ability of a company to make a distribution, there is no requirement to identify those profits and losses that are realised and those that are unrealised in the relevant accounts. The only time the directors need to form a view on whether profits are realised or not is when they wish to use them to make a distribution. The directors often use a Statement of Total Recognised Gains and Losses to help them to determine distributable profits.

Apart from clarifying a couple of specific points in relation to revaluation of fixed assets (s. 841) and dividends in kind (ss. 845 and 846; see below), the Act delegates to the accounting industry the task of establishing standards and practices for determining when a profit or loss is and when it is not realised by s. 853(4):

> 'References to "realised profits" and "realised losses", in relation to a company's accounts, are to such profits or losses of the company as fall to be treated as realised in accordance with principles generally accepted at the time when the accounts are prepared, with respect to the determination for accounting purposes of realised profits or losses.'

Profits received by the company in cash or as some other asset (provided the cash value of that asset can be realised with reasonable certainty) are treated as 'realised' for accounting purposes (see Financial Reporting Standard (FRS) 18 at paragraph 28) (FRSs are part of UK GAAP).

The ascertainment of distributable profits can be a very complex process. It involves far more than simply checking the company's profit and loss account. It is even sometimes the case that amounts reported outside the profit and loss account are available for distribution. Detailed consideration can be found in the guidance on determination of realised profits for the purposes of distributions issued as a technical release by the Institute of Chartered Accountants in February 2008.

6.3 Additional limit on distributions by public company: net asset test

In addition to distributions having to come out of profits available for the purpose in accordance with s. 830, s. 831 states that a public company may only make a distribution up to the amount by which its net assets exceed the aggregate of its called-up share capital and undistributable reserves.

Undistributable reserves are listed in s. 831(4) as:

- the share premium account (see Case Example 9.3 above);
- the capital redemption account;
- the amount by which its accumulated, unrealised profits (so far as not previously utilised by capitalisation) exceed its accumulated, unrealised losses (so far as not previously written off in a reduction or reorganisation of capital duly made) (note that if the losses exceed profits this will be a net unrealised loss);
- any other reserve the company is prohibited from distributing by any enactment or by its Articles.

The effect of this additional limit is that a public company's net unrealised losses must be deducted from its net realised profits (the company's 'profits available for the purpose of distribution' pursuant to s. 830) to determine whether or not the company may make a distribution in accordance with the Act. Again, exactly what is and what is not an 'unrealised loss' for these purposes is determined by generally accepted accounting practice (see s. 853(4)).

6.4 Distributions in kind

If authorised by the Articles, dividends may be made 'in kind'. Distributions to shareholders often take a non-cash form, such as the transfer of an asset from a subsidiary to its parent. Even a distribution by a company to a sister company (a company with which it shares a parent company) will be treated as a distribution to its shareholder for the purposes of s. 829 and could potentially also be a transfer of capital to a shareholder (*Aveling Barford Ltd v Perion Ltd* [1989] BCLC 626).

Sections 845, 846 and 851(2) of the 2006 Act clarify the previously uncertain legal position relating to the transfer of an asset to a shareholder (or any company controlled by its shareholder) where the market value of the asset is higher than the value of the asset in the company's balance sheet, the asset's 'book value'.

Transfer of an asset at book value

It is not uncommon for a company to transfer assets to its parent company at book value. If the market value of the asset is the same as its book value, there is no distribution and no unlawful return of capital: the company has received full value for the asset. If, however, the market value of the asset is more than the book value, in the absence of specific statutory provisions otherwise, transfer at book value would be a distribution of the amount by which the market value of the asset exceeded the book value, the company having in effect made a gift of the difference to its shareholder.

CASE EXAMPLE 9.6

Company A Ltd bought a piece of property in 2000 for £100,000. The value of the property in the accounts (or 'books') of Company A Ltd is £100,000 (book value). In 2008 the market value of the property has risen to £150,000. Company A Ltd transfers the property to its parent company for £100,000. In the absence of specific statutory provisions otherwise, this would be a disguised distribution of £50,000, the company having, in effect, given the shareholder £50,000 of company money. If such a transaction were to take place when the company did not have distributable profits at least equal to the difference between the book price and the market price the company would, without more, have made an unlawful distribution.

Sections 845, 846 and 851 provide relief in specific circumstances thereby ensuring that such a transaction is not an unlawful distribution and will not be regarded as a transfer of capital contrary to the common law principle in *Flitcroft's* case, by reason of the market value and the book value being different.

If, as in Case Example 9.6, the property is transferred at book value, provided the company has distributable profits, the amount of the distribution will be taken to be zero (ss. 845(2)(a) and 845(2)). There will be no distribution for the purposes of s. 829, or the common law. It is s. 851(2) that takes away the danger of the transfer being regarded as a transfer of capital to a shareholder contrary to the common law prohibition.

Transfer of an asset at above book value

If property is transferred at above book value, again, subject to the company having distributable profits, the amount of the distribution will be taken to be zero. Also, s. 845(3) provides that, solely for the purpose of meeting the precondition for the application of s. 845(2) that a company has distributable profits, the distributable profits of the company may be treated as increased by the amount by which the price paid for the asset exceeds its book value.

Transfer of an asset at below book value

If the asset is transferred for a consideration less than its book value, s. 845 operates to render the amount of the distribution equal only to the shortfall versus book value (rather than the difference between the actual consideration and market value). For the distribution to be in accordance with the Act, this shortfall will need to be covered by distributable profits.

Finally, s. 846 allows a company with a revalued asset in its balance sheet, so that it is showing an unrealised profit in its accounts, to treat that profit as a realised profit. The concession applies only for the purposes of a distribution by way of transfer of that particular revalued asset.

TEST YOUR KNOWLEDGE 9.4

(a) What restriction does s. 830 place on the payment of dividends?
(b) What is the significance of accumulated in the definition of 'profits available for the purpose' in s. 830?
(c) What is the effect of the additional restriction on payment of dividends by a public company imposed by s. 831?
(d) Is transfer of an asset at book value by a subsidiary to its parent company ever a distribution?

6.5 Remedies for payment of unlawful distributions

Unlawful payment of distributions is not a criminal offence. Section 847(2) provides a civil remedy against shareholders and s. 847(3) preserves the common law and equitable remedies available against a shareholder who receives a distribution made unlawfully to him. Common law and equity also potentially provide remedies against the directors involved in the making of such payments. Additionally, unless a company is entitled to rely on the small or dormant company exemption from audit, the relevant accounts by which a distribution has been justified will have been reviewed by the company's auditor and an audit report signed. If it can be established that the unlawfulness of the distribution has resulted from negligence or breach of contract by the auditor, a company may be able to claim damages from its auditor. (Auditor liability is considered in chapter 11.) The following sections explore the potential liability of directors and shareholders in more detail.

Remedies available against the directors

Although the 2006 Act is silent in relation to the liability of directors who pay company capital to shareholders or make unlawful distributions, it is clear from *Flitcroft's* case that the directors at the time of the payment are jointly and severally liable to compensate the company for the whole amount paid. This was applied in *Bairstow v Queen's Moat Houses* [2001] 2 BCLC 531 even though the directors did not know that the distributions were unlawful. *Bairstow* also made it clear that the liability of the directors is not limited to cases where distributions are demonstrably made out of capital, and applies whether or not the company is insolvent. The degree of fault required for a director to be liable for payment of an unlawful distribution is unclear. One view is that liability is strict subject to the potential for the court to grant relief pursuant to s. 1157 if it appears to the court that the director acted honestly and reasonably and having regard to the circumstances of the case ought fairly to be excused.

Remedies available against a shareholder

Remedies against a shareholder arise both under s. 847 and pursuant to the common law principle that payment of an unlawful distribution is a misapplication of corporate funds.

The s. 847 statutory remedy

Section 847(1) makes a shareholder liable to repay any sum received in contravention of the statutory distribution rules if at the time the distribution was made he knew, or had reasonable grounds for believing, the distribution was made in contravention of the statutory distribution rules.

Common law and equitable remedies

A sharcholder who receives a distribution that contravenes the common law prohibition on distributions out of capital or (due to s. 847(3)) the statutory rules may be required to repay the sum received to the company based on the imposition of a constructive trust (*Precision Dippings Ltd v Precision Dippings Marketing Ltd* [1986] Ch 447 (CA)). This will be a more effective remedy than recovery pursuant to s. 847 because it is a proprietary remedy. If the shareholder becomes bankrupt or insolvent after the imposition of the constructive trust, the constructive trust funds will not be available to the other creditors of the shareholder. The circumstances in which a constructive trust will be imposed on a shareholder may not be exactly the same as those in which a repayment would be ordered under s. 847.

A constructive trust may be imposed where the shareholder has knowledge of the facts and is not a *bona fide* purchaser for value without notice of the wrongful payment.

A further basis on which the company may be able to recover unlawfully paid sums is if the sum can be traced and either an action for money had and received established at common law, or an equitable proprietary claim (based on *Re Diplock* [1948] Ch 465 (CA) established). (These topics are usually covered in Trust courses.)

TEST YOUR KNOWLEDGE 9.5

(a) Is unlawful payment of dividends a criminal offence?
(b) Are directors liable to compensate the company for unlawfully paid dividends?
(c) What is the potential liability of a shareholder under s. 847?
(d) Is knowledge that a dividend is paid in contravention of the Companies Act 2006 a precondition of shareholder liability under s. 847?

7 Shareholder last principle on a winding up

Shareholders have no claim to return of their contribution in a winding up until all creditor claims have been satisfied (Insolvency Act 1986, ss. 107 and 143(1)). This supports the principle that the share capital sum is there to provide a buffer for creditors against poor trading and is not to be returned to shareholders ahead of creditors being paid.

8 A broader concept of capital maintenance?

8.1 Gratuitous payments to non-shareholders

Capital maintenance rules regulate the transfer of value to shareholders. It is interesting to consider the extent to which the law regulates gratuitous transfers of value by a company to persons other than shareholders. The most obvious example of a gratuitous transfer of value is a gift, but any activity that takes value out of the company for no apparently good commercial reason could be characterised as a 'disguised gift'.

Examples of uncommercial arrangements are:

- sale of company property at an undervalue (below market value);
- purchase of property by the company at an overvalue (above market value);
- payment of excessive directors' fees;
- payment of excessive employees' wages;
- excessive payment for goods or services; and
- corporate gifts delivering no benefit to the company commensurate with cost.

8.2 The 'cakes and ale case law'

Cases as recently as *Barclays Bank v British and Commonwealth Holdings plc* [1996] BCLC 1, appear to support the existence of a principle that 'no company may make truly gratuitous dispositions of its assets'. This line of cases has been dubbed the 'cakes and ale case law' (see McGuinness, 2007), as it can be traced back to Bowen LJ's often quoted words from *Hutton v West Cork Railway Co* (1883) Ch D 654 (CA).

> 'The law does not say that there are to be no cakes and ale, but there are to be no cakes and ale except such as are required for the benefit of the company.'

The principle has been criticised by Ferran (1999), who argues that 'the principle that a company cannot give away its capital is not part of English company law'. It appears to remain good law in Canada (McGuinness, 2007) and the issue is best regarded as moot in English law. What seems to be clear is that a principle that truly gratuitous dispositions are unlawful is not needed as other legal principles adequately regulate the mischief it addresses, whether the decision to make the gratuitous payment is made by the directors or the shareholders. Whether or not there is a general principle prohibiting gratuitous payments, a number of legal principles and specific legal rules are available to regulate gifts and 'disguised gift' transactions:

1. If the payments are authorised by directors, the company can challenge the directors based on breaches of their directors' duties.
2. Breaches by the company and directors of specific provisions of the 2006 Act such as long service agreements, asset/loan etc., transactions with directors.
3. If the transaction has been authorised by shareholders, a minority can seek relief by:
   - derivative action on behalf of the company based on breach of duty by a director that the shareholders are prepared to condone (especially if those directors are shareholders purporting to condone the transaction);
   - unfair prejudice petition; or
   - assertion of the improper purpose principle (*Re Halt Garage (1964) Ltd* [1982] 3 All ER 1016).
4. If the transaction takes place in the twilight zone, the liquidator can challenge it based on it being:
   - a voidable preference pursuant to Insolvency Act 1986, s. 239;
   - an invalid floating charge pursuant to Insolvency Act 1986, s. 245;
   - a transfer at an undervalue (TUV) pursuant to Insolvency Act 1986, s. 238; or
   - a liquidator can enforce breaches of directors' duties using Insolvency Act 1986, s. 212.
5. A liquidator can apply for contribution orders based on wrongful or fraudulent trading (ss. 213 and 214 of the Insolvency Act 1986).

Each of these legal principles and rules is considered at the appropriate place in this book.

8.3 Political donations

The making of political donations and incurring of political expenditure by a company is specifically regulated by the Companies Act 2006 (ss. 366–379), although companies may make political donations of up to £5,000 in any 12-month period without complying with the statutory provisions (s. 378). Also, donations and subscriptions to trade unions other than to the union's political fund are not political contributions and all-party parliamentary groups are not political organisations for the purposes of the statutory provisions (ss. 374–376).

Subject to the foregoing, no political donations or expenses are permitted unless authorised by both the shareholders of the company and, if the company is part of a group, by the shareholders of the ultimate holding company (s. 366). A wholly-owned subsidiary company is not required to pass such a resolution (but the parent company must) (s. 366). Shareholder approval has been required since 2000.

A resolution generally authorising such has effect for four years or such shorter period as the Articles require or the directors determine (s. 368). All directors are jointly and severally liable to repay any payments or expenses incurred without authorisation and compensate the company for any consequent loss or damage (s. 369), and there are special provisions governing the rights of shareholders to enforce the directors' liabilities (ss. 370–373).

9 Financial assistance for the purchase of its own shares

9.1 Background to the current rules

The provision of financial assistance by a company for the acquisition of its own shares by another person was first prohibited in 1928 to deal with two perceived mischiefs:

- manipulation of a company's share price brought about by the company providing assistance for the purchase of its shares;

- use of an acquired company's assets to pay off the debt incurred to buy the company.

The second mischief explains why the prohibition applies to assistance provided after (s. 678(3)), as well as before or at the same time as (s. 678(1)), the acquisition of shares takes place. According to Lord Greene MR, the practice, following the end of the First World War, of a financier taking out a short-term loan (sometimes called a bridging loan) to finance the acquisition of shares in a company and then using the assets of that company to repay the loan 'gave rise to great dissatisfaction and, in some cases, great scandals' (*R v GM Holdings Ltd* [1942] Ch 235 at 239).

In fact, the practice Lord Greene describes is not uncommon today and is not regarded as contentious. It is quite acceptable, and within the law, for one company to borrow significantly to finance the acquisition of another company and, following acquisition, to cause the acquired company to pay out as much as it can by way of lawful dividend to its new parent to enable the parent to pay back as much of its acquisition borrowings as possible. The legality of this is assured by s. 681(2), taking 'a distribution of a company's assets by way of dividend lawfully made' outside the statutory prohibition.

Also, if the acquired company has a lot of cash or readily realisable assets, loans from the subsidiary to the parent can be put in place enabling the parent company to pay back acquisition-borrowings. This may, however, be caught by the prohibition. The fact that such a loan is innocuous, yet it is not clear whether or not it would be caught by the statutory prohibition, is but one way in which the provisions prohibiting financial assistance are unsatisfactory.

9.2 Typical examples of financial assistance

Typical examples of a company providing financial assistance for the purchase of its shares are:

- Company A plc lends money to X and X uses that money to buy shares in Company A plc.
- Company B plc guarantees a loan made by Bank E to Y and Y uses the borrowed money to buy shares in Company B plc.
- Z borrows money from Bank F and uses it to buy Company C Ltd. Z then uses the resources of Company C Ltd to repay the loan monies to Bank F.

9.3 What is prohibited?

By ss. 678 and 679 it is not lawful for:

- a public company;
- to give financial assistance;
- directly or indirectly;
- for the purpose of acquisition of its shares or shares in its private holding company;
- either before or at the same time as the acquisition;
- or for the purpose of reducing or discharging a liability incurred for the purpose of the acquisition.

Financial assistance is defined very widely in s. 677. The section lists specific examples of ways in which financial assistance can be given and also contains generic language, as follows:

- gift, guarantee, security, indemnity, release, waiver and loan;
- any other financial assistance given by the company where the net assets of the company are reduced to a material extent by the giving of the assistance or the company has no net assets (s. 677(d)).

The prohibition now applies only to public companies (see 10.8 below). This means that if a public company is acquired and the parent company wishes to use its assets to reduce or discharge a liability incurred for the purpose of the acquisition, even if the acquired company is not able to pay money to the parent as dividends, the acquired company can be re-registered as a private company, following which there is no prohibition on it providing financial assistance.

9.4 Limits and exceptions to the prohibition

The main limits to the prohibition are the 'principal purpose' and 'incidental part' carve-outs.

The 'principal purpose' carve-out

If the company's principal purpose in giving assistance is not to give it for the purpose of acquisition of shares, or to reduce or discharge any liability incurred for the purpose of the acquisition of shares, and the assistance is given in good faith in the interests of the company, it is not prohibited (ss. 678(2)(a), (4)(a) and 679(2)(a), (4)(a)).

The 'incidental part' carve-out

If the giving of the assistance for the acquisition of shares, or to reduce or discharge any liability incurred for the purpose of the acquisition of shares, is only an incidental part of some larger purpose of the company and the assistance is given in good faith in the interests of the company, it is not prohibited (ss. 678(2)(b), (4)(b) and 679(2)(b), (4)(b)).

The scope of these carve-outs was considered in *Brady v Brady* [1989] AC 755 (HL). The narrow approach taken has been fiercely criticised and seems at odds with the more liberal approach generally taken to exceptions operating in the context of criminal offences (although the case was in fact a civil case in which one party sought specific performance of an agreement which included the provision of financial assistance). Nonetheless, notwithstanding the proposal to replace the words 'principal purpose' with 'predominant reason', the 2006 Act retains the old language.

CASE LAW 9.2

Brady v Brady [1989] AC 755 (HL)

Two brothers were unable to run the family company together. To save the company from being run down they made arrangements to split the businesses of the company with one brother, Robert, to run the soft drinks side and the other brother, Jack, to run the road haulier business. Arrangements were put in place which included the original company providing financial assistance to a new company to allow the new company to purchase shares in the old company. Jack sued Robert for specific performance of the agreement but Robert argued that the agreement provided for the giving of unlawful financial assistance and was therefore void and unenforceable. Jack argued that the 'incidental part of some larger purpose' exception applied.

Held: The financial assistance did not fall within the incidental part exception (though specific performance was granted based on other grounds). The purpose of the assistance was to acquire shares even if that was not the reason for assistance 'reason is not the same as purpose'; and 'larger is not the same thing as "more important"'. *Per* Lord Oliver: 'The purpose and the only purpose of the financial assistance is and remains that of enabling the shares to be acquired and the financial or commercial advantages flowing from the acquisition, whilst they may form the reason for forming the purpose of providing assistance, are a by-product of it rather than an independent purpose of which the assistance can properly be considered to be an incident.'

Exceptions to the prohibition contained in ss. 681 and 682 are detailed. In addition to the particularly important exception noted above of a dividend lawfully made, s. 681 removes from the prohibition allotment of bonus shares and reductions of capital and redemption or purchase of shares in accordance with the Act. The main arrangements excluded by s. 682 are arrangements by which employees acquire shares. Section 682 exceptions are conditional upon the company's net assets not being reduced or any such reduction being provided out of distributable profits.

9.5 Criminal sanctions for contravention

Section 680 states that if the company contravenes the prohibition on the giving of financial assistance, the company and every officer of the company in default commits an offence. The company is liable to a fine and officers are liable to up to 12 months' imprisonment or a fine, or both.

9.6 Civil remedies for breach

The Act does not specify the civil consequences of the company contravening the prohibition and providing unlawful financial assistance. The consequences must be found in the cases and the approach of the judges has changed over time. It is necessary to consider the position of the following:

- the company giving the unlawful financial assistance;
- the person purchasing the shares;
- any third party involved such as a bank lending money to the purchaser of the shares the guarantee of which by the company amounts to unlawful financial assistance; and
- the directors of the company.

The current position can be summarised as:

- An agreement between the purchaser and the company for the provision of unlawful financial assistance is void and unenforceable by either party (*Brady v Brady* [1989] AC 755 (HL)).
- If the agreement to provide unlawful financial assistance and the agreement to purchase shares form a single composite transaction and the financial assistance provisions cannot be severed from the agreement so as to leave an enforceable agreement, the entire agreement will be unlawful and unenforceable by the company or the purchaser (*South Western Mineral Water Co Ltd v Ashmore* [1967] 1 WLR 1110).
- Connected transactions are not tainted by the unlawfulness of the unlawful financial assistance so that, for example, a purchaser cannot avoid an obligation to buy shares relying on the argument that the company has agreed to provide unlawful financial assistance in relation to the purchase (unless the two are one composite agreement).
- Any agreement by which the unlawful financial assistance is to be given is void and unenforceable (*Heald v O'Connor* [1971] WLR 497).
- The directors are liable to the company for breach of duty.
- If company assets have been transferred by way of financial assistance, the company may be able to recover those assets based on the recipient holding the assets on constructive trust arising as a result of the breaches of fiduciary duty by the directors.

9.7 Private companies and financial assistance

The Companies Act 2006 prohibition on financial assistance does not apply to private companies. Commentators have questioned the impact on the common law position of simply excluding private companies from the scope of the *statutory* prohibition.

Essentially, common law capital maintenance principles expounded in the nineteenth century in the context of undeveloped accounting principles and practices have not been developed because statutory developments have, in large part, removed the need for recourse to the common law. Accordingly, there is no specific common law prohibition on financial assistance, but any financial assistance by a private company will need to comply with the general principles of capital maintenance outlined in this chapter. For example, if an existing shareholder were to be given company funds to buy shares in the company at a time when the company had no distributable profits, it would be an unlawful distribution. If the sum was a return of capital, that would be an unlawful return of capital. Where the decision to provide the funds is taken by directors, the duties they owe to the company will also regulate behaviour.

Financial assistance must remain in place for public companies because of the need for English law to continue to reflect the 2nd EU Company Law Directive. The UK would like to see significant reform or removal of the prohibition on financial assistance from EU law altogether.

TEST YOUR KNOWLEDGE 9.6

(a) What was the mischief that the laws prohibiting financial assistance were designed to address and is this behaviour still regarded as a mischief today?
(b) Give three typical examples of a company providing financial assistance for the purchase of its shares.
(c) Explain the two principal carve-outs from prohibited financial assistance.
(d) Who is potentially criminally liable when a company gives financial assistance for the purchase of its own shares?
(e) What is the legal basis for the liability of directors in relation to the giving of financial assistance?
(f) What step might be taken to prevent the use of the assets of a recently acquired public company to reduce a liability incurred for the purpose of the acquisition from being financial assistance?

CHAPTER SUMMARY

- Capital maintenance is essentially two principles now found in the Companies Act 2006:
  - a limited company having a share capital may not reduce its share capital except as authorised by statute (s. 617);
  - distributions of a company's assets to its members, whether in cash or otherwise, may only be made out of profits available for the purpose (s. 830 and see also s. 831 in relation to public companies).
- Public limited companies (only) are required to have a minimum share capital of £50,000 or Euro equivalent paid up as to at least 25 per cent nominal value in cash (ss. 761, 763, 584 and 586).
- Reduction of share capital is prohibited both at common law and by statute except as permitted by statute, (*Trevor v Whitworth* (1887); s. 617).
- A private company may reduce share capital by the solvency statement route (ss. 641–644) or court approval route (ss. 641 and 645–651) and may acquire or redeem its own shares out of capital, (ss. 687, 690 and 709–723).
- A public company may reduce share capital only by the court approval route (ss. 641 and 645–651; *Ex parte Westburn Sugar Refineries Ltd* (1951)) and may acquire or redeem its own shares only out of profits or the proceeds of a new issue.
- Companies may only pay distributions out of profits available for the purpose (*Re Exchange Banking Co, Flitcroft's Case* (1882); s. 830) Public companies must also take unrealised losses into account when calculating profits, (s. 831).
- Transfer of assets to sister companies may be a distribution (*Aveling Barford Ltd v Perion Ltd* (1989); ss. 845, 846 and 851).
- Remedies for payment of unlawful distributions are available against directors (jointly and severally liable) (*Re Exchange Banking Co, Flitcroft's Case* (1882); *Bairstow v Queen's Moat Houses* (2001)) and shareholders (pursuant to both statute and case law), *Precision Dippings Ltd v Precision Dippings Marketing Ltd* (1986)).
- Shareholders have no claim to a company's assets until creditors have been paid in full, (Insolvency Act 1986, ss. 107 and 143(1))
- A public company may not provide financial assistance for purchase of its own shares (ss. 678 and 679) subject to criminal sanctions (s. 680) and civil remedies for breach (*Brady v Brady* (1989); *South Western Mineral Water Co Ltd v Ashmore* (1967); *Heald v O'Connor* (1971)).
- Statutory prohibition of financial assistance was abolished for private companies by the Companies Act 2006 (the behaviour is principally regulated by directors' duties).

10 Loan capital

■ CONTENTS

1 Debentures
2 Secured creditors: fixed and floating charges

■ INTRODUCTION

This chapter examines the law governing secured borrowing by a company. The meaning of debenture is considered and different types of debentures identified before fixed and floating charges, the two most common forms of security created by companies, are examined in depth.

1 Debentures

The term **debenture** is used to refer to a range of documents acknowledging or establishing different types of debts where, for our purposes, the company is the borrower and the debenture holder is the lender.

In *Levy v Abercorris Slate and Slab Co* (1887) 37 ChD 260, it was stated that debenture 'means a document which either creates a debt or acknowledges it ... [there is no] precise legal definition of the term, it is not either in law or commerce a strictly technical term, or what is called a term of art.'

1.1 Types of debentures

Debentures may be put in place between the company and one other person on an individual lender basis. A number of unique debentures of this type may exist at one time. This type of debenture is put in place where a company enters into a secured borrowing arrangement with a bank. A loan is put in place secured by a charge (fixed, floating, or both), on specified company property. The document evidencing this arrangement is usually in the form of a deed or formal documents executed by the company. The sum borrowed and the terms governing repayment of the borrowed sum and payment of interest will be set out in the document, as will the terms creating the charge and providing for enforcement in the event of the company defaulting (i.e. failing to comply with any terms of the loan).

Note that even if no charge is provided for (i.e. even if the document evidences an unsecured loan), it is still a debenture, known sometimes as a **bare debenture** or **naked debenture**. That said, in practice the term debenture is more often used to refer to a document establishing a secured loan. A common form of debenture was the subject of judicial scrutiny in the leading case of *Re Spectrum Plus Ltd* [2005] 2 BCLC 269, considered below.

A bare debenture is not an instrument a copy of which is required to be sent to the Registrar of Companies or kept by the company pursuant to s. 860 or s. 875, nor will it appear on the register of charges a company is required to keep under the Companies Act 2006, s. 876. Similarly, particulars of a bare debenture do not have to be registered with the Registrar of Companies pursuant to s. 860. Rather, it is prescribed particulars of any **charge** created by a debenture that need to be registered with the Registrar of Companies (s. 860), copies of only **secured debentures** need to be kept pursuant to s. 875, and the charges create or acknowledge by a debenture instrument need to be entered on a company's register of charges.

Debentures are also put in place on a collective basis. Corporate bonds or debenture stock issued by a company are debentures and those who hold them are called debenture holders. These instruments – generically loan securities – are not shares in the company but evidence of loans to the company. Yet, like share issues, a corporate bond issue or an issue of debenture stock is a way in which a company can raise money in the capital markets. Being securities, debenture stock is subject to the Companies Act prohibition on a private company offering securities to the public. If offered to the public or traded on a regulated market, debenture stock is subject to the FSMA 2000 and the Prospectus Rules (see chapter 7).

Debenture stock has been said to differ from individual debentures in form only, rather than in substance (*Re Herring* [1908] 2 Ch 493). The Companies Act 2006 states expressly that where the term 'debenture' is used in the Act, that term should be read to include collective debentures:

> 'In the Companies Acts 'debenture' includes debenture stock, bonds and any other securities of a company, whether or not constituting a charge on the assets of the company.' (s. 738)

Beyond categorisation into individual and collective debentures, debentures can be categorised into different types based on a number of other characteristics such as whether or not they are:

- secured or unsecured debentures (see earlier paragraphs of this section);
- bearer or registered debentures;
- permanent or redeemable debentures; or
- convertible or non-convertible debentures.

Bearer or registered debentures

Bearer debentures are **negotiable instruments** the rights in relation to which can be transferred by physical delivery. The bearer, or holder, of the instrument at any time is the debenture holder. The name of the holder of a bearer debenture is not reflected in a register of debentures.

Permanent or redeemable debentures

Permanent debentures do not specify a date or event on which the sum lent to the company becomes repayable.

Convertible or non-convertible debentures

A convertible debenture is a debenture containing an option to convert it, typically into an equity or preference share (as specified), at a specified rate of conversion and after a certain period of time.

1.2 Use of a trust deed

Debenture stock is usually structured as an interest under a trust. A professional trust corporation is appointed to be a debenture trustee by a trust deed which sets out the details of the loan, the security and the trust, including provisions establishing and governing:

- issue of the stock;
- payment of interest and repayment by the company;
- a charge over specified company property; and
- powers and duties of the trustee.

The debenture trustee holds the benefit of the promise, or 'covenant', made by the company on trust for all of the debenture stockholders and it is common for debenture trust deeds to provide for stockholders to be paid proportionately. Stockholders hold a certificate evidencing their rights. The benefit of setting debenture stock up in this way is that there is one charge securing one large loan rather than the company having to execute a large number of small charges securing small loans. Rights of the stockholders are centralised in the trustee allowing for more cost effective enforcement of debenture stockholders' rights.

TEST YOUR KNOWLEDGE 10.1

(a) What is a debenture?
(b) Identify five characteristics on the basis of which debentures can be categorised.
(c) What is debenture stock?
(d) What are the advantages of using a trust deed to structure debenture stock?

2 Secured creditors: fixed and floating charges

Secured creditors are those who, in addition to having a contractual right to sue the company for the return of any money owed to them, have taken a property interest in one or more items of the company's property as security for the credit they have made available to the company.

The existence of a property right becomes important when the company is unable to pay its debts. The holder of the property or asset has the right to take possession of the asset in certain circumstances and doing so remove it from the assets available to the liquidator to liquidate and distribute among those creditors who have only contractual rights against the company (unsecured creditors). In this way, the property interest – the security – reduces the risk to the secured creditor of not getting its money back. By reducing risk, security facilitates the lending of money (see *Re Brightlife Ltd* [1987] Ch 200). As we shall see, not all property right holders have the right to take possession of the charged property. Fixed charge holders do, but floating charge holders do not (although the rights of floating charge holders are greater than those of unsecured creditors).

2.1 Reasons to distinguish fixed and floating charges

When we study winding up (part 5) we shall need to understand both the rights of secured creditors *vis-à-vis* other creditors and the rights of different types of secured creditors. In this context it is critically important to classify charges into fixed and floating charges, an important distinction for at least three key reasons.

First, when a company is being wound up there is, in effect, a statutory partial overriding of the property rights of a floating charge holder. Insolvency legislation provides for liquidation expenses, preferential debts and a statutory 'prescribed part' amount to be deducted from the proceeds of sale of property subject to a floating charge before the proceeds are available to pay the debt owed to the floating charge holder. No similar overriding occurs in relation to fixed charge holders. This is why it is said that fixed charges are outside the statutory order of distribution provided for in Chapter VIII of the Insolvency Act 1986.

Second, all floating charges created by companies are registrable, whereas not all fixed charges are (fixed charges over shares or non-book debts, for example, are not registrable). Because a registrable but ununregistered charge is void against a liquidator, it is sometimes very important to know whether or not a charge is a fixed or floating charge to determine its registrability.

Third, a floating charge is vulnerable to avoidance pursuant to the Insolvency Act 1986, s. 245, whereas a fixed charge is not (see avoidance of transactions in part 5).

For these three key reasons, among others, it is essential to know how to decide whether a particular security interest is a fixed or floating charge. Also for these reasons, banks go out of their way to characterise charges as fixed charges, seeking to establish the much stronger rights of a fixed charge holder in the event of a winding-up, when in reality the charge in question is operated as a floating charge.

2.2 Fixed charges

A **fixed charge** (also sometimes called a specific charge) is a property interest in specific property preventing the owner of the property from selling the property or otherwise dealing with it without first either:

- paying back the sum secured against it; or
- obtaining the consent of the charge holder.

A fixed charge is created by a deed or other charge document, called a debenture, usually at the same time the loan is made or a credit facility (e.g. an overdraft facility) is put in place.

The rights of the fixed charge holder will be determined by the language of the charge document which stipulates what the charge holder may do in relation to the charged property and in what circumstances. Typically, the fixed charge holder has the right to take possession of the charged property, sell it and, from the proceeds of sale, recover the secured sum and costs reasonably incurred. Any surplus proceeds are returned to the company. Additionally, or alternatively, the charge will empower the charge holder to appoint a receiver to take possession of the property on its behalf. The charge holder is empowered to take these steps only if and when certain events occur, such as the company defaulting on payment of one or more repayments, or the company entering into liquidation. Figures 10.1 and 10.2 illustrate how fixed charges work.

No simple legal definition of a fixed charge exists. It is a non-possessory security that is not a floating charge. Non-possessory means that the person who benefits from the charge does not have possession of the charged property. Possession remains with the company. This is the reason why it is important to have a public register of charges so that third parties, by consulting the register, are able to discover whether or not a piece of property owned and in the possession of the company is subject to any of the registrable charges. Note, however, that while all floating charges are registrable, not all fixed charges are registrable. Fixed charges on shares and non-book debts, for example, are not registrable.

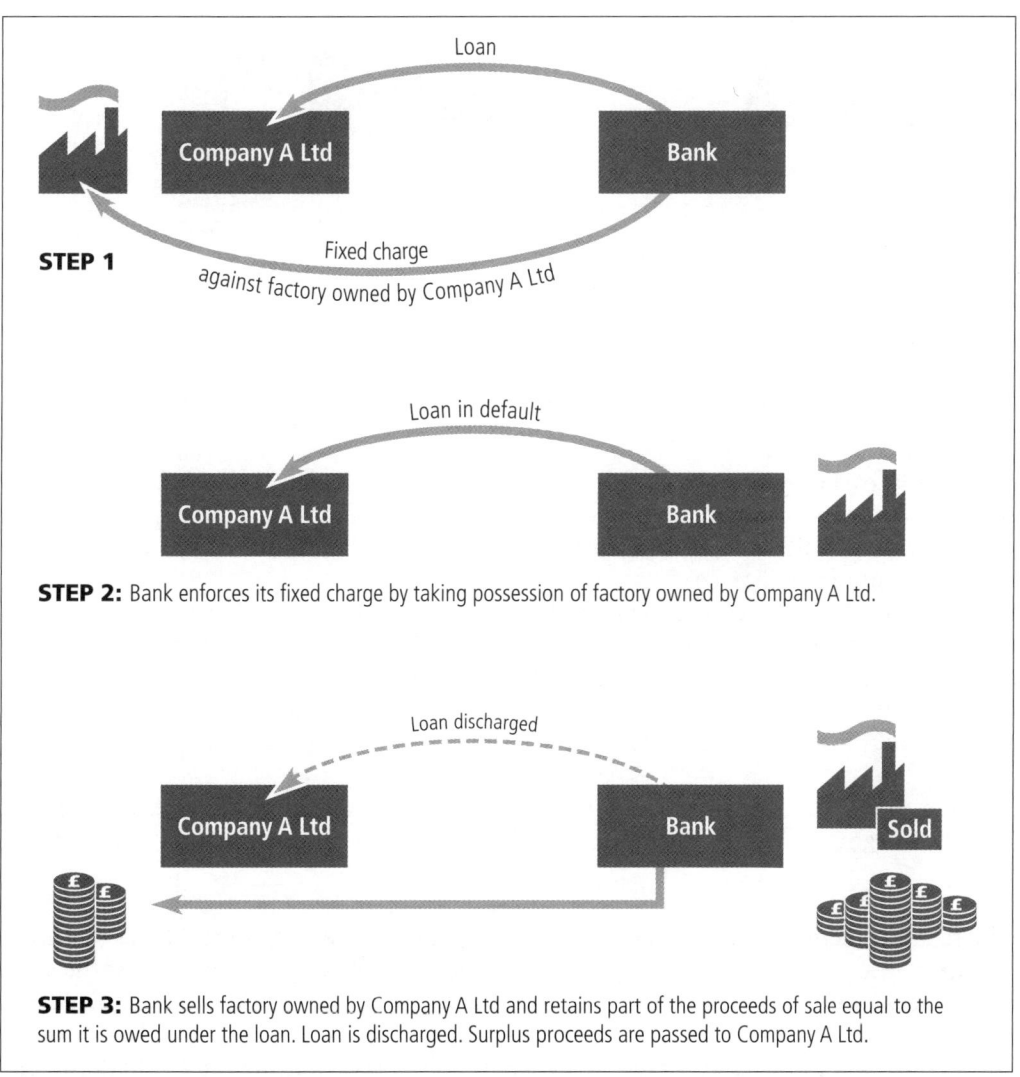

FIGURE 10.1 Fixed charge against real property: stages of enforcement

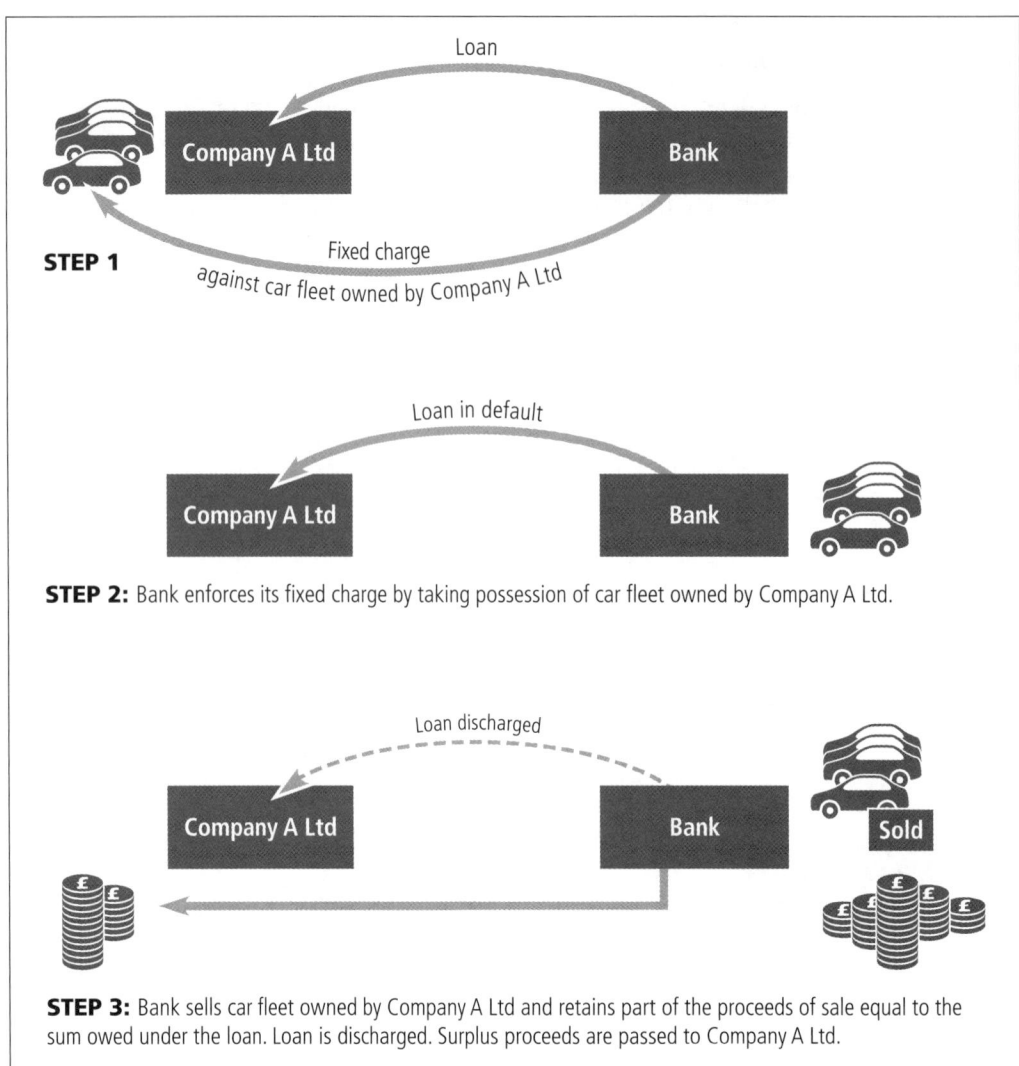

FIGURE 10.2 Fixed charge against personal property: stages of enforcement

The essence of a fixed charge is that control over dealing with the charged property rests with the bank/lender/creditor/chargee/charge holder. In contrast, property subject to a floating charge may be dealt with (usually sold) by the company in the ordinary course of business without seeking the consent of the chargee.

The meaning of fixed charge has been explored in several significant cases in the past 20 years in which liquidators and the Inland Revenue (now HM Revenue & Customs) have sought to challenge charges described on their face as fixed charges, arguing that they are, in reality, floating charges. In *Re Spectrum Plus Ltd* [2005] 2 AC 680 (HL), Lord Scott emphasised that it is the substance of the rights created and not the form that determines the nature of the charge.

> 'the label of "fixed" or "specific" (which I take to be synonymous in this context) cannot be decisive if the rights created by the debenture, properly construed, are inconsistent with that label.'

Before the relevant sections of the Enterprise Act 2002 came into effect, unpaid taxes of a company that went into winding-up were payable as preferential debts. This is no longer the case, but it was the case when the facts of the four major cases exploring the line between fixed and floating charges arose. Accordingly, the taxing authorities were keen to establish that the form of security scrutinised in the cases were floating charges thereby requiring the liquidator to pay the unpaid taxes out of the proceeds of sale of the charged assets before applying any of those proceeds to pay back the charge holder.

The four leading cases in which a charge named on its face as a fixed charge was examined to determine what rights the parties intended to create and whether or not, as a matter of law, those rights constituted a fixed or a floating charge are:

- *Siebe Gorman & Co Ltd v Barclays Bank Ltd* [1979] 2 Lloyds Rep 142 (overruled in *Re Spectrum*).
- *Re New Bullas Trading Ltd* [1994] 1 BCLC 485 (PC) (overruled in *Agnew*).
- *Agnew v Commissioner of Inland Revenue (Re Brumark Investments Ltd)* [2001] 2 AC 710 (PC) (approved in *Re Spectrum*).
- *Re Spectrum Plus Ltd* [2005] 2 AC 680 (HL).

The leading authority, *Re Spectrum*, a test case on a widely used standard form of debenture, is discussed at section 3.4 below when we examine charges over book debts.

2.3 Floating charges

Justice Hoffmann (as he then was) explained the role played by **floating charges** in *Re Brightlife Ltd* [1987] Ch 200. He highlighted the tension between the rights of floating chargeholders and unsecured creditors, stating that responsibility for balancing these competing interests lies with the legislature, not the courts:

'The floating charge was invented by Victorian lawyers to enable manufacturing and trading companies to raise loan capital on debentures. It could offer the security of a charge over the whole of the company's undertaking without inhibiting its ability to trade. But the mirror image of these advantages was the potential prejudice to the general body of creditors, who might know nothing of the floating charge but find that all the company's assets, including the very goods which they had just delivered on credit, had been swept up by the debenture holder. The public interest requires a balancing of the advantages to the economy of facilitating the borrowing of money against the possibility of injustice to unsecured creditors. These arguments for and against the floating charge are matters for Parliament rather than the courts and have been the subject of public debate in and out of Parliament for more than a century.

Parliament has responded, first, by restricting the right of the holder of a floating charge and secondly, by requiring public notice of the existence and enforcement of the charge.'

In *Re Yorkshire Woolcombers Association Ltd* (1903), Romer LJ described three key characteristics of a floating charge. A floating charge, he stated, is:

- a charge upon all of a certain class of assets present and future,
- which class is, in the ordinary course of the company's business, changing from time to time,
- in relation to which charged assets, until steps are taken to enforce the charge, the company can carry on business in the ordinary way including removing a charged asset from the security.

In *Agnew v Commissioner of Inland Revenue (Re Brumark Investments Ltd)* [2001] 2 AC 710 (PC) Lord Millett stressed it is the third of these characteristics that is the essential feature of a floating charge and distinguishes a floating charge from a fixed charge. A fixed charge may have one or both of the first characteristics listed above but may not have the third.

Figures 10.3 and 10.4 illustrate how a floating charge may be put in place against a single class of assets or a number of different classes of assets. It is common for floating charges to be put in place against 'all the assets and business of the company'. This is referred to as a general floating charge. The great attraction and benefit of a floating charge is that the company can continue to use the charged assets of the company, buying and selling them in the ordinary course of business, without recourse to the charge holder, until, that is, the charge crystallises. Until crystallisation, the property interest of the chargee simply floats above the assets, hence the name 'floating charge'.

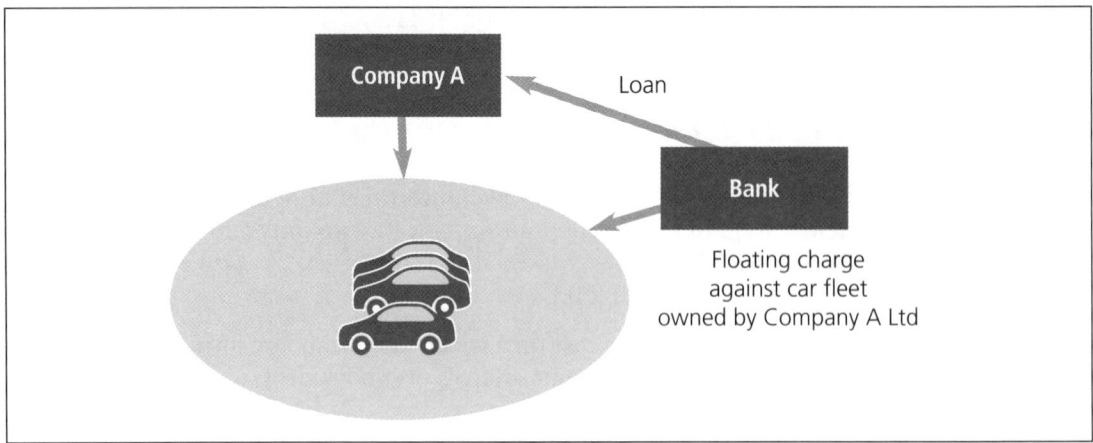

FIGURE 10.3 Floating charge against single class of assets

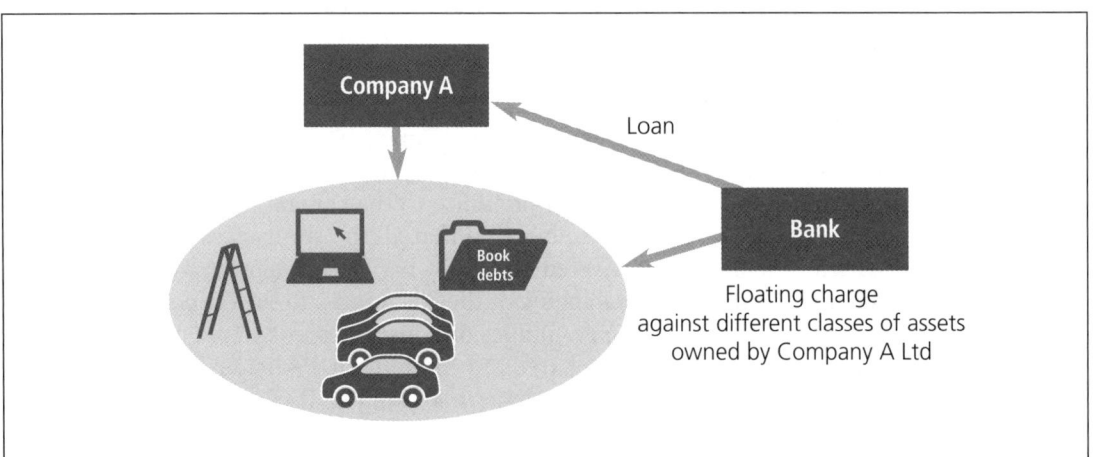

FIGURE 10.4 Floating charge against different classes of assets

Crystallisation of a floating charge

On **crystallisation**, a floating charge becomes a fixed charge. The right of the company to deal with the charged assets in the ordinary course of business ceases and the rights of the charge holder/bank are essentially those stated for a fixed charge holder above, except that if the company is being wound up those rights are subject to the Insolvency Act provisions overriding them.

Also, do not think that because a floating charge becomes a fixed charge at the point of crystallisation it is thereby taken outside the statutory insolvency law provisions applicable to floating charges. Although it is possible to provide in a floating charge that it will crystallise in circumstances that occur before the commencement of a winding up, Parliament has acted to neutralise the effect of such provisions by providing in the Insolvency Act 1986 that for the purposes of a winding up, 'floating charge' is defined as, 'a charge which, *as created*, was a floating charge' (s. 251) (emphasis added). Consequently, provided the charge started its life as a floating charge, it is treated as a floating charge in a winding up.

When does crystallisation occur?

Crystallisation of a floating charge occurs on/when:

- appointment of a receiver;
- the company goes into liquidation;
- the company ceases to carry on business/sells its business;
- a notice of conversion being given (if the charge document gives the charge holder/bank the right to convert the charge from floating to fixed on giving notice); or

- an event occurs which, under the terms of the charge document, causes 'automatic crystallisation'.

The freedom of the parties to stipulate the crystallisation events was supported by Hoffmann J in *Re Brightlife Ltd* [1987] Ch 200 subject to statutory provisions that cannot be contracted out of.

TEST YOUR KNOWLEDGE 10.2

(a) Identify three key reasons why it is important to distinguish a fixed charge from a floating charge.
(b) What is the most essential characteristic of a fixed charge?
(c) Explain the tension that exists between the rights of a floating charge holder and a company's unsecured creditors.
(d) Which three characteristics of a floating charge were identified in *Re Yorkshire Woolcombers Association Ltd?*
(e) Is the description given to a charge in the instrument creating it determinative of the nature of the charge?
(f) Does the holder of a crystallised floating charge have the same rights as the holder of a fixed charge?

2.4 Charges over book debts

Book debts are sums receivable, either immediately or at some date in the future, by a company. 'Receivables' are significant assets of a company and book debts are a very important type of receivable. They can be either sold (assigned) to raise capital for the company (the sale price), or charged as security for a loan made to the company. A charge over book debts is registrable with the Registrar of Companies pursuant to s. 860 of the Companies Act 2006, whether it is a fixed or floating charge, yet there is no definition of book debt in the Companies Act 2006.

Consequently, the definition of book debt has been litigated, for example, in the context of one party seeking to establish that a charge over a debt is not registrable because the debt is not a book debt. A fixed charge on a non-book debt does not fall within the list in s. 860 of charges that need to be registered and, accordingly, is not registrable. In contrast, a floating charge on any property of the company, including book debts, is registrable. In *Independent Automatic Sales Ltd v Knowles & Foster* [1962] 1 WLR 974, Buckley J considered whether or not the debts in question were book debts. If they were, the charges were registrable, and, as they had not been registered, were void against the liquidator.

'*Shipley v Marshall* [(1863) 14 CBNS 566], I think, establishes that, if it can be said of a debt arising in the course of a business and due or growing due to the proprietor of that business that such a debt would or could in the ordinary course of such a business be entered in well-kept books relating to that business, that debt can properly be called a book debt whether it is in fact entered in the books of the business or not.'

CASE EXAMPLE 10.1

Company A Ltd manufactures shoes and sells them to wholesaler customers. The customers to whom it sells shoes in December 2006 are B, C, D, E and F. The customers it sells to in January 2007 are D, E, F, G and H. The terms of supply provide for the price to be paid within 45 days of invoice. The sums owed to Company A Ltd are recorded in its books of account as assets. These assets are called 'book debts' and they are choses in action. When the debtor pays the invoiced sum, the book debt is extinguished and the cash payment is deposited in the bank account of Company A Ltd. If a debtor/customer does not pay the sum due by the due date, the Company can sue the debtor to recover the debt. Company A Ltd's list of book debts is constantly changing.

CASE EXAMPLE 10.1 continued

Book Debts of Company A Ltd	
1 January 2007	1 February 2007
B owes £10,000	D owes £15,000
C owes £5,000	E owes £1,000
D owes £1,000	F owes £1,000
E owes £1,000	G owes £6,000
F owes £1,000	H owes £9,000

In January 2007, wholesaler B pays the invoice for the shoes it has bought from Company A Ltd in December 2006 by sending Company A Ltd a cheque for £10,000. The book debt owed by wholesaler B ceases to exist and does not appear in the list of book debts of Company A Ltd on 1 February 2007. Company A Ltd has, in its place, a cheque. Company A Ltd deposits the cheque in its bank account. Company A Ltd uses the money in the bank account in the ordinary course of running the business, to pay bills, employee wages, taxes, etc.

Fixed charges over book debts

Charges over book debts are usually floating charges. It is theoretically possible to have a fixed charge over book debts but the charge holder/bank must control the property charged.

CASE LAW 10.1

Re Spectrum Plus Ltd [2005] 2 AC 680 (HL)

A standard form charge used widely by banks to take security over book debts, present and future, of a company, was expressed on its face to be a specific charge, meaning a fixed charge. The Inland Revenue challenged the nature of the charge, seeking to have it declared to be a floating charge so that the proceeds of sale of the book debts in the hands of the liquidator had to be used to pay off preferred debts (which, when the facts of the case arose, included unpaid taxes, although this is no longer the case). The charge provided that the company could not deal with uncollected book debts. It also required the proceeds of the book debts (the sums paid by the book debtors to the company extinguishing the book debt) to be paid into the company's current account with the bank. Provided the overdraft limit on that account was not exceeded, the company could draw sums freely out of the bank account and use the sums for its business purposes.

Held: The document created a floating charge not a fixed charge. The account into which the proceeds of the book debts was to be paid was not a 'blocked account', that is, one that the company could not draw on without the consent of the chargee bank and therefore the company was free to deal with the proceeds of the book debts in the ordinary course of its business. This did not give the bank the control over the charged asset that is required to establish a fixed charge.

Following *Re Spectrum Plus Ltd* (2005), the leading case on the defining features of a fixed charge and which involved a charge over book debts, there are three stages to the control needed for a charge over book debts to be a fixed charge:

- The company must not be able to sell or use the book debts as security without the consent of the charge holder/bank (so no using the charged book debts for receivables financing).
- The sum paid to the company by the book debtors must be paid into an account specified by the charge holder/bank.

- The proceeds in the bank account must be useable by the company only with the consent of the chargee/bank (it must be a 'blocked account'): essentially, the chargee/bank must control withdrawals from the bank account into which the book debt receipts are paid, both in theory and in practice.

Note that although not strictly needed for the decision in the case, the court in *Re Spectrum* did not consider that a court should confine its concern to the language of the documentation creating the charge but should also consider how the charge was operated in practice. Lord Scott, referring to the words of Lord Millet in *Agnew v Commissioner of Inland Revenue (Re Brumark Investments Ltd)* [2001] 2 AC 710 (PC) said, 'it was not enough to provide in the debenture for an account to be blocked, if it was not in fact operated as a blocked account'. Where, therefore, the language of the document gives the chargee bank control over the bank account but as a matter of fact that control is not exercised, the charge will not be a fixed charge.

TEST YOUR KNOWLEDGE 10.3

(a) What is a book debt?
(b) Is it possible to have a fixed charge over book debts?
(c) Which characteristic of a fixed charge is the most difficult to comply with when a charge is put in place over book debts?
(d) If an instrument creating a charge states that the company cannot dispose of or otherwise deal with the book debts, is this sufficient to establish the level of control required for a charge to be fixed in nature?

2.5 Registration and avoidance of charges

Charges created by a company may need to be registered with the Registrar of Companies to protect the chargeholder and charges over land may need to be registered additionally with HM Land Registry (charges on registered land) or at the Land Charges Department (charges on unregistered land). Every company is required by the Companies Act 2006 to keep a copy of every instrument creating a charge over the company's property and must make those copies available for inspection (s. 859P). The requirement for a company to maintain a register of charges has been abolished.

Registration with the Registrar of Companies

The rules for registering charges with the Registrar of Companies changed significantly in April 2013 as a result of the Companies Act 2006 (Amendment of Part 25) Regulations 2013, which repealed ss. 860–892 of the Companies Act 2006, replacing them with ss. 859A–R. The new rules apply only to charges created on or after the date on which the new rules entered into effect. The aims of the changes are to streamline procedures and reduce costs, particularly by enabling electronic filing, to clarify which charges need to be registered (basically all) for the charge holder's rights to be protected, to have a single scheme for all UK-registered companies (Scotland included) and to expand the information about the security provided by companies and in the public domain, i.e. available to third parties.

The new rules do not clarify the operation of the doctrine of constructive notice in relation to the registration of charges, and, in particular, in relation to negative charge clauses in registered charges. To do so was characterised as potentially interfering with property rights which is beyond the powers of amendment conferred on the Secretary of State by ss. 894(1) and 1292(1) of the Companies Act 2006. The effect of registration on priority is addressed below, in section 2.6.

The criminal penalty for non-registration no longer exists and, technically, the statutory provisions no longer make registration a legal obligation. The unenforceability of unregistered charges, however, means that registration remains essential to protect the charge holder's property interest. Charges are now registered in one place, not with the three Registrars depending upon the place of incorporation of the company.

Charge is defined in s. 859A(7) to include a mortgage, and all charges may be registered other than those listed in s. 859A(6). Charges on cash deposits connected with leases of land and charges made by members of Lloyds are the only two charges listed as not registrable but provision is made for specified types of charges to be excepted by provisions in other statutes.

The documents to be delivered to register a charge are a statement of particulars and a certified copy of the document creating the charge (which can be delivered as a pdf) (s. 859A). The contents of the statement of particulars (s. 859D) are:

- the registered name and number of the company;
- the date of creation of the charge and (if applicable) the date of acquisition of the property or undertaking concerned;
- where the charge is created or evidenced by an instrument:
  - the name of each of the persons in whose favour the charge has been created;
  - whether the instrument is expressed to contain a floating charge and, if so, whether it is expressed to cover all the property and undertaking of the company;
  - whether any of the terms of the charge prohibit or restrict the company from creating further security that will rank equally with or ahead of the charge;
  - whether (and if so, a short description of) any land, ship, aircraft or intellectual property that is registered or required to be registered in the United Kingdom, is subject to a charge (which is not a floating charge) or fixed security included in the instrument;
  - whether the instrument includes a charge (which is not a floating charge) or fixed security over any tangible or corporeal property, or any intangible or incorporeal property, not described in the foregoing bulletpoint; and
- where the charge is not created or evidenced by an instrument:
  - a statement that there is no instrument creating or evidencing the charge;
  - the names of each of the persons in whose favour the charge has been created;
  - the nature of the charge;
  - a short description of the property or undertaking charged; and
  - the obligations secured by the charge.

A charge may be registered within 21 days beginning with the day after the date of creation of the charge (which is set out clearly for the purposes of registration in s. 859E) or any extended period ordered by the court under s. 859F(3). If a company acquires property subject to a charge, however, no time limit is specified within which that charge may be registered to preserve its enforceability.

On registration of a charge, the Registrar of Companies gives a certificate of registration. A certificate is conclusive evidence that the requirements of the Act as to registration have been complied with (s. 859I(6)), and the decision to issue a certificate cannot be judicially reviewed (*R v Registrar of Companies, ex parte Central Bank of India* [1986] QB 1114).

If a charge is not registered in the time provided the court may extend the time to register the charge. Under the old rules, late registration was only granted subject to the standard proviso, known as the 'Joplin' proviso, that registration was without prejudice to the rights of parties acquired during the period between the date by which the charge should have been registered and the date of its actual registration (*Re Joplin Brewery Co Ltd* [1902] 1 Ch 79). It was also settled practice that a court would not make an order under extending time for registration if the application was made after winding up of the company has commenced, and there is no reason to expect these practices to change.

Failure to register a charge within the initial or extended time period renders the charge void (so far as any security on the company's property or undertaking is conferred by it) against a liquidator, administrator or creditor of the company. Even if a second charge holder knew of the creation of the prior unregistered charge, the prior charge is still void against the second charge holder (*Re Monolithic Building Co* [1915] Ch 643).

The obligation to repay the money secured by the charge continues (i.e. the loan secured by the charge is not void) and, by s. 859H(4), the money secured becomes repayable immediately. Even an unregistered charge is valid and can be enforced against the company when the company is a going concern (though subsequent registered charges will take priority). *Smith (Administrator of Coslett (Contractors) Ltd) v Bridgend County Borough Council* [2001] 1 All ER 292 decided that, in the event of insolvency, an unregistered registrable charge is void against a company. In effect, on a winding up, the creditor becomes an unsecured creditor. Also, s. 874 states that when a charge becomes void for want of registration, the money secured becomes immediately repayable.

When a registered charge is released, property subject to the registered charge has ceased to form part of the company's property, or the debt for which the registered charge was given has been paid, in whole or in part, the company sends the information required by s. 859L to the Registrar of Companies. The Registrar of Companies will enter a statement of satisfaction or release, as the case may be, on the register.

Registration of charges over land

In addition to registration with the Registrar of Companies, a charge over registered land owned by the company must be registered in the Land Registry pursuant to the Land Registration Act 2002 and a charge over unregistered land must be registered with the Land Charges Department pursuant to the Land Charges Act 1972.

TEST YOUR KNOWLEDGE 10.4

(a) Identify four places where a charge created by a company may need to be registered.
(b) What is the time within which charges need to be registered with the Registrar of Companies?
(c) What are the consequences of failure to register a charge with the Registrar of Companies?
(d) What steps should a company take when a registered charge is released?

2.6 Priority of charges

Provided charges have been properly registered with the Registrar of Companies pursuant to s. 859A, the following basic rules apply to determine the priority of charges:

- Fixed charges rank in order of the time at which they are created: the first in time takes priority over all subsequent fixed charges over the same property.
- Fixed charges establish stronger rights than floating charges and a later-in-time fixed charge ranks in priority over an earlier floating charge (*Re Castell & Brown Ltd* [1898] 1 Ch 315).

Except that if the subsequent fixed charge holder had actual knowledge, at the time its charge was entered into, that the pre-existing floating charge expressly prohibited the company from creating a subsequent charge with priority, the pre-existing floating charge will take priority over the subsequent fixed charge (*Siebe Gorman & Co Ltd v Barclays Bank Ltd* [1979] 2 Lloyds Rep 142 which remains good law on this point). Such a clause is known as a 'negative pledge'. A negative pledge principally operates as a contractual right between the company and the first charge holder. The 2013 rules governing registration of charges are deliberately silent about their effect on priorities. An early draft of the regulations specified that registration was constructive notice to subsequent charge holders. This clarification was rejected as it was seen as interfering with property rights which there is no power to do using the powers in the Companies Act 2006 to enact delegated legislation. The effect of the register remains a question of common law. The governing common law principle is that registration is constructive notice to those who should be reasonably expected to search the register. Subject to the potential for a special fact scenario to exist indicating that it was not reasonable for him to search the register, and provided that the fact that registration is not compulsory is not permitted to undermine the constructive notice doctrine, a subsequent charge holder will now have constructive notice of a negative pledge clause. Accordingly, a pre-existing floating charge with a negative pledge clause will normally take priority not only over a subsequent floating charge but also over a subsequent fixed charge.

- Floating charges rank in order of time of creation: the first in time takes priority over all subsequent floating charges over the same property (*Re Benjamin Cope & Sons Ltd* [1914] 1 Ch 800).
- A floating charge over specific assets may rank in priority to an earlier floating charge expressed to be a charge over all the assets and undertaking of the company ('a general floating charge') if power is reserved to the company in the earlier charge to create a later charge having priority (*Re Automatic Bottle Makers Ltd* [1926] Ch 412).

Figures 10.5–10.7 illustrate the operation of these rules.

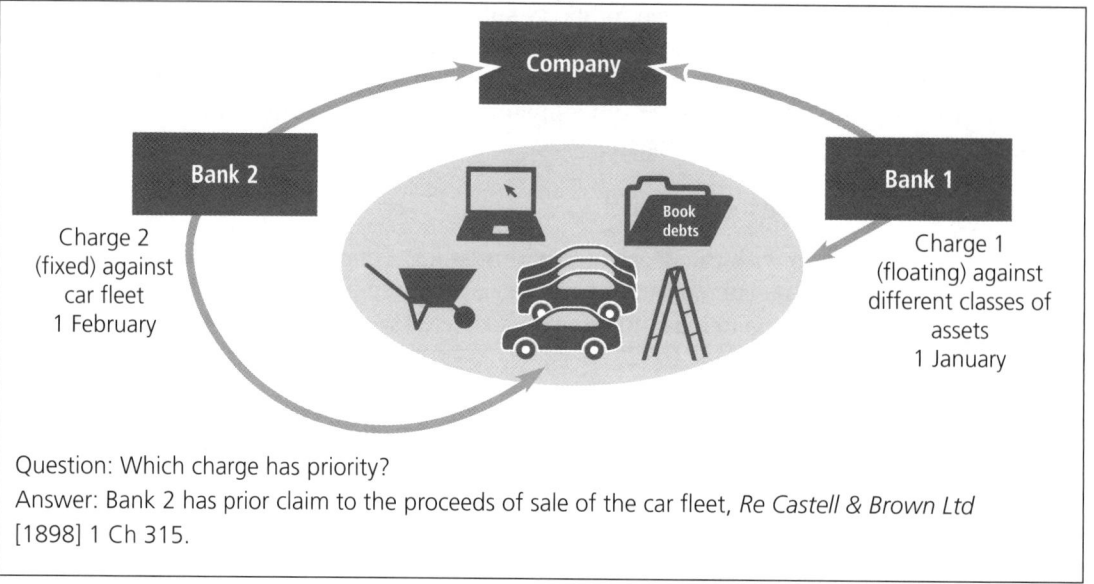

FIGURE 10.5 Priority of charges: fixed and floating charges

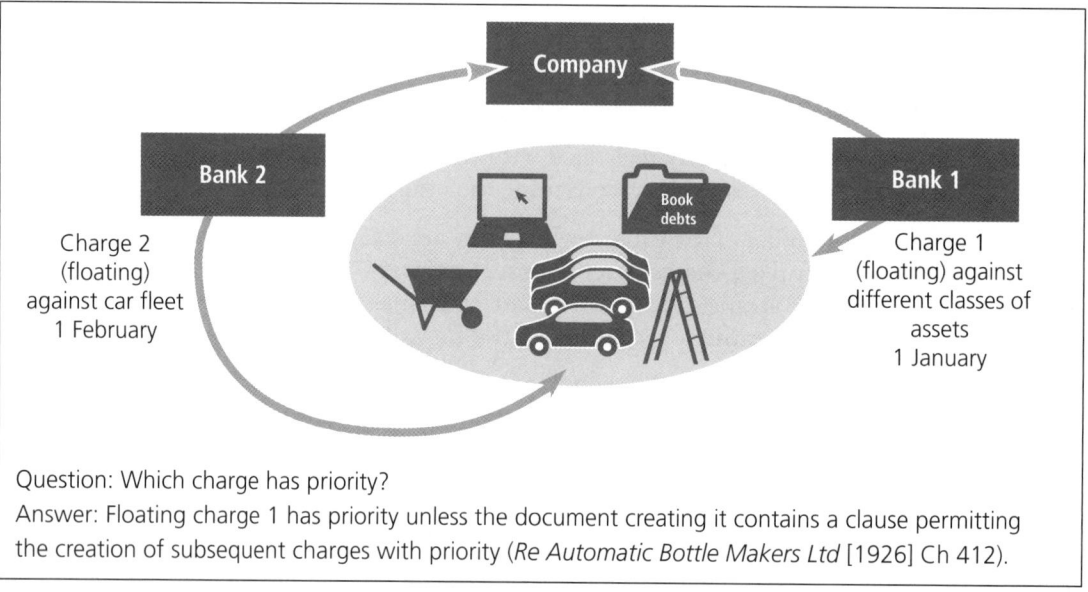

FIGURE 10.6 Priority of charges: two floating charges

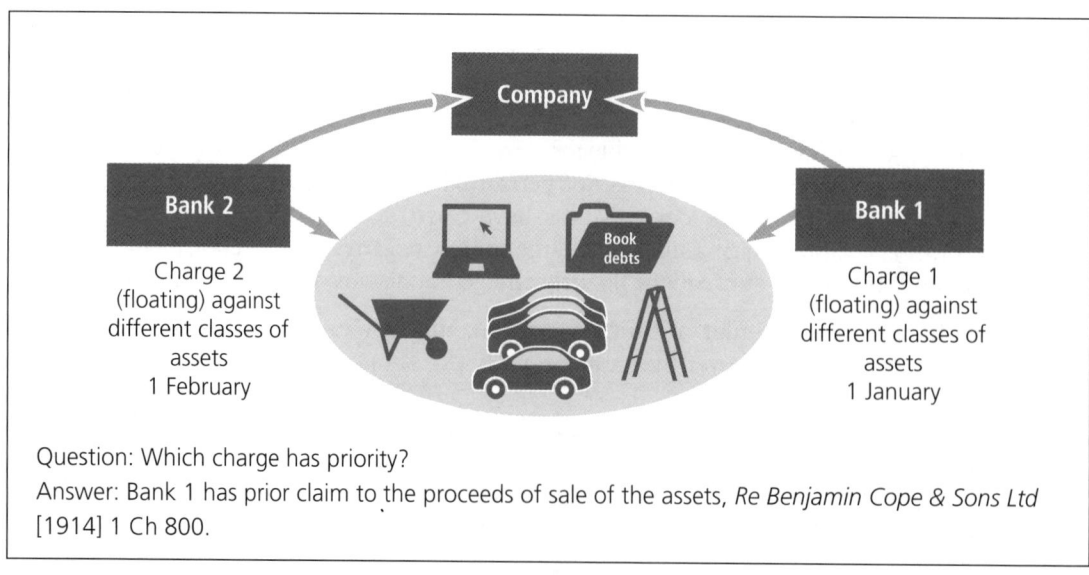

FIGURE 10.7 Priority of charges: two general floating charges

2.7 Fixed and floating charges compared and contrasted

The key differences between a fixed and floating charge are:

1 Whilst the floating charge remains floating (before crystallisation), the company/charger remains free to deal with the charged property in the ordinary course of business.
2 Various statutory rules relating to validity and priority are worded to apply to one form of security (e.g. floating charges) but not the other, including:
   - floating charge property proceeds are available to pay the expenses of winding up, preferential debts and a statutory 'prescribed' part is set aside for unsecured creditors out of them;
   - the liquidator may treat certain floating charges as invalid pursuant to s. 245 of the Insolvency Act 1986.
3 Priority of charges against the same property: the floating nature of the floating charge until it crystallises, results in it being treated differently from a fixed charge in determining priority of charges.

Note that it is common for banks to take both a fixed charge and a floating charge in the same document thereby seeking to combine the priority advantages of the fixed charge with the flexibility of the floating charge. It is instructive to look at the language actually used in such documents. In *Re Spectrum*, for example, the charge was expressed in the following language:

> ' "A specific charge [of] all book debts and other debts ... now and from time to time due or owing to [*Spectrum*]" (para 2(v)) and "A floating security [of] its undertaking and all its property assets and rights whatsoever and wheresoever present and/or future including those for the time being charged by way of specific charge pursuant to the foregoing paragraphs if and to the extent that such charges as aforesaid shall fail as specific charges but without prejudice to any such specific charges as shall continue to be effective" (para 2(vii)).'

TEST YOUR KNOWLEDGE 10.5

(a) When is it necessary to establish the order of priority of charges?
(b) What are the three basic rules governing the priority of properly-registered fixed and floating charges?
(c) What is a negative pledge clause?
(d) Does registration of a charge give a subsequent charge holder constructive notice of a negative pledge clause in the earlier charge?

CHAPTER SUMMARY

- A debenture is a document which either creates a debt or acknowledges it.
- Debentures can be categorised based on a number of characteristics including: individual debentures or debenture stock; secured or unsecured debentures; bearer or registered debentures; permanent or redeemable debentures; and convertible or non-convertible debentures.
- Debenture stock is usually structured as a series of interests under a trust.
- The debenture trustee holds the benefit of the company's covenant and any charge over property on trust for the debenture stockholders.
- Secured creditors have an interest in the company's property in addition to contractual rights.
- On crystallisation, a floating charge becomes a fixed charge although a charge that started its life as a floating charge is treated as a floating charge in a winding up even if it has crystallised (Insolvency Act 1986, s. 251).
- A debt arising in the course of a business that would or could in the ordinary course of business be entered in well-kept books relating to that business is a book debt (*Independent Automatic Sales Ltd v Knowles & Foster* (1962)).

- Charges over book debts are almost always floating charges due to the difficulty of satisfying the requirement of control over the property required to establish a fixed charge (*Re Spectrum* (2005)).
- Charges created by a company need to be registered with the Registrar of Companies to be enforceable (s. 859A), and charges over land may need to be registered at the Land Registry or at the Land Charges Department.
- An unregistered charge which is registrable with the Registrar of Companies is void against the liquidator, administrator and other creditors of the company.
- Priority of charges:
  - Fixed charges rank in order of the time at which they are created.
  - A later-in-time fixed charge ranks in priority over an earlier floating charge, (*Re Castell & Brown Ltd* [1898] 1 Ch 315), unless the fixed charge holder has actual or constructive knowledge of a negative pledge clause.
  - Floating charges rank in order of time of creation, (*Re Benjamin Cope & Sons* Ltd [1914] 1 Ch 800).
  - A floating charge over specific assets may rank in priority to an earlier general floating charge if power is reserved to the company in the earlier charge to create a later charge having priority (*Re Automatic Bottle Makers Ltd* [1926] Ch 412).
- Fixed and floating charges compared:
  - Whilst the floating charge remains floating the company is free to deal with the charged property in the ordinary course of business.
  - Floating charge property proceeds are available to pay the expenses of winding up, preferential debts and a statutory 'prescribed' part is set aside for unsecured creditors out of them.
  - Liquidator may treat certain floating charges as invalid pursuant to s. 245 of the Insolvency Act 1986.
  - Fixed charges ordinarily take priority over floating charges regardless of when created.

PART 2 CASE QUESTIONS

Return to the opening case at the start of this part and re-read it. Think generally about the issues it raises, the law in relation to which has been covered in the chapters in this part, before attempting to answer the following questions.

1. What types of funding could Growing Well Ltd consider putting in place in 2006 and from which sources if it wished to remain a private company?
2. Sketch out the steps the company would have to go through to issue the preference shares to Frederick.
3. What does the fact that the company was able to pay off Frederick's preference shares without his consent tell us about the rights attached to those shares?
4. Discuss the extent to which the security for the £1.25 million loan is likely to be effective.
5. What change would have to be made to the company's registration before it could make an IPO?
6. Outline the stages to be gone through in the IPO.
7. Have any criminal offences been committed by Charles or Frederick? Have any civil offences been committed by Charles or Frederick?
8. What additional restrictions apply to the payment of dividends from the company becoming a public company?

PART THREE

Company management and shareholder remedies

■ LIST OF CHAPTERS

11 Directors, shareholders and the division of powers
12 Directors' duties
13 Minority shareholder protection

■ OVERVIEW

Part 3 covers a wide range of topics. Chapter 11 explains the division of powers between the two key organs of government of a company, the shareholders and the board of directors. Focus is then turned to explore the appointment, removal, disqualification and remuneration of directors. Also included in this chapter are the functions, roles, authority and liability of the company secretary and the auditor.

Chapter 12 explores the general duties owed by a director to the company, dividing the duties into those designed to bring about good corporate governance and those designed to deter directors from acting in their own self-interest or in the interests of other than the company in relation to which they are in a fiduciary relationship. The provisions in the Companies Act 2006 regulating specific types of transactions and arrangements between the company and its directors are also examined.

In exploring minority shareholder protection, chapter 13 distinguishes between wrongs done to the company, in relation to which the correct claimant is the company, and wrongs done by the company to shareholders, the correct claimant in relation to which is the shareholder (the company is the respondent). The statutory derivative action provided for in the Companies Act 2006, s. 260 is covered here. The right of a shareholder to bring a petition complaining that the affairs of the company have been conducted in a manner that is unfairly prejudicial to his interests, or, alternatively, to petition the court for a winding up order on the ground that it is just and equitable to order that the company be wound up are also examined.

■ LEARNING OUTCOMES

After reading part 3 you should be able to:

- Explain the division of power between the board of directors and the general meeting.
- Explain the purpose and extent of directors' duties including to whom directors owe their duties.

- Understand the regulation of directors contracting with their companies.
- Understand and advise on the remedies and reliefs for breach of duty.
- Understand and explain the concept, role and responsibilities of the company secretary.
- Understand and explain the concept, role and liabilities of the company auditor and the audit requirement.
- Apply the rule in *Foss v Harbottle*: the proper claimant principle.
- Understand the need for and process to bring a statutory derivative claim (s. 260).
- Advise on the circumstances in which personal and representative actions by shareholders may be brought and the process for unfairly prejudicial conduct petitions (s. 994).
- Explain the relevance of just and equitable winding up petitions (Insolvency Act 1986, s. 122).

PART 3 CASE STUDY

Blossom plc (Blossom) offers plant maintenance services to corporate clients. Until recently it had four directors all of whom worked full-time for the company: Orlando, Nile, Moira and Larry. It also has a full-time company secretary, Joel. Dramatic growth in the last 18 months has resulted in a restructuring of roles which has caused high levels of executive stress.

Orlando is unhappy with his new role as Head of Marketing. He agreed to take the role only because Joel agreed to add a clause to his service contract guaranteeing him three years in the new role with the right to return to his old role at the end of that time. Joel issued a new service contract to Orlando reflecting these terms.

Nile, the Finance Director, has been experiencing personal financial difficulties since he took up gambling over a year ago to relieve his stress levels. At a meeting with Blossom's bankers six months ago, Brasher Bank (Brasher) suggested to Nile that he ask Blossom for a loan to reduce his personal overdraft with Brasher. At a subsequent board meeting, Moira, Orlando and Larry agreed that Blossom should lend Nile £15,000. After the meeting, Joel called Brasher and told Brasher that Blossom had agreed to lend £15,000 to Nile and that Brasher could transfer £15,000 from Blossom's account to Nile's account, which Brasher did.

Moira found that after assuming her new position as Head of Sales she spent most of her time managing new recruits rather than working with customers. Six months ago she informed Nile, Orlando and Larry that if Blossom did not recruit a training manager immediately, she would be looking for another job. Moira was subsequently offered a job by Customerled plc, a significant client of Blossom, at a salary 50% higher than her salary from Blossom and Customerled plc paid her a £25,000 introductory bonus. On recruiting Moira, Customerled plc wrote to Blossom exercising its right to terminate its agreement for services with Blossom by giving three months' notice. Moira is now happy working for Customerled plc. Her role involves performing the services Customerled plc contracted out to Blossom when Moira worked for Blossom.

Joel has been working long hours and, believing that he deserved some special treatment, he ordered a massage machine in the name of Blossom from Pummel plc for £30,000. He had the massage machine installed in his garage. The invoice for the machine has not yet been paid.

Blossom is not performing well. Orlando has agreed to leave the company with one year's pay and Joel and Nile sign a cheque for that amount.

Blossom's shareholders have discovered the above events and have lost faith in the board of directors. They wish to appoint a new team. Sally, the majority shareholder, owns 55% of the shares. She wishes to 'draw a line', look forward and does not want Blossom to become embroiled in litigation. The minority shareholder, Teresa, believes that Blossom should sue Orlando, Nile, Moira, Larry and Joel.

11

Directors, shareholders and the division of powers

■ **CONTENTS**

1 Shareholders as a governing organ of the company
2 The board of directors as a governing organ of the company
3 Directors
4 The company secretary
5 The auditor

■ **INTRODUCTION**

The key organs of governance of a company are the board of directors and the shareholders. As a governing organ or body of the company, the shareholders are often referred to as 'the shareholders in general meeting'. This description is accurate for public companies because decision-making by public company shareholders must take place by resolutions being passed at a shareholders' meeting (s. 281(2)). However, the terminology is not appropriate for private companies, because there is no requirement for a private company to hold shareholders' meetings and private company shareholders may make decisions without meetings, by written resolution (s. 281(1)).

In this chapter, the shareholders and the board of directors are considered as organs of governance of a company and the division of powers between them is examined. Directors are then subject to scrutiny, including types, appointment and removal, remuneration, retirement, removal and vacation from office and disqualification under the Company Directors Disqualification Act 1986. The law governing the appointment, qualifications and role and responsibilities of the company secretary is then set out, before confirming the current legal position on the right of the company secretary to bind the company to contracts. Finally, the statutory rules governing the audit of company annual reports and accounts contained in Part 16 of the Companies Act 2006 (ss. 475–539) are examined as are the general contract and tort law principles governing auditor liability and the extent to which the general civil law principles are overridden and supplemented by the statutory rules relating to auditor liability.

1 Shareholders as a governing organ of the company

1.1 Introduction

The role of shareholders in the governance of any given company is established by a combination of:

- constitutional rules of the company (the Articles of Association);
- statute law (the Companies Act 2006 and the Insolvency Act 1986); and
- cases recognising the power of the shareholders in certain circumstances.

Shareholders are sometimes referred to as 'residual controllers' of the company. Four main points support this:

- The law requires certain fundamental decisions to be made by the shareholders.
- While the Articles normally entrust management to the board of directors, they also usually reserve a right for shareholders to direct the board by special resolution on any specified matter.

- If the board is unable to act, power will revert to the shareholders.
- Shareholders have the right to remove directors from office.

It is important to distinguish clearly between a shareholder acting as part of the decision-making governance body of the company and a shareholder acting in an individual capacity to enforce his or her personal rights. The rights and obligations of a shareholder acting in his or her personal capacity are dealt with in chapter 5, where we consider the rights of a shareholder to enforce provisions in the Articles, and again in chapter 13. They are not considered further in this chapter.

Shareholders in closely-held companies

The role played by shareholders in a closely-held company is typically very different from the role played by shareholders of a company with dispersed ownership. Closely-held companies are usually 'owner-managed'. The practical difficulty here is that decision-making can be very informal. Very often, the major shareholders are the directors, who are also the executives/managers of the company. The shareholder/director/manager individual is usually focused on running the business of the company, not figuring out in which capacity the law requires him to take particular decisions. He has no practical concern to 'get the legal paperwork right'. Compared to the procedures in place for public companies, the law provides simpler, less formal procedures for decisions to be made by shareholders (essentially no need for annual general meetings and the option to make written resolutions) and boards of directors of private companies.

Shareholders in listed companies

The scenario outlined above is in stark contrast to a large public company with shares traded on a stock market in which the main, indeed virtually sole, interest of shareholders is to see the price of their shares increase and receive adequate dividends on their shares. Consider, for example, individuals who own shares in a banking company, such as Lloyds Banking Group plc. They may be shareholders as a result of having been customers/members of an organisation acquired by Lloyds Banking Bank plc, such as Halifax, when it was a mutual building society. When the building society became a bank, customers were offered the choice of cash or shares in the new registered company and many opted to become shareholders.

Invitations to shareholder meetings, received through the post, are often regarded by shareholders of dispersed ownership companies as akin to junk mail. Little or no interest is shown in filling out the proxy form enclosed with the invitation empowering another to exercise their vote at the meeting on the proposed resolutions also included with the invitation to the meeting. Consequently, attendance at shareholder meetings is very poor. In all, the governance of the company is wholly entrusted by such shareholders to the board of directors.

Large proportions of the shares of listed companies are owned by 'institutional shareholders', such as banks and insurance companies, who manage pools of funds on behalf of investors, or are held as assets within pension plans. Company pension funds are owned by trustees on behalf of the members of the pension plan and the trustees appoint investment advisers and investment managers who manage the portfolio of shares owned by the fund. Invitations to meetings go to the investment managers. Institutional investors have faced severe criticism over the years for their failure to take their role as shareholders seriously and for failing to exert adequate influence over boards of directors of the companies in which they invest. Laws and the Stewardship Code have recently been put in place in an attempt to improve shareholder engagement in the governance of listed companies.

 TEST YOUR KNOWLEDGE 11.1

(a) Identify three places to look for the rules establishing the role of shareholders in the governance of a company.

(b) Identify four points supporting the assertion that the shareholders are the 'residual controllers' of registered companies.

(c) Why are shareholders less likely to be engaged in listed companies than in closely-held companies?

1.2 Division of powers in the Articles

Article 3 of both the Model Articles for Private Companies Limited by Shares and those for Public Companies establishes the board of directors as the principal organ of management of the company:

> 'Subject to the articles, the directors are responsible for the management of the company's business, for which purpose they may exercise all the powers of the company.'

In addition to being expressly subject to the company's other Articles, this power is also subject to the provisions of the Companies Act 2006.

Article 4 of both the Model Articles for Private Companies Limited by Shares and for Public Companies establishes a reserve power for the shareholders:

> 'The shareholders may, by special resolution, direct the directors to take, or refrain from taking, specified action.'

Attempts by shareholders to usurp board powers by passing ordinary resolutions or acting in any other way inconsistently with the Articles will not succeed.

CASE LAW 11.1

Automatic Self Cleansing v Cuninghame [1906] 2 Ch 34

Powers of general management were vested in the board subject to directions from the shareholders by extraordinary resolution. The shareholders passed an ordinary resolution directing the board to sell the company's business. The directors objected to the sale.

Held: the board of directors could lawfully refuse to comply as direction by ordinary resolution was insufficient. On a true construction of the Articles the shareholders were only competent to intervene by extraordinary general meeting.

[Note that extraordinary resolutions are no longer provided for in the Companies Act 2006. They required 75 per cent support and had to be passed at an extraordinary general meeting.]

CASE LAW 11.2

John Shaw & Sons (Salford) Ltd v Shaw [1935] 2 KB 113 (CA)

Articles vested general powers of management in 'permanent directors'. The permanent directors resolved to institute legal proceedings against three 'ordinary directors' who were shareholders. The shareholders passed a resolution to discontinue the company's legal proceedings.

Held: The shareholders had no power to overrule the decision of the permanent directors. The options available to the shareholder were to change the Articles, or to remove the board of directors.

The decision whether or not a company should commence legal action in given circumstances is part of the general management of the company so will ordinarily be vested in the board of directors pursuant to Article 3. The applicability of the basic rule against usurpation by shareholders to the decision to litigate or not was confirmed in *Breckland Group Holdings Ltd v London & Suffolk Properties Ltd* [1989] BCLC 100. Harman J restrained the majority shareholder from taking any further action in litigation commenced by the shareholder without authority of the board until a board meeting could be held at which it could be resolved whether to continue or discontinue the legal action.

1.3 Statutory powers of shareholders

The statutory powers given to shareholders are mainly in the Companies Act 2006 but also arise from the Insolvency Act 1986.

Powers given to shareholders by the Companies Act 2006

The main powers given to shareholders by the Companies Act 2006 are:

- to amend the company's constitution (s. 21(1));
- to resolve to reregister the company, e.g. from private to public, or vice versa (ss. 90 and 97);
- to remove directors by ordinary resolution (s. 168);
- to approve directors' service contracts if employment is guaranteed for more than two years (s. 188(2));
- to approve substantial property transactions (s. 190(1)) and loans (s. 197) between the company and a director;
- to approve compensation to a director for loss of office (s. 217);
- to ratify directors' breaches of duty (s. 239);
- to authorise political donations in excess of £5,000 (s. 366);
- to approve appointment of the company auditor (s. 489(4));
- to authorise the board to allot shares (s. 551) (board power to allot is automatic for a private company with only one class of shares, s. 550);
- to disapply pre-emption rights (ss. 569–571);
- to reduce share capital (s. 641(1));
- to authorise the company to purchase its own shares (ss. 694, 701);
- to approve a payment out of capital for redemption or other acquisition of a company's own shares (s. 716).

Note that while the shareholders have a statutory power to remove directors (s. 168), shareholders have no *statutory* power to appoint directors (appointment is governed by the Articles of Association).

Power given to shareholders by the Insolvency Act 2006

The main power given to shareholders by the Insolvency Act 1986 is to decide, by special resolution, to wind up the company voluntarily (s. 84(1)).

1.4 Default powers of shareholders

Management power will revert to the shareholders in circumstances where the board is unable to act.

 **CASE LAW 11.3**

Barron v Potter [1914] 1 Ch 895

A company had two directors and the Articles gave directors power to appoint additional directors. One director would not attend any board meeting at which the other was present.

Held: A general resolution appointing an additional director was valid. *Per* Warrington J: 'If directors having certain powers are unable or unwilling to exercise them ... there must be some power in the company to do itself that which under other circumstances would be otherwise done ... in my opinion the company in general meeting has power to make the appointment.'

TEST YOUR KNOWLEDGE 11.2

(a) Which Model/default Articles allocate powers to the board of directors and the shareholders and what do those Articles state?
(b) Who may appoint directors and where is the power to appoint to be found?
(c) Where does management power reside in a company the board of directors of which is unable to act and which case establishes this?

2 The board of directors as a governing body of the company

We now turn to look at the board of directors as an organ of governance of the company and the powers vested in the directors *collectively*.

2.1 Powers of the board

As stated above, Article 3 of both the Model Articles for Private Companies Limited by Shares and those for public companies establishes the board of directors as the principal organ of management of the company:

> 'Subject to the articles, the directors are responsible for the management of the company's business, for which purpose they may exercise all the powers of the company.'

When considering these powers and the exercise of them, it is essential to view the board of directors as a body distinct from the individual directors making it up. It is the board *collectively* that is entrusted by the Articles with the responsibility to manage the company and it is the board collectively, as an organ of government of the company, that is empowered to exercise all the powers of the company for this purpose. Sir George Mellish LJ made this point clearly in *Re Marseilles Extension Railway Company, ex parte Credit Foncier and Mobilier of England* (1871) LR 7 Ch App 161 (CA) (cited in Mayson, French and Ryan, 2012–13).

> 'It appears to me, that a director is simply a person appointed to act as one of a board, with power to bind the company when acting as a board, but having otherwise no power to bind them.'

The collective nature of the responsibility of the board is also emphasised in the first principle of the UK Corporate Governance Code (2012):

> 'Every company should be headed by an effective board, which is *collectively* responsible for the long-term success of the company.' (emphasis added)

Although the Model Articles do not contain any particular limitation, it is not uncommon for the Articles to limit the general allocation of management and powers to the board of directors by, typically, requiring shareholder approval before certain powers of the company may be exercised. An example would be an article providing that shareholder approval in advance is required before £1 million or more can be borrowed by the company.

It is always essential to check a company's Articles to be aware of any such limitation. If the power is exercised without first obtaining shareholder approval, the board and every director involved in the decision is acting outside his authority. Section 40 of the Companies Act 2006 operates in such a case in favour of a person dealing with the company in good faith. The powers of the board of directors are deemed, in that person's favour, to be free of any such limitation. The consequences of the board and individual directors acting outside their authority and the operation and effect of s. 40 are considered in chapter 6 where we look at binding the company.

2.2 Delegation and authorisation

In the course of management of a company, company powers are not only exercised by the board of directors. Delegation of power is essential if a company is to be run efficiently. Article 5 of both the Model Articles for Private Companies Limited by Shares and those for public companies empowers the board of directors to delegate any power conferred on it by the Articles.

> '5 (1) Subject to the Articles, the directors may delegate any of the powers which are conferred on them under the Articles—
> (a) to such person or committee;
> (b) by such means (including by power of attorney);
> (c) to such an extent;
> (d) in relation to such matters or territories; and
> (e) on such terms and conditions; as they think fit.
> (2) If the directors so specify, any such delegation may authorise further delegation of the directors' powers by any person to whom they are delegated.
> (3) The directors may revoke any delegation in whole or part, or alter its terms and conditions.'

The board's power to delegate is broad. From the perspective of knowing who is authorised to exercise which power, it would be ideal if the board passed resolutions approving lists of powers delegated to named individuals. Ideals, however, are all too often unrealistic and in most companies the practice of documenting delegation is very poor. Note that subsection (2) of Model Article 5 allows a cascade of delegation by enabling any person to whom the board has delegated powers in turn to delegate those powers.

All too often it is unclear whether or not an individual director, executive or employee has the authority to exercise a particular power. The governing area of law here is agency law. A person to whom the board delegates power to change the legal position of the company is an **agent** of the company. Evidence of express actual agency is often missing, so it is necessary to examine the fact of the situation to determine whether or not the individual has implied actual authority or even ostensible (also known as apparent) authority to exercise the power in question. The operation of agency principles in the company context is examined in chapter 6. Board decision-making (i.e. how the board of directors exercises the powers conferred on it) is examined in part 4.

TEST YOUR KNOWLEDGE 11.3

(a) Does Model Article 3 vest company powers in individual directors?
(b) Which principle of the UK Corporate Governance Code (June 2010) emphasises the collective nature of board membership and what does it say?
(c) Where is the power of the board of directors to delegate company powers typically found and to whom is the board permitted to delegate?

3 Directors

3.1 Definition and types of directors

Most **directors** are appointed in accordance with the Articles of the company, their details are recorded by the company in the register of directors (s. 162) and their appointment is notified to the Registrar of Companies (s. 167). There is no doubt as to the status of such individuals; they are directors for all legal purposes.

Occasionally, however, individuals behave openly like directors without the formalities of appointment having taken place (*de facto* directors). A different but related situation is where an individual does not patently behave as a director but gives directions and instructions which the actual directors follow (a shadow director). In both situations the question often arises of the extent of application of the law applicable to formally appointed directors. In particular, are *de facto* and/or shadow directors for the purposes of owing directors' duties to the company?

In the following paragraphs we examine different types of directors. The legal starting point is s. 250(1) of the Companies Act 2006.

> 'In the Companies Acts 'director' includes any person occupying the position of director, by whatever name called'.

De jure directors

Directors appointed in accordance with the Articles of association are **de jure directors**.

De facto directors

Directors who have not been legally appointed, including where a purported appointment is irregular, but nevertheless openly assume the position of director, despite a lack of authority and right to act, are **de facto directors**. The concept of *de facto* director has been recently considered by the Supreme Court in *Revenue and Customs Commissioners v Holland* [2010] UKSC 51 (SC), a case involving an alleged breach of trust by an allegedly *de facto* director. The majority of the court confirmed that a person is only a *de facto* director if he or she has assumed responsibility, that is, has 'opted in' to the role of director of a company. Lord Collins stated, 'for almost 150 years *de facto* directors in English law were persons who had been appointed as directors, but whose appointment was defective, or had come to an end, but who acted or continued to act as directors.'

De facto directors are capable of coming within the definition of director in s. 250. In its 1998 Consultation Paper on company directors (No. 153), the Law Commission explained the approach to be taken to determining whether or not a particular statutory provision extends beyond *de jure* directors.

> 'The meaning of "director" varies according to the context in which it is to be found, and it is a matter of construction whether a particular section covers a person who is a *de facto* director.'

The courts must examine the statute and determine, as a matter of statutory interpretation, the intention of the legislature and the meaning and effect of the particular provision of the Act in question.

Shadow directors

The 2006 Act states that, '... **shadow director**, in relation to a company, means a person in accordance with whose directions or instructions the directors of the company are accustomed to act' (s. 251(1)). Note, however, that if the directors of a company act on the advice of another individual given in a professional capacity, this will not be enough to render that individual a shadow director.

Shadow directors are not prohibited by law and no penalty attaches to occupying the status of shadow director. They are expressly referred to in a number of provisions of the Companies Act 2006, such as in s. 170(5) which provides that the general duties of directors apply to shadow directors, 'where, and to the extent that, the corresponding common law rules or equitable principles so apply'. Where the Act does not expressly refer to shadow directors, the courts will need to ascertain the meaning and effect of the statutory provision to determine whether or not it extends to shadow directors.

Executive and non-executive directors

'Executive director' is not a legally defined term but is used to refer to a director who usually has extensive powers delegated to him because of the role he performs in the company and who almost certainly has a service contract with the company. His service contract will be separate from his appointment as a director.

Non-executive directors (NEDs) are essentially directors who do not have an employment contract and have no executive management responsibilities within the company. Most large companies have both types of directors on their boards and both have overall and equal responsibility for the leadership of the company. In the words of the Law Commission, speaking in the context of core company law:

> 'Non-executive directors are subject to the same legal framework as their executive counterparts. Accordingly, their position can be somewhat invidious in many cases where they are expected to act without the executives' day to day decision making power and detailed knowledge of the business. The duty of care owed by non-executive directors would also appear to be the same as that expected of executive directors. However the non-executive is likely to have to do less than an executive director to discharge his duty.' (Consultation Paper No. 153)

The UK Corporate Governance Code (June 2012) draws a distinction between executive directors and non-executive directors (NEDs), and places important reliance on NEDs. The role of NEDs is set out in paragraph A.4 and following paragraphs of the Code.

Paragraph A.4 of the Code states:

'Main Principle
As part of their role as members of a unitary board, non-executive directors should constructively challenge and help develop proposals on strategy.

Supporting Principles
Non-executive directors should scrutinise the performance of management in meeting agreed goals and objectives and monitor the reporting of performance. They should satisfy themselves on the integrity of financial information and that financial controls and systems of risk management are robust and defensible. They are responsible for determining appropriate levels of remuneration of executive directors and have a prime role in appointing and, where necessary, removing executive directors, and in succession planning.

Code Provisions
A.4.1. The board should appoint one of the independent non-executive directors to be the senior independent director to provide a sounding board for the chairman and to serve as an intermediary for the other directors when necessary. The senior independent director should be available to shareholders if they have concerns which contact through the normal channels of chairman, chief executive or other executive directors has failed to resolve or for which such contact is inappropriate.
A.4.2. The chairman should hold meetings with the non-executive directors without the executives present. Led by the senior independent director, the non-executive directors should meet without the chairman present at least annually to appraise the chairman's performance and on such other occasions as are deemed appropriate.
A.4.3. Where directors have concerns which cannot be resolved about the running of the company or a proposed action, they should ensure that their concerns are recorded in the board minutes. On resignation, a non-executive director should provide a written statement to the chairman, for circulation to the board, if they have any such concerns.'

The UK Corporate Governance Code (June 2012) further distinguishes between NEDs and independent NEDs.

> 'The board should include an appropriate combination of executive and non-executive directors (and, in particular, independent non-executive directors) such that no individual or small group of individuals can dominate the board's decision taking.'

The code provisions state that, except for smaller companies, at least 50 per cent of the board should be independent NEDs (B.1.2). Independence is a question of whether the director is independent in character and judgement, based on whether there are relationships or circumstances which are likely to affect, or could appear to affect, the director's judgement (see UK Corporate Governance Code (June 2012) Provision B.1.1).

Nominee directors

Nominee director is not a legal term but is usually used to describe a director who, in practice, is expected to act in accordance with some understanding or arrangement which creates an obligation or mutual expectation of loyalty to someone other than the company as a whole. A nominee director must not, however, put the interests of this principal above those of the company (*Scottish Co-operative Wholesale Society v Meyer* [1959] AC 324).

Managing director

Table A made specific reference to appointing a member of the board to be a managing director. The Model Articles do not mention managing director. The term used to be legally important because of cases indicating the breadth of authority an individual given the title would be regarded by the courts as having.

TEST YOUR KNOWLEDGE 11.4

(a) How do you establish who the directors of a company are at any point in time?
(b) Distinguish between a *de facto* director and a shadow director.
(c) What is the approach taken by a court to determine whether or not a particular statutory provision is applicable to a *de facto* or shadow director?
(d) Compare and contrast executive and non-executive directors.

3.2 Appointment and numbers

The Companies Act 2006 is silent on how directors are to be appointed (except for providing that special notice must be given of any intention to appoint, at the removal meeting, a director in place of a director to be removed pursuant to s. 168). The Act requires the names and details of each new director, with his signed consent to act as a director, to be notified to the Registrar (s. 167), who must keep a register, and the company must also maintain a register of directors (s. 162).

Both registers are open to public inspection, but under the 2006 Act even though a director's residential address must be disclosed to both the Registrar and the company, it is protected from public inspection (ss. 240–242). This is achieved by a director providing both his residential address and a service address (which will often be the company's registered address) to the company and the registrar. The registers that the public can inspect contain only the service address. Before the 2006 Act a director could only protect his residential address if he could demonstrate that he was at serious risk of violence or intimidation.

Rules regarding appointment of directors are normally set out in the Articles and both the Model Articles for Private Companies Limited by Shares (art. 17) and those for public companies (art. 20) provide for directors to be appointed either by ordinary resolution or by a decision of the directors. Where the number of appointed directors is less than a quorum to hold a directors' meeting, the Model Articles provide that the appointed director or directors may appoint sufficient number of directors to make up a quorum (art. 11 for both private and public companies). The Model Articles for Public Companies provide for a director appointed by the directors to retire at the next AGM, the practice being for him to be reappointed by the shareholders, and for all directors to retire every three years, although they may be, and regularly are, reappointed (art. 21).

If the Articles do not expressly deal with appointment, the default Articles will apply unless excluded (the relevant Table A for companies registered under pre-2006 statutes, the Model Articles for Private Companies Limited by Shares or Public Companies, as the case may be, for companies registered under the 2006 Act). Furthermore, the shareholders have inherent power to appoint directors by general resolution (*Link Agricultural Property Ltd v Shanahan* (1998) 28 ACSR 498). This would be important in the unusual circumstance of Articles not dealing with appointment and exclusion of the default Articles. Where Articles deal with appointment but do not mention the rights of shareholders, it is a question of construction of the particular language of the Articles to determine whether or not this inherent power has been excluded.

Number of directors

A private company must have at least one director and a public company must have a minimum of two (s. 154) but no statutory maximum number of directors is set for either private or public companies. There are no provisions governing the numbers of directors in the Model Articles for Private Companies Limited by Shares or those for public companies. Companies with Premium Listings on the Main Market of the London Stock Exchange are subject to the UK Corporate Governance Code which states, as part of the B.1. supporting principle:

> 'The board should be of sufficient size that the requirements of the business can be met and that changes to the board's composition and that of its committees can be managed without undue disruption, and should not be so large as to be unwieldy.'

Who can be a director?

A director need not be an individual. A company, for example, may be a director of another company. The Act does, however, require every company to have at least one director who is a natural person (s. 155). Consequently, if a company is a sole director company, that director must be an individual. The main categories of persons not permitted to act as a director are:

- A person who has not attained the age of 16 (s. 157). Directors who were not yet 16 when this provision came into effect on 1 October 2008, ceased to be directors from that date.
- A bankrupt person (unless he secures permission of the court) (Company Directors Disqualification Act 1986 (CDDA), s. 11).
- Persons disqualified by the court under the CDDA or subject to an undertaking in lieu.

In addition to statutory disqualifications, the Articles may extend the list of persons disqualified from being a director or may impose conditions on those who are directors. Historically, directors were typically required to own a specified number of shares in the company, but this is no longer a common requirement. In practice, directors of private companies are often major shareholders, if not the sole shareholder, and in large companies directors often own shares (and/or share options) acquired as part of their remuneration or incentive packages.

3.3 Removal and retirement of directors

Statutory provisions

Unlike appointment of directors, in relation to which it confines itself largely to disclosure obligations, the Companies Act 2006 contains a very important provision entitling shareholders to remove one, several or all directors (s. 168(1)).

> 'A company may by ordinary resolution at a meeting remove a director before the expiration of his period of office, notwithstanding anything in any agreement between it and him.'

A meeting is required for the statutory power of removal to be exercised and this is the case even for private companies: the written resolution procedure cannot be used to remove a director pursuant to s. 168. Section 168(2) states that special notice must be given of a resolution to remove a director. This means that the company must receive notice that the removal resolution is to be moved, from the shareholder proposing the resolution, at least 28 days before the meeting to consider it is held.

On receipt of notice of an intended resolution to remove a director, the company must send a copy to the director concerned. The director may require the company to circulate written representations to the shareholders and is also entitled to address the meeting at which the resolution is to be considered, s. 169.

The shares held by a director may carry additional voting rights when his removal is being sought. It may therefore be possible for the director to use such additional voting rights to defeat the wishes of controlling shareholders (*Bushell v Faith* [1970] AC 1099). There is no provision for weighted voting rights in the model Articles and they are prohibited for listed companies by the Listing Rules made pursuant to the FSMA.

The final point to note is that s. 168(5) states that removal under s. 168(1) does not prejudice any right the director may have to compensation for early termination of a service contract.

Articles

The Articles of a company usually state grounds for automatic retirement of directors and art. 18 of the Model Articles for Private Companies Limited by Shares and Article 22 of those for public companies do just that, essentially providing for a director to cease to hold office if he:

- ceases to be a director by virtue of any provision of the Companies Act 2006 or is prohibited from being a director by law;
- is bankrupted or makes a composition with his creditors;
- is physically or mentally incapable of acting as a director;
- has notified the company that he is resigning or retiring from office.

Article 21 of the Model Articles for Public Companies further provides for:

- a director appointed by the directors to retire at the next AGM, the practice being for him to be reappointed by the shareholders at that AGM; and
- all directors to retire every three years ('retirement by rotation'), although directors may be, and regularly are, reappointed.

UK Corporate Governance Code (June 2012)

Under main principle B.7 of The UK Corporate Governance Code (June 2012), 'All directors should be submitted for re-election at regular intervals, subject to continued satisfactory performance.' Code provision B.7.1 states:

'All directors of FTSE 350 companies should be subject to annual election by shareholders. All other directors should be subject to election by shareholders at the first annual general meeting after their appointment, and to re-election thereafter at intervals of no more than three years. Non-executive directors who have served longer than nine years should be subject to annual re-election.'

TEST YOUR KNOWLEDGE 11.5

(a) Where are the rules governing appointment of directors to be found?
(b) What is the minimum number of directors that a registered company must have?
(c) Identify the three main categories of persons who are prohibited from being directors of a registered company.

3.4 Director disqualification orders and undertakings

Disqualification has become an important means of enforcing directors' duties. Director disqualification is now a key source of much of the modern law of directors' duties.

Under the CDDA, subject to the power to accept undertakings in lieu (see below), the court may (and in proceedings under ss. 6 and 9A must) make an order in the terms of s. 1 disqualifying the defendant from acting in various capacities including that of director in the following defined circumstances:

- Where a person is convicted of an indictable offence in connection with the promotion, formation, management, liquidation or striking off of a company, or with the receivership or management of a company's property (s. 2).
- Where a person has been persistently in default in relation to provisions of companies legislation requiring returns or accounts to be filed with the registrar of companies (ss. 3 and 5).
- Where it appears that a person has been guilty of an offence of fraudulent trading (Companies Act, s. 993) or any other fraud in relation to the company (s. 4).
- Where he is or has been a director of a company which has become insolvent and his conduct as a director of that company (either taken alone or taken together with his conduct as a director of any other company or companies) makes him unfit to be concerned in the management of a company (s. 6).

- Where he is or has been a director of a company and his conduct (as revealed in the course of the exercise of certain specified powers of investigation) makes him unfit to be concerned in the management of a company (s. 8).
- Where he is a director of a company that has committed a breach of competition law and his conduct as a director of that company makes him unfit to be concerned in the management of a company (s. 9A)
- Where a declaration of liability is made against a person or director under the fraudulent (s. 213) or wrongful (s. 214) trading provisions of the Insolvency Act 1986 (s. 10).

A disqualification order is an order that for the period specified in the order the person shall not be a director of a company, act as a receiver of a company's property or in any way, whether directly or indirectly, be concerned or take part in the promotion, formation or management of a company unless (in each case) he has the leave of the court (CDDA, s. 1(1)). A disqualified person could not, for example, be a company secretary.

The period of disqualification can be anything up to 15 years depending on the seriousness of the misconduct. In the case of s. 6, if the director's conduct is found to make him unfit, the court must disqualify him for at least two years. The majority of disqualification orders are made on the application of the Secretary of State under ss. 6 and 8. Under both provisions, the court is required by s. 9 to have regard to the matters listed in Schedule 1 of the Act in determining the question of unfitness.

The option to accept disqualification undertakings in lieu of a disqualification order was introduced in 2000 (see CDDA, ss. 1A, 7(2A), 8(2A), 8A and 9B). Essentially, the Secretary of State can accept an undertaking if it appears to him that it is expedient in the public interest that he should do so instead of applying or proceeding with an application to court for a disqualification order. The option to accept undertakings is limited to where disqualification is being considered under s. 6 (insolvency and unfit director), s. 8 (following a company investigation) and s. 9A (breach of competition law).

It is a criminal offence to act in contravention of a disqualification order or undertaking in lieu (s.13). The punishment is up to two years imprisonment and an unlimited fine.

TEST YOUR KNOWLEDGE 11.6

(a) Identify seven circumstances in which a disqualification order may be sought.
(b) In which circumstances *must* (rather than may) a court make a disqualification order?
(c) What is the effect of a disqualification order?
(d) When is the Secretary of State entitled to accept a disqualification undertaking in lieu of seeking a disqualification order?

3.5 Remuneration of directors

Directors' terms of service and remuneration have attracted a great deal of attention in recent years. It is in relation to remuneration in particular that boards of directors may be most keenly tempted to behave not in the best interests of the company, but rather in their own best interests. The importance of the topic is underlined by the fact that one of the five sections of the main principles of the UK Corporate Governance Code (June 2012), Section D, is dedicated to directors' remuneration (see final section below).

The law set out in this section (3.5) applied as at February 2013. Reform of the law relating to director remuneration was under consideration as this text was being finalised. The reforms are relevant to quoted companies (as defined in s. 385).

The Enterprise and Regulatory Reform Bill 2012 (as drafted immediately prior to the report stage in the House of Lords), amends various sections of the Companies Act 2006 and adds new sections, including the following:

- A new section 439A will contain detailed rules providing for the members of quoted companies to approve the company's directors' remuneration policy.

- Sections 226A–226F, will state that a quoted company may not make a remuneration payment or a payment for loss of office to a director (past, present or future) unless the payment is consistent with the approved directors' remuneration policy, or is approved by resolution of the members.

Any payment in contravention will have 'no effect', will be held by the recipient on trust, and any director who authorised the payment will be jointly and severally liable to indemnify the company. The Bill also includes amendments to the powers of the Secretary of State to make regulations governing the contents of directors' remuneration reports (s.421) and provides for information (the remuneration policy and payments to directors who leave the company) to appear on the company's website (s. 430). New draft regulations containing detailed requirements as to the information about remuneration to be disclosed by companies in their remuneration reports were due to be published in Spring 2013.

Directors as directors, employees and independent contractors

It is important to realise that a director who works for a company beyond attending and preparing for meetings of the board of directors and committees of the board will have two relationships with the company. He will be:

1. a director, which is an 'office', governed by trust principles as developed in the corporate environment; and
2. either:
   - an employee, which is a contractual relationship supplemented by employment law as developed in the corporate environment; or
   - an independent contractor (if the non-board-related services are part-time or occasional and do not render him an employee), which is also a contractual relationship.

Directors are not employees of the company simply because they have been appointed as a director. Family-owned companies often appoint the spouse and/or grown-up children, or other relatives of the person who runs the business, to be directors and those individuals do not play any role in the company apart from being a director (a role to which they often pay little attention). Clearly, they are not employees of the company. Non-executive directors of large companies are also not employees of the company. They are paid directors' fees and are reimbursed expenses incurred in the performance of the role of director.

On the other hand, a person who works full-time running the family-owned company, or an executive director of a large company, is an employee of the company. A large company will negotiate and enter into a service contract with each of its executives, executive directors included. Due to the potential for self-interested action by board members, directors' service contracts and remuneration are subject to laws and regulations designed to inhibit excess. Small companies often do not formalise employee relationships with its directors, by the company and the director/employees signing written service contracts.

A legal grey area exists where directors perform occasional or part-time services for a company beyond those strictly required of a director. The terms on which the services are rendered should be agreed and clearly documented and this is likely to establish the director as an independent contractor with the company, rather than an employee. If the services are such as to bring the director within the definition of employee, however, he will be an employee. If terms have not been clearly agreed, to be entitled to payment for services the director will need to establish that the services performed were not merely performance of the role of director.

Payment for performing the role of director

Without more, directors are not entitled to be paid for their services to the company as directors because the office of director was historically aligned in law with that of a trustee, who is not entitled to payment. If either the Articles permit payment or the shareholders approve payment, the company can pay its directors and the sums paid are sometime called directors' fees but are also called remuneration. It is standard practice for Articles to authorise the payment of directors' fees, and the Model Articles for Private Companies Limited by Shares (art. 19(2)) and those for public companies (art. 23) provide that directors are entitled to such remuneration as the directors determine for their services to the company as directors.

Payment on termination of office

Payments by way of compensation for loss of office as a director, or loss of any other office or employment held by a director, must not be made unless the payment does not exceed £200 (s. 221), or it has been approved by ordinary resolution of the shareholders (s. 217). Note that this requirement does not apply to payments made pursuant to a legal obligation or by way of damages for breach of a legal obligation or settlement of any claim related to a legal obligation (s. 220). This takes payment in lieu of notice under a service contract and other payments provided for under a service or other contract out of the s. 217 prohibition.

Payment for non-director services provided as an independent contractor

The trustee-like nature of the role of director also precludes the company from paying remuneration for services beyond services as a director unless payment is authorised by the Articles or the shareholders. Again, the Model Articles for Private Companies Limited by Shares (art. 19) and those for public companies (art. 23) provide that in addition to payment for services as a director, directors are entitled to such remuneration as the directors determine for 'any other service which they undertake for the company'.

Where a director has performed additional services but the procedure by which the Articles require payment to be determined has not been gone through (under the Model Articles that is determination by the directors), the House of Lords decision in *Guinness plc v Saunders* [1990] 2 AC 663 (HL), appears to preclude a successful **quantum meruit** claim by a director.

CASE LAW 11.4

***Guinness plc v Saunders* [1990] 2 AC 663 (HL)**
The Articles of Guinness plc provided that remuneration for work outside the scope of the ordinary duties of a director had to be fixed by the board of directors as a whole. Mr Ward was a director who performed work outside the normal scope and was given special remuneration of £5.2 million by a committee of the board. The committee had no authority to make the payment which Mr Ward was ordered to repay to the company. Mr Ward argued that a *quantum meruit* sum was owed to him.

Held: Where parties to a contract have agreed how remuneration is to be determined the court will not award a *quantum meruit* even if the agreement has not been implemented. The court considered the relevant Articles as terms embodied in a contract between Mr Ward and the company (a contract separate from the s. 33 contract).

The general principle that a person who has performed services requested and freely accepted by another is entitled to a *quantum meruit* payment has no application where the amount of the payment has been contractually agreed, nor where a mechanism for the determination of the payment amount has been specified in a contract. As a director is not entitled to payment unless the Articles authorise it, the only time a director is able to contemplate a *quantum meruit* claim is if the Articles authorise payment. Whilst a provision in the Articles simply stating that a director is entitled to be paid for additional service would leave open a *quantum meruit* claim, the moment the power to determine the remuneration is allocated to the directors (as in the Model Articles), or any other procedure for determination of the amount is stipulated in the Articles, no *quantum meruit* claim would succeed if the mechanism for determination of payment had not been adhered to.

Where the Model Articles apply, the director whose remuneration is being determined must not participate as a director in the board of directors' decision nor will he count towards quorum because he has a conflict of interest (art. 14 (private companies) and art. 16 (public companies)).

Service contracts

Model Articles 19 (for private companies) and 23 (for public companies) also apply to permit the directors to determine remuneration payable pursuant to directors' service contracts (also known as contracts of employment). Again, individual directors are normally precluded by the Articles from voting to approve their own service contracts because they have a conflict of interest (see Model Articles 14 (for private companies) and 16 (for public companies)).

Statutory protections in relation to service contracts and remuneration

Due to the potential for mutual self-interested action by directors, who could otherwise award each other long-term service contracts and excessively generous compensation packages and other remuneration, statutory protections have been enacted in relation to directors' service contracts and remuneration generally to protect shareholders and creditors.

Note that in addition to statutory requirements, section D of the main principles of the UK Corporate Governance Code (June 2012) specifically addresses director remuneration (see below).

Shareholder approval of long-term director service contracts

Section 188 requires shareholder approval in advance of directors' service contracts (as defined in s. 227; see below) with a guaranteed term of longer than two years. A copy of the entire proposed contract must be available for inspection by shareholders or, in the case of a written resolution, sent to shareholders before the shareholders' resolution is passed (s. 188(5)). Technically, it is only the provision of the contract relating to its length that must be approved (s. 188(2)). The consequences of failure to secure shareholder approval are that:

- the provision is void to the extent of the contravention so that, if longer, the contract term becomes two years; and
- the contract is deemed to contain a term entitling the company to terminate the contract at any time by giving reasonable notice.

Note, if the company is a listed company incorporated in the UK, approval by shareholders of long-term incentive plans for directors is mandated by the Listing Rules (LR 9.4).

Shareholder inspection of director service contracts

Companies are required to keep copies of directors' service contracts, or, if the contract is not in writing, a written memorandum setting out the terms of the contract, make them available for inspection by shareholders without charge, and provide copies to shareholders on request. Failure to do so is a criminal offence by every director, officer or manager in default (ss. 228–229). As an anti-avoidance provision, service contract is defined to include the terms of appointment of a person as a director and a contract for the performance of the ordinary duties of a director (s. 227(2)).

Public disclosure of director remuneration

The law requiring public disclosure of directors' remuneration becomes more demanding as one moves along the spectrum from small companies, through 'other unquoted companies' and quoted companies, to companies with officially listed securities.

Small companies
The small companies regime effectively removes small companies from any requirement to disclose director remuneration to the public. Information in the notes to the accounts can be deleted from the accounts filed with the registrar of companies (see the Small Companies and Groups (Accounts and Directors' Report) Regulations 2008 (SI 2008/409)).

Unquoted companies
The notes to the annual accounts of unquoted companies must state the total remuneration paid to all directors as a single figure, the amount paid to the highest paid director and the total sum paid as compensation for loss of office (s. 412 and the Large and Medium-sized Companies and Groups (Accounts and Reports) Regulations 2008 (SI 2008/410), reg. 8 and sch. 5). This information is filed with the registrar of companies as part of the accounts.

Quoted companies

As with unquoted companies, the notes to the annual accounts of quoted companies must state the total remuneration paid to all directors as a single figure. Further detailed disclosure relevant to directors' remuneration is mandated in an annual directors' remuneration report that the directors of a quoted company are required to prepare (ss. 420–422 and the Large and Medium-sized Companies and Groups (Accounts and Reports) Regulations 2008 (SI 2008/410), reg. 11 and sch. 8). The company's auditors must audit the auditable part of the remuneration report and state in their audit report whether or not that part has been properly prepared in accordance with the 2006 Act (s. 497).

Companies with officially listed securities

In addition to being subject to the rules in the Companies Act 2006 for quoted companies, a UK company with officially listed securities (whether a Premium listing or a Standard listing) is required by the Listing Rules to disclose yet further directors' remuneration information in its annual report and accounts (see Listing Rule 9.8).

Those companies with Premium listings, i.e. those subject to the UK Corporate Governance Code (2012), are required by the Listing Rules to comply with the Code or explain in their annual report and accounts the extent of their non compliance and reasons for not complying (LR 9.8.6 R (UK companies) and LR 9.8.7.R (overseas companies)). The Code itself requires further disclosures in the annual report and accounts. These last disclosures (such as where an executive director serves as a non-executive director elsewhere, whether or not the director will retain the earnings and, if so, what the remuneration is), are required by the Code but are backed up by a Listing Rule requirement to disclose any non-compliance with the Code's obligation to disclose. The line between law and self-regulation is definitely blurred here.

UK Corporate Governance Code (2012) principles

Remuneration of directors is covered in detail in Section D of the main principles and Schedule A of the UK Corporate Governance Code (2012) (see Appendix 3). Two main principles deal respectively with the level and components of remuneration (D1) and the procedure for fixing the remuneration packages of individual directors (D2).

Main Principle D1 states:

'Levels of remuneration should be sufficient to attract, retain and motivate directors of the quality required to run the company successfully, but a company should avoid paying more than is necessary for this purpose. A significant proportion of executive directors' remuneration should be structured so as to link rewards to corporate and individual performance.'

It is supplemented by Code Provision D.1.5 which provides:

'Notice or contract periods should be set at one year or less. If it is necessary to offer longer notice or contract periods to new directors recruited from outside, such periods should reduce to one year or less after the initial period.'

The part of the Code (D2) addressing the procedure for fixing the remuneration package for individual directors is very clear; see Appendix 3.

Note in particular the composition of the remuneration committee (Code provision D.2.1) and the clear distinction drawn between remuneration of executive and non-executive directors (Code provisions D.2.2 and D.2.3).

TEST YOUR KNOWLEDGE 11.7

(a) Where are the rules governing payment of directors for performing the role of director to be found and what do they normally state?

(b) Is a company permitted to enter into a service contract with a director for a term in excess of one year? What are the consequences if it does?

(c) How would your answer to (b) differ if the period stated was in excess of two years?

4 The company secretary

The role of the company secretary developed significantly over the course of the twentieth century causing Lord Denning MR, in 1971, to reject the assertion that the secretary 'fulfils a very humble role' and to comment, in *Panorama Developments (Guildford) Ltd v Fidelis Furnishing Fabrics Ltd* [1971] 2 QB 711), that:

> 'A company secretary is a much more important person nowadays … He is an officer of the company with extensive duties and responsibilities.'

In the twenty-first century, the statutory rules governing company secretaries are to be found in Part 12 of the Companies Act 2006 (ss. 270–280) and the responsibilities of the company secretary are recognised in the supporting principles and code provisions contained in Section B of the main principles of the UK Corporate Governance Code (June 2012). A company with a premium listing of equity shares on the London Stock Exchange is required to make a statement in its annual report of how it has applied the main principles and, if it has not, explaining why it has not complied with the Code.

4.1 Requirement to have a company secretary and keep a register

A private company is not required to have a company secretary (s. 270). Where a private company takes advantage of this exemption, anything authorised or required to be sent to the secretary may be sent to the company itself. Anything authorised or required to be done by the secretary may be done by a director or a person authorised by the directors.

A public company, however, must have a company secretary (s. 271) and may have more than one, in which event they are joint secretaries (s. 275(2)). A register of secretaries must be kept containing the name and a service address of the secretary and the register must be kept available for inspection (s. 275).

If a company fails to appoint a secretary, keep a register or keep the register open to inspection, the company and every officer of the company who is in default commits an offence.

The Secretary of State may give a company that appears to have failed to appoint a secretary a direction under the Companies Act 2006, s. 272 stating that the company appears to be in breach and the steps required to be taken and the time within which they must be taken.

4.2 Appointment and qualifications

The role of company secretary carries significant responsibilities. Section 273 reflects this by imposing a duty on directors of public companies that is designed to ensure that a person appointed to be a secretary is appropriately qualified. Note also UK Governance Code Provision B.5.2, which provides:

> 'Both the appointment and removal of the company secretary should be a matter for the board as a whole.'

Section 273 requires the directors of a public company to take reasonable steps to ensure that the secretary is a person who appears to them to have:

- the requisite knowledge and experience to discharge the functions of company secretary; and
- one or more of the qualifications listed in s. 273(2) of the Act.

Note that these requirements are cumulative. It is not enough to be qualified in accordance with s. 273(2). The company secretary also needs to appear to have the requisite knowledge and, crucially, experience. The qualifications are set out in s. 273(2) as supplemented by s. 273(3):

> 'Section 273 Qualifications of secretaries of public companies …
> (2) The qualifications are—
>   (a) that he has held the office of secretary of a public company for at least three of the five years immediately preceding his appointment as secretary;
>   (b) that he is a member of any of the bodies specified in subsection (3);

(c) that he is a barrister, advocate or solicitor called or admitted in any part of the United Kingdom;
(d) that he is a person who, by virtue of his holding or having held any other position or his being a member of any other body, appears to the directors to be capable of discharging the functions of secretary of the company.

(3) The bodies referred to in subsection (2)(b) are—
(a) the Institute of Chartered Accountants in England and Wales;
(b) the Institute of Chartered Accountants of Scotland;
(c) the Association of Chartered Certified Accountants;
(d) the Institute of Chartered Accountants in Ireland;
(e) the Institute of Chartered Secretaries and Administrators;
(f) the Chartered Institute of Management Accountants;
(g) the Chartered Institute of Public Finance and Accountancy.'

Notice must be given to the Registrar of Companies within 14 days of a person becoming or ceasing to be its secretary (s. 276).

4.3 Role and responsibilities

The secretary is the chief administrative officer of the company (*Panorama Developments (Guildford) Ltd v Fidelis Furnishing Fabrics Ltd* [1971] 2 QB 711 *per* Salmon LJ). His functions are not defined in the Act. They are administrative rather than of a business nature, as stated in *Re Maidstone Buildings Provisions Ltd* [1971] 1 WLR 1085:

'a secretary ... is not concerned in the management [of] the company. Equally, I think he is not concerned in carrying on the business of the company ... a person who holds the office of secretary may in some other capacity be concerned in the management of the company's business.'

Supporting principle B.5 of the UK Corporate Governance Code (June 2010) states some of the responsibilities of the company secretary:

'Under the direction of the chairman, the company secretary's responsibilities include ensuring good information flows within the board and its committees and between senior management and non-executive directors, as well as facilitating induction and assisting with professional development as required.

The company secretary should be responsible for advising the board through the chairman on all governance matters.'

Code provision B.5.2 adds:

'All directors should have access to the advice and services of the company secretary, who is responsible to the board for ensuring that board procedures are complied with.'

Although the precise role and responsibilities of a secretary will vary from company to company, a list of the core responsibilities of the secretary will include some or all of the following:

- advising on and securing best practice compliance with the Companies Acts and other company regulation particularly listed company obligations;
- providing independent advice to the board on all governance matters, facilitating the induction and professional development and evaluation of directors;
- facilitating the flow of information to the board and its committees, and particularly to the NEDs;
- advising on and coordinating preparation of shareholder circulars, financial statements and annual report;
- organising all aspects of company meetings, such as the AGM (including minuting) and written resolutions;
- maintaining good relations with shareholders and facilitating meetings where necessary;
- managing shareholder activism issues on behalf of the board;

- advising on and securing best practice compliance with the company's constitution;
- maintaining the company statutory books and registers;
- ensuring compliance with requirements to file documents and information with the Registrar of Companies;
- organising all aspects of board meetings (including minuting);
- maintaining the record-keeping system of the company; and
- administering employee and executive share and share option schemes.

TEST YOUR KNOWLEDGE 11.8

(a) Which companies are required to have a company secretary?
(b) Of what must the directors of a public company satisfy themselves before appointing an individual to the role of company secretary?
(c) Describe the role of the company secretary.
(d) Identify ten functions a company secretary is likely to fulfil.

4.4 Authority to bind the company

The leading case on the power of a secretary to bind the company to contracts is *Panorama Developments (Guildford) Ltd v Fidelis Furnishing Fabrics Ltd* [1971] 2 QB 711.

CASE LAW 11.5

***Panorama Developments (Guildford) Ltd v Fidelis Furnishing Fabrics Ltd* [1971] 2 QB 711**

The secretary of a company ordered cars for hire. They were in fact for his personal use and the question arose as to whether or not the company, on whose behalf he ostensibly placed the orders, was bound by the hire contracts and therefore liable to pay the hire charges. Held: the secretary had ostensible authority to enter into the car hire contracts and the company was bound to pay the hire charges.

LJ Salmon stated: 'As regards matters concerned with administration, in my judgment, the secretary has ostensible authority to sign contracts on behalf of the company ... Whether the secretary would have any authority to sign a contract relating to the commercial management of the company, for example, a contract for the sale or purchase of goods in which the company deal, does not arise for decision in the present case and I do not propose to express any concluded opinion upon the point ...'

The principle is, then, that in addition to any express actual authority, a secretary has authority to bind the company as to matters concerned with administration, including contracts relating to administration. This authority may be implied actual or ostensible authority in nature (see chapter 6 for an analysis of the authority of company agents and officers).

Where the office of secretary is vacant or the secretary is not capable of acting, an assistant or deputy secretary is authorised to do anything required or authorised to be done by the secretary (s. 274).

Finally, note that a provision requiring or authorising a thing to be done by or to a director and the secretary is not satisfied by being done by or to the same person acting as both director and secretary (s. 280).

4.5 Company secretary as an officer of the company

The term 'officer' is frequently used in the Companies Act 2006. Where it is used in a provision imposing criminal liability, officer is defined, by s. 1121(2), to mean any director, manager or secretary of the company as well as any person treated as an officer for the purposes of the particular offence. Accordingly, a company secretary is exposed to liability under a long list of statutory provisions.

> **TEST YOUR KNOWLEDGE 11.9**
>
> (a) Is a company secretary authorised to bind the company to any contracts?
> (b) Is a company secretary authorised to bind a company to a contract for the acquisition of new manufacturing equipment?
> (c) Is a company secretary an officer of the company?
> (d) What are the consequences of a company secretary being an officer of the company for the purposes of s. 1121(2)?

5 The auditor

5.1 The audit requirement

The general requirement to have a company's annual accounts audited is set out in CA 2006, s. 475. For this purpose, the annual accounts includes the directors' report and, for quoted companies, the directors' remuneration report.

A company's auditor is required to make an independent report (the 'auditor's report') to the company's shareholders as to whether, in his opinion:

- the company's annual accounts have been properly prepared in accordance with the Companies Act 2006 and the relevant reporting framework (s. 495);
- the company's accounts give a true and fair view of the company's state of affairs and the profit or loss of the company for (in respect of the profit and loss account) or at the end of (in respect of the balance sheet) the financial year (s. 495);
- the information given in the directors' report is consistent with the accounts (s. 496); and
- the directors' remuneration report has been prepared in accordance with the Act (s. 497).

An auditor's report may be qualified or unqualified. 'Qualified' means that the report does not state the auditor's unqualified opinion that the accounts have been properly prepared in accordance with the Companies Act 2006 (s. 539).

Important exemptions from audit exist for dormant and small companies (s. 475). More than two-thirds of companies delivering accounts to the Registrar take advantage of the audit exemption.

- A dormant company for the purposes of audit exemption is essentially a company with no significant accounting transactions, i.e. no entries in the accounting records for the financial year in question (s. 480).
- A small company for the purposes of audit exemption (s. 477, updated by regulation and s. 478) essentially means a private company with less than:
  - £6.5m annual turnover; and
  - £36.26m balance sheet.

If the company is to take advantage of the audit exemption, the balance sheet must contain, above the signature line, the following statements made by the directors (s. 475(3)):

- The members have not required the company to obtain in audit of its accounts for the year in question in accordance with section 476.
- The directors acknowledge their responsibilities for complying with the requirements of the Companies Act 2006 with respect to accounting records and the preparation of accounts.

Even if the company would otherwise be entitled to exemption, members representing no less than 10 per cent nominal value of the share capital, or any class of it, may give notice requiring the company to have its accounts audited (s. 476).

5.2 Appointment and removal of auditors

The rules governing the appointment and removal of auditors are set out in chapters 2 (appointment) and 4 (removal) of Part 16 of the Companies Act 2006.

Appointment

A company must appoint auditors for each financial year unless, in the case of a private company, the directors reasonably resolve not to appoint auditors on the ground that audited accounts are unlikely to be required (ss. 485 and 489), that is, the company is likely to be entitled to take advantage of the dormant or small company audit exemption described above.

The 'period for appointing auditors' is essentially 28 days from the end of the period allowed, in relation to private companies, for sending out copies of the annual accounts for the previous financial year to shareholders (s. 485), and, in relation to public companies, the accounts meeting at which the annual accounts and reports for the previous year are laid.

A private company's first auditors can be, and usually are, appointed by the directors. Subsequently, the auditors are appointed by ordinary resolution of the shareholders (either at a meeting or by written resolution). If no auditor has been appointed at the end of the period for appointing auditors, the auditor in office will be deemed to have been reappointed, unless (s. 487):

(a) he was appointed by the directors; or
(b) the company's Articles require actual reappointment; or
(c) notice that the auditor should not be reappointed is received from members representing at least 5 per cent of voting rights (s. 488); or
(d) the members have resolved that he should not be reappointed; or
(e) the directors have resolved that no auditor or auditors should be appointed for the financial year in question.

A public company's directors usually appoint the first auditor with subsequent appointment being made by the shareholders at an accounts meeting. No default reappointment provisions exist for public companies: the auditors cease to hold office at the end of the next accounts meeting of the company.

In default of appointment of an auditor where an auditor is required, the Secretary of State may appoint an auditor to fill the vacancy (ss. 486 and 490).

To advance the cause of auditor independence by increased transparency, the Secretary of State is empowered to make provisions by regulation for securing the disclosure of:

- the terms of appointment, including remuneration, of auditors (s. 493); and
- the nature of any services provided for a company by its auditors or its associates and the amount of any remuneration receivable in respect of those services (s. 494).

Removal and resignation

An auditor may only be removed from office before the expiration of his term by ordinary resolution at a meeting (s. 510), special notice of which resolution has been given by the proposing shareholder(s) to the company in accordance with s. 511. Notice of the passing of such a resolution must be sent to the Registrar of Companies within 14 days (s. 512). Note that this in only one of two situations (the other being removal of a director) in which a private company is required to hold a meeting as the written resolution procedure is not available.

An auditor may resign by depositing a notice in writing at the company's registered office which terminated the appointment with immediate effect (s. 516). The company must then send a copy of both notices to the Registrar of Companies within 14 days (s. 517).

Along with his resignation, the auditor of a quoted company must deposit a statement of the circumstances connected with his resignation. The auditor of an *unquoted* company is only required to deposit such a statement if he considers there are circumstances in connection with his ceasing to hold office that need to be brought to the attention of members or creditors (s. 519).

A s. 519 notice must be sent by the company to any person entitled to receive a copy of the accounts or the company may apply to court for an order that the auditor is using s. 519 to secure needless publicity for defamatory matter (s. 520). In the absence of notice that the company has made an application to court under s. 520, the auditor is required to send his s. 519 notice to the Registrar of Companies.

Where an auditor resigns before the end of his term, the company is also required to send a copy of the resignation and s. 519 notice to the Secretary of State or the person authorised by the Secretary of State to receive such notices (the 'audit authority') (s. 523).

In relation to a company with listed securities or in whose financial position there is a major public interest (s. 525(3)) the audit authority is required to inform the Secretary of State or the person authorised by the Secretary of State to receive such notices (the 'accounting authority') of a resignation and notice of circumstances (s. 524).

A resigning auditor may also deposit a requisition for a company meeting for the purposes of considering his resignation and the circumstances connected with his resignation (s. 518). The company is required to convene such a meeting (s. 518(5)).

Website publication of audit concerns

Shareholders of a quoted company representing at least 5 per cent of voting rights may ask the company, and the company is required to, publish on its website a statement relating to the audit of the company's accounts or any circumstances connected with an auditor of the company ceasing to hold office that they wish to raise at the next accounts meeting (s. 527).

> **TEST YOUR KNOWLEDGE 11.10**
>
> (a) Which companies are entitled to exemption from audit?
> (b) How is an auditor appointed and for how long does the appointment last?
> (c) Describe the process by which an auditor may be removed before the expiry of his term of office.
> (d) Describe the process by which an auditor of a quoted company may resign before the end of this term and state to whom a copy of his resignation and notice of circumstances must be sent and by whom.

5.3 Duties and rights

The principal duties of an auditor are set out in s. 498. In preparing his report required under s. 495 the auditor must carry out such investigations as will enable him to form an opinion as to whether:

- adequate accounting records have been kept;
- the company's accounts are in agreement with the accounting records;
- whether the directors' remuneration report is in agreement with the accounting records.

If the auditor is of the opinion that adequate records have not been kept, or the company's accounts are not in agreement with the accounting records or the directors' remuneration report is not in agreement with the accounting records, he must state that fact in his report.

If the auditor fails to obtain all the information and explanations which, to the best of his knowledge and belief, are necessary for the purposes of his audit, he shall state that fact in his report. Further, if:

- the requirements of regulations under s. 412 (disclosure of directors' benefits: remuneration, pensions and compensation for loss of office) are not complied with in the annual accounts; or
- in the case of a quoted company, the requirements of regulations under s. 421 as to information forming the auditable part of the directors' remuneration report are not complied with in that report;
- the auditor must include in his report, so far as he is reasonably able to do so, a statement giving the required particulars. Finally, if the directors of the company have prepared accounts and reports in accordance with the small companies regime and in the auditor's opinion they were not entitled so to do, the auditor shall state that fact in his report.

The auditor's report must state the name of the auditor and be signed and dated (s. 503). Where the auditor is not an individual but a firm, or LLP etc., the report must be signed by the senior statutory auditor.

TEST YOUR KNOWLEDGE 11.11

(a) On what is the auditor required to express his opinion in the auditor's report?
(b) What must an auditor do if the he is of the opinion that adequate accounting records have not been kept?
(c) What must an auditor do if the he is of the opinion that the directors' remuneration report is not in agreement with the accounting records?
(d) What must an auditor do if required information about director remuneration and associated payments is not contained in the annual accounts or directors' remuneration report?

5.4 Auditor liability

Rather than operating, as they have in the past, as unincorporated partnerships, firms of auditors are increasingly incorporated as limited liability partnerships (LLPs). Indeed, it was the large accountancy firms that pushed for adoption of the LLP structure in the UK (in 2000). The LLP structure provides the opportunity for accounting professionals to combine the tax treatment of a partnership with the benefits of both incorporation and, crucially, limited liability.

The liability of the auditor is governed principally by contract and tort law. A contract for audit services will be entered into between the company and the auditors, i.e., the LLP, usually on the standard terms of engagement of the LLP. The potential liability of the firm (i.e. the LLP) for breach of contract is supplemented by tort law.

Both the LLP and the individual auditors who conduct the audit on behalf of the LLP may find themselves liable in tort for negligently performed services and, in particular, for negligent or fraudulent misrepresentation. To whom they may find themselves liable has been the focus of much debate and whether or not third parties may rely on audit reports is considered below. Statutory rules in Chapter 6 of Part 16 of the Companies Act 2006 (ss. 532–538) override and supplement the basic civil law principles that would otherwise govern auditor liability.

Auditor liability to the company

Auditor liability to the company arises principally in contract law. The contract between the auditor and the company will in almost every case impose a contractual obligation to perform services under the contract with reasonable care and skill. Liability may also arise in tort, most likely for negligence based on a lack of reasonable care and, as indicated, this liability may attach to individual auditors as well as to the audit firm or LLP of which the individual auditor is a member or by whom he or she is employed. Individuals providing services on behalf of an LLP will be liable only for their own negligence, not the negligence of other members or employees of the LLP.

Statute places a significant restriction on the agreement that can be reached by the parties to an audit contract in relation to liability for the audit services to be performed. Provisions in any contract with the company (or in the Articles of a company), exempting or limiting the liability of an auditor, or providing an indemnity against any liability of an auditor, in relation to the audit of accounts are void (s. 532). This is subject to two exceptions:

- A company may now agree to limit the liability of its auditors by:
  - using a 'liability limitation agreement', as that term is used in the Act (ss. 534–538); and
  - complying with the Companies (Disclosure of Auditor Remuneration and Liability Limitation Agreements) Regulations 2008 (SI 2008/489).
- A company may indemnify an auditor in relation to the liabilities arising out of successfully defending himself in proceedings (s. 533).

The Financial Reporting Council (FRC) has published guidance in 2008 on what is and what is not permitted in relation to auditor liability limitation agreements (Guidance on Auditor Liability Limitation Agreements, June 2008, accessible on the FRC website). Auditor liability and the importance of auditors being permitted to limit their liability was also the subject of a 2008 EU Commission recommendation (Commission Recommendation of 5 June 2008 concerning the limitation of the civil liability of statutory auditors and audit firms, 2008/473/EC) which stresses the increasing trend of litigation and lack of sufficient insurance cover faced by auditors. The aim of the recommendation is to protect European capital markets by ensuring that audit firms remain available to carry out audits on companies listed in the EU.

Auditor liability to third parties

Auditor liability to third parties is governed by tort law. Consider an investor who relies on the audited, published accounts of a company to buy the shares of the company only to lose money because the accounts did not present a true and fair view of the finances of the company, and to discover that the auditor was negligent in not discovering and flagging this. The liability of the auditor in such a case is governed by tort rules on liability for economic loss arising from negligent misstatement, the leading case on which is *Hedley Byrne & Co Ltd v Heller & Partners Ltd* [1964] AC 465 (HL).

Auditor liability for third party economic loss was considered and settled in *Caparo Industries Ltd v Dickman* [1990] 2 AC 605 (HL). Basically, the House of Lords decided that an auditor owes a duty of care to the company, a limited duty of care to shareholders of the company (limited to protection of their shareholder rights) and only owes a duty of care to third parties (and a wider duty to shareholders), where a special relationship exists between the auditor and the third party in question. Reasonable foresight of loss by a third party is not sufficient to establish a special relationship/auditor liability to a third party.

Subsequent cases have described the need to establish a 'special relationship' pursuant to *Caparo* as the need to show that there has been an assumption of responsibility to the third party by the auditor. In the absence of an express assumption of responsibility, the type of parties to whom courts may be willing to find that responsibility has been assumed are believed to be parent companies and directors.

Auditor criminal liability

An auditor is exposed to potential criminal liability under the Companies Act 2006, s. 507, essentially in two situations as follows:

1. If he knowingly or recklessly causes an auditor's report on the annual accounts to include a matter that is misleading, false or deceptive in a material particular, (s. 507(1)).
2. If he knowingly or recklessly causes an auditor's report on the annual accounts to omit one of the following statements:
   - that the company's accounts do not agree with the accounting records (s. 507(2)(a)); or
   - that necessary information and explanations have not been obtained (s. 507(2)(b)); or
   - that directors wrongly took advantage of the exemption from the obligation to prepare group accounts (s. 507(2)(c)).

TEST YOUR KNOWLEDGE 11.2

(a) What are the benefits from a liability perspective of an accountancy firm changing from operating as a partnership to operating as a limited liability partnership?

(b) To whom does an auditor owe a duty of care in tort law to avoid pure economic loss resulting from the negligent performance of an audit of a company?

(c) In which two situations is an auditor exposed to criminal liability under the Companies Act 2006?

CHAPTER SUMMARY

- Shareholders are the residual controllers of the company as the result of the Articles of Association, statute law (the Companies Act 2006 and the Insolvency Act 1986) and cases recognising their power in certain circumstances.
- The board of directors is responsible for the management of the company's business, for which purpose they may exercise all the powers of the company (Model Article 3).

- Types of directors include *de jure* directors, *de facto* directors, shadow directors, executive and non-executive directors (some of whom are independent and some are not) and nominee directors.
- A private company must have at least one director and a public company two directors.
- Rules regarding appointment and the quorum of directors are normally set out in the Articles as the Act does not govern quorum or appointment but confines itself largely to disclosure obligations.
- A director may be removed by ordinary resolution at a meeting (s. 168(1)).
- The Company Directors Disqualification Act 1986 empowers the Secretary of State in defined circumstances to apply to the court for an order disqualifying the defendant from being concerned or taking part in the promotion, formation or management of a company, or to take undertakings in lieu.
- In addition to holding the office of director, a director who performs additional work will be either an employee or an independent contractor and remuneration for each must be considered separately.
- The Act regulates payments on termination of office (s. 217) and the length of service contracts (s. 188) so that the right to remove directors is not priced out of existence by the directors.
- The rules on disclosure of board remuneration have been tightened over the years and are increasingly onerous, depending on whether the company is a small, unquoted, quoted or has listed securities.
- Public companies must have a company secretary; private companies need not.
- Directors of a public company are required to take reasonable steps to ensure that the secretary is a person who appears to them to have the requisite knowledge and experience to discharge the functions of company secretary, and one or more of the qualifications listed in of the Companies Act 2006.
- The precise role and responsibilities of a secretary will vary from company to company but will normally include those listed at pp. 220–221 above.
- A company secretary has the authority to bind the company as regards matters concerned with administration. See *Panorama Developments (Guildford) Ltd v Fidelis Furnishing Fabrics Ltd* (1971).
- A company secretary is an officer of the company as defined by s. 1121(2) for the purposes of the Act imposing criminal liability, typically on 'any officer in default'.
- A company's annual accounts, including its directors' report and (for quoted companies) the directors' remuneration report must be audited (s. 475) unless the company is dormant (s. 477) or entitled to the small company exemption from audit (s. 477).
- All non-exempt companies must appoint auditors for each financial year (ss. 485 and 489) and after the first auditors (who are usually appointed by the directors) auditors are appointed by ordinary resolution of the shareholders.
- Removal from office is by ordinary resolution at a meeting (s. 510), special notice of which resolution has been given by the proposing shareholder(s) to the company in accordance with s. 511.
- An auditor resigns by depositing a notice in writing at the company's registered office (s. 516) and (unless it is not required) a statement of the circumstances connected with his resignation (s. 519).
- The auditor is required to make an independent report, the 'auditor's report' to the company's shareholders on all annual accounts (s. 495), principally that the accounts give a true and fair view of the company at the end of its financial year and of the profit and loss for the financial year.
- Civil liability to the company is principally in contract law, and to third parties may arise under tort law although in *Caparo Industries Ltd v Dickman* (1990) the House of Lords decided that an auditor owes a duty of care to third parties only where a special relationship exists between the auditor and the third party in question.
- Criminal liability is provided for in s. 507 where an auditor knowingly or recklessly omits required information from, or causes any matter that is misleading, false or deceptive to be included in an auditor's report.

12 Directors' duties

■ CONTENTS

1. Legal duties of directors
2. Legislative reform of directors' duties
3. To whom do directors owe their duties?
4. Corporate governance duties
5. Conflict of interest duties of directors
6. Directors contracting with their companies
7. Remedies
8. Relief from liability, indemnification, exclusion of liability and insurance

■ INTRODUCTION

The legal duties of directors are an essential part of the legal corporate governance framework. Classification of directors' duties into corporate governance duties and conflict of interest duties, depicted in Figure 12.1, is artificial but, it is suggested, helpful. Students regularly fail to differentiate between a director who is acting in his role as a director, such as attending a board meeting and participating in decision-making of the board, and a director who is not purporting to act as a director, but is acting on his own behalf (his personal role), such as negotiating amendments to his service contract with the company, or contracting personally with a customer of the company. In both roles, a director is subject to all the duties of a director, it is just that certain duties are more relevant to one role than the other.

1 Legal duties of directors

1.1 Control of director conflict of interest

The primary role of directors' duties is to discourage individuals empowered to manage companies from acting in their own self-interest or in the interest of persons other than the company. It is because the directors of a company are empowered to alter the legal position of the company and in doing so are entrusted to act in the best interests of the company that they are subject to fiduciary obligations. You will come across fiduciary responsibility in agency, partnership and trust law. As a fundamental legal concept underpinning English law, it is not confined to trustees, partners and agents.

CASE LAW 12.1

***York Building Co v MacKenzie* (1795) 3 Pat 378**
He that is entrusted with the interest of others cannot be allowed to make the business an object of interest to himself; because from the frailty of nature, one who has the power will be too readily seized with the inclination to use the opportunity for serving his own interest at the expense of those for whom he is entrusted.

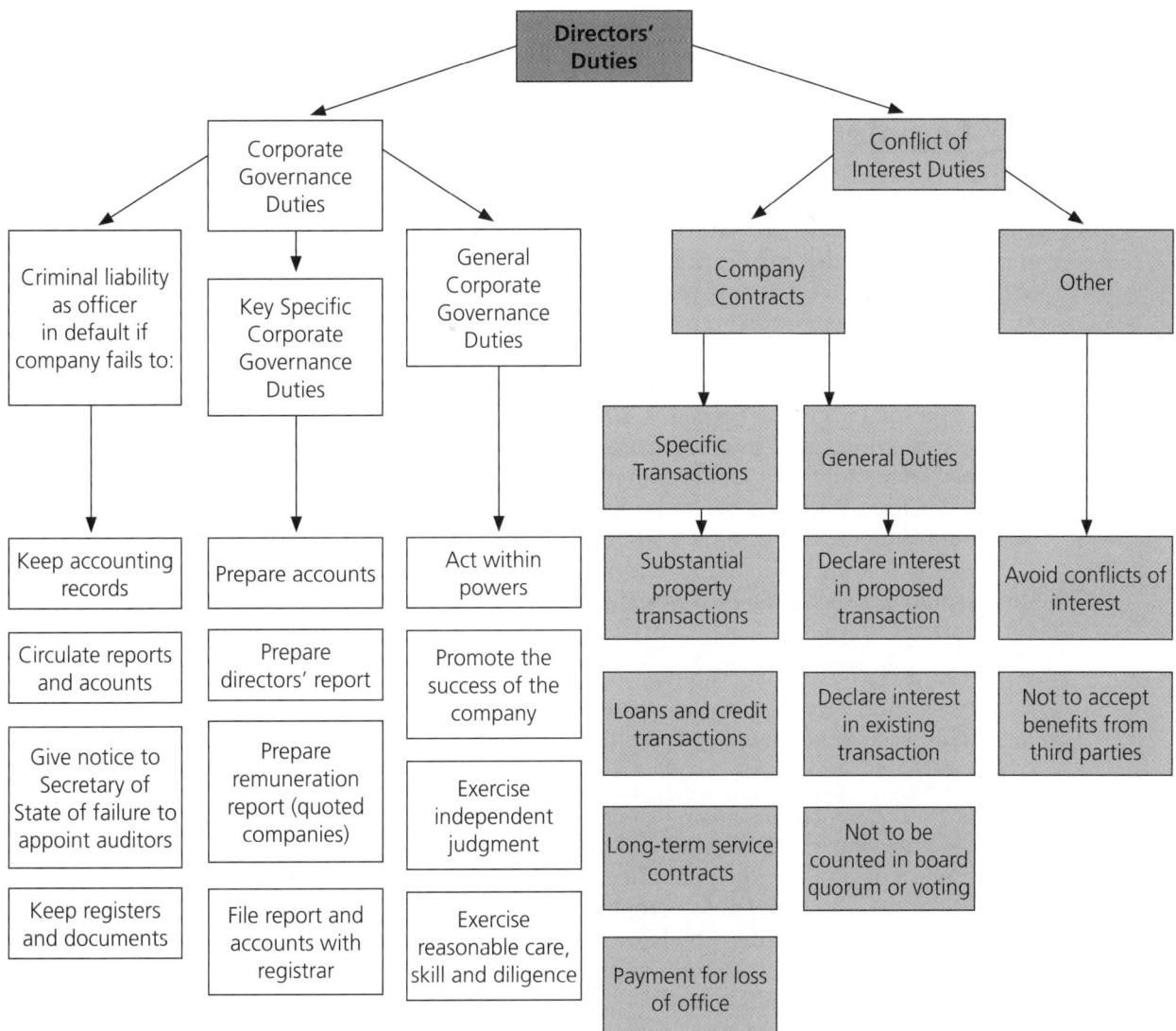

FIGURE 12.1 Categorisation of directors' duties

Protecting rights, particularly property rights, and establishing standards for conscience when individuals are entrusted to protect the rights of third parties are regarded as proper matters for the civil law courts. Conflict of interest has long been discouraged by the courts and stringent remedies awarded against transgressors.

1.2 Control of corporate governance behaviour

In contrast to controlling conflict of interest, the courts have not considered it their role to create incentives for good management. To do so would inevitably draw judges into making judgments about the reasonableness of business decisions, a role they acknowledge they have no particular competence to play. Only relatively recently has the law given any meaningful content to what are termed here 'corporate governance duties' of directors, a development shaped by legislative intervention. The approach of the law is to require directors to arrive at decisions by satisfactory processes rather than to review the substance of management decisions.

The legislature enacts law in response to government proposals to use law as a tool to drive behaviours considered desirable to achieve government policy. Better corporate governance is regarded as desirable to achieve greater economic productivity with higher levels of employment, making the UK economy stronger and, ultimately, benefiting society. Although socioeconomic policy and debate as to what that policy should be and consideration of the role company law does, could and should play are beyond the scope of this book, it is essential to be aware that these issues form the backdrop to the framework of legal corporate governance of which directors' duties form an important part. Before turning to examine corporate governance duties in detail, we shall consider directors' duties generally, including legislative reform and to whom the duties are owed.

2 Legislative reform of directors' duties

Directors' general duties were developed over time by the courts and remained case-based until the Companies Act 2006. Although complete codification of the duties has been discussed a number of times, the 'codification' achieved by the 2006 Act is incomplete. The general duties are stated in the Act, but past cases must be relied upon to give meaning to the words in the statute and no attempt has been made to state the remedies for breach in the statute.

In contrast, statutory provisions regulating specific transactions between a director and the company were first introduced in 1928. Prompted by financial scandals, the statutory provisions were significantly enhanced in 1980, which marked the high tide of statutory regulation of directors' conflicts of interest. Company loans above a minimal amount to directors, for example, were prohibited and criminalised. The law has receded from this high water mark. The prohibition on loans, for example, has been removed and replaced with a shareholder approval requirement.

After the passing of the 2006 Act, Margaret Hodge articulated two aims of the reform of directors' duties. A third aim is found in the Law Commission's consultation paper on directors' duties:

- providing clarity and accessibility;
- aligning what is good for the company with what is good for society at large;
- keeping legal regulation to the minimum necessary to safeguard stakeholders' legitimate interests.

At this point it remains too early to tell whether the law on directors' duties is now clearer, easier to understand and more accessible than the old law. Feedback from industry suggests a greater awareness of the duties of directors, but it is not clear that this translates into understanding of what is required to comply with them. Certainly, the headline duties are drawn together in one place in the Act. However, the statutory provisions far from comprehensively cover all issues relevant to a directors' liability for breach of duty. It is likely that in many situations directors will continue to need to seek legal advice to understand their legal duties and the procedures available to avoid incurring liability.

At the same time, although the concept of **enlightened shareholder value** enshrined in the s. 172 duty requires directors to 'have regard to' the interests of the plurality of stakeholders when taking business decisions, this duty is performed in a boardroom of individuals appointed and removable by shareholders who owe their duties to the company, the interests of which are the interests of the shareholders as a whole (s. 172(1)). Again, it is premature to comment on the extent to which the new directors' duties will bring about a change for the good of society in the way directors make decisions. The extent to which greater emphasis will be placed on the interests of non-shareholder stakeholders, including 'the community and the environment' (s. 172(1)(d)) and 'the likely consequences of any decisions in the long term' (s. 172(1)(a)), remains to be seen.

With regard to keeping legal regulation to the minimum necessary to safeguard stakeholders' legitimate interests, the Companies Act 2006 was drafted in light of the need, emphasised by the Law Commission, to strike a balance between 'necessary regulation and freedom for directors to make business decisions'.

3 To whom do directors owe their duties?

3.1 Directors' duties are owed to the company

The statutory general duties of directors are owed by each individual director to the company (s. 170(1)). Consequently, any action for breach of duty vests in the company (*Foss v Harbottle* (1843) 2 Hare 461). Without more, a director does not owe duties to individual shareholders or to other stakeholders in the company (*Percival v Wright* [1902] 2 Ch 421).

When considering the conflict of interest duties of directors it is sufficient to require the director to act in the interests of 'the company' as the company's interests can be contrasted with the directors' own self-interest or the interest of a person external to the company. When considering the corporate governance duties of directors, however, it becomes necessary to penetrate further and ask what is meant by the 'interests of the company'.

3.2 Enlightened shareholder value

The interests of the shareholders as a whole are the paramount consideration of the directors. This is captured in s. 172 which requires directors to act in the way they consider to be most likely to promote the success of the company 'for the benefit of its members as a whole' (members meaning shareholders for our purposes). In performing this duty, however, the directors must have regard to the interests of other stakeholders, particularly those listed in s. 172(1).

> 'A director of a company must act in the way he considers, in good faith, would be most likely to promote the success of the company for the benefit of its members as a whole, and in doing so have regard (amongst other matters) to –
> (a) the likely consequences of any decision in the long term,
> (b) the interests of the company's employees,
> (c) the need to foster the company's business relationships with suppliers, customers and others,
> (d) the impact of the company's operations on the community and the environment,
> (e) the desirability of the company maintaining a reputation for high standards of business conduct, and
> (f) the need to act fairly as between members of the company.

The requirement to take various interests into account as part of acting for the benefit of the shareholders as a whole enshrines the concept of 'enlightened shareholder value.'
This is illustrated in Figure 12.2.

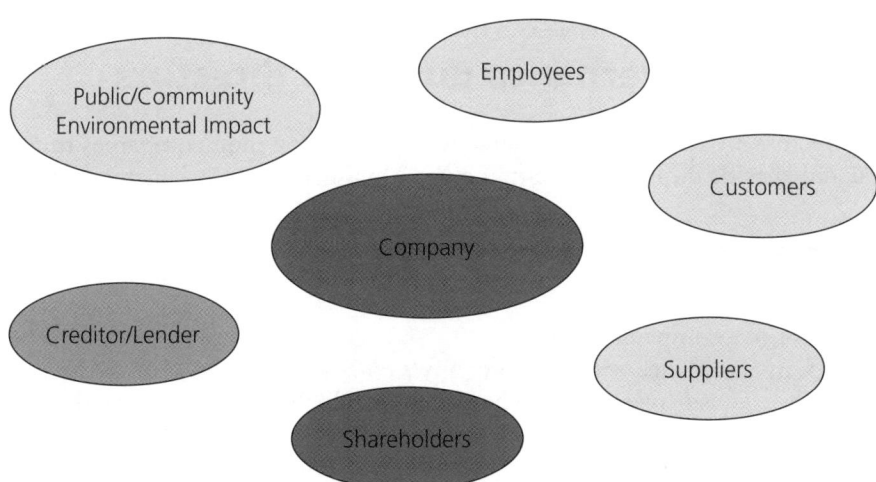

FIGURE 12.2 Enlightened shareholder value and s. 172

3.3 The interests of creditors

The extent to which directors are required to take the interests of creditors into account when they are managing the company is a very important issue. Creditors are not listed alongside other obvious stakeholders in s. 172(1). Instead, s. 172(3) makes the duty to promote the success of the company 'for the benefit of its members as a whole' subject to 'any enactment or rule of law requiring directors, in certain circumstances, to consider or act in the interests of creditors of the company'.

The interests of creditors predominate when there is no residual wealth left in the company, that is, when shareholder equity has been dissipated, usually by poor trading (see chapters 8 and 9). At that point, the economic owners of the company are the creditors: all the company has it owes to them. As the financial health of a company deteriorates, the directors need increasingly to focus on the interests of the creditors when they take decisions because the interests of the company become increasingly aligned with the interests of its creditors (*Facia Footwear Ltd v Hinchcliffe* [1998] 1 BCLC 218).

At the point of insolvency, or at some point approaching insolvency (the courts have not established agreed upon wording as to the point at which the need to prioritise creditors' interests is triggered), it is not a question of the directors owing a duty to its creditors, the duty remains owed to the company. The duty simply needs to be performed with different priorities in mind. The duty remains enforceable against the directors only by the company but note that the shareholders cannot ratify what would otherwise be a breach of duty (*Sycotex Pty Ltd v Balser* (1993) 13 ACSR 766).

The common law and equitable principles requiring directors, in certain circumstances, to consider or act in the interests of creditors, preserved by s. 172(3), have not had to be developed in case law in recent years due to the enactment of the Insolvency Act 1986, s. 214. Section 214 applies when a company is being wound up. It exposes directors to court orders to contribute to the assets of the company if knowing, or in circumstances in which they ought to have known, that the company had no reasonable prospect of not going into insolvent liquidation, they continued to trade or otherwise took steps not in the interests of creditors. (Section 214 is considered in part 5.)

TEST YOUR KNOWLEDGE 12.1

(a) To whom does a director owe his directors' duties?
(b) Explain the term 'enlightened shareholder value'.
(c) When, and to what extent, are directors required to take the interests of creditors into account when they are managing the company?

4 Corporate governance duties of directors

The duties directors are required to discharge when managing their companies may be divided into general and specific duties. The main focus of this section is the general duties.

4.1 Duty to act within powers (s. 171)

'171 Duty to act within powers
 A director of a company must—
 (a) act in accordance with the company's constitution, and
 (b) only exercise powers for the purposes for which they are conferred.'

The first general duty set out in the 2006 Act contains two limbs. The first limb, the duty to act in accordance with the company's constitution, places any director who acts outside his actual powers in breach of duty. A third party may be entitled to rely on ostensible authority of a director to enforce a contract against a company. This does not preclude an action for breach of duty being brought by the company against the director. Also, s. 40 may operate to make an agreement binding on the company when the directors have acted outside their powers. Section 40 does not however, affect any liability incurred by a director by reason of exceeding his powers, a point confirmed in s. 40(5) (see chapter 6).

CASE EXAMPLE 12.1

A company's Articles require loans in excess of £200,000 to be approved in advance by the shareholders. Without shareholder approval the board unanimously resolves to enter into a loan with a third party for £500,000 and the loan is entered into. Each member of the board is in breach of s. 171.

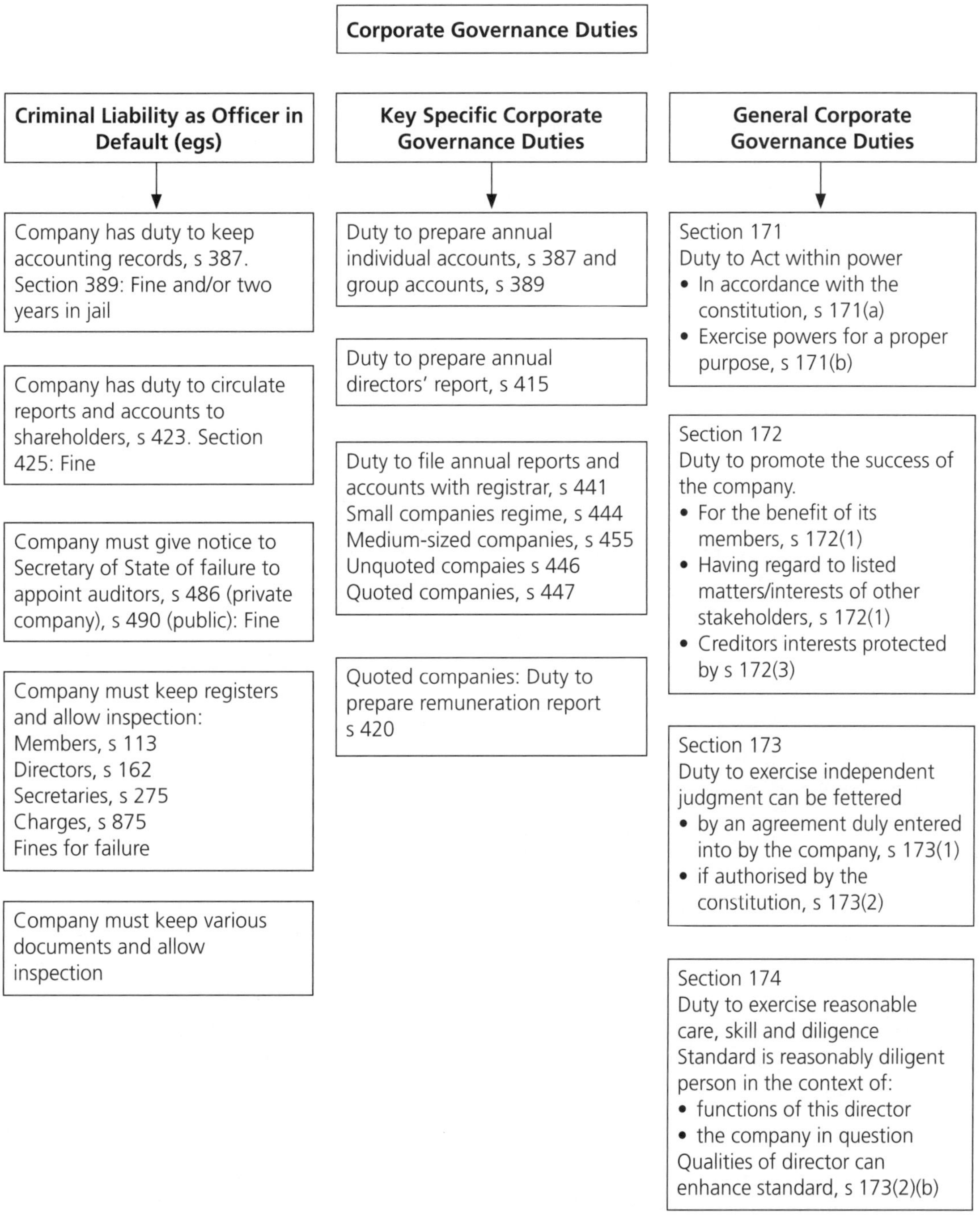

Corporate Governance Duties

Criminal Liability as Officer in Default (egs)

- Company has duty to keep accounting records, s 387. Section 389: Fine and/or two years in jail
- Company has duty to circulate reports and accounts to shareholders, s 423. Section 425: Fine
- Company must give notice to Secretary of State of failure to appoint auditors, s 486 (private company), s 490 (public): Fine
- Company must keep registers and allow inspection:
  Members, s 113
  Directors, s 162
  Secretaries, s 275
  Charges, s 875
  Fines for failure
- Company must keep various documents and allow inspection

Key Specific Corporate Governance Duties

- Duty to prepare annual individual accounts, s 387 and group accounts, s 389
- Duty to prepare annual directors' report, s 415
- Duty to file annual reports and accounts with registrar, s 441
  Small companies regime, s 444
  Medium-sized companies, s 455
  Unquoted compaies s 446
  Quoted companies, s 447
- Quoted companies: Duty to prepare remuneration report s 420

General Corporate Governance Duties

- **Section 171**
  Duty to Act within power
  - In accordance with the constitution, s 171(a)
  - Exercise powers for a proper purpose, s 171(b)

- **Section 172**
  Duty to promote the success of the company.
  - For the benefit of its members, s 172(1)
  - Having regard to listed matters/interests of other stakeholders, s 172(1)
  - Creditors interests protected by s 172(3)

- **Section 173**
  Duty to exercise independent judgment can be fettered
  - by an agreement duly entered into by the company, s 173(1)
  - if authorised by the constitution, s 173(2)

- **Section 174**
  Duty to exercise reasonable care, skill and diligence
  Standard is reasonably diligent person in the context of:
  - functions of this director
  - the company in question
  Qualities of director can enhance standard, s 173(2)(b)

FIGURE 12.3 Directors' Corporate Governance Duties

The second limb of s. 171 is based on *Re Smith & Fawcett* [1942] Ch 304, *per* Greene MR.

> '[Directors] must exercise their discretion *bona fide* in what they consider – not what a court may consider – is in the interests of the company, and not for any collateral purpose.'

The duty to exercise powers for a proper purpose has been particularly relevant in relation to directors issuing shares (*Hogg v Cramphorn Ltd* [1967] Ch 254 and *Howard Smith v Ampol Petroleum Ltd* [1974] AC 821 (PC)), but is not confined to such decisions. It has been applied, for example, to the power to refuse to register a transfer of shares (*Re Smith & Fawcett Ltd* [1942] Ch 304 (CA), and to the power to enter into a management agreement (*Lee Panavision v Lee Lighting Ltd* [1992] BCLC 22 (CA)).

 **CASE LAW 12.2**

***Hogg v Cramphorn Ltd* [1967] Ch 254**

In an effort to forestall a takeover bid it considered not to be in the interests of the company, the board of directors of Cramphorn Ltd issued shares with special voting rights to trustees of a scheme set up for the benefit of employees.

Held: Even though it was accepted that the board had acted in good faith and the directors believed it was in the best interests of the company not to be taken over by Mr Baxter, the power to issue shares had been exercised for an improper purpose, the primary purpose having been to prevent Mr Baxter's bid from succeeding. (Note that the court adjourned proceedings to give the shareholders opportunity to ratify the breach by ordinary resolution, which it did. The new shares were not, and could not have been voted.)

The irrelevance of the finding in *Hogg v Cramphorn* (1967) that the directors were acting *bona fide* in what they believed to be the best interests of the company demonstrated that the duty to exercise powers for a proper purpose was different from the duty to act *bona fide* in what they consider to be the interests of the company. There is an objective element to the court's assessment of what is a proper purpose and what is not. How the courts approach the task of determining what is proper and what is not was addressed by Lord Wilberforce in *Howard Smith v Ampol* [1974] AC 821 (PC).

 **CASE LAW 12.3**

***Howard Smith v Ampol Petroleum Ltd* [1974] AC 821 (PC)**

Rival takeover offers were received for Miller Ltd. Miller's board of directors favoured the bid of Howard Smith but it was unlikely to succeed as the other bidder, Ampol, already owned 55 per cent of the shares in Miller Ltd. The board issued shares to Howard Smith with two purposes in mind: 1) to provide Miller with capital, which it needed, and 2) to convert Ampol's stake to a minority interest. The directors were not motivated by self-interest or the desire to retain control.

Held: On the evidence, the substantial purpose for which the power was exercised was to convert Ampol's interest in the company from a majority to a minority shareholding. The power to allot share had therefore been improperly exercised and the allotment of shares was set aside.

In the course of his judgment Lord Wilberforce set out the following steps a court should take when determining whether or not there has been a breach of what is now s. 171(b):

- Ascertain, on a fair view, the nature of the power.
- Define the limits within which it may be exercised.
- Examine the substantial purpose for which it was exercised.
- Reach a conclusion whether the exercise was proper or not.

In reaching its conclusion, Lord Wilberforce continued, the court 'will necessarily give credit to the *bona fide* opinion of the directors, if such is found to exist, and will respect their judgement as to matters of management; having done this, the ultimate conclusion has to be as to the side of a fairly broad line on which the case falls'.

4.2 Duty to promote the success of the company (s. 172)

The s. 172 statutory duty to promote the success of the company is set out in 3.2. Like the s. 171 duty to act within powers, it is based on *Re Smith & Fawcett* [1942] Ch 304. In that case the court spoke in terms of directors acting *bona fide* in what they consider to be not what a court may consider to be, in the interests of the company. Section 172, however, is couched in different language, stating that directors must act in the way they consider, in good faith, would be most likely to promote the success of the company. The section also includes guidance as to how directors should go about performing the duty (see section 3.2 above).

Focusing on the basis on which courts will find a breach of this duty, pre-2006 case law established that the court will not ask whether or not the decision is objectively in the interests of the company: the duty is subjective (*Regentcrest plc v Cohen* [2001] BCC 494 (Ch), a point reflected in the language of s. 172 and confirmed in recent cases (see *Re Southern Counties Fresh Foods Ltd* [2011] EWHC 1370, *Cobden Investments Ltd v RWM Langport Ltd* [2008] EWHC 2810 and *Re West Coast Capital (Lios) Ltd* [2008] CSOH 72 per Lord Glennie).

In some circumstances, however, the courts have introduced an objective dimension into consideration of whether or not the duty has been breached. For example, where there is evidence that a director did not stop to consider the interests of the company at all. In such a case, if no intelligent and honest person in the position of the director of the company concerned could in the circumstances have reasonably believed he was acting in the interests of the company, the courts will find that the duty has been breached. Pennycuick J stated this test clearly in *Charterbridge Corporation Ltd v Lloyds Bank* Ltd [1970] Ch 62.

> 'The proper test, I think ... must be whether an intelligent and honest man in the position of a director of the company concerned, could, in the whole of the existing circumstances have reasonably believed that... [his actions] ... were for the benefit of the company.'

Whether or not this test survives the enactment of s. 172 is unclear.

The next question posed by s. 172 is, if directors have not taken into account the various matters listed in s. 172(1) (the matters can be seen in section 3.2 above), will a court hold the directors to be in breach of s. 172 on the basis of a procedural failing notwithstanding them being in good faith and considering that they have acted in the way most likely to promote the success of the company? There is evidence that boards are being advised that a safe practice to avoid the potential for procedural-based liability pursuant to this section is to minute that the matters listed in s. 172, and other relevant factors, have been considered before a major decision is entered into, bringing about the 'tick-box' defensive board room practices it was hoped to avoid. The requirement for directors to take into account the matters listed in s. 172, looked at from a different perspective, can be seen as providing boards with a defence to actions against directors for breach of s. 172 instituted by shareholders convinced board decisions have not served their interests.

Finally, a controversial aspect of the duty to act *bona fide* in the interests of the company that now attaches to s. 172 is the extent to which the duty imposes on directors a duty to disclose breaches of fiduciary duty. It is settled that if he considers it to be in the interests of the company to know, a director is under a duty to disclose to the company a breach of fiduciary duty by another director. In *Item Software (UK) Ltd v Fassihi* [2005] 2 BCLC 91 (CA), the court went further and held that a director was in breach of his duty to the company by failing to disclose his own earlier breach of fiduciary duty.

4.3 Duty to exercise independent judgment (s. 173)

> '173 Duty to exercise independent judgment
> (1) A director of a company must exercise independent judgment.
> (2) This duty is not infringed by his acting—
>   (a) in accordance with an agreement duly entered into by the company that restricts the future exercise of discretion by its directors, or
>   (b) in a way authorised by the company's constitution.'

Case law establishes that directors are prohibited from fettering their discretion in the exercise of their powers, meaning that they must not enter into agreements with third parties as to how they will exercise their discretion. Whilst s. 173 is based on this duty, it is not clear how far the restatement of the duty in positive terms 'must exercise independent judgment' might have changed the common law position. The important exception to the prohibition at common law is captured in s. 173(2)(a), which must be read in conjunction with s. 172 (section 3.2 above).

The result is that if a director acts in accordance with a contract binding on the company and thereby does not exercise independent discretion, no breach of s. 173 occurs. Rather, a breach of s. 172 may have occurred. If the directors who caused the company to enter into the contract did not consider, in good faith, entry into the contract, and the implicit fettering of future directors' discretion the contract entails, would be most likely to promote the success of the company.

As the Court of Appeal pointed out in *Fulham Football Club Ltd v Cabra Estates plc* [1994] 1 BCLC 363, to preclude directors from making contracts by which they bind themselves to the future exercise of their powers in a particular manner, when the contract taken as a whole is manifestly for the benefit of the company, would prevent companies from entering into contracts which are commercially beneficial to them. The position is summed up in the head note to *Thorby v Goldberg* (1964) 112 CLR 597, a High Court of Australia case.

> 'If, when a contract is negotiated on behalf of a company, the directors *bona fide* think it in the interests of the company as a whole that the transaction should be entered into and carried into effect they may bind themselves by the contract to do whatever is necessary to effectuate it.'

The issue of exercising independent judgement can be particularly difficult for a nominee director who, without more, must not simply follow the instructions of the shareholder who has appointed him. Provided the interests of the appointing shareholder and the company coincide, no practical difficulty arises. When the interests of the shareholder who has appointed them and the company do not coincide, many nominee directors fail to appreciate that, as a member of the board, they are required to exercise independent judgement.

In *Scottish Co-operative Wholesale Society Ltd v Meyer* [1959] AC 324 (HL), the Scottish Co-operative Wholesale Society Ltd (SCWS) formed a private company with Meyer & Lucas (the defendants). Meyer and Lucas were the managing directors and SCWS appointed three of its own directors to the new company's board. SCWS commenced a business in competition with the company, and in the context of an action based on the affairs of the company having been conducted in a manner oppressive to some part of the members (the predecessor section to a s. 994 unfair prejudice petition), Lord Denning commenting on the nominee directors, stated, 'They probably thought that "as nominees" of the co-operative society their first duty was to the co-operative society. In this they were wrong.'

Lord Denning again addressed the duty of a nominee director in *Boulting v ACTT* [1963] 2 QB 606.

> 'take a nominee director, that is, a director of a company who is nominated by a large shareholder to represent his interests. There is nothing wrong in it. It is done every day. Nothing wrong, that is, so long as the director is left free to exercise his best judgment in the interests of the company which he serves. But if he is put upon terms that he is bound to act in the affairs of the company in accordance with the directions of his patron, it is beyond doubt unlawful.'

Section 173(2)(b) appears to be particularly pertinent to nominee directors as it contemplates a director being able to avoid breach of s. 173 if the company's constitution permits him not to exercise independent judgement. This seems to permit language in the Articles, or an appropriate special resolution, providing for a nominee director to represent his nominating shareholder and authorising him to represent the interests of that shareholder. As much as this could lift from a nominee director the threat of being found in breach of s. 173, the general duties are cumulative, and there is no similar way around the duty in s. 172, to act in good faith to promote the success of the company for the benefit of its shareholders as a whole. Notwithstanding s. 173(2)(b), where the interests of a nominating shareholder diverge from the interests of the company, the nominee director remains in a commercially unrealistic and consequently legally precarious position.

A further point arising out of the positive formulation of this duty is its effect on the ability of directors to delegate the exercise of their powers so that another person exercises the discretion or judgement which, in the absence of delegation of the power, would need to be exercised by the director. The common law principle is that a person to whom a power has been granted cannot delegate that power unless the grant empowers him to do so (*Cartmell's Case* (1874) LR 9). The articles grant the directors their powers (see Model Article 3) and invariably grant them the power to delegate any of their powers (see Model Article 5). Delegation is essential for the operation of large companies and s. 173(2)(b) indicates that if authorised by the company's constitution, delegation will not, in itself, be an infringement of s. 173. When deciding to delegate, selecting the delegate and supervising and reviewing the performance of the delegate, it is important for directors to act in accordance with all of their duties, including the need to comply with s 172 (above) and to act with the care and skill required by s. 174 (below). In large companies, with multiple levels of delegation, this will require the board to satisfy itself that there are adequate supervision and review systems in place at all levels in the company.

Finally, the positive formulation of the duty also raises the question of the right of directors to rely on the judgement of others in taking decisions. Directors can and in many cases must take advice from experts before taking decisions. This will not be a breach of s. 173 provided the director considers the advice and then, having taken the advice into account, makes his own decision. Again, other duties come into play when the director is deciding whether or not advice is required and when selecting advisers.

4.4 Duty to exercise reasonable care, skill and diligence (s. 174)

'174 Duty to exercise reasonable care, skill and diligence
  (1) A director of a company must exercise reasonable care, skill and diligence.
  (2) This means the care, skill and diligence that would be exercised by a reasonably diligent person with—
      (a) the general knowledge, skill and experience that may reasonably be expected of a person carrying out the functions carried out by the director in relation to the company, and
      (b) the general knowledge, skill and experience that the director has.'

The common law standard of care, skill and diligence owed by directors to their companies was developed before the modern law of negligence evolved. The degree of attendance to the affairs of the company required was negligible. In *Re Cardiff Saving Bank, Marquis of Bute* [1892] 2 Ch 100, for example, a director of a bank attended only one board meeting in the 39 years for which he was president yet was held not be in breach of duty. The standard of care required was largely subjective.

In his first instance judgment in *Re City Equitable Fire Insurance Co Ltd* [1925] Ch 407, Romer J reviewed the authorities and stated that a director is not required to exhibit a greater degree of skill than may reasonably be expected from a person of his knowledge and experience. Although this case was not overruled in the years leading up to the enactment of the 2006 Act, courts had begun to work round it, preferring the statement of duty set out in s. 214 of the Insolvency Act 1986.

Re D'Jan (of London) Ltd [1994] 1 BCLC 561

Mr D'Jan, a director of a small company, failed, before signing it, to read an insurance proposal form that had been filled out by the company's insurance broker.

Held (by Hoffmann LJ sitting in the Chancery Division at first instance): The duty of a director at common law is accurately stated in s. 214 of the Insolvency Act 1986. The document was a very simple document asking a few questions that Mr D'Jan was the best person to answer and in failing to read the form he did not show reasonable diligence and was therefore in breach of his duty to the company. The court has a discretionary power (now s. 1157 of the Companies Act 2006) to relieve a director wholly or in part from liability for breach of duty if the court considers he acted honestly and reasonably and ought fairly to be excused and that section contemplates that conduct may be reasonable for the purposes of the section despite amounting to lack of care at common law. His breach was not gross, it could have happened to any busy man, although this is not enough to excuse it. At the relevant time the company was solvent and prosperous and the company is and was owned by Mr D'Jan and his wife. Mr D'Jan was excused for some but not all of the liability.

This was not the first case in which Hoffmann LJ had chosen not to apply the *Re City Equitable* subjective standard of care. His approach is now reflected in s. 174. The standard described in s. 174(2)(a) is essentially an objective standard of care. Although it has been described as a 'universal standard', the standard is applied to the facts of each particular case (*Re Barings plc (No. 5)* [1999] 1 BCLC 433, see below). In particular:

- the functions/role in the management of the company to be carried out by the particular director must be taken into account;
- the nature of its business and size of the particular company in question must be taken into account;
- the actual knowledge, skills and experience of the director can only enhance the level of care, skill and diligence required to satisfy the duty (s. 174(2)(b)) ('and' linking them indicates that subsections (a) and (b) are cumulative).

An experienced business accountant, for example, will be expected to show a higher level of skill in relation to financial matters than a person who does not hold himself out as having financial skills. A financial director will be expected to have the special skills expected of a person in that role (*Re Brian D Pierson (Contractors) Ltd* [2001] 1 BCLC 275).

Section 174 is modelled on s. 214(4) of the Insolvency Act 1986, which deals with wrongful trading by directors. In addition to wrongful trading cases providing guidance on the application of this duty, cases involving disqualification of directors pursuant to the Company Directors Disqualification Act 1986 often involve assessment of whether or not a director has discharged this duty. Indeed, the duty of care skill and diligence has largely been developed and clarified in director disqualification cases, such as in *Re Barings plc (No. 5)* [1999] 1 BCLC 433 (confirmed on appeal [2000] 1 BCLC 523 (CA)). That case is one of a number of cases resulting from the unauthorised trading of Nick Leeson, an employee of a subsidiary of Barings plc, which drove one of the bank's principal operating subsidiaries into insolvency. Although relevant, a finding of breach of duty of care is not sufficient to establish a case for disqualification.

 **CASE LAW 12.5**

***Re Barings plc (No. 5), Secretary of State for Trade and Industry v Baker* [1999] 1 BCLC 433**

Disqualification orders were sought by the Secretary of State for Trade and Industry against former directors of a principal operating subsidiary of Barings plc based on their failure to institute and monitor appropriate internal management controls which resulted in Nick Leeson, a trader in its Singapore office, having sole control of both the settlement or 'back' office and the dealing or 'front' offices of the bank in Singapore. This situation continued notwithstanding an internal audit proposal that the bank should separate the roles. The issue before the court was whether the conduct of the directors was such as to make them 'unfit to be concerned in the management of a company' for the purposes of s. 6 of the Company Directors Disqualification Act 1986.

Held: The directors had failed properly to monitor and control Leeson's activities even though they had management responsibility for those activities. They had failed to investigate a fictitious transaction discovered by internal auditors; perform any proper examination of the subsidiary's profitability; remove responsibility for both the front and back offices from Leeson; and ensure that the trading positions in Singapore were properly managed. Parker J held that the directors were incompetent to such a degree as to make them unfit to be directors and disqualified them for six years.

In the course of his judgment, Parker J stated: 'each director owes duties to the company to inform himself about its affairs and to join with his co-directors in supervising and controlling them'. He summarised the relevant duties of directors:

'In summary, the following general propositions can, in my judgment, be derived from the authorities to which I was referred in relation to the duties of directors:
(i) Directors have, both collectively and individually, a continuing duty to acquire and maintain a sufficient knowledge and understanding of the company's business to enable them properly to discharge their duties as directors.

CASE LAW 12.5 *continued*

(ii) Whilst directors are entitled (subject to the Articles of Association of the company) to delegate particular functions to those below them in the management chain, and to trust their competence and integrity to a reasonable extent, the exercise of the power of delegation does not absolve a director from the duty to supervise the discharge of the delegated functions.

(iii) No rule of universal application can be formulated as to the duty referred to in (ii) above. The extent of the duty, and the question whether it has been discharged, must depend on the facts of each particular case, including the director's role in the management of the company.'

The duty of diligence was emphasised in *Lexi Holdings plc v Luqman* [2009] EWCA Civ 117, a case in which the failure of two directors, who were sisters of a dishonest co-director, to attend to the affairs of the company, was sufficient breach of duty for the court to hold them liable to the company, alongside their brother, for monies which had, in effect, been stolen by him from the company.

4.5 Key specific corporate governance duties

The 2006 Act sometimes imposes specific duties directly on directors and sometimes on the company. Where obligations imposed on the company are backed by criminal liability of both the company and its officers (a term that includes directors, s. 1121(2)), they give officers of the company an incentive to ensure that the obligations are fulfilled. These obligations therefore serve a similar function to duties. Criminal liability for default is not absolute: directors will only be liable for default if they are personally in default.

Key specific corporate governance duties and company obligations are referenced in Figures 12.1 and 12.3 above and can be looked up in the Companies Act 2006.

TEST YOUR KNOWLEDGE 12.2

(a) Which four general duties of a director are most relevant when a director is deciding whether to support a board resolution or not?
(b) Is a nominee director entitled to put the interests of his nominator ahead of the interests of the company?
(c) What is the test to determine whether or not a director has demonstrated the standard of care, skill and diligence required by s. 174?
(d) Would you describe the test at question (c) as an objective or subjective test?

5 Conflict of interest duties

5.1 Introduction

Conflict of interest duties are the duties imposed on directors primarily to discourage them from acting not only in their own self-interest but also in the interest of any person other than the company, including a person to whom they may also owe a duty. The duty in s. 173 to exercise independent judgement, is also often very relevant to a director faced with duties both to the company and a third party (often the director's nominating shareholder).

As stated above, corporate governance duties and conflict of interest duties are not mutually exclusive. Where a director acts in his own self-interest or in the interest of another person to whom he owes a duty, he will very often also be in breach of a corporate governance duty. (The same is less likely in reverse, however; there is not the same likelihood that a breach of corporate governance duty will also entail a breach of a conflict of interest duty.)

The essential learning point is that directors' duties are cumulative. A single act can be evidence of breach of a number of different duties. Section 179 states clearly: 'more than one of the general duties may apply in any given case'.

The general duties regulating self-interested actions by directors fall into two categories: disclosure duties in relation to contracts with the company (ss. 177 and 182) on the one hand, and the duties to avoid conflicts of interests (s. 175) and not to take benefits from third parties (s.176), on the other. Additional statutory provisions govern specific types of contracts directors enter into with their companies, mandating shareholder approval in advance. These statutory provisions are not strictly speaking directors' duties but if they are not complied with, the remedies the company has against directors are similar to those available for breach of the general directors' duties. An overview of conflict of interest duties and the key statutory provisions governing directors contracting with their companies can be seen in Figure 12.4.

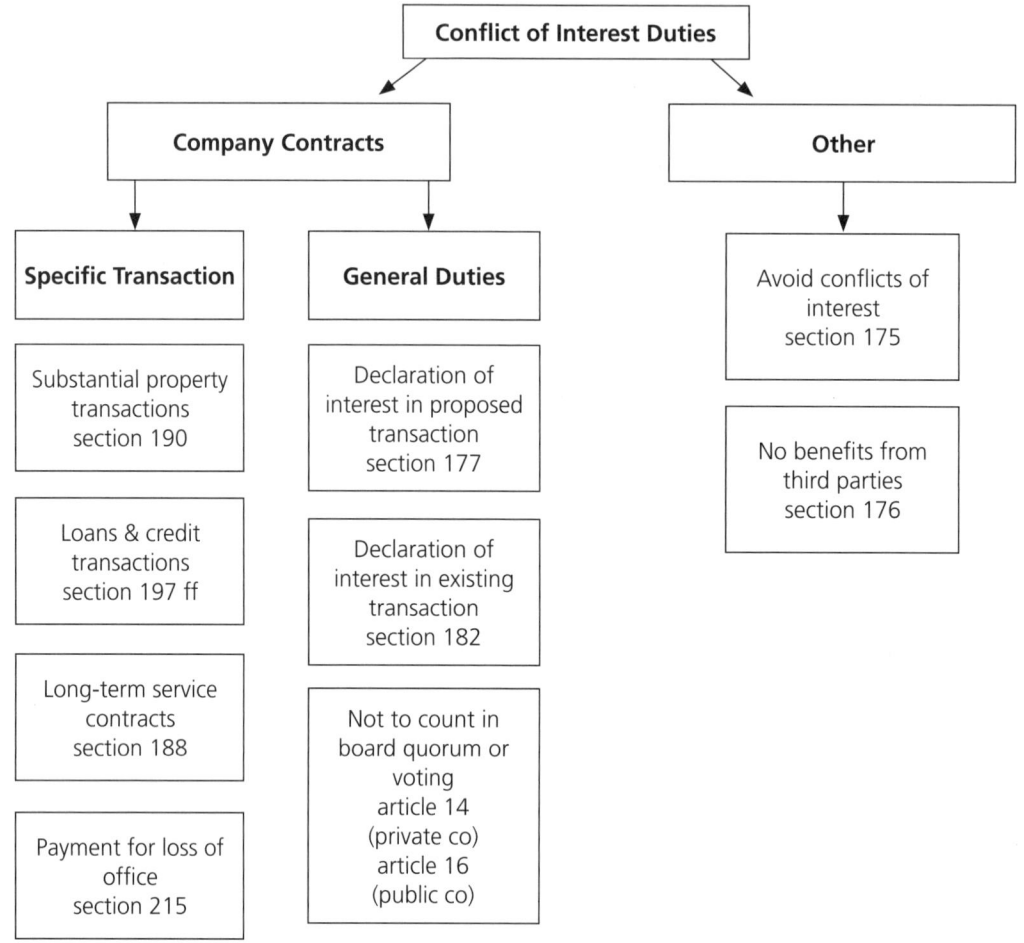

FIGURE 12.4 Directors' conflict of interest duties

5.2 Directors' conflicts of interest

Directors' conflicts of interests are governed by two general duties, the duty to avoid conflicts of interest (s. 175) and the duty not to accept benefits from third parties (s. 176).

Duty to avoid conflicts of interest

'175 Duty to avoid conflicts of interest
(1) A director of a company must avoid a situation in which he has, or can have, a direct or indirect interest that conflicts, or possibly may conflict, with the interests of the company.

(2) This applies in particular to the exploitation of any property, information or opportunity (and it is immaterial whether the company could take advantage of the property, information or opportunity).
(3) This duty does not apply to a conflict of interest arising in relation to a transaction or arrangement with the company.
(4) This duty is not infringed—
   (a) if the situation cannot reasonably be regarded as likely to give rise to a conflict of interest; or
   (b) if the matter has been authorised by the directors.
(5) Authorisation may be given by the directors—
   (a) where the company is a private company and nothing in the company's constitution invalidates such authorisation, by the matter being proposed to and authorised by the directors; or
   (b) where the company is a public company and its constitution includes provision enabling the directors to authorise the matter, by the matter being proposed to and authorised by them in accordance with the constitution.
(6) The authorisation is effective only if—
   (a) any requirement as to the quorum at the meeting at which the matter is considered is met without counting the director in question or any other interested director, and
   (b) the matter was agreed to without their voting or would have been agreed to if their votes had not been counted.
(7) Any reference in this section to a conflict of interest includes a conflict of interest and duty and a conflict of duties'.

A director of a company is quite likely, at some point in his directorship, to find himself in a situation in which his duty to advance the interests of the company comes into conflict with his personal interest or a duty he owes to another person. An example of a situation with the potential to give rise to a conflict is where a director wishes to take up an opportunity that has been offered to but declined by the company. Other examples are where a director is on two or more boards of directors and one company is a major customer, supplier or competitor of the other.

Multiple directorships are common in the UK, especially among NEDs of large quoted companies. Consequently, the power to authorise conflict situations and thereby remove them from the statutory duty of a director to avoid a situation in which he has, or can have, a direct or indirect interest that conflicts, or possibly may conflict, with the interests of the company is of great practical importance.

Director authorisation

Section 175 permits the board to authorise conflicts of interest. This is in contrast to the pre-2006 Act law, which reserved the power to authorise conflicts of interest to the shareholders unless the Articles provided otherwise (which they regularly did). The conditions for availability of s. 175(5) authorisation are different for private and public companies.

Private company director authorisation of conflicts
The s. 175(5) power of directors to authorise conflicts is automatic for private companies registered on or after 1 October 2008, provided nothing in its Articles invalidates such authorisation (s. 175(5)(a)). Important transitional provisions state that director authorisation will only apply to private companies incorporated before that date where the shareholders have resolved (before, on or after 1 October 2008) that authorisation may be given in accordance with s. 175(5) (see para 47(3) of sch. 4 to the Companies Act 2006 Fifth Commencement Order (SI 2007/3495)).

Public company director authorisation of conflicts
The board of a public company is only permitted to authorise conflicts pursuant to s. 175(5) if the Articles include a provision enabling the directors to do so.

Entry into force of s. 175 was delayed until 1 October 2008 to enable private companies to consider the matter and, if they so required, amend their Articles to provide that director authorisation pursuant to s. 175(5) was not permitted. Public companies, on the other hand, were to consider providing in their Articles that directors may authorise conflicts pursuant to s. 175(5).

Conditions for effective director authorisation

Section 175(6) governs the conditions of effective director authorisation. Any requirement as to the quorum at the meeting at which the matter is considered must be met without counting the director in question or any other interested director, and the matter must be agreed to without their voting or it must be the case that it would have been agreed to if their votes had not been counted. Note also that authorisation must be obtained in advance of acting in what would otherwise be a conflict of interest matter. When deciding whether or not to authorise a conflict, a director must, of course, act in accordance with all of the duties he owes to the company. For example, if he votes to authorise a conflict when he does not consider, in good faith, that the authorisation would be most likely to promote the success of the company, he will be in breach of s. 172.

What is a conflict of interest?

The 2006 Act contains no definition of 'conflict of interest'. When, then, will a conflict of interest exist for the purposes of the s. 175 duty?

- Section 175(7) spells out that a conflict of interest includes a conflict of interest and duty and a conflict of duties.
- Section 175(3) provides that a conflict arising in relation to a transaction or arrangement with the company is not a conflict covered by s. 175 (regulation of these transactions and the scope of s. 175(3) are considered below).
- Section 175(1) refers to the duty to avoid a situation in which the director has, or can have, a direct or indirect interest that conflicts, or possibly may conflict, with the interests of the company, yet s. 175(4) states that the duty does not apply if the situation cannot reasonably be regarded as likely to give rise to a conflict of interest.
- Section 175(2) reinforces that the duty applies in particular to the exploitation of any property, information or opportunity.
- Section 175(2) goes on to state that it is immaterial whether the company could take advantage of the property, information or opportunity, yet again, it is difficult to reconcile this with the duty not applying if the situation cannot reasonably be regarded as likely to give rise to a conflict of interest (s. 175(4)).

Beyond the clues in s. 175 as to when a conflict of interest will exist, it is instructive to examine pre-2006 Act conflict of interest cases to have a sense of when a director will be found to have a conflict of interest for the purposes of s. 175. Many cases have concerned directors diverting corporate opportunities to themselves then leaving the company to pursue those opportunities.

Corporate opportunities and directors ceasing to hold office

Section 170(2) specifically provides that a person who ceases to be a director continues to be subject to the duty in s. 175, 'as regards the exploitation of any property, information or opportunity of which he became aware at a time when he was a director'. What is not always clear is whether such exploitation is, as a matter of fact, a conflict of interest. Two types of cases dealing with directors who leave companies and take up opportunities the companies consider they should not have exploited for their own benefit are where a director leaves deliberately in order to acquire an opportunity previously sought by and for the company, and where a director is forced out of a company. In relation to the first of these scenarios, the law is strictly applied.

 **CASE LAW 12.6**

Canadian Aero Service Ltd v O'Mally (1973) 40 DLR (3d) 371
Two directors, the president and vice-president of the company, tried to obtain a contract on behalf of the company and were active participants in the negotiations. They then resigned, formed a new company and acquired the contract for the new company.

 **CASE LAW** **12.6** *continued*

Held: the directors were liable to account to their former company for the profits made. This was a diversion of a maturing business opportunity that the company was actively pursuing. Laskin J stated that even after his resignation a director is precluded from exploiting the opportunity, 'where the resignation may fairly be said to have been prompted or influenced by a wish to acquire for himself the opportunity sought by the company, or where it was his position with the company rather than a fresh initiative that led him to the opportunity which he later acquired'.

In contrast, there may be no conflict where a director performs services for a customer of the company in competition with the company, even while he is a director, if he is in the process of being forced out of the company. Starting from the principle illustrated in *London and Mashonaland Exploration Co Ltd v New Mashonaland Exploration Co Ltd* [1891] WN 165 that there is no completely rigid rule that a director may not be involved in the business of a company which is in competition with another company of which he is a director, the Court of Appeal in *Plus Group Ltd v Pyke* [2002] 2 BCLC 201 (CA) considered it possible for a director's duty to be 'reduced to vanishing point' on the facts because he had been squeezed out of any management role in the company. In those circumstances, a director who set up a new company to compete with the company and performed services for a major client of the company, was held not to be in breach of duty.

In *Foster Bryant Surveying Ltd v Bryant & Savernake Property Consultants Ltd* [2007] 2 BCLC 239 (CA), the Court of Appeal explored the duty of a director between resigning (he was effectively forced out of a company) and his resignation taking effect in the context of a customer of the company wishing to continue to secure the services of the director. Rix LJ's judgment is worth reading for its clear review of the 'corporate opportunity' authorities. He focused on the need for a link between the resignation and the obtaining of the business by the director, i.e. the resignation must be part of a dishonest plan. He stated that the standards of loyalty, good faith and the no-conflict rule should be tested in each case by many factors, i.e. a fact-intensive investigation was required to determine liability for breach. Among the factors to be considered are:

- position or office held;
- the nature of the corporate opportunity;
- its ripeness;
- its specificity;
- the director's or managerial officer's relation to it;
- the amount of knowledge possessed;
- the circumstances in which it was obtained;
- whether it was special or even private;
- time as a factor in the continuation of fiduciary duty where the alleged breach occurs after termination of the relationship with the company;
- the circumstances under which the relationship was terminated, that is whether by retirement or resignation or discharge.

Note the willingness of the court in this case to engage in in-depth factual analysis when applying the conflict of interest rules to determine whether or not a conflict actually existed. This approach is in stark contrast with the approach in old cases asserting the necessity for fiduciary obligations to be applied strictly, regardless of whether or not the principal suffered a loss, to protect the principal, 'as no court is equal to the examination and ascertainment of the truth in much the greater number of cases' (*per* Lord Eldon LC in *Ex parte James* 8 Ves 337).

The strict principle that a fiduciary may not benefit from a corporate opportunity even where the company could not have benefited from the opportunity itself has been applied to company directors in what was the leading case on conflict of interest before the 2006 Act, *Regal (Hastings) Ltd v Gulliver* [1967] 2 AC 134.

Regal (Hastings) Ltd v Gulliver [1967] 2 AC 134

The board of directors of Regal (Hastings) Ltd, acting together and honestly, bought shares in a subsidiary of the company set up to facilitate the sale of the company's business. Regal (Hastings) Ltd had been given the option to acquire the shares but lacked the finances to do so. On the subsequent sale of the company and the partly-owned subsidiary, the directors made profits on their shares in the subsidiary company. The new owners of the company brought proceedings against the directors to recover those profits.

Held: The directors had not disclosed their intention to acquire the shares to the shareholders and obtained the approval of the shareholders to their action. Accordingly, the directors were in breach of the duty not to make a secret profit.

The reference in s. 175 to it being immaterial whether the company could take advantage of the property, information or opportunity alleged to have been exploited by the director can be traced back to this case. Yet later cases, such as *Foster Bryant*, showed the willingness of the courts to take a 'common sense and merits based approach ... which reflects the equitable principles at the root of these issues' (*per* Rix LJ). As we have seen, this more flexible approach is reflected in s. 175 insofar as s. 175(4)(a) states that the duty is not infringed if the situation 'cannot reasonably be regarded as likely to give rise to a conflict of interest'. It is clear that *Regal (Hastings) Ltd v Gulliver* would be decided in the same way were it to come to court today and s. 175 applied to determine whether or not the directors were liable to account for the profits they made based on a breach of the duty not to put themselves in a position in which their personal interest and the interests of the company conflicted.

A further strict application of the rule occurred in *Bhullar v Bhullar* [2003] 2 BCLC 241 (CA), a case in which two directors of a small company which was not currently developing any further land, bought land in which the company would otherwise have been interested, for development by themselves personally. Although he approved the following quotation from the dissenting judgment of Lord Upjohn in the leading case of *Boardman v Phipps* [1967] 2 AC 46 (HL), Jonathan Parker LJ went on to find the directors liable for breach of duty as, 'reasonable men looking at the facts would think there was a real sensible possibility of conflict'.

> 'The phrase "possibly may conflict" requires consideration. In my view it means that the reasonable man looking at the relevant facts and circumstances of the particular case would think that there was a real sensible possibility of conflict, not that you could imagine some situation arising which might, in some conceivable possibility in events not contemplated as real sensible possibilities by any reasonable person, result in a conflict.'

5.3 Duty not to accept benefits from third parties

'176 Duty not to accept benefits from third parties
(1) A director of a company must not accept a benefit from a third party conferred by reason of—
(a) his being a director, or
(b) his doing (or not doing) anything as director.
(2) A 'third party' means a person other than the company, an associated body corporate or a person acting on behalf of the company or an associated body corporate.'

The second general directors' duty aimed at protecting the company from a director acting in his own self-interest or in the interest of any person other than the company is the duty not to accept benefits from third parties. Section 176 is based on and operates in relation to directors in place of the equitable principle that fiduciaries must not accept bribes or secret commissions (see *AG of Hong Kong v Reid* [1994] 1 AC 324 (PC) but note that in relation to the remedy available where a bribe has been taken, this case has not been followed and has been criticised by the Court of Appeal in *Sinclair Investments (UK) Ltd v Versailles Trade Finance Ltd* [2011] EWCA

Civ 347). The section is broader than bribes and secret commissions, extending to any kind of benefit, whether financial or non-financial. Every breach of this section will fall within the duty to avoid conflicts of interest in s. 175, but note that acceptance of benefits from third parties has clearly been singled out as behaviour that other directors cannot be entrusted to monitor and approve as, unlike s. 175, s. 176 contains no provision for board authorisation. The uncertainty as to the scope of s. 176 will make it unclear in some cases whether the director authorisation under s. 175(4)(b) will be of *practical* benefit.

Unless provisions in the Articles permit such (s. 180(4)(b)), third party benefits must be approved by the shareholders if a director is to avoid liability. This power of the shareholders to approve receipt of third party benefits is preserved by s. 180(4)(a). The exception of any benefit that cannot reasonably be regarded as likely to give rise to a conflict of interests is an important one as it takes reasonable corporate hospitality out of the realm of breach. A final point to note is that s. 170(2)(b) specifically provides that a person who ceases to be a director continues to be subject to this duty 'as regards things done or omitted by him before he ceased to be a director'.

TEST YOUR KNOWLEDGE 12.3

(a) Does the duty to avoid conflicts of interest apply to a conflict of interest arising in relation to a director entering into a contract with the company?
(b) Who may authorise a directors' conflict of interest?
(c) Would *Regal (Hastings) Ltd v Gulliver* (1967) be decided the same way today? Do you believe it should be?

6 Directors contracting with their companies

The Companies Act 2006 imposes on directors a duty to declare interests in proposed and existing company contracts to the board of directors (ss. 177 and 182). It also requires shareholder approval for four specific types of transactions directors may enter into with their companies.

6.1 Statutory declaration of interest to the board of directors

'177 Duty to declare interest in proposed transaction or arrangement
  (1) If a director of a company is in any way, directly or indirectly, interested in a proposed transaction or arrangement with the company, he must declare the nature and extent of that interest to the other directors.
  (2) The declaration may (but need not) be made—
    (a) at a meeting of the directors, or
    (b) by notice to the directors in accordance with—
      (i) section 184 (notice in writing), or
      (ii) section 185 (general notice).
  (3) If a declaration of interest under this section proves to be, or becomes, inaccurate or incomplete, a further declaration must be made.
  (4) Any declaration required by this section must be made before the company enters into the transaction or arrangement.
  (5) This section does not require a declaration of an interest of which the director is not aware or where the director is not aware of the transaction or arrangement in question. For this purpose a director is treated as being aware of matters of which he ought reasonably to be aware.
  (6) A director need not declare an interest—
    (a) if it cannot reasonably be regarded as likely to give rise to a conflict of interest;
    (b) if, or to the extent that, the other directors are already aware of it (and for this purpose the other directors are treated as aware of anything of which they ought reasonably to be aware); or
    (c) if, or to the extent that, it concerns terms of his service contract that have been or are to be considered—

(i) by a meeting of the directors, or
(ii) by a committee of the directors appointed for the purpose under the company's constitution.

182 Declaration of interest in existing transaction or arrangement

(1) Where a director of a company is in any way, directly or indirectly, interested in a transaction or arrangement that has been entered into by the company, he must declare the nature and extent of the interest to the other directors in accordance with this section. This section does not apply if or to the extent that the interest has been declared under section 177 (duty to declare interest in proposed transaction or arrangement).'

The 2006 Act requires a director to declare his interest in any transaction or arrangement the company proposes to enter into (s. 177) or has already entered into (s. 182) to the other directors. The details of how and when such declarations must be made have changed (see s. 177, set out above and similar subsections in s. 182).

CASE EXAMPLE 12.2

Dan is a director of E Company Ltd. Dan also owns all of the shares of Company S Ltd. Company E Ltd proposes to enter into a purchase agreement with Company S Ltd. Dan must declare his interest in Company S Ltd to the directors of Company E Ltd before the companies enter into the contract unless he can establish that his interest cannot reasonably be regarded as likely to give rise to a conflict of interest (unlikely in this case) or that the other directors are already aware of it or ought reasonably to be aware of it.

If the company enters into the transaction or arrangement, a director who fails to declare his interest commits a criminal offence (s. 183). Of greater interest are the civil consequences of failure to comply. Sections 177 and 182 are silent as to the civil consequences of failure to comply with them, although the 2006 Act does contain the general statement that the consequences of breach of the directors' general duties are the same as would apply if the corresponding common law or equitable principle applied (s. 178(1)).

The problem is that there was no common law or equitable principle requiring a director to declare his interest to the board: ss. 177 and 182 could be seen as amended re-enactments of a prior statutory provision which had no civil consequences. Section 170(3) of the Act, however, states that, 'The general duties are bases on certain common law rules and equitable principles as they apply in relation to directors and have effect in place of those rules and principles as regards the duties owed to a company by a director'. Accordingly, the statutory duty of a director to declare his interest in a company contract to the other directors appears to operate in place of the duty of a director to make disclosure of his interest to the company (which was the shareholders). On this basis, failure to declare an interest in accordance with s. 177 or 182 has the same consequences as failure to disclose to the shareholders had, and the contract is voidable by the company. Depending on the facts, a director may also be liable to account to the company for any profits made.

If s. 177 is complied with, the contract will not be voidable by the company as a result of not having been approved by the shareholders (s. 180(1). Again, however, the Act is silent as to whether or not a director who makes a declaration to the other directors is protected against the company seeking an account of profits made by the director from the contract. The implication is that he is protected but the situation may be a little more involved than simply a director making a profit from a contract with his company.

Consider Case Example 12.3.

CASE EXAMPLE 12.3

Erin became a director of F Company Ltd in 2000. At the first board meeting she attended she learned that F Company Ltd was planning to expand into selling MP3 players in the medium term and was looking for a major supplier to open discussions with. In 2001 she was called by MiCo Ltd, an MP3 player manufacturer that was in trouble financially. It was looking for new customers and wanted to discuss establishing a contract to supply F Company Ltd. Erin told MiCo Ltd that F Company Ltd was not ready to enter the MP3 player market. She expressed interest in purchasing an interest in MiCo Ltd. Erin bought shares in MiCo Ltd giving her 25 per cent of the issued shares. In 2006, F Company Ltd proposed to enter into a contract with MiCo Ltd for the supply of MP3 players. Erin declared to the other directors that she had a 25 per cent interest in MiCo Ltd. A supply contract was entered into between F Company Ltd and MiCo Ltd. MiCo Ltd made healthy profits from the contract and Erin has received dividends of £100,000 from MiCo Ltd for the last two years (compared to £100 in each of 2001–5). Another director of F Company Ltd discovers that Erin was approached by MiCo Ltd in 2001 and is angry that Erin did not inform the board of the approach as the company might have been able to get into the MP3 player market sooner.

Can F Company Ltd sue Erin for breach of s. 175?
Does s. 175(3) prevent such an action?

In Case Example 12.3 Erin is only able to make the profit from the contract with the company because of a conflict of interest (MiCo Ltd approaching her in 2001) which she resolved in favour of herself (by not informing F Company Ltd of the approach and purchasing an interest in MiCo Ltd herself). Surely, s. 175(3) does not protect Erin from being pursued for an account of profits the potential for which arose because of the 2001 breach of s. 175. Section 175(3) does not apply to 'a conflict of interest arising in relation to a transaction or arrangement with the company'. It should not protect a director where the benefit of a conflict of interest is crystallised by a transaction or arrangement with the company. The scope of s. 175(3) is, however, far from clear and the question posed in the example above must be regarded as moot.

A company's Articles will invariably include provisions expressly addressing the permitted participation of a director who has an interest in a company contract in the board meeting at which the contract is considered. The Model Articles provide that when a board decision is concerned with an actual or proposed transaction or arrangement with the company in which a director is interested, a director is not to be counted as participating in the decision-making process for quorum, voting or agreement purposes (Model Articles, art. 14(1) (private companies) and art. 16(1) (public companies)). The Model Articles do not contain language removing the exposure of a director to being made to account for profits made out of a contract with the company, provided he has declared his interest to the directors in accordance with s. 177. This contrasts with Table A which invariably contained such language.

6.2 Shareholder approval of specified transactions

Shareholder approval is required for:

- substantial property transactions (ss. 190–196);
- loans, quasi-loans and other credit transactions (ss. 197–214);
- long-term service agreements (s. 188);
- payments for loss of office (s. 215).

The relationship between the provisions on specific types of transactions and the general duties of directors is expressly addressed in s. 180. Compliance with the general duties does not remove the need for shareholder approval required by the specific provisions (s. 180(3)). Compliance with the relevant specific provision, however, removes the requirement to comply with the general duties to avoid conflicts of interest (s. 175) and not to accept benefits from third parties (ss. 176 and 180(2)).

Substantial property transactions

If a director of a company or its holding company (a parent company and any parent of its parent company are holding companies) or a person connected with him acquires or disposes of a substantial non-cash asset from or to the company, the arrangement must be approved in advance by shareholders or the acquisition or disposal must be conditional on such approval being obtained (s. 190).

CASE EXAMPLE 12.4

A director buys a second-hand executive car from the company for £25,000. This may be an acquisition of a substantial non-cash asset by a director from the company for which shareholder approval is required in advance or the contract must be conditional upon such approval being obtained. The test in s. 191(2)(a) must be applied: does the value of the car exceed 10 per cent of the company's net asset value?

CASE EXAMPLE 12.5

A director sells a flat he owns to the company for £200,000. This is a sale of a substantial non-cash asset by a director to the company. Shareholder approval is required in advance or the contract must be conditional upon such approval being obtained.

CASE EXAMPLE 12.6

A director of Company A Ltd sells a boat for £140,000 to Company S Ltd, which is a subsidiary of Company A Ltd. This is a sale of a substantial non-cash asset to a company by a director of its holding company. Approval is required in advance by the shareholders of Company A Ltd or the contract must be conditional upon such approval being obtained.

The key points to note about the governing provisions in ss. 190–196 of the Companies Act 2006 are:

1. Approval is required in advance (s. 190(1)) (although if not secured, affirmation within a reasonable time after the transaction has been entered into precludes avoidance of the transaction (s. 196)).
2. Approval must be by shareholder general resolution (s. 190(1)).
3. An asset is a substantial asset if its value exceeds £5,000 and exceeds either:
   - 10 per cent of the company's net asset value (based on annual accounts); or
   - £100,000 (s. 191(2)).
4. A person can be connected with a director based on a number of relationships including (but not limited to) being a (s. 252):
   - family member (s. 253), which includes a spouse, children and parents, but not sibling, aunts and uncles, nephews, nieces or grandparents
   - business partner
   - company, at least 20 per cent of the shares of which are owned by, or at least 20 per cent of the votes of which are controlled by, the director and persons connected with him.
5. Transactions between a company and its parent or wholly-owned subsidiary or between two wholly-owned subsidiaries of one parent company are excluded from the requirement (s. 192).

6   Transactions between a company and a director in his character as a shareholder of the company are excluded from the requirement (s. 192).

An example of a transaction with a director in his character as a shareholder would be a distribution made to a shareholder, who was also a director, in the form of an asset rather than cash (a distribution *in specie*).

Loans, quasi-loans and other credit transactions

A company may not make a loan to a director of the company or its holding company unless the transaction has been approved in advance by shareholders (s. 197(1)(a)). The same applies to a company guarantee of a loan provided to the director by a third party and the provision by the company of security in relation to such a loan. For public companies, the circumstances in which shareholder approval is required are expanded to also cover:

- loans and guarantees to a person connected with the director;
- a broader range of financial transactions with directors and persons connected with them: quasi loans, credit transactions and guarantees or security provided in relation to credit transactions.

The governing provisions (ss. 197–214) are detailed and what follows is simply intended to capture some of the key points:

- Approval is required in advance (s. 197 *et al.*) (although if not secured, affirmation within a reasonable time after the transaction has been entered into precludes avoidance of the transaction (s. 214)).
- Approval must be by shareholder general resolution.
- No approval is required if the aggregate value of the transaction and any other relevant transactions does not exceed £10,000.
- Advances up to £50,000 provided to a director to fund expenditure on company business are excepted (s. 204).

Long-term service contracts

Section 188 requires shareholder approval in advance of directors' service contracts (as defined in s. 227) of longer than two years. A copy of the entire proposed contract must be available for inspection by shareholders or, in the case of a written resolution, sent to shareholders before the shareholders' resolution is passed (s. 188(5)). Technically, it is only the provision of the contract relating to its length that must be approved (s. 188(2)), and the consequences of failure to secure shareholder approval are that:

- the provision is void to the extent of the contravention so that the contract can run for a maximum of two years; and
- the contract is deemed to contain a term entitling the company to terminate the contract at any time by giving reasonable notice.

Payment for loss of office

Non-contractual payments by way of compensation to a director for loss of office as director or any other office or employment, in excess of £200, must be approved by ordinary resolution of the shareholders (ss. 217 and 221). A memorandum setting out the particulars of the proposed payment must be available to the shareholders.

Note that this requirement does not apply to payments made pursuant to a legal obligation or by way of damages for breach of a legal obligation or settlement of any claim related to a legal obligation (s. 220). This takes payment in lieu of notice under a service contract and other payments provided for under a service contract outside the requirement for shareholder approval in s. 217. This area of law will be affected by proposed reform of the law governing directors' remuneration.

TEST YOUR KNOWLEDGE 12.4

(a) To whom is a director required to declare his interest in a contract the company proposes to enter into or to which it is already a party?
(b) Where are the rules governing the right of a director to vote on a contract with the company in which he has an interest to be found?
(c) Identify four types of transaction between a director and the company for which shareholder approval in advance is required.

7 Remedies

Codification of the remedies for breach of directors' duties was a step too far for the reform process and the remedies potentially available for breach of s. 174, a common law based duty, and ss. 171–173 and 175–177, the equity-based duties, are the same as would apply if the corresponding common law rule or equitable principle applied (s. 178(1)). Given that the remedies for failure to obtain shareholder approval for substantial transactions, loans and other credit arrangements between a director and the company are set out in the statute it would not have been too difficult to set out the remedies for breach of the general duties. The approach taken, however, leaves the remedies flexible and able to evolve. Unfortunately, this flexibility is secured at the price of not achieving the clarity and accessibility the statutory statement of directors' duties was supposed to deliver.

7.1 Remedies for breach of duty to exercise reasonable care, skill and diligence (s. 174)

The duty to exercise reasonable care, skill and diligence is a common law duty rather than an equitable duty. Consequently, the usual remedy available to the company against a director who is found to be in breach will be damages for breach of duty. Damages will be based on tort principles. Accordingly, the company must be able to show:

- loss to the company that is not too remote;
- a causal link between the breach and the company's loss (*Cohen v Selby* [2001] 1 BCLC 176).

7.2 Remedies for breach of the equity-based duties (ss. 171–173 and 175–177)

With the exception of the duty to exercise reasonable care, skill and diligence, the general duties of directors are equity-based, for which equitable remedies may be available. Equitable remedies are never available as of right. The company must satisfy the conditions for the court to grant relief sought. Your equity or trusts studies will assist you to understand equitable remedies for breach of duty. Essentially, depending on the circumstances, four potential remedies are available to the company, as follows:

- return of property a director has received in breach of duty;
- confiscation/account of profits a director has made as a result of breach of duty;
- rescission of contracts made in breach of duty; or
- equitable compensation.

Return of property received in breach of duty

A director may be ordered to restore to the company property transferred to him in breach of fiduciary duty. This remedy is based on ordinary trust principles – the director holds such property as constructive trustee (*Harrison (JJ) (Properties) Ltd v Harrison* [2001] 1 BCLC 162) for the company. The Court of Appeal in *Sinclair Investments (UK) Ltd v Versailles Trade Finance Ltd* [2011] EWCA Civ 347 has, however, emphasised that a proprietary remedy, by way of constructive trust, will not be available where the property sought by the company was never owned by the company (nor is it the traceable proceeds of property once owned by the company). This means that the court will not impose a constructive trust on money or other property received by a director from a third party. Accordingly, the decision of the Privy Council in AG of *Hong Kong v Reid* [1994] 1 AC 324 (PC) can no longer be considered to be good law. A director who receives a bribe will simply be personally liable to account to the company for the profit he has made as a result of receiving the bribe.

Account of profits made as a result of breach of duty

A director may be ordered to account to the company for any profits he has made as a result of the breach of duty. The principal object of an account of profits is to deter directors from breaching their duties and not to compensate the company for loss (*United Pan-Europe Communications NV v Deutsche Bank AG* [2000] 2 BCLC 461). Accordingly, the director may be made to account even if the company has suffered no loss, and even if the company could not have made the profit itself, as was the case in *Regal (Hastings) Ltd v Gulliver* [1967] 2 AC 134.

> 'The rule of equity which insists on those, who by use of a fiduciary position make a profit, being liable to account for that profit, in no way depends on fraud, or absence of *bona fides*; or upon such questions and considerations as whether the profit would or should otherwise have gone to the plaintiff, or whether the profiteer was under a duty to obtain the source of the profit for the plaintiff, or whether he took a risk or acted as he did for the benefit of the plaintiff, or whether the plaintiff had in fact been damaged or benefited by his action. The liability arises from the mere fact of the profit having, in the stated circumstances, been made. The profiteer, however honest or well-intentioned, cannot escape the risk of being called upon to account.'

Rescission of contracts made in breach of duty

A contract made in breach of fiduciary duty may be voidable at the option of the company. Each party must return any property transferred by the other pursuant to the contract. This may be relatively straightforward where the contract is between the director and the company but where the contract is between the company and a third party, rescission may not be possible due to the effect it would have on the third party. Rescission may be awarded if the third party has requisite knowledge of the breach of duty (*Logicrose Ltd v Southend UFC Ltd* [1988] 1 WLR 1256).

Equitable compensation

A director may be ordered to pay equitable compensation to the company for loss the company has suffered as a result of the breach of duty. Equitable compensation is different from damages for breach of contract or compensation for a tort. It is closer to an indemnification. There must still be a causal connection between the breach and the loss. The importance of causation in determining equitable compensation was made clear by Lord Brown-Wilkinson's judgment in *Target Holdings Limited v Redferns* [1996] 1 AC 421 (HL), a case in which the House of Lords quashed the Court of Appeal's order that a solicitor in breach of fiduciary duty must compensate his client for losses that had not been caused by the breach. The losses would have been suffered even had there been no breach of duty and therefore were not recoverable as equitable compensation for the breach of duty.

> 'At common law there are two principles fundamental to the award of damages. First that the defendant's wrongful act must cause the damage complained of. Second that the plaintiff is to be put "in the same position as he would have been in if he had not sustained the wrong for which he is now getting his compensation or reparation". Although … in many ways equity approaches liability for making good a breach of trust from a different starting point, in my judgment those two principles are applicable as much in equity as at common law. Under both systems liability is fault based: the defendant is only liable for the consequences of the legal wrong he has done to the plaintiff and to make good the damage caused by such wrong.'

7.3 Remedies for failure to obtain shareholder approval for specific transactions

In contrast to the remedies for breach of the general duties of directors, when a contract is entered into without securing statutorily required shareholder approval the remedies available against directors are set out in the 2006 Act. Section 195 (relating to substantial property transactions with directors) and s. 213 (relating to loans, quasi-loans and credit transactions) provide that:

1. The transaction is voidable at the instance of the company.
2. A director may be required to:
   - account to the company for any benefit or profit made from the transaction; and
   - indemnify the company for any loss or damages resulting from the transaction.

Liability extends not only to the director who enters into the transaction, but also to any director of the company who has authorised the transaction is also liable to account for any profit he has made and is jointly and severally liable to indemnify the company for any loss or damage resulting from the transaction (ss. 195(4)(d) and 213(4)(d)). A director could be liable even if, rather than taking any active part in authorising it, he has merely acquiesced in the transaction. A director who authorised the transaction may defend himself against liability by proving that at the time the arrangement was entered into he did not know the relevant circumstances constituting the contravention (ss. 195(7) and 213(7)).

7.4 Removal from office

Where a director is in breach of duty, the shareholders may decide to remove him as a director either pursuant to any power to do so in the Articles or pursuant to s. 168. The company may also seek to terminate any service contract he has with the company.

The rights of the director in relation to his service contract are principally governed by employment law. In particular it will be a matter of construction of the service contract whether or not the behaviour of the director is sufficient to allow termination for cause. Company law simply provided for service contracts of longer than two years' duration entered into without securing shareholder approval, as required by s. 188, to be terminated by reasonable notice.

TEST YOUR KNOWLEDGE 12.5

(a) Have the remedies for breach of directors' duties been codified? Where are the rules establishing the remedies to be found?
(b) What are the remedies for breach of the duty of care, skill and diligence in s. 174?
(c) Identify the four key equitable remedies available for breach of fiduciary duty.

8 Relief from liability, indemnification, exclusion of liability and insurance

8.1 Relief from liability

We have seen above that directors may be able to obtain authorisation in advance for what would otherwise be a breach of duty. This authorisation may be obtained from:

- directors in relation to conflicts of interest (s. 175(5));
- shareholders, as allowed by any rule of law (s. 180(4));
- a provision in the Articles of the company (s. 180(4)).

We have also seen that disclosure to the board in accordance with s. 177 will protect a director's contract with the company, or one in which he has an interest, from being set aside (s. 180(1)(b)).

In this section we focus on post-breach relief. After a breach, a director may be able to obtain relief from the consequences of his breach by:

- ratification by the shareholders pursuant to s. 239;
- court-granted relief pursuant to s. 1157.

Shareholder ratification (s. 239)

The starting point at common law and in equity, based on majority rule and the proper plaintiff principle, is that a breach of duty by a director can be ratified after the event by the shareholders by general resolution. Section 239 is a new provision which applies to ratification of a director's conduct amounting to negligence, default, breach of duty or breach of trust in relation to the company. In effect, it provides for ratification by:

- general resolution of shareholders; or
- unanimous consent of shareholders.

The votes of the director whose behaviour is being voted on (if he is a member) and any member connected with him are disregarded for the purposes of s. 239. Sub-section 239(7) states that s. 239 does not affect any other enactment or rule of law imposing additional requirements for valid ratification or any rule of law as to acts that are incapable of being ratified by the company. In doing so it preserves the uncertainty that exists regarding limits on the ratification power of shareholders.

Even if a breach is apparently ratified by a disinterested majority, as required by and in accordance with s. 239, it may be possible to use s. 239(7) to argue that the apparent ratification is ineffective. This issue could very well arise in the context of a shareholder seeking permission to continue a derivative claim (considered in chapter 17) as the court is precluded from giving such permission if the act complained of has been ratified (s. 263(2)(c)(ii)).

Court-granted relief (s. 1157)

A court that finds a director liable in respect of negligence, default, breach of duty or breach of trust may relieve the director from liability either wholly or in part if the court finds that the director acted honestly and reasonably having regard to the circumstances of the case (s. 1157). The test to be applied was stated in *Re Duomatic Ltd* [1969] 2 Ch 365 at 377.

> '[Was the director] … acting in the way in which a man of affairs dealing with his own affairs with reasonable care and circumspection could reasonably be expected to act in such a case.'

An example of when the court will exercise this power is Re *D'Jan (of London) Ltd* [1994] 1 BCLC 561 (considered above). In *Re D'Jan*, the court held that the predecessor to s. 1157 contemplated that conduct may be reasonable for the purposes of that section despite amounting to lack of care at common law.

8.2 Indemnification, exclusion of liability and insurance

Subject to three important exceptions, s. 232 renders void any provision which, in connection with negligence, default, breach of duty or breach of trust in relation to the company, purports to:

- exempt a director to any extent from any liability that would otherwise attach to him; or
- directly or indirectly provide a director with an indemnity to any extent against any liability

Section 232 does not prevent a company from:

- purchasing and maintaining liability insurance for its directors (s. 233);
- indemnifying a director against liability he incurs to third parties (subject to limits in relation to criminal liability and proceedings) (s. 234);
- indemnifying a director of a company that is a corporate occupational pension scheme trustee against liability he incurs in connection with the company's activities as trustee of the scheme (subject to limits in relation to criminal liability and proceedings) (s. 235).

Also, to avoid arguments that they are exclusions of liability, otherwise lawful provisions in a company's Articles dealing with conflict of interest are expressly excluded from the s. 232 prohibition (s. 232(4)).

TEST YOUR KNOWLEDGE 12.6

(a) Identify three potential sources of authorisation for an act that would otherwise be a breach of directors' duty.
(b) Identify two ways of obtaining relief after the event when a breach of directors' duty has occurred.
(c) In what circumstances may a court grant relief to a director from the consequences of breach of directors' duty?

CHAPTER SUMMARY

- Directors' general duties were developed by the courts until the Companies Act 2006 reduced them to statutory general duties. They are supplemented by provisions of the Act regulating particular types of arrangement between a director and the company: substantial non-cash asset transactions (ss. 190–196), loans and similar arrangements (ss. 197–214); long-term service contracts (s. 188) and payments for loss of office (s. 215).
- Directors' duties are owed to *the company* and to no other person.
- Four general duties are particularly relevant when directors take decisions:
    - duty to act within powers (s. 171);
    - duty to promote the success of the company (s. 172);
    - duty to exercise independent judgment (s. 173);
    - duty to exercise reasonable skill, care and diligence (s. 174).
- Directors are in a fiduciary relationship to their companies the principal fiduciary duties of a director being:
    - to avoid conflicts of interest (s. 175);
    - not to accept benefits from third parties (s. 176).
- Directors contracting with their companies are regulated by the duty to declare interest in proposed and existing transactions or arrangements (ss. 177 and 182) and the provisions of the Act requiring shareholder approval in advance of:
    - substantial property transaction (ss. 190–196);
    - loans and similar arrangements to directors (ss. 197–214);
    - long term service contracts (s. 188);
    - payment for loss of office (s. 215).
- Remedies for breach of duty are still found in case law and are fiduciary remedies except that for breach of the duty of care, skill and diligence damages is the basic, common law, remedy.
- The directors or shareholders may in some circumstances authorise or ratify acts or breaches by individual directors. Ratification is now governed by s. 239 which disregards the votes of the interested director or any member connected with him.
- The court may grant relief from liability for breach if it considers a director to have acted honestly and reasonably having regard to the circumstances of the case (s. 1157).

Minority shareholder protection 13

■ CONTENTS

1 The rule in *Foss v Harbottle*
2 Statutory derivative claims
3 Personal and representative actions by shareholder
4 Unfairly prejudicial conduct petitions
5 Just and equitable winding up petitions
6 Company investigations

■ INTRODUCTION

In the opening section of this chapter, we examine the rule that the company is the proper claimant in proceedings in which a wrong is alleged to have been done to a company (the 'proper claimant rule', or rule in *Foss v Harbottle*) and limits of that rule. We then look at the circumstances in which shareholders may commence, and will be permitted to continue, a **derivative claim** to enforce directors' duties on behalf of the company. We move on to consider the personal rights of a shareholder to sue in his own name for legal wrongs done to him in a personal capacity, to make good losses he has suffered, including, potentially, reflective losses. We then examine petitions based on a company's affairs having been conducted in a manner that is unfairly prejudicial to the interests of the shareholders (s. 994 petitions) and their relationship to just and equitable winding up petitions. The chapter closes with a look at the work of the CIB.

1 The rule in *Foss v Harbottle*

We have seen that the company is a separate legal entity from its shareholders and consequently has legal rights and liabilities. If its rights are infringed by a person failing to perform a contract they have entered into with the company, for example, the company may sue to enforce its rights under the contract. We also know that the decision to litigate rests with the board of directors as part of the general powers of management of the company. From this perspective, it makes sense to have a basic rule, known as the rule in *Foss v Harbottle*, that in any legal proceedings in which a wrong is alleged to have been done to a company, the proper claimant is the company.

CASE LAW 13.1

Foss v Harbottle (1843) 2 Hare 461
The plaintiffs, Foss and Turton, were shareholders in a company formed to buy land for use as a pleasure park. The defendants were the other directors and shareholders of the company. The plaintiff shareholders alleged that the defendants had defrauded the company in a number of ways, including some of the defendants selling land belonging to them to the company at an exorbitant price. The plaintiffs sought an order that the defendants make good the losses to the company.

# CASE LAW 13.1 continued

Held, dismissing the action: In any action in which a wrong is alleged to have been done to a company, the proper claimant is the company and as the company was still in existence, it was possible to call a general meeting and therefore there was nothing to prevent the company from dealing with the matter.

Although logical on its face, the rule has presented enormous difficulty to courts over the years.

1.1 Majority rule and the business judgment rule

Quite apart from reflecting the separate personality doctrine, the proper claimant principle also reflects two sentiments that nineteenth-century courts felt towards companies. First, is the reluctance of the courts to become involved in business decisions. As Lord Eldon stated in *Carlen v Drury* (1812) 1 Ves & B 149: 'The court is not to be required on every occasion to take the management of every playhouse and brewhouse in the Kingdom.'

Second, is the fear felt by the courts of a multiplicity of legal actions arising from differences among shareholders. Courts have held strong to the principle that disputes among members of a company should be resolved by the members themselves, according to the internal decision-making process provided by the company constitution and the Companies Acts (*MacDougall v Gardiner* (1875-76) LR 1 (CA)). Internal rules usually provided for majority rule, and the rule in *Foss v Harbottle* (1843) subjected minority shareholders to the rule of the majority shareholder.

1.2 Limits to the proper claimant principle

The courts were compelled to recognise limits to the rule in *Foss v Harbottle* (1843). First, the rule is not relevant where a shareholder is exercising a personal right (see below), such as enforcing the right set out in the Articles of Association to attend company meetings. Although this may look as if the shareholder is enforcing the duty of the directors to act in accordance with the constitution of the company, it is in fact an action by a shareholder *against the company* to enforce the statutory contract in the Articles.

Second, the rule in *Foss v Harbottle* was not applied if a minority shareholder complained to the court about action by the company for which more than a simple majority was needed, as in *Edwards v Halliwell* [1950] 2 All ER 1064, which is a trade union case, but the principle is applicable to companies.

# CASE LAW 13.2

Edwards v Halliwell [1950] 2 All ER 1064

The constitution of a trade union provided that contributions were not to be altered until a ballot vote of members had been taken and a two-thirds majority in favour obtained. Contributions were increased following a resolution supported by a simple majority. Two members sued seeking a declaration that the resolution was invalid.

Held: Where a matter cannot be sanctioned by a simple majority of the members of the company but only by some special majority, an individual member is not prevented from suing by the rule in *Foss v Harbottle*.

Third, and the principal area in which the rule presented difficulties, was where those who control the company and, in particular, the decision to sue or not sue a person who has legally wronged the company, are themselves the wrongdoers. The most important limit to the rule, *which was the only true exception to the rule in Foss v Harbottle*, came to be referred to as 'fraud on the minority'. Where directors, who were also majority shareholders, had perpetrated a fraud on the company, a minority shareholder was permitted to commence an action based on a wrong done to the company to secure a remedy for the company. The action was called a 'derivative action'.

Cook v Deeks [1916] 1 AC 554 (PC)

Three directors obtained a contract in their own name to the exclusion of the company in breach of fiduciary duty (now s. 175). As holders of 75 per cent of the shares, they secured a resolution declaring the company had no interest in the contract.

Held: the contract belonged in equity to the company and the directors could not use their shares to vest it in themselves. In these circumstances, where the board and majority shareholders were not willing to commence an action, minority shareholders could bring an action on behalf of the company.

The Companies Act 2006 has replaced the common law derivative action with a statutory derivative claim in ss. 260–264 (considered below). All circumstances in which permission to continue a derivative action is granted may now be seen as exceptions to the proper claimant principle.

TEST YOUR KNOWLEDGE 13.1

(a) State the rule in *Foss v Harbottle*.
(b) Why is it believed that historically the courts have been so strict in the application of the rule in *Foss v Harbottle*?
(c) What has superseded the principal common law exception to the rule in *Foss v Harbottle* set out in *Cooks v Deeks* (1916)?

CASE EXAMPLE 13.1

Proper claimant principle

It is helpful to illustrate how the proper claimant principle, and the exception to it, works by analysing a hypothetical scenario.

Directors as wrongdoers

Consider a company with two directors. They find out informally that planning permission will be granted for a piece of land owned by the company. They keep this information to themselves and buy the land from the company at a price representing its value without planning permission which is far lower than its value with planning permission.

In these circumstances, the directors cannot act as a decision-making organ of the company and decide to sell the land to themselves because they are conflicted out. Articles normally provide that they cannot vote on the decision of the company to sell the land to them, and, even if the Articles did not say this, and the directors cause the company to sell the land to them, they are in breach of ss. 172, 175 and 190, as they have not acted to promote the success of the company (s. 172), have used information obtained as directors to personal advantage (s. 175), and have failed to obtain the approval of the shareholders (s. 190). Consequently, the transaction will be voidable by the company, the directors will be liable to account for any profits they have made and must indemnify the company against any losses caused by the breach of duty.

CASE EXAMPLE 13.1 *continued*

Although the directors, as the board, ordinarily have the power to decide whether or not to commence any legal action, in these circumstances control of the decision to litigate transfers to the shareholders. The shareholders, as a decision-making organ of the company, decide whether or not the company will sue the directors. The legal proceedings are still brought by the company, in the name of the company, seeking a remedy for the company.

Majority shareholders as wrongdoers

Staying with Case Example 13.1, the company has three shareholders, each owning one third of the shares. Two of the shareholders are the directors. Because the wrongdoers are directors, who are not going to sue themselves, the decision to litigate or not has reverted to the shareholders. Does this help the company if the wrongdoers are also shareholders?

Shareholders take most decisions by ordinary resolution, which encompasses majority rule (see chapter 14). In Case Example 13.1, the wrongdoers own a majority of the shares and, as majority shareholders, they are able to pass or defeat ordinary resolutions. Are they, therefore, permitted to:

- Pass an ordinary resolution approving the sale of the land pursuant to s. 190?
- Pass an ordinary resolution ratifying the breach pursuant to s. 239?
- Defeat a proposed resolution to sue the directors to recover the land?
- Have any legal action commenced by the minority shareholder stopped because he is not the proper claimant?

The answer to the second question is no. On a resolution to ratify his breach of directors' duty, the votes of both the director/shareholder and any person connected with him are disregarded (s. 239(4)). Curiously, there is no similar provision in s. 190 requiring the votes of the director to be discounted on a resolution to approve a substantial asset transaction which leaves the matter moot and the answer to the first question depends on the approach the court takes to statutory interpretation. A literal approach would suggest that all shareholders can vote, as the section does not state otherwise, whereas s. 239 does state otherwise. A purposive approach may suggest otherwise.

Turning to the third question, a resolution to sue the directors, if defeated, could be characterised as an indirect decision of the company to ratify a breach of duty, thereby bringing it within s. 239, which requires the directors' votes to be disregarded. It is surprising that the answers to questions one and three are not clear-cut.

The answer to the fourth question is that, provided the minority shareholder brings the legal action as a claim under s. 260, a statutory derivative claim, the action will not be stopped based on him not being the proper claimant.

2 Statutory derivative claims

The statutory derivative claim is the only proceeding by which a minority shareholder can commence legal action in respect of a cause of action vested in the company, seeking relief on behalf of the company, to remedy a wrong done to the company. The 2006 Act has expanded the grounds on which a derivative claim may be brought but requires the permission of the court to continue the claim.

Increased emphasis on good corporate governance in the interests of all stakeholders in companies, the enshrinement of 'enlightened shareholder value' in s. 172 of the 2006 Act and the placing of the derivative claim on a statutory footing have come together to raise the question of the extent to which shareholder remedies may be used to enforce better management of companies in the interests of all stakeholders. Minority shareholders may challenge, or threaten to challenge, management decisions as having been taken in breach of duty by commencing a derivative claim. This has raised the spectre of minority shareholders who support public interest groups using the law to influence board decision-making in favour of public interest groups.

There is no evidence of this use of s. 260. Indeed, as at February 2013, permission to continue had been granted in only four cases (*Kiani v Cooper* [2010] BCC 463; *Stainer v Lee & Others* [2010] EWHC 1539; *Hughes v Weiss* [2012] EWHC 2363 and *Parry v Bartlett & Another* [2011] EWHC 3146).

2.1 Grounds for claim

A statutory derivative claim may be brought only in respect of a cause of action arising from an actual or proposed act or omission involving negligence, default, breach of duty or breach of trust by a director of the company. The cause of action may be against the director or another person or both (s. 260(3)). Note that the exposure of third parties to a s. 260 claim will depend on dishonest assistance and knowing receipt as the courts have developed these concepts in the context of breaches of duty by directors.

2.2 Claim procedure

The parties

The claimant in a s. 260 derivative claim is the shareholder. Note that because the shareholder is bringing the action to secure relief for the company, the company must be made a defendant to the claim along with the directors and any third parties against whom relief is sought. The claimant need not necessarily be a minority shareholder, although permission to continue will be given to a majority shareholder only in exceptional circumstances (*Cinematic Finance Ltd v Ryder* [2010] EWHC 3387). Nor is it necessary for the directors whose behaviour is being complained of to control a majority of the shareholder votes, although, again, permission will be granted only in exceptional circumstances (*Stimpson v Southern Private Landlords Association* [2010] BCC 387 (Ch D)). Permission to continue was refused in both of the cases cited in this paragraph.

Application for permission to continue claim

Once the claim form has been issued, an application must be made to the court for permission to continue the claim (s. 261(1)). The shareholder will submit written evidence with this application supporting his statement of claim and the defendants may submit evidence in answer to the claim. The shareholder is precluded from taking any further steps in the proceedings until the court has given permission for the claim to continue. A two stage process exists by which the court decides whether or not to permit the claim to continue. In practice, however, a claimant often simply issues a claim and serves an application for permission to continue to which the defendants to the claim are made respondents. The first hearing is then treated as both stages 1 and 2 and in at least one case the court has refused to support an objection to combining the stages in this way (see *Stimpson v Southern Landlords Association* [2010] BCC 387).

Stage 1
The court must be satisfied that the particulars of the claim and the evidence submitted to support it disclose a *prima facie* case. If no *prima facie* case is made out, the court must dismiss the application and make any consequential order it considers appropriate (s. 261(2)). If the court does not dismiss the application, the application moves to stage 2.

Stage 2
Stage 2 involves a hearing of the application for permission to continue the claim. Here, again, the court must refuse permission to continue if:

- a person acting in accordance with the s. 172 duty to promote the success of the company would not seek to continue the claim (s. 263(2)(a)); or
- the act or omission has been authorised (ahead of time) or ratified (after the event) by the company (s. 263(2)(b) and (c)).

The court does not have to decide that a hypothetical director would consider the claim worth pursuing. Rather, permission to continue must be refused if, on the balance of probabilities, such a director would decide not to pursue the claim. This test has been interpreted to mean that only if no director acting in accordance with s. 172 would seek to continue the claim will the courts consider themselves bound to refuse permission to continue (*Franbar Holdings Ltd v Patel* [2008] BCC 885 (Ch D) and *Iesini Westrip Holdings Ltd* [2010] BCC 420).

The second ground for obligatory refusal preserves the difficult issue of which acts and omissions of directors the shareholders can authorise or ratify and which they cannot. This is a controversial area which s. 239 of the Companies Act 2006 has gone some way to clarifying. Uncertainty remains, however, because, even in relation to ratification, s. 239(7) preserves 'any other enactment or rule of law imposing additional requirements for valid ratification or any rule of law as to acts that are incapable of being ratified by the company'. *Cook v Deeks* [1916] 1 AC 554 (PC) (see above) is the authority for the proposition that ratification will be invalid where it amounts to expropriation of the company's property by the majority shareholder.

In relation to authorisation, as noted in the context of directors' duties, the Companies Act 2006 does not make clear how far an interested shareholder may vote to authorise a transaction for which the Act requires shareholder approval. The principle in *Cook v Deeks* should, arguably, be extended to any case in which the transaction for which authorisation is sought would amount to an expropriation of company property. In such a case, the court would surely be permitted to find that, as a matter of law, the transaction had not been authorised so that the court must refuse permission for a minority shareholder to continue a statutory derivative claim.

If the court is not compelled to refuse permission, it must take into account the following when deciding whether or not to grant permission to continue (s. 263(3)):

- whether or not the claimant is acting in good faith in seeking to continue the claim (*Nurcombe v Nurcombe* [1985] 1 WLR 370);
- the importance that a person acting in accordance with s. 172 would attach to continuing the claim;
- whether or not the act or omission could be, and in the circumstances would be likely to be, authorised or ratified by the company;
- whether the company has decided not to pursue the claim;
- whether the act or omission in question is one in respect of which the shareholder could pursue an action in his own right (this would most likely be under s. 994) rather than on behalf of the company (*Barrett v Duckett* [1995] 1 BCLC 243);
- any evidence before it of the views of shareholders who have no personal interest in the matter (*Smith v Croft (No. 2)* [1988] Ch 114).

In relation to the first point, *Nurcombe v Nurcombe* [1985] 1 WLR 370 is an example of the courts being alert to attempts by claimants to use the derivative claim where they have already received a remedy for the wrong done. Such a claimant will be regarded as not acting in good faith in bringing the derivative claim.

CASE LAW 13.4

Nurcombe v Nurcombe [1985] 1 WLR 370

The first defendant (D1) in the derivative action was a director and the major shareholder of the company which was the second defendant (D2). The remaining shares were held by the claimant who was the former wife of D1. In earlier matrimonial proceedings by the claimant for financial provision it had become clear that D1 had diverted the considerable benefit of a contract for the purchase of certain land from the company to a company owned by his second wife. The judge in the matrimonial proceedings took into account that D1 had made a substantial profit out of his dealings in respect of the land and the lump sum awarded to his first wife, the claimant, in the matrimonial proceedings had reflected this. The claimant brought the derivative action, as a minority shareholder, on behalf of the company seeking payment by D1 to the company of the profit on the property transaction which she alleged he had diverted from the company in breach of his fiduciary duty as a director.

Held: Dismissing the action, P had abandoned her right to bring a minority shareholder's action by obtaining, in the matrimonial proceedings, the benefit of a lump sum award based on the inclusion of the profit from the property transaction in the first defendant's assets.

More recently, a claimant who is seeking to use a s. 260 action to, in effect, obtain double recovery in relation to a wrongdoing by a director will not be granted permission to continue (*Keay & Loughrey* [2010] JBL 151). Note that the last but one point in the list above is narrower than the common law principle established in *Barrett v Duckett* [1995] 1 BCLC 243, that a derivative action would not be permitted to proceed where an alternative adequate remedy was available, and in *Parry v Bartlett* the court held that the existence of an alternative remedy under s. 994 was only a factor to be taken into account, not an absolute bar to the grant of permission to continue. Lastly, in relation to the final point in the list, a derivative action was struck out in *Smith v Croft (No. 2)* (1988) because a majority of the independent shareholders' votes would have been cast against allowing the action to proceed and there was no evidence to suggest that they would be cast for other than reasons genuinely thought to be for the company's advantage.

Permission to continue and discontinuance

If the court gives permission for a derivative claim to continue, the claim continues much like any other action with remedies available that would be available in a case brought by the company against its directors. In its report on Shareholder Remedies (No. 246), the Law Commission recommended that the consent of the court should be a prerequisite to any subsequent discontinuance of a derivative action. This recommendation reflected concern that the claimant and the directors could collude, with the claimant being bought off by the directors which, even at a premium from the perspective of the shareholder, would in many cases cost the directors far less than their liability were the claim to proceed to judgment. Such arrangements would be unlikely to be in the interests of the company. This recommendation has not been adopted. It may be, however, that when judges grant permission to continue, they use the power given to the court in s. 261(4)(a), 'to continue the claim on such terms as it think fit', to order that the claim cannot be discontinued without the court's permission.

2.3 Costs

A derivative claim is brought by a shareholder for the benefit of the company. The shareholder is an agent acting on behalf of the company (*per* Lord Denning MR in *Wallersteiner*; see also *Re Sherborne Park Residents Co Ltd* [1986] 2 BCC 99, 528 considered below). For this reason, the court is usually prepared to grant a costs order, typically applied for early on in proceedings, that the claimant shall be indemnified by the company against his liability for costs of both the derivative claim and the application for permission to continue, whether the claim is successful or not.

The authority for such an order, now reflected in the Civil Procedure Rules (CPR 19.9E), is *Wallersteiner v Moir (No. 2)* [1975] QB 373. Note that it is only as valuable as the creditworthiness of the company, as it does not provide the shareholder with any form of property interest to secure the sum payable by the company (*Qayoumi v Oakhouse Property Holdings plc* [2003] 1 BCLC 352). Note that the courts in both *Stainer v Lee* and *Kiani v Cooper* made capped costs indemnity orders, evidencing awareness of the danger of imposing a potentially large financial obligation on companies.

TEST YOUR KNOWLEDGE 13.2

(a) In respect of which causes of action is it possible to commence a statutory derivative cause of action?
(b) Who may commence a derivative cause of action?
(c) In which circumstances is a court required to refuse permission to continue a s. 260 claim?
(d) Identify six factors the court is required to consider before deciding whether or not to exercise its discretion to grant permission for a s. 260 claim to continue.

3 Personal and representative actions by shareholders

3.1 Personal and representative actions

Shareholders may bring legal actions asserting their personal rights as shareholders. The rule in *Foss v Harbottle* is not relevant to these actions. The company is the defendant.

In many situations, the rights of more than one shareholder may have been denied. Generally, civil procedure rules in English law are not designed to facilitate group actions. That said, the Civil Procedure Rules (CPR) offer three procedural mechanisms for the management of group claims. (CPR) 19.6 provides for legal action to be commenced by one or more persons who have the same interest as representatives of any other persons who have that interest. In the case of *Wood v Odessa Waterworks Co* [1889] LR 42 Ch D 636, a shareholder brought an action on behalf of himself and other shareholders, all in their personal capacity. This is known as a representative action. Representative actions have been supplemented by the availability of group litigation orders (GLOs) where claims give rise to 'common or related issues' of fact or law (*CPR 19.10*), and another alternative to the representative action is for individual claims to be joined and consolidated under Civil Procedure Rules (CPR 7.3 and 19.1).

CASE LAW 13.5

***Wood v Odessa Waterworks Co* [1889] LR 42 Ch D 636**
The rights of the shareholders in respect of a division of the profits of the company were governed by provisions in the Articles of Association. A shareholder, on behalf of himself and all other shareholders, brought action for an injunction to restrain the company from acting on a resolution on the ground that it contravened the Articles of Association of the company.

Held *per* Stirling J: 'What I have to determine is, whether that which is proposed to be done is in accordance with the Articles of Association as they stand, and, in my judgment, it is not, and therefore the Plaintiff is entitled to an injunction so far as relates to the payment of dividends.'

The precise scope of the personal rights of shareholders is not completely clear. When we examined the rights of shareholders to sue to enforce provisions of the Articles of Association, we saw that there is disagreement as to precisely which rights set out in the Articles of Association may be enforced as personal rights by shareholders (see chapter 5). The importance of defining the strict legal rights of shareholders has been eclipsed by the availability of the very popular unfairly prejudicial conduct petition under s. 994 of the Companies Act 2006, for which a very wide range of remedies may be granted by the court (see s. 996). Section 994 petitions can be brought to protect the 'interests' of one or more shareholders. The concept of 'interests' is broader than 'rights' and therefore s. 994 petitions can be successfully brought in fact situations in which no strict legal rights of a shareholder have been infringed. (See section 5 below.)

Confusion often arises where a given fact situation gives rise to both a right of the company to sue its directors and a right of the shareholder to sue the company. Examples are when directors abuse the power to allot shares, or allot shares without first respecting the pre-emption rights of existing shareholders.

An improper exercise of powers is a breach of duty by the directors (s. 171). It is a wrong done to the company for which the company can sue the directors for a remedy against the directors. It is also a breach of the Articles of Association and an individual shareholder can sue the company for acting inconsistently with the Articles (through the agency of its directors). *Re Sherborne Park Residents Co Ltd* [1986] 2 BCC 99 528 is just such a case. The report is of a hearing of a motion (a preliminary hearing for a specific order, in this case an order for costs) in what would today be a s. 994 case brought by an individual shareholder.

CASE LAW 13.6

Re Sherborne Park Residents Co Ltd [1986] 2 BCC 99528

A shareholder in a residential leaseholders' management company objected to a planned allotment of shares by the directors and commenced what would now be a s. 994 unfairly prejudicial conduct petition. By notice of motion, the shareholder sought an indemnity for costs order against the company arguing that the action was a 'derivative' action because the facts complained of involved a breach of fiduciary duty by the directors.

Held: The court declined to make the costs order. Hoffmann J, stated that the allotment was alleged to be an improper and unlawful exercise of the powers granted to the board by the Articles of Association and that whilst this was a breach of directors' duty owed to the company, the true basis of the action was that the alleged abuse of fiduciary powers was an infringement of the petitioner's rights as a member under the Articles. A shareholder in such an action might sue as representative of himself and other shareholders who had identical interests but he did not in substance assert a right which belonged to the company alone. In a derivative action, the only true plaintiff is the company. The availability in derivative claims of costs orders indemnifying a claimant against the costs of the action whether the action is won or lost, is based on the shareholder being in a relationship with the company analogous to agent and principal for the purpose of bringing the action. That was not the case here.

3.2 Reflective loss

If a company suffers a loss which significantly diminishes its assets, shareholders are likely to experience a reduction in the value of their shares. If these losses are caused by a breach of duty owed to the company the position is clear: the company is the proper claimant and can sue for the breach. The shareholder cannot sue because the duty is not owed to him. Where, however, in addition to the company being owed a duty, the shareholder is also owed a duty by the wrongdoer, the principle that the shareholder has no right to sue to recover purely 'reflective loss' comes into play and is referred to as the 'no reflective loss principle' (*Day v Cook* [2002] 1 BCLC 1). (The shareholders' loss of share value reflects the loss suffered by the company and for this reason is called reflective loss).

Where there is a breach of a duty owed to both the company and the shareholder, if the shareholder's loss is reflective loss, the shareholder cannot recover it because the company's claim 'will always trump that of the shareholder' (*per* Arden, LJ in *Day v Cook* [2002] 1 BCLC 1). This is because otherwise double recovery (i.e. by the company and the shareholder) will occur, or, if the action were to be allowed on a first-come-first-served basis, a shareholder could recover at the expense of the company. Lord Millett stated the justification for the principle succinctly in *Johnson v Gore Wood & Co* [2001] 2 AC 1 (HL), the leading case on reflective loss.

> 'Justice to the defendant requires the exclusion of one claim or the other; protection of the interests of the company's creditors requires that it is the company which is allowed to recover to the exclusion of the shareholder.'

In *Johnson v Gore Wood* (2001), Lord Bingham summarised the law in three principles:

> '(1) Where a company suffers loss caused by a breach of duty owed to it, only the company may sue in respect of that loss. No action lies at the suit of a shareholder suing in that capacity and no other to make good a diminution in the value of the shareholder's shareholding where that merely reflects the loss suffered by the company. A claim will not lie by a shareholder to make good a loss which would be made good if the company's assets were replenished through action against the party responsible for the loss, even if the company, acting through its constitutional organs, has declined or failed to make good that loss. So much is clear from *Prudential Assurance Co Ltd v Newman Industries Ltd (No. 2)* [1982] Ch 204 ...

(2) Where a company suffers loss but has no cause of action to sue to recover that loss, the shareholder in the company may sue in respect of it (if the shareholder has a cause of action to do so), even though the loss is a diminution in the value of the shareholding.
...
(3) Where a company suffers loss caused by a breach of duty to it, and a shareholder suffers a loss separate and distinct from that suffered by the company caused by breach of a duty independently owed to the shareholder, each may sue to recover the loss caused to it by breach of the duty owed to it but neither may recover loss caused to the other by breach of the duty owed to that other.'

Only one true exception appears to exist to the no reflective loss principle. Where the company is unable to pursue its claim against the defendant because of the defendant's wrongdoing, a shareholder will be permitted to bring an action to recover reflective loss (*Giles v Rhind* [2003] 1 BCLC 1 (CA)).

CASE LAW 13.7

Giles v Rhind [2003] 1 BCLC 1 (CA)

Giles and Rhind were the principal shareholders and directors of Surrey Hills Foods Ltd (SHF). Rhind, having sold his shares and left the company, in breach of an obligation of confidence owed both to the company and to Giles, set up a business in competition with SHF, caused the company's major customer to move its business to his new company and thereby brought about the insolvency of SHF. SHF commenced proceedings against Rhind which it was unable to continue when it went into administrative receivership because it could not afford to provide security for the costs of the defendant as ordered by the court. The action was discontinued on the basis of a consent order by which SHF was precluded from bringing any further action against Rhind. Giles therefore commenced an action against Rhind seeking damages for breach of the obligation of confidence owed personally to him. He claimed, amongst other heads of damage, the diminution in the value of his shares in SHF. Rhind argued that this was reflective loss which was not recoverable based on the no reflective loss principle. Rhind won at first instance. Giles appealed.

Held: The appeal was allowed. Giles could continue his action. *Per* Waller LJ, 'Even in relation to that part of the claim for diminution which could be said to be reflective of the company's loss, since, if the company had no cause of action to recover that loss the shareholder could bring a claim, the same should be true of a situation in which the wrongdoer has disabled the company from pursuing that cause of action.'

Although *Giles v Rhind* has been followed (see *Perry v Day* [2005] 2 BCLC 405), the Court of Appeal in *Gardner v Parker* [2004] 2 BCLC 554 has made it clear that the case is authority for a very narrow exception to the no reflective loss principle. Only if the company is unable to sue the wrongdoer 'because of the very wrongdoing of which complaint was being made', will a shareholder not be barred from recovering reflective loss. The Court of Appeal confirmed the narrowness of the exception again, in *Webster v Sandersons Solicitors (A Firm)* [2009] EWCA Civ 830.

TEST YOUR KNOWLEDGE 13.3

(a) What is a representative action?
(b) Why is the rule in *Foss v Harbottle* not relevant where a shareholder brings an action based on his personal rights?
(c) Describe a situation that could result in both a claim by a company against its directors for breach of duty and a claim by a shareholder for breach of his personal rights.
(d) What is the 'no reflective loss' principle?

4 Unfairly prejudicial conduct petitions

4.1 Introduction

The unfair prejudice petition in s. 994 has existed since 1980 when it replaced an 'oppressive behaviour'-based remedy introduced in 1948. Between 1948 and 1980 only a couple of cases were reported in which oppressive behaviour had been successfully established. The unfair prejudice petition allows petitions to be made based on a much wider range of fact situations and remedies are awarded in a far higher proportion of cases than under the predecessor section. Consequently, s. 994 petitions are extremely popular.

The right to petition is set out in s. 994(1).

> '994 (1) A member of a company may apply to the court by petition for an order under this Part on the ground—
> (a) that the company's affairs are being or have been conducted in a manner that is unfairly prejudicial to the interests of members generally or of some part of its members (including at least himself), or
> (b) that an actual or proposed act or omission of the company (including an act or omission on its behalf) is or would be so prejudicial.'

4.2 Petitioners and respondents

Who may petition?

Members of a company, the shareholders for our purposes, are entitled to petition for an order under s. 994. This clearly includes registered members, which means those individuals whose names are entered on the company's register of members as the legal owners of shares. By s. 994(2) member includes persons to whom shares in the company have been transferred or transmitted by operation of law. Problems may arise if the board of directors has power to refuse to register a person as owner of shares, as is common in private companies. A shareholder can complain of conduct that pre-dates his registration, yet a former shareholder cannot present a s. 994 petition even in respect of conduct that occurred while he was a member. The case that decided the last point, *Re a Company (No. 00330 of 1991)* [1991] BCLC 597, has attracted criticism.

The Secretary of State can present a petition (s. 995) and this is most likely to occur following an investigation into a company pursuant to the Companies Act 1985 (see final section of this chapter).

Who may be a respondent?

In theory, any person may be made a respondent to a s. 994 petition. A person against whom a remedy is sought must be made a respondent and remedies are usually sought against the controlling shareholders/directors of the company. The company will also be made a respondent, albeit on a nominal basis, even where no remedy is sought against it and any shareholder whose interests may be affected by the remedy sought should also be joined (*Re a Company (No. 005287 of 1985)* [1986] BCLC 68). Remedies may also be sought against more remote respondents such as ex-shareholders (liability cannot be avoided by a person transferring his shares) or a third party company controlled by the controlling shareholders.

In *Gamlestaden Fastigheter AB v Baltic Partners Ltd* [2007] UKPC 26, a shareholder who petitioned the court pursuant to the Jersey equivalent of s. 994 was held to be entitled to pursue his petition and the claim was not struck out simply because, the company being insolvent and the shareholder also being a creditor of the company, the benefit of any order would benefit the shareholder only in his capacity as a creditor, and not as a shareholder. The shareholder had *locus standi* as long as the relief would be of real value to him in facilitating recovery of some part of his investment, whether loan capital or share capital. Unusually, the remedy sought in this case was payment to the company by the wrongdoer directors.

4.3 The behaviour complained of

The company's affairs

The complaint must be about the conduct of the company's affairs, not the affairs of a director in his private capacity or a shareholder in his private capacity. A wide interpretation has been given to the affairs of the company. In *Re City Branch Group Ltd* [2005] 1 WLR 3505, for example, the conduct of the affairs of a subsidiary company were regarded as conduct of the company's affairs.

Examples of shareholders acting in their private capacity occurred in *Re Unisoft Group Ltd (No. 3)* [1994] 1 BCLC 609 and *Re Leeds United Holdings plc* [1996] 2 BCLC 545. In both cases the petition was dismissed because the behaviour complained of was breach by a shareholder of a shareholders' agreement relating to the rights of the shareholder to transfer shares in the company.

Unfairly prejudical conduct

The conduct complained of must be 'both prejudicial ... and also unfairly so' (*Re a Company (No. 005685) ex parte Schwartz (No. 2)* [1989] BCLC 427). Prejudice must be 'harm in a commercial sense, not in a merely emotional sense' (*Re Unisoft Group Ltd (No. 3)* [1994] 1 BCLC 609).

Slade J made it clear in *Re Bovey Hotel Ventures Ltd (1981)* (unreported) (quoted with approval by Nourse J in *R v A Noble & Sons (Clothing) Ltd* [1983] BCLC 273 and in subsequent cases), that the court will apply an objective test to determine whether or not conduct has unfairly prejudiced the petitioning shareholder's interests.

> 'The test of unfairness must, I think, be an objective, not a subjective, one. In other words it is not necessary for the petitioner to show that the persons who have *de facto* control of the company have acted as they did in the conscious knowledge that this was unfair to the petitioner or that they were acting in bad faith; the test, I think, is whether a reasonable bystander observing the consequences of their conduct, would regard it as having unfairly prejudiced the petitioner's interests.'

Trivial or technical infringements of the Articles will not be regarded as unfair (*Re Saul D Harrison & Sons plc* (1995)), and if the behaviour complained of can be brought to an end by the petitioning shareholder exercising his votes, the behaviour will not be considered unfair (*Re Baltic Real Estate Ltd (No. 2)* [1993] BCLC 503).

4.4 The interests of members

The behaviour complained of in the petition must evidence the company's affairs being conducted in a manner that is unfairly prejudicial to the 'interests of members generally or some part of the members' (s. 994(1)(a)).

Interests of members as members

The interests protected must be the interests of members as members or of shareholders as shareholders, although this requirement should not be approached too narrowly. The Privy Council has shown, for example, that where the remedy sought would simply bring relief to a shareholder as a creditor of the company rather than as a shareholder, the court may be prepared to treat the shareholders' interests as a creditor as interests for the purposes of the petition (*Gamlestaden Fastigheter AB v Baltic Partner Ltd* [2008] 1 BCLC 468 (PC)). In *Gamlestaden* the petitioner was a shareholder in a joint venture in which the joint venturers had agreed in a joint venture agreement to advance loan capital to the joint venture company as well as to subscribe for shares. Delivering the judgment of the Privy Council, Lord Scott stated:

> 'the investor ought not to be precluded from the grant of relief under [section 994] on the ground that the relief would benefit the investor only as loan creditor and not as member.'

Rights and interests

'Interests' are wider than strict legal rights. To understand the range of behaviour that may be included in s. 994 petitions it is helpful to place behaviour in three (overlapping) categories.

First, shareholders have certain personal rights as shareholders, the exact range of which is, as we have seen, unclear. Breaches of a shareholder's personal rights as a shareholder are included in s. 994 petitions as evidence of the company's affairs being conducted in a manner that is unfairly prejudicial to the petitioning shareholder.

> **CASE EXAMPLE 13.2**
>
> A company declares a dividend and then refuses to pay the share of the dividend due to one particular shareholder. This would be a breach of the contractual right of a shareholder to his share of a declared dividend. This infringement of the shareholder's legal rights could be included in a s. 994 petition.

Second, a company has certain rights, such as the right to insist on its directors acting in accordance with their duties, which, as we have also seen, are not rights that are directly actionable by a shareholder. However, behaviour amounting to a breach of duty owed to the company may be included in a s. 994 petition as evidence of the company's affairs being conducted in a manner that is unfairly prejudicial to the petitioning shareholder.

> **CASE EXAMPLE 13.3**
>
> The board of directors terminates a minority shareholder director's directorship in accordance with the power to do so in the Articles and excludes him from management of the company. This could be a breach of directors' duties if the directors take these actions because they have fallen out with the minority shareholder, rather than because they believe that to do so is likely to promote the success of the company. Nonetheless, the minority shareholder could include this behaviour in his s. 994 petition as evidence of the company's affairs being conducted in a manner unfairly prejudicial to his interests.

In the second example the minority shareholder will be asserting unfair prejudice to his interests, rather than any strict legal right.

Third, although 'a company is an association of persons for an economic purpose, usually entered into with legal advice and some degree of formality' (*O'Neill v Phillips* (1999) HL *per* Lord Hoffmann) and that, accordingly, in most cases, a breach of rights is required for conduct to be unfair, behaviour may amount to evidence of a company's affairs being conducted in a manner unfairly prejudicial to the interests of the petitioning sharcholder even if it neither infringes his strict legal rights nor breaches a right of the company.

The 'rights-based approach' is supplemented by an 'interests-based approach' and it is necessary to ask: has the majority acted or is it proposing to act in a manner which equity would regard as contrary to good faith? (*Re Guidezone Ltd* [2000] 2 BCLC 321, *per* Parker J), in which case a s. 994 petition operates to give relief on an equitable basis. Hoffmann J, as he then was, confirmed this interests-based approach in *Re a Company (No. 00477 of 1986)* [1986] BCLC 376.

> 'the court must take into account that the interests of a member are not necessarily limited to his strict legal rights under the company's constitution ... The use of the word "unfairly"... like the use of the words "just and equitable" ... enables the court to have regard to wider equitable considerations.'

Circumstances in which an 'interests-based' equitable approach is appropriate

Many petitions which today would be brought under s. 994 were, prior to 1980, brought as petitions for the court to wind up the company on just and equitable grounds. The leading case on just and equitable winding up is *Ebrahimi v Westbourne Galleries Ltd* [1973] AC 360 (HL), which has been endorsed as authority for how the court approaches the exercise of its equitable jurisdiction under s. 994.

CASE LAW 13.8

Ebrahimi v Westbourne Galleries Ltd [1973] AC 360 (HL)

N & E were partners in an unincorporated business. They incorporated a company and transferred the assets of the partnership to it. Initially, they were equal shareholders and were both directors. The company paid the directors remuneration rather than paying dividends. N's son joined the company as a director and shareholder. E was now one of three directors and owned one-third of the company's shares. After a disagreement, E was removed from office under what is now Companies Act 2006, s. 168, deprived of his salary and deprived of his role in the management of the company. E presented a petition for the company to be wound up on the ground that it was just and equitable to do so.

Held: the company was ordered to be wound up. The company had been formed on the assumption that E would participate in its management and receive a salary. The exercise of the company's strict legal right to remove him from office breached an implied agreement or mutual understanding that E would be a full-time working director. In the circumstances such breach was unjust and inequitable. Lord Wilberforce stated that company law recognises that behind the corporate entity there are individuals with rights, expectations and obligations among themselves which are not necessarily submerged in the company structure. He stated that a company's structure is defined by the Act and by the Articles by which members agree to be bound and that in most companies and in most contexts, this definition is sufficient and exhaustive, whether the company is large or small. But, he emphasised, 'The winding-up jurisdiction is an equitable jurisdiction. It does not entitle one party to disregard the obligation he assumes by entering a company but *it does, as equity always does, enable the court to subject the exercise of legal rights to equitable considerations*; considerations, that is, of a personal character arising between one individual and another, which may make it unjust, or inequitable, to insist on legal rights, or to exercise them in a particular way' (emphasis added).

Lord Wilberforce described the typical circumstances in which the court is called upon to provide relief under s. 994 based on behaviour that does not amount to an infringement of the petitioning shareholder's strict legal rights, and set out what have come to be referred to as the '*Ebrahimi* factors' that are likely to be present before the court will grant such equitable relief. The *Ebrahimi* factors should not be regarded as written in stone. Lord Wilberforce introduced them with a reminder that it would be impossible, and wholly undesirable, to define the circumstances in which equitable considerations may arise. Those circumstances, he stated, typically may include one, or probably more, of the following elements:

- An association formed or continued on the basis of a personal relationship, involving mutual confidence – this element will often be found where a pre-existing partnership has been converted into a limited company.
- An agreement or understanding that all or some of the shareholders shall participate in the conduct of the business (may be evidenced by the manner in which profits are distributed).
- Restriction on the transfer of the members' interests in the company, so that if confidence is lost, or one member is removed from management, he cannot take out his stake and go elsewhere.

In *O'Neill v Phillips* (1999) Lord Hoffmann explained the partnership law parentage of the equitable principles in evidence in successful s. 994 petitions.

'Company law has developed seamlessly from the law of partnership, which was treated by equity ... as a contract of good faith. One of the traditional roles of equity, as a separate jurisdiction, was to restrain the exercise of strict legal rights in relationships in which it considered that this would be contrary to good faith. These principles have, with appropriate modification, been carried over into company law ... [It follows] that there will be cases in which equitable considerations make it unfair for those conducting the affairs of the company to rely upon their strict legal powers.'

Lord Hoffmann also stressed that in exercising its discretion, the court must strike a balance between the breadth of its discretion and the principle of legal certainty. The way in which the equitable principles operate are, in his view, 'tolerably well settled'.

O'Neill v Phillips [1999] 1 WLR 1092

Phillips (P) owned all of the shares of a company. He transferred 25 per cent of his shares to O'Neill (O), a company employee, and promoted O to the board. P retired from the board and O was appointed managing director of the company. The company was initially profitable and although O was only strictly entitled to one quarter of the dividends, P waived a third of his dividend entitlement so that dividends were shared equally between P and O. Preliminary discussions took place with a view to O increasing his stake to 50 per cent, but no formal agreement was reached. A financial downturn followed. P resumed command of the company and although O remained on the board his status was reduced to that of a branch manager. As O was no longer managing director, P decided that O would receive only his salary and one quarter of any dividends. O petitioned under what is now s. 994 alleging that there was an 'implied agreement' giving rise to a legitimate expectation that he would receive an equal share of the company's profits and an increase to a 50 per cent shareholding.

Held: O's petition for relief would not succeed. While there might be circumstances in which equitable considerations would make it unfair for a controlling shareholder to rely on his strict legal powers, this was not such a case. O had not been excluded from management nor, on the evidence, had P unconditionally promised that O would receive an equal share of profits for all time or an increased shareholding.

Typical lawful conduct that may form the basis of a successful petition

The following conduct may be lawful yet be evidence of the affairs of the company being conducted in a manner unfairly prejudicial to the interests of the petitioning shareholder:

- removal of the petitioner as a director;
- denying the petitioner a role in the management of the company (in *Richards v Lundy* [2000] 1 BCLC 376, the petitioner had been unfairly excluded from management as a director and employee where the company was in substance a quasi-partnership);
- mismanagement of the company's assets (see *Re Elgindata Ltd* [1991] BCLC 959 and *Re Macro (Ipswich) Ltd* [1994] 2 BCLC 354);
- payment of excessive remuneration to directors (see *Re Cumana Ltd* [1986] BCLC 430 (CA));
- non-payment of dividends or payment of derisory dividends (in *Re Sam Weller & Sons Ltd* [1990] BCLC 80, the company failed to increase dividends for 37 years despite increasing profits).

Unlawful conduct that has formed the basis of a successful petition

The following unlawful conduct has been successfully included in s. 994 petitions as evidence of the affairs of the company being conducted in a manner unfairly prejudicial to the interests of the petitioning shareholder:

- directors exercising powers for an improper purpose (see *Re Cumana Ltd* (1986), in which a rights issue was timed for when the minority shareholder had no funds);
- breach of statutory pre-emption rights (now found in s. 561) (as in *Re a Company (No. 005134 of 1986), ex parte Harries* [1989] BCLC 383);

- refusal to pay declared dividend (as in *Grace v Biagioli* [2006] 2 BCLC 70);
- diversion of company business to a majority shareholder in breach of fiduciary duty (as in *Re London School of Electronics* [1986] Ch 211).

TEST YOUR KNOWLEDGE 13.4

(a) Who is entitled to commence a s. 994 petition?
(b) Who are the respondents in a s. 994 petition?
(c) What type of behaviour can be complained about in a s. 994 petition?
(d) What is meant by the phrase 'interests of members' in s. 994(1)(a)?

4.5 Remedies and costs

On a s. 994 petition the court has power to 'make such order as it thinks fit for giving relief in respect of the matters complained of' (s. 996(1)). Section 996(2) then contains a non-exhaustive list of orders the court may make. Although the court may order the winding up of the company on a s. 994 petition, pursuit of such an order introduces complications and petitioners are discouraged from seeking such an order on a s. 994 petition. The relationship between a s. 994 petition and a petition to wind up the company on the basis that it is just and equitable for it to be wound up is examined in section 5.3 below.

Buy-out orders

The most important remedy, listed at s. 996(2)(g), is an order 'for the purchase of the shares of the company by other members or by the company itself and, in the case of a purchase by the company itself, the reduction of the company's share capital accordingly'. In *Grace v Biagioli* (2006) a buy-out was described as the usual order to make.

> 'In most cases, the usual order to make will be the one requiring the respondents to buy out the petitioning shareholder at a price to be fixed by the court. This is normally the most appropriate order to deal with intra-company disputes involving small private companies.'

CASE LAW 13.10

Grace v Biagioli [2006] 2 BCLC 70 (CA)

Members of a company each took responsibility for developing and managing its business in various countries. The petitioner (P) was responsible for starting up and developing business in France. The other members became unhappy because the French business was not very profitable. Dividends were declared but it was decided to withhold P's dividend and pay an equivalent sum to the other members as management fees. P presented a petition under what is now s. 994 seeking a buy-out order. It was argued that buy-out relief was not appropriate as any unfair prejudice could be remedied by ordering payment of the dividends.

Held: P was locked into a company where relationships had soured and there were likely to be further disputes in the future. The appropriate remedy was an order that he be bought out at a fair valuation.

Buy-outs have a number of benefits:

- The possibility of future difficulties between shareholders is removed.
- They allow an otherwise locked-in minority to extract his share of the value of the business: to 'exit'.
- The company and its business are preserved for the benefit of the respondent shareholders.
- The company is free from the claims of the petitioning shareholder.

It is important to understand the effect on a s. 994 petition of the respondent having offered or, as a result of the petition being presented, offering to buy out the petitioning shareholder. Essentially, if the respondent makes a reasonable offer to buy the petitioner out of the company, the petitioner will be expected to accept the offer (*O'Neill v Phillips* (1999) *per* Lord Hoffmann).

> 'If the respondent to a petition has plainly made a reasonable offer, then the exclusion as such will not be unfairly prejudicial and he will be entitled to have the petition struck out.'

If the offer is made only after the petition has been made and costs have been incurred by the petitioner, the respondent will also need to make a reasonable offer in relation to costs.

Fair valuation of shares

A reasonable offer to buy out the petitioner, and a court order that the respondent or the company (or, potentially a third party) buy out the petitioning shareholders' shares, will be based on a fair valuation of those shares. Both the time at which the shares are to be valued and the basis on which they are to be valued are important aspects of fair value.

Timing of the share valuation

There are three potential dates for the valuation of the petitioning shareholders' shares: the date of the petition, the date of the trial and the date of the final order in the petition. Generally, the appropriate date will be the date of the order in the petition, that is, the date on which the shares are ordered to be purchased. Where, however, the conduct complained of has reduced or depreciated the value of the shares as measured at that date, their value will need to be adjusted to restore the petitioning shareholders' position (*Profinance Trust SA v Gladstone* [2002] 1 BCLC 141).

Basis of the share valuation

Valuation of a private company is a notoriously difficult task as alternative valuation methods exist. Because valuation is not an exact science and potential exists for a low valuation or, contrarily, a high valuation to be presented as objectively arrived at, it is extremely important that the valuation is made by an independent valuer. Even once the company has been valued it is necessary to allocate that value to the share interests held by different shareholders in the company. Assuming, as is common, the company has only one class of shares (and assuming that the company has not been valued on a 'net assets on break-up' value but as a 'going concern'), the two bases for the valuation of shareholdings are a *pro rata* valuation and a discounted valuation.

A *pro rata* valuation simply means allocation of an equal value to each share. The value of a shareholders' stake in the company is, on this basis, the value of a share multiplied by the number of shares he owns. In a small company, however, individual shareholders typically own significant shareholdings. It is not uncommon for one shareholder to own a block of shares which confers on him voting control of the company (50% + 1 vote). It is standard practice in valuing a block of shares in a company for the purpose of a sale between a willing buyer and seller to discount the *pro rata* value of a minority holding to reflect the absence of control, hence the term 'discounted value'. A minority shareholding may confer the power to block special resolutions which is referred to as 'negative control' (25 per cent) and a minority shareholding conferring negative control ordinarily would not be discounted to the same extent as a shareholding of less than 25 per cent.

The key question to determine the correct basis of valuation in a s. 994 petition is whether or not it is appropriate on the facts to discount the value of the petitioning shareholders' stake below a *pro rata* valuation because it is a minority stake and, as such, the petitioning shareholder was never in a position to exercise much or any control over the company. The rule of thumb (although it will not always be the case) on a petition based on unfair exclusion from management will be for shares to be given a *pro rata* valuation (*Re Bird Precision Bellow Ltd* [1984] 3 All ER 44). In exclusion from management petitions, the very point of the relief is that the petitioner had been in a position to exercise control alongside the other shareholders until the other shareholders began to assert their strict legal rights contrary to the understanding that formed the basis on which the company had been run prior to the unfairly prejudicial conduct of which the petitioner is complaining.

In *O'Neill v Phillips* [1999] 1 WLR 1092, Lord Hoffman set out a five-point guide to what constitutes a reasonable offer such that the court will strike out a petition if it is not accepted:

- The offer must be to purchase the petitioner's shares at a fair value: ordinarily at a *pro rata* valuation.
- If the value is not agreed, it must be determined by a competent expert.
- The value should be determined by an expert as an expert, not by a more complex procedure.
- Both parties should have access to information about the company which bears on the value of the shares and both should have the right to make submissions to the expert.
- The respondent should be given a reasonable opportunity to make a costs offer before becoming obliged to pay costs.

Costs

The special costs rules that apply to derivative claims do not apply to s. 994 petitions because the rationale for making the company indemnify the claimant shareholder is not present. In s. 994 petitions the petitioning shareholder is seeking a remedy for himself, not the company (see *Re Sherborne Park Residents Co Ltd* (1986)).

Controllers of a company will not be permitted to use the assets of the company to pay the legal costs of defending a s. 994 petition which is essentially brought against them, even though the company has been joined as a respondent (*Re a Company (No. 001126 of 1992)* [1993] BCC 325, and *Re Milgate Developments Ltd* [1993] BCLC 291).

TEST YOUR KNOWLEDGE 13.5

(a) Which orders may be made by a court under s. 996 when a s. 994 petition is successful?
(b) What is the most popular order made under s. 996?
(c) What is a reasonable offer to buy such that the court will expect such an offer to be accepted by the petitioner?
(d) Compare and contrast a *pro rata* valuation and a discounted valuation of shares. Is it ever appropriate to use a discounted valuation method in a s. 994 petition?

5 Just and equitable winding up petitions

5.1 Who may apply

Section 124 of the Insolvency Act 1986 provides that a company, its directors, any creditor, the liquidator or a **contributory** of at least six months' standing may petition the court for a winding up order. One of the grounds on which the court may order a winding up is that the court 'is of the opinion that it is just and equitable that the company should be wound up' (s. 122(1)(g)).

Contributory is defined in s. 79 of the Insolvency Act 1986 to mean a person liable to contribute to the assets of the company if it is wound up. A shareholder with partly-paid shares clearly falls within the definition of contributory. Although a shareholder with fully paid up shares would appear not to fall within the definition, such a shareholder has been held to be a contributory provided he has a sufficient interest in the winding up (*Re Rica Gold Washing Co Ltd* (1879) 11 Ch D 36). Basically, a shareholder with fully paid-up shares must prove that there will be a surplus in which he will share to be able to bring a petition.

5.2 Foundation of the jurisdiction

The circumstances in which a court will order a winding up on just and equitable grounds were considered by the House of Lords in the leading case of *Ebrahimi v Westbourne Galleries Ltd* (1973) (see above). Having reviewed the authorities Lord Wilberforce described the foundation of the jurisdiction.

> 'The foundation of it all lies in the words "just and equitable" and, if there is any respect in which some of the cases may be open to criticism, it is that the courts may sometimes have

been too timorous in giving them full force. The words are a recognition of the fact that a limited company is more than a mere legal entity, with a personality in law of its own: that there is room in company law for recognition of the fact that behind it, or amongst it, there are individuals, with rights, expectations and obligations *inter se* which are not necessarily submerged in the company structure. That structure is defined by the Companies Act and by the Articles of association by which shareholders agree to be bound. In most companies and in most contexts, this definition is sufficient and exhaustive, equally so whether the company is large or small. The "just and equitable" provision does not, as the respondents suggest, entitle one party to disregard the obligation he assumes by entering a company, nor the court to dispense him from it. It does, as equity always does, enable the court to subject the exercise of legal rights to equitable considerations; considerations, that is, of a personal character arising between one individual and another, which may make it unjust, or inequitable, to insist on legal rights, or to exercise them in a particular way.'

As we have seen, *Ebrahimi* is now a leading case on the approach to be taken by courts on s. 994 petitions. It is important to understand the relationship between s. 124 and s. 994 petitions.

5.3 Relationship with unfair prejudice claims

Ebrahimi was decided when shareholders did not have the right to petition the court for a remedy based on unfairly prejudicial conduct of the company's affairs (s. 994). Since 1980, when the unfairly prejudicial conduct petition was introduced, many petitioners who, prior to 1980, would have made a winding up petition on just and equitable grounds now choose to seek relief pursuant to ss. 994–996.

Three questions are of critical importance to a shareholder:

- May the court order a winding up on a s. 994 petition?
- May the court make an alternative order to a winding up order on a s. 124 petition?
- Is a shareholder entitled to a winding up order pursuant to a s. 124 petition if he could obtain an adequate remedy under s. 994?

May the court order a winding up on a s. 994 petition?

Although the court technically has power to make a winding up order pursuant to a s. 994 petition, courts will not do so unless asked to make such an order (see *Re Full Cup International Trading Ltd* [1995] BCC 682). The effect of asking for a winding up order, even in the alternative, is to trigger the Insolvency Act 1986, s. 127, which results in the company being unable to carry on business from the date the petition is presented. Again, as a matter of practice, the court will, unless the petitioner can convince it not to, make an order overriding s. 127 so that the company can continue to trade.

The learning point here is that s. 994 is not intended to be used by a person who is seeking to wind up the company. A shareholder seeking a winding up order should petition the court under s. 124 of the Insolvency Act 1986.

May the court make an alternative order to a winding up order on a s. 124 petition?

The powers of the court under a s. 124 application are set out in s. 125. Again, while technically it may make 'any order that it thinks fit', it is not the practice of the court to provide a remedy different from a winding up on a s. 124 petition.

Is a shareholder entitled to a winding up order pursuant to a s. 124 petition if he could obtain an adequate remedy under s. 994?

The right of a shareholder to a winding up order where an alternative remedy is available is dealt with in s. 125(2)(b).

> '125 Powers of court on hearing of petition
> (1) On hearing a winding-up petition the court may dismiss it, or adjourn the hearing conditionally or unconditionally, or make an interim order, or any other order that it thinks fit; ...

(2) If the petition is presented by members of the company as contributories on the ground that it is just and equitable that the company should be wound up, the court, if it is of opinion—

(a) that the petitioners are entitled to relief either by winding up the company or by some other means, and

(b) that in the absence of any other remedy it would be just and equitable that the company should be wound up, shall make a winding-up order; but this does not apply if the court is also of the opinion both that some other remedy is available to the petitioners and that they are acting unreasonably in seeking to have the company wound up instead of pursuing that other remedy.'

Essentially, even if a winding up order would otherwise be available, the court will not order the company wound up if the court is of the opinion that both:

- 'some other remedy is available'; and
- the shareholder is acting unreasonably in seeking to have the company wound up.

Consequently, even if the shareholder could make an application under s. 994, this is not sufficient ground for the court to deny a winding up order (see *Re a Company (No. 001363 of 1988) ex parte S-P* [1989] BCLC 579).

The key consideration is whether or not the shareholder is acting reasonably in seeking a winding up order, which involves consideration of all the facts of the case. A typical scenario is that the petitioner has been made or, as a result of presentation of the winding up petition, is made, an offer to purchase his shares in the company. Courts consider whether or not the shareholder is acting unreasonably in refusing to accept the offer. Where it appears that it would be unreasonable for the petitioner to refuse to be bought out, the court may stay (suspend) the winding up petition for the details of the purchase to be worked out, in this way protecting the petitioner from the defendant adopting bad faith tactics in the share sale negotiations, as in *Re a Company (No. 002567 of 1982)* [1983] 1 WLR 927.

 **CASE LAW 13.12**

Re a Company (No. 002567 of 1982) [1983] 1 WLR 927

T and C were partners in an unincorporated business. They formed a company to run the business and T and C were the directors and shareholders. Later, R joined the company with the result that T, C and R were all salaried directors owning one third of the company's shares and receiving equal remuneration *qua* directors. No dividends were paid. T was removed from office as a director, deprived of his employment and any say in the management of the company's affairs, and the company stopped paying him his remuneration. T petitioned the court under the Insolvency Act 1986 for the winding-up of the company on the just and equitable ground citing a breakdown of mutual trust and confidence.

Held: the winding up petition would be stayed pending finalisation of the purchase of shares subject to which it would be dismissed. This was not because the petition lacked merit but because in the court's view the petitioner was unreasonable in refusing the respondents' (C and R's) offer to purchase his shares at a value reached by machinery which met all his reasonable objections. (*Obiter*) A case where what is alleged is unfair exclusion from the management of the company's affairs in breach of an express or implied agreement that the member will be allowed to participate in management and be paid remuneration falls within the scope of section [994(1)] even though the member's strict rights *qua* member are not affected. Per Vinelott J: 'It seems to me unlikely that the legislature could have intended to exclude from the scope of section [994] a shareholder in the position of Mr Ebrahimi in *Ebrahimi v Westbourne Galleries Ltd* [1973] AC 360.'

6 Company investigations

The Secretary of State for Business, Innovation and Skills has broad powers to investigate companies pursuant to Part XIV of the Companies Act 1985 (as amended). This jurisdiction was not included within the remit of the 1998 Company Law Review. Consequently, the governing provisions have not been consolidated into the Companies Act 2006 but remain, and are expected to remain, in the 1985 Act.

The powers are in practice exercised by the Companies Investigations Branch (CIB), part of the Insolvency Service. Although the powers are granted in wide terms, the CIB will generally investigate a company only where it has reasonable grounds to suspect fraud, serious misconduct, or material irregularity in the conduct of its affairs – approximately 75 per cent of investigations are begun because fraud is suspected.

Most investigations are carried out pursuant to s. 477 by requiring companies or 'any person' to produce documents and information. Investigators may be empowered to enter premises and search for documents and information. These investigations are confidential.

Less common but more comprehensive are investigations by inspectors appointed pursuant to ss. 431 and 432 to investigate and report to the Secretary of State on the affairs of a company. The appointment of an inspector is a publicly announced event and traditionally their reports had to be published. An amendment introduced in 1989 now permits appointment of inspectors on the basis of non-publication of the report (s. 432(2A) inserted by the Companies Act 1989). Investigations may result in a decision not to take further action. Where action is taken it is typically one or more of the following:

- a petition pursuant to s. 124A of the Insolvency Act 1986 for the winding up of the company;
- prosecutions being undertaken (often by the Serious Fraud Squad);
- a petition pursuant to the Company Directors Disqualification Act 1986 for disqualification of one or more directors on the grounds of unfitness;
- (less commonly), a petition for relief under s. 994 based on the company's affairs having been conducted in a manner unfairly prejudicial to its members' interests.

The findings in published reports may also encourage shareholders, creditors and other parties to bring civil actions.

TEST YOUR KNOWLEDGE 13.6

(a) Who may petition the court for a winding up under s. 124?
(b) Did the court order a winding up in *Ebrahimi v Westbourne Galleries* (1973) and would such an order be made today?
(c) Will the court order a winding up on just and equitable grounds if an alternative remedy is available?

CHAPTER SUMMARY

- The rule in *Foss v Harbottle* (the proper claimant principle) states that in any legal proceedings in which a wrong is alleged to have been done to a company, the proper claimant is the company.
- The rule directly arises from application by the courts of majority rule and the business judgement rule.
- The rule does not apply where a shareholder is exercising a personal right; the action complained of is action by the company for which more than a simple majority is needed, (*Edwards v Halliwell* (1950)); or a statutory derivative action may be pursued (s. 260) (replacing the common law exception where those who controlled the majority shareholder vote were the wrongdoers (*Cook v Deeks* (1916)).
- Grounds for statutory derivative claims are actual or proposed acts or omissions involving negligence, default, breach of duty or breach of trust by a director of the company (s. 260).
- The claim is issued followed by an application to the court for permission to continue disclosing a *prima facie* case (s. 261(1)).

- Permission to continue must be refused if a person acting in accordance with the s. 172 duty to promote the success of the company would not seek to continue the claim (s. 263(2)(a)); or there has been authorisation or ratification of the act complained of (s. 263(2)(b) and (c)).
- The court must consider a list of factors before exercising its discretion to permit the claim to continue (s. 263(3)).
- Claimants will ordinarily be entitled to an order of indemnity in relation to costs, regardless of the outcome of the litigation (*Wallersteiner v Moir (No 2)* (1975)) based on the theory that the claimant is in effect bringing the claim as an agent of the company.
- Legal actions asserting the personal rights of a shareholders are personal actions and, if the rights of more than one shareholder have been denied or breached, legal action may be brought by one or more shareholders on behalf of all similarly injured shareholders: a 'representative action' (CPR 19.6). Cases may be consolidated (CPR 19.1) and Group Legal Orders are available (CPR 19.10).
- The no reflective loss principle denies a shareholder the right to assert personal rights where his loss simply reflects a loss incurred by the company (*Johnson v Gore Wood & Co* (2001)).
- Where the company is unable to pursue its claim against the defendant because of the defendant's wrongdoing, a shareholder will be entitled to bring a personal action as an exception to the no reflective loss principle (*Giles v Rhind* [2003] 1 BCLC 1 (CA)).
- A shareholder may petition the court for an order on the ground that *the company's affairs* have been conducted in a manner that is *unfairly prejudicial to one or more shareholders' interests*.
- A remedy is usually sought against the controlling shareholders/directors of the company, most commonly for an order to buy out the petitioner's shares in the company.
- The conduct complained of must be both prejudicial and unfairly so (*Re a Company (No. 005685) ex parte Schwartz (No. 2)* (1989)). The test of unfairness is objective, not subjective (*Re Bovey Hotel Ventures Ltd* (1981))
- Prejudice must be harm in a commercial sense, not in a merely emotional sense (*Re Unisoft Group Ltd (No. 3)* (1994)).
- Shareholders' interests protected by s. 994 are wider than strict legal rights.
- The interests protected in quasi-partnership cases can be equitable in nature (*Ebrahimi v Westbourne Galleries Ltd* (1973); *O'Neill v Phillips* [1999]).
- The court has power to make such order as it thinks fit for giving relief.
- The court may order a winding up on the petition of (among others) a contributor (which a shareholder is likely to be) if it is of the opinion that it is just and equitable to do so (s. 122(1)(g) of the 1986 Act).
- It is not the practice of the court to provide a remedy different from a winding up on a s. 124 petition.
- The availability of a s. 994 application is not sufficient ground for the court to deny a winding up order (see *Re a Company (No. 001363 of 1988) ex parte S-P* (1989)).
- The Secretary of State for Business, Innovation and Skills has broad powers to investigate companies pursuant to Pt. XIV of the Companies Act 1985 (as amended).
- The powers are in practice exercised by the Companies Investigations Branch.
- Reasonable grounds to suspect fraud, serious misconduct or material irregularity in the conduct of its affairs is generally required for an investigation to be initiated.

PART 3 CASE QUESTIONS

Return to the opening case at the start of this part and re-read it. Think generally about the issues it raises, the law in relation to which has been covered in the chapters in this part, before attempting to answer the following questions.

1 Is Joel, the company secretary, authorised to agree the new clauses in Orlando's service contract? Are the new clauses binding on Blossom plc?
2 What rights and remedies does Blossom plc have in relation to Nile arising out of the £15,000 loan to Nile?
3 Does Blossom plc have any rights or remedies against Moira or Customerled plc arising out of Moira's change of employment?
4 Is Blossom plc bound to pay Pummel plc for the massage machine? Does Blossom plc have any rights in relation to Joel in relation to the massage machine?
5 What rights, if any, does Blossom plc have against Larry?
6 Can Sally and Teresa remove Nile and Larry as directors and, if so, what process is required? What would be the effect of removing Nile and Larry as directors on their service contracts with the company?
7 Can Teresa insist that Blossom plc commence legal proceedings?
8 Can Teresa commence a derivative action and if so, is she likely to be able to continue such an action?
9 Is Teresa able to commence a s. 994 petition? If so, is she likely to succeed? What remedy would it be appropriate to ask the court to award?

PART FOUR

Meetings and resolutions

■ LIST OF CHAPTERS

14 Members' meetings and decision-making
15 Directors' meetings and decision-making

■ OVERVIEW

This, the shortest part of the text, focuses on the fundamental question of how decisions are made by the members, or shareholders, of a company on the one hand, and the board of directors of a company on the other. In relation to private companies, following recent deregulation, the need to hold meetings is very limited.

Chapter 14 considers the members, or shareholders. It covers the convening and conduct of meetings of the company and meetings of particular classes of shareholders before turning to examine the types of resolutions that may be passed. The final section of chapter 14 addresses shareholder engagement, a topic that has attracted a great deal of attention in recent years.

Chapter 15 focuses on the board of directors, covering, in turn, board meetings and board decision-making. The law here is principally contained in a company's Articles of Association.

■ LEARNING OUTCOMES

After reading this part you should be able to:

- Understand the importance of, and the processes surrounding, company meetings.
- Understand and apply the law and procedure around company resolutions and how company decisions are made.
- Explain the concepts and rights of corporate representatives and proxies.
- Understand the importance of, and growing emphasis on, shareholder engagement.
- Understand the importance of, and the process around, board meetings and how directors make decisions.

PART 4 CASE STUDY

The annual general meeting of Landing plc is to take place on 1 June 2013. Sue, the company secretary, sends out notices on 16 May 2013. Included with the notice are the texts of a number of proposed resolutions, including a resolution to remove one of the directors, David, before his term of office expires and a resolution to amend the Articles of Association. The notice is also accompanied by a form for appointing a proxy.

The notice is received by all ten shareholders of the company. Alice, who owns 500 shares in Landing plc, receives the notice the day before she leaves for a three-week vacation. She completes the proxy form, appointing her brother, Mark, scans the form and emails it to the company secretary. She calls her brother and instructs him to vote against both of the proposed resolutions referenced above.

Mark himself owns 500 shares in Landing plc. He wishes to vote in favour of the two resolutions. Mark attends the AGM and is informed that he cannot exercise the votes attached to his sister's shares. Both resolutions are voted on by a show of hands and four out of the six shareholders of the company in attendance at the meeting support the resolutions.

The board of Landing plc need to decide whether or not to commit the company to a £3 million contract with Takeoff plc. The language of a board resolution is emailed to four of the five directors. Brian, one of the directors, is left out because he is trekking in Nepal. All four directors reply, two supporting entry into the contract and two opposing it. The chairman of the board, Colin, tells Sue that he has a casting vote and therefore, as he supports entry into the contract, the two of them can sign the contract with Takeoff plc.

Members' meetings and decision-making

■ CONTENTS

1 Company meetings
2 Records of meetings and resolutions
3 Company resolutions and decisions
4 Corporate representatives
5 Proxies
6 Shareholder engagement

■ INTRODUCTION

This chapter focuses on the members, or shareholders. It covers the convening and conduct of meetings of the company (all shareholders) and meetings of particular classes of shareholders, before turning to examine the types of resolutions that may be passed by shareholders and how such resolutions may be passed. The law governing resolutions and meetings is found in Part 13 of the Companies Act 2006 (ss. 281–361). The chapter ends with a section on shareholder engagement.

The relevant provisions of the Companies Act 2006 were amended with effect from 3 August 2009, most extensively in their application to companies with listed equity shares, by the Companies (Shareholders' Rights) Regulations (SI 2009/1632) (the 2009 Regulations), which implemented the Shareholder Rights Directive (2007/36/EC). Although some of the changes are of general application, most apply only to companies with listed equity shares reflecting the principal aim of the directive 'to help facilitate the exercise of basic shareholders' rights and solve problems in the cross-border exercise of such rights, particularly voting rights, in respect of companies traded on regulated markets' (see the explanatory memorandum to the 2009 Regulations). The changes relevant to companies traded on regulated markets do not apply to companies the shares of which are traded on AIM.

1 Company meetings

Rules governing shareholder meetings (also called company meetings) are an important part of shareholder decision-making. Although a company with only one shareholder may hold a properly constituted meeting (s. 318(1)), apart from sole member companies, and unless the Articles require a higher number, two shareholders (or corporate representatives or member proxies) present at a meeting are a **quorum** (s. 318(2)). This means that if only one person attends a meeting, even if they are the representative or **proxy** (see section 7 below) for more than one member, the meeting is not properly constituted and no business can be conducted.

Adjournment of meetings is not dealt with in the Act, except that s. 332 provides that a resolution passed at an adjourned meeting is treated as having been passed on the date on which it was in fact passed and not on any earlier date. If the Articles are silent, a decision to adjourn may be taken at a meeting. The Model Articles (art. 41 for private companies, and art. 33 for public companies, which are identical) provide for adjournments.

Both sets of Model Articles provide that the chairman may adjourn a meeting if, within half an hour of the planned start, there is no quorum. He must adjourn a meeting if directed to do so by the meeting, and may adjourn a meeting if the meeting consents or appears necessary to protect the safety of any person attending the meeting or to ensure the at business of the meeting is conducted in an orderly manner. The chairman must state the time and place to which the meeting is adjourned or that the directors are to decide such.

1.1 Annual general meetings

Every public company must hold an **annual general meeting (AGM)** within six months of the end of its financial year. If the company fails to do so, a criminal offence is committed by every director and the company secretary (s. 336). At least 21 days' notice of an AGM, stating that it is an AGM, must be given (s. 307(2)) to all shareholders and directors (s. 310), unless all shareholders entitled to attend and vote agree to shorter notice (s. 337(2)).

The rules for **general meetings** set out below apply to AGMs with a number of key differences:

- The minimum notice of meeting period for AGMs is 21 days rather than 14 days for other general meetings (or, in the case of companies with listed shares, the opportunity to allow 14 days' notice).
- Unanimous consent to short notice is required for an AGM rather than 90 per cent (for private companies) or 95 per cent (for public companies) consent to short notice for general meetings.
- Notice of shareholders' resolutions to be moved at the AGM are required to be circulated by the company if requested by shareholders with 5 per cent of the voting rights or 100 shareholders (s. 338).
- In the case of companies with listed shares, 100 shareholders or shareholders with 5 per cent of the voting rights may request the company to include in the business to be dealt with at an AGM any matter which is not defamatory of any person, or frivolous or vexatious (s. 338A) and companies are required to circulate notice of any such matter, either in the same way as it gives notice of the AGM or as soon as reasonably practicable afterwards (s. 340A).
- If an AGM notice is sent out more than six weeks before the meeting it must include a statement about the right of shareholders to requisition a resolution or other matter at the meeting (s. 337).

Main principle E2 of the UK Corporate Governance Code (September 2012) emphasises the role of the AGM and the supporting code provisions supplement the provisions of the Companies Act governing AGMs:

'E.2 Constructive Use of the AGM

Main Principle

The board should use the AGM to communicate with investors and to encourage their participation.

Code Provisions

E.2.1 At any general meeting, the company should propose a separate resolution on each substantially separate issue, and should, in particular, propose a resolution at the AGM relating to the report and accounts. For each resolution, proxy appointment forms should provide shareholders with the option to direct their proxy to vote either for or against the resolution or to withhold their vote. The proxy form and any announcement of the results of a vote should make it clear that a 'vote withheld' is not a vote in law and will not be counted in the calculation of the proportion of the votes for and against the resolution.

E.2.2 The company should ensure that all valid proxy appointments received for general meetings are properly recorded and counted. For each resolution, where a vote has been taken on a show of hands, the company should ensure that the following information is given at the meeting and made available as soon as reasonably practicable on a website which is maintained by or on behalf of the company:
- the number of shares in respect of which proxy appointments have been validly made;
- the number of votes for the resolution;
- the number of votes against the resolution; and
- the number of shares in respect of which the vote was directed to be withheld.

E.2.3 The chairman should arrange for the chairmen of the audit, remuneration and nomination committees to be available to answer questions at the AGM and for all directors to attend.

E.2.4 The company should arrange for the Notice of the AGM and related papers to be sent to shareholders at least 20 working days before the meeting.'

1.2 General meetings

The directors may call a general meeting (s. 302) and are required to call a general meeting if holders of at least 5 per cent of the voting rights of shareholders having a right to vote at general meetings request (in writing or electronic form) that the directors do so (ss. 303 and 304). Five per cent has been substituted for the previous figure of 10 per cent by the Companies (Shareholders' Rights) Regulations 2009 (SI 2209/1632), reg. 4. If the directors fail to call a general meeting within 21 days of such a request, or to hold the meeting within 28 days of the request, the shareholders who made the request may call a meeting and hold it within three months of the request, in which event their reasonable expenses are reimbursable by the company (s. 305).

Companies with listed shares are required to make certain information available in advance of meetings, from the date of notice of any meetings, on its website (s. 311). The information is:

- the matters set out in the notice of the meeting;
- the total numbers of:
  - shares in the company, and
  - shares of each class
- in respect of which members are entitled to exercise voting rights at the meeting;
- the totals of the voting rights that members are entitled to exercise at the meeting in respect of the shares of each class; and
- members' statements, members' resolutions and members' matters of business received by the company after the first date on which notice of the meeting is given.

All shareholders and directors are entitled to receive notice of every general meeting unless the Articles provide otherwise (s. 310). At least 14 days' notice of a meeting must be given unless shareholders holding not less than 90 per cent (for a private company) or 95 per cent (for a public company) of the nominal value of the shares held by those entitled to attend and vote at the meeting agree to shorter notice. A notice must state the general nature of the business to be dealt with, as well as the time, date and place of the meeting (s. 311). If notice is given of a meeting, any accidental failure to give notice to one or more shareholders will not render the notice invalid (s. 313).

Notice of a meeting must also include, with reasonable prominence, a statement informing the member of his rights to appoint a proxy, whether the right is simply that stated in s. 324 or a more extensive right provided for in the Articles.

Note that for a resolution to be passed as a **special resolution** at a meeting, the text of the resolution and the intention to propose it as a special resolution must have been included in the notice of the meeting (s. 283(6)). This requirement of notice of a special resolution is not to be confused with **special notice**, which is considered below.

Shareholders with at least 5 per cent of the voting rights of shareholders eligible to vote on the proposed matter may require the company to circulate a statement of up to 1,000 words relating to a proposed resolution or any other business to be dealt with at the meeting (s. 314). A similar right exists in relation to **written resolutions** (s. 293).

Special notice is required of four resolutions:

- to remove a director pursuant to s. 168;
- to appoint someone in his place at the removal meeting;
- to remove an auditor (s. 511); and
- to appoint a new auditor (s. 515).

Special notice must be given by the shareholder to the company of his intention to move the resolution and must be not less than 28 days before the date of the meeting at which the resolution is to be voted on (s. 312). Be sure to distinguish special notice of a resolution given by a shareholder to the company from notice of a meeting given by a company to shareholders.

Additional rules apply to notices of meetings sent by companies with listed shares, which notices must now include (s. 311):

- details of a website where other information is available;
- details of how to attend and vote at the meeting; and
- details of the right to ask questions at the meeting.

The default notice period for general meetings of companies with listed shares is now 21 days. It is possible for this to be reduced to 14 days if both a special resolution is passed at the AGM approving the shortening of the notice period to 14 days and the company allows shareholders to vote by electronic means accessible to all shareholders (s. 307A).

Shareholders of companies with listed shares who attend a general meeting have the right to ask questions at the meetings (s. 319A). This right is subject to a number of exceptions which are not precisely defined. A question need not be answered if:

- to do so would interfere unduly with the preparation for the meeting;
- to do so would involve the disclosure of confidential information;
- the answer has already been given on a website in the form of an answer to a question; or
- it is undesirable in the interests of the company or the good order of the meeting that the question be answered.

1.3 Class meetings

Class meetings are meetings of the holders of a class of shares in a company. The rights of the holders to attend meetings will be set out in the Articles or the resolution authorising the directors to issue the shares. Section 334 states that, subject to four exceptions, the rules in the Act applicable to general meetings apply 'with necessary modifications' in relation to class meetings.

The first two exceptions are general in nature: the right of shareholders to require directors to call a meeting (ss. 303–305) does not apply to class meetings and the power of the court under s. 306 to order a meeting does not apply to class meetings.

The third and fourth exceptions are relevant only to class meetings in connection with variation of class rights. Special quorum rules apply to such meetings, superseding the quorum of two set out in s. 318, and any holder of the class of shares in question may demand a **poll** (see section 3.2 below) at such a meeting, displacing the rule for general meetings in s. 321. The quorum for class meetings in connection with variation of class rights is two persons present holding at least one third in nominal value of the issued shares of the class in question. For an adjourned meeting, the quorum is reduced to one person present holding shares of the class in question (s. 334(4)). Variation of class rights is discussed in chapter 8.

1.4 Court-ordered meetings

If it is impracticable for a meeting to be called or conducted in accordance with the Articles of the company or the 2006 Act, the court may, on application by a director or any shareholder who would be entitled to vote at the meeting, or of its own volition, order a meeting to be called, held and conducted in any manner the court thinks fit (s. 306).

TEST YOUR KNOWLEDGE 14.1

(a) What is the default quorum for a company meeting and where is the default rule found?
(b) Which companies are required to hold annual general meetings?
(c) Identify five ways in which the rules governing the holding of an AGM differs from other general meetings.
(d) When may and when must the directors convene a general meeting?
(e) What is the minimum period of notice required for an AGM and a general meeting?
(f) Identify four resolutions for which special notice is required.

2 Records of meetings and resolutions

The requirements relating to records of meetings and resolutions are set out in chapter 6 of Part 13 of the Act. The requisite records must be kept for at least ten years (s. 355) and records for the past ten years must be available for inspection (s. 358). The required records are:

- copies of all resolutions of members passed otherwise than at general meetings;
- minutes of all proceedings of general meetings; and
- details of decisions of a sole member provided to the company in accordance with s. 357.

Minutes are a written record of business transacted at a meeting which constitute a permanent record of proceedings.

3 Company resolutions and decisions

Shareholders exercise their powers by taking decisions and the rules governing how decisions are to be taken are determined by a combination of the Articles, statute and common law. The 2006 Act requires shareholder resolutions in a number of situations and shareholder decisions are usually taken by resolutions in accordance with the provisions of the Act (ss. 281–299). The common law is, however, preserved, which leaves open the potential for shareholder decisions to be effective even if they are made otherwise than by passing a resolution (s. 281(4)(a)). The common law may also override the statutory rules as to the circumstances in which a resolution is or is not treated as having been passed and undermine the statutory rules insofar as the common law may preclude a person from alleging that a resolution has not been duly passed (s. 281(4)(b) and (c)). The common law rules are considered after the statutory rules.

3.1 Resolutions

The 2006 Act states that resolutions of the shareholders of a public company must be passed at shareholders' meetings held and conducted in accordance with the 2006 Act for which notice has been given in accordance with the Act (ss. 281(2) and 301). Private company shareholders must pass resolutions either at similarly conforming shareholders' meetings or by written resolution (s. 288(1)).

It is only possible to determine whether or not a resolution has been validly passed if we know:

- which shareholders have the right to vote;
- the proportion of votes needed to pass the resolution; and
- how votes are to be counted.

3.2 Voting rights

A company must have at least one class of shares that carry the right to vote. Unless the Articles provide otherwise, every share carries one vote on every resolution put to shareholders (s. 284), except in a vote by show of hands, when, regardless of the number of shares he owns, a shareholder has only one vote (see voting methods below). Articles may provide for weighted voting rights which can give rise to surprising outcomes. The decision in *Bushell v Faith* [1970] AC 1099 (HL) has rendered s. 168, by which shareholders may remove a director by ordinary resolution, a presumptive rather than mandatory rule of law, and the decision in *Amalgamated Pest Control v McCarron* [1995] 1 QdR 583 permitted incorporators to use weighted voting rights to give a less than 25 per cent minority shareholder a veto on any special resolution.

Even where a company has different classes of shares, the starting point is that all shares carry the right to one vote. The Articles or resolution authorising allotment may state that a certain class of shares carries the right to vote on resolutions on matters affecting the rights of the class. Even if it is not stated expressly that these are the only voting rights attaching to the shares, the court may use the principle of exhaustion of rights to construe such a provision in the Articles as excluding any other voting rights (see *Re Bradford Investments Ltd* [1991] BCLC 224 and section 8.2).

Proportion of votes needed to pass resolutions

The two basic types of resolution passed by shareholders are **ordinary resolutions** and special resolutions. Ordinary resolutions must be passed by not less than a simple majority (50 per cent +1) (s. 282) and special resolutions must be passed by not less than 75 per cent (s. 283). Provisions of the Companies Act 2006 mandating shareholder approval of certain acts or empowering shareholders usually require a special resolution or a general resolution.

Curiously, s. 282 appears to have inadvertently changed the law in relation to the right of the chairman of a shareholders' meeting to have a casting vote. The chairman is usually a director of the company who may or may not be a shareholder. Nonetheless, traditionally, it was common for Articles to provide for the chairman to have a casting vote in the event of an equality of votes for and against an ordinary resolution and regulation 50 of Table A contained just such a provision. Without more, s. 282 overrides an article giving the chairman a casting vote.

This outcome has been partly reversed by a provision in The Companies Act 2006 (Commencement No. 5, Transitional Provisions and Savings) Order 2007) (SI 2007/3495), which provides that companies whose Articles contained a provision giving the chairman a casting vote immediately before 1 October 2007 may continue to rely on that article, notwithstanding s. 282. Companies incorporated after 1 October 2007 may not rely on such a provision in their Articles, nor can such a provision be introduced by a company that did not have such a provision before 1 October 2007.

Companies with listed shares are not permitted to give a casting vote to the chairman of the meeting (see reg. 22 of the 2009 Regulations).

Voting methods

Three different voting methods are used to pass resolutions. Two are used at shareholders' meetings and the third, available to private companies only, is used for written resolutions.

Vote on a show of hands

A vote on a show of hands is very simple. It is based on shareholders in attendance at a meeting raising their hands to indicate support for, or opposition to, a resolution put to the meeting. A resolution passed on a show of hands is a general resolution if it is passed by not less than a simple majority of the shareholders (including duly appointed proxies) who vote on the resolution (being eligible to do so). It is a special resolution if passed by not less than 75 per cent of shareholders (including duly appointed proxies) who vote on the resolution (being eligible to do so).

STOP AND THINK 14.1

Ten shareholders attend a meeting and are eligible to vote on a resolution. Six shareholders raise their hands in support of the resolution. The resolution has been passed as a general resolution.

If only three shareholders had raised their hands in support, the chairman of the meeting would have been required to ask those who wished to vote against the resolution to raise their hands. If only two shareholders voted against the resolution, the resolution would have been passed as a general resolution because a simple majority (three) of those who voted (five) supported it. If three or more shareholders had voted against the resolution, it would not have been passed.

Poll vote

A poll vote is not based on the number of shareholders who vote, but on the voting rights of the shareholders who vote. A resolution passed on a poll is a general resolution if passed by shareholders representing not less than a simple majority of the total voting rights of shareholders who vote (in person or by proxy) on the resolution. It is a special resolution if passed by shareholders representing not less than 75 per cent of the total voting rights of shareholders who vote (in person or by proxy) on the resolution. A person with more than one vote is under no obligation to cast all his votes or to cast those he uses in the same way (s. 322).

All companies are permitted to make provision in their article to allow shareholders to cast votes on a poll in advance of a meeting (s. 322A). This right is not expected to become popular in the UK where the appointment of proxies is well established.

STOP AND THINK 14.2

The same ten shareholders as appeared in Stop and Think 14.1 attend the same meeting and are eligible to vote on the resolution. There is a call for a poll vote on the resolution. Nine of the shareholders own ten ordinary shares each. The tenth shareholder owns 910 ordinary shares in the company. The number of votes that can potentially be cast at the meeting is 1,000. The six shareholders who passed the general resolution in Stop and Think 14.1 each have ten shares. They vote in favour of the resolution. They represent only 6 per cent of the voting rights of shareholders who could vote. The holder of 910 shares votes against the resolution. The resolution is not passed. If the holder of 910 votes attended the meeting but decided to abstain from voting in the poll vote, the six shareholders could pass the resolution as a general resolution.

Quoted companies and poll votes

Where a poll is taken by a quoted company that is not a traded company for the purposes of the 2009 Regulations (such as a quoted company traded on NASDAQ), the company must make available on its website (s. 341):

- the date of the meeting;
- the text of the resolution;
- the number of votes cast in favour; and
- the number of votes cast against.

Where the company is a traded company, the following additional information is required:

- the number of votes validly cast;
- the proportion of the company's issued share capital (determined at the time at which the right to vote is determined under s. 360B(2)) represented by those votes; and
- the number of abstentions (if counted).

Members holding 5 per cent of the voting rights or 100 members holding voting rights may require a quoted company to obtain in independent report on a poll vote and post the report on its website (ss. 342–351). The independent assessor retained to write the report must determine and report whether or not, in his opinion, giving reasons:

- the procedures adopted in connection with the poll or polls were adequate;
- the votes cast (including proxy votes) were fairly and accurately recorded and counted;
- the validity of members' appointments of proxies was fairly assessed;
- the notice of the meeting complied with s. 325 (notice of meeting to contain statement of rights to appoint proxy); and
- s. 326 (company-sponsored invitations to appoint proxies) was complied with in relation to the meeting.

Written resolution vote

A written resolution is based not on the number of shareholders who actually vote or on the voting rights of the shareholders who actually vote, but on the voting rights of all shareholders eligible to vote. The date for determining eligibility to vote on a written resolution is the date on which the written resolution is sent to shareholders (ss. 289 and 290). Essentially, copies of a proposed written resolution are sent to shareholders who sign the copy of the resolution and return it to the company, although any signed or otherwise authenticated document referencing the resolution and indicating the shareholder's agreement to it, sent or emailed to the company, suffices (s. 296).

In one respect, voting on a written resolution is calculated in the same way as on a poll vote: it is the proportion of votes held by those shareholders who support and oppose the resolution that counts. Calculation of votes differs from a poll vote, however, in that a written resolution must be passed by shareholders representing no less than a simple majority (for an ordinary resolution) or no less than 75 per cent (for a special resolution) of the total voting rights of eligible shareholders. In contrast, a poll vote is based on the voting rights of only those shareholders who are in attendance at the meeting (in person or by proxy) and who actually vote on the particular resolution.

As indicated above, written resolutions can only be used by private companies (s. 288) and even private companies may not use the written resolution procedure to remove a director pursuant to s. 168 or to remove an auditor before expiry of his term of office (s. 288(2)).

A new s. 285A has been introduced into the Companies Act 2006 by the 2009 Regulations stating that, in relation to a resolution required or authorised by an enactment, if a private company's Articles provide that a shareholder has a different number of votes in relation to a resolution when it is passed as a written resolution and when it is passed on a poll taken at a meeting, the provision about how many votes a shareholder has in relation to the resolution passed on a poll is void, and a shareholder has the same number of votes in relation to the resolution when it is passed on a poll as when it is passed as a written resolution.

3.3 The *Duomatic* principle and informal unanimous consent

The principle that the shareholders of a company may unanimously reach a decision without the need for compliance with formal procedures is known as the 'Duomatic principle' although the principle was established long before it was applied in *Re Duomatic Ltd* [1969] 2 Ch 365. Lord Davey referred to the principle in *Salomon* to confirm that the company was bound by the purchase of the boot manufacturing business because the unanimous agreement of the shareholders of the company was an inevitable inference from the circumstance. The principle was applied in the very simple circumstances of *Re Express Engineering Works Ltd* [1920] 1 Ch 466 (CA).

CASE LAW 14.1

Re Express Engineering Works Ltd [1920] 1 Ch 466 (CA)
The purchase of property paid for by the issue of debentures had been approved by resolution of the five directors of the company at a directors' meeting. All directors in attendance at the meeting were disqualified from acting because they were all interested in the seller of the property, so the directors' resolution was ineffective. The directors were also the shareholders of the company. The liquidator of the company argued that the issue of the debentures was invalid.

Held: The court refused to set the debentures aside. The meeting was a directors' meeting but it might be considered a general meeting. If the five persons present had said 'We will now constitute this a general meeting' it would have been within their powers to do so and it appeared to Lord Sterndale MR that that was in fact what they did and the company was bound by the unanimous agreement of the shareholders.

The principle has been applied in a wide range of circumstances, including when different types of resolutions would otherwise have been required, such as a special resolution (*Cane v Jones* [1980] 1 WLR 1451). Mummery LJ described the principle in the following terms in *Euro Brokers Holdings Ltd v Monecor (London) Ltd* [2003] BCLC 506 (CA).

> '[The Duomatic principle] ... is a sound and sensible principle of company law allowing the members of the company to reach an agreement without the need for strict compliance with formal procedures, where they exist only for the benefit of those who are agreed not to comply with them. What matters is the unanimous assent of those who ultimately exercise power over the affairs of the company through their right to attend and vote at a general meeting. It does not matter whether the formal procedures in question are stipulated for in the Articles of association, in the Companies Acts or in a separate contract between the members of the company concerned. What matters is that all the members have reached an agreement. If they have they cannot be heard to say that they are not bound by it because the formal procedures were not followed. The position is treated in the same way as if the agreed formal procedure had been followed.'

3.4 Judicial constraint on the exercise of voting rights by a shareholder

Tension exists between two lines of cases relevant to the exercise of shareholder voting rights. There is no principle that the position of shareholder gives rise to fiduciary obligations to the company but the range of decisions in relation to which a shareholder is required to think beyond his own self interest is unclear.

The *Allen v Gold Reefs of West Africa Ltd* [1900] 1 Ch 656 (CA) line of cases focuses on when voting shareholders are exercising a power conferred on majorities enabling them to bind minorities. They apply the general principles of law and equity applicable to such powers and require a shareholder to exercise his votes *bona fide* for the benefit of the company. With the exception of Oliver J (as he then was) in *Re Halt Garage (1964) Ltd* [1982] 3 All ER 1016 explaining the decision in *Hutton v West Cork Railway Co* (1883) Ch D 654 (CA) as an application of these general principles, cases asserting the requirement that a shareholder must exercise his votes *bona fide* for the benefit of the company appear to be confined to cases amending the Articles.

In contrast, a number of cases, reaching back to *Pender v Lushington* (1877) 6 Ch D 70, have emphasised the unrestrained right of a shareholder to vote in his own individual interest. In the words of Sir George Jessel MR in *Pender*:

'There is, if I may say so, no obligation on a shareholder of a company to give his vote merely with a view to what other persons may consider the interests of the company at large. He has a right, if he thinks fit, to give his vote from motives or promptings of what he considers his own individual interest.'

Subsequent cases have stressed the individual property nature of the voting rights attaching to shares. In *Re Astec (BSR) plc* [1998] 2 BCLC 556, Johnathon Parker J stated:

'The starting point is the proposition that in general the right of a shareholder to vote his shares is a right of property which the shareholder is free to exercise in what he regards as his own best interests. He is not obliged to cast his vote in what others may regard as the best interests of the general body of shareholders, or in the best interests of the company as an entity in its own right.'

Northern Counties Securities Ltd v Jackson & Steeple Ltd [1974] 2 All ER 625 seems to be the high water mark of this approach. The question in issue was whether or not shareholders would be in contempt of court if they voted against a resolution that had to be passed if the company was to comply with an undertaking it had given to the court. Walton LJ (sitting in the Chancery Division) held that not even a shareholder who was also a director was required to vote in anything other than his own interest.

'When a shareholder is voting for or against a particular resolution he is voting as a person owing no fiduciary duty to the company and who is exercising his own right of property, to vote as he thinks fit. ... a shareholder who casts his vote in general meeting is not casting it as an agent of the company in any shape or form. His act therefore, in voting as he pleases, cannot in any way be regarded as an act of the company.'

In *Re Unisoft Group Ltd (No. 3)* [1994] 1 BCLC 609, Harman J attempted to reconcile the *Allen* and *Pender* lines of cases by asserting the freedom of the shareholder in strong terms but emphasising the distinction between the act of a shareholder in voting for or against a resolution and the resolution itself.

'It is important to remember that shareholders' rights to deal with or vote their shares are separate from the rights of the company as a corporate entity and shareholders' relationships with it. Shareholders are entitled to sell their shares, to vote their shares, to take any course they like in general meeting without regard to any other person's rights or position. In my judgment the law is that a shareholder may act with malice in voting his shares against a particular resolution and there can be no objection to that.'

Where self-interested voting behaviour results in a special resolution to amend the Articles, it is the special resolution which is an act of the corporate entity, Harman J appears to be saying, that may be challenged as not *bona fide* for the benefit of the company. Harman J's analysis implicitly emphasises the substantive rights of minority shareholders. Although it is a valiant attempt to reconcile apparently irreconcilable case law, his approach is difficult to reconcile with the language of the *Allen* cases.

TEST YOUR KNOWLEDGE 14.2

(a) For how long are records of company meetings and resolutions required to be kept?
(b) How can company decisions be taken apart from by resolutions passed at duly convened meetings?
(c) What proportion of votes is needed to pass general and special resolutions?
(d) Which companies are entitled to use the written resolution procedure?

4 Corporate representatives

A corporate representative is an individual who has been authorised by resolution of the directors of a company (Company A) to represent Company A at any meeting of a company of which Company A is a shareholder (s. 323). The individual is then empowered to exercise the same powers on behalf of the company as if it were an individual member of the company, i.e. from the company's perspective, the corporate representative is, for all intents and purposes, the member/shareholder and has the full rights of the corporate shareholder he or she represents.

Where a shareholder appoints more than one corporate representative, the corporate representatives are permitted to vote in different ways from one another in respect of different blocks of shares (s. 323 as amended).

5 Proxies

A shareholder is entitled to appoint another person as his proxy to exercise all or any of his rights to attend, speak and vote at a meeting of the company (s. 324). Proxies are entitled to vote on votes by a show of hands as well as on poll vote.

The availability of proxy voting has been expanded and the rules improved by the 2009 Regulations. A clear statement of the obligation of a proxy has been introduced as a new s. 324A to the Act:

> 'A proxy must vote in accordance with any instructions given by the member by whom the proxy is appointed.'

The changes to the proxy rules applicable to all companies essentially allow proxies for more than one shareholder to cast votes both for and against a resolution where their instructions from different shareholders requires such. Some of the changes apply only to traded companies (as defined) which must provide an electronic address for the return of proxies and, although the appointment and termination of a proxy's authority must be in writing, for these purposes, writing includes by electronic communication (ss. 327 and 333A).

6 Shareholder engagement

6.1 Electronic communications

As seen in the previous sections, the Shareholder Rights Directive has reinforced the importance of electronic communication with shareholders. All companies are now expected to have websites on which basic information must be displayed and are permitted to provide facilities for electronic voting on resolutions ahead of meetings.

Traded companies for the purposes of the 2009 Regulations must put in place arrangements for shareholders to communicate with them electronically by providing an electronic address (i.e. an email address) for the receipt of proxies.

6.2 UK Stewardship Code

In July 2010, the Financial Reporting Council (FRC) first published the UK Stewardship Code. The first version of the code was based on the code on the responsibilities of institutional investors issued by the Institutional Shareholders Committee (ISC). Now in its second iteration, as of September 2012, the Stewardship Code complements the UK Corporate Governance Code (September 2012). The FRC encourages the institutional investors at which it is aimed to comply on a 'comply or explain' basis, but, unlike the UK Corporate Governance Code (September 2012), no legal obligation exists to comply or explain compliance with the UK Stewardship Code (September 2012). The FRC does, however, monitor compliance. Analysis of the code's provisions is beyond the scope of this book. The UK Stewardship Code can be found on the FRC website.

TEST YOUR KNOWLEDGE 14.3

(a) What powers may be exercised by a corporate representative?
(b) What rights may a shareholder appoint a proxy to exercise?
(c) In which circumstance may a proxy vote both for and against a resolution?
(d) Which companies must permit proxies to be appointed by lodging a proxy form electronically?

CHAPTER SUMMARY

- Companies may have annual general meetings, general meetings, class meetings and court-ordered meetings.
- Public companies are required to hold AGMs (s. 336).
- Records of resolutions and meetings must be kept for at least ten years.
- Companies take decisions primarily by passing resolutions at meetings (ss. 281 and 301). Only private companies may use the written resolution procedure (s. 288).
- The *Duomatic* principle permits companies to make binding decisions informally with unanimous shareholder consent.
- Judicial constraints have been developed on the exercise of voting rights by a shareholder in the context of amendment of the Articles but not otherwise (*Allen v Gold Reefs of West Africa* (1900)).
- A corporate representative is empowered to exercise the same powers on behalf of the company as if it were an individual member of the company (s. 323).
- A proxy is entitled to exercise all or any of the rights of the appointing member to attend, speak and vote at a meeting of the company (s. 324).
- A proxy may vote both for and against a resolution if his instructions so require.
- European level developments have encouraged electronic communications to promote cross-border share ownership.
- The FRC UK Stewardship Code (September 2012) promotes institutional shareholder engagement.

15 Directors' meetings and decision-making

■ **CONTENTS**

1 Sole director companies
2 Board meetings
3 Board decisions
4 UK Corporate Governance Code (September 2012)

■ **INTRODUCTION**

After a brief word on sole director companies, this chapter examines the Model Article provisions governing the holding of board meetings and how boards of directors are empowered to take binding decisions, both at board meetings and outside board meetings.

1 Sole director companies

This chapter is not relevant to companies that have only one director and no provision in its Articles requiring it to have more directors. Article 7(2) of the Model Articles for Private Companies Limited by Shares allows such a director to take decisions without regard to any of the provisions of the Articles relating to directors' quorums and decision-making.

As we have seen in chapter 11, public companies can never be sole director companies as they are required to have at least two directors (s. 154). All sole director companies are private companies.

2 Board meetings

The convening and conduct of board meetings is not governed by the Companies Act 2006 but by a company's Articles of Association. The Model Article provisions are considered here, but it is possible for these default/Model rules to be replaced, in whole or in part, or supplemented, by rules chosen for the company.

Board meetings of a public or private company may be called by any director by giving notice to the other directors (Model Articles, art. 9 (private company), art. 8 (public company)). The company secretary of a public company must call a board meeting if a director so requests (art. 8(2)).

The notice provisions of Table A (the predecessor default Articles to the Model Articles) were often amended to meet the specific requirements of companies, and this practice is expected to continue in relation to the Model Articles. The notice provisions in the Model Articles are brief. Notice must be given to each director, but need not be in writing nor given to a director who has waived his or her entitlement to notice (art. 9(3) and (4) (private companies); art. 8(5) and (6) (public companies)).

Notices must simply state the proposed date, time and place and, if the directors are not expected to be in the same place, how the directors are expected to communicate with one another (art. 9(2) (private companies); art. 8(4) (public companies)).

> **TEST YOUR KNOWLEDGE 15.1**
>
> (a) Where are the rules governing board meetings to be found?
> (b) Who may call a board meeting?
> (c) In which circumstances is there no requirement to give notice of a board meeting to a director?
> (d) What information must be included in notice of a board meeting?

3 Board decisions

Statute also does not regulate board decision-making. Establishing the rules for how the board of directors is to take decisions is an important part of the Articles of both private and public companies. The rules are contained in Part 2 of both the Model Articles for Private Companies Limited by Shares and those for public companies, both of which are set out in Appendices 2 and 3.

The Model Articles establish the quorum, that is, the number of directors who must be present before decisions may be taken or any other business conducted at a meeting of directors. The Model Article provisions are straightforward: the quorum may be fixed from time to time by a decision of the directors, must never be less than two and, unless otherwise fixed, is two (art. 11 (private companies), art. 10 (public companies)). Both sets of Model Articles allow directors at meetings without a quorum to appoint further directors and call a general meeting to enable shareholders to appoint further directors (art. 11).

3.1 Public companies

The Model Articles for Public Companies provisions governing the taking of decisions by the board are relatively straightforward. Article 7(1) provides that, subject to the Articles, decisions of the directors must be taken:

- at a directors' meeting (at which resolutions are passed by a majority of those participating with every director having one vote unless the Articles provide otherwise (art. 13)); or
- in the form of a directors' written resolution (which require the *unanimous* support of all directors (art. 18)) (emphasis added).

Be careful not to confuse directors' written resolutions with written resolutions of private companies, a form of shareholder resolution permitted only by private companies and governed by the Companies Act 2006, ss. 288–300.

3.2 Private companies

The private company Model Articles governing the taking of decisions by the board are not drafted as clearly as those for public companies. This is the legacy of the consultative process which saw the draft Model Articles amended on more than one occasion. The end result provides less informality than originally proposed, the original proposal having been in line with the deregulatory theme for private companies of the Companies Act 2006. The final language of art. 7 is:

> 'The general rule about decision making by directors is that any decision of the directors must be either a majority decision at a meeting or a decision taken in accordance with article 8.'

Article 8 then provides for unanimous decision-making outside board meetings. Unanimous informal decisions may be arrived at in a number of ways. Article 8(1) states:

> 'A decision of the directors is taken in accordance with this article when all eligible directors indicate to each other by any means that they share a common view on a matter.'

Alternatively, a unanimous informal decision may be taken in the form of a resolution in writing, copies of which have been signed by all eligible directors or to which each eligible director has indicated his or her agreement.

It is clear that majority decisions of directors outside board meetings will *not* be effective in any circumstances except where a specific provision permitting majority decisions to be taken outside directors' meetings appears in the Articles of Association of the company.

3.3 Chairman's casting vote

In the event of an equal number of votes on a particular resolution, the chairman or other director chairing a board meeting will have a casting vote (art. 13 (private company), art. 14 (public company)). Historically, this default/Model article has been amended.

3.4 Conflicts of interest

Rules relating to participation of an individual director who is interested in a matter on which the board is taking a decision are not considered here. They are addressed in chapter 12, in the context of directors' duties.

4 UK Corporate Governance Code (September 2012)

Although the law does not lay down how regularly it is appropriate for directors to meet, the UK Corporate Governance Code (September 2012) addresses the regularity of board meetings in Code Provision A.1.1. Disclosure of the number of board meetings and attendance is provided for by DTR 7.2.7 and Code Provision A.1.2. The Code states:

'A.1.1	The board should meet sufficiently regularly to discharge its duties effectively. There should be a formal schedule of matters specifically reserved for its decision. The annual report should include a statement of how the board operates, including a high level statement of which types of decisions are to be taken by the board and which are to be delegated to management.
A.1.2	The annual report should identify the chairman, the deputy chairman (where there is one), the chief executive, the senior independent director and the chairmen and members of the board committees. It should also set out the number of meetings of the board and its committees and individual attendance by directors.'

DTR 7.2.7 Simply requires disclosure of the composition and operation of the board and its committees in corporate governance statements.

TEST YOUR KNOWLEDGE 15.2

(a) Where are the rules governing the quorum required for a board meeting found and how may a quorum be set?
(b) How may decisions of the board of directors of public companies be taken?
(c) How may decisions of the board of directors of private companies be taken?
(d) What happens if there is an equality of votes on either side of a board resolution?

CHAPTER SUMMARY

- Rules governing the convening of board meetings are found in the Articles.
- Unless otherwise fixed a quorum is two (art. 11 (private companies) and art. 10 (public companies)).
- Directors may make decisions at board meetings and the Model Articles provide for decisions at meetings to be by majority vote.
- The Articles, including the Model Articles, usually give the chairman a casting vote (art. 13 (private companies) and art. 14 (public companies)).

- Written resolutions may be taken by public companies but must be unanimous (art. 18).
- Informal decision-making by private companies is permitted by the Model Articles but must be unanimous (art. 8).

PART 4 CASE QUESTIONS

Return to the opening case at the start of this part and re-read it. Think generally about the issues it raises, the law in relation to which has been covered in the chapters in this part, before attempting to answer the following questions.

1. Has the annual general meeting been properly convened?
2. Is Alice's appointment of a proxy valid? If Alice's appointment of Mark to be her proxy is valid, could he vote her shares differently from the way he votes his own shares?
3. Has the resolution to remove David been properly proposed? If not, what steps should have been taken?
4. Has the resolution to amend the Articles been passed?
5. Was Sue correct to omit Brian from communication of the proposed board resolution?
6. Does Colin have a casting vote and, if so, is it relevant?
7. Has the board resolution been properly passed?

PART **FIVE**

Company restructuring and winding up

■ LIST OF CHAPTERS

16 Company restructuring
17 Takeovers
18 Corporate rescue
19 Winding up and company dissolution

■ OVERVIEW

The laws and statutory procedures covered in part 5 are relevant to a number of very different practical situations in which companies or corporate groups find themselves. These situations may be grouped under four headings:

- mergers and acquisitions (sometimes called takeovers) of companies where a change of control occurs;

- restructuring, including demerging, a financially healthy company or corporate group where no change of control occurs;

- corporate rescue activity where a company is in financial difficulty;

- winding up a company.

Winding up aside, these activities frequently involve making changes to the company's shareholdings, to its debt, or both.

The laws and statutory procedures relating to company restructuring have grown up piecemeal over time with the consequence that the law does not map neatly onto practical situations. Company restructuring statutory procedures can usually be applied to a number of very different practical situations. For example, the scheme of arrangement procedure in Part 26 of the Companies Act 2006 can be used to effect such diverse activities as a takeover, a tax-effective return of capital to shareholders, and a compromise with creditors in an effort to stave off insolvency.

Frequently, a company is faced with a number of legal options to choose from, and it must select the procedure best suited to its circumstances and aims. For example, a company in financial difficulty may need to restructure its debt. Depending upon how cooperative its creditors are and how complex the restructuring of the debt is, the company may simply pursue renegotiation with its creditors or it may use one or a combination of: the company voluntary arrangement procedure in Part I of the Insolvency Act 1986, the Part 26 scheme of arrangement procedure in the Companies Act 2006 and the administration procedure in Part II and Schedule B1 of the Insolvency Act 1986.

■ LEARNING OUTCOMES

After reading this part you should be able understand and explain:

- When section 110 schemes of reconstruction are available and when and how they are typically used.

- When Part 26 schemes of arrangement are available and when and how they are typically used.

- When the Companies Act 2006, s. 900 extends the powers of the court in relation to a Part 26 scheme of arrangement.

- The role and scope of application of the City Code on Takeovers and Mergers, the role and legal status of the Panel on Takeovers and Mergers (the Panel) and the availability of judicial review of Panel decisions.

- The object and effect of a company voluntary arrangement (CVA) and the procedure to put one in place.

- The availability, object and effect of a small company moratorium and the procedure to put one in place.

- Administration, how administrators are appointed, the objectives and effect of administration and how administration comes to an end.

- The different types of liquidation.

- Compulsory winding up (including grounds), the role of the liquidator and the liquidator's principal powers.

PART 5 CASE STUDY

Vesuvius FC is a football club owned by Vesuvius FC Ltd, a private company limited by shares (Vesuvius). Vesuvius has not played well for the last two seasons even though it spent £100 million on new players for the 2009/10 season. Narrowly avoiding relegation in the 2008/9 season, it experienced a reduction in ticket sales and sponsorship income in the 12 months to April 2010. As the season was coming to a disappointing close, Vesuvius was locked in protracted discussions with Her Majesty's Revenue & Customs (HMRC) over £15 million overdue PAYE and VAT payments.

In April 2009, FoulBrew Ltd entered into a three-year exclusive beer supply agreement with Vesuvius. At any one time beer supplied by FoulBrew Ltd worth approximately £20,000 is kept in stock at Vesuvius' stadium.

The major shareholder of Vesuvius, Nelson, has a floating charge over all the assets and business of Vesuvius to secure £100 million in loans. Goal Bank plc has a fixed charge over the stadium to secure a £60 million loan. Vesuvius has an unsecured overdraft facility of £10 million with Home Bank plc, which is drawn down to its limit, and Home Bank has asked Vesuvius to grant it a fixed charge over the stadium to secure the existing and future overdrawn sums. Nelson, who is governed by his love of football, not his head, is prepared to lend Vesuvius a further £10 million but also wants a fixed charge against the stadium. The stadium is believed to be worth in the order of £50 million.

Company restructuring

16

■ CONTENTS

1 Insolvency Act 1986, s. 110 schemes of reconstruction
2 Part 26 schemes of arrangement
3 Part 26, Part 27 and the Cross-Border Merger Regulations: plc mergers and divisions

■ INTRODUCTION

In this chapter we examine two key statutory procedures by which the structure of a company or a group of companies may be changed or restructured. The emphasis is on restructuring of the shareholdings of a company or corporate group, rather than simply debt restructuring. The two statutory procedures examined are schemes of arrangement under Part 26 of the Companies Act 2006 and schemes of reconstruction, also known as demerger schemes, under the simpler Insolvency Act 1986, s. 110 procedure.

We considered in chapter 8 the ways in which the rights attached to particular shares may be varied and the share capital of a company increased and decreased. In chapter 17 we consider the legal framework governing changes of control, or **takeovers**. The statutory processes considered here are used where the processes already considered, or a takeover bid, are not available, the requirements are too cumbersome, the conditions are unlikely to be fulfilled or there is other good reason to choose one of the statutory schemes. Tax considerations are extremely important in restructuring activity and may lead to a restructuring proposal that can only by achieved using one legal process rather than another.

1 Insolvency Act 1986, s. 110 schemes of reconstruction

1.1 Availability and usage

The most common use of the Insolvency Act 1986, s. 110 (a s. 110 scheme of reconstruction, or 'demerger scheme') is by a company wishing to demerge one or more of its businesses. The demerger may be a preliminary step in the sale of one or more of its businesses to another company or it may be part of an internal reconstruction of a corporate group designed to deliver commercial and tax advantages. For example, demergers can be used to unlock shareholder value, that is, to overcome the strict rules on maintenance of capital so that shareholders can lawfully receive capital from the company.

Demergers can be achieved by a number of routes. The tax benefits of using a s. 110 scheme of reconstruction, coupled with the greater expense and longer timeframe for putting a Part 26 scheme of arrangement in place, make s. 110 schemes very attractive. Section 110 cannot, however, be used if a compromise is sought with creditors. A Part 26 scheme of arrangement or a voluntary arrangement is required instead.

A s. 110 scheme necessarily entails the winding up of the original, transferor company. However, do not be misled into thinking that it is a corporate rescue procedure. Section 110 is designed for use where the company is solvent and applies only to a company that is being *voluntarily* wound up. Two types of voluntary winding up exist: a **members' voluntary winding up** and a **creditors' voluntary winding up** (see chapter 19). A company in creditors' voluntary winding up is not necessarily solvent but, subject to this potential for voluntary winding up of an insolvent company, most companies wound up voluntarily are solvent.

A typical s. 110 demerger is effected by the company transferring its assets to two (or more) newly-created companies in return for shares in those companies. The shares in the new companies are distributed to the shareholders of the original, now parent, company in proportion to their shareholdings in the original company and the original company is then wound up. The shareholders may continue to own the two companies or one of them may be sold off.

1.2 The s. 110 procedure

The procedure to put a s. 110 scheme in place is to hold a general meeting at which special resolutions are proposed:

- to wind up the company (a members' voluntary winding up);
- to appoint a **liquidator**;
- to approve a s. 110 scheme of reconstruction; and
- to authorise the liquidator to enter into and carry out the s. 110 scheme of reconstruction.

If any shareholder does not vote in favour of the s. 110 scheme, s. 111 gives him the right, by giving notice in writing within seven days after the passing of the resolution, to require the liquidator to buy out his shares. The liquidator should therefore also be authorised by resolution at the general meeting to buy out shareholders pursuant to s. 111. The manner by which the liquidator may raise money to do so must be stated in the authorising resolution.

A general meeting will not be necessary where the company is a private company as the written resolution procedure can be used. Following the passing of the resolutions, the merger can be effected in accordance with the reconstruction agreement.

1.3 Dissenting shareholder protection

In addition to providing for a dissenting shareholder to insist on being bought out (at a price to be agreed or determined by arbitration), s. 111 also provides for a shareholder who neither supports the scheme nor agrees to be bought out, to stop a scheme going forward by giving notice to the liquidator (again, within seven days after the passing of the resolution), to abstain from carrying the resolution into effect.

A shareholder cannot be deprived of the rights afforded by s. 111 by a provision in the company's Articles of Association (*Payne v The Cork Company Ltd* [1900] 1 Ch 308). Subject to this right of dissenting shareholders, the scheme is binding on all members of the company (s. 110(5)).

1.4 Creditor protection

A creditor of the company who is unhappy with a scheme may have negotiated contractual provisions in its loan agreements that are triggered by such a reconstruction. In the absence of such contractual, or 'self-help', remedies, the only route available to a creditor to stop a s. 110 scheme from progressing is to petition the court for a compulsory winding up order. To secure a winding up order a creditor must demonstrate either that it is just and equitable to wind up the company or that the company is unable to pay its debts (as that phrase is defined in the Insolvency Act 1986, s. 123). Even if one of these grounds can be established, the decision to order a winding up or not is in the discretion of the court (s. 122). If a court orders the company to be wound up within a year of the special resolution authorising a s. 110 scheme, the special resolution is not valid unless sanctioned (approved) by the court (s. 110(6)).

STOP AND THINK 16.1

Steps can be taken to reduce significantly the risk of a special resolution authorising a s. 110 scheme of reconstruction being stopped by a dissenting shareholder or rendered invalid by a court-ordered winding up within a year of its passage. One commonly adopted step is to incorporate a new 'holding' company (Holdco) to own the company (or parent company of the group) to be reconstructed. Holdco issues its own shares to the shareholders of the company in return for their shares in the company. It is Holdco that then enters into voluntary winding up and effects a s. 110 scheme. Holdco has no creditors which virtually removes the risk of a court ordered winding up. The s. 110 special resolution can be passed more than seven days before a winding up resolution so that the shareholder dissent period has expired before the winding up commences.

TEST YOUR KNOWLEDGE 16.1

(a) What is the most common use of the s. 110 scheme of reconstruction?
(b) Can s. 110 be used if a compromise is sought with creditors?
(c) Which shareholder resolutions are required to put a typical section 110 scheme of demerger in place?

2 Part 26 schemes of arrangement

2.1 Availability and usage

The statutory procedure set out in Part 26 of the Companies Act 2006, called the **scheme of arrangement** procedure, exists to facilitate changes being made to the rights of creditors or shareholders without securing the unanimous approval of those affected by the changes. Section 895 states that Part 26 applies where a compromise or arrangement is proposed between a company and its creditors, or any class of them, and its members, or any class or them. Accordingly, a Part 26 scheme of arrangement can be used:

- to restructure debt, with or without changes to shareholdings; or
- to restructure the rights of shareholders, with or without changes to the rights of creditors.

If a Part 26 scheme of arrangement is to be used to effect a compromise by the company and its creditors and/or its shareholders of any rights and liabilities between them, there must be an accommodation by each side. A unilateral release of rights by one group, for example, is not a compromise and will not amount to an arrangement and therefore, cannot be achieved by a Part 26 scheme of arrangement (*Re Savoy Hotel Ltd* [1981] 3 All ER 346; *Re NFU Development Trust Ltd* [1973] 1 All ER 135). Where such a release is part of a wider arrangement, however, such as the release of claims against one company in return for the substitution of claims against a new company, the procedure can be used (see *In the matter of Bluebrook Ltd* [2009] EWHC 2114 (Ch) and *Re Uniq plc* [2011] EWHC 749 (Ch)).

An arrangement involving a change in the shareholders but no change in the rights of those shareholders or any creditors (such as a takeover), while not a compromise, can be an arrangement for Part 26 purposes: not all arrangements involve compromise (*Re T & N Ltd (No. 3)* [2007] 1 BCLC 563).

The procedure for a Part 26 scheme of arrangement to be put in place is cumbersome, expensive and slow, resulting in their use being confined to complex restructurings or situations where no other procedure is available. That said, Part 26 schemes of arrangement are regularly used in all three of the non-winding up situations identified in the introduction to this part:

- mergers and acquisitions (sometimes called takeovers) of companies;
- restructuring, including demerging, a financially healthy company or corporate group; or

- corporate rescue activity where a company is in financial difficulty.

Part 26 schemes are regularly used to effect takeovers, including takeovers of companies with shares listed on a stock exchange such as the London Stock Exchange. In fact, they have become the most favoured method by which to structure a takeover of a company with listed shares. Where a private sale or acquisition is negotiated, a Part 26 scheme may be used to effect a reconstruction to merge or demerge companies and businesses and bring about other changes to improve the commercial benefits of the sale or acquisition, including effectively managing the tax implications.

Examples of when a Part 26 scheme of arrangement might be used to restructure a financially healthy company are:

- to return capital to shareholders;
- to divide or demerge a company (typically a family-owned company) when a founder member or other large shareholder dies or retires;
- in anticipation of a disposal, that is, all or a part of the company or group being taken over or sold to a third party;
- in anticipation of an acquisition of a company or business by the company or group; or
- to remove minority shareholders.

Turning finally to the use of Part 26 schemes of arrangement by companies in financial difficulty, Part 26 is not restricted to compromises with creditors *before* a company becomes subject to a formal rescue or winding up procedure. Administrators can also use the Part 26 scheme of arrangement procedure within the context of an administration as can liquidators in the course of a winding up, although use of Part 26 by the liquidator of a company in involuntary liquidation is rare.

The liquidator of a company being voluntarily wound up may have to use the Part 26 procedure to change the rights of creditors because the scheme of reconstruction procedure in s. 110 of the Insolvency Act 1986 cannot be used to effect such a compromise.

 STOP AND THINK 16.2

Notwithstanding its complexity, a Part 26 scheme may be the only option available in the circumstances to achieve the desired goal. A good illustration is use of a Part 26 scheme of arrangement to squeeze shareholders out of a company where only 75 per cent of the shareholders approve of a takeover of the company. This is less than the 90 per cent support that would be required were a takeover bid to be made, making a takeover by way of a Part 26 scheme of arrangement achievable where a takeover bid would fail for lack of 90 per cent support. This is one (though usually not the only) reason to structure a company takeover as a Part 26 scheme of arrangement.

2.2 The Part 26 procedure

The Part 26 procedure involves two applications to court, one before and one after the summoning of separate meetings of those classes of creditors and shareholders who would be affected were the proposed scheme of arrangement to be implemented.

The first stage in the procedure is an application to the court for an order that meetings be summoned of every affected class of shareholders and creditors for the purpose of securing approval of the proposed scheme (s. 896(1)). This application is usually made by the company or the administrator on behalf of the company, as the case may be, although it can also be made by any creditor, shareholder or liquidator (s. 896(2)). The application is made by issuing a claim form in the Companies Court and is usually heard by a registrar of the court rather than by a judge. The fairness of the scheme is not considered at this stage (*Re Hawk Insurance Company Ltd* [1922] 2 Ch 723). The registrar may, however, decide not to order the meetings, if, for example, it considers there is such a level of opposition to the scheme that the scheme would not be approved by the shareholders or creditors as the case may be (*Re Savoy Hotel Limited* [1981] Ch 351).

The court-ordered meetings must then be summoned. The court order will direct the manner in which notice of each meeting is to be given and the length of notice required. Notice is usually directed to be given in one of two ways: by sending notice to those entitled to receive notice or by advertisement. A notice sent to a creditor or shareholder must include, and an advertisement must indicate, where and how those entitled to attend a meeting may obtain a free copy of an explanatory statement.

Section 897(2) states that the statement must explain:

- the effect of the compromise or arrangement;
- any interests of the directors of the company; and
- the effect of the compromise or arrangement on those interests.

Where the scheme of arrangements affects the rights of debenture holders, the information relevant to directors must also be given for any trustees of those debentures (s. 897(3)). Directors and trustees are under a duty, default in relation to which is punishable by fine, to notify the company of any matters relevant to themselves necessary to enable the company to provide the information it is required to include in the explanatory statement (s. 898).

The scheme of arrangement must be approved by a majority in number, representing 75 per cent in value of the class of creditors or shareholders, as the case may be, voting, either in person or by proxy, at the duly summoned meeting (s. 899(1)). Only if approved by this majority at each of the court-ordered meetings can the court sanction (i.e. approve) the scheme.

Identification of the different classes of shareholders and creditors, that is, recognising when a sub-group of shareholders or creditors needs to be regarded as unique and therefore a separate class and accorded a separate meeting, is often difficult in relation to Part 26 schemes. The case law in which this issue is raised is extensive. If a sub-group feels it ought to have a separate meeting and convinces the court of this, the court will not sanction the scheme without the requisite majority approval by that sub-group at a separate meeting (see below).

The test to determine whether a sub-group is a separate class or not for the purposes of what is now Part 26 was stated by Bowen LJ in *Sovereign Life Assurance Co v Dodd* [1892] 2QB 573:

> 'What is the proper construction of [the] statute? It makes the majority of the creditors or of a class of creditors bind the minority; it exercises a most formidable compulsion upon dissentient, or would-be dissentient, creditors; and it therefore requires to be construed with care, so as not to place in the hands of some of the creditors the means and opportunity of forcing dissentients to do that which it is unreasonable to require them to do, or of making a mere jest of the interests of the minority.
>
> ... The word "class" is vague, and to find out what is meant by it we must look at the scope of the section, which is a section enabling the Court to order a meeting of a class of creditors to be called. It seems plain that we must give such a meaning to the term 'class' as will prevent the section being so worked as to result in confiscation and injustice, and that it must be confined to those persons whose rights are not so dissimilar as to make it impossible for them to consult together with a view to their common interest.'

The third stage in the Part 26 procedure is the second application to the court, asking the court to sanction the approved scheme of arrangement. The court may (not must) sanction the scheme. As explained by Astbury J in *Re Anglo-Continental Supply Co Ltd* [1922] 2 Ch 723, it is the role of the court to exercise its discretion:

> 'In exercising its power of sanction ... the Court will see: First, that the provisions of the statute have been complied with. Secondly, that the class was fairly represented by those who attended the meeting and that the statutory majority are acting *bona fide* and are not coercing the minority in order to promote interests adverse to those of the class whom they purport to represent, and, Thirdly, that the arrangement is such as a man of business would reasonably approve ...'

If a Part 26 procedural requirement has not been satisfied, the court will not sanction the scheme. Also, if a reduction in capital is a feature of the scheme, the further legal procedures governing capital reduction must be complied with (ss. 641, 645–653) and a court will not sanction a scheme where they have not been complied with. Note, however, that if the court has, by oversight, sanctioned a scheme that involves an unlawful capital reduction, the scheme will not be invalidated on this ground (*British & Commonwealth Holdings Ltd v Barclays Bank* [1996] 1 WLR 1). If a matter that may have caused shareholders or creditors to vote differently has not been disclosed, the court may not sanction the scheme (*Re Jessel Trust Ltd* [1985] BCLC 119).

The test to be applied to determine the reasonableness of the approval was stated by Maugham J in *Re Dorman Long & Co Ltd* [1934] 1 Ch 635.

> '[The court must be satisfied that] the proposal is such that an intelligent and honest man, a member of the class concerned, acting in respect of his interests might reasonably approve [the scheme].'

The role of the court is not to substitute its judgment for that of the requisite majority and courts have endorsed the words in *Buckley on the Companies Acts*, that ' ... the court will be slow to differ from the meeting.' The key concern of the court is to be satisfied that the shareholders and creditors have acted in good faith and that the majority has voted in a class meeting to promote their interests as members of that class, rather than to promote other interests, such as to promote their interests as members of a different class of shareholders, or, possibly, their interests as creditors (*Carruth v ICI* [1937] AC 707).

A court order sanctioning the scheme has no effect until a copy has been delivered to the registrar of companies (s. 899(4)). When the order takes effect it is binding on all creditors, shareholders and the company (or, as appropriate, the administrator, liquidator and all contributories of the company) (s. 899(3)).

2.3 Section 900 reconstructions and amalgamations

Section 900 extends the powers of the court on a Part 26 application by empowering the court to order a broad range of matters, either by including them in the order approving the scheme of arrangement or in a separate order. The broader powers are available and may be exercised by the court to provide for matters which are necessary to secure the full and effective carrying out of a proposed 'reconstruction or amalgamation'.

The broader powers are available only when a Part 26 scheme of arrangement:

- includes or is connected with a scheme of reconstruction of any company or companies or the amalgamation of any two or more companies; and
- involves the transfer of the whole or any part of the undertaking or property of a company concerned in the scheme to another company.

The absence of not only a definite legal meaning but also a definite commercial meaning for the terms 'reconstruction' and 'amalgamation' was noted by Buckley J in *Re South African Supply and Cold Storage Co* [1904] 2 Ch 268:

> 'Neither of these words, "reconstruction" and "amalgamation", has any definite *legal* meaning. Each is a commercial and not a legal term, and, even as a commercial term, there is no exact definite meaning. In each case one has to decide whether the transaction is such that, in the meaning of commercial men, it is one which is comprehended in the term "reconstruction" or "amalgamation".'

Buckley J went on to provide a description of a reconstruction which remains influential today and which is therefore set out here in full. It was relied on by Mann J in the Chancery Division in *Re Mytravel Group Plc* [2004] EWHC 2741 (the point was not in issue on appeal) and by Millett J in *Re Courage Group's Pension Schemes* [1987] 1 WLR 495:

> 'What does "reconstruction" mean? To my mind it means this. An undertaking of some definite kind is being carried on, and the conclusion is arrived at that it is not desirable to kill that undertaking, but that it is desirable to preserve it in some form, and to do so, not by selling it to an outsider who shall carry it on – that would be a mere sale – but in some altered form to continue the undertaking in such a manner as that the persons now carrying it on will substantially continue to carry it on. It involves, I think, that substantially the same business shall be carried on and substantially the same persons shall carry it on. But it does not involve that all the assets shall pass to the new company or resuscitated company, or that

all the shareholders of the old company shall be shareholders in the new company or resuscitated company. Substantially the business and the persons interested must be the same. Does it make any difference that the new company or resuscitated company does or does not take over the liabilities? I think not. I think it is none the less a reconstruction because from the assets taken over some part is excepted provided that substantially the business is taken, and it is immaterial whether the liabilities are taken over by the new or resuscitated company or are provided for by excepting from the scheme of reconstruction a sufficient amount to answer them. It is not, therefore, vital that either the whole assets should be taken over or that the liabilities would be taken over. You have to see whether substantially the same persons carry on the same business; and if they do, that, I conceive, is a reconstruction.'

The term is not confined to the transfer of business from one company to one other entity: the transfer of part of the business of a company to one company and part to another company can be a reconstruction. (*Fallon v Fellows* [2001] STC 1409). Rather, 'The essential character of a corporate reconstruction is that substantially the same business is carried on and substantially the same persons continue to carry it on ...' (per Millett J in *Re Courage Group's Pension Schemes* [1987] 1 WLR 495).

Examples of matters the court may order under s. 900 include:

- the transfer of the business or undertaking (including liabilities) of one company to another;
- the allotting of shares or debentures of one company to another person;
- that legal claims against a company be continued against the company to whom the business is being transferred; or
- the dissolution of a company without a winding up.

TEST YOUR KNOWLEDGE 16.2

(a) Identify the three basic stages in a Part 26 procedure.
(b) What is it that s. 897 requires an explanatory notice delivered to those entitled to attend a court-ordered meeting to explain?
(c) How does the court approach the question of whether a sub-group of creditors or shareholders is a separate class or not?
(d) What is the essential character of a corporate reconstruction for s. 900 purposes?

3 Part 26, Part 27 and the Cross-Border Merger Regulations: plc mergers and divisions

Where an application under Part 26 of the Companies Act 2006 involves the 'merger or division' of a public (rather than a private) company, the court must not sanction the scheme unless the requirements of Part 27 have been complied with. 'Merger' and 'division' for Part 27 purposes are defined narrowly in ss. 904 and 919 respectively. The acquisition of the shares of one company by another is not a merger for Part 27 purposes. Nor, without more, is the acquisition of the business of one company by another company.

A merger for Part 27 purposes essentially has three characteristics:

1. the acquisition of the business (i.e. the assets and liabilities that make up the undertakings, of one public company (the transferor) by another public company (the transferee));
2. the consideration for the transfer of the business is shares in the transferee company;
3. the transferor company is dissolved, otherwise then by a winding up process, so that the consideration shares in the transferee are receivable by the shareholders of the transferor company.

The merger described above is called a 'merger by absorption'. A 'merger by formation of a new company' is also governed by Part 27. Such a merger entails at least two public companies transferring their businesses to a new company (which may or may not be a public company).

Part 27 implements the 3rd and 6th EU Company Law Directives ((78/855/EEC) and (82/891/EEC)) and for this reason is confined to mergers and divisions involving UK companies only. The 10th EU Company Law Directive, which governs mergers between companies in different member states (2005/56/EC), has been implemented in the UK by the Companies (Cross-Border Mergers) Regulations 2007 (SI 2007/2974). These Regulations apply to similarly defined mergers except that they apply to mergers involving limited liability companies, whether public or private, but only where the parties are in more than one Member State.

It is extremely unusual for mergers or divisions as defined in Part 27 to take place in the UK. Accordingly, it is not necessary to say any more about Part 27 or the Companies (Cross-Border Merger) Regulations 2007.

CHAPTER SUMMARY

- Section 110 schemes of reconstruction:
  - are most commonly used by a company seeking to demerge one or more of its businesses typically to unlock shareholder value or as a preliminary step in a sale of one or more of its businesses;
  - can only be used if the company is to be voluntarily wound up;
  - cannot be used if a compromise is sought with creditors;
  - various special resolutions are required to put a typical s. 110 scheme of demerger in place;
  - the written resolution procedure can be used by private companies to pass the required resolutions;
  - dissident shareholders are protected when a s. 110 scheme of reconstruction is proposed by having the right to request that they be bought out or to stop the scheme being implemented (s. 111);
  - creditors that do not have pre-negotiated protections when a section 110 scheme of reconstruction is proposed may petition the court for a winding up under s. 123.
- Part 26 schemes of arrangement:
  - may be used in mergers and acquisitions of companies, in the restructuring of financially healthy companies or as part of a corporate rescue package;
  - the three basic stages in a Part 26 procedure are an application to court for an order that meetings be summoned, the holding of court-ordered meetings at each of which the proposed scheme is approved by the requisite majority and a further application to the court to sanction the approved scheme;
  - the test to determine whether a sub-group of creditors or shareholders needs to be carved out as a separate class is whether or not the rights of the larger group are so dissimilar as to make it impossible for them to consult together with a view to their common interest (*Sovereign Life Assurance Co v Dodd* [1892] 2 QB 573);
  - the court's powers under Part 26 are extended under s. 900 only if the proposed scheme includes or is connected with a scheme of reconstruction of any company or companies or the amalgamation of any two or more companies; and involves the transfer of the whole or part of the undertaking or property of a company to another company;
  - the essential character of a corporate reconstruction for s. 900 purposes is that substantially the same business is carried on and substantially the same persons continue to carry it on (*In re Courage Group's Pension Schemes* [1987] 1 WLR 495).
- Part 27 and the Cross-Border Merger Regulations impose additional requirements before schemes of arrangement involving mergers (as defined) can be sanctioned but are of very limited practical relevance in the UK.

Takeovers

CONTENTS

1. The City Code and the EU Takeover Directive
2. Methods of restructuring and takeovers
3. Takeovers, mergers, acquisitions and disposals
4. Scope of application of the City Code
5. Part 26 scheme of arrangement takeovers
6. The nature and purpose of the City Code
7. The City Code General Principles
8. Outline of the basic takeover bid process
9. Minority shareholder treatment
10. Key additional legal rules and problem areas in takeovers
11. The system for regulating takeovers

INTRODUCTION

The focus of this chapter is the **City Code on Takeovers and Mergers** (the City Code). The City Code was first introduced in 1968 in response to the emergence of hostile takeover bids for companies with shares listed on stock exchanges in the US and the UK. The current version of the City Code was published on 19 September 2011. The principal changes introduced are set out in section 7 of this chapter.

According to neoclassical economic theory, or the efficient market hypothesis, hostile takeovers occur because the target company, while not necessarily in financial difficulty, is economically underperforming due to poor management. From this perspective, hostile takeovers are efficiency-enhancing transactions in the market for corporate control. An alternative view is that hostile takeovers undermine the ability of boards to take a long-term approach to building the businesses they run. Instead, it is argued, boards must constantly ensure that their share price increases in the short term and that dividend levels are maintained to insulate the company from an opportunistic hostile takeover. The absence of consensus on the benefits and shortcomings of hostile takeovers contributed to the difficulty experienced reaching pan-European agreement on the EU Takeover Directive.

1 The City Code and the EU Takeover Directive

Of all the EU Member States, the UK has the greatest experience of hostile takeovers. Consequently, the EU Takeover Directive (2004/25/EC) was strongly influenced by the City Code. EU-wide consensus on how takeovers should be regulated was hard to reach and took 15 years to achieve, with the result that a number of the provisions of the Takeover Directive are the product of political compromise. The Takeover Directive establishes a minimum (rather than a maximum) regime of protection for shareholders of companies with shares listed on a regulated market, (essentially a main stock exchange in the EU), when a third party seeks to acquire control of the company. Member states are able to opt out of certain provisions of the Takeover Directive.

Before the Directive was adopted and subsequently implemented in the UK by what is now Part 28 of the Companies Act 2006, the UK system of takeover regulation was a system of 'self-regulation' by the Panel on Takeovers and Mergers (the Panel), based on the City Code. The regime was widely believed to work well. The 'minimum protection' nature of the EU Takeover Directive entitles individual Member States to maintain higher levels of protection for shareholders than those provided for in the Takeover Directive. Consequently, the UK has been able to preserve the pre-Directive regime largely intact. The current UK law regulating takeovers is applicable in a broader range of circumstances than the EU Directive requires and is more comprehensive in its provisions.

2 Methods of restructuring and takeovers

2.1 Methods of restructuring

The legal procedures considered in the previous chapter on restructuring are often used to effect changes to the ownership of the shares of one or more companies. In most instances, however, those restructurings are internal: the ultimate control of the company or corporate group remains unchanged. In contrast, the City Code regulates only real rather than technical changes of control of companies.

2.2 Change of control

The City Code applies in a range of situations in which a purchaser acquires control of a company. Its precise scope is technical and detailed. Contrary to popular belief, it is not confined to the takeover of companies with shares listed on the London Stock Exchange. In limited circumstances, it may even apply to the acquisition of control of a private company (see section 5 below).

The concept of 'control' of a company is not a simple one. Clearly a person owning 100 per cent of the voting shares of a company controls the company. A person who owns shares with sufficient voting rights to pass special resolutions also clearly has control of the company. Few would doubt that a person who owns shares with sufficient voting rights to pass ordinary resolutions controls a company, given that this delivers the right to appoint and remove directors.

The point in the aggregation of voting shares in a company at which a person can exercise effective control over a company is a matter of fact. The definition of control in the City Code for the purposes of triggering a mandatory offer to all shareholders to be made by a person who has acquired that level of control is 30 per cent.

The EU Takeover Directive, while offering a partial definition, leaves the definition of control for mandatory offer purposes to be determined by each Member State. The partial definition of control set out in the Takeover Directive refers to ownership of shares carrying 30 per cent or more of the voting rights of a company. The Directive expressly provides that this is to be treated as control irrespective of whether or not it gives control as a matter of fact. While many Member States have defined control for this purpose at 30 per cent or thereabouts, others have set it significantly higher. Poland, for example, has set the trigger at ownership of shares carrying 66 per cent of the voting rights of a company.

This chapter considers the operation of the City Code in the typical situation to which it was designed to apply i.e. a purchaser seeking to obtain ownership of sufficient voting shares of a company, the shares of which are listed on the London Stock Exchange, to exercise control of the company, against the wishes of the target company's board of directors. Before turning to this, the following paragraphs place such a 'hostile takeover' in the broad context of changes of corporate control.

3 Takeovers, mergers, acquisitions and disposals

Most companies do not have shares held by a large number of shareholders and their shares are not listed on a stock exchange. Acquisitions and disposals of these companies typically take place following an approach being made by or to a purchaser who is interested in buying the company and negotiation of the terms of a share purchase agreement. The share purchase agreement is negotiated between the purchaser and either the board of the parent company (the seller) of the company to be acquired (the target company) or, where the target is owned by individuals, the shareholders of the target company. Even though a change of control of the company occurs, the term 'takeover' is not typically used to describe these transactions. Nor is the term 'merger' typically used, even where the purchaser is a company and the target, on becoming owned by the purchaser company, in one sense, 'merges' into it (or, at least, becomes a subsidiary in the corporate group). The language typically used to describe such transactions is 'sale', 'disposal', 'purchase' or 'acquisition'. Note that companies with shares traded on a stock exchange frequently agree to sell substantial parts of their business, or one or more of the different businesses they operate, by private sale agreement. Typically, the parent company negotiates and sells the shares of one or more of the subsidiaries through which the businesses to be disposed of are operated.

For a number of commercial reasons, including the tax implications, a disposal or acquisition may be structured as a sale of the underlying business of the target company to the purchaser. A business sale agreement, rather than a share purchase agreement, is then negotiated. Business sale agreements are legally more complex than share sale agreements because each of the assets and liabilities of the target business to be acquired needs to be assigned to the purchaser. Again, these transactions are not usually described as 'takeovers'. Whilst the term 'merger' is sometimes used, the typical language used is 'sale', 'disposal', 'purchase' or 'acquisition'.

As can be seen, change of control of an undertaking (company or business) may be achieved by a range of legal procedures and methods. The term 'takeover', however, is typically used to describe acquisition of *sufficient* shares in a widely-held company, which shares are usually listed on a stock exchange, to exercise control of the company. The terms 'takeover offer' or 'takeover bid' usually refer to an offer to *all* shareholders of a widely-held company to acquire their shares. These terms are usually used in this narrower sense because the City Code requires a takeover offer to be made to *all* shareholders. Use of the term 'takeover' is not confined to a 'hostile' takeover bid. It is used even if the offer to purchase is welcomed and approved by the board of the target company.

4 Scope of application of the City Code

The City Code is essentially a shareholder protection measure. Consequently, it applies to changes of control resulting from the purchase of shares, not to direct purchases of underlying businesses. It applies where there is an offer to acquire, or an attempt to gain a controlling interest (defined as an interest in shares carrying 30 per cent or more of the voting rights), in:

- a company with shares traded on a regulated market in the UK (primarily companies with shares listed on the London Stock Exchange); or
- any other UK public company with its central management and control in the UK.

The takeover of a plc with shares listed on the Alternative Investment Market (AIM) or any other UK stock market will be subject to the City Code *if its central management and control is in the UK*. For the purposes of the City Code the UK includes the Channel Isles and the Isle of Man.

A takeover offer may be recommended to the shareholders by the target company's board (a recommended bid) or not (a hostile bid). The takeover process unfolds very differently depending on which of these it is. If the takeover is welcomed by the board of directors of the target company, this opens up the potential to structure the acquisition in the most commercially sensible and tax-efficient manner.

5 Part 26 scheme of arrangement takeovers

Part 26 schemes of arrangement (see chapter 16) are used to effect about half of all takeovers subject to the City Code. Recognising this development, the Panel has drafted special rules for this type of takeover. These are set out in Appendix 7 to the City Code. They are a popular choice to effect recommended takeovers, not hostile takeovers. This is due to their flexibility (including the ability to gain 100 per cent ownership where only 75 per cent of shareholders wish to sell their shares), and the tax benefits that can be secured.

Although each takeover scheme of arrangement is unique, a typical takeover involves the shareholders of the target company surrendering their shares in the target company (which are cancelled) and receiving shares in the **offeror** company which are issued to them in return for the target company allotting fully paid-up shares to the offeror. This results in the target company becoming a subsidiary of the offeror.

TEST YOUR KNOWLEDGE 17.1

(a) Does the EU Takeover Directive lay down a maximum or minimum level of protection for shareholders that Member States must implement?
(b) What is meant by the term 'change of control' of a company?
(c) How do most companies change hands?
(d) Is a takeover bid made to the shareholders of a PLC with shares traded on the Alternative Investment Market governed by the City Code?
(e) What is a hostile takeover bid?
(f) Why are Part 26 schemes of arrangement popular to effect takeovers?

6 The nature and purpose of the City Code

The nature and purpose of the City Code is stated clearly in its introduction:

> 'The Code is designed principally to ensure that shareholders are treated fairly and are not denied an opportunity to decide on the merits of a takeover and that shareholders of the same class are afforded equivalent treatment by an offeror. The Code also provides an orderly framework within which takeovers are conducted. In addition, it is designed to promote, in conjunction with other regulatory regimes, the integrity of the financial markets.
>
> The Code is not concerned with the financial or commercial advantages or disadvantages of a takeover. These are matters for the company and its shareholders. Nor is the Code concerned with those issues, such as competition policy, which are the responsibility of government and other bodies.'

7 The City Code General Principles

The City Code is not simply a set of rules. The rules are underpinned by six General Principles which also form part of the Code. The General Principles are the same as the general principles set out in art. 3 of the EU Takeover Directive. They are brief and it is helpful to set them out in full. In the General Principles, the target is referred to as the **offeree** company, shares are referred to as 'securities' and shareholders are referred to as 'holders of securities'.

1. All holders of the securities of an offeree company of the same class must be afforded equivalent treatment; moreover, if a person acquires control of a company, the other holders of securities must be protected.
2. The holders of the securities of an offeree company must have sufficient time and information to enable them to reach a properly informed decision on the bid; where it advises the holders of securities, the board of the offeree company must give its views on the effects of implementation of the bid on employment, conditions of employment and the locations of the company's places of business.
3. The board of an offeree company must act in the interests of the company as a whole and must not deny the holders of securities the opportunity to decide on the merits of the bid.
4. False markets must not be created in the securities of the offeree company, of the offeror company or of any other company concerned by the bid in such a way that the rise or fall of the prices of the securities becomes artificial and the normal functioning of the markets is distorted.

5 An offeror must announce a bid only after ensuring that he/she can fulfil in full any cash consideration, if such is offered, and after taking all reasonable measures to secure the implementation of any other type of consideration.
6 An offeree company must not be hindered in the conduct of its affairs for longer than is reasonable by a bid for its securities.

The rules are interpreted and applied by the Panel in the spirit of these principles.

The changes made to the City Code in September 2011 were principally designed to protect target companies from what were perceived as tactical advantages available to the bidder. The key changes were:

- A target is required to identify all potential offerors of which it is aware when it makes a possible offer announcement. This will typically occur where the Panel requires an announcement because of market speculation or an untoward price movement resulting from an approach by an offeror.
- Public identification of an offeror by the target company triggers a fixed, 28 day 'put up or shut up' period (PUSU) (which can be extended by the Panel on request from the target, and generally has been) during which the offeror must make an announcement that it has either a firm intention to make a bid or no intention to make a bid.
- Break fees and various other offer-related arrangements are prohibited.
- Greater information is required in offer documents including about deal financing and plans for the target and about the fees of advisers in relation to the takeover.

8 Outline of the basic takeover bid process

This section describes how a simple takeover of a publicly traded company is conducted in accordance with the City Code. Before deciding to acquire control of another company (the target), the purchaser (the offeror) conducts due diligence based on publicly available information (unless the target company board cooperates) and makes confidential enquiries. The offeror may decide to make a firm offer for the target company and then approach the target company board or may approach the target company board before it has made a decision, i.e., it may approach the target company board to discuss a possible offer.

The 2011 revisions to the City Code have tightened up the rules applicable at the early stage in the takeover process, before a 'firm intention to make an offer' is announced (Rule 2.7). In circumstances specified in Rule 2.2, including where there are rumours of a takeover in the market or untoward movements in the target company's share price or confidential negotiations regarding a takeover require more than a small core team to be aware of the discussions, an unambiguous announcement must be made, identifying the offeror, which is called a 'possible offer announcement' (Rule 2.4). This announcement triggers a 28 day 'put up or shut up' period which can be extended only by the Panel at the request of the target (Rule 2.6). During this period the offeror is required to make a 'firm intention announcement' (Rule 2.7) or a 'no intention to bid' announcement (Rule 2.8). If it makes a no intention to bid announcement, the offeror and any person acting in concert with it is banned from making an offer for the target within the following six months (Rule 2.8).

A firm intention announcement (Rule 2.7) is, in effect, the announcement of an offer. It must include specified information including the price and other terms of the offer. Subject to any permitted preconditions to the making of the offer that may have been announced, a firm intention announcement effectively binds the offeror to make the described offer. If the offer is recommended, the firm intention announcement will be a joint announcement of the offeror and the target company and will include the target company board's recommendation of the offer. In any event, after the firm intention announcement, the target company must send copies 'promptly' to all shareholders.

A firm intention announcement initiates the **offer period**. An **offer document** containing the contractual offer to purchase the shares in the company must be posted on the target company's website and sent to all shareholders within 28 days of the announcement. The City Code specifies minimum information to be included in this document. The offer must remain open for at least 21 days and the expiry of the initial offer period is called the 'first closing day'. In a hostile takeover, the target company board has 14 days from publication of the offer document to send out its first defence document to shareholders.

Most offers are conditioned on the offer being accepted by holders of a specified proportion of the shares in the target company for which the offer is made: the 'acceptance condition'. This proportion is usually 90 per cent because if 90 per cent of the shares for which an offer is made and 90 per cent of their voting rights are acquired, an offeror can compel holders of the remaining 10 per cent to sell their shares (s. 979). The acceptance level achieved must be announced on the business day following the first closing day. If the acceptance condition has not been satisfied by the first closing day, an extension of the offer will usually be made. An offer can be extended for up to 60 days from publication of the offer document. If the acceptance condition has not been satisfied by day 60, the offer will lapse unless the offeror decides to proceed based on the actual acceptance level. An offeror is not permitted to proceed unless he has secured over 50 per cent of the voting rights in the target. If the offer lapses, the takeover fails and the offeror cannot make another offer for at least a further 12 months.

If the acceptance condition is satisfied on day 60 (or the condition is, where permitted, waived), the offer must remain open for a further 14 days, until day 74, and may remain open for longer. If the offeror has secured acceptances from shareholders holding 90 per cent or more of the voting rights attached to the shares for which the offer was made and 90 per cent or more of the value of those shares he will probably wish to exercise his right to acquire the outstanding shares. A notice to acquire the outstanding shares compulsorily must be served by the offeror within three months of the offer closing. Alternatively, although the offeror may be comfortable with a small cohort of minority shareholders, minority shareholders in a company in which the offeror owns and controls 90 per cent or more of the shares and voting rights can individually insist on being bought out by the offeror on the terms of the takeover offer (see section 9.2).

An offer must state that it will lapse if the takeover either is referred to the Competition Commission or the EU Commission decides to initiate a Phase II merger investigation. It may also be subject to additional conditions above and beyond an acceptance condition. If the offeror has shares listed on the London Stock Exchange, for example, the takeover is likely to be a class 1 transaction for the purposes of the Listing Rules and the offer will be made conditional on approval of the takeover by the offeror shareholders. These conditions must be satisfied within 21 days of the offer being declared unconditional as to acceptances, that is, based on a maximum offer period (60 day), by the 81st day after publication of the offer document.

Rule 31 requires the consideration for their shares to be posted to target shareholders not more than 14 days following the offer becoming wholly unconditional: on the timetable above, no later than 95 days after the publication of the offer document.

This is a very simple illustration of the basic timetable of an offer. Takeovers are rarely so straightforward. The terms of an offer are often revised, for example. Revision of the terms of the offer is permitted up until the 46th day after publication of the offer document. The City Code rules are detailed, discretions can be exercised by the Panel and delays and difficulties invariably arise. Also, a range of laws in addition to the City Code come into play in takeovers.

Some of the key additional legal rules typically applicable to takeovers and the laws applicable to a sample of practices typically encountered in takeovers are discussed in section 10 below.

9 Minority shareholder treatment

An important aspect of the shareholder protection delivered by the City Code is the protection of minority shareholders. Minority shareholders are protected in particular by the mandatory offer requirement in Rule 9. Section 983 of the Companies Act 2006 supplements the City Code and implements Article 16 of the EU Takeover Directive by providing each minority shareholder with sell-out rights.

9.1 Mandatory offers on acquisition of a controlling stake

Rule 9 requires a person who acquires shares carrying 30 per cent or more of the voting rights in a company to make a cash offer to all other shareholders at no less than the highest price paid for the shares already acquired. The reason for this is that in practice control of a company can be exercised by a person owning 30 per cent of its shares. The acquisition of that control is very valuable and the purchaser, therefore, will be prepared to pay a price premium for the shares delivering that control. The mandatory bid requirement supports the purpose of the City Code to ensure that shareholders of the same class are afforded equivalent treatment by an offeror.

The effect of the mandatory offer requirement is to ensure that the price premium for control is shared among all the shareholders. Control for the purposes of triggering a mandatory offer is not defined in the EU Takeover Directive, but is left to be defined by Member States (see section 3.2).

9.2 Sell-out rights

If, when the offer period closes, the offeror, already owns or has the right to acquire shares in the company amounting to 90 per cent or more of the value of the voting shares and carrying 90 per cent or more of the voting rights of the company, s. 983 gives each shareholder the right to require the offeror to buy him out at the same price and otherwise subject to the same terms as the takeover offer.

Note that the 90 per cent threshold trigger for minority sell-out rights is different from the 90 per cent threshold trigger for the s. 979 right of the offeror to buy out minority shareholders. The minority shareholder's right to compel acquisition of his shares is triggered based on the entire ownership rights of the offeror in the company. Essentially, the offeror must have 90 per cent of the voting shares and 90 per cent of the voting rights in the company, whether he owned those shares before the takeover offer or as a result of it. In contrast, the buy-out right of the offeror is triggered based on the success of the takeover offer – the offeror must secure acceptance from the holders of 90 per cent or more of the shares to which the offer relates. Where the purchaser is seeking 100 per cent control of the target, this test operates as a disincentive to **stakebuilding** prior to making a takeover offer.

10 Key additional legal rules and problem areas in takeovers

Legal requirements above and beyond compliance with the City Code apply to takeovers. Precisely which legal rules apply will depend on the circumstances, including the legal character of the parties involved. Two sets of supplementary legal rules that almost invariably come into play are commented on below, before turning to a sample of practices regularly encountered in takeovers and the laws relevant to those practices.

10.1 FCA Listing Rules, Disclosure and Transparency Rules and Prospectus Rules

In many takeovers, one or more of the companies involved are subject to and will need to comply with the relevant provisions of the FCA Listing Rules, Disclosure and Transparency Rules and Prospectus Rules. Where the offeror company has a primary listing of its equity shares on the London Stock Exchange, for example, it will need to comply with Rule 7 of the Listing Rules, which requires shareholder approval of a class 1 transaction, which a takeover usually will be. The disclosure provisions of the City Code are materially supplemented in most takeovers by the disclosure requirements of the aforementioned FCA rules.

10.2 Competition law

Both domestic and EU level competition laws apply in the UK and one or the other if not both are often engaged in a takeover situation. Beyond this, takeovers involving foreign companies and/or having international effects outside the EU, may trigger the competition laws of other countries, not uncommonly the USA.

Competition laws and procedures relevant to the takeover transaction itself need to be considered, such as the need for pre-notification to the EU Commission under the EU Merger Regulation (139/2004/EC), or, where the takeover does not have a 'community dimension' bringing it within the scope of the EU Merger Regulation, the benefit to be secured from notification to the Office of Fair Trading to mitigate the uncertainty of a referral to the Competition Commission under the Enterprise Act 2002. Additionally, and not to be overlooked, is analysis of the effect of the change of control on the agreements operated by each party. Although compliant with competition law beforehand, agreements may become problematic from a competition law perspective as a result of the takeover and necessary amendments should be anticipated and actioned.

10.3 Insider dealing in shares of both parties

Insider dealing is a temptation that may present itself during a takeover when a potentially wide range of personnel of companies and their advisers are privy to market-sensitive information. The law governing insider dealing is considered in chapter 7.

10.4 Creating a false market in the offeror's shares

The consideration, or one of the consideration options, offered to target company shareholders invariably includes shares in the offeror. The value of the offeror's shares is therefore very important. This opens up the potential for the market price of offeror shares to be artificially inflated.

The law regulating behaviour designed to enhance the price of the offeror's shares includes the Companies Act 2006, s. 678 (prohibition on a public company providing financial assistance for the purchase of its own shares) and s. 397 and Part VIII (the market abuse provisions) of the Financial Services and Markets Act 2000 (see rule 19). The FCA and the Panel work closely together to prevent market abuse relating to takeovers.

In 1986, to make Guinness plc's takeover offer for Distillers look more attractive than a rival offer, Guinness executives established a scheme to support Guinness's share price. This involved Guinness rewarding those involved in the scheme, including Pipetec, for buying and retaining Guinness shares and indemnifying them against any losses they might incur. The conduct of the takeover was regarded as scandalous. A government investigation by the Department of Trade and Industry (now BIS) into the takeover, published 11 years after the event, concluded that the takeover had succeeded in part due to the share support scheme. The takeover resulted in criminal prosecutions and extensive civil actions in the courts (the reason why publication of the Government report was delayed). The Panel found that Guinness had breached the City Code and Guinness was required to pay c. £85 million in compensation to Distillers' shareholders.

10.5 Concert parties acquiring a stake in the target

Offerors are limited in the proportion of shares, or stake, in a target company it can own before it must make a takeover offer to all shareholders (see, 'change of control', above). Attempts to avoid triggering a bid are sometimes made by arranging for a stake in the target company to be built up by a number of persons acting in concert with the offeror, known as a **concert party**. The City Code is drafted to trigger a mandatory offer when control is acquired by persons acting in concert. It is therefore important to know who might be regarded as acting in concert with an offeror.

10.6 Defensive action by the target company board

Board directors are in a conflict of interest position when a hostile takeover offer is made or anticipated. They are likely to lose their position as directors and their job as executive employees of the company if the bid succeeds. It is difficult to reconcile their self-interests with those of the company. Yet directors are not always motivated by self-interest when they consider a takeover not to be in the interests of the company. As mentioned at the beginning of this chapter, one view of hostile takeovers is that they undermine the ability of management to build prosperity based on long-term planning. This was echoed in the words of the outgoing chairman of Cadbury after the successful takeover of the company by Kraft in February 2010 following a takeover battle: 'At the end of the day, there were simply not enough shareholders prepared to take a long-term view of Cadbury and prepared to forgo short-term gain for longer-term prosperity.'

The 'enlightened' aspect of shareholder value enshrined in the s. 172 duty of a director requiring directors to have regard to the matters listed in that section, which include, among others, the likely consequences of any decision in the long term and the interests of the company's employees, appears to vanish in a takeover. The divergence of the immediate interests of shareholders (to secure the highest offer for their shares as possible) and other stakeholders in the company is reinforced where the shares in the target are held by hedge funds and other short-term funds. It was reported in the press that close to 25 per cent of the shares in Cadbury were purchased by such funds during the 19-week takeover battle.

The third General Principle (set out above) and Rule 21 of the City Code require directors to play a neutral role. Essentially, once the directors have notice of a firm intention to make an offer they are unable to take any action to frustrate the takeover offer or deny shareholders the opportunity to decide on its merits. In particular, Rule 21 prohibits the board, unless shareholder approval is obtained, from issuing any shares, granting any options in relation to shares or issuing convertible bonds or subscription rights, selling or acquiring or agreeing to sell or dispose of assets of a material amount; or entering into contracts otherwise than in the ordinary course of business. The EU Takeover Directive provides for board neutrality in art. 9.2, but, to secure political consensus, this is an optional principle that Member States are permitted to opt out of: in some Member States defence tactics are permitted.

A **poison pill** is a device to frustrate future takeovers that is put in place often long before a takeover situation arises. The right to enforce an agreement amounting to a poison pill was considered by the House of Lords in *Criterion Properties plc v Stratford UK Properties LLC* [2006] 1 BCLC 729 (HL). Criterion was contractually obliged to buy out a shareholder at an inflated price on the occurrence of a range of events, including a change of control of the company. The case provides no binding authority on the ability of the board of a company to legally commit a company to a poison pill arrangement. The House of Lords identified that question as a matter of considerable public importance before going on to remit the case to the court of first instance to be decided on the basis of whether or not the particular directors who signed the agreement had authority to do so.

10.7 Break fees and non-solicitation agreements

Since September 2011, break fees and other deal protection measures such as non-solicitation agreements are no longer permitted under the City Code. A break fee (also called an inducement fee) is a sum payable on the occurrence of specified events (such as recommendation by the target board of a higher competing offer) by a target company to a potential offeror pursuant to an agreement entered into between the target company and the potential offeror. A non-solicitation undertaking entails the target company agreeing not to solicit offers from other parties. Break fees and non-solicitation undertakings were typically included in confidentiality agreements entered into between the offeror and the target in a non-hostile takeover. Other commitments typically entered into in deal 'implementation agreements' have also been prohibited since September 2011, although co-operation on competition law matters is still permitted.

TEST YOUR KNOWLEDGE 17.2

(a) Summarise the six General Principles underpinning the City Code and set out in the EU Takeover Directive.
(b) What is the rationale for the Rule 9 requirement that a person who obtains 30 per cent or more of the voting rights in a company must make a cash offer to all other shareholders?
(c) Compare and contrast the triggers for the s. 979 right of the offeror to buy out minority shareholders (buy-out rights) and the right of a minority shareholder to insist that he be bought out under s. 983 (sell-out rights).
(d) Identify two sets of supplementary legal rules that almost invariably come into play on a takeover.

11 The system for regulating takeovers

11.1 Composition and funding of the Panel

The Panel on Takeovers and Mergers is independent of the Government. It is made up of up to 22 individuals regarded as having expertise in takeovers, most of whom work or have worked in organisations engaged in takeovers, such as merchant banks, law and accountancy firms, investment management firms and large publicly-traded companies. Panel members also sit on Panel committees, the most important of which are the Code Committee and the Hearings Committee. The Panel is supported by the Executive which conducts the day-to-day work of takeover regulation.

The Panel is funded by companies and organisations involved in takeovers. Its principal income comes from charges levied on takeovers (the PTM levy) and on documents reviewed in the course of takeovers (document charges).

11.2 Role of the Panel

The Panel issues and makes rulings on the interpretation, application and effect of the City Code. It can require a person to provide it with documents and information and also issues directions to restrain breaches and otherwise secure compliance with the City Code and imposes sanctions on those who breach the City Code or fail to comply with directions issued by the Panel. Finally, the Panel may order those in breach of the City Code to pay such compensation as it thinks just and reasonable.

The Panel also cooperates and shares information with bodies performing similar functions in other EU Member States, the FCA and, subject to the caveat that they must be exercising functions of a public nature, bodies performing functions similar to itself and the FCA in other countries.

The Panel publishes annual reports, available on its website, which summarise the Panel's work in any given year and provide takeover statistics. In the year to 31 March 2009, for example, 104 firm intentions to make an offer were made resulting in 88 successful takeovers.

11.3 Statutory empowerment of the Panel

The Panel's functions are put on a statutory footing by Part 28 of the Companies Act 2006 where the City Code is referred to as 'the rules'. The Panel's statutory footing extends to all of its work in relation to takeovers, not just those takeovers the UK is required by the EU Takeover Directive to regulate.

The Panel is authorised to make rules in relation to 'transactions ... that have or may have, directly or indirectly, an effect on the ownership or control of companies' (s. 943(2)(a)(iii)). The Panel's rulings on the interpretation, application or effect of the rules are given binding legal effect by s. 945(2), and Panel directions to restrain breaches and secure compliance with the rules are given legal effect by s. 946. Any rule conferring power on the Panel to impose sanctions for breach of the code or failure to comply with Panel directions given to secure compliance with the code is given legal effect by s. 952 and any rule conferring the power to order a person to pay compensation is given legal effect by s. 954.

Finally, where there has been a breach of a requirement set out in the rules, including a disclosure requirement, the Panel is statutorily empowered to make an application to the court in relation to which the court may make any order it thinks fit to secure compliance (s. 955). However, the 2006 Act states clearly that contravention of a rule-based requirement or a disclosure requirement does not give rise to any action for breach of statutory duty (s. 956).

In relation to sanctions, s. 952 requires the Panel to prepare, consult on and publish a compliance policy statement. This statement must include its policy as to the amount of any financial penalty that may be imposed. When exercising its power to impose a sanction the Panel is required to have regard to the policy statement in force when a breach or failure occurred (s. 952(8)), to the seriousness of the breach or failure, to the extent to which the breach was deliberate or reckless and to whether the person to be sanctioned is an individual (s. 952(4)).

11.4 Panel Committees and the Takeover Appeal Board

The Panel is required to have a rule-making committee (s. 943). In practice this committee is called the Code Committee. The rules must also provide for a Panel decision to be subject to review by a Hearings Committee (s. 951).

A right of appeal against a decision of the Hearing Committee to an independent tribunal, the 'Takeover Appeal Board', must also be set out in the rules (s. 951(3)). The chairman and deputy chairman of the Takeover Appeal Board are ordinarily persons who have held high judicial office and, as at May 2010, were Lord Steyn (former member of the judicial House of Lords) and Sir Martin Nourse (one-time Lord Justice). They appoint the remaining members of the Board and are themselves appointed by the Master of the Rolls.

11.5 Review of Panel decisions

Litigation has not been common in relation to takeovers in the UK. This record may indicate that the Panel has been doing a good job, a widely-accepted view which is part of the explanation. Limited judicial review of Panel decisions is largely the result of the history and origins of the City Code coupled with judicial endorsement of an explicit policy to deter tactical litigation to delay and frustrate takeovers which has made judicial review available only in extremely narrow circumstances and only after the fact.

Established in 1968, the City Code and the Panel operated as a private institution for over 20 years before the public nature of its functions was judicially acknowledged and performance of those functions confirmed to be subject to judicial review. In *R v Panel on Takeovers and Mergers, ex parte Datafin plc* [1987] 1 All ER 564 (CA)), Sir John Donaldson praised the Panel as a 'truly remarkable body'. He stated that, while its decisions were subject to judicial review, people were entitled to assume the validity of the Panel's rules and decisions unless and until they were quashed by the court. This part of his judgment has been superseded by Part 28 of the Companies Act 2006 which now confers legal validity on the Panel's rules, rulings, directions and sanctions.

It was with the following words that the then Master of the Rolls confirmed that the courts could not be used to delay takeovers:

> 'I should expect the relationship between the panel and the court to be historic rather than contemporaneous. I should expect the court to allow contemporary decisions to take their course, considering the complaint and intervening, if at all, later and in retrospect by declaratory orders which would enable the panel not to repeat any error and would relieve individuals of the disciplinary consequences of any erroneous finding of breach of the rules. This would provide a workable and valuable partnership between the courts and the panel in the public interest ...'

This appreciation of the importance of avoiding delay was confirmed in the recent Companies Court case of *Re Expro International Group plc* [2008] EWHC 154 in which the court refused to adjourn the hearing of an application to sanction a Part 26 scheme of arrangement to effect a takeover where the adjournment was requested 'to see how events unfold', and, basically, to give a potential rival bidder time to try (again) to mount a rival bid.

A hands-off approach to judicial review is enshrined in Part 28 of the Companies Act, allaying fears that the effectiveness of the Panel and the City Code would be undermined by placing them on a statutory footing. Specifically, the details of procedure, evidence and powers of the Hearings Committee are a matter for the Panel which may be contained in the Rules (s. 951(4)) and, very importantly, the circumstances and conditions subject to which appeals may be made to the Takeover Appeal Board are also matters for the Panel to set out in the rules (s. 951(3)). As at February 2013, two appeals have been decided by the Board, Eurotunnel (2007) (which was unsuccessful) and Principle Capital Investment Trust plc (PCIT) (2010) (also an unsuccessful appeal). PCIT was an appeal from a decision to sanction three individuals for operating an undisclosed concert party with the intention of avoiding making a mandatory offer, in breach of Rule 9 and for failing to assist the Panel by continuing to conceal material facts.

In summary, a two-stage review process in relation to Panel decisions is set out in the 2006 Act: internal review by the Hearing Committee and, from there, independent review by the Takeover Appeal Board. As far as possible, review will not be allowed to hold up takeover timetables. Court review is primarily to clarify the rules for future benefit and to alleviate the disciplinary consequences of breaches, i.e., will continue to be subject to the very narrow approach outlined in *Datafin*. Note also that s. 961 exempts the Panel and its members from liability for damages for anything done in connection with the discharge of its functions except in the case of bad faith or behaviour that is unlawful under s. 6(1) of the Human Rights Act 1998, i.e., an act incompatible with rights under the European Convention on Human Rights would be actionable.

TEST YOUR KNOWLEDGE 17.3

(a) Outline briefly the key functions of the Panel on Takeovers and Mergers.
(b) Describe the two-stage review process for Panel decisions.
(c) Explain the decision in *R v Panel on Takeovers and Mergers, ex parte Datafin plc* [1987] 1 All ER 564 (CA).

CHAPTER SUMMARY

- The Takeover Directive lays down a minimum level of protection for shareholders in the event of a takeover that Member States must implement, allowing the higher level of protection applicable in the UK in the form of the City Code to continue in operation.
- The point in the aggregation of voting shares in a company at which a person can exercise effective control over a company is a matter of fact. The partial definition of control in the Takeover Directive is ownership of shares carrying 30 per cent or more of the voting rights.
- Control of most unlisted companies changes hands as a result of a share purchase agreement negotiated between the target shareholder and the purchaser.
- The City Code applies where there is an offer to acquire, or an attempt to gain a controlling interest (defined as an interest in shares carrying 30 per cent or more of the voting rights), in a company with shares traded on a regulated market in the UK, or any other UK public company with its central management and control in the UK.
- A takeover bid made to the shareholders of a PLC with shares traded on the Alternative Investment Market will be governed by the City Code if its central management and control is in the UK.
- A hostile takeover bid is a bid which is not recommended by the board of directors of the target company.
- Where a takeover bid is recommended, the share acquisition can be structured as efficiently as possible and Part 26 schemes of arrangement are popular to effect recommended takeovers. Part 26 also allows a takeover to succeed with less than 90 per cent acceptance by shareholders.
- Six General Principles underpin the City Code and are also set out in the EU Takeover Directive. They are essentially:
  - equivalent treatment of shareholders;
  - shareholder should be able to make properly informed decision on a bid;
  - target company board defense tactics are prohibited;
  - no false markets in takeover bid shares;
  - offeror must be in a position to complete any bid made; and
  - target companies to be protected from protracted takeover attempts.
- A person who obtains 30 per cent or more of the voting rights in a company is believed to have effective control so that a cash offer to all other shareholders at the highest price paid for the already-acquired shares advances the first principle – equality of treatment of shareholders.
- Section 979 gives to the offeror the right to buy out minority shareholders (buy-out rights) and s. 983 gives to minority shareholder the right to insist that they be bought out by the offeror (sell-out rights) in each case subject to the offeror achieving ownership or the right to own 90 per cent of those shares/voting rights specified. The 90 per cent triggers are calculated very differently in either case.
- FCA Listing Rules, Disclosure and Transparency Rules and Prospectus Rules and Competition Law almost invariably come into play on a takeover.
- Common practices encountered in takeovers and the key legal rules that come into play in relation to each include:
  - insider dealing in shares of both parties;
  - creating a false market in the offeror's shares;
  - concert parties acquiring a stake in the target;
  - defensive action by the target company board; and
  - break fees.

- The key functions of the Panel on Takeovers and Mergers (the Panel) are to:
  - issue and make rulings on the interpretation, application and effect of the City Code;
  - require a person to provide it with documents and information;
  - issue directions to restrain breaches and otherwise secure compliance with the City Code;
  - impose sanctions on those who breach the City Code or fail to comply with directions issued by the Panel; and
  - order those in breach of the City Code to pay such compensation as it thinks just and reasonable.
- The Panel was placed on a statutory footing by what is now Part 28 of the Companies Act 2006.
- The power of the courts to review the decisions of the Panel was confirmed in *R v Panel on Takeovers and Mergers, ex parte Datafin plc* [1987] 1 All ER 564 (CA). This review operates retrospectively so that takeover timetables are not delayed.
- Panel decisions are subject to internal review by the Hearing Committee and, from there, independent review by the Takeover Appeal Board.

18 Corporate rescue

■ CONTENTS

1 Company voluntary arrangements
2 The small company moratorium
3 Administration

■ INTRODUCTION

This chapter is relevant to companies in financial difficulties. When a company experiences financial difficulty it may struggle to pay its debts as they fall due or to service its debt, that is, make interest payments, capital repayments, and/or meet certain covenants, or conditions, specified in its loan agreements. The situation may deteriorate rapidly into one in which there is no reasonable prospect that the company can avoid going into insolvent **liquidation**, or in which an individual creditor considers it has no option but to seek a winding up order.

It is important that directors and officers of companies understand the options available to facilitate a corporate rescue, that is, the procedures that can be utilised to allow a breathing space to take stock of the situation and to restructure the company's debt (and, sometimes, the shareholder arrangements) to give the company or group the best chance to trade its way back to financial good health.

The law and procedures outlined in this chapter are designed to facilitate restructuring of the rights of creditors and, sometimes, shareholders of a company in financial difficulties. Each of the three procedures examined is governed by the Insolvency Act 1986 and the Insolvency Rules 1986, both of which have been extensively amended, principally by the Insolvency Act 2000 and the Enterprise Act 2002, to facilitate corporate rescue and to make the law operate more fairly in relation to unsecured creditors. The resulting legal framework looks like this:

- Company voluntary arrangements (Part I, ss. 1–7).
- Small company moratorium and company voluntary arrangement (Part I, s. 1A (only) and Schedule A1).
- Administration (Part II, s. 8 (only) and Schedules B1 and 1).
- Winding up (Part IV, ss. 73–219) (see chapter 19).

Due to the emphasis now placed on administration, receivership is far less important than it used to be and is not covered in this book.

1 Company voluntary arrangements

Part 1 of the Insolvency Act 1986 contains a procedure by which a company may put in place a composition in satisfaction of its debts, or a scheme of arrangement of its affairs, that binds all unsecured creditors even though not all of them agree to its terms. A preferential creditor or secured creditor is not bound unless it agrees with the proposal (s. 4(3)). The proposal, approval and implementation of such a composition or scheme, called a **company voluntary arrangement (CVA)**, must comply with ss. 1–7. A CVA proposal may be made to the company and its creditors either by its directors (s. 1(1)) or by the administrator or liquidator of the company (s. 1(3)). A successful end to administration is often brought about by putting in place a CVA.

Where a company is not in administration or liquidation, in the period leading up to the approval of the CVA, as Part 1 contains no moratorium on enforcement, creditors may seek to enforce their debts. A procedure for putting in place a CVA which includes a moratorium is available for small companies (see section 2 below) but as it is not relevant to a company in administration or liquidation and is cumbersome, it is not very popular. The unavailability of a moratorium makes CVAs unattractive and unpopular outside of administration. Government proposals to address this by legislating for a restructuring moratorium were consulted on and responses published in May 2011 but this reform ran into difficulties and has not been implemented.

A CVA proposal must provide for a nominee to supervise its implementation (s. 1(2)). The nominee must be a qualified insolvency practitioner (s. 1(2)). The person who carries out the functions of the nominee is referred to as a supervisor (s. 7). Where the proposal is made by an administrator or liquidator, he or she will often (though not always) be the supervisor.

If the CVA is proposed by the directors, they must give the supervisor notice of the CVA proposal setting out its terms and a statement of affairs of the company (which will give details of its creditors, debts, other liabilities and assets) (s. 2(3)). Within 28 days of such notice the supervisor must submit a report to the court (s. 2(2)) stating:

- whether, in his opinion, the proposed CVA 'has a reasonable prospect of being approved and implemented';
- whether, in his opinion, meetings of the company and its creditors should be summoned to consider the proposal; and
- proposed dates, times and places for such meetings.

Assuming the supervisor's report is positive, and unless the court directs otherwise, the meetings are then summoned by the supervisor to consider the proposal. If the company is in administration or liquidation, no report to the court is required under s. 2, but meetings of the shareholders and creditors must be summoned to consider the proposal. Every creditor of the company of whose claims and address the supervisor is aware must be invited to the creditors' meeting (s. 3(3)) and all meetings must be conducted in accordance with the Insolvency Rules 1986. At the creditors' meeting, the proposal must be approved by a majority of three-quarters or more in value of creditors present (in person or by proxy). The shareholders can approve the proposal by a simple majority on a poll of those present in person or by proxy. The outcome of each meeting must be reported to the court by the chairman of the meeting and notices of the result given in accordance with the Insolvency Rules 1986.

The shareholders and creditors may decide to approve the proposed CVA with or without amendments. The CVA takes effect if the proposal is approved at both the shareholders' meeting and the creditors' meeting. If it is approved only at the meeting of the creditors, or there is a difference in what is approved by the shareholders and what is approved by the creditors, the CVA takes effect as approved by the creditors subject to the right of a member, within 28 days, to make an application to court, whereupon the court may make such order as it thinks fit (s. 4A).

Any shareholder or creditor who believes that the CVA unfairly prejudices the interests of a creditor or shareholder or that there has been some material irregularity at or in relation to one or more meetings, may, within 28 days, apply to the court for an order revising or revoking the CVA or directing a further meeting or meetings (s. 6). HMRC applied to the court under s. 6 in the administration of Portsmouth City FC (*HMRC v Portsmouth City Football Club Limited (in administration) and others* [2010] EWHC 2013 (Ch)) (see table at end of chapter).

The CVA binds all creditors of the company (except preferential and secured creditors who disagree with it), as if they were parties to the CVA (s. 5), and creditors cannot commence legal proceedings to enforce a debt owing to them unless the company fails to perform the CVA. During the implementation of the CVA, either the supervisor or a person dissatisfied with his actions may apply to court and the court may make such order as it thinks fit (s. 7). Note that it was held in *Re TXU Europe Group plc* [2011] EWHC 2072 that a distribution of company assets to its members which is unlawful under the Companies Act 2006 is not made lawful simply because it is provided for or facilitated by a CVA. When the CVA comes to an end, the supervisor submits a report to the shareholders and the creditors.

An example of a CVA is a company agreeing to pay £100,000 per year for each of three years to the supervisor for distribution to creditors. If the company fails to pay the agreed sum to the supervisor or the CVA has in some other way not been implemented in accordance with its terms, the CVA is deemed to have come to an end (s. 7B). On the CVA coming to an end, the company becomes liable to the creditor for any sum that had been payable under the CVA but was not in fact paid.

> **TEST YOUR KNOWLEDGE 18.1**
>
> (a) What is a company voluntary arrangement?
> (b) If the company is not in administration or liquidation, what must the nominee or supervisor send to the court within 28 days of receiving notice of the terms of a proposed CVA?
> (c) State the proportion of creditors needed to approve a CVA proposal.
> (d) What is the effect of a CVA?

2 The small company moratorium

A procedure allowing small companies to obtain a stay or moratorium in the enforcement of its debts to give it time to put a CVA in place was introduced into the Insolvency Act 1986 by the Insolvency Act 2000. The procedure, set out in detail in Schedule A1 to the 1986 Act, is only relevant to CVAs put in place by the directors of a company. It is not needed by an administrator or liquidator.

The procedure is available only to directors of *small* companies defined to be those companies satisfying two out of three of the following conditions (from s. 382(3) Companies Act 2006 (as amended)):

Turnover	Not more than £6.5 million
Balance sheet total	Not more than £3.26 million
Employees	Not more than 50 employees

A number of companies in specialist sectors such as banking and insurance are precluded from using the procedure and the procedure cannot be used if it has been used in the previous 12 months.

The directors send a document setting out the terms of the proposed CVA and a statement of the company's affairs to the nominee of the proposed CVA who submits to the directors a prescribed-form statement indicating whether or not, in his opinion:

- the proposed CVA 'has a reasonable prospect of being approved and implemented';
- the company is likely to have sufficient funds available to it during the proposed moratorium to enable it to carry on its business; and
- meetings of the company and its creditors should be summoned to consider the CVA proposal.

The moratorium comes into force when the following documents are filed with the court (sch. A1, para. 7):

- document setting out the terms of the proposed CVA;
- statement of the company's affairs;
- statement that the company is eligible for a moratorium;
- statement from the nominee that he has given his consent to act;
- statement from the nominee that in his opinion:
  - the proposed CVA 'has a reasonable prospect of being approved and implemented';
  - the company is likely to have sufficient funds available to it during the proposed moratorium to enable it to carry on its business; and
  - meetings of the company and its creditors should be summoned to consider the CVA proposal.

When the moratorium comes into effect, the directors must notify the nominee, who must advertise the moratorium and notify the registrar, the company and any creditor who has petitioned for the winding up of the company (sch. A1, paras. 9 and 10).

A moratorium initially lasts no more than 28 days (para. 8). An extension of up to a further two months may be approved by meetings of the shareholders and creditors during that initial period (para. 32).

A moratorium usually ends at the end of the day on which the meeting of shareholders or creditors (whichever is later) is held at which the proposed CVA is approved. If meetings of the shareholders and creditors have not been summoned, the moratorium will end on the expiry of the initial period. If meetings have been summoned to take place but for some reason do not, the moratorium will end on the day the latest meeting was summoned to take place. Other events on which a moratorium will end include the nominee's withdrawal of consent to act, by order of the court and by decision of one or both of the meetings of shareholders and creditors.

The nominee must advertise the coming to an end of a moratorium and notify the court, the registrar, the company and any petitioning creditor (para. 11).

During the moratorium, no legal proceedings to enforce debts against the company may be commenced, no winding up petition may be presented and no winding up resolution may be passed. No administrator or administrative receiver may be appointed, no security may be enforced against the company's property and no meetings may be held without the consent of the nominee (para. 12).

TEST YOUR KNOWLEDGE 18.2

(a) Explain why a small company moratorium may be thought necessary.
(b) How does a small company moratorium usually end?
(c) Identify five consequences of a small company moratorium being in effect.

3 Administration

The administration procedure in the Insolvency Act 1986 was significantly revised by the Enterprise Act 2002, which focused administration on corporate rescue: the principal objective of an **administrator** is to rescue the company as a going concern (sch. B1, para. 3). Administration has taken the place of administrative receivership in most cases. Only in exceptional circumstances will a provision in a floating charge entered into on or after 15 September 2003 (the date on which the relevant provisions of the Enterprise Act 2002 came into effect), purporting to give the charge holder the right to appoint an administrative receiver, be effective. Moreover, even where a creditor has the right under a pre-15 September 2003 floating charge to appoint an administrative receiver, an administrator is often appointed instead. It remains unclear, however, how far corporate rescue has been enhanced by the 2002 Act changes.

The rules governing administration and the powers of an administrator are found in Schedules B1 and 1 of the Insolvency Act 1986. Unless otherwise stated, paragraph references are to Schedule B1.

3.1 Purpose of administration

Paragraph 3 of Schedule B1 sets out three objectives of administration in order of priority. The administrator is required to perform his functions to achieve the first objective unless he thinks that this is not reasonably practicable to achieve. Only then may he pursue the second objective and only if he thinks that too is not reasonably practicable to achieve is he required to work towards the third objective. The three objectives are to:

- rescue the company as a going concern;
- achieve a better result for the company's creditors as a whole than would be likely if the company were wound up (without first being in administration);
- make a distribution to one or more secured or preferential creditors.

The administrator is also required to perform his functions as quickly and efficiently as reasonably possible.

3.2 Commencement of administration

An administrator may be appointed by order of the court or, quickly, straightforwardly and without a court application or hearing, by the company, the company's directors, or the holder of a qualifying floating charge.

Out of court appointments

Appointment by the company or its directors

Neither the company nor the directors may appoint an administrator if the company is in liquidation or a winding up petition is pending, an administrative receiver is in office or an administration application remains to be disposed of by the court. To prevent administration being used whenever a company hits financially rough waters, this route into administration is also unavailable if the company has had the benefit of a moratorium (or interim moratorium) within the previous 12 months.

Subject to this, and at least five days' written notice of intention to make an appointment having been given to holders of qualifying floating charges and any person entitled to appoint an administrative receiver (para. 26), a copy of which notice must be filed with the court, the administration commences when the company or directors have filed a notice of appointment in prescribed form with the court (paras. 29 and 31). As soon as it is practicable to do so, the administrator must be given notice that the notice of appointment has been filed with the court. An interim moratorium operates between the notice of intention being filed with the court and the appointment of the administrator (see below).

Appointment by a floating charge holder

A floating charge 'qualifies' for the purposes of appointing an administrator if it:

- states that para. 14 of Schedule B1 applies to the floating charge;
- purports to empower the holder to appoint an administrator; or
- purports to empower the holder to appoint an administrative receiver.

The floating charge must relate to the whole or substantially the whole of the company's property, or, it, together with other security held by the charge holder, must meet this requirement (para. 14). At least two business days' notice of intention to make an appointment must be given to the holder of any prior floating charge (or their written consent obtained) and no appointment may be made if an administrative receiver is already in office, if, following the presentation of a winding up petition, the court has already appointed a provisional liquidator or the company is already in liquidation (paras. 8 and 15). Again, an interim moratorium operates between the notice of intention being filed with the court and the appointment of the administrator (see below).

Subject to this, the administration commences when the holder of the qualifying charge has filed a notice of appointment in the prescribed form with the court (paras. 18 and 19).

Content of prescribed form notice of appointment

The prescribed form notice of appointment contains:

- a notice of appointment identifying the administrator;
- a statutory declaration that:
  - the charge holder making the appointment is the holder of a qualifying floating charge in respect of the company's property;
  - each floating charge relied on is enforceable on the date of the appointment;
  - the appointment is in accordance with Schedule B1;
- a statement by the administrator:
  - that he consents to the appointment;
  - that in his opinion the purpose of administration is reasonably likely to be achieved.

Again, as soon as it is practicable to do so, the administrator must be given notice that the notice of appointment has been filed with the court. A pending winding up petition is suspended on the appointment of an administrator for the duration of the administration. Note that if the only reason why a floating charge holder cannot appoint an administrator is because the company is in liquidation, the charge holder may make an administration application to the court (para. 37).

Appointment by order of the court

Administration applications
An application for an **administration order** may be made to the court by the company, its directors, any creditor of the company, or, if the company is in liquidation, the liquidator.

Notice of administration application
As soon as reasonably practicable after the making of an administration application, it must be notified to any person who has appointed or is entitled to appoint an administrative receiver, or who is the holder of a qualifying floating charge entitled to appoint an administrator.

Grounds for grant of an administration order
An order of the court appointing a person to be an administrator may be made only if the court is satisfied (para. 11) that:

- the company is or is likely to become unable to pay its debts; and
- the administration order is reasonably likely to achieve the purpose of administration.

The first condition need not be satisfied if the applicant could appoint an administrator because he is the holder of a qualifying floating charge (para. 35).

Timing and effect of an administration order
A court-ordered administration takes effect at the time appointed by the order or, if the order is silent, when the order is made (para. 13).

On the making of an administration order:

- a pending winding up petition will be dismissed;
- if an administrative receiver has been appointed he will vacate office; and
- the administrator may require a receiver of part of the company's property to vacate office.

The interim moratorium

Paragraph 44 provides for an interim moratorium in relation to insolvency and other legal process (see below) to operate between the making of an administration application to the court and the administration order taking effect (or the court refusing to grant an administration order). An interim moratorium also operates when an administrator is appointed out of court, between the notice of intention to appoint being filed with the court and the appointment taking effect.

3.3 Effect of administration

Upon appointment an administrator must send notice of his appointment to the company and every creditor of whom he is aware. He must publish his appointment in *The Gazette* and notify the Registrar. While a company is in administration, every business document and all the company's websites must state the name of the administrator and that the affairs, business and property of the company are being managed by him (para. 45). Business document, for these purposes, means a hard copy or electronic:

- invoice;
- order for goods or services;
- business letter; or
- order form.

Effect on insolvency proceedings and other legal process

When a company is in administration a moratorium on insolvency proceedings and other legal process operates. The company cannot be put into liquidation (except pursuant to a public interest petition to do so) (para. 42) and, without the consent of the administrator or permission of the court (para. 43):

- No step may be taken to enforce any security over the company's assets.
- No administrative receiver may be appointed.
- No property may be repossessed under a hire purchase agreement.
- No landlord may exercise the right of forfeiture by re-entry.

- No legal process may be commenced or continued against the company whether civil or criminal.
- No step may be taken to enforce any legal judgment against the company.

The precise scope of legal process for the purposes of the moratorium has been litigated a number of times and the court has adopted a purposive approach, interpreting the term very broadly. The moratorium applies to all potential claimants, not just creditors (see *Biosource Technologies Inc v Axis Genetics plc* [2000] 1 BCLC 286). Quasi-judicial proceedings are included, such as arbitrations (*Bristol Airport plc v Powdrill* [1990] BCLC 585), as are criminal proceedings (*Re Rhondda Waste Disposal Ltd* [2000] BCC 653). Note also that cases such as *Re Lomax Leisure Ltd* [1999] 2 BCLC 126 holding that the right of forfeiture of a landlord did not amount to enforcement of security and therefore the exercise of the right of forfeiture was not prohibited by those words are no longer important because express language has been introduced into para. 43 stating that no landlord may exercise the right of forfeiture.

The basis on which the court should exercise its discretion to permit what is otherwise not allowed has also come before the courts. The court must have regard to all the circumstances and seek to balance all the 'legitimate' interests, including in an appropriate case the public interest.

Effect on directors

The appointment of an administrator has no automatic effect on the holding of office by the directors, who remain subject to all the duties and obligations of directors but an administrator may remove and appoint directors (paragraph 61). By para. 64, however, a company or an officer of a company in administration may not, without the consent of the administrator, exercise a power which could be exercised so as to interfere with the exercise of the administrator's powers: in effect, the powers of the directors of a company are suspended upon the appointment of the administrator.

Effect on employees

Administration does not bring employment contracts with the company automatically to an end. The administrator will review the employees' contracts and decide whether or not to terminate them and make employees redundant. If an administrator adopts a contract of employment, the wages or salary of the employees from the point of adoption forward are afforded priority, sometimes called 'super-priority' over the wages and expenses of the administrator as well as the claims of floating charge holders. This super-priority extends to liabilities under all contracts entered into by the administrator. The fact that employees have not been made redundant in the first 14 days of an administration cannot be argued to constitute adoption or evidence relevant to adoption for these purposes (para. 99).

Effect on contracts

Administration does not bring contracts with the company automatically to an end. Without more, they remain in place but cannot be enforced without the consent of the administrator or the permission of the court. Many commercial contracts automatically terminate or provide the other party with the right to terminate them in the event of administration (and other insolvency events) so many contractors will seek to terminate or renegotiate the terms of contracts, introducing tighter payment provisions such as cash on delivery or supplying with a retention of title clause (if not doing so already). Liabilities under any contract the administrator enters into will attract the super-priority referred to in the previous paragraph.

Effect on property

Whilst the property of the company remains vested in the company, the administrator has the power to manage the property, including the powers set out in Schedule 1 to 'take possession of, collect and get in the property of the company …' and sell or otherwise dispose of it. An administrator may dispose of and take actions in relation to property subject to a floating charge as if it were not subject to the charge (para. 70).

3.4 The role and powers of administrators

An administrator must be an authorised insolvency practitioner and is an officer of the court. He has power to do 'anything necessary or expedient for the management of the affairs, business and property of the company' (para. 59) and Schedule 1 to the 1986 Act lists 23 broad-ranging powers of administrators. He acts as an agent of the company (para. 69). The administrator must perform his functions in the interests of the company's creditors as a whole with the objective of rescuing the company as a going concern. Only if he thinks that this is not reasonably practicable to achieve should he seek 'to achieve a better result for the company's creditors as a whole than would be likely if the company were wound up' and, failing the reasonable practicability of that, aim to realise property in order to make a distribution to one or more secured or preferential creditors (para. 3).

An administrator must circulate a statement as to how he intends to conduct the administration within eight weeks of appointment (para. 49) and, unless there is no prospect of a return to unsecured creditors other than from the prescribed part, invite the creditors to an initial meeting to approve the proposals (para. 51). Proposals are approved by 50 per cent by value of creditors in attendance. If proposals are not approved the administrator must report this to the court and seek directions. The court may make such order as it thinks fit, including a winding up order (para. 55). During the administration an administrator must send reports to creditors every six months outlining progress.

3.5 Ending the administration

Paragraphs 76–86 of Schedule B1 govern how administration ends (more accurately referred to as when the appointment of the administrator ceases).

Automatic ending

An administrator is required to perform his functions as quickly and efficiently as is reasonably practicable (para. 4) and, in this spirit, the appointment of an administrator ceases to have effect automatically one year from taking effect. The appointment may be extended by order of the court or, for no more than six months and once only, with the consent of the creditors. Consent for these purposes means consent of each secured creditor and unsecured creditors owed at least 50 per cent by value of the debt held by unsecured creditors, who reply to an invitation to give or withhold consent. If, however, there is unlikely to be any sum to distribute to unsecured creditors beyond the prescribed amount, consent of the unsecured creditors is not required: only the secured creditors need consent unless the administrator thinks that a distribution to preferential creditors may be made, in which event the consent of preferential creditors owed 50 per cent of the value of preferential debt held by preferential creditors who reply to an invitation to give or withhold consent is also required.

Creditor application to court to end the administration

A creditor may apply to the court for an order that the administrator's appointment shall cease to have effect on the ground that the applicant for an administration order or the person who appointed the administrator has an improper motive (para. 81).

Administrator application to court to end the administration

An administrator shall make an application for the appointment to cease if he thinks the purpose of the administration cannot be achieved or the company should not have entered administration or a creditors' meeting requires him to make the application. A court-appointed administrator must also make such an application if he thinks that the purpose of the administration has been sufficiently achieved (para. 79).

Termination where objective achieved

Where an administrator has been appointed outside court and the administrator thinks that the purpose of the administration has been sufficiently achieved, his appointment will cease on the filing of a notice in prescribed form to that effect with the court and the registrar. A copy of the notice must be sent to every creditor known to the administrator (para. 80). As indicated above, a court-appointed administrator in this position must apply to court for an order that his appointment shall cease (para. 79).

Public interest winding up

If the court makes a winding up order following a petition by the Secretary of State pursuant to s. 124A for a winding up order on public interest grounds, the court will ordinarily order that the administrator's appointment shall cease to have effect.

Conversion to a creditors' voluntary winding up

Where an administrator appointed by court order thinks that the total amount which a secured creditor is likely to receive has been paid or set aside and that a distribution will be made to unsecured creditors, he may send the registrar a notice that para. 83 applies. The notice must be sent to all known creditors and filed with the court. The appointment will cease when the registrar registers the notice and the company is then wound up as if a resolution to voluntarily wind up the company had been passed (para. 83). If no person is nominated to be the liquidator by the creditors, the administrator becomes the liquidator. This is a very popular way for administrations to end.

Dissolution of the company

If the administrator thinks that the company has no property to distribute to creditors he is required to send a notice to that effect to the registrar and three months after the notice is registered by the registrar, the company is deemed to be dissolved (para. 84).

STOP AND THINK 8.1

'Pre-pack administrations' are a method by which the business of a company in financial difficulty is prepared for sale to a new company before the appointment of an administrator with the intention that the sale will be made by the administrator immediately after the company goes into administration. This can keep adverse publicity to a minimum. Creditors can feel as if they have no real choice but to accept the pre-negotiated package. More than this, although a business may be pre-packed and sold to a new company that is independent of the directors and secured creditors of the old company, what difficulties can you think of that may arise if the business is pre-packed and sold to either the directors or to a floating charge holder of the old company?

TEST YOUR KNOWLEDGE 18.3

(a) What are the three objectives of administration, in order of priority?
(b) Identify two routes by which an administrator may be appointed.
(c) Who is a qualifying floating charge holder for the purposes of appointing an administrator?
(d) What is the effect of appointment of an administrator on a winding up petition?
(e) How does administration affect the employees and contracts of the company?
(f) What is meant by the term 'super-priority'?

 **CASE EXAMPLE 18.1**

Portsmouth Football Club

Portsmouth Football Club, a Premier League club relegated to the Championship League at the end of the 2009–10 season, can be used to illustrate the interplay between administration, CVAs and compulsory winding up, including the effect of the appointment of an administrator on a winding up petition. The club has had the misfortune to see three companies that have owned it go into administration – in 1998, 2010 and again in 2012.

Portsmouth City Football Club Limited (Pompey)
Winding up and Administration Time Line

	Pompey failed to make scheduled payments to Her Majesty's Revenue & Customs (HMRC) as they fell due.
23 December 2009	HMRC filed a winding up petition in the High Court.
	Ongoing negotiations between HMRC and Pompey to arrive at a settlement in relation to £7.5 million in unpaid taxes (unpaid PAYE deductions from wages, NI contributions and VAT).
19 January 2010	High Court dismissed an application from Pompey for the winding up petition to be struck out. Pompey had seven days to lodge an appeal against the order.
10 February 2010	Winding up petition hearing. Court granted Pompey a nine-day adjournment requiring them to present a detailed financial breakdown of the state of the company (a 'statement of affairs'), within seven days with HMRC to have two days to examine the document. Winding up petition to be heard on the first available date after 19 February 2010.
	Provisional date for hearing winding up petition fixed for 1 March 2010.
26 February 2010	Pompey entered into administration when Portpin Ltd, a British Virgin Isles company believed to have connections with Pompey's owner, appointed an administrator (in fact, three individuals were appointed to be joint administrator) pursuant to two charges held over Pompey assets. The appointment of the joint administrator suspended the winding up petition.
2 March 2010	High Court hearing of HMRC application for the court to consider the validity of the appointment of the joint administrator. Court ordered a hearing of the validity of the appointment of the joint administrator and ordered the production of documentary evidence of the charges.
11 March 2010	Having received documentation (including two debentures) proving the validity of the appointment of the joint administrator, HMRC withdrew its winding up petition and signed a consent order conditional upon the holding of a provisional creditors' meeting.
25 March 2010	Provisional creditors' meeting held.

 **CASE EXAMPLE 18.1** *continued*

19 April 2010	Joint administrator publishes a letter to all known creditors, together with:
	Formal notice of a creditors' meeting pursuant to para. 51 of the Insolvency Act 1986 to be held on 6 May 2010.
	Statement setting out the proposals of the joint administrator to achieve the purpose of the administration pursuant to para. 49, Schedule B1.
	Proof of debt form.
	Proxy form.
	Resolutions to be voted on at the meeting were summarised as:
	Administrator to be authorised to draft a CVA proposal to be circulated to creditors.
	Creditors committee to be constituted.
	Administrators to be discharged from liability.
	Administration to be closed by the purpose being sufficiently achieved in accordance with para. 80, Schedule B1 by the company being placed into CVA.
	If CVA not approved, administrators to be able to exit via a creditors' voluntary liquidation (CVL), compulsory liquidation or dissolution as appropriate.
	Administrators to be authorised to achieve a sale of the business assets of the company in any manner they deem fit.
6 May 2010	Creditors' meeting held lasting five hours pursuant to Schedule B1, para. 51 of the Insolvency Act 1986.
	Pompey debts disclosed to stand at £135 million.
	Resolutions approved (with modifications) by a majority of creditors, including resolution that the club should move from administration to liquidation via a CVA.
	Meeting to be convened to approve the CVA. Approval must be supported by 75 per cent in value of the creditors. HMRC may have more than 25 per cent of the debt.
17 June 2010	CVA approved by 81% by value of creditors. HMRC not allowed votes for c. £13 million debt and CVA provided for 100% payment of 'football creditors' but 20 pence in the £1 for other creditors.
	HMRC lodged an appeal against the amount allowed as its debt on the vote and applied for the approval to be revoked or suspended based on unfair prejudice and material irregularity, under section 6 of the Insolvency Act 1986 and rule 1.17 of the Insolvency Rules 1986.
5 August 2010	*HMRC v Portsmouth City Football Club Limited (in administration) and others* [2010] EWHC 2013 (Ch)
	The High Court dismissed HMRC's claim.
24 October 2010	The business and assets (principally the Club) are sold to a new company Portsmouth Football Club (2010) Ltd.
18 January 2011	Creditors' meeting resolved that Pompey move from administration to compulsory liquidation.
10 February 2011	Order of the court granted for Pompey to move to compulsory liquidation.

 **CASE EXAMPLE 18.1** *continued*

24 February 2011	Completion of the Pompey's Company Voluntary Arrangement and exit from Administration. Liquidation commences.
1 June 2011	Liquidators sells all of the shares in Portsmouth Football Club (2010) Ltd to Convers Sports Intiatives plc
24 January 2012	HMRC issue a winding up petition against Portsmouth Football Club (2010) Ltd for £1.6 million in unpaid taxes.
13 February 2012	Portsmouth Football Club (2010) Ltd goes into administration – again … the winding up petition was withdrawn and the company remained in administration as at February 2013.

CHAPTER SUMMARY

- A CVA is a composition in satisfaction of a company's debts, or a scheme of arrangement of its affairs, that binds all affected company creditors even though not all of them agree to its terms.
- A CVA must be approved by a simple majority of the shareholders and also by a majority in excess of three-quarters in value of creditors present (in person or by proxy) at a meeting called for the purpose of approving the CVA.
- Failure by the company to make a payment due under a CVA brings it to an end.
- CVAs are usually put in place after a company has gone into administration because of the lack of statutory moratorium for the period it takes to put a CVA in place for a company that is not in administration.
- The small company moratorium is designed to protect small companies from legal actions while steps are taken to put a CVA in place.
- The small company moratorium is not a popular procedure.
- Administration is designed primarily to rescue the company as a going concern (Insolvency Act 1986 Schedule B1, para. 3). Administrators can be appointed out of court by directors or a qualifying floating charge holder or by the court.
- A pending winding up petition is suspended or dismissed on appointment of an administrator.
- An administrator is required to perform his functions as quickly as possible in the interests of the company's creditors as a whole with the objective of rescuing the company as a going concern.
- Administrations automatically end one year after taking effect unless they are extended by the court or, with the consent of creditors, for a further maximum of six months.
- Many administrations end by the company's business being sold as a 'pre-pack' or the company going into creditors' voluntary liquidation.

19 Winding up and company dissolution

■ **CONTENTS**

1. Sources of insolvency law
2. Types of winding up
3. Property not available to a liquidator
4. Order of distribution of assets
5. Company dissolution
6. Prohibition on the re-use of insolvent company names
7. Disclaiming onerous property
8. Challenging pre-liquidation transactions
9. Swelling the company's assets: personal contributions

■ **INTRODUCTION**

This chapter is about winding up and dissolution of a company. Before a company ceases to exist, its affairs should be wound up. Winding up and liquidation mean the same thing. Essentially, in a winding up any assets the company has are sold to turn them into cash, which is distributed to meet the company's liabilities. The name of the company is then removed by the Registrar from the register of companies and at that point the company ceases to exist. Most companies cease to exist without being formally wound up. If a company ceases to trade, has no assets and stops making the required annual returns to the Registrar, for example, the Registrar may remove its name from the register of companies.

When a solvent company is wound up, all creditors are paid in full and the surplus is shared between the shareholders in accordance with their class rights. The shareholders may decide to wind up a company voluntarily and share out its residual wealth by passing a special resolution (Insolvency Act 1986, s. 84).

The situation is very different if a company is insolvent. The board of a company struggling to pay its debts, including interest payments on its loans, will try to renegotiate the terms of loans and other credit arrangements to reach a voluntary compromise or settlement or composition (a range of terms are used) with its creditors to give the company a breathing space to trade itself back into financial good health. In addition to informal efforts, the three statutory legal processes available to a company in financial difficulties to try to avoid the need to liquidate and dissolve the company (company voluntary arrangements, the small company moratorium and administration) have been dealt with in the previous chapter.

If efforts to renegotiate legal agreements with its creditors fail and none of the corporate rescue processes in the previous chapter is successful, a company is likely to enter liquidation (i.e. is wound up). This chapter focuses on companies entering into insolvent winding up. We briefly consider the sources of insolvency law and the different types of winding up, before looking at the assets available for distribution, the statutory order of distribution, completion of the winding up and the prohibition on the use of insolvent company names.

Finally, we cover the steps and applications a liquidator may take to avoid certain pre-winding up transactions and swell the assets available for distribution.

1 Sources of insolvency law

The main statute governing winding up is the Insolvency Act 1986, as amended most significantly for our purposes by the Enterprise Act 2002. The main regulations are the Insolvency Rules 1986. The Companies Act 2006 also contains provisions important to winding up and a host of other Acts and statutory instruments are relevant, prompting Goode (2005) to comment:

> 'It has to be said that the structure of English insolvency legislation does not display a particularly rational structure or scheme of arrangement ... Overall the Insolvency Act and the Insolvency Rules have become a legislative morass through which even the experienced practitioner cannot pick his way without difficulty.'

In an effort to address this state of affairs, the Insolvency Service (an executive agency of BIS), is working on a project to 'reduce the regulatory and administrative burdens that exist for users of insolvency legislation'.

2 Types of winding up

A company may be wound up whether it is solvent or insolvent. Two types of winding up exist: voluntary winding up and compulsory winding up.

2.1 Voluntary winding up

A **voluntary winding up** is commenced by the passing of a special resolution by the shareholders (Insolvency Act 1986, s. 84(1)(b)). A voluntary winding up will be:

- a members' voluntary winding up, if a statutory declaration of solvency (that they are of the opinion that the company will be able to pay its debts in full within a specified time of no more than 12 months) has been made by the directors in accordance with s. 89; or
- a creditors' voluntary winding up, if no such statutory declaration has been made (s. 90), or, if a declaration of solvency has been made, but subsequently the liquidator disagrees with the declaration and is of the opinion that the company will be unable to pay its debts in full within the specified period (s. 96).

2.2 Compulsory winding up

A **compulsory winding up** is commenced by presentation of a petition to the court followed by an order of the court (Insolvency Act 1986, ss. 122 and 124).

The grounds on which a court may order that a company be wound up are set out in s. 122:

> '(1) A company may be wound up by the court if—
> (a) the company has by special resolution resolved that the company be wound up by the court,
> (b) being a public company which was registered as such on its original incorporation, the company has not been issued with a trading certificate under section 761 of the Companies Act 2006 (requirement as to minimum share capital) and more than a year has expired since it was so registered,
> (c) it is an old public company, within the meaning of Schedule 3 to the Companies Act 2006 (Consequential Amendments, Transitional Provisions and Savings) Order 2009,
> (d) the company does not commence its business within a year from its incorporation or suspends its business for a whole year, ...
> (f) the company is unable to pay its debts,
> (fa) at the time at which a moratorium for the company under section 1A comes to an end, no voluntary arrangement approved under Part I has effect in relation to the company.
> (g) the court is of the opinion that it is just and equitable that the company should be wound up.'

In addition, the Secretary of State may petition for winding up on the grounds of public interest (s. 124A).

The principal grounds on which a company may be wound up by the court are:

- the company is unable to pay its debts (s. 122(1)(f)); and
- the court is of the opinion that it is just and equitable that the company should be wound up (s. 122(1)(g)).

Creditors typically present a petition seeking a winding up on the first ground whereas minority shareholders typically seek a winding up on the second ground.

2.3 Insolvent winding up

The focus of this chapter is insolvent winding up, which can be either voluntary or compulsory. A company is insolvent when it is unable to pay its debts. What is meant by 'unable to pay its debts' is a much debated question. A number of situations in which a company will be deemed to be unable to pay its debts are set out in s. 123(1) and (2). The winding up of an insolvent company is commenced either by the company itself passing a special resolution to commence a creditors' voluntary winding up or by a winding up petition being presented to the court, most commonly by a creditor who is owed £750 or more and has served an unpaid statutory demand on the company (s. 123(1)(a)), or a creditor who has secured a judgment for any sum owed to him and execution of that judgment has failed (s. 123(1)(b)).

2.4 Commencement of winding up

A voluntary winding up is deemed to commence at the time of the passing of the resolution for voluntary winding up (section 86) and an involuntary winding up is in almost all cases deemed to commence at the time of the presentation of the petition for winding up (s. 129(2)).

2.5 Effects of a winding up order or appointment of a liquidator

Once a winding up order has been made (in a compulsory winding up), or a liquidator has been put in place (in a creditors' voluntary winding up):

- The powers of the board of directors cease.
- No person may commence or continue any legal actions against the company without the leave of the court.
- Control of the assets of the company passes to the liquidator.

In a compulsory winding up, the initial liquidator is the official receiver. The liquidator exercises statutory powers as an agent for the company (*Knowles v Scott* [1891] 1 Ch 717).

2.6 Role of the liquidator

The liquidator's role is to collect or 'get in' the assets, convert them into cash and distribute the proceeds in satisfaction of the company's liabilities **pari passu**. *Pari passu* means that the money available for distribution will be paid to creditors in proportion to the size of their valid (known as 'admitted') claims against the company. This principle cannot be excluded by contract but it does have a number of exceptions.

Company A Ltd (in liquidation) has admitted unsecured creditor claims of £2,000 made up of £500 owed to each of B, C, D and E. The liquidator gets in all the company's assets and realises only £1,000. Ignoring expenses and in the absence of preferential and secured creditors, the £1,000 will be distributed *pari passu*, or 'rateably' among the unsecured creditors, by paying £250 to each of B, C, D and E. This is referred to as '50 pence in the pound'. The amount received per pound is

CASE EXAMPLE 9.1 continued

arrived at by dividing the sum available to distribute by the total sum owing, 1,000/2000 = 0.5 or 50 pence per pound. If B, C, D and E had been owed £1,000 each, they still would have received £250 each but this would be 25 pence in the pound arrived at by dividing the £1000 available for distribution by the £4,000 owed.

CASE EXAMPLE 9.2

Company F Ltd (in liquidation) has admitted unsecured creditor claims of £2,000 made up of £1,000 owed to G, £500 owed to H and £250 owed to each of I and J. The liquidator gets in all the company's assets and realises only £1,000. Ignoring expenses and in the absence of preferential and secured creditors, that £1,000 will be distributed *pari passu*, or 'rateably', among the unsecured creditors as follows:

Creditor	Is owed £	Receives £
G	1000	500
H	500	250
I	250	125
J	250	125
Total	2000	1000

This is referred to as a payment of '50 pence in the pound'.

Pari passu is not applied to the combined claims of secured and unsecured creditors because secured creditors have property rights, or 'rights *in rem*', in relation to property in the possession of the company. The existence of creditor property rights in the company's property means that the liquidator must take the property to which those rights attach out of the company's general assets and distribute them between holders of property rights in those assets: the secured creditors. The statutory order of distribution of assets that must be applied by a liquidator in an insolvent winding up is considered later in this chapter.

Collecting in the assets includes:

- bringing any actions vested in the company, such as actions for breach of contract against a third party;
- disclaiming onerous contracts and property (Insolvency Act 1986 ss. 178–182);
- avoiding specific types of transactions that can be avoided pursuant to the Insolvency Act 1986 (ss. 238, 239, 244 and 245);
- making applications to recover contributions from officers and others pursuant to the Insolvency Act 1986 (ss. 212–214).

These matters are considered in detail in the following sections.

TEST YOUR KNOWLEDGE 19.1

(a) What are the two types of voluntary winding up and how are they commenced?
(b) Name the two principal grounds on which a court may make a compulsory winding up order.
(c) When are a voluntary and involuntary winding up deemed to commence?

3 Property not available to a liquidator

If somebody other than the company has a proprietary interest in property or assets in the possession of the company, that property will not be available to the liquidator to the extent of the third party's proprietary interest.

3.1 Property or assets subject to fixed charges

Property or assets subject to fixed charges are outside the statutory order of distribution. The fixed charge holding creditor is entitled to take possession of the charged asset, sell it and take from the proceeds of sale what is owed to him and expenses (the additional amounts the proceeds may be used to meet will usually be stated in the charge or loan document). If the asset is insufficient to pay the sum secured, the charge holder will, unless he has a second security, become an unsecured creditor for the outstanding amount of his debt.

It is common for banks to take a fixed charge in relation to specific assets and a floating charge on a broad range of the company's assets in which event, if the specific assets do not provide enough money to pay the sum owed to the bank, the bank becomes a floating charge holding secured creditor for the remainder. If, however, the proceeds of sale exceed the sums due to the fixed charge holder, the surplus amount must be paid to the liquidator.

3.2 Property or assets subject to retention of title

A simple **retention of title clause** is a clause in a contract of sale between a seller and buyer (the company) which specifies that legal title, i.e., ownership, of the goods sold shall not pass to the buyer/company until the goods have been paid for.

In its most simple form such a clause is effective and relatively unproblematic. If a company goes into liquidation at a time when goods have been delivered to it but it has not paid for those goods, the goods are not owned by the company, but remain the property of the seller who is entitled to recover the goods from the liquidator: i.e. the goods do not form part of the property of the company for distribution to creditors. A liquidator will release such goods provided they can be shown to have been supplied on terms that include an enforceable retention of title clause and the invoice for them has not been paid. It is in these circumstances that arguments often arise about the precise terms of the contract of sale.

Retention of title clauses are often more complex than that considered immediately above. The buyer/company is often given power in the sale contract to sell the goods or use them to manufacture other products and the retention of title clause purports to establish proprietary interest in the proceeds of sale or in the products produced using the original goods.

Essentially, if the goods have been mixed with other goods or materials to produce a product and/or effort has been expended by the buyer/company in producing the new product, the seller is unlikely to be able to claim the product. It may be able to claim them if they remain recognisable or can be detached from the other goods, but unless this is the case, or the clause has been registered under the Companies Act 2006 as a charge which covers the new products, the seller's claim will fail (*Re Peachdart Ltd* [1984] Ch 131 and *Borden (UK) Ltd v Scottish Timber Products Ltd* [1979] 3 All ER 961).

Similarly, a clause which purports to establish a claim to the proceeds of sale of goods that have been resold is likely to be treated as a charge on book debts which is void unless registered under the Companies Act 2006. Note that the *Romalpa Case* (*Aluminium Industrie Vaassen BV v Romalpa Aluminium* [1976] 2 All ER 552) is not authority for the proposition that proceeds of sale may be recovered pursuant to such a clause. Although the proceeds were recovered in that case, the Court of Appeal did not consider the specific issue.

3.3 Property or assets held on trust

Property or assets impressed with a trust, including a constructive trust, are not property of the company and are not available to the liquidator for distribution. When assets are held by the company on express trust, the position should be clear. Sometimes, however, the court uses the concept of constructive trust as a remedial device which means that it is not always clear whether particular property is subject to a constructive trust or not: the proprietary interest of a third party is not acknowledged until the issue has been argued in the court, often between the liquidator and the third party claiming the proprietary interest. This is a very complex area of law that is evolving and remains uncertain.

> **TEST YOUR KNOWLEDGE 19.2**
>
> (a) Is property subject to a floating charge available to a liquidator for distribution?
> (b) What is a retention of title clause?
> (c) Can a supplier rely on a retention of title clause in a supply contract to claim from a liquidator the proceeds of resale of goods it has supplied to the company but not been paid for?
> (d) Is property impressed with a trust available to a liquidator for distribution?

4 Order of distribution of the assets

Having got in the assets and realised them, the role of the liquidator is to distribute the assets among the creditors and (if any money is left) the shareholders, in accordance with the statutory order of distribution.

The order in which a liquidator is required to distribute the proceeds of sale of the property of an insolvent company, the 'statutory order of distribution' is governed by:

- Insolvency Act 1986, principally ss. 115, 175, 176A and 386 and Sch. 6 (as amended);
- Companies Act 2006, s. 1282;
- Insolvency Rules 1986 (SI 1986/1925) (also as amended);
- Insolvency Act 1986 (Prescribed Part) Order 2003 (SI 2003/2097).

The order of payment resulting from these provisions is shown in Table 19.1.

TABLE 19.1 Statutory order of distribution on an insolvent winding up

Expenses of liquidation
Preferential debts *pari passu*
Debts secured by floating charges put in place before 15 September 2003 to be paid out of the proceeds of the property subject to the charges
Prescribed part of the proceeds of sale of property subject to floating charges put in place on or after 15 September 2003 to be set aside for unsecured creditors
Debts secured by floating charges put in place on or after 15 September 2003 to be paid out of the proceeds of the property subject to the charges
Ordinary unsecured creditors *pari passu*
Deferred creditors *pari passu*
Shareholders (the 'shareholder last' principle)

Significant changes introduced by s. 251 of the Enterprise Act 2002 were brought into effect on 15 September 2003 (which explains why this date appears in the list above). Essentially, in relation to floating charges entered into on or after 15 September 2003 only, in return for changes that were good for floating charge holders (including reducing the range of preferential debts), the proceeds that would otherwise be available to floating charge holders are subject to deduction of a 'prescribed part' to be set aside for the benefit of unsecured creditors (Insolvency Act 1986, s. 176A).

Calculation of the prescribed part is governed by the Prescribed Part Order referenced above. The prescribed part is calculated by taking:

- 50 per cent of the first £10,000 net assets of the company; and
- 20 per cent of any net assets of the company exceeding £10,000;
- subject to the prescribed part not exceeding £600,000.

Net assets of the company for these purposes means the sum remaining after payment of liquidation expenses and preferential debts. Neither fixed nor floating charge holders are permitted to participate in the prescribed part in respect of any unsecured part of their debts *(Re Permacell Finesse Limited (in liquidation)* [2008] BCC 208 (floating charge holder) and *Re Airbase (UK) Limited* [2008] EWHC 124 (Ch) (fixed and floating charge holder), unless they surrender their entire security and participate in the winding up as an unsecured creditor *(PAL SC Realisations 2007 Ltd v Inflexion Fund 2 Limited Partnership* [2010] EWHC 2850). The fixed and floating charge holders will be counted as an unsecured creditor for the purposes of sharing any non-prescribed part of the remaining distributable funds.

If more than one charge exists in relation to company property, a liquidator must work out the priority of the charges as this will affect the order of distribution. You should refresh your knowledge of fixed and floating charges from chapter 10 before attempting the following question.

TEST YOUR KNOWLEDGE 19.3

Assuming that each has been properly registered, put the following charges over the specified assets of Company B Ltd in order of priority:

	Charge	Date created
1	Floating charge over all assets	1 January 2004
2	Floating charge over car fleet	1 January 2005
3	Fixed charge over freehold premises	1 January 2006
4	Floating charge over freehold premises	1 January 2007

Remember that you only need to prioritise charges attached to the same property.

5 Company dissolution

A company (i.e. the separate corporate personality) continues to exist throughout the winding up process. A company ceases to exist only by the act of removal of the name of the company from the register at Companies House (Insolvency Act 1986, ss. 201ff). Removal from the register is the point of dissolution of the company. All legal relationships the company has with any person, including its shareholders, are terminated on dissolution. If the company owns any property on dissolution the property passes to the Crown as **bona vacantia** (Companies Act 2006, s. 1012).

Dissolution does not solely occur following a winding up. Winding up is an expensive process and is often avoided for that very reason. Removal from the register may take place:

- By the Registrar of Companies striking the company off the register after an advertisement in *The Gazette*. The Registrar may exercise this administrative power if his enquiries suggest the company has ceased to carry on business (Companies Act 2006, s. 1000).
- By the Registrar of Companies if he has reasonable cause to believe that no liquidator is acting or the affairs of the company have been fully wound up and required returns have not been made for six months (Companies Act 2006, s. 1001).
- On application by the company three months after publication of the application to remove in *The Gazette* (Companies Act 2006, s. 1003).
- Automatically, three months after the Registrar of Companies has been notified a voluntary winding up procedure is complete (Insolvency Act 1986, s. 201).
- Automatically, three months after the Registrar of Companies has been notified a compulsory winding up procedure is complete (Insolvency Act 1986, s. 205).

- Automatically, three months after application by the official receiver (who is the liquidator of the company) for early dissolution because it appears to him that (i) the realisable assets of the company are insufficient to cover the expenses of liquidation and (ii) no further investigation into the company is necessary (Insolvency Act 1986, s. 202).
- On completion of administration: three months after notification to the Registrar by an administrator that there is nothing to distribute to creditors (Insolvency Act 1986, Schedule B1, para. 84(6)).
- By order of the court in relation to various circumstances such as reconstructions and amalgamations (Companies Act 2006, s. 900(2)(d)).
- Pursuant to an Act of Parliament such as an Act providing for the takeover of one bank by another or a merger of banks.

In limited circumstances, a company that has been removed from the register may be restored (Companies Act 2006 ss. 1024–1042). In addition to administrative restoration to reverse a striking-off by the Registrar pursuant to ss. 1000 and 1001 (s. 1024), a court may, on application within six years of removal, order restoration to enable legal proceedings for damages for death or personal injury to be brought against the company (ss. 1029 and 1030). The general effect of an order by the court for restoration to the register is that the company is deemed to have continued in existence as if it had not been removed from the register (s. 1032). This step is sometimes necessary to access liability insurance cover of the dissolved company.

TEST YOUR KNOWLEDGE 19.4

(a) When does a company cease to exist?
(b) Identify nine situations resulting in the removal of the name of a company from the register.
(c) Why might it be appropriate for a company to be restored to the register?
(d) What is the effect of a court order for restoration?

6 Prohibition on the re-use of insolvent company names

Section 216 of the Insolvency Act 1986 prohibits a person who was a director of a company that has gone into insolvent liquidation from being a director of, or otherwise being involved in the following five years in the management of, a company or a business with a prohibited name. A prohibited name is a name so similar to the name by which the insolvent company was known as to suggest an association with the insolvent company. The name by which a company is or was known for these purposes may be either its company name or its business name.

A person who contravenes s. 216 is criminally liable and may be imprisoned or fined, or both. Section 217 renders the director personally liable, jointly and severally with the company, for all the debts and liabilities of the new company or business incurred whilst he was involved with it in contravention of s. 216. Sections 216 and 217 are drafted to apply broadly. Customers do not have to have been deceived or misled nor is it necessary to show that assets have been transferred between the relevant companies. The sections impose personal liability beyond the morally culpable 'phoenix syndrome' scenario.

In *Ad Valorem Factors Ltd v Ricketts* [2004] 1 All ER 894 (CA), Mummery LJ gave guidance as to how a court will go about deciding whether or not a name is a prohibited name for s. 216 purposes and rejected arguments that sections 216 and 217 should be given a purposive interpretation to narrow their range of application.

CASE LAW 19.1

***Ad Valorem Factors Ltd v Ricketts* [2004] 1 All ER 894 (CA)**

The defendant had been a director of Air Component Co Ltd, which had gone into insolvent liquidation. He was then a director of Air Equipment Co Ltd and it also went into insolvent liquidation. An assignee of a debt owed to Air Equipment Co Ltd sought to recover the debt from the defendant on the basis that the name of the second company was a prohibited name within s. 216 of the Insolvency Act 1986 and that therefore the defendant was personally liable for the debts of the second company pursuant to s. 217.

Held: The second company name was so similar to the name by which the insolvent company was known as to suggest an association with the first company and was therefore a prohibited name. Mummery LJ stated:

'It is necessary, of course, to make a comparison of the names of the two companies in the context of all the circumstances in which they were actually used or likely to be used: the types of product dealt in, the locations of the business, the types of customers dealing with the companies and those involved in the operations of the two companies'.

That being the conclusion, the court had no discretion to exercise and the director was personally liable for the debts of the second company. This was so even if the second company was not a 'phoenix syndrome' case.

Mummery LJ's rejection in *Ad Valorem Factors Ltd* of a purposive interpretation to narrow the range of application of sections 216 and 217 has been confirmed in a number of subsequent cases. In *First Independent Factors and Finance Ltd v Mountford* [2008] 2 BCLC 297, for example, Lewison J stated:

'In my judgment it is not a permissible method of interpreting the rule to allow the ill-defined metaphorical idea of a "phoenix" to distort the meaning of the rule. As the Court of Appeal pointed out in *Ricketts v Ad Valorem Factors Ltd*, the statute ... should not be given a distorted interpretation in order to confine it to "phoenix cases"'.

STOP AND THINK 19.1

The **phoenix syndrome** describes the setting up of a company with a similar name to, and running essentially the same business that had been run by, a company that has gone into insolvent liquidation having run up significant debts, its assets having been transferred to the second company. The imagery is of a new company arising out of the flames of its financially burnt-out predecessor. Businessmen who engage in this behaviour have little respect for the creditors (including consumers) of the companies they sequentially set up and abandon and are said to exploit the privileges of limited liability. Section 216 is part of the response of the law to the phenomenon of phoenix companies, though it is of more general application.

TEST YOUR KNOWLEDGE 19.5

(a) What is a prohibited name for the purposes of s. 216 Companies Act 2006?
(b) What are the consequences of contravention of s. 216?
(c) To what situation is the term 'phoenix syndrome' applied?
(d) Why is s. 216 not restricted to phoenix syndrome scenarios?

7 Disclaiming onerous property

The Insolvency Act 1986, ss. 178–182 permit a liquidator to disclaim onerous property. The definition of onerous property for these purposes is set out in s. 178(3). It includes:

- 'any unprofitable contract'; and
- 'any other property of the company which is unsaleable or not readily saleable or is such that it may give rise to liability to pay money or perform any other onerous act.'

The act of disclaiming, effected by service of a notice and which is not lost by the taking of possession of property by the liquidator or the passage of time, brings to an end, from the date of the disclaimer, the rights, interests and liabilities of the company in or in respect of the property disclaimed. Any person who suffers a loss or damage as a result of the disclaimer is deemed a creditor of the company to the extent of the loss or damage and may prove for that loss or damage in the winding up.

The leading cases on what is and what is not an unprofitable contract are *Re SSSL Realisations (2002) Ltd* [2007] 1 BCLC 29 and *Re Celtic Extraction Ltd* [1999] 2 BCLC 555 which make it clear that the test for disclaimer is not financial disadvantage. The question to be asked is whether or not continued performance of the contract may be detrimental to creditors – the continuation of the contract must not prefer one prospective creditor (the other party to the contract) to other creditors because monies are, in effect, appropriated to them.

8 Challenging pre-liquidation transactions

Fair dealing provisions in the Insolvency Act 1986 permit a liquidator (or administrator) to reverse certain transactions regarded by the law to be detrimental to creditors and the collective nature of the winding up process because they undermine the *pari passu* principle. The power of the court to make orders in relation to some of these arrangements is very wide, going beyond the power to set aside a transaction. In relation to extortionate credit transactions, for example, the court has the option to order that the transaction remain in place but with varied terms.

The transactions examined in this part of the chapter are 'pre-liquidation' transactions entered into up to two years before the winding up commences. The Insolvency Act 1986 classifies these transactions into four types:

- transactions at an undervalue (s. 238);
- preferences (s. 239);
- invalid floating charges (s. 245); and
- extortionate credit transactions (s. 244).

The statutory provisions protect creditors by legally overriding attempts, in the run-up to a winding up, by directors and major shareholders of a company, to put particular persons (individuals or companies) in a more advantageous position than that in which they would otherwise find themselves. The person intended to benefit from the arrangement in question may be a director or major shareholder of the company or, as is often the case, a person who is related or linked in some way to a director or major shareholder. In relation to three of the four types of arrangements, the statute uses the 'connected person' concept to make it easier to successfully challenge an arrangement benefiting a person connected with the company.

Each type of transaction is dealt with below, followed by an examination of the concept of a 'connected person'.

8.1 Transactions at an undervalue (s. 238)

The liquidator (or administrator) may apply to the court for an order and the court may make 'such order as it thinks fit for restoring the position to what it would have been if the company had not entered into' a transaction at an undervalue (TUV) with any person. Transaction at an undervalue is defined in s. 238(4):

'a company enters into a transaction with a person at an undervalue if –
(a) the company makes a gift to that person or otherwise enters into a transaction with a person on terms that provide for the company to receive no consideration, or
(b) the company enters into a transaction with that person for a consideration the value of which, in money or money's worth, is significantly less than the value, in money or money's worth, of the consideration provided by the company.'

In the only House of Lords decision, *Philips v Brewin Dolphin Bell Lawrie Ltd* [2001] 1 WLR 143, Lord Scott regarded as useful the following breakdown of the statutory requirement provided by Millet J when analysing the requirements of s. 238(4)(b) in *Re MC Bacon Ltd* [1990] BCLC 324 at 340.

'To come within that paragraph the transaction must be
(i)   entered into by the company;
(ii) for a consideration;
(iii) the value of which measured in money or money's worth;
(iv) is significantly less than the value;
(v)   also measured in money or money's worth;
(vi) of the consideration provided by the company.'

A classic example of a transaction at an undervalue as defined in s. 238(4) would be the sale by a company of an executive BMW company car with a second hand market value of £40,000, to a director or, indeed, to any person, for, let us say, £10,000. Gifts are also regarded as transactions at an undervalue so that if the BMW car were given to somebody, the gift would also be vulnerable to challenge under s. 238. Before the 1986 Act, transactions at an undervalue were regulated as 'fraudulent conveyances' but the new terminology makes it clear that it is not necessary to prove fraud.

How much, you may ask, would have to be paid for the BMW car in our example for the sum paid to fall outside the language 'significantly less than the value' of the car and the transaction not to be open to challenge as a transaction at an undervalue? No clear rule of thumb is stated in the sparse case law on s. 238. Whilst the specific issue of what proportionate shortfall in value amounts to a significant undervalue was not discussed in *Philips v Brewin Dolphin Bell Lawrie* Ltd [2001] 1 WLR 143, the transaction in that case was held to be at an undervalue where the consideration receivable by the company was approximately 60 per cent of the value of the consideration given by the company.

Lord Scott of Foscote focused on the importance of valuing consideration at a realistic appraisal of actual value rather than a speculative estimate of value. This was important because part of the consideration given to the company in the case was the value of another agreement, which had to be ascertained. The 'collateral' contract was described as being 'a precarious thing' at the time the transaction was entered into, and its value 'speculative'. Where the consideration offered is speculative and precarious, the House of Lords held that it is for the party seeking to rely on the value to prove it.

Even if a transaction is at an undervalue, the liquidator must establish two further conditions to successfully challenge a transaction under s. 238:

- The transaction must have been entered into at a relevant time which means within the two years ending with the commencement of the insolvency (which in most cases means the presentation of the winding-up petition to the court); and
- At the time the transaction was entered into the company must have been unable to pay its debts as they fell due or to have become unable to do so as a result of the transaction.

Finally, even if the liquidator can establish these two conditions, no order will be made if the court is satisfied that s. 238(5) applies and the company entered into the transaction:

- in good faith;
- for the purpose of carrying on its business; and
- reasonable grounds existed for believing that the transaction would benefit the company.

At this point, however, it is for the party seeking to rely on s. 238(5) to resist the making of an order, to prove that the requirements of s. 238(5) are satisfied.

If the transaction is entered into with a connected person (a concept examined in detail below), the requirement that at the time the transaction was entered into the company must have been unable to pay its debts as they fell due, or to have become unable to do so as a result of the transaction, is assumed to have been satisfied and the burden of proof, to show that at the time of the transaction the company was solvent, lies with the party resisting the order.

It is noteworthy that a transaction at an undervalue can sometimes be challenged under s. 423 of the Insolvency Act as a transaction defrauding creditors.

TEST YOUR KNOWLEDGE 19.6

(a) What is a transfer at an undervalue?
(b) What is the relevant time for the purposes of a liquidator challenging a TUV?
(c) Is it always necessary for a liquidator to establish that the company was insolvent at the time the TUV was entered into or became insolvent as a result of entering into the TUV?
(d) What is the statutory defence available to a company that has otherwise entered into a challengable TUV?

8.2 Preferences (s. 239)

The conditions for a liquidator's successful application under s. 239 are as follows:

Factual preference

The company must have given a factual preference. This has two dimensions:

- Person dimension: the preference must have been given to a creditor, surety or guarantor of the company.
- Effect dimension: the preference must have put that person in a better position in the event of insolvent liquidation.

An example of a factual preference is the granting of a charge to an unsecured creditor, whether that charge is fixed or floating, for no consideration. Another example is the premature repayment of an unsecured loan (*Re Exchange Travel Ltd (No. 3)* [1996] 2 BCLC 524 and *Wills v Corfe Joinery Ltd* [1998] 2 BCLC 75). Unsurprisingly, the debt is often due to a director.

Relevant time

The preference must have been granted at a relevant time. Relevant time has two dimensions:

- Temporal dimension: the preference must have been given within two years for a connected person, six months for others, of the commencement of insolvency.
- Financial dimension: the company must have been insolvent at the time of the grant or have become insolvent as a result of the grant.

Insolvency commences on the presenting of a petition in a compulsory winding up and on the passing of the winding up resolution in a voluntary winding up.

Desire

In granting the preference, the company must have been influenced by a desire to put the preferred person in a better position in the event of the company going into insolvent liquidation. Two key points to remember are:

- Desire is presumed to have existed if the preference has been granted to a connected person. It can, however, be rebutted (*Re Fairway Magazines Ltd* [1993] BCLC 643).
- We do not desire every necessary consequence of our actions (*Re MC Bacon Ltd* [1990] BCLC 324, especially *per* Millet J (as he then was):

  'A man is taken to intend the necessary consequences of his actions, so that an intention to grant a security to a creditor necessarily involves an intention to prefer that creditor ...

A man is not to be taken as desiring all the necessary consequences of his actions. Some consequences may be of advantage to him and be desired by him; others may not affect him and be matters of indifference to him; while still others may be positively disadvantageous to him and not be desired by him, but regarded by him as the unavoidable price of obtaining the desired advantages... a transaction will not be set aside... unless the company positively wished to improve the creditor's position in... liquidation').

Re MC Bacon Ltd [1990] BCLC 324

A company with an unsecured overdraft facility was trading near to its overdraft limit when it lost a major customer. The company's bank demanded a fixed and floating charge security for existing unsecured liabilities on the overdraft and any future advances as a pre-condition to continuing support. The company's directors caused the company to grant security in response to the bank's demands. The liquidator applied to set aside the Bank's security under s. 239.

Held *per* Millett J: The company had not been 'influenced by a desire' to prefer the bank. The company/directors desired to do everything necessary to stay in business and turn the company around. Their thinking was, either we give the bank security or they call in the overdraft. The preference was therefore the 'unavoidable price of obtaining the desired advantages'. The company directors did not positively wish to improve the bank's position.

Consequences

The liquidator may apply for such order as the court thinks fit for restoring the position to the pre-preference position. Unlike a transfer at an undervalue, a voidable preference need not diminish the assets of the company. The reason why the preference is unacceptable is because it undermines the *pari passu* principle. Where the preference is a release from an obligation, such as a guarantee, the court may order that a person is under a new or revived guarantee obligation. Where the preference is the grant of a charge, the court will often set aside the charge and when a creditor has been repaid early, the court will order that the sum be paid back to the company with the creditor left to prove for the debt in the winding up.

TEST YOUR KNOWLEDGE 19.7

(a) To whom must a preference have been given for it to be challengeable?
(b) What is the essential ingredient of a preference for the purposes of s. 239?
(c) What are the relevant times for the purposes of s. 239 and why is there more than one time period?
(d) Explain the concept of 'desire' in relation to a s. 239 preference and contrast it with intention.

8.3 Invalid floating charges (s. 245)

Section 245 enables a liquidator to avoid a floating charge in certain defined circumstances. No application to the court is required. The circumstances bringing a floating charge within s. 245 are as follows:

Floating charges

Section 245 is relevant only if a floating charge has been granted. Remember that a charge called a fixed or specific charge on its face may, in reality, be a floating charge and therefore challengeable (see *Re Spectrum Plus*). A fixed charge (in substance) cannot be challenged pursuant to s. 245. A floating charge may also be challenged in a s. 239 application.

Relevant time

The floating charge must have been granted at a relevant time. Relevant time has two dimensions:

- Temporal dimension: the preference must have been given within two years for a connected person, 12 months for others, of the commencement of insolvency.
- Financial dimension: the company must have been insolvent at the time of the grant or have become insolvent as a result of the grant unless the floating charge is granted in favour of a connected person in which case insolvency at the time of the grant is not relevant.

Consequences

A floating charge falling within s. 245 is invalid except as to money paid or goods and services supplied to the company at the same time as, or after the creation of the charge (s. 245(2)). The meaning of this subsection has been explored in cases involving:

- Overdraft facilities: where a floating charge is granted to secure an overdraft facility and money has been paid in and out of the account both before and after the grant (such as *Re Yeovil Glove Co Ltd* [1965] Ch 148).
- 'Structured transactions': where money is paid in the context of transactions deliberately structured to appear as if money has been paid on or after creation of the charge. In these cases the court looks at the substance of the transaction, not simply the form (see, for example, *Re GT Whyte & Co Ltd* [1983] BCLC 311).

CASE LAW 19.3

***Re Yeovil Glove Co Ltd* [1965] Ch 148**

The company's bank extended an overdraft facility to it on 1 February 2006. On 1 August 2006, when the company was already overdrawn by £50,000, it granted a floating charge to its bank as security for sums advanced both in the past and to be advanced in the future. After 1 August 2006, the bank made further advances totalling £50,000 to the company and the company paid £70,000 into the account.

The winding up of the company was commenced on 1 December 2006 at which point the balance on the overdraft stood at £30,000 overdrawn (£50,000 + £50,000 less £70,000). The question arose whether that £30,000 represented pre-charge advances, post-charge advances or a combination of the two.

Held: The court applied *Clayton's* case ('first in, first out') to movements on the bank account, so that payments into the account were treated as repaying advances in the order in which those advances had been made, that is, the earliest advances were deemed to be repaid to the bank first. On the simplified facts above, the post-charge repayments (£70,000) were treated as repaying the first £70,000 of advances which covered all pre-charge unsecured advances and £20,000 of the post-charge advances. It followed that the £30,000 outstanding to the bank was lent to the company after the creation of the charge and therefore s. 245 did not make the floating charge void to that extent, it being 'money paid ... after the creation of the charge' within s. 245(2). Note that the facts have been simplified in the extreme for the purposes of this case summary.

CASE LAW 19.4

***Re GT Whyte & Co Ltd* [1983] BCLC 311**

The company's bank made an unsecured loan to the company. Later, when the company was close to being wound up, the bank demanded repayment in full. The company repaid the loan out of the little cash it had remaining and immediately borrowed the money from the bank again but this time on a secured basis: the company granted the bank a floating charge to secure the sum lent. In form, the money had been paid at the same time as the creation of the charge. Held: The floating charge was set aside. The intention of the company was not relevant to s. 245. In substance, the transaction simply involved the substitution of an unsecured loan by a secured loan and as no new money had been paid, the sum was not money paid on or after the creation of the charge.

The effect of the grant of late security on unsecured creditors is illustrated in Figure 19.1.

- Each creditor is owed £20,000. 5 × £20,000 = £100,000
- Company X goes into insolvent liquidation with assets of £50,000
- Each creditor receives £10,000 (50 pence in the pound): 'pari passu'

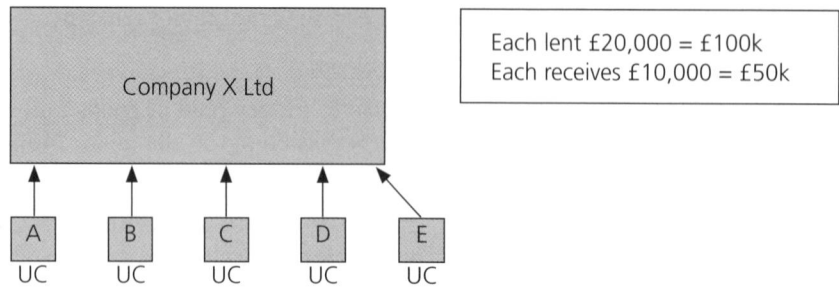

Three months before the winding up of Company X Ltd commences, a floating charge is granted to E

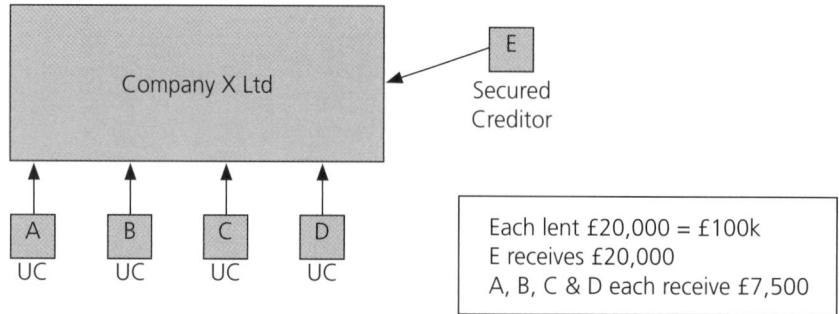

- E now receives £20,000 first
- A, B, C & D now each receive only £7,500 (30/80 × £20,000)
- The liquidator will examine the circumstance of the grant of the floating charge to see if it is void to any extent pursuant to s. 245

FIGURE 19.1 The effect of grant of a late security on unsecured creditors and distribution of the company's assets in a winding up

 **TEST YOUR KNOWLEDGE 19.8**

(a) Does a liquidator apply to the court to challenge a floating charge under s. 245?
(b) What are the relevant times for the purposes of s. 245 and why are they not the same as for s. 239?
(c) Is it always necessary for a liquidator to establish that the company was insolvent at the time the charge was entered into?
(d) To what extent is a floating charge avoided under s. 245?

8.4 Extortionate credit transactions (s. 244)

In addition to the three avoidance provisions dealt with above, where a company, within three years of the commencement of its winding up, has been a party to a transaction involving the provision of credit to the company, or still is a party to such, the liquidator may apply to the court for an order if the transaction is or was extortionate. The concept of connected persons is not used in this provision. The test to determine whether or not a transaction is or was extortionate is contained in s. 244(3).

'(3) For the purposes of this section a transaction is extortionate if, having regard to the risk accepted by the person providing the credit –
   (a) the terms of it are or were such as to require grossly exorbitant payments to be made (whether unconditionally or in certain contingencies) in respect of the provision of the credit, or
   (b) it otherwise grossly contravened ordinary principles of fair dealing and it shall be presumed, unless the contrary is proved, that a transaction with respect to which an application is made, under this section is or, as the case may be, was extortionate.'

Note that the burden of proof is reversed, being placed on the party arguing that the transaction is not extortionate. Details of how this section works can be found in insolvency law textbooks.

8.5 Connected persons

As we have seen, the rules governing the avoidance of pre-liquidation transactions apply more strictly where the other party to the transaction is connected to the company. Apart from the time limit being extended (from six or twelve months to two years), the burden of proof may be reversed (for example in relation to proof of the company's solvency at the time of a transaction at an undervalue), or an otherwise required condition may not need to be proved (for example the insolvency of the company at the time a late floating charge is granted).

This tightening of the provisions in relation to connected persons was introduced in 1986 on the recommendation of the Cork Committee following its review of insolvency laws. Consequently, the concept of being connected to a company for the purposes of the avoidance of pre-liquidation transactions is different from, and must not be confused with, the different concept of being connected to a director for the purposes of directors' breaches of duty (which is dealt with in ss. 251–256 of the Companies Act 2006).

Who, then, is a connected person? Section 249 provides that a person is connected with a company if he is:

- a director of the company
- an associate of:
  - the company; or
  - a director of the company.

Director, in this context, includes a shadow director. Connected persons can be represented diagrammatically as in Figure 19.2.

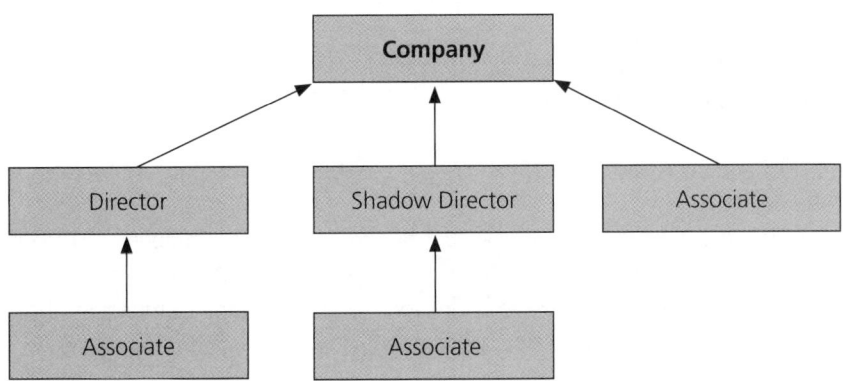

FIGURE 19.2 Connected persons for the purposes of the fair dealing provisions of the Insolvency Act 1986

Although s. 249 is short, it raises the question of the meaning of 'associate'. Associate is defined in s. 435 and, in contrast to s. 249, the definition is detailed and complex. Two key aspects of associate, relative and control, are defined very widely. Unlike the approach taken in other jurisdictions, such as Australia, an attempt is made in s. 435 to define these aspects exhaustively.

Relative, defined in s. 435(8), includes brothers, sisters, uncles, aunts, nephews, nieces, lineal ancestors and descendants, half-blood relationships, adopted and stepchildren, and former spouses. Control, important in deciding both whether or not two companies are associated and whether or not a company is associated with an individual, is essentially 30 per cent voting power over the company (or any company with control over the company), or evidence that the board acts in accordance with instructions (see s. 435(10)).

Table 19.2 conveys some of the complexity of ascertaining whether or not a person is an associate of a company.

TABLE 19.2 Persons who are associates of a company

Company A is an associate of its directors and its directors' associates who are:	Company A is an associate of Company B if:
1 His: ■ Spouse ■ Relatives (very widely defined in s. 435(8)) ■ Relatives' spouses ■ Spouse's relatives ■ Spouse's relatives' spouses ■ Business partners ■ Business partners' relatives ■ Business partners' spouses (not business partners' relatives' spouses!) ■ Employees (note, these are employed by him personally, not the employees of the company of which he is a director) ■ Employers (includes any company of which he is a director or secretary) ■ Beneficiaries (and their associates) of certain trust of which he is a trustee 2 And any: ■ Company controlled by him ■ Company controlled by him together with his associates	■ Both companies are controlled by the same person ■ A person has control of Company A and his associates have control of Company B ■ A person has control of Company A and he and his associates together have control of Company B ■ Both companies are controlled by the same group of persons (for these purposes, any person in a group can be replaced by an associate)

As Table 19.2 indicates, the definition of connected person is far-ranging.

 STOP AND THINK 19.2

Two directors of Company A each own 25 per cent of the shares of Company B. Are Company A and Company B connected?

You may be surprised to learn that Company B is not an associate of Company A. The directors are not associated simply because they are both directors of Company A, and, consequently, the companies are not connected. If, however, the directors, together control Company A, then the two companies are connected because the same group of persons controls both.

9 Swelling the company's assets: personal contributions

The Insolvency Act 1986 provides a liquidator with power to seek orders from the court arising out of a number of types of behaviour, including:

- **misfeasance** by officers of the company (s. 212);
- **wrongful trading** (s. 214); and
- **fraudulent trading** (s. 213).

The objective of the liquidator is usually to obtain funds from individual directors (though it can be from others) to add to the funds of the company available for distribution to creditors.

9.1 Misfeasance proceedings (s. 212)

If it appears to the liquidator that an officer of the company (principally the directors but also the company secretary) has misapplied or retained or become accountable for any money or other property of the company or been guilty of any misfeasance or breach of any fiduciary or other duty in relation to the company, the liquidator may make an application to the court for the conduct of that person to be examined (s. 212). In addition to the liquidator, a creditor or other contributory may also make an application to the court under s. 212 but only with the leave of the court (s. 212(5)). Section 212 is simply a procedural provision enabling the liquidator to bring an underlying cause of action; it does not create any new causes of action.

Many reported cases concerning breaches of directors' duties are s. 212 misfeasance applications by liquidators. The court can compel the officer to repay, restore or account for the money or property or any part of it or contribute such sum to the company's assets by way of compensation as the court thinks just (s. 212(3)). Not being a distinct cause of action, the court in *Re Eurocruit Europe Ltd (In Liquidation)* [2007] EWHC 1433 (Ch) held that a claim under s. 212 does not have a limitation period distinct from the limitation period applicable to the underlying claim.

9.2 Wrongful trading (s. 214)

A liquidator may make an application to the court for an order arising out of wrongful trading by directors (note that company secretaries are not exposed to potential liability under s. 214 unless they also perform the role of director; see below). It is helpful to set out the first three subsections of the wrongful trading section of the Insolvency Act 1986.

'(1) Subject to subsection (3) below, if in the course of the winding up of a company it appears that subsection (2) of this section applies in relation to a person who is or has been a director of the company, the court, on the application of the liquidator, may declare that that person is to be liable to make such contribution (if any) to the company's assets as the court thinks proper.
(2) This subsection applies in relation to a person if:
  (a) the company has gone into insolvent liquidation,
  (b) at some time before the commencement of the winding up, that person knew or ought to have concluded that there was no reasonable prospect that the company would avoid going into insolvent liquidation, and
  (c) that person was a director of the company at that time ...
(3) The court shall not make a declaration under this section with respect to any person if it is satisfied that ... that person took every step with a view to minimising the potential loss to the company's creditors as ... he ought to have taken.'

Sub-section 4 sets out the test to determine whether or not a director ought to have known or concluded or taken steps for the purposes of subsections (2) and (3). The test has been adopted and replicated in s. 174 of the Companies Act 2006 as the test of reasonable care, skill and diligence generally expected of a director.

The main points to note about s. 214 are that only the liquidator may make an application, and the company must be in liquidation and factually insolvent for an application to be successful. Only directors can be made liable, although note that it is expressly provided in the section that director included shadow director (s. 214(7)).

Basically, if a director knew or ought to have concluded that there was no reasonable prospect that the company would avoid going into insolvent liquidation but continued to incur debts, he risks being ordered to make a contribution to the company's assets in a subsequent liquidation. It is not enough that the directors knew or ought to have known that the company was insolvent. Many businesses trade through financially difficult times when they are unable to pay their debts as they fall due to reach financial health at a future date. In *Re Hawkes Hill Publishing Co Ltd* [2007] BCC 937, Lewison J, unwilling to find that the directors had wrongfully traded, stressed that having the opportunity to trade the company to financial good health where the prospect of such is reasonable is particularly important in the early years of a new business: 'picking over the bones of a dead company in a courtroom is not always fair to those who struggled to keep going in the reasonable (but ultimately misplaced) hope that things would get better.'

In determining what facts a director ought to have known, the conclusions he ought to have reached and the steps which he ought to have taken, the test applied is the same as that for determining whether or not there has been a breach of the directors' general duty in s. 174, the duty to exercise reasonable care, skill and diligence (see chapter 12). If proper books and records have not been kept which, if kept, would have shown that there was no reasonable prospect that the company would avoid going into insolvent liquidation, it will be held that a director 'ought to have known'.

It is a defence for a director to show that he took every step he ought to have taken with a view to minimising the potential loss to the company's creditors (s. 214((3)). An example of a situation in which the court could not make an order because s. 214 (3) has been complied with would be where the directors had advised all existing creditors and each potential new creditor of the risks it might be undertaking in advancing credit or further credit.

9.3 Fraudulent trading (s. 213)

Section 213 is not a commonly used provision because of the need to plead and prove fraud. Far more applications are made under s. 214, for wrongful trading.

> '(1) If in the course of the winding up of a company it appears that any business of the company has been carried on with intent to defraud creditors of the company or creditors of any other person, or for any fraudulent purpose, the following has effect.
>
> (2) The court, on the application of the liquidator may declare that any persons who were knowingly parties to the carrying on of the business in the manner above-mentioned are to be liable to make such contributions (if any) to the company's assets as the court thinks proper.'

Points to note in relation to fraudulent trading are that only a liquidator may make an application, liability under the section is not confined to directors; any persons may be required to make a contribution to the company's assets, and actual dishonesty, involving real moral blame, is required (*Re Patrick and Lyon Ltd* [1933] Ch 786). It is not enough to show that the company continued to run up debts when the directors knew it was factually insolvent. There has to be 'intent to defraud creditors' and *Morphitis v Bernasconi and Others* [2003] Ch 552 (CA) establishes that a fraudulent misrepresentation made to a single creditor may not be enough to establish that the business of the company had been carried on with intent to defraud creditors of the company.

CHAPTER SUMMARY

- Two types of winding up exist – voluntary winding up (either members' voluntary winding up (s. 84) or creditors' voluntary winding up (ss. 84 and 90) and compulsory winding up which occurs most commonly when a company is unable to pay its debts (s. 122(1)(f)) or if the court is of the opinion that it is just and equitable that the company should be wound up.
- The main effects of winding up are as follows:
  - the powers of the board cease;
  - the liquidator exercises statutory powers as agent of company, (*Knowles v Scott* (1891));
  - there can be no commencement or continuance of legal action against the company without leave of the court;
  - onerous contracts and property may be disclaimed by the company, ss. 178–182.
- The key duties and powers of liquidator are to 'get in' all assets of the company, convert them to cash and distribute the proceeds, (s. 143(1)).
- Proceeds are to be distributed *pari passu* subject to, in particular:
  - property rights of third parties including secured creditors (distinguish fixed and floating charges);
  - statutory order of distribution.

- Four key types of pre-liquidation transactions can be challenged.
- Transfers at an undervalue (s. 238):
  - liquidator may apply to the court for an order.
  - must establish all elements to succeed:
    - there must be a TUV
    - at a relevant time
      - temporal dimension: two years ending with onset of insolvency; same period for connected persons as any other person.
      - financial dimension: company insolvent at time of transaction or as a result; presumption of insolvency if entered into with a connected person
  - defence: entered into in good faith and reasonable grounds for believing it would benefit the company.
- Preferences (s. 239):
  - liquidator may apply to the court for an order.
  - must establish all elements to succeed:
    - there must be an actual preference;
    - person dimension: company's creditors or surety or guarantor;
    - effect dimension: must have been put in a better position in the event of insolvent liquidation, e.g. fixed or floating charge;
    - at a relevant time:
      - temporal dimension: two years for a connected person; six months for others
      - financial dimension: company insolvent at time or as a result
  - desire: company influenced by a desire to put the person in a better position in the event of the company going into insolvent liquidation: We do not desire every necessary consequence of our actions (*Re MC Bacon Ltd* (1990)). Desire presumed if to a connected person.
- Invalid floating charges (s. 245):
  - liquidator need not apply to court;
  - liquidator may avoid a floating charge if and to the extent it meets certain conditions;
  - must establish all elements to succeed:
  - floating charge granted – note 'fixed charges' may, in reality, be floating charges and therefore challengeable;
  - at a relevant time:
    - Temporal dimension: two years if to a connected person; 12 months if to another
    - Financial dimension: insolvent or becomes so (s. 245(4)), but solvency is not relevant if a connected person.
  - Consequence: floating charge is invalid except as to money paid or goods and service supplied to the company *at the same time as, or after the creation of, the charge (Re Yeovil Glove Co Ltd (1965))*
- Extortionate credit transactions (s. 244): A liquidator may apply to the court for an order if, having regard to the risk, a transaction entered into within three years of the commencement of the winding up (whether the other party is connected to the company or not) provided for grossly exorbitant payments to be made or otherwise grossly contravened ordinary principles of fair dealing.
- Three key provisions relevant to personal liability:
  - misfeasance restorations and contributions (s. 212): essentially enforcement of breaches of directors' duties by application to the court by the liquidator;
  - fraudulent trading contributions (s. 213): available only where there is an 'intent to defraud creditors' (which is narrowly defined) by any persons who were knowingly parties to the carrying on of the business for this purpose;
  - wrongful trading contributions (s. 214): arising from negligence-based liability more broadly available than fraudulent trading but limited to directors.

PART FIVE CASE QUESTIONS

Return to the opening case at the start of this part and re-read it. Think generally about the issues it raises, the law in relation to which has been covered in the chapters in this part, before attempting to answer the following questions.

1. HMRC decides that Vesuvius is not going to agree an acceptable rescheduling of payment of its outstanding taxes. What steps can and should HMRC take?
2. If HMRC petitions the court for a winding up order, could the court make such an order?
3. What if any action could Vesuvius or Nelson take in response to an HMRC winding up petition?
4. What must be established for a floating charge holder to appoint an administrator?
5. If Vesuvius were wound up, what if any property may not be available to the liquidator to distribute to creditors?
6. In what order of distribution would a liquidator distribute the assets of Vesuvius?
7. If Nelson were to lend Vesuvius a further £10 million and secure it by a fixed charge against the stadium, would this charge be effective in the event of a liquidator? (Consider in particular what additional information you may need to give a definite answer to this question).
8. If Vesuvius entered administration, what steps might FoulBrew Ltd take (or wish it had put itself in a position to take) to protect itself?
9. What decisions must an administrator take in relation to the contracts for Vesuvius' players?
10. If, when requested to do so, Vesuvius had granted Home Bank a charge to secure the existing and future overdraft and, two months later, gone into liquidation, by which time the overdraft had increased to £15 million, what steps or actions might a liquidator take in relation to that charge? Consider the situation if the charge were:
    (i) a fixed charge; and
    (ii) a floating charge.

APPENDIX 1
Model Articles for Private Companies by Shares

INDEX TO THE ARTICLES

PART 1
INTERPRETATION AND LIMITATION OF LIABILITY
1. Defined terms
2. Liability of members

PART 2
DIRECTORS
DIRECTORS' POWERS AND RESPONSIBILITIES
3. Directors' general authority
4. Shareholders' reserve power
5. Directors may delegate
6. Committees

DECISION-MAKING BY DIRECTORS
7. Directors to take decisions collectively
8. Unanimous decisions
9. Calling a directors' meeting
10. Participation in directors' meetings
11. Quorum for directors' meetings
12. Chairing of directors' meetings
13. Casting vote
14. Conflicts of interest
15. Records of decisions to be kept
16. Directors' discretion to make further rules

APPOINTMENT OF DIRECTORS
17. Methods of appointing directors
18. Termination of director's appointment
19. Directors' remuneration
20. Directors' expenses

PART 3
SHARES AND DISTRIBUTIONS
SHARES
21. All shares to be fully paid up
22. Powers to issue different classes of share
23. Company not bound by less than absolute interests
24. Share certificates
25. Replacement share certificates
26. Share transfers
27. Transmission of shares
28. Exercise of transmittees' rights
29. Transmittees bound by prior notices

DIVIDENDS AND OTHER DISTRIBUTIONS
30. Procedure for declaring dividends
31. Payment of dividends and other distributions
32. No interest on distributions
33. Unclaimed distributions
34. Non-cash distributions
35. Waiver of distributions

CAPITALISATION OF PROFITS
36. Authority to capitalise and appropriation of capitalised sums

PART 4
DECISION-MAKING BY SHAREHOLDERS
ORGANISATION OF GENERAL MEETINGS
37. Attendance and speaking at general meetings
38. Quorum for general meetings
39. Chairing general meetings
40. Attendance and speaking by directors and non-shareholders
41. Adjournment

VOTING AT GENERAL MEETINGS
42. Voting: general
43. Errors and disputes
44. Poll votes
45. Content of proxy notices
46. Delivery of proxy notices
47. Amendments to resolutions

PART 5
ADMINISTRATIVE ARRANGEMENTS
48. Means of communication to be used
49. Company seals
50. No right to inspect accounts and other records
51. Provision for employees on cessation of business

DIRECTORS' INDEMNITY AND INSURANCE
52. Indemnity
53. Insurance

PART 1 INTERPRETATION AND LIMITATION OF LIABILITY

Defined terms

1. In the articles, unless the context requires otherwise—
    "articles" means the company's articles of association;
    "bankruptcy" includes individual insolvency proceedings in a jurisdiction other than England and Wales or Northern Ireland which have an effect similar to that of bankruptcy;
    "chairman" has the meaning given in article 12;
    "chairman of the meeting" has the meaning given in article 39;
    "Companies Acts" means the Companies Acts (as defined in section 2 of the Companies Act 2006), in so far as they apply to the company;
    "director" means a director of the company, and includes any person occupying the position of director, by whatever name called;
    "distribution recipient" has the meaning given in article 31;
    "document" includes, unless otherwise specified, any document sent or supplied in electronic form;
    "electronic form" has the meaning given in section 1168 of the Companies Act 2006;
    "fully paid" in relation to a share, means that the nominal value and any premium to be paid to the company in respect of that share have been paid to the company;
    "hard copy form" has the meaning given in section 1168 of the Companies Act 2006;
    "holder" in relation to shares means the person whose name is entered in the register of members as the holder of the shares;
    "instrument" means a document in hard copy form;
    "ordinary resolution" has the meaning given in section 282 of the Companies Act 2006;
    "paid" means paid or credited as paid;
    "participate", in relation to a directors' meeting, has the meaning given in article 10;
    "proxy notice" has the meaning given in article 45;
    "shareholder" means a person who is the holder of a share;
    "shares" means shares in the company;
    "special resolution" has the meaning given in section 283 of the Companies Act 2006;
    "subsidiary" has the meaning given in section 1159 of the Companies Act 2006;
    "transmittee" means a person entitled to a share by reason of the death or bankruptcy of a shareholder or otherwise by operation of law; and
    "writing" means the representation or reproduction of words, symbols or other information in a visible form by any method or combination of methods, whether sent or supplied in electronic form or otherwise.
    Unless the context otherwise requires, other words or expressions contained in these articles bear the same meaning as in the Companies Act 2006 as in force on the date when these articles become binding on the company.

Liability of members

2. The liability of the members is limited to the amount, if any, unpaid on the shares held by them.

PART 2 DIRECTORS

DIRECTORS' POWERS AND RESPONSIBILITIES

Directors' general authority

3. Subject to the articles, the directors are responsible for the management of the company's business, for which purpose they may exercise all the powers of the company.

Shareholders' reserve power

4.— (1) The shareholders may, by special resolution, direct the directors to take, or refrain from taking, specified action.

(2) No such special resolution invalidates anything which the directors have done before the passing of the resolution.

Directors may delegate

5.— (1) Subject to the articles, the directors may delegate any of the powers which are conferred on them under the articles—
  (a) to such person or committee;
  (b) by such means (including by power of attorney);
  (c) to such an extent;
  (d) in relation to such matters or territories; and
  (e) on such terms and conditions; as they think fit.

(2) If the directors so specify, any such delegation may authorise further delegation of the directors' powers by any person to whom they are delegated.

(3) The directors may revoke any delegation in whole or part, or alter its terms and conditions.

Committees

6.— (1) Committees to which the directors delegate any of their powers must follow procedures which are based as far as they are applicable on those provisions of the articles which govern the taking of decisions by directors.

(2) The directors may make rules of procedure for all or any committees, which prevail over rules derived from the articles if they are not consistent with them.

DECISION-MAKING BY DIRECTORS

Directors to take decisions collectively

7.— (1) The general rule about decision-making by directors is that any decision of the directors must be either a majority decision at a meeting or a decision taken in accordance with article 8.

(2) If—
  (a) the company only has one director, and
  (b) no provision of the articles requires it to have more than one director, the general rule does not apply, and the director may take decisions without regard to any of the provisions of the articles relating to directors' decision-making.

Unanimous decisions

8.— (1) A decision of the directors is taken in accordance with this article when all eligible directors indicate to each other by any means that they share a common view on a matter.

(2) Such a decision may take the form of a resolution in writing, copies of which have been signed by each eligible director or to which each eligible director has otherwise indicated agreement in writing.

(3) References in this article to eligible directors are to directors who would have been entitled to vote on the matter had it been proposed as a resolution at a directors' meeting.

(4) A decision may not be taken in accordance with this article if the eligible directors would not have formed a quorum at such a meeting.

Calling a directors' meeting

9.— (1) Any director may call a directors' meeting by giving notice of the meeting to the directors or by authorising the company secretary (if any) to give such notice.

(2) Notice of any directors' meeting must indicate—

(a) its proposed date and time;
(b) where it is to take place; and
(c) if it is anticipated that directors participating in the meeting will not be in the same place, how it is proposed that they should communicate with each other during the meeting.

(3) Notice of a directors' meeting must be given to each director, but need not be in writing.

(4) Notice of a directors' meeting need not be given to directors who waive their entitlement to notice of that meeting, by giving notice to that effect to the company not more than 7 days after the date on which the meeting is held. Where such notice is given after the meeting has been held, that does not affect the validity of the meeting, or of any business conducted at it.

Participation in directors' meetings

10.— (1) Subject to the articles, directors participate in a directors' meeting, or part of a directors' meeting, when—
(a) the meeting has been called and takes place in accordance with the articles, and
(b) they can each communicate to the others any information or opinions they have on any particular item of the business of the meeting.

(2) In determining whether directors are participating in a directors' meeting, it is irrelevant where any director is or how they communicate with each other.

(3) If all the directors participating in a meeting are not in the same place, they may decide that the meeting is to be treated as taking place wherever any of them is.

Quorum for directors' meetings

11.—(1) At a directors' meeting, unless a quorum is participating, no proposal is to be voted on, except a proposal to call another meeting.

(2) The quorum for directors' meetings may be fixed from time to time by a decision of the directors, but it must never be less than two, and unless otherwise fixed it is two.

(3) If the total number of directors for the time being is less than the quorum required, the directors must not take any decision other than a decision—
(a) to appoint further directors, or
(b) to call a general meeting so as to enable the shareholders to appoint further directors.

Chairing of directors' meetings

12.—(1) The directors may appoint a director to chair their meetings.
(2) The person so appointed for the time being is known as the chairman.
(3) The directors may terminate the chairman's appointment at any time.
(4) If the chairman is not participating in a directors' meeting within ten minutes of the time at which it was to start, the participating directors must appoint one of themselves to chair it.

Casting vote

13.—(1) If the numbers of votes for and against a proposal are equal, the chairman or other director chairing the meeting has a casting vote.

(2) But this does not apply if, in accordance with the articles, the chairman or other director is not to be counted as participating in the decision-making process for quorum or voting purposes.

Conflicts of interest

14.—(1) If a proposed decision of the directors is concerned with an actual or proposed transaction or arrangement with the company in which a director is interested, that director is not to be counted as participating in the decision-making process for quorum or voting purposes.

(2) But if paragraph (3) applies, a director who is interested in an actual or proposed transaction or arrangement with the company is to be counted as participating in the decision-making process for quorum and voting purposes.

(3) This paragraph applies when—
   (a) the company by ordinary resolution disapplies the provision of the articles which would otherwise prevent a director from being counted as participating in the decision-making process;
   (b) the director's interest cannot reasonably be regarded as likely to give rise to a conflict of interest; or
   (c) the director's conflict of interest arises from a permitted cause.

(4) For the purposes of this article, the following are permitted causes—
   (a) a guarantee given, or to be given, by or to a director in respect of an obligation incurred by or on behalf of the company or any of its subsidiaries;
   (b) subscription, or an agreement to subscribe, for shares or other securities of the company or any of its subsidiaries, or to underwrite, sub-underwrite, or guarantee subscription for any such shares or securities; and
   (c) arrangements pursuant to which benefits are made available to employees and directors or former employees and directors of the company or any of its subsidiaries which do not provide special benefits for directors or former directors.

(5) For the purposes of this article, references to proposed decisions and decision-making processes include any directors' meeting or part of a directors' meeting.

(6) Subject to paragraph (7), if a question arises at a meeting of directors or of a committee of directors as to the right of a director to participate in the meeting (or part of the meeting) for voting or quorum purposes, the question may, before the conclusion of the meeting, be referred to the chairman whose ruling in relation to any director other than the chairman is to be final and conclusive.

(7) If any question as to the right to participate in the meeting (or part of the meeting) should arise in respect of the chairman, the question is to be decided by a decision of the directors at that meeting, for which purpose the chairman is not to be counted as participating in the meeting (or that part of the meeting) for voting or quorum purposes.

Records of decisions to be kept

15. The directors must ensure that the company keeps a record, in writing, for at least 10 years from the date of the decision recorded, of every unanimous or majority decision taken by the directors.

Directors' discretion to make further rules

16. Subject to the articles, the directors may make any rule which they think fit about how they take decisions, and about how such rules are to be recorded or communicated to directors.

APPOINTMENT OF DIRECTORS

Methods of appointing directors

17.—(1) Any person who is willing to act as a director, and is permitted by law to do so, may be appointed to be a director—
   (a) by ordinary resolution, or
   (b) by a decision of the directors.

(2) In any case where, as a result of death, the company has no shareholders and no directors, the personal representatives of the last shareholder to have died have the right, by notice in writing, to appoint a person to be a director.

(3) For the purposes of paragraph (2), where 2 or more shareholders die in circumstances rendering it uncertain who was the last to die, a younger shareholder is deemed to have survived an older shareholder.

Termination of director's appointment

18. A person ceases to be a director as soon as—
  (a) that person ceases to be a director by virtue of any provision of the Companies Act 2006 or is prohibited from being a director by law;
  (b) a bankruptcy order is made against that person;
  (c) a composition is made with that person's creditors generally in satisfaction of that person's debts;
  (d) a registered medical practitioner who is treating that person gives a written opinion to the company stating that that person has become physically or mentally incapable of acting as a director and may remain so for more than three months;
  (e) by reason of that person's mental health, a court makes an order which wholly or partly prevents that person from personally exercising any powers or rights which that person would otherwise have;
  (f) notification is received by the company from the director that the director is resigning from office, and such resignation has taken effect in accordance with its terms.

Directors' remuneration

19.—(1) Directors may undertake any services for the company that the directors decide.
  (2) Directors are entitled to such remuneration as the directors determine—
    (a) for their services to the company as directors, and
    (b) for any other service which they undertake for the company.
  (3) Subject to the articles, a director's remuneration may—
    (a) take any form, and
    (b) include any arrangements in connection with the payment of a pension, allowance or gratuity, or any death, sickness or disability benefits, to or in respect of that director.
  (4) Unless the directors decide otherwise, directors' remuneration accrues from day to day.
  (5) Unless the directors decide otherwise, directors are not accountable to the company for any remuneration which they receive as directors or other officers or employees of the company's subsidiaries or of any other body corporate in which the company is interested.

Directors' expenses

20. The company may pay any reasonable expenses which the directors properly incur in connection with their attendance at—
  (a) meetings of directors or committees of directors,
  (b) general meetings, or
  (c) separate meetings of the holders of any class of shares or of debentures of the company, or otherwise in connection with the exercise of their powers and the discharge of their responsibilities in relation to the company.

PART 3 SHARES AND DISTRIBUTIONS

SHARES

All shares to be fully paid up

21.—(1) No share is to be issued for less than the aggregate of its nominal value and any premium to be paid to the company in consideration for its issue.
  (2) This does not apply to shares taken on the formation of the company by the subscribers to the company's memorandum.

Powers to issue different classes of share

22.—(1) Subject to the articles, but without prejudice to the rights attached to any existing share, the company may issue shares with such rights or restrictions as may be determined by ordinary resolution.

(2) The company may issue shares which are to be redeemed, or are liable to be redeemed at the option of the company or the holder, and the directors may determine the terms, conditions and manner of redemption of any such shares.

Company not bound by less than absolute interests

23. Except as required by law, no person is to be recognised by the company as holding any share upon any trust, and except as otherwise required by law or the articles, the company is not in any way to be bound by or recognise any interest in a share other than the holder's absolute ownership of it and all the rights attaching to it.

Share certificates

24.—(1) The company must issue each shareholder, free of charge, with one or more certificates in respect of the shares which that shareholder holds.
(2) Every certificate must specify—
  (a) in respect of how many shares, of what class, it is issued;
  (b) the nominal value of those shares;
  (c) that the shares are fully paid; and
  (d) any distinguishing numbers assigned to them.
(3) No certificate may be issued in respect of shares of more than one class.
(4) If more than one person holds a share, only one certificate may be issued in respect of it.
(5) Certificates must—
  (a) have affixed to them the company's common seal, or
  (b) be otherwise executed in accordance with the Companies Acts.

Replacement share certificates

25.—(1) If a certificate issued in respect of a shareholder's shares is—
  (a) damaged or defaced, or
  (b) said to be lost, stolen or destroyed, that shareholder is entitled to be issued with a replacement certificate in respect of the same shares.
(2) A shareholder exercising the right to be issued with such a replacement certificate—
  (a) may at the same time exercise the right to be issued with a single certificate or separate certificates;
  (b) must return the certificate which is to be replaced to the company if it is damaged or defaced; and
  (c) must comply with such conditions as to evidence, indemnity and the payment of a reasonable fee as the directors decide.

Share transfers

26.—(1) Shares may be transferred by means of an instrument of transfer in any usual form or any other form approved by the directors, which is executed by or on behalf of the transferor.
(2) No fee may be charged for registering any instrument of transfer or other document relating to or affecting the title to any share.
(3) The company may retain any instrument of transfer which is registered.
(4) The transferor remains the holder of a share until the transferee's name is entered in the register of members as holder of it.
(5) The directors may refuse to register the transfer of a share and, if they do so, the instrument of transfer must be returned to the transferee with the notice of refusal unless they suspect that the proposed transfer may be fraudulent.

Transmission of shares

27.—(1) If title to a share passes to a transmittee, the company may only recognise the transmittee as having any title to that share.
(2) A transmittee who produces such evidence of entitlement to shares as the directors may properly require—

(a) may, subject to the articles, choose either to become the holder of those shares or to have them transferred to another person, and
(b) subject to the articles, and pending any transfer of the shares to another person, has the same rights as the holder had.

(3) But transmittees do not have the right to attend or vote at a general meeting, or agree to a proposed written resolution, in respect of shares to which they are entitled, by reason of the holder's death or bankruptcy or otherwise, unless they become the holders of those shares.

Exercise of transmittees' rights

28.—(1) Transmittees who wish to become the holders of shares to which they have become entitled must notify the company in writing of that wish.
(2) If the transmittee wishes to have a share transferred to another person, the transmittee must execute an instrument of transfer in respect of it.
(3) Any transfer made or executed under this article is to be treated as if it were made or executed by the person from whom the transmittee has derived rights in respect of the share, and as if the event which gave rise to the transmission had not occurred.

Transmittees bound by prior notices

29. If a notice is given to a shareholder in respect of shares and a transmittee is entitled to those shares, the transmittee is bound by the notice if it was given to the shareholder before the transmittee's name has been entered in the register of members.

DIVIDENDS AND OTHER DISTRIBUTIONS

Procedure for declaring dividends

30.—(1) The company may by ordinary resolution declare dividends, and the directors may decide to pay interim dividends.
(2) A dividend must not be declared unless the directors have made a recommendation as to its amount. Such a dividend must not exceed the amount recommended by the directors.
(3) No dividend may be declared or paid unless it is in accordance with shareholders' respective rights.
(4) Unless the shareholders' resolution to declare or directors' decision to pay a dividend, or the terms on which shares are issued, specify otherwise, it must be paid by reference to each shareholder's holding of shares on the date of the resolution or decision to declare or pay it.
(5) If the company's share capital is divided into different classes, no interim dividend may be paid on shares carrying deferred or non-preferred rights if, at the time of payment, any preferential dividend is in arrear.
(6) The directors may pay at intervals any dividend payable at a fixed rate if it appears to them that the profits available for distribution justify the payment.
(7) If the directors act in good faith, they do not incur any liability to the holders of shares conferring preferred rights for any loss they may suffer by the lawful payment of an interim dividend on shares with deferred or non-preferred rights.

Payment of dividends and other distributions

31.—(1) Where a dividend or other sum which is a distribution is payable in respect of a share, it must be paid by one or more of the following means—
(a) transfer to a bank or building society account specified by the distribution recipient either in writing or as the directors may otherwise decide;
(b) sending a cheque made payable to the distribution recipient by post to the distribution recipient at the distribution recipient's registered address (if the distribution recipient is a holder of the share), or (in any other case) to an address specified by the distribution recipient either in writing or as the directors may otherwise decide;

(c) sending a cheque made payable to such person by post to such person at such address as the distribution recipient has specified either in writing or as the directors may otherwise decide; or

(d) any other means of payment as the directors agree with the distribution recipient either in writing or by such other means as the directors decide.

(2) In the articles, "the distribution recipient" means, in respect of a share in respect of which a dividend or other sum is payable—

(a) the holder of the share; or

(b) if the share has two or more joint holders, whichever of them is named first in the register of members; or

(c) if the holder is no longer entitled to the share by reason of death or bankruptcy, or otherwise by operation of law, the transmittee.

No interest on distributions

32. The company may not pay interest on any dividend or other sum payable in respect of a share unless otherwise provided by—

(a) the terms on which the share was issued, or

(b) the provisions of another agreement between the holder of that share and the company.

Unclaimed distributions

33.—(1) All dividends or other sums which are—

(a) payable in respect of shares, and

(b) unclaimed after having been declared or become payable, may be invested or otherwise made use of by the directors for the benefit of the company until claimed.

(2) The payment of any such dividend or other sum into a separate account does not make the company a trustee in respect of it.

(3) If—

(a) twelve years have passed from the date on which a dividend or other sum became due for payment, and

(b) the distribution recipient has not claimed it, the distribution recipient is no longer entitled to that dividend or other sum and it ceases to remain owing by the company.

Non-cash distributions

34.—(1) Subject to the terms of issue of the share in question, the company may, by ordinary resolution on the recommendation of the directors, decide to pay all or part of a dividend or other distribution payable in respect of a share by transferring non-cash assets of equivalent value (including, without limitation, shares or other securities in any company).

(2) For the purposes of paying a non-cash distribution, the directors may make whatever arrangements they think fit, including, where any difficulty arises regarding the distribution—

(a) fixing the value of any assets;

(b) paying cash to any distribution recipient on the basis of that value in order to adjust the rights of recipients; and

(c) vesting any assets in trustees.

Waiver of distributions

35. Distribution recipients may waive their entitlement to a dividend or other distribution payable in respect of a share by giving the company notice in writing to that effect, but if—

(a) the share has more than one holder, or

(b) more than one person is entitled to the share, whether by reason of the death or bankruptcy of one or more joint holders, or otherwise, the notice is not effective unless it is expressed to be given, and signed, by all the holders or persons otherwise entitled to the share.

CAPITALISATION OF PROFITS

Authority to capitalise and appropriation of capitalised sums

36.—(1) Subject to the articles, the directors may, if they are so authorised by an ordinary resolution—
  (a) decide to capitalise any profits of the company (whether or not they are available for distribution) which are not required for paying a preferential dividend, or any sum standing to the credit of the company's share premium account or capital redemption reserve; and
  (b) appropriate any sum which they so decide to capitalise (a "capitalised sum") to the persons who would have been entitled to it if it were distributed by way of dividend (the "persons entitled") and in the same proportions.
(2) Capitalised sums must be applied—
  (a) on behalf of the persons entitled, and
  (b) i n the same proportions as a dividend would have been distributed to them.
(3) Any capitalised sum may be applied in paying up new shares of a nominal amount equal to the capitalised sum which are then allotted credited as fully paid to the persons entitled or as they may direct.
(4) A capitalised sum which was appropriated from profits available for distribution may be applied in paying up new debentures of the company which are then allotted credited as fully paid to the persons entitled or as they may direct.
(5) Subject to the articles the directors may—
  (a) apply capitalised sums in accordance with paragraphs (3) and (4) partly in one way and partly in another;
  (b) make such arrangements as they think fit to deal with shares or debentures becoming distributable in fractions under this article (including the issuing of fractional certificates or the making of cash payments); and
  (c) authorise any person to enter into an agreement with the company on behalf of all the persons entitled which is binding on them in respect of the allotment of shares and debentures to them under this article.

PART 4 DECISION-MAKING BY SHAREHOLDERS

ORGANISATION OF GENERAL MEETINGS

Attendance and speaking at general meetings

37.—(1) A person is able to exercise the right to speak at a general meeting when that person is in a position to communicate to all those attending the meeting, during the meeting, any information or opinions which that person has on the business of the meeting.
(2) A person is able to exercise the right to vote at a general meeting when—
  (a) that person is able to vote, during the meeting, on resolutions put to the vote at the meeting, and
  (b) that person's vote can be taken into account in determining whether or not such resolutions are passed at the same time as the votes of all the other persons attending the meeting.
(3) The directors may make whatever arrangements they consider appropriate to enable those attending a general meeting to exercise their rights to speak or vote at it.
(4) In determining attendance at a general meeting, it is immaterial whether any two or more members attending it are in the same place as each other.
(5) Two or more persons who are not in the same place as each other attend a general meeting if their circumstances are such that if they have (or were to have) rights to speak and vote at that meeting, they are (or would be) able to exercise them.

Quorum for general meetings

38. No business other than the appointment of the chairman of the meeting is to be transacted at a general meeting if the persons attending it do not constitute a quorum.

Chairing general meetings

39.—(1) If the directors have appointed a chairman, the chairman shall chair general meetings if present and willing to do so.

(2) If the directors have not appointed a chairman, or if the chairman is unwilling to chair the meeting or is not present within ten minutes of the time at which a meeting was due to start—
  (a) the directors present, or
  (b) (if no directors are present), the meeting, must appoint a director or shareholder to chair the meeting, and the appointment of the chairman of the meeting must be the first business of the meeting.

(3) The person chairing a meeting in accordance with this article is referred to as "the chairman of the meeting".

Attendance and speaking by directors and non-shareholders

40.—(1) Directors may attend and speak at general meetings, whether or not they are shareholders.

(2) The chairman of the meeting may permit other persons who are not—
  (a) shareholders of the company, or
  (b) otherwise entitled to exercise the rights of shareholders in relation to general meetings, to attend and speak at a general meeting.

Adjournment

41.—(1) If the persons attending a general meeting within half an hour of the time at which the meeting was due to start do not constitute a quorum, or if during a meeting a quorum ceases to be present, the chairman of the meeting must adjourn it.

(2) The chairman of the meeting may adjourn a general meeting at which a quorum is present if—
  (a) the meeting consents to an adjournment, or
  (b) it appears to the chairman of the meeting that an adjournment is necessary to protect the safety of any person attending the meeting or ensure that the business of the meeting is conducted in an orderly manner.

(3) The chairman of the meeting must adjourn a general meeting if directed to do so by the meeting.

(4) When adjourning a general meeting, the chairman of the meeting must—
  (a) either specify the time and place to which it is adjourned or state that it is to continue at a time and place to be fixed by the directors, and
  (b) have regard to any directions as to the time and place of any adjournment which have been given by the meeting.

(5) If the continuation of an adjourned meeting is to take place more than 14 days after it was adjourned, the company must give at least 7 clear days' notice of it (that is, excluding the day of the adjourned meeting and the day on which the notice is given)—
  (a) to the same persons to whom notice of the company's general meetings is required to be given, and
  (b) containing the same information which such notice is required to contain.

(6) No business may be transacted at an adjourned general meeting which could not properly have been transacted at the meeting if the adjournment had not taken place.

VOTING AT GENERAL MEETINGS

Voting: general

42. A resolution put to the vote of a general meeting must be decided on a show of hands unless a poll is duly demanded in accordance with the articles.

Errors and disputes

43.—(1) No objection may be raised to the qualification of any person voting at a general meeting except at the meeting or adjourned meeting at which the vote objected to is tendered, and every vote not disallowed at the meeting is valid.

(2) Any such objection must be referred to the chairman of the meeting, whose decision is final.

Poll votes

44.—(1) A poll on a resolution may be demanded—
- (a) in advance of the general meeting where it is to be put to the vote, or
- (b) at a general meeting, either before a show of hands on that resolution or immediately after the result of a show of hands on that resolution is declared.

(2) A poll may be demanded by—
- (a) the chairman of the meeting;
- (b) the directors;
- (c) two or more persons having the right to vote on the resolution; or
- (d) a person or persons representing not less than one tenth of the total voting rights of all the shareholders having the right to vote on the resolution.

(3) A demand for a poll may be withdrawn if—
- (a) the poll has not yet been taken, and
- (b) the chairman of the meeting consents to the withdrawal.

(4) Polls must be taken immediately and in such manner as the chairman of the meeting directs.

Content of proxy notices

45.—(1) Proxies may only validly be appointed by a notice in writing (a "proxy notice") which—
- (a) states the name and address of the shareholder appointing the proxy;
- (b) identifies the person appointed to be that shareholder's proxy and the general meeting in relation to which that person is appointed;
- (c) is signed by or on behalf of the shareholder appointing the proxy, or is authenticated in such manner as the directors may determine; and
- (d) is delivered to the company in accordance with the articles and any instructions contained in the notice of the general meeting to which they relate.

(2) The company may require proxy notices to be delivered in a particular form, and may specify different forms for different purposes.

(3) Proxy notices may specify how the proxy appointed under them is to vote (or that the proxy is to abstain from voting) on one or more resolutions.

(4) Unless a proxy notice indicates otherwise, it must be treated as—
- (a) allowing the person appointed under it as a proxy discretion as to how to vote on any ancillary or procedural resolutions put to the meeting, and
- (b) appointing that person as a proxy in relation to any adjournment of the general meeting to which it relates as well as the meeting itself.

Delivery of proxy notices

46.—(1) A person who is entitled to attend, speak or vote (either on a show of hands or on a poll) at a general meeting remains so entitled in respect of that meeting or any adjournment of it, even though a valid proxy notice has been delivered to the company by or on behalf of that person.

(2) An appointment under a proxy notice may be revoked by delivering to the company a notice in writing given by or on behalf of the person by whom or on whose behalf the proxy notice was given.

(3) A notice revoking a proxy appointment only takes effect if it is delivered before the start of the meeting or adjourned meeting to which it relates.

(4) If a proxy notice is not executed by the person appointing the proxy, it must be accompanied by written evidence of the authority of the person who executed it to execute it on the appointor's behalf.

Amendments to resolutions

47.—(1) An ordinary resolution to be proposed at a general meeting may be amended by ordinary resolution if—
  (a) notice of the proposed amendment is given to the company in writing by a person entitled to vote at the general meeting at which it is to be proposed not less than 48 hours before the meeting is to take place (or such later time as the chairman of the meeting may determine), and
  (b) the proposed amendment does not, in the reasonable opinion of the chairman of the meeting, materially alter the scope of the resolution.

(2) A special resolution to be proposed at a general meeting may be amended by ordinary resolution, if—
  (a) the chairman of the meeting proposes the amendment at the general meeting at which the resolution is to be proposed, and
  (b) the amendment does not go beyond what is necessary to correct a grammatical or other non-substantive error in the resolution.

(3) If the chairman of the meeting, acting in good faith, wrongly decides that an amendment to a resolution is out of order, the chairman's error does not invalidate the vote on that resolution.

PART 5 ADMINISTRATIVE ARRANGEMENTS

Means of communication to be used

48.—(1) Subject to the articles, anything sent or supplied by or to the company under the articles may be sent or supplied in any way in which the Companies Act 2006 provides for documents or information which are authorised or required by any provision of that Act to be sent or supplied by or to the company.

(2) Subject to the articles, any notice or document to be sent or supplied to a director in connection with the taking of decisions by directors may also be sent or supplied by the means by which that director has asked to be sent or supplied with such notices or documents for the time being.

(3) A director may agree with the company that notices or documents sent to that director in a particular way are to be deemed to have been received within a specified time of their being sent, and for the specified time to be less than 48 hours.

Company seals

49.—(1) Any common seal may only be used by the authority of the directors.

(2) The directors may decide by what means and in what form any common seal is to be used.

(3) Unless otherwise decided by the directors, if the company has a common seal and it is affixed to a document, the document must also be signed by at least one authorised person in the presence of a witness who attests the signature.

(4) For the purposes of this article, an authorised person is—
  (a) any director of the company;
  (b) the company secretary (if any); or
  (c) any person authorised by the directors for the purpose of signing documents to which the common seal is applied.

No right to inspect accounts and other records

50. Except as provided by law or authorised by the directors or an ordinary resolution of the company, no person is entitled to inspect any of the company's accounting or other records or documents merely by virtue of being a shareholder.

Provision for employees on cessation of business

51. The directors may decide to make provision for the benefit of persons employed or formerly employed by the company or any of its subsidiaries (other than a director or former director or shadow director) in connection with the cessation or transfer to any person of the whole or part of the undertaking of the company or that subsidiary.

DIRECTORS' INDEMNITY AND INSURANCE

Indemnity

52.—(1) Subject to paragraph (2), a relevant director of the company or an associated company may be indemnified out of the company's assets against—
 (a) any liability incurred by that director in connection with any negligence, default, breach of duty or breach of trust in relation to the company or an associated company,
 (b) any liability incurred by that director in connection with the activities of the company or an associated company in its capacity as a trustee of an occupational pension scheme (as defined in section 235(6) of the Companies Act 2006),
 (c) any other liability incurred by that director as an officer of the company or an associated company.
 (2) This article does not authorise any indemnity which would be prohibited or rendered void by any provision of the Companies Acts or by any other provision of law.
 (3) In this article—
 (a) companies are associated if one is a subsidiary of the other or both are subsidiaries of the same body corporate, and
 (b) a "relevant director" means any director or former director of the company or an associated company.

Insurance

53.—(1) The directors may decide to purchase and maintain insurance, at the expense of the company, for the benefit of any relevant director in respect of any relevant loss.
 (2) In this article—
 (a) a "relevant director" means any director or former director of the company or an associated company,
 (b) a "relevant loss" means any loss or liability which has been or may be incurred by a relevant director in connection with that director's duties or powers in relation to the company, any associated company or any pension fund or employees' share scheme of the company or associated company, and
 (c) companies are associated if one is a subsidiary of the other or both are subsidiaries of the same body corporate.

APPENDIX 2
Model Articles for Public Companies

INDEX TO THE ARTICLES

PART 1
INTERPRETATION AND LIMITATION OF LIABILITY
1. Defined terms
2. Liability of members

PART 2
DIRECTORS
DIRECTORS' POWERS AND RESPONSIBILITIES
3. Directors' general authority
4. Members' reserve power
5. Directors may delegate
6. Committees

DECISION-MAKING BY DIRECTORS
7. Directors to take decisions collectively
8. Calling a directors' meeting
9. Participation in directors' meetings
10. Quorum for directors' meetings
11. Meetings where total number of directors less than quorum
12. Chairing directors' meetings
13. Voting at directors' meetings: general rules
14. Chairman's casting vote at directors' meetings
15. Alternates voting at directors' meetings
16. Conflicts of interest
17. Proposing directors' written resolutions
18. Adoption of directors' written resolutions
19. Directors' discretion to make further rules

APPOINTMENT OF DIRECTORS
20. Methods of appointing directors
21. Retirement of directors by rotation
22. Termination of director's appointment
23. Directors' remuneration
24. Directors' expenses

ALTERNATE DIRECTORS
25. Appointment and removal of alternates
26. Rights and responsibilities of alternate directors
27. Termination of alternate directorship

PART 3
DECISION-MAKING BY MEMBERS
ORGANISATION OF GENERAL MEETINGS
28. Members can call general meeting if not enough directors
29. Attendance and speaking at general meetings
30. Quorum for general meetings
31. Chairing general meetings
32. Attendance and speaking by directors and non-members
33. Adjournment

VOTING AT GENERAL MEETINGS
34. Voting: general
35. Errors and disputes
36. Demanding a poll
37. Procedure on a poll
38. Content of proxy notices
39. Delivery of proxy notices
40. Amendments to resolutions

RESTRICTIONS ON MEMBERS' RIGHTS
41. No voting of shares on which money owed to company

APPLICATION OF RULES TO CLASS MEETINGS
42. Class meetings

PART 4
SHARES AND DISTRIBUTIONS
ISSUE OF SHARES
43. Powers to issue different classes of share
44. Payment of commissions on subscription for shares

INTERESTS IN SHARES
45. Company not bound by less than absolute interests

SHARE CERTIFICATES
46. Certificates to be issued except in certain cases
47. Contents and execution of share certificates
48. Consolidated share certificates
49. Replacement share certificates

SHARES NOT HELD IN CERTIFICATED FORM
50. Uncertificated shares
51. Share warrants

PARTLY PAID SHARES
52. Company's lien over partly paid shares
53. Enforcement of the company's lien
54. Call notices
55. Liability to pay calls
56. When call notice need not be issued
57. Failure to comply with call notice: automatic consequences
58. Notice of intended forfeiture
59. Directors' power to forfeit shares
60. Effect of forfeiture
61. Procedure following forfeiture
62. Surrender of shares

TRANSFER AND TRANSMISSION OF SHARES
63. Transfers of certificated shares
64. Transfer of uncertificated shares
65. Transmission of shares
66. Transmittees' rights
67. Exercise of transmittees' rights
68. Transmittees bound by prior notices

CONSOLIDATION OF SHARES
69. Procedure for disposing of fractions of shares

DISTRIBUTIONS
70. Procedure for declaring dividends
71. Calculation of dividends
72. Payment of dividends and other distributions
73. Deductions from distributions in respect of sums owed to the company
74. No interest on distributions
75. Unclaimed distributions
76. Non-cash distributions
77. Waiver of distributions

CAPITALISATION OF PROFITS
78. Authority to capitalise and appropriation of capitalised sums

PART 5
MISCELLANEOUS PROVISIONS
COMMUNICATIONS
79. Means of communication to be used
80. Failure to notify contact details

ADMINISTRATIVE ARRANGEMENTS
81. Company seals
82. Destruction of documents
83. No right to inspect accounts and other records
84. Provision for employees on cessation of business

DIRECTORS' INDEMNITY AND INSURANCE
85. Indemnity
86. Insurance

PART 1 INTERPRETATION AND LIMITATION OF LIABILITY

Defined terms

1. In the articles , unless the context requires otherwise—
    "alternate" or "alternate director" has the meaning given in article 25;
    "appointor" has the meaning given in article 25;
    "articles" means the company's articles of association;
    "bankruptcy" includes individual insolvency proceedings in a jurisdiction other than England and Wales or Northern Ireland which have an effect similar to that of bankruptcy;
    "call" has the meaning given in article 54;
    "call notice" has the meaning given in article 54;
    "certificate" means a paper certificate (other than a share warrant) evidencing a person's title to specified shares or other securities;
    "certificated" in relation to a share, means that it is not an uncertificated share or a share

in respect of which a share warrant has been issued and is current;
"chairman" has the meaning given in article 12;
"chairman of the meeting" has the meaning given in article 31;
"Companies Acts" means the Companies Acts (as defined in section 2 of the Companies Act 2006), in so far as they apply to the company;
"company's lien" has the meaning given in article 52;
"director" means a director of the company, and includes any person occupying the position of director, by whatever name called;
"distribution recipient" has the meaning given in article 72;
"document" includes, unless otherwise specified, any document sent or supplied in electronic form;
"electronic form" has the meaning given in section 1168 of the Companies Act 2006;
"fully paid" in relation to a share, means that the nominal value and any premium to be paid to the company in respect of that share have been paid to the company;
"hard copy form" has the meaning given in section 1168 of the Companies Act 2006;
"holder" in relation to shares means the person whose name is entered in the register of members as the holder of the shares, or, in the case of a share in respect of which a share warrant has been issued (and not cancelled), the person in possession of that warrant;
"instrument" means a document in hard copy form;
"lien enforcement notice" has the meaning given in article 53;
"member" has the meaning given in section 112 of the Companies Act 2006;
"ordinary resolution" has the meaning given in section 282 of the Companies Act 2006;
"paid" means paid or credited as paid;
"participate", in relation to a directors' meeting, has the meaning given in article 9;
"partly paid" in relation to a share means that part of that share's nominal value or any premium at which it was issued has not been paid to the company;
"proxy notice" has the meaning given in article 38;
"securities seal" has the meaning given in article 47;
"shares" means shares in the company;
"special resolution" has the meaning given in section 283 of the Companies Act 2006;
"subsidiary" has the meaning given in section 1159 of the Companies Act 2006;
"transmittee" means a person entitled to a share by reason of the death or bankruptcy of a shareholder or otherwise by operation of law;
"uncertificated" in relation to a share means that, by virtue of legislation (other than section 778 of the Companies Act 2006) permitting title to shares to be evidenced and transferred without a certificate, title to that share is evidenced and may be transferred without a certificate; and
"writing" means the representation or reproduction of words, symbols or other information in a visible form by any method or combination of methods, whether sent or supplied in electronic form or otherwise.
Unless the context otherwise requires, other words or expressions contained in these articles bear the same meaning as in the Companies Act 2006 as in force on the date when these articles become binding on the company.

Liability of members

2. The liability of the members is limited to the amount, if any, unpaid on the shares held by them.

PART 2 DIRECTORS

DIRECTORS' POWERS AND RESPONSIBILITIES

Directors' general authority

3. Subject to the articles, the directors are responsible for the management of the company's business, for which purpose they may exercise all the powers of the company.

Members' reserve power

4.— (1) The members may, by special resolution, direct the directors to take, or refrain from taking, specified action.
   (2) No such special resolution invalidates anything which the directors have done before the passing of the resolution.

Directors may delegate
5.— (1) Subject to the articles, the directors may delegate any of the powers which are conferred on them under the articles—
   (a) to such person or committee;
   (b) by such means (including by power of attorney);
   (c) to such an extent;
   (d) in relation to such matters or territories; and
   (e) on such terms and conditions; as they think fit.
   (2) If the directors so specify, any such delegation may authorise further delegation of the directors' powers by any person to whom they are delegated.
   (3) The directors may revoke any delegation in whole or part, or alter its terms and conditions.

Committees

6.— (1) Committees to which the directors delegate any of their powers must follow procedures which are based as far as they are applicable on those provisions of the articles which govern the taking of decisions by directors.
   (2) The directors may make rules of procedure for all or any committees, which prevail over rules derived from the articles if they are not consistent with them.

DECISION-MAKING BY DIRECTORS

Directors to take decisions collectively

7. Decisions of the directors may be taken—
   (a) at a directors' meeting, or
   (b) in the form of a directors' written resolution.

Calling a directors' meeting

8.— (1) Any director may call a directors' meeting.
   (2) The company secretary must call a directors' meeting if a director so requests.
   (3) A directors' meeting is called by giving notice of the meeting to the directors.
   (4) Notice of any directors' meeting must indicate—
      (a) its proposed date and time;
      (b) where it is to take place; and
      (c) if it is anticipated that directors participating in the meeting will not be in the same place, how it is proposed that they should communicate with each other during the meeting.
   (5) Notice of a directors' meeting must be given to each director, but need not be in writing.
   (6) Notice of a directors' meeting need not be given to directors who waive their entitlement to notice of that meeting, by giving notice to that effect to the company not more than 7 days after the date on which the meeting is held. Where such notice is

given after the meeting has been held, that does not affect the validity of the meeting, or of any business conducted at it.

Participation in directors' meetings

9.— (1) Subject to the articles, directors participate in a directors' meeting, or part of a directors' meeting, when—
  (a) the meeting has been called and takes place in accordance with the articles, and
  (b) they can each communicate to the others any information or opinions they have on any particular item of the business of the meeting.
 (2) In determining whether directors are participating in a directors' meeting, it is irrelevant where any director is or how they communicate with each other.
 (3) If all the directors participating in a meeting are not in the same place, they may decide that the meeting is to be treated as taking place wherever any of them is.

Quorum for directors' meetings

10.—(1) At a directors' meeting, unless a quorum is participating, no proposal is to be voted on, except a proposal to call another meeting.
 (2) The quorum for directors' meetings may be fixed from time to time by a decision of the directors, but it must never be less than two, and unless otherwise fixed it is two.

Meetings where total number of directors less than quorum

11.—(1) This article applies where the total number of directors for the time being is less than the quorum for directors' meetings.
 (2) If there is only one director, that director may appoint sufficient directors to make up a quorum or call a general meeting to do so.
 (3) If there is more than one director—
  (a) a directors' meeting may take place, if it is called in accordance with the articles and at least two directors participate in it, with a view to appointing sufficient directors to make up a quorum or calling a general meeting to do so, and
  (b) if a directors' meeting is called but only one director attends at the appointed date and time to participate in it, that director may appoint sufficient directors to make up a quorum or call a general meeting to do so.

Chairing directors' meetings

12.—(1) The directors may appoint a director to chair their meetings.
 (2) The person so appointed for the time being is known as the chairman.
 (3) The directors may appoint other directors as deputy or assistant chairmen to chair directors' meetings in the chairman's absence.
 (4) The directors may terminate the appointment of the chairman, deputy or assistant chairman at any time.
 (5) If neither the chairman nor any director appointed generally to chair directors' meetings in the chairman's absence is participating in a meeting within ten minutes of the time at which it was to start, the participating directors must appoint one of themselves to chair it.

Voting at directors' meetings: general rules

13.—(1) Subject to the articles, a decision is taken at a directors' meeting by a majority of the votes of the participating directors.
 (2) Subject to the articles, each director participating in a directors' meeting has one vote.
 (3) Subject to the articles, if a director has an interest in an actual or proposed transaction or arrangement with the company—
  (a) that director and that director's alternate may not vote on any proposal relating to it, but
  (b) this does not preclude the alternate from voting in relation to that transaction or arrangement on behalf of another appointor who does not have such an interest.

Chairman's casting vote at directors' meetings

14.—(1) If the numbers of votes for and against a proposal are equal, the chairman or other director chairing the meeting has a casting vote.

(2) But this does not apply if, in accordance with the articles, the chairman or other director is not to be counted as participating in the decision-making process for quorum or voting purposes.

Alternates voting at directors' meetings

15. A director who is also an alternate director has an additional vote on behalf of each appointor who is—
(a) not participating in a directors' meeting, and
(b) would have been entitled to vote if they were participating in it.

Conflicts of interest

16.—(1) If a directors' meeting, or part of a directors' meeting, is concerned with an actual or proposed transaction or arrangement with the company in which a director is interested, that director is not to be counted as participating in that meeting, or part of a meeting, for quorum or voting purposes.

(2) But if paragraph (3) applies, a director who is interested in an actual or proposed transaction or arrangement with the company is to be counted as participating in a decision at a directors' meeting, or part of a directors' meeting, relating to it for quorum and voting purposes.

(3) This paragraph applies when—
(a) the company by ordinary resolution disapplies the provision of the articles which would otherwise prevent a director from being counted as participating in, or voting at, a directors' meeting;
(b) the director's interest cannot reasonably be regarded as likely to give rise to a conflict of interest; or
(c) the director's conflict of interest arises from a permitted cause.

(4) For the purposes of this article, the following are permitted causes—
(a) a guarantee given, or to be given, by or to a director in respect of an obligation incurred by or on behalf of the company or any of its subsidiaries;
(b) subscription, or an agreement to subscribe, for shares or other securities of the company or any of its subsidiaries, or to underwrite, sub-underwrite, or guarantee subscription for any such shares or securities; and
(c) arrangements pursuant to which benefits are made available to employees and directors or former employees and directors of the company or any of its subsidiaries which do not provide special benefits for directors or former directors.

(5) Subject to paragraph (6), if a question arises at a meeting of directors or of a committee of directors as to the right of a director to participate in the meeting (or part of the meeting) for voting or quorum purposes, the question may, before the conclusion of the meeting, be referred to the chairman whose ruling in relation to any director other than the chairman is to be final and conclusive.

(6) If any question as to the right to participate in the meeting (or part of the meeting) should arise in respect of the chairman, the question is to be decided by a decision of the directors at that meeting, for which purpose the chairman is not to be counted as participating in the meeting (or that part of the meeting) for voting or quorum purposes.

Proposing directors' written resolutions

17.—(1) Any director may propose a directors' written resolution.
(2) The company secretary must propose a directors' written resolution if a director so requests.
(3) A directors' written resolution is proposed by giving notice of the proposed resolution to the directors.
(4) Notice of a proposed directors' written resolution must indicate—
(a) the proposed resolution, and
(b) the time by which it is proposed that the directors should adopt it.

(5) Notice of a proposed directors' written resolution must be given in writing to each director.

(6) Any decision which a person giving notice of a proposed directors' written resolution takes regarding the process of adopting that resolution must be taken reasonably in good faith.

Adoption of directors' written resolutions

18.—(1) A proposed directors' written resolution is adopted when all the directors who would have been entitled to vote on the resolution at a directors' meeting have signed one or more copies of it, provided that those directors would have formed a quorum at such a meeting.

(2) It is immaterial whether any director signs the resolution before or after the time by which the notice proposed that it should be adopted.

(3) Once a directors' written resolution has been adopted, it must be treated as if it had been a decision taken at a directors' meeting in accordance with the articles.

(4) The company secretary must ensure that the company keeps a record, in writing, of all directors' written resolutions for at least ten years from the date of their adoption.

Directors' discretion to make further rules

19. Subject to the articles, the directors may make any rule which they think fit about how they take decisions, and about how such rules are to be recorded or communicated to directors.

APPOINTMENT OF DIRECTORS

Methods of appointing directors

20. Any person who is willing to act as a director, and is permitted by law to do so, may be appointed to be a director—
(a) by ordinary resolution, or
(b) by a decision of the directors.

Retirement of directors by rotation

21.—(1) At the first annual general meeting all the directors must retire from office.

(2) At every subsequent annual general meeting any directors—
(a) who have been appointed by the directors since the last annual general meeting, or
(b) who were not appointed or reappointed at one of the preceding two annual general meetings, must retire from office and may offer themselves for reappointment by the members.

Termination of director's appointment

22. A person ceases to be a director as soon as—
(a) that person ceases to be a director by virtue of any provision of the Companies Act 2006 or is prohibited from being a director by law;
(b) a bankruptcy order is made against that person;
(c) a composition is made with that person's creditors generally in satisfaction of that person's debts;
(d) a registered medical practitioner who is treating that person gives a written opinion to the company stating that that person has become physically or mentally incapable of acting as a director and may remain so for more than three months;
(e) by reason of that person's mental health, a court makes an order which wholly or partly prevents that person from personally exercising any powers or rights which that person would otherwise have;
(f) notification is received by the company from the director that the director is resigning from office as director, and such resignation has taken effect in accordance with its terms.

Directors' remuneration

23.—(1) Directors may undertake any services for the company that the directors decide.
    (2) Directors are entitled to such remuneration as the directors determine—
        (a) for their services to the company as directors, and
        (b) for any other service which they undertake for the company.
    (3) Subject to the articles, a director's remuneration may—
        (a) take any form, and
        (b) include any arrangements in connection with the payment of a pension, allowance or gratuity, or any death, sickness or disability benefits, to or in respect of that director.
    (4) Unless the directors decide otherwise, directors' remuneration accrues from day to day.
    (5) Unless the directors decide otherwise, directors are not accountable to the company for any remuneration which they receive as directors or other officers or employees of the company's subsidiaries or of any other body corporate in which the company is interested.

Directors' expenses

24. The company may pay any reasonable expenses which the directors properly incur in connection with their attendance at—
    (a) meetings of directors or committees of directors,
    (b) general meetings, or
    (c) separate meetings of the holders of any class of shares or of debentures of the company, or otherwise in connection with the exercise of their powers and the discharge of their responsibilities in relation to the company.

ALTERNATE DIRECTORS

Appointment and removal of alternates

25.—(1) Any director (the "appointor") may appoint as an alternate any other director, or any other person approved by resolution of the directors, to—
        (a) exercise that director's powers, and
        (b) carry out that director's responsibilities, in relation to the taking of decisions by the directors in the absence of the alternate's appointor.
    (2) Any appointment or removal of an alternate must be effected by notice in writing to the company signed by the appointor, or in any other manner approved by the directors.
    (3) The notice must—
        (a) identify the proposed alternate, and
        (b) in the case of a notice of appointment, contain a statement signed by the proposed alternate that the proposed alternate is willing to act as the alternate of the director giving the notice.

Rights and responsibilities of alternate directors

26.—(1) An alternate director has the same rights, in relation to any directors' meeting or directors' written resolution, as the alternate's appointor.
    (2) Except as the articles specify otherwise, alternate directors—
        (a) are deemed for all purposes to be directors;
        (b) are liable for their own acts and omissions;
        (c) are subject to the same restrictions as their appointors; and
        (d) are not deemed to be agents of or for their appointors.
    (3) A person who is an alternate director but not a director—
        (a) may be counted as participating for the purposes of determining whether a quorum is participating (but only if that person's appointor is not participating), and

(b) may sign a written resolution (but only if it is not signed or to be signed by that person's appointor).

No alternate may be counted as more than one director for such purposes.

(4) An alternate director is not entitled to receive any remuneration from the company for serving as an alternate director except such part of the alternate's appointor's remuneration as the appointor may direct by notice in writing made to the company.

Termination of alternate directorship

27. An alternate director's appointment as an alternate terminates—
   (a) when the alternate's appointor revokes the appointment by notice to the company in writing specifying when it is to terminate;
   (b) on the occurrence in relation to the alternate of any event which, if it occurred in relation to the alternate's appointor, would result in the termination of the appointor's appointment as a director;
   (c) on the death of the alternate's appointor; or
   (d) when the alternate's appointor's appointment as a director terminates, except that an alternate's appointment as an alternate does not terminate when the appointor retires by rotation at a general meeting and is then re-appointed as a director at the same general meeting.

PART 3 DECISION-MAKING BY MEMBERS

ORGANISATION OF GENERAL MEETINGS

Members can call general meeting if not enough directors

28. If—
   (a) the company has fewer than two directors, and
   (b) the director (if any) is unable or unwilling to appoint sufficient directors to make up a quorum or to call a general meeting to do so, then two or more members may call a general meeting (or instruct the company secretary to do so) for the purpose of appointing one or more directors.

Attendance and speaking at general meetings

29.—(1) A person is able to exercise the right to speak at a general meeting when that person is in a position to communicate to all those attending the meeting, during the meeting, any information or opinions which that person has on the business of the meeting.
   (2) A person is able to exercise the right to vote at a general meeting when—
      (a) that person is able to vote, during the meeting, on resolutions put to the vote at the meeting, and
      (b) that person's vote can be taken into account in determining whether or not such resolutions are passed at the same time as the votes of all the other persons attending the meeting.
   (3) The directors may make whatever arrangements they consider appropriate to enable those attending a general meeting to exercise their rights to speak or vote at it.
   (4) In determining attendance at a general meeting, it is immaterial whether any two or more members attending it are in the same place as each other.
   (5) Two or more persons who are not in the same place as each other attend a general meeting if their circumstances are such that if they have (or were to have) rights to speak and vote at that meeting, they are (or would be) able to exercise them.

Quorum for general meetings

30. No business other than the appointment of the chairman of the meeting is to be transacted at a general meeting if the persons attending it do not constitute a quorum.

Chairing general meetings

31.—(1) If the directors have appointed a chairman, the chairman shall chair general meetings if present and willing to do so.
    (2) If the directors have not appointed a chairman, or if the chairman is unwilling to chair the meeting or is not present within ten minutes of the time at which a meeting was due to start—
        (a) the directors present, or
        (b) (if no directors are present), the meeting, must appoint a director or member to chair the meeting, and the appointment of the chairman of the meeting must be the first business of the meeting.
    (3) The person chairing a meeting in accordance with this article is referred to as "the chairman of the meeting".

Attendance and speaking by directors and non-members

32.—(1) Directors may attend and speak at general meetings, whether or not they are members.
    (2) The chairman of the meeting may permit other persons who are not—
        (a) members of the company, or
        (b) otherwise entitled to exercise the rights of members in relation to general meetings, to attend and speak at a general meeting.

Adjournment

33.—(1) If the persons attending a general meeting within half an hour of the time at which the meeting was due to start do not constitute a quorum, or if during a meeting a quorum ceases to be present, the chairman of the meeting must adjourn it.
    (2) The chairman of the meeting may adjourn a general meeting at which a quorum is present if—
        (a) the meeting consents to an adjournment, or
        (b) it appears to the chairman of the meeting that an adjournment is necessary to protect the safety of any person attending the meeting or ensure that the business of the meeting is conducted in an orderly manner.
    (3) The chairman of the meeting must adjourn a general meeting if directed to do so by the meeting.
    (4) When adjourning a general meeting, the chairman of the meeting must—
        (a) either specify the time and place to which it is adjourned or state that it is to continue at a time and place to be fixed by the directors, and
        (b) have regard to any directions as to the time and place of any adjournment which have been given by the meeting.
    (5) If the continuation of an adjourned meeting is to take place more than 14 days after it was adjourned, the company must give at least 7 clear days' notice of it (that is, excluding the day of the adjourned meeting and the day on which the notice is given)—
        (a) to the same persons to whom notice of the company's general meetings is required to be given, and
        (b) containing the same information which such notice is required to contain.
    (6) No business may be transacted at an adjourned general meeting which could not properly have been transacted at the meeting if the adjournment had not taken place.

VOTING AT GENERAL MEETINGS

Voting: general

34. A resolution put to the vote of a general meeting must be decided on a show of hands unless a poll is duly demanded in accordance with the articles.

Errors and disputes

35.—(1) No objection may be raised to the qualification of any person voting at a general meeting except at the meeting or adjourned meeting at which the vote objected to is tendered, and every vote not disallowed at the meeting is valid.

(2) Any such objection must be referred to the chairman of the meeting whose decision is final.

Demanding a poll

36.—(1) A poll on a resolution may be demanded—
(a) in advance of the general meeting where it is to be put to the vote, or
(b) at a general meeting, either before a show of hands on that resolution or immediately after the result of a show of hands on that resolution is declared.
(2) A poll may be demanded by—
(a) the chairman of the meeting;
(b) the directors;
(c) two or more persons having the right to vote on the resolution; or
(d) a person or persons representing not less than one tenth of the total voting rights of all the members having the right to vote on the resolution.
(3) A demand for a poll may be withdrawn if—
(a) the poll has not yet been taken, and
(b) the chairman of the meeting consents to the withdrawal.

Procedure on a poll

37.—(1) Subject to the articles, polls at general meetings must be taken when, where and in such manner as the chairman of the meeting directs.
(2) The chairman of the meeting may appoint scrutineers (who need not be members) and decide how and when the result of the poll is to be declared.
(3) The result of a poll shall be the decision of the meeting in respect of the resolution on which the poll was demanded.
(4) A poll on—
(a) the election of the chairman of the meeting, or
(b) a question of adjournment, must be taken immediately.
(5) Other polls must be taken within 30 days of their being demanded.
(6) A demand for a poll does not prevent a general meeting from continuing, except as regards the question on which the poll was demanded.
(7) No notice need be given of a poll not taken immediately if the time and place at which it is to be taken are announced at the meeting at which it is demanded.
(8) In any other case, at least 7 days' notice must be given specifying the time and place at which the poll is to be taken.

Content of proxy notices

38.—(1) Proxies may only validly be appointed by a notice in writing (a "proxy notice") which—
(a) states the name and address of the member appointing the proxy;
(b) identifies the person appointed to be that member's proxy and the general meeting in relation to which that person is appointed;
(c) is signed by or on behalf of the member appointing the proxy, or is authenticated in such manner as the directors may determine; and
(d) is delivered to the company in accordance with the articles and any instructions contained in the notice of the general meeting to which they relate.
(2) The company may require proxy notices to be delivered in a particular form, and may specify different forms for different purposes.
(3) Proxy notices may specify how the proxy appointed under them is to vote (or that the proxy is to abstain from voting) on one or more resolutions.
(4) Unless a proxy notice indicates otherwise, it must be treated as—
(a) allowing the person appointed under it as a proxy discretion as to how to vote on any ancillary or procedural resolutions put to the meeting, and
(b) appointing that person as a proxy in relation to any adjournment of the general meeting to which it relates as well as the meeting itself.

Delivery of proxy notices

39.—(1) Any notice of a general meeting must specify the address or addresses ("proxy notification address") at which the company or its agents will receive proxy notices relating to that meeting, or any adjournment of it, delivered in hard copy or electronic form.

(2) A person who is entitled to attend, speak or vote (either on a show of hands or on a poll) at a general meeting remains so entitled in respect of that meeting or any adjournment of it, even though a valid proxy notice has been delivered to the company by or on behalf of that person.

(3) Subject to paragraphs (4) and (5), a proxy notice must be delivered to a proxy notification address not less than 48 hours before the general meeting or adjourned meeting to which it relates.

(4) In the case of a poll taken more than 48 hours after it is demanded, the notice must be delivered to a proxy notification address not less than 24 hours before the time appointed for the taking of the poll.

(5) In the case of a poll not taken during the meeting but taken not more than 48 hours after it was demanded, the proxy notice must be delivered—
   (a) in accordance with paragraph (3), or
   (b) at the meeting at which the poll was demanded to the chairman, secretary or any director.

(6) An appointment under a proxy notice may be revoked by delivering a notice in writing given by or on behalf of the person by whom or on whose behalf the proxy notice was given to a proxy notification address.

(7) A notice revoking a proxy appointment only takes effect if it is delivered before—
   (a) the start of the meeting or adjourned meeting to which it relates, or
   (b) (in the case of a poll not taken on the same day as the meeting or adjourned meeting) the time appointed for taking the poll to which it relates.

(8) If a proxy notice is not signed by the person appointing the proxy, it must be accompanied by written evidence of the authority of the person who executed it to execute it on the appointor's behalf.

Amendments to resolutions

40.—(1) An ordinary resolution to be proposed at a general meeting may be amended by ordinary resolution if—
   (a) notice of the proposed amendment is given to the company secretary in writing by a person entitled to vote at the general meeting at which it is to be proposed not less than 48 hours before the meeting is to take place (or such later time as the chairman of the meeting may determine), and
   (b) the proposed amendment does not, in the reasonable opinion of the chairman of the meeting, materially alter the scope of the resolution.

(2) A special resolution to be proposed at a general meeting may be amended by ordinary resolution, if—
   (a) the chairman of the meeting proposes the amendment at the general meeting at which the resolution is to be proposed, and
   (b) the amendment does not go beyond what is necessary to correct a grammatical or other non-substantive error in the resolution.

(3) If the chairman of the meeting, acting in good faith, wrongly decides that an amendment to a resolution is out of order, the chairman's error does not invalidate the vote on that resolution.

RESTRICTIONS ON MEMBERS' RIGHTS

No voting of shares on which money owed to company

41. No voting rights attached to a share may be exercised at any general meeting, at any adjournment of it, or on any poll called at or in relation to it, unless all amounts payable to the company in respect of that share have been paid.

APPLICATION OF RULES TO CLASS MEETINGS

Class meetings

42. The provisions of the articles relating to general meetings apply, with any necessary modifications, to meetings of the holders of any class of shares.

PART 4 SHARES AND DISTRIBUTIONS

ISSUE OF SHARES

Powers to issue different classes of share

43.—(1) Subject to the articles, but without prejudice to the rights attached to any existing share, the company may issue shares with such rights or restrictions as may be determined by ordinary resolution.

(2) The company may issue shares which are to be redeemed, or are liable to be redeemed at the option of the company or the holder, and the directors may determine the terms, conditions and manner of redemption of any such shares.

Payment of commissions on subscription for shares

44.—(1) The company may pay any person a commission in consideration for that person—
  (a) subscribing, or agreeing to subscribe, for shares, or
  (b) procuring, or agreeing to procure, subscriptions for shares.
(2) Any such commission may be paid—
  (a) in cash, or in fully paid or partly paid shares or other securities, or partly in one way and partly in the other, and
  (b) in respect of a conditional or an absolute subscription.

INTERESTS IN SHARES

Company not bound by less than absolute interests

45. Except as required by law, no person is to be recognised by the company as holding any share upon any trust, and except as otherwise required by law or the articles, the company is not in any way to be bound by or recognise any interest in a share other than the holder's absolute ownership of it and all the rights attaching to it.

SHARE CERTIFICATES

Certificates to be issued except in certain cases

46.—(1) The company must issue each member with one or more certificates in respect of the shares which that member holds.
(2) This article does not apply to—
  (a) uncertificated shares;
  (b) shares in respect of which a share warrant has been issued; or
  (c) shares in respect of which the Companies Acts permit the company not to issue a certificate.
(3) Except as otherwise specified in the articles, all certificates must be issued free of charge.
(4) No certificate may be issued in respect of shares of more than one class.
(5) If more than one person holds a share, only one certificate may be issued in respect of it.

Contents and execution of share certificates

47.—(1) Every certificate must specify—
    (a) in respect of how many shares, of what class, it is issued;
    (b) the nominal value of those shares;
    (c) the amount paid up on them; and
    (d) any distinguishing numbers assigned to them.
(2) Certificates must—
    (a) have affixed to them the company's common seal or an official seal which is a facsimile of the company's common seal with the addition on its face of the word "Securities" (a "securities seal"), or
    (b) be otherwise executed in accordance with the Companies Acts.

Consolidated share certificates

48.—(1) When a member's holding of shares of a particular class increases, the company may issue that member with—
    (a) a single, consolidated certificate in respect of all the shares of a particular class which that member holds, or
    (b) a separate certificate in respect of only those shares by which that member's holding has increased.
(2) When a member's holding of shares of a particular class is reduced, the company must ensure that the member is issued with one or more certificates in respect of the number of shares held by the member after that reduction. But the company need not (in the absence of a request from the member) issue any new certificate if—
    (a) all the shares which the member no longer holds as a result of the reduction, and
    (b) none of the shares which the member retains following the reduction, were, immediately before the reduction, represented by the same certificate.
(3) A member may request the company, in writing, to replace—
    (a) the member's separate certificates with a consolidated certificate, or
    (b) the member's consolidated certificate with two or more separate certificates representing such proportion of the shares as the member may specify.
(4) When the company complies with such a request it may charge such reasonable fee as the directors may decide for doing so.
(5) A consolidated certificate must not be issued unless any certificates which it is to replace have first been returned to the company for cancellation.

Replacement share certificates

49.—(1) If a certificate issued in respect of a member's shares is—
    (a) damaged or defaced, or
    (b) said to be lost, stolen or destroyed, that member is entitled to be issued with a replacement certificate in respect of the same shares.
(2) A member exercising the right to be issued with such a replacement certificate—
    (a) may at the same time exercise the right to be issued with a single certificate or separate certificates;
    (b) must return the certificate which is to be replaced to the company if it is damaged or defaced; and
    (c) must comply with such conditions as to evidence, indemnity and the payment of a reasonable fee as the directors decide.

SHARES NOT HELD IN CERTIFICATED FORM

Uncertificated shares

50.—(1) In this article, "the relevant rules" means—
    (a) any applicable provision of the Companies Acts about the holding, evidencing of title to, or transfer of shares other than in certificated form, and

(b) any applicable legislation, rules or other arrangements made under or by virtue of such provision.
(2) The provisions of this article have effect subject to the relevant rules.
(3) Any provision of the articles which is inconsistent with the relevant rules must be disregarded, to the extent that it is inconsistent, whenever the relevant rules apply.
(4) Any share or class of shares of the company may be issued or held on such terms, or in such a way, that—
   (a) title to it or them is not, or must not be, evidenced by a certificate, or
   (b) it or they may or must be transferred wholly or partly without a certificate.
(5) The directors have power to take such steps as they think fit in relation to—
   (a) the evidencing of and transfer of title to uncertificated shares (including in connection with the issue of such shares);
   (b) any records relating to the holding of uncertificated shares;
   (c) the conversion of certificated shares into uncertificated shares; or
   (d) the conversion of uncertificated shares into certificated shares.
(6) The company may by notice to the holder of a share require that share—
   (a) if it is uncertificated, to be converted into certificated form, and
   (b) if it is certificated, to be converted into uncertificated form, to enable it to be dealt with in accordance with the articles.
(7) If—
   (a) the articles give the directors power to take action, or require other persons to take action, in order to sell, transfer or otherwise dispose of shares, and
   (b) uncertificated shares are subject to that power, but the power is expressed in terms which assume the use of a certificate or other written instrument, the directors may take such action as is necessary or expedient to achieve the same results when exercising that power in relation to uncertificated shares.
(8) In particular, the directors may take such action as they consider appropriate to achieve the sale, transfer, disposal, forfeiture, re-allotment or surrender of an uncertificated share or otherwise to enforce a lien in respect of it.
(9) Unless the directors otherwise determine, shares which a member holds in uncertificated form must be treated as separate holdings from any shares which that member holds in certificated form.
(10) A class of shares must not be treated as two classes simply because some shares of that class are held in certificated form and others are held in uncertificated form.

Share warrants

51.—(1) The directors may issue a share warrant in respect of any fully paid share.
(2) Share warrants must be—
   (a) issued in such form, and
   (b) executed in such manner, as the directors decide.
(3) A share represented by a share warrant may be transferred by delivery of the warrant representing it.
(4) The directors may make provision for the payment of dividends in respect of any share represented by a share warrant.
(5) Subject to the articles, the directors may decide the conditions on which any share warrant is issued. In particular, they may—
   (a) decide the conditions on which new warrants are to be issued in place of warrants which are damaged or defaced, or said to have been lost, stolen or destroyed;
   (b) decide the conditions on which bearers of warrants are entitled to attend and vote at general meetings;
   (c) decide the conditions subject to which bearers of warrants may surrender their warrant so as to hold their shares in certificated or uncertificated form instead; and
   (d) vary the conditions of issue of any warrant from time to time, and the bearer of a warrant is subject to the conditions and procedures in force in relation to it, whether or not they were decided or specified before the warrant was issued.

(6) Subject to the conditions on which the warrants are issued from time to time, bearers of share warrants have the same rights and privileges as they would if their names had been included in the register as holders of the shares represented by their warrants.

(7) The company must not in any way be bound by or recognise any interest in a share represented by a share warrant other than the absolute right of the bearer of that warrant to that warrant.

PARTLY PAID SHARES

Company's lien over partly paid shares

52.—(1) The company has a lien ("the company's lien") over every share which is partly paid for any part of—
  (a) that share's nominal value, and
  (b) any premium at which it was issued, which has not been paid to the company, and which is payable immediately or at some time in the future, whether or not a call notice has been sent in respect of it.

(2) The company's lien over a share—
  (a) takes priority over any third party's interest in that share, and
  (b) extends to any dividend or other money payable by the company in respect of that share and (if the lien is enforced and the share is sold by the company) the proceeds of sale of that share.

(3) The directors may at any time decide that a share which is or would otherwise be subject to the company's lien shall not be subject to it, either wholly or in part.

Enforcement of the company's lien

53.—(1) Subject to the provisions of this article, if—
  (a) a lien enforcement notice has been given in respect of a share, and
  (b) the person to whom the notice was given has failed to comply with it, the company may sell that share in such manner as the directors decide.

(2) A lien enforcement notice—
  (a) may only be given in respect of a share which is subject to the company's lien, in respect of which a sum is payable and the due date for payment of that sum has passed;
  (b) must specify the share concerned;
  (c) must require payment of the sum payable within 14 days of the notice;
  (d) must be addressed either to the holder of the share or to a person entitled to it by reason of the holder's death, bankruptcy or otherwise; and
  (e) must state the company's intention to sell the share if the notice is not complied with.

(3) Where shares are sold under this article—
  (a) the directors may authorise any person to execute an instrument of transfer of the shares to the purchaser or a person nominated by the purchaser, and
  (b) the transferee is not bound to see to the application of the consideration, and the transferee's title is not affected by any irregularity in or invalidity of the process leading to the sale.

(4) The net proceeds of any such sale (after payment of the costs of sale and any other costs of enforcing the lien) must be applied—
  (a) first, in payment of so much of the sum for which the lien exists as was payable at the date of the lien enforcement notice,
  (b) second, to the person entitled to the shares at the date of the sale, but only after the certificate for the shares sold has been surrendered to the company for cancellation or a suitable indemnity has been given for any lost certificates, and subject to a lien equivalent to the company's lien over the shares before the sale for any money payable in respect of the shares after the date of the lien enforcement notice.

(5) A statutory declaration by a director or the company secretary that the declarant is a director or the company secretary and that a share has been sold to satisfy the company's lien on a specified date—
   (a) is conclusive evidence of the facts stated in it as against all persons claiming to be entitled to the share, and
   (b) subject to compliance with any other formalities of transfer required by the articles or by law, constitutes a good title to the share.

Call notices

54.—(1) Subject to the articles and the terms on which shares are allotted, the directors may send a notice (a "call notice") to a member requiring the member to pay the company a specified sum of money (a "call") which is payable in respect of shares which that member holds at the date when the directors decide to send the call notice.

(2) A call notice—
   (a) may not require a member to pay a call which exceeds the total sum unpaid on that member's shares (whether as to the share's nominal value or any amount payable to the company by way of premium);
   (b) must state when and how any call to which it relates it is to be paid; and
   (c) may permit or require the call to be paid by instalments.

(3) A member must comply with the requirements of a call notice, but no member is obliged to pay any call before 14 days have passed since the notice was sent.

(4) Before the company has received any call due under a call notice the directors may—
   (a) revoke it wholly or in part, or
   (b) specify a later time for payment than is specified in the notice, by a further notice in writing to the member in respect of whose shares the call is made.

Liability to pay calls

55.—(1) Liability to pay a call is not extinguished or transferred by transferring the shares in respect of which it is required to be paid.

(2) Joint holders of a share are jointly and severally liable to pay all calls in respect of that share.

(3) Subject to the terms on which shares are allotted, the directors may, when issuing shares, provide that call notices sent to the holders of those shares may require them—
   (a) to pay calls which are not the same, or
   (b) to pay calls at different times.

When call notice need not be issued

56.—(1) A call notice need not be issued in respect of sums which are specified, in the terms on which a share is issued, as being payable to the company in respect of that share (whether in respect of nominal value or premium)—
   (a) on allotment;
   (b) on the occurrence of a particular event; or
   (c) on a date fixed by or in accordance with the terms of issue.

(2) But if the due date for payment of such a sum has passed and it has not been paid, the holder of the share concerned is treated in all respects as having failed to comply with a call notice in respect of that sum, and is liable to the same consequences as regards the payment of interest and forfeiture.

Failure to comply with call notice: automatic consequences

57.—(1) If a person is liable to pay a call and fails to do so by the call payment date—
   (a) the directors may issue a notice of intended forfeiture to that person, and
   (b) until the call is paid, that person must pay the company interest on the call from the call payment date at the relevant rate.

(2) For the purposes of this article—
   (a) the "call payment date" is the time when the call notice states that a call is payable, unless the directors give a notice specifying a later date, in which case the "call payment date" is that later date;

(b) the "relevant rate" is—
  (i) the rate fixed by the terms on which the share in respect of which the call is due was allotted;
  (ii) such other rate as was fixed in the call notice which required payment of the call, or has otherwise been determined by the directors; or
  (iii) if no rate is fixed in either of these ways, 5 per cent per annum.

(3) The relevant rate must not exceed by more than 5 percentage points the base lending rate most recently set by the Monetary Policy Committee of the Bank of England in connection with its responsibilities under Part 2 of the Bank of England Act 1998(**2**).

(4) The directors may waive any obligation to pay interest on a call wholly or in part.

Notice of intended forfeiture

58. A notice of intended forfeiture—
  (a) may be sent in respect of any share in respect of which a call has not been paid as required by a call notice;
  (b) must be sent to the holder of that share or to a person entitled to it by reason of the holder's death, bankruptcy or otherwise;
  (c) must require payment of the call and any accrued interest by a date which is not less than 14 days after the date of the notice;
  (d) must state how the payment is to be made; and
  (e) must state that if the notice is not complied with, the shares in respect of which the call is payable will be liable to be forfeited.

Directors' power to forfeit shares

59. If a notice of intended forfeiture is not complied with before the date by which payment of the call is required in the notice of intended forfeiture, the directors may decide that any share in respect of which it was given is forfeited, and the forfeiture is to include all dividends or other moneys payable in respect of the forfeited shares and not paid before the forfeiture.

Effect of forfeiture

60.—(1) Subject to the articles, the forfeiture of a share extinguishes—
  (a) all interests in that share, and all claims and demands against the company in respect of it, and
  (b) all other rights and liabilities incidental to the share as between the person whose share it was prior to the forfeiture and the company.

(2) Any share which is forfeited in accordance with the articles—
  (a) is deemed to have been forfeited when the directors decide that it is forfeited;
  (b) is deemed to be the property of the company; and
  (c) may be sold, re-allotted or otherwise disposed of as the directors think fit.

(3) If a person's shares have been forfeited—
  (a) the company must send that person notice that forfeiture has occurred and record it in the register of members;
  (b) that person ceases to be a member in respect of those shares;
  (c) that person must surrender the certificate for the shares forfeited to the company for cancellation;
  (d) that person remains liable to the company for all sums payable by that person under the articles at the date of forfeiture in respect of those shares, including any interest (whether accrued before or after the date of forfeiture); and
  (e) the directors may waive payment of such sums wholly or in part or enforce payment without any allowance for the value of the shares at the time of forfeiture or for any consideration received on their disposal.

(4) At any time before the company disposes of a forfeited share, the directors may decide to cancel the forfeiture on payment of all calls and interest due in respect of it and on such other terms as they think fit.

Procedure following forfeiture

61.—(1) If a forfeited share is to be disposed of by being transferred, the company may receive the consideration for the transfer and the directors may authorise any person to execute the instrument of transfer.
  (2) A statutory declaration by a director or the company secretary that the declarant is a director or the company secretary and that a share has been forfeited on a specified date—
    (a) is conclusive evidence of the facts stated in it as against all persons claiming to be entitled to the share, and
    (b) subject to compliance with any other formalities of transfer required by the articles or by law, constitutes a good title to the share.
  (3) A person to whom a forfeited share is transferred is not bound to see to the application of the consideration (if any) nor is that person's title to the share affected by any irregularity in or invalidity of the process leading to the forfeiture or transfer of the share.
  (4) If the company sells a forfeited share, the person who held it prior to its forfeiture is entitled to receive from the company the proceeds of such sale, net of any commission, and excluding any amount which—
    (a) was, or would have become, payable, and
    (b) had not, when that share was forfeited, been paid by that person in respect of that share, but no interest is payable to such a person in respect of such proceeds and the company is not required to account for any money earned on them.

Surrender of shares

62.—(1) A member may surrender any share—
    (a) in respect of which the directors may issue a notice of intended forfeiture;
    (b) which the directors may forfeit; or
    (c) which has been forfeited.
  (2) The directors may accept the surrender of any such share.
  (3) The effect of surrender on a share is the same as the effect of forfeiture on that share.
  (4) A share which has been surrendered may be dealt with in the same way as a share which has been forfeited.

TRANSFER AND TRANSMISSION OF SHARES

Transfers of certificated shares

63.—(1) Certificated shares may be transferred by means of an instrument of transfer in any usual form or any other form approved by the directors, which is executed by or on behalf of—
    (a) the transferor, and
    (b) (if any of the shares is partly paid) the transferee.
  (2) No fee may be charged for registering any instrument of transfer or other document relating to or affecting the title to any share.
  (3) The company may retain any instrument of transfer which is registered.
  (4) The transferor remains the holder of a certificated share until the transferee's name is entered in the register of members as holder of it.
  (5) The directors may refuse to register the transfer of a certificated share if—
    (a) the share is not fully paid;
    (b) the transfer is not lodged at the company's registered office or such other place as the directors have appointed;
    (c) the transfer is not accompanied by the certificate for the shares to which it relates, or such other evidence as the directors may reasonably require to show the transferor's right to make the transfer, or evidence of the right of someone other than the transferor to make the transfer on the transferor's behalf;
    (d) the transfer is in respect of more than one class of share; or
    (e) the transfer is in favour of more than four transferees.

(6) If the directors refuse to register the transfer of a share, the instrument of transfer must be returned to the transferee with the notice of refusal unless they suspect that the proposed transfer may be fraudulent.

Transfer of uncertificated shares

64. A transfer of an uncertificated share must not be registered if it is in favour of more than four transferees.

Transmission of shares

65.—(1) If title to a share passes to a transmittee, the company may only recognise the transmittee as having any title to that share.
  (2) Nothing in these articles releases the estate of a deceased member from any liability in respect of a share solely or jointly held by that member.

Transmittees' rights

66.—(1) A transmittee who produces such evidence of entitlement to shares as the directors may properly require—
  (a) may, subject to the articles, choose either to become the holder of those shares or to have them transferred to another person, and
  (b) subject to the articles, and pending any transfer of the shares to another person, has the same rights as the holder had.
  (2) But transmittees do not have the right to attend or vote at a general meeting in respect of shares to which they are entitled, by reason of the holder's death or bankruptcy or otherwise, unless they become the holders of those shares

Exercise of transmittees' rights

67.—(1) Transmittees who wish to become the holders of shares to which they have become entitled must notify the company in writing of that wish.
  (2) If the share is a certificated share and a transmittee wishes to have it transferred to another person, the transmittee must execute an instrument of transfer in respect of it.
  (3) If the share is an uncertificated share and the transmittee wishes to have it transferred to another person, the transmittee must—
  (a) procure that all appropriate instructions are given to effect the transfer, or
  (b) procure that the uncertificated share is changed into certificated form and then execute an instrument of transfer in respect of it.
  (4) Any transfer made or executed under this article is to be treated as if it were made or executed by the person from whom the transmittee has derived rights in respect of the share, and as if the event which gave rise to the transmission had not occurred.

Transmittees bound by prior notices

68. If a notice is given to a member in respect of shares and a transmittee is entitled to those shares, the transmittee is bound by the notice if it was given to the member before the transmittee's name has been entered in the register of members.

CONSOLIDATION OF SHARES

Procedure for disposing of fractions of shares

69.—(1) This article applies where—
  (a) there has been a consolidation or division of shares, and
  (b) as a result, members are entitled to fractions of shares.
  (2) The directors may—
  (a) sell the shares representing the fractions to any person including the company for the best price reasonably obtainable;

(b) in the case of a certificated share, authorise any person to execute an instrument of transfer of the shares to the purchaser or a person nominated by the purchaser; and
(c) distribute the net proceeds of sale in due proportion among the holders of the shares.
(3) Where any holder's entitlement to a portion of the proceeds of sale amounts to less than a minimum figure determined by the directors, that member's portion may be distributed to an organisation which is a charity for the purposes of the law of England and Wales, Scotland or Northern Ireland.
(4) The person to whom the shares are transferred is not obliged to ensure that any purchase money is received by the person entitled to the relevant fractions.
(5) The transferee's title to the shares is not affected by any irregularity in or invalidity of the process leading to their sale.

DISTRIBUTIONS

Procedure for declaring dividends

70.—(1) The company may by ordinary resolution declare dividends, and the directors may decide to pay interim dividends.
(2) A dividend must not be declared unless the directors have made a recommendation as to its amount. Such a dividend must not exceed the amount recommended by the directors.
(3) No dividend may be declared or paid unless it is in accordance with members' respective rights.
(4) Unless the members' resolution to declare or directors' decision to pay a dividend, or the terms on which shares are issued, specify otherwise, it must be paid by reference to each member's holding of shares on the date of the resolution or decision to declare or pay it.
(5) If the company's share capital is divided into different classes, no interim dividend may be paid on shares carrying deferred or non-preferred rights if, at the time of payment, any preferential dividend is in arrear.
(6) The directors may pay at intervals any dividend payable at a fixed rate if it appears to them that the profits available for distribution justify the payment.
(7) If the directors act in good faith, they do not incur any liability to the holders of shares conferring preferred rights for any loss they may suffer by the lawful payment of an interim dividend on shares with deferred or non-preferred rights.

Calculation of dividends

71.—(1) Except as otherwise provided by the articles or the rights attached to shares, all dividends must be—
(a) declared and paid according to the amounts paid up on the shares on which the dividend is paid, and
(b) apportioned and paid proportionately to the amounts paid up on the shares during any portion or portions of the period in respect of which the dividend is paid.
(2) If any share is issued on terms providing that it ranks for dividend as from a particular date, that share ranks for dividend accordingly.
(3) For the purposes of calculating dividends, no account is to be taken of any amount which has been paid up on a share in advance of the due date for payment of that amount.

Payment of dividends and other distributions

72.—(1) Where a dividend or other sum which is a distribution is payable in respect of a share, it must be paid by one or more of the following means—
(a) transfer to a bank or building society account specified by the distribution recipient either in writing or as the directors may otherwise decide;

(b) sending a cheque made payable to the distribution recipient by post to the distribution recipient at the distribution recipient's registered address (if the distribution recipient is a holder of the share), or (in any other case) to an address specified by the distribution recipient either in writing or as the directors may otherwise decide;

(c) sending a cheque made payable to such person by post to such person at such address as the distribution recipient has specified either in writing or as the directors may otherwise decide; or

(d) any other means of payment as the directors agree with the distribution recipient either in writing or by such other means as the directors decide.

(2) In the articles, "the distribution recipient" means, in respect of a share in respect of which a dividend or other sum is payable—
  (a) the holder of the share; or
  (b) if the share has two or more joint holders, whichever of them is named first in the register of members; or
  (c) if the holder is no longer entitled to the share by reason of death or bankruptcy, or otherwise by operation of law, the transmittee.

Deductions from distributions in respect of sums owed to the company

73.—(1) If—
  (a) a share is subject to the company's lien, and
  (b) the directors are entitled to issue a lien enforcement notice in respect of it, they may, instead of issuing a lien enforcement notice, deduct from any dividend or other sum payable in respect of the share any sum of money which is payable to the company in respect of that share to the extent that they are entitled to require payment under a lien enforcement notice.

(2) Money so deducted must be used to pay any of the sums payable in respect of that share.

(3) The company must notify the distribution recipient in writing of—
  (a) the fact and amount of any such deduction;
  (b) any non-payment of a dividend or other sum payable in respect of a share resulting from any such deduction; and
  (c) how the money deducted has been applied.

No interest on distributions

74. The company may not pay interest on any dividend or other sum payable in respect of a share unless otherwise provided by—
  (a) the terms on which the share was issued, or
  (b) the provisions of another agreement between the holder of that share and the company.

Unclaimed distributions

75.—(1) All dividends or other sums which are—
  (a) payable in respect of shares, and
  (b) unclaimed after having been declared or become payable, may be invested or otherwise made use of by the directors for the benefit of the company until claimed.

(2) The payment of any such dividend or other sum into a separate account does not make the company a trustee in respect of it.

(3) If—
  (a) twelve years have passed from the date on which a dividend or other sum became due for payment, and
  (b) the distribution recipient has not claimed it, the distribution recipient is no longer entitled to that dividend or other sum and it ceases to remain owing by the company.

Non-cash distributions

76.—(1) Subject to the terms of issue of the share in question, the company may, by ordinary resolution on the recommendation of the directors, decide to pay all or part of a dividend or other distribution payable in respect of a share by transferring non-cash assets of equivalent value (including, without limitation, shares or other securities in any company).

(2) If the shares in respect of which such a non-cash distribution is paid are uncertificated, any shares in the company which are issued as a non-cash distribution in respect of them must be uncertificated.

(3) For the purposes of paying a non-cash distribution, the directors may make whatever arrangements they think fit, including, where any difficulty arises regarding the distribution—
  (a) fixing the value of any assets;
  (b) paying cash to any distribution recipient on the basis of that value in order to adjust the rights of recipients; and
  (c) vesting any assets in trustees.

Waiver of distributions

77. Distribution recipients may waive their entitlement to a dividend or other distribution payable in respect of a share by giving the company notice in writing to that effect, but if—
  (a) the share has more than one holder, or
  (b) more than one person is entitled to the share, whether by reason of the death or bankruptcy of one or more joint holders, or otherwise, the notice is not effective unless it is expressed to be given, and signed, by all the holders or persons otherwise entitled to the share.

CAPITALISATION OF PROFITS

Authority to capitalise and appropriation of capitalised sums

78.—(1) Subject to the articles, the directors may, if they are so authorised by an ordinary resolution—
  (a) decide to capitalise any profits of the company (whether or not they are available for distribution) which are not required for paying a preferential dividend, or any sum standing to the credit of the company's share premium account or capital redemption reserve; and
  (b) appropriate any sum which they so decide to capitalise (a "capitalised sum") to the persons who would have been entitled to it if it were distributed by way of dividend (the "persons entitled") and in the same proportions.

(2) Capitalised sums must be applied—
  (a) on behalf of the persons entitled, and
  (b) in the same proportions as a dividend would have been distributed to them.

(3) Any capitalised sum may be applied in paying up new shares of a nominal amount equal to the capitalised sum which are then allotted credited as fully paid to the persons entitled or as they may direct.

(4) A capitalised sum which was appropriated from profits available for distribution may be applied—
  (**2**)
  1998 c.11. Back [2]
  (a) in or towards paying up any amounts unpaid on existing shares held by the persons entitled, or
  (b) in paying up new debentures of the company which are then allotted credited as fully paid to the persons entitled or as they may direct.

(5) Subject to the articles the directors may—
  (a) apply capitalised sums in accordance with paragraphs (3) and (4) partly in one way and partly in another;

(b) make such arrangements as they think fit to deal with shares or debentures becoming distributable in fractions under this article (including the issuing of fractional certificates or the making of cash payments); and
(c) authorise any person to enter into an agreement with the company on behalf of all the persons entitled which is binding on them in respect of the allotment of shares and debentures to them under this article.

PART 5 MISCELLANEOUS PROVISIONS

COMMUNICATIONS

Means of communication to be used

79.—(1) Subject to the articles, anything sent or supplied by or to the company under the articles may be sent or supplied in any way in which the Companies Act 2006 provides for documents or information which are authorised or required by any provision of that Act to be sent or supplied by or to the company.
(2) Subject to the articles, any notice or document to be sent or supplied to a director in connection with the taking of decisions by directors may also be sent or supplied by the means by which that director has asked to be sent or supplied with such notices or documents for the time being.
(3) A director may agree with the company that notices or documents sent to that director in a particular way are to be deemed to have been received within a specified time of their being sent, and for the specified time to be less than 48 hours.

Failure to notify contact details

80.—(1) If—
(a) the company sends two consecutive documents to a member over a period of at least 12 months, and
(b) each of those documents is returned undelivered, or the company receives notification that it has not been delivered, that member ceases to be entitled to receive notices from the company.
(2) A member who has ceased to be entitled to receive notices from the company becomes entitled to receive such notices again by sending the company—
(a) a new address to be recorded in the register of members, or
(b) if the member has agreed that the company should use a means of communication other than sending things to such an address, the information that the company needs to use that means of communication effectively.

ADMINISTRATIVE ARRANGEMENTS

Company seals

81.—(1) Any common seal may only be used by the authority of the directors.
(2) The directors may decide by what means and in what form any common seal or securities seal is to be used.
(3) Unless otherwise decided by the directors, if the company has a common seal and it is affixed to a document, the document must also be signed by at least one authorised person in the presence of a witness who attests the signature.
(4) For the purposes of this article, an authorised person is—
(a) any director of the company;
(b) the company secretary; or
(c) any person authorised by the directors for the purpose of signing documents to which the common seal is applied.
(5) If the company has an official seal for use abroad, it may only be affixed to a document if its use on that document, or documents of a class to which it belongs, has been authorised by a decision of the directors.

(6) If the company has a securities seal, it may only be affixed to securities by the company secretary or a person authorised to apply it to securities by the company secretary.

(7) For the purposes of the articles, references to the securities seal being affixed to any document include the reproduction of the image of that seal on or in a document by any mechanical or electronic means which has been approved by the directors in relation to that document or documents of a class to which it belongs.

Destruction of documents

82.—(1) The company is entitled to destroy—
- (a) all instruments of transfer of shares which have been registered, and all other documents on the basis of which any entries are made in the register of members, from six years after the date of registration;
- (b) all dividend mandates, variations or cancellations of dividend mandates, and notifications of change of address, from two years after they have been recorded;
- (c) all share certificates which have been cancelled from one year after the date of the cancellation;
- (d) all paid dividend warrants and cheques from one year after the date of actual payment; and
- (e) all proxy notices from one year after the end of the meeting to which the proxy notice relates.

(2) If the company destroys a document in good faith, in accordance with the articles, and without notice of any claim to which that document may be relevant, it is conclusively presumed in favour of the company that—
- (a) entries in the register purporting to have been made on the basis of an instrument of transfer or other document so destroyed were duly and properly made;
- (b) any instrument of transfer so destroyed was a valid and effective instrument duly and properly registered;
- (c) any share certificate so destroyed was a valid and effective certificate duly and properly cancelled; and
- (d) any other document so destroyed was a valid and effective document in accordance with its recorded particulars in the books or records of the company.

(3) This article does not impose on the company any liability which it would not otherwise have if it destroys any document before the time at which this article permits it to do so.

(4) In this article, references to the destruction of any document include a reference to its being disposed of in any manner.

No right to inspect accounts and other records

83. Except as provided by law or authorised by the directors or an ordinary resolution of the company, no person is entitled to inspect any of the company's accounting or other records or documents merely by virtue of being a member.

Provision for employees on cessation of business

84. The directors may decide to make provision for the benefit of persons employed or formerly employed by the company or any of its subsidiaries (other than a director or former director or shadow director) in connection with the cessation or transfer to any person of the whole or part of the undertaking of the company or that subsidiary.

DIRECTORS' INDEMNITY AND INSURANCE

Indemnity

85.—(1) Subject to paragraph (2), a relevant director of the company or an associated company may be indemnified out of the company's assets against—
- (a) any liability incurred by that director in connection with any negligence, default, breach of duty or breach of trust in relation to the company or an associated company,

(b) any liability incurred by that director in connection with the activities of the company or an associated company in its capacity as a trustee of an occupational pension scheme (as defined in section 235(6) of the Companies Act 2006),
(c) any other liability incurred by that director as an officer of the company or an associated company.

(2) This article does not authorise any indemnity which would be prohibited or rendered void by any provision of the Companies Acts or by any other provision of law.

(3) In this article—
(a) companies are associated if one is a subsidiary of the other or both are subsidiaries of the same body corporate, and
(b) a "relevant director" means any director or former director of the company or an associated company.

Insurance

86.—(1) The directors may decide to purchase and maintain insurance, at the expense of the company, for the benefit of any relevant director in respect of any relevant loss.

(2) In this article—
(a) a "relevant director" means any director or former director of the company or an associated company,
(b) a "relevant loss" means any loss or liability which has been or may be incurred by a relevant director in connection with that director's duties or powers in relation to the company, any associated company or any pension fund or employees' share scheme of the company or associated company, and
(c) companies are associated if one is a subsidiary of the other or both are subsidiaries of the same body corporate.

EXPLANATORY NOTE
(This note is not part of the Regulations)
These Regulations, made under section 19 of the Companies Act 2006 (c.46), prescribe model forms of articles of association for—
(a) private companies limited by shares (regulation 2 and Schedule 1),
(b) private companies limited by guarantee (regulation 3 and Schedule 2), and
(c) public companies (regulation 4 and Schedule 3).
These model articles will automatically form the articles of association for companies formed under the Companies Act 2006 which, on their formation, either do not register their own articles of association with the registrar of companies under that Act, or, if they do so, do not exclude the model articles in whole or in part (section 20 of the 2006 Act). Other companies are free to adopt the model articles in whole or in part.

An Impact Assessment has not been produced for these Regulations as they have only a negligible impact on the costs of business, charities or voluntary bodies.

APPENDIX 3
The UK Corporate Governance Code

GOVERNANCE AND THE CODE

1. The purpose of corporate governance is to facilitate effective, entrepreneurial and prudent management that can deliver the long-term success of the company.
2. The first version of the UK Corporate Governance Code (the Code) was produced in 1992 by the Cadbury Committee. Its paragraph 2.5 is still the classic definition of the context of the Code:

   Corporate governance is the system by which companies are directed and controlled. Boards of directors are responsible for the governance of their companies. The shareholders' role in governance is to appoint the directors and the auditors and to satisfy themselves that an appropriate governance structure is in place. The responsibilities of the board include setting the company's strategic aims, providing the leadership to put them into effect, supervising the management of the business and reporting to shareholders on their stewardship. The board's actions are subject to laws, regulations and the shareholders in general meeting.
3. Corporate governance is therefore about what the board of a company does and how it sets the values of the company, and is to be distinguished from the day to day operational management of the company by full-time executives.
4. The Code is a guide to a number of key components of effective board practice. It is based on the underlying principles of all good governance: accountability, transparency, probity and focus on the sustainable success of an entity over the longer term.
5. The Code has been enduring, but it is not immutable. Its fitness for purpose in a permanently changing economic and social business environment requires its evaluation at appropriate intervals.
6. The new Code applies to accounting periods beginning on or after 1 October 2012 and applies to all companies with a Premium listing of equity shares regardless of whether they are incorporated in the UK or elsewhere.

PREFACE

1. The FRC's review of the implementation of the Code in 2011 reinforced the two principal conclusions reported in the preface to the 2010 edition. First, that much more attention needed to be paid to following the spirit of the Code as well as its letter. Secondly, that the impact of shareholders in monitoring the Code could and should be enhanced by better interaction between the boards of listed companies and their shareholders. The UK Stewardship Code, which provides guidance on good practice for investors, should be seen as a companion piece to this Code.
2. Nearly two decades of constructive usage have enhanced the prestige of the Code. Indeed, it seems that there is almost a belief that complying with the Code in itself constitutes good governance. The Code, however, is of necessity limited to being a guide only in general terms to principles, structure and processes. It cannot guarantee effective board behaviour because the range of situations in which it is applicable is much too great for it to attempt to mandate behaviour more specifically than it does. Boards therefore have a lot of room within the framework of the Code to decide for themselves how they should act.
3. To follow the spirit of the Code to good effect, boards must think deeply, thoroughly and on a continuing basis about their overall tasks and the implications of these for the roles of their individual members. Absolutely key in this endeavour are the leadership of the chairman of a board, the support given to and by the CEO, and the frankness and openness of mind with which issues are discussed and tackled by all directors.
4. The challenge should not be underrated. To run a corporate board successfully is extremely demanding. Constraints on time and knowledge combine with the need to maintain

mutual respect and openness between a cast of strong, able and busy directors dealing with each other across the different demands of executive and non-executive roles. To achieve good governance requires continuing and high quality effort.

5. The Code's function should be to help boards discharge their duties in the best interests of their companies. In recent reviews of the Code, the FRC has focused on changing the 'tone' of the Code by making limited but significant changes to signal the importance of the general principles which should guide board behaviours. It is to be hoped that these changes will promote greater clarity and understanding with regard to the tasks of a board and that communication with shareholders will be more effective as a result.

6. Chairmen are encouraged to report personally in their annual statements how the principles relating to the role and effectiveness of the board (in Sections A and B of the Code) have been applied. Not only will this give investors a clearer picture of the steps taken by boards to operate effectively but also, by providing fuller context, it may make investors more willing to accept explanations when a company chooses to explain rather than to comply with one or more provisions. Above all, the personal reporting on governance by chairmen as the leaders of boards might be a turning point in attacking the fungus of 'boiler-plate' which is so often the preferred and easy option in sensitive areas but which is dead communication.

7. While in law the company is primarily accountable to its shareholders, and the relationship between the company and its shareholders is also the main focus of the Code, companies are encouraged to recognise the contribution made by other providers of capital and to confirm the board's interest in listening to the views of such providers insofar as these are relevant to the company's overall approach to governance.

Financial Reporting Council
September 2012

THE MAIN PRINCIPLES OF THE CODE

Section A: Leadership

Every company should be headed by an effective board which is collectively responsible for the long-term success of the company.

There should be a clear division of responsibilities at the head of the company between the running of the board and the executive responsibility for the running of the company's business. No one individual should have unfettered powers of decision.

The chairman is responsible for leadership of the board and ensuring its effectiveness on all aspects of its role.

As part of their role as members of a unitary board, non-executive directors should constructively challenge and help develop proposals on strategy.

Section B: Effectiveness

The board and its committees should have the appropriate balance of skills, experience, independence and knowledge of the company to enable them to discharge their respective duties and responsibilities effectively.

There should be a formal, rigorous and transparent procedure for the appointment of new directors to the board.

All directors should be able to allocate sufficient time to the company to discharge their responsibilities effectively.

All directors should receive induction on joining the board and should regularly update and refresh their skills and knowledge.

The board should be supplied in a timely manner with information in a form and of a quality appropriate to enable it to discharge its duties.

The board should undertake a formal and rigorous annual evaluation of its own performance and that of its committees and individual directors.

All directors should be submitted for re-election at regular intervals, subject to continued satisfactory performance.

Section C: Accountability

The board should present a fair, balanced and understandable assessment of the company's position and prospects.

The board is responsible for determining the nature and extent of the significant risks it is willing to take in achieving its strategic objectives. The board should maintain sound risk management and internal control systems.

The board should establish formal and transparent arrangements for considering how they should apply the corporate reporting, risk management and internal control principles and for maintaining an appropriate relationship with the company's auditors.

Section D: Remuneration

Levels of remuneration should be sufficient to attract, retain and motivate directors of the quality required to run the company successfully, but a company should avoid paying more than is necessary for this purpose.

A significant proportion of executive directors' remuneration should be structured so as to link rewards to corporate and individual performance.

There should be a formal and transparent procedure for developing policy on executive remuneration and for fixing the remuneration packages of individual directors. No director should be involved in deciding his or her own remuneration.

Section E: Relations With Shareholders

There should be a dialogue with shareholders based on the mutual understanding of objectives. The board as a whole has responsibility for ensuring that a satisfactory dialogue with shareholders takes place.

The board should use the AGM to communicate with investors and to encourage their participation.

SECTION A: LEADERSHIP

A.1: The Role of the Board

Main Principle
Every company should be headed by an effective board which is collectively responsible for the long-term success of the company.

Supporting Principles
The board's role is to provide entrepreneurial leadership of the company within a framework of prudent and effective controls which enables risk to be assessed and managed. The board should set the company's strategic aims, ensure that the necessary financial and human resources are in place for the company to meet its objectives and review management performance. The board should set the company's values and standards and ensure that its obligations to its shareholders and others are understood and met.

All directors must act in what they consider to be the best interests of the company, consistent with their statutory duties[2].

Code Provisions

A.1.1. The board should meet sufficiently regularly to discharge its duties effectively. There should be a formal schedule of matters specifically reserved for its decision. The annual report should include a statement of how the board operates, including a high level statement of which types of decisions are to be taken by the board and which are to be delegated to management.

A.1.2. The annual report should identify the chairman, the deputy chairman (where there is one), the chief executive, the senior independent director and the chairmen and

---

[2] For directors of UK incorporated companies, these duties are set out in the Sections 170 to 177 of the Companies Act 2006.

members of the board committees[3]. It should also set out the number of meetings of the board and those committees and individual attendance by directors.

A.1.3. The company should arrange appropriate insurance cover in respect of legal action against its directors.

A.2: DIVISION OF RESPONSIBILITIES

Main Principle
There should be a clear division of responsibilities at the head of the company between the running of the board and the executive responsibility for the running of the company's business. No one individual should have unfettered powers of decision.

Code Provision

A.2.1 The roles of chairman and chief executive should not be exercised by the same individual. The division of responsibilities between the chairman and chief executive should be clearly established, set out in writing and agreed by the board.

A.3: THE CHAIRMAN

Main Principle
The chairman is responsible for leadership of the board and ensuring its effectiveness on all aspects of its role.

Supporting Principle
The chairman is responsible for setting the board's agenda and ensuring that adequate time is available for discussion of all agenda items, in particular strategic issues. The chairman should also promote a culture of openness and debate by facilitating the effective contribution of non-executive directors in particular and ensuring constructive relations between executive and non-executive directors.

The chairman is responsible for ensuring that the directors receive accurate, timely and clear information. The chairman should ensure effective communication with shareholders.

Code Provisions

A.3.1. The chairman should on appointment meet the independence criteria set out in B.1.1 below. A chief executive should not go on to be chairman of the same company. If exceptionally a board decides that a chief executive should become chairman, the board should consult major shareholders in advance and should set out its reasons to shareholders at the time of the appointment and in the next annual report[4].

A.4: NON-EXECUTIVE DIRECTORS

Main Principle
As part of their role as members of a unitary board, non-executive directors should constructively challenge and help develop proposals on strategy.

Supporting Principles
Non-executive directors should scrutinise the performance of management in meeting agreed goals and objectives and monitor the reporting of performance. They should satisfy themselves on the integrity of financial information and that financial controls and systems of risk management are robust and defensible. They are responsible for determining appropriate levels of remuneration of executive directors and have a prime role in appointing and, where necessary, removing executive directors, and in succession planning.

Code Provisions

A.4.1. The board should appoint one of the independent non-executive directors to be the senior independent director to provide a sounding board for the chairman and to serve

---

3 Provisions A.1.1 and A.1.2 overlap with FSA Rule DTR 7.2.7 R; Provision A.1.2 also overlaps with DTR 7.1.5 R (see Schedule B).
4 Compliance or otherwise with this provision need only be reported for the year in which the appointment is made.

as an intermediary for the other directors when necessary. The senior independent director should be available to shareholders if they have concerns which contact through the normal channels of chairman, chief executive or other executive directors has failed to resolve or for which such contact is inappropriate.

A.4.2. The chairman should hold meetings with the non-executive directors without the executives present. Led by the senior independent director, the non-executive directors should meet without the chairman present at least annually to appraise the chairman's performance and on such other occasions as are deemed appropriate.

A.4.3. Where directors have concerns which cannot be resolved about the running of the company or a proposed action, they should ensure that their concerns are recorded in the board minutes. On resignation, a non-executive director should provide a written statement to the chairman, for circulation to the board, if they have any such concerns.

SECTION B: EFFECTIVENESS

B.1: The Composition of the Board

Main Principle
The board and its committees should have the appropriate balance of skills, experience, independence and knowledge of the company to enable them to discharge their respective duties and responsibilities effectively.

Supporting Principles
The board should be of sufficient size that the requirements of the business can be met and that changes to the board's composition and that of its committees can be managed without undue disruption, and should not be so large as to be unwieldy.

The board should include an appropriate combination of executive and non-executive directors (and, in particular, independent non-executive directors) such that no individual or small group of individuals can dominate the board's decision taking.

The value of ensuring that committee membership is refreshed and that undue reliance is not placed on particular individuals should be taken into account in deciding chairmanship and membership of committees.

No one other than the committee chairman and members is entitled to be present at a meeting of the nomination, audit or remuneration committee, but others may attend at the invitation of the committee.

Code Provisions

B.1.1. The board should identify in the annual report each non-executive director it considers to be independent[5]. The board should determine whether the director is independent in character and judgement and whether there are relationships or circumstances which are likely to affect, or could appear to affect, the director's judgement. The board should state its reasons if it determines that a director is independent notwithstanding the existence of relationships or circumstances which may appear relevant to its determination, including if the director:
- has been an employee of the company or group within the last five years;
- has, or has had within the last three years, a material business relationship with the company either directly, or as a partner, shareholder, director or senior employee of a body that has such a relationship with the company;
- has received or receives additional remuneration from the company apart from a director's fee, participates in the company's share option or a performance-related pay scheme, or is a member of the company's pension scheme;
- has close family ties with any of the company's advisers, directors or senior employees;
- holds cross-directorships or has significant links with other directors through involvement in other companies or bodies;
- represents a significant shareholder; or
- has served on the board for more than nine years from the date of their first election.

---

[5] A.3.1 states that the chairman should, on appointment, meet the independence criteria set out in this provision, but thereafter the test of independence is not appropriate in relation to the chairman.

B.1.2. Except for smaller companies[6], at least half the board, excluding the chairman, should comprise non-executive directors determined by the board to be independent. A smaller company should have at least two independent non-executive directors.

B.2: Appointments to the Board

Main Principle

There should be a formal, rigorous and transparent procedure for the appointment of new directors to the board.

Supporting Principles

The search for board candidates should be conducted, and appointments made, on merit, against objective criteria and with due regard for the benefits of diversity on the board, including gender.

The board should satisfy itself that plans are in place for orderly succession for appointments to the board and to senior management, so as to maintain an appropriate balance of skills and experience within the company and on the board and to ensure progressive refreshing of the board.

Code Provisions

B.2.1. There should be a nomination committee which should lead the process for board appointments and make recommendations to the board. A majority of members of the nomination committee should be independent non-executive directors. The chairman or an independent non-executive director should chair the committee, but the chairman should not chair the nomination committee when it is dealing with the appointment of a successor to the chairmanship. The nomination committee should make available its terms of reference, explaining its role and the authority delegated to it by the board[7].

B.2.2. The nomination committee should evaluate the balance of skills, experience, independence and knowledge on the board and, in the light of this evaluation, prepare a description of the role and capabilities required for a particular appointment.

B.2.3. Non-executive directors should be appointed for specified terms subject to re-election and to statutory provisions relating to the removal of a director. Any term beyond six years for a non-executive director should be subject to particularly rigorous review, and should take into account the need for progressive refreshing of the board.

B.2.4. A separate section of the annual report should describe the work of the nomination committee[8], including the process it has used in relation to board appointments. This section should include a description of the board's policy on diversity, including gender, any measurable objectives that it has set for implementing the policy, and progress on achieving the objectives. An explanation should be given if neither an external search consultancy nor open advertising has been used in the appointment of a chairman or a non-executive director. Where an external search consultancy has been used, it should be identified in the annual report and a statement made as to whether it has any other connection with the company.

B.3: Commitment

Main Principle

All directors should be able to allocate sufficient time to the company to discharge their responsibilities effectively.

Code Provisions

B.3.1. For the appointment of a chairman, the nomination committee should prepare a job specification, including an assessment of the time commitment expected, recognising the need for availability in the event of crises. A chairman's other significant commitments should be disclosed to the board before appointment and included in the annual report. Changes to such commitments should be reported to the board as they arise, and their impact explained in the next annual report.

---

6 A smaller company is one that is below the FTSE 350 throughout the year immediately prior to the reporting year.
7 The requirement to make the information available would be met by including the information on a website that is maintained by or on behalf of the company.
8 This provision overlaps with FSA Rule DTR 7.2.7 R (see Schedule B).

B.3.2. The terms and conditions of appointment of non-executive directors should be made available for inspection[9]. The letter of appointment should set out the expected time commitment. Non-executive directors should undertake that they will have sufficient time to meet what is expected of them. Their other significant commitments should be disclosed to the board before appointment, with a broad indication of the time involved and the board should be informed of subsequent changes.

B.3.3. The board should not agree to a full time executive director taking on more than one non-executive directorship in a FTSE 100 company nor the chairmanship of such a company.

B.4: Development

Main Principle
All directors should receive induction on joining the board and should regularly update and refresh their skills and knowledge.

Supporting Principles
The chairman should ensure that the directors continually update their skills and the knowledge and familiarity with the company required to fulfil their role both on the board and on board committees.

The company should provide the necessary resources for developing and updating its directors' knowledge and capabilities.

To function effectively all directors need appropriate knowledge of the company and access to its operations and staff.

Code Provisions

B.4.1. The chairman should ensure that new directors receive a full, formal and tailored induction on joining the board. As part of this, directors should avail themselves of opportunities to meet major shareholders.

B.4.2. The chairman should regularly review and agree with each director their training and development needs.

B.5: Information and Support

Main Principle
The board should be supplied in a timely manner with information in a form and of a quality appropriate to enable it to discharge its duties.

Supporting Principles
The chairman is responsible for ensuring that the directors receive accurate, timely and clear information. Management has an obligation to provide such information but directors should seek clarification or amplification where necessary.

Under the direction of the chairman, the company secretary's responsibilities include ensuring good information flows within the board and its committees and between senior management and non-executive directors, as well as facilitating induction and assisting with professional development as required.

The company secretary should be responsible for advising the board through the chairman on all governance matters.

Code Provisions

B.5.1. The board should ensure that directors, especially non-executive directors, have access to independent professional advice at the company's expense where they judge it necessary to discharge their responsibilities as directors. Committees should be provided with sufficient resources to undertake their duties.

---

9 The terms and conditions of appointment of non-executive directors should be made available for inspection by any person at the company's registered office during normal business hours and at the AGM (for 15 minutes prior to the meeting and during the meeting).

B.5.2. All directors should have access to the advice and services of the company secretary, who is responsible to the board for ensuring that board procedures are complied with. Both the appointment and removal of the company secretary should be a matter for the board as a whole.

B.6: Evaluation

Main Principle

The board should undertake a formal and rigorous annual evaluation of its own performance and that of its committees and individual directors.

Supporting Principles

Evaluation of the board should consider the balance of skills, experience, independence and knowledge of the company on the board, its diversity, including gender, how the board works together as a unit, and other factors relevant to its effectiveness.

The chairman should act on the results of the performance evaluation by recognising the strengths and addressing the weaknesses of the board and, where appropriate, proposing new members be appointed to the board or seeking the resignation of directors.

Individual evaluation should aim to show whether each director continues to contribute effectively and to demonstrate commitment to the role (including commitment of time for board and committee meetings and any other duties).

Code Provisions

B.6.1. The board should state in the annual report how performance evaluation of the board, its committees and its individual directors has been conducted.

B.6.2. Evaluation of the board of FTSE 350 companies should be externally facilitated at least every three years. The external facilitator should be identified in the annual report and a statement made as to whether they have any other connection with the company.

B.6.3. The non-executive directors, led by the senior independent director, should be responsible for performance evaluation of the chairman, taking into account the views of executive directors.

B.7: Re-election

Main Principle

All directors should be submitted for re-election at regular intervals, subject to continued satisfactory performance.

Code Provisions

B.7.1. All directors of FTSE 350 companies should be subject to annual election by shareholders. All other directors should be subject to election by shareholders at the first annual general meeting after their appointment, and to re-election thereafter at intervals of no more than three years. Non-executive directors who have served longer than nine years should be subject to annual re-election. The names of directors submitted for election or re-election should be accompanied by sufficient biographical details and any other relevant information to enable shareholders to take an informed decision on their election.

B.7.2. The board should set out to shareholders in the papers accompanying a resolution to elect a non-executive director why they believe an individual should be elected. The chairman should confirm to shareholders when proposing re-election that, following formal performance evaluation, the individual's performance continues to be effective and to demonstrate commitment to the role.

SECTION C: ACCOUNTABILITY

C.1: Financial And Business Reporting

Main Principle

The board should present a fair, balanced and understandable assessment of the company's position and prospects.

Supporting Principle

The board's responsibility to present a fair, balanced and understandable assessment extends to interim and other price-sensitive public reports and reports to regulators as well as to information required to be presented by statutory requirements.

The board should establish arrangements that will enable it to ensure that the information presented is fair, balanced and understandable.

Code Provisions

C.1.1. The directors should explain in the annual report their responsibility for preparing the annual report and accounts, and state that they consider the annual report and accounts, taken as a whole, is fair, balanced and understandable and provides the information necessary for shareholders to assess the company's performance, business model and strategy. There should be a statement by the auditor about their reporting responsibilities[10].

C.1.2. The directors should include in the annual report an explanation of the basis on which the company generates or preserves value over the longer term (the business model) and the strategy for delivering the objectives of the company[11].

C.1.3. The directors should report in annual and half-yearly financial statements that the business is a going concern, with supporting assumptions or qualifications as necessary[12].

C.2: Risk Management and Internal Control[13]

Main Principle

The board is responsible for determining the nature and extent of the significant risks it is willing to take in achieving its strategic objectives. The board should maintain sound risk management and internal control systems.

Code Provision

C.2.1. The board should, at least annually, conduct a review of the effectiveness of the company's risk management and internal control systems and should report to shareholders that they have done so[14]. The review should cover all material controls, including financial, operational and compliance controls.

C.3: Audit Committee and Auditors[15]

Main Principle

The board should establish formal and transparent arrangements for considering how they should apply the corporate reporting and risk management and internal control principles and for maintaining an appropriate relationship with the company's auditors.

Code Provisions

C.3.1. The board should establish an audit committee of at least three, or in the case of smaller companies[16] two, independent non-executive directors. In smaller companies the company chairman may be a member of, but not chair, the committee in addition to the independent non-executive directors, provided he or she was considered independent on appointment as chairman. The board should satisfy itself that at least one member of the audit committee has recent and relevant financial experience[17].

---

10 This requirement may be met by the disclosures about the audit scope and responsibilities of the auditor included, or referred to, in the auditor's report pursuant to the requirements of ISA (UK and Ireland) 700, 'The Auditor's Report on Financial Statements'. Copies are available from the FRC website.

11 It would be desirable if the explanation were located in the same part of the annual report as the Business Review required by Section 417 of the Companies Act 2006. Guidance as to the matters that should be considered in an explanation of a business model is provided in 'Reporting Statement: Operating And Financial Review'. Copies are available from the FRC website.

12 'Going Concern and Liquidity Risk: Guidance for Directors of UK Companies 2009' suggests means of applying this part of the Code. Copies are available from the FRC website.

13 'Internal Control: Guidance to Directors' suggests means of applying this part of the Code. Copies are available from the FRC website.

14 In addition FSA Rule DTR 7.2.5 R requires companies to describe the main features of the internal control and risk management systems in relation to the financial reporting process.

15 'Guidance on Audit Committees' suggests means of applying this part of the Code. Copies are available from the FRC website.

16 See footnote 6.

17 This provision overlaps with FSA Rule DTR 7.1.1 R (see Schedule B).

C.3.2. The main role and responsibilities of the audit committee should be set out in written terms of reference[18] and should include:
- to monitor the integrity of the financial statements of the company and any formal announcements relating to the company's financial performance, reviewing significant financial reporting judgements contained in them;
- to review the company's internal financial controls and, unless expressly addressed by a separate board risk committee composed of independent directors, or by the board itself, to review the company's internal control and risk management systems;
- to monitor and review the effectiveness of the company's internal audit function;
- to make recommendations to the board, for it to put to the shareholders for their approval in general meeting, in relation to the appointment, re-appointment and removal of the external auditor and to approve the remuneration and terms of engagement of the external auditor;
- to review and monitor the external auditor's independence and objectivity and the effectiveness of the audit process, taking into consideration relevant UK professional and regulatory requirements;
- to develop and implement policy on the engagement of the external auditor to supply non-audit services, taking into account relevant ethical guidance regarding the provision of non-audit services by the external audit firm; and to report to the board, identifying any matters in respect of which it considers that action or improvement is needed and making recommendations as to the steps to be taken; and
- to report to the board on how it has discharged its responsibilities.

C.3.3. The terms of reference of the audit committee, including its role and the authority delegated to it by the board, should be made available[19].

C.3.4. Where requested by the board, the audit committee should provide advice on whether the annual report and accounts, taken as a whole, is fair, balanced and understandable and provides the information necessary for shareholders to assess the company's performance, business model and strategy.

C.3.5. The audit committee should review arrangements by which staff of the company may, in confidence, raise concerns about possible improprieties in matters of financial reporting or other matters. The audit committee's objective should be to ensure that arrangements are in place for the proportionate and independent investigation of such matters and for appropriate follow-up action.

C.3.6. The audit committee should monitor and review the effectiveness of the internal audit activities. Where there is no internal audit function, the audit committee should consider annually whether there is a need for an internal audit function and make a recommendation to the board, and the reasons for the absence of such a function should be explained in the relevant section of the annual report.

C.3.7. The audit committee should have primary responsibility for making a recommendation on the appointment, reappointment and removal of the external auditors. FTSE 350 companies should put the external audit contract out to tender at least every ten years. If the board does not accept the audit committee's recommendation, it should include in the annual report, and in any papers recommending appointment or re-appointment, a statement from the audit committee explaining the recommendation and should set out reasons why the board has taken a different position.

C.3.8. A separate section of the annual report should describe the work of the committee in discharging its responsibilities[20]. The report should include:
- the significant issues that the committee considered in relation to the financial statements, and how these issues were addressed;
- an explanation of how it has assessed the effectiveness of the external audit process and the approach taken to the appointment or reappointment of the external auditor, and information on the length of tenure of the current audit firm and when a tender was last conducted; and
- if the external auditor provides non-audit services, an explanation of how auditor objectivity and independence is safeguarded.

---

18 This provision overlaps with FSA Rules DTR 7.1.3 R (see Schedule B).
19 See footnote 7.
20 This provision overlaps with FSA Rules DTR 7.1.5 R and 7.2.7 R (see Schedule B).

SECTION D: REMUNERATION

D.1: The Level and Components of Remuneration

Main Principle
Levels of remuneration should be sufficient to attract, retain and motivate directors of the quality required to run the company successfully, but a company should avoid paying more than is necessary for this purpose. A significant proportion of executive directors' remuneration should be structured so as to link rewards to corporate and individual performance.

Supporting Principle
The performance-related elements of executive directors' remuneration should be stretching and designed to promote the long-term success of the company.
The remuneration committee should judge where to position their company relative to other companies. But they should use such comparisons with caution, in view of the risk of an upward ratchet of remuneration levels with no corresponding improvement in performance.
They should also be sensitive to pay and employment conditions elsewhere in the group, especially when determining annual salary increases.

Code Provisions
D.1.1. In designing schemes of performance-related remuneration for executive directors, the remuneration committee should follow the provisions in Schedule A to this Code.
D.1.2. Where a company releases an executive director to serve as a non-executive director elsewhere, the remuneration report[21] should include a statement as to whether or not the director will retain such earnings and, if so, what the remuneration is.
D.1.3. Levels of remuneration for non-executive directors should reflect the time commitment and responsibilities of the role. Remuneration for non-executive directors should not include share options or other performance-related elements. If, exceptionally, options are granted, shareholder approval should be sought in advance and any shares acquired by exercise of the options should be held until at least one year after the non-executive director leaves the board. Holding of share options could be relevant to the determination of a non-executive director's independence (as set out in provision B.1.1).
D.1.4 The remuneration committee should carefully consider what compensation commitments (including pension contributions and all other elements) their directors' terms of appointment would entail in the event of early termination. The aim should be to avoid rewarding poor performance. They should take a robust line on reducing compensation to reflect departing directors' obligations to mitigate loss.
D.1.5 Notice or contract periods should be set at one year or less. If it is necessary to offer longer notice or contract periods to new directors recruited from outside, such periods should reduce to one year or less after the initial period.

D.2 Procedure

Main Principle
There should be a formal and transparent procedure for developing policy on executive remuneration and for fixing the remuneration packages of individual directors. No director should be involved in deciding his or her own remuneration.

Supporting Principles
The remuneration committee should consult the chairman and/or chief executive about their proposals relating to the remuneration of other executive directors. The remuneration committee should also be responsible for appointing any consultants in respect of executive director remuneration. Where executive directors or senior management are involved in advising or supporting the remuneration committee, care should be taken to recognise and avoid conflicts of interest.

---

21 As required for UK incorporated companies under the Large and Medium-Sized Companies and Groups (Accounts and Reports) Regulations 2008.

The chairman of the board should ensure that the company maintains contact as required with its principal shareholders about remuneration.

Code Provisions

D.2.1 The board should establish a remuneration committee of at least three, or in the case of smaller companies[22] two, independent non-executive directors. In addition the company chairman may also be a member of, but not chair, the committee if he or she was considered independent on appointment as chairman. The remuneration committee should make available its terms of reference, explaining its role and the authority delegated to it by the board[23]. Where remuneration consultants are appointed, a statement should be made available[24] of whether they have any other connection with the company.

D.2.2 The remuneration committee should have delegated responsibility for setting remuneration for all executive directors and the chairman, including pension rights and any compensation payments. The committee should also recommend and monitor the level and structure of remuneration for senior management. The definition of 'senior management' for this purpose should be determined by the board but should normally include the first layer of management below board level.

D.2.3 The board itself or, where required by the Articles of Association, the shareholders should determine the remuneration of the non-executive directors within the limits set in the Articles of Association. Where permitted by the Articles, the board may however delegate this responsibility to a committee, which might include the chief executive.

D.2.4 Shareholders should be invited specifically to approve all new long-term incentive schemes (as defined in the Listing Rules[25]) and significant changes to existing schemes, save in the circumstances permitted by the Listing Rules.

SECTION E: RELATIONS WITH SHAREHOLDERS

E.1: Dialogue with Shareholders

Main Principle
There should be a dialogue with shareholders based on the mutual understanding of objectives. The board as a whole has responsibility for ensuring that a satisfactory dialogue with shareholders takes place.[26]

Supporting Principles
Whilst recognising that most shareholder contact is with the chief executive and finance director, the chairman should ensure that all directors are made aware of their major shareholders' issues and concerns.
The board should keep in touch with shareholder opinion in whatever ways are most practical and efficient.

Code Provisions

E.1.1. The chairman should ensure that the views of shareholders are communicated to the board as a whole. The chairman should discuss governance and strategy with major shareholders. Non-executive directors should be offered the opportunity to attend scheduled meetings with major shareholders and should expect to attend meetings if requested by major shareholders. The senior independent director should attend sufficient meetings with a range of major shareholders to listen to their views in order to help develop a balanced understanding of the issues and concerns of major shareholders.

E.1.2. The board should state in the annual report the steps they have taken to ensure that the members of the board, and in particular the non-executive directors, develop an

---

22 See footnote 6.
23 This provision overlaps with FSA Rule DTR 7.2.7 R (see Schedule B).
24 See footnote 7.
25 Listing Rules LR 9.4; available at http://fsahandbook.info/FSA/html/handbook/LR/9/4.
26 Nothing in these principles or provisions should be taken to override the general requirements of law to treat shareholders equally in access to information.

understanding of the views of major shareholders about the company, for example through direct face-to-face contact, analysts' or brokers' briefings and surveys of shareholder opinion.

E.2: Constructive Use of the AGM

Main Principle
The board should use the AGM to communicate with investors and to encourage their participation.

Code Provisions
E.2.1. At any general meeting, the company should propose a separate resolution on each substantially separate issue, and should in particular propose a resolution at the AGM relating to the report and accounts. For each resolution, proxy appointment forms should provide shareholders with the option to direct their proxy to vote either for or against the resolution or to withhold their vote. The proxy form and any announcement of the results of a vote should make it clear that a 'vote withheld' is not a vote in law and will not be counted in the calculation of the proportion of the votes for and against the resolution.

E.2.2. The company should ensure that all valid proxy appointments received for general meetings are properly recorded and counted. For each resolution, where a vote has been taken on a show of hands, the company should ensure that the following information is given at the meeting and made available as soon as reasonably practicable on a website which is maintained by or on behalf of the company:
- the number of shares in respect of which proxy appointments have been validly made;
- the number of votes for the resolution;
- the number of votes against the resolution; and
- the number of shares in respect of which the vote was directed to be withheld.

E.2.3. The chairman should arrange for the chairmen of the audit, remuneration and nomination committees to be available to answer questions at the AGM and for all directors to attend.

E.2.4. The company should arrange for the Notice of the AGM and related papers to be sent to shareholders at least 20 working days before the meeting.

Schedule A: The design of performance-related remuneration for executive directors

The remuneration committee should consider whether the directors should be eligible for annual bonuses. If so, performance conditions should be relevant, stretching and designed to promote the long-term success of the company. Upper limits should be set and disclosed. There may be a case for part payment in shares to be held for a significant period.

The remuneration committee should consider whether the directors should be eligible for benefits under long-term incentive schemes. Traditional share option schemes should be weighed against other kinds of long-term incentive scheme. Executive share options should not be offered at a discount save as permitted by the relevant provisions of the Listing Rules.

In normal circumstances, shares granted or other forms of deferred remuneration should not vest, and options should not be exercisable, in less than three years. Directors should be encouraged to hold their shares for a further period after vesting or exercise, subject to the need to finance any costs of acquisition and associated tax liabilities.

Any new long-term incentive schemes which are proposed should be approved by shareholders and should preferably replace any existing schemes or, at least, form part of a well considered overall plan incorporating existing schemes. The total rewards potentially available should not be excessive.

Payouts or grants under all incentive schemes, including new grants under existing share option schemes, should be subject to challenging performance criteria reflecting the company's objectives, including non-financial performance metrics where appropriate. Remuneration incentives should be compatible with risk policies and systems.

Grants under executive share option and other long-term incentive schemes should normally be phased rather than awarded in one large block.

Consideration should be given to the use of provisions that permit the company to reclaim variable components in exceptional circumstances of misstatement or misconduct.

In general, only basic salary should be pensionable. The remuneration committee should consider the pension consequences and associated costs to the company of basic salary increases and any other changes in pensionable remuneration, especially for directors close to retirement.

Schedule B: Disclosure of corporate governance arrangements

Corporate governance disclosure requirements are set out in three places:
- FSA Disclosure and Transparency Rules sub-chapters 7.1 and 7.2 (which set out certain mandatory disclosures);
- FSA Listing Rules 9.8.6 R, 9.8.7 R, and 9.8.7A R (which includes the 'comply or explain' requirement); and
- The UK Corporate Governance Code (in addition to providing an explanation where they choose not to comply with a provision, companies must disclose specified information in order to comply with certain provisions).

These requirements are summarised below. The full text of Disclosure and Transparency Rules 7.1 and 7.2 and Listing Rules 9.8.6 R, 9.8.7 R, 9.8.7A R are contained in the relevant chapters of the FSA Handbook.

The Disclosure and Transparency Rules sub-chapters 7.1 and 7.2 apply to issuers whose securities are admitted to trading on a regulated market (this includes all issuers with a Premium or Standard listing). The Listing Rules 9.8.6 R, 9.8.7 R and 9.8.7A R and UK Corporate Governance Code apply to issuers of Premium listed equity shares only.

There is some overlap between the mandatory disclosures required under the Disclosure and Transparency Rules and those expected under the UK Corporate Governance Code. Areas of overlap are summarised in the Appendix to this Schedule. In respect of disclosures relating to the audit committee and the composition and operation of the board and its committees, compliance with the relevant provisions of the Code will result in compliance with the relevant Rules.

Disclosure and Transparency Rules

Sub-chapter 7.1 of the Disclosure and Transparency Rules concerns audit committees or bodies carrying out equivalent functions.

DTR 7.1.1 R and 7.1.3 R set out requirements relating to the composition and functions of the committee or equivalent body:
- DTR 7.1.1 R states than an issuer must have a body which is responsible for performing the functions set out in DTR 7.1.3 R, and that at least one member of that body must be independent and at least one member must have competence in accounting and/or auditing.
- DTR 7.1.2 G states that the requirements for independence and competence in accounting and/or auditing may be satisfied by the same member or by different members of the relevant body.
- DTR 7.1.3 R states that an issuer must ensure that, as a minimum, the relevant body must:
    1. monitor the financial reporting process;
    2. monitor the effectiveness of the issuer's internal control, internal audit where applicable, and risk management systems;
    3. monitor the statutory audit of the annual and consolidated accounts;
    4. review and monitor the independence of the statutory auditor, and in particular the provision of additional services to the issuer.

DTR 7.1.5 R sets out what disclosure is required. Specifically:
- DTR 7.1.5 R states that the issuer must make a statement available to the public disclosing which body carries out the functions required by DTR 7.1.3 R and how it is composed.
- DTR 7.1.6 G states that this can be included in the corporate governance statement required under sub-chapter DTR 7.2 (see below).
- DTR 7.1.7 G states that compliance with the relevant provisions of the UK Corporate Governance Code (as set out in the Appendix to this Schedule) will result in compliance with DTR 7.1.1 R to 7.1.5 R.

Sub-chapter 7.2 concerns corporate governance statements. Issuers are required to produce a corporate governance statement that must be either included in the directors' report (DTR 7.2.1 R); or in a separate report published together with the annual report; or on the issuer's website, in which case there must be a cross-reference in the directors' report (DTR 7.2.9 R).

DTR 7.2.2 R requires that the corporate governance statements must contain a reference to the corporate governance code to which the company is subject (for companies with a Premium listing this is the UK Corporate Governance Code). DTR 7.2.3 R requires that, to the extent that it departs from that code, the company must explain which parts of the code it departs from and the reasons for doing so. DTR 7.2.4 G states that compliance with LR 9.8.6 R (6) (the 'comply or explain' rule in relation to the UK Corporate Governance Code) will also satisfy these requirements.

DTR 7.2.5 R, DTR 7.2.7 R and DTR 7.2.10 R set out certain information that must be disclosed in the corporate governance statement:

> DTR 7.2.5 R states that the corporate governance statement must contain a description of the main features of the company's internal control and risk management systems in relation to the financial reporting process. DTR 7.2.10 R states that an issuer which is required to prepare a group directors' report within the meaning of Section 415(2) of the Companies Act 2006 must include in that report a description of the main features of the group's internal control and risk management systems in relation to the process for preparing consolidated accounts. · DTR 7.2.6 R states that the corporate governance statement must contain the information required by paragraph 13(2)(c), (d), (f), (h) and (i) of Schedule 7 to the Large and Medium-sized Companies and Groups (Accounts and Reports) Regulations 2008 (SI 2008/410) where the issuer is subject to the requirements of that paragraph. · DTR 7.2.7 R states that the corporate governance statement must contain a description of the composition and operation of the issuers administrative, management and supervisory bodies and their committees. DTR 7.2.8 G states that compliance with the relevant provisions of the UK Corporate Governance Code (as set out in the Appendix to this Schedule) will satisfy these requirements.

Listing Rules

Listing Rules 9.8.6 R (for UK incorporated companies) and 9.8.7 R (for overseas incorporated companies) state that in the case of a company that has a Premium listing of equity shares, the following items must be included in its annual report and accounts:

- a statement of how the listed company has applied the Main Principles set out in the UK Corporate Governance Code, in a manner that would enable shareholders to evaluate how the principles have been applied;
- a statement as to whether the listed company has: -complied throughout the accounting period with all relevant provisions set out in the UK Corporate Governance Code; or -not complied throughout the accounting period with all relevant provisions set out in the UK Corporate Governance Code, and if so, setting out:
    i. those provisions, if any, it has not complied with;
    ii. in the case of provisions whose requirements are of a continuing nature, the period within which, if any, it did not comply with some or all of those provisions; and
    iii. the company's reasons for non-compliance.

The UK Corporate Governance Code

In addition to the 'comply or explain' requirement in the Listing Rules, the Code includes specific requirements for disclosure which must be provided in order to comply. These are summarised below.

The annual report should include:
- a statement of how the board operates, including a high level statement of which types of decisions are to be taken by the board and which are to be delegated to management (A.1.1);
- the names of the chairman, the deputy chairman (where there is one), the chief executive, the senior independent director and the chairmen and members of the board committees (A.1.2);

- the number of meetings of the board and those committees and individual attendance by directors (A.1.2);
- where a chief executive is appointed chairman, the reasons for their appointment (this only needs to be done in the annual report following the appointment) (A.3.1);
- the names of the non-executive directors whom the board determines to be independent, with reasons where necessary (B.1.1);
- a separate section describing the work of the nomination committee, including the process it has used in relation to board appointments; a description of the board's policy on diversity, including gender; any measurable objectives that it has set for implementing the policy, and progress on achieving the objectives. An explanation should be given if neither external search consultancy nor open advertising has been used in the appointment of a chairman or a non-executive director. Where an external search consultancy has been used it should be identified and a statement made as to whether it has any other connection with the company (B.2.4);
- any changes to the other significant commitments of the chairman during the year (B.3.1);
- a statement of how performance evaluation of the board, its committees and its directors has been conducted (B.6.1). Where an external facilitator has been used, they should be identified and a statement made as to whether they have any other connection to the company (B.6.2);
- an explanation from the directors of their responsibility for preparing the accounts and a statement that they consider that the annual report and accounts, taken as a whole, is fair, balanced and understandable and provides the information necessary for shareholders to assess and provide the company's performance, business model and strategy. There should also be a statement by the auditor about their reporting responsibilities (C.1.1);
- an explanation from the directors of the basis on which the company generates or preserves value over the longer term (the business model) and the strategy for delivering the objectives of the company (C.1.2);
- a statement from the directors that the business is a going concern, with supporting assumptions or qualifications as necessary (C.1.3);
- a report that the board has conducted a review of the effectiveness of the company's risk management and internal controls systems (C.2.1);
- where there is no internal audit function, the reasons for the absence of such a function (C.3.6);
- where the board does not accept the audit committee's recommendation on the appointment, reappointment or removal of an external auditor, a statement from the audit committee explaining the recommendation and the reasons why the board has taken a different position (C.3.7);
- a separate section describing the work of the audit committee in discharging its responsibilities, including: the significant issues that it considered in relation to the financial statements, and how these issues were addressed; an explanation of how it has assessed the effectiveness of the external audit process and the approach taken to the appointment or reappointment of the external auditor, including the length of tenure of the current audit firm and when a tender was last conducted; and, if the external auditor provides non-audit services, an explanation of how auditor objectivity and independence is safeguarded (C.3.8);
- a description of the work of the remuneration committee as required under the Large and Medium-Sized Companies and Groups (Accounts and Reports) Regulations 2008, including, where an executive director serves as a non-executive director elsewhere, whether or not the director will retain such earnings and, if so, what the remuneration is (D.1.2);
- where remuneration consultants are appointed they should be identified and a statement made as to whether they have any other connection with the company (D.2.1); and

- the steps the board has taken to ensure that members of the board, and in particular the non-executive directors, develop an understanding of the views of major shareholders about their company (E.1.2).

The following information should be made available (which may be met by placing the information on a website that is maintained by or on behalf of the company):
- the terms of reference of the nomination, audit and remuneration committees, explaining their role and the authority delegated to them by the board (B.2.1, C.3.3 and D.2.1); and
- the terms and conditions of appointment of non-executive directors (B.3.2) (see footnote 9 on page 13).

The board should set out to shareholders in the papers accompanying a resolution to elect or re-elect directors:
- sufficient biographical details to enable shareholders to take an informed decision on their election or re-election (B.7.1);
- why they believe an individual should be elected to a non-executive role (B.7.2); and
- on re-election of a non-executive director, confirmation from the chairman that, following formal performance evaluation, the individual's performance continues to be effective and to demonstrate commitment to the role (B.7.2).

The board should set out to shareholders in the papers recommending appointment or reappointment of an external auditor:
- if the board does not accept the audit committee's recommendation, a statement from the audit committee explaining the recommendation and from the board setting out reasons why they have taken a different position (C.3.6).

Additional guidance

The FRC publishes guidance on going concern, risk management and internal control and audit committees, which contain further suggestions as to information that might usefully be disclosed in the statement that the business is a going concern (C.1.3), the statement on the board's review of the company's risk management and internal control systems (C.2.1) and the report of the audit committee (C.3.8) respectively. This guidance is available on the FRC website.

APPENDIX

OVERLAP BETWEEN THE DISCLOSURE AND TRANSPARENCY RULES AND THE UK CORPORATE GOVERNANCE CODE

DISCLOSURE AND TRANSPARENCY RULES	UK CORPORATE GOVERNANCE CODE
D.T.R 7.1.1 R Sets out minimum requirements on composition of the audit committee or equivalent body.	**Provision C.3.1** Sets out recommended composition of the audit committee.
D.T.R 7.1.3 R Sets out minimum functions of the audit committee or equivalent body.	**Provision C.3.2** Sets out the recommended minimum terms of reference for the audit committee.
D.T.R 7.1.5 R The composition and function of the audit committee or equivalent body must be disclosed in the annual report *DTR 7.1.7 R states that compliance with Code provisions A.1.2, C.3.1, C.3.2 and C.3.3 will result in compliance with DTR 7.1.1 R to DTR 7.1.5 R.*	**Provision A.1.2** The annual report should identify members of the board committees. **Provision C.3.3** The annual report should describe the work of the audit committee. Further recommendations on the content of the audit committee report are set out in the FRC Guidance on Audit Committees.
D.T.R 7.2.5 R The corporate governance statement must include a description of the main features of the company's internal control and risk management systems in relation to the financial reporting process. *While this requirement differs from the requirement in the UK Corporate Governance Code, it is envisaged that both could be met by a single internal control statement.*	**Provision C.2.1** The Board must report that a review of the effectiveness of the risk management and internal control systems has been carried out. Further recommendations on the content of the internal control statement are set out in the Turnbull Guidance.
DTR 7.2.7 R The corporate governance statement must include a description of the composition and operation of the administrative, management and supervisory bodies and their committees. *DTR 7.2.8 R states that compliance with Code provisions A.1.1, A.1.2, A.4.6, B.2.1 and C.3.3 will result in compliance with DTR 7.2.7 R.*	This requirement overlaps with a number of different provisions of the Code: **A.1.1**: the annual report should include a statement of how the board operates. **A.1.2**: the annual report should identify members of the board and board committees. **B.2.4**: the annual report should describe the work of the nomination committee. **C.3.3**: the annual report should describe the work of the audit committee. **D.2.1**: a description of the work of the remuneration committee should be made available. *[Note: in order to comply with DTR 7.2.7 R this information will need to be included in the corporate governance statement].*

Glossary

abbreviated accounts The brief accounts that a company which qualifies as small or medium-sized may file with the Registrar of Companies.

administration order A court order which gives power to manage the business to the administrator.

administrative receiver A receiver and manager appointed by the holder of a pre-15 September 2003 floating charge, which appointment results in his taking control of the whole or substantially the whole of the undertaking of the company. Now largely replaced by administrators.

administrative restoration A procedure introduced under the Companies Act 2006 whereby the Registrar of Companies may restore a company to the register without the need for a court order, provided certain criteria are met.

agent A person with authority to alter the legal position of another person which other person is known as the principal.

administrator An insolvency practitioner appointed by the court under an administration order.

allotment Shares in a company are taken to be allotted when a person acquires the unconditional right to be included in the company's register of members in respect of the shares.

Alternative Investment Market (AIM) The market for smaller companies operated by the London Stock Exchange. Companies on the AIM market are not listed on the Official List and are not subject to the Listing Rules, but are controlled by separate AIM Rules.

annual general meeting (AGM) A general meeting of the members which, following the year of the company's incorporation, must for public limited companies be held in each calendar year within six months of the financial year end. Under the Companies Act 2006, only public companies and those private limited companies with an express requirement in the Articles are required to hold AGMs.

annual return A document in prescribed form which every registered company is required to file with the Registrar of Companies on an annual basis pursuant to the Companies Act 2006, s. 854, containing basic information about the company accurate as of the return date which is normally the anniversary of the incorporation of the company.

Articles of Association The regulations governing a company's internal management – the rights of shareholders, the conduct of meetings and the appointment, removal and powers of directors. Separate Model Articles for public and private limited companies come into effect from 1 October 2009 and will be the default Articles to the extent that companies incorporated after this date do not exclude or modify them.

asset shielding A term used in the company context to describe the effect of incorporation whereby the assets of a company are protected from exposure to the creditors of a member or shareholder (i.e. a creditor of a shareholder cannot seek to enforce a judgment debt against a shareholder by legal execution against the assets of the company of which the judgment debtor is a shareholder). Also called 'entity shielding' or 'affirmative asset partitioning'.

bare debenture An unsecured debenture. Also called a 'naked debenture'.

BIS The Department of Business, Innovation and Skills (formerly BERR and the DTI), the government department responsible for company law (amongst other things) of which The Insolvency Service is an executive agency.

bona fide In good faith.

bona vacantia Property without an apparent owner legal title in which is vested in the Crown. In practice the Treasury has power to grant such property to the person who appears to have the most meritorious claim.

bonus issue Fully paid shares of the same class issued free of charge to existing shareholders in proportion to their existing holding. Also referred to as a capitalisation issue.

book debts A debt arising in the course of a business that would or could in the ordinary course of business be entered in well-kept books relating to that business.

branch Part of an overseas company with a permanent place of business in Great Britain with its own management and delegated responsibility. A branch business must be registered with the Registrar of Companies.

certificated A paper-based system of holding shares, represented by share certificates.

certificate of incorporation The document issued by the Registrar of Companies on the registration of a company under the Companies Act 2006 (or a predecessor statute).

charge A legal or equitable property interest in some or all of the assets of the company created to secure a loan to the company or to secure some other right against the company.

charitable incorporated organisation A corporate vehicle for charities provided for by the Companies Act 2011 which is registered with the Charity Commission rather than with the Registrar of Companies.

class right A right attaching to a class of share, the most common being the right to receive a dividend, the right to receive a return of capital on a winding up and the right to vote in general meeting. The precise range of attributes of a share that may amount to class rights is moot.

City Code on Takeovers and Mergers A set of principles and rules designed principally to ensure that shareholders are treated fairly and are not denied an opportunity to decide on the merits of a takeover and that shareholders of the same class are afforded equivalent treatment by an offeror. It provides an orderly framework within which takeovers are conducted and is designed to promote the integrity of the financial markets. The FSMA 2000 placed the City Code on a statutory footing.

class meeting A meeting of the holders of a class of a company's shares. Class meetings are held whenever the rights of the holder are to be varied by an action proposed by the company.

common seal The seal of a company; a device used for making an impressed mark upon a document so as to authenticate it.

community interest company (CIC) A corporate entity to encourage the provision of products and services to benefit community, social and environmental needs. Companies wishing to qualify for CIC status are required to satisfy the community interest test.

company limited by guarantee In a company limited by guarantee the members of which agree to contribute a specified amount towards the payment of its debts and the expenses of winding up while they are members or within one year after ceasing to be members.

company voluntary arrangement A composition in satisfaction of a company's debts, or a scheme of arrangement of its affairs, that binds all affected company creditors even though not all of them agree to its terms, entered into under and in accordance with the procedure in Part 1 of the Insolvency Act 1986.

compulsory liquidation or compulsory winding up The winding up of a company by order of the court.

concert party In relation to a takeover, the offeror and those acting in concert with the offeror, meaning persons who pursuant to an agreement or understanding (whether formal or informal), co-operate to obtain or consolidate control of a company or frustrate the successful outcome of an offer for a company.

connected persons A person connected with the company, defined for the purposes of challenging pre-liquidation transactions pursuant to the Insolvency Act 1986, in section 249 of the 1986 Act as a director of the company or an associate of either the company or a director of the company. Not to be confused with a person connected with a director for the purposes of Part 10 of the Companies Act 2006 (such as for the purpose of deciding whether or not a person connected with a director has entered into a transaction with the company for which shareholder approval is required) defined in s. 252 of the 2006 Act.

continuing obligations Part of the Listing Rules and Disclosure and Transparency Rules. The regulations and obligations which listed companies have to comply with once they have been admitted to the Official List.

contributory The holder of a partly paid share who is required to pay the unpaid element on his shares on a winding up. This term is given a broader meaning for the purposes of a person being permitted to petition the court for a winding up order under the Insolvency Act 1986, s. 124.

corporate governance The system by which companies are directed and controlled. Corporate governance is concerned with how the company is structured and controlled internally to ensure that the business is run lawfully and ethically.

creditor A person to whom a debt is owed.

creditors' voluntary winding up A voluntary winding up where no statutory declaration of solvency has been made by the directors, or, if a declaration of solvency has been made, subsequently, the liquidator disagrees with the declaration and is of the opinion that the company will be unable to pay its debts in full within the specified period.

CREST An electronic holding and settlement system in which legal title to a dematerialised share is recorded and by which share transfer are made. Shares held and transferred in this way are called 'dematerialised'.

crystallisation On crystallisation, a floating charge becomes a fixed charge.

cumulative dividend If any dividend due is not paid, it accrues to the shareholder and is payable with the next dividend due at the next payment date. Usually associated with preference shares.

debenture A document which either creates a debt or acknowledges it. Usually, though by no means always, a debenture is secured.

deed A formal document conforming with the requirements of a deed set out in the Law of Property (Miscellaneous Provisions) Act 1989 and, in the case of a registered company, executed as a deed in accordance with the Companies Act 2006, s. 44.

***de facto* director** A person who has not been properly appointed but who is occupying the position of a director.

***de jure* director** A person who has not only been properly appointed but who has satisfied the legal formalities that have to be observed by directors.

derivative claim A claim brought by a member under the Companies Act 2006, ss 260–269 against a director for an actual or proposed act or omission involving negligence, breach of duty or breach of trust by a director of a company. The claim is brought by the member for and on behalf of the company itself.

director Any person occupying the position of a director by whatever name he is called.

disqualification (voluntary) undertaking An out of court procedure whereby a director accepts a binding undertaking not, without the consent of the court, to act as a director for a defined disqualification period, in lieu of a disqualification order under the Company Director Disqualification Act 1986.

distributable profits Profits within the company which may be used to pay dividends.

dividend A payment made to members out of a company's distributable profits, in proportion to their shareholding.

dormant company A company which has no significant accounting transactions during a financial year.

enlightened shareholder value The doctrine enshrined in the Companies Act 2006, s. 172, whereby although directors must act in the way they consider, in good faith, would be most likely to promote the success of the company *for the benefit of its members as a whole*, in performing this duty they must have regard to the interests of other stakeholders and the long term consequences of any decision.

estoppel In the context of the authority of an agent, estoppel is the doctrine upon which ostensible authority is based, that a person who induces another person, by representation, to change his position in reliance on the representation, cannot subsequently deny the truth of his representation; he is estopped from such denial.

European Economic Interest Group (EEIG) A legal entity separate from its members at least two members of which must be from different Member States and all members of which must carry on business within the European Union (EU) with their principal administration within the EU and, if not an individual, be an entity formed in accordance with the laws of a Member State with their registered offices in the EU.

equity share capital The issued share capital of a company excluding any part of that capital that, neither as respects dividends nor as respects capital, carries any right to participate beyond a specified amount in a distribution.

extraordinary general meeting (EGM) Before the Companies Act 2006, a term used to describe any general meeting held by a company which was not an AGM. While it is not used in the 2006 Act an EGM may still be referred to in company's

Articles which have not been updated to reflect 2006 Act changes.

fiduciary duty A duty owed by a fiduciary to his principal, an example of which is a director, who owes fiduciary duties to his company, arising out of the fiduciary nature of the relationship. The root of all fiduciary duties is the obligation of a fiduciary to act in good faith and not to allow any conflict to arise between his self interest or any duty he may owe to any third party and the duty he owes to his principal, i.e. the company. The principal fiduciary duties owed by a director to the company are now set out in Part 10 of the Companies Act 2006.

final dividend Dividend paid in respect of the financial year-end.

Financial Reporting Council (FRC) An independent non-governmental regulatory body that publishes (amongst other things) the UK Code of Corporate Governance and the UK Stewardship Code.

Financial Conduct Authority (FCA) An independent non-governmental regulatory body given a wide range of rule-making, investigatory and enforcement powers by the Financial Services and Markets Act 2000 (FSMA 2000) as amended by the Financial Services Act 2012. As the UK Listing Authority it maintains the Official List.

fixed charge A property interest in specified property preventing the owner of the property from selling or otherwise dealing with it without first either paying back the sum secured against it or obtaining the consent of the chargeholder. Also called a specific charge.

floating charge A charge upon all of a certain class of assets present and future which class is, in the ordinary course of the company's business, changing from time to time in relation to which charged assets, until steps are taken to enforce the charge, the company can carry on business in the ordinary way including removing a charged asset from the security.

forfeiture If the owner of partly paid shares fails to pay on a call or according to the schedule of payments, the shares can be forfeited. This happens rarely.

founder shares Shares issued to the founders or promoter of a company which may carry enhanced rights over other classes of share.

fraudulent trading For the purposes of s. 213 of the Insolvency Act 1986, the carrying on of the business of the company with intent to defraud creditors of the company or creditors of any other person, or for any fraudulent purpose.

Gazette, The The London, Edinburgh and/or Belfast *Gazette* published by The Stationery Office which comes out every business day and in which formal announcements concerning companies are made, such as when a winding up order is made or when a winding up resolution is passed.

general meeting A meeting of the members of a company.

grant of probate A legal document issued following a person's death where the deceased has a valid will. The grant of probate of a will is a legal document issued by the Probate Registry or Probate Office after the will has been proved and is evidence of the executor's authority to act as personal representative.

grant of representation The collective description of probate and letters of administration.

holding company A company having one or more subsidiary companies, i.e. holding a majority of voting rights or the right to appoint or remove a majority of directors in one or more other companies.

incorporation The process by which a legal entity, separate from its owners and managers, is formed

inside information Information of a precise nature in relation to a company with listed securities which is not generally available. If such information were generally available, it would be likely to have a significant effect on the share price of the company.

insider dealing The use of information which is not publicly available so as to unreasonably disadvantage investors in securities in ways which are either criminalised or subject to civil penalty.

Insolvency Service An executive agency of BIS established and operating under the Insolvency Acts 1986 and 2000 and Company Directors Disqualifications Act 1986 made up of 38 Official Receivers' offices throughout the UK.

institutional shareholders Owners and asset managers with equity holdings in UK listed companies, including (but not limited to) pension fund managers, insurance companies, and investment managers.

interim dividend Dividend paid during the year.

issued share capital The shares of a company that have been issued, including those taken on the formation of the company by those who subscribed to the Memorandum of Association.

judgment creditor A creditor who has sued the company owing him money and obtained judgment from the court in his favour against the company.

letter of allotment Written confirmation that shares have been allotted to an individual.

letter of administration A document issued following a person's death where the deceased did not have a valid will. In non-contentious cases the Probate Registry or Office will issue a letter of administration to a person entitled to act as personal representative in respect of the deceased.

lien A form of possessory security, being the right to hold the property of another as security for the performance of an obligation, although an equitable (distinct from a common law) lien can exist independently of possession. If provided for in the Articles, a company may have a lien in relation to those of its shares that are partly paid for any part of the nominal value or premium that has not been paid.

limited company A company the liability of whose members to contribute to the company to enable it to pay its debts is limited.

limited liability partnership A body corporate the liability of whose members is limited and formed by registration under the Limited Partnerships Act 2000. Has the organisational flexibility of a partnership and is taxed as a partnership.

limited partnership A partnership having one or more but not all limited partners i.e. sleeping partners whose liability in the event of the partnership's insolvency is limited to the amount that such partner has agreed to contribute.

liquidation The winding up of a company.

liquidator The person who undertakes the liquidation of a company and who must be a qualified insolvency practitioner.

listed company This term is not defined in statute. If you use it, it is essential to state the meaning you have given to it and the purpose for which you are using it. In the Glossary to the FCA Handbook it is defined as a company that has any class of its securities listed, i.e. included on an official list. Whilst this definition applies to the use of the term in the Listing Rules it does not apply to the use of the term in the Disclosure or Prospectus Rules.

Listing Regime A set of rules, called the Listing Rules, made by the FCA, as the UK Listing Authority, setting out the obligations that must be complied with to obtain admission of securities to the Official List, and the continuing obligations of companies with listed securities.

market abuse A generic term that covers two categories of behaviour: insider dealing and market manipulation which together describe behaviour in relation to securities or investments traded on a UK market which amount to misuse of information, disseminating misleading or false information and market distortion.

member A shareholder becomes a member when his name is entered in the register of members.

members' voluntary winding up The solvent winding up of a company pursuant to a special resolution passed by its members, the directors having made a statutory declaration of solvency.

Memorandum of Association Under the Companies Act 2006, a document containing historical details of the initial subscribers for shares and their agreement to form a company. Previously, a document setting out the basic details of a company: name, place of incorporation, objects, liability of the members and authorised share capital

mens rea The state of mind required for a crime to be committed which forms part of the definition of the particular crime.

misfeasance For Insolvency Act 1986, s. 212 purposes, where an officer of the company has misapplied or retained or become accountable for any money or other property of the company or been guilty of any misfeasance or breach of any fiduciary or other duty in relation to the company.

Model Articles The default Articles which, by operation of the Companies Act 2006, s. 20, form part, or all, of the Articles of a registered company on its formation as a result of failure of the incorporators to register bespoke Articles . Three sets of Model Articles have been prescribed by regulation by the Secretary of State pursuant to the power in s. 19 of the 2006 Act: Model Articles for Private Companies Limited by Shares, Model Articles for Private Companies Limited by Guarantee and Model Articles for Public Companies.

Model Code A code, published as part of the Listing Regime, which governs dealing in securities by directors and other 'persons discharging managerial responsibility' to avoid the possibility of insider dealing and other market abuse.

naked debenture An unsecured debenture. Also called a 'bare debenture'.

negotiable instrument Property which may be transferred by simple delivery or by delivery with endorsement (usually by way of a signature).

nominal value The value attached to a share when it is issued. The nominal value of a share need not bear any correlation to the market value of that share.

nominee shareholder A person, group of people or company whose name appears on a company register of members instead of the beneficial owner.

non-executive director (NED) A director who is not an employee of the company and who has no executive responsibilities.

objects clause The clause in an old style Memorandum of Association which sets out the business(es) the company proposes to carry on. Under the Companies Act 2006, the objects clause of pre-2006 Act companies has become a provision of the Articles of Association. A company incorporated under the 2006 Act may but need not have an objects clauses in its Articles.

Official Receiver A civil servant in the Insolvency Service and an officer of the court. The first liquidator of any company subject to compulsory winding up.

off-market purchase The purchase by a company of its own shares when such shares are not dealt with on a market.

off-the-shelf company A company which has already been registered by a third party such as a formation agent. The new owners purchase the company from the third party and adapt its details for their own needs.

offeree A company in respect of which an offer has been, or potentially may be, made to which the City Code on Takeovers and Mergers applies. Also known as the target or target company.

offeror A person (whether a company or an individual) who makes or is considering making an offer to which the City Code on Takeovers and Mergers applies. Also known as a bidder.

Official List The list maintained by the FCA as UK Listing Authority pursuant to FSMA 2000, s. 74(1) being a list of securities issued by companies for the purpose of being traded on a UK regulated market (the most important of which markets for equity shares is the Main Market of the London Stock Exchange).

ordinary resolution A resolution of the shareholders of a company passed by a simple majority of 50% plus one vote.

ordinary shares Shares other than shares that as respects dividends and capital carry a right to participate only up to a specified amount in a distribution.

ostensible authority The authority that one can assume a person purporting to be an agent has based on a representation made by a person authorised by the company. Also known as apparent authority.

overseas company A company incorporated outside the UK.

paid-up capital The amount of issued capital which has actually been paid. (Shares are not always paid in full at the time they are taken up.)

partnership The relationship which subsists between persons carrying on a business in common with a view of profit.

pari passu The principle that all unsecured creditors in a winding up share the assets available to unsecured creditors of the company on an equal footing.

passing off A common law tort actionable by a claimant who is the owner of goodwill (sometimes referred to as an unregistered trade mark or reputation attached to a good or service) when another person has made a misrepresentation which leads or is likely to lead to its product or service being associated with the claimant thereby deceiving the public and resulting in damage to the goodwill of the claimant.

personal representative An executor or administrator who administers a deceased person's estate.

phoenix company A new company formed with a name the same as or similar to that of a company that has gone into insolvent liquidation having the same director(s) as the failed company and running essentially the same business that had been run by the failed company the assets of which have been transferred to the second company.

poison pill A device or strategy to frustrate a takeover of the company which is sometimes put in place long before a takeover situation arises.

poll A vote in writing at a general meeting where shareholders or their proxies vote in proportion to their shareholding.

pre-emption rights The rights of existing shareholders to be offered new shares first in proportion to their existing shareholding.

preference shares Shares giving the holder preferential rights, usually in respect of dividends and/or return of capital on a winding up.

preferential creditors Creditors entitled to receive payment on a winding up in advance of the floating charge holders and unsecured creditors.

premium The amount paid for a share over and above the nominal value when it is allotted by the company.

price-sensitive information Information which would, if made public, be likely to have a significant effect on the price of particular securities.

prima facie On the face of it; at first sight.

primary market a market for new issues of securities.

private company A registered company that is not a public company.

pro rata Rateably. In proportion.

promoter A person who undertakes to form a company and who takes all or some of the necessary steps to achieve that end.

public limited company A company which is registered as a public company the name of which ends with the letters plc (or the names represented by those letters in full).

prospectus A document containing information about the company and its shares which enables prospective investors to decide whether or not to invest.

proxy A person appointed by a member entitled to vote at a general meeting to attend the meeting and vote in his place. The proxy can speak at the meeting and vote on a show of hands and on a poll. The proxy need not be a member of the company.

qualifying floating charge holder A floating charge entered into after 15 September 2003 which comprises a charge over the whole or substantially all of the company's property, the holder of which has the right under the Enterprise Act 2002 to appoint an administrator out of court.

qualifying person An individual who is a member of the company, a representative of a corporation, appointed under the Companies Act 2006, s. 323 for the purposes of that meeting or a proxy of a member appointed for that meeting.

quantum meruit The sum due to a person who has performed services for which no remuneration or means of calculating remuneration has been agreed but for which it was implied that payment would be made.

quorum The minimum number of people necessary for the transaction of business at a general meeting or board meeting.

receiver A person appointed under a debenture or other instrument secured over the assets of a company. In the event that the company defaults under the terms of the debenture or other instrument, the receiver is appointed to manage and realise the secured assets for the benefit of the charge holder.

recognised investment exchange (RIE) An investment exchange recognised by the FCA under Part XVIII of the FSMA 2000. The most important is the London Stock Exchange plc.

redeemable shares Shares that will be redeemed by the company at their nominal or par value at some stated date in the future.

redemption The process of redeeming (buying back) redeemable shares.

registered office The address of the office of a company to which formal notices and legal documents should be addressed and sent.

Registrar of Companies The registrar of companies for England and Wales, Scotland or Northern Ireland, as the case may require, to whom documents are sent to form a company and to whom the necessary returns are made during the lifetime of a company.

register of members A statutory register of information, it is the definitive list of members of a company.

resolution The formal way in which a decision of the shareholders or the directors is proposed and passed.

retention of title clause A clause that may be inserted into a contract for the sale of goods providing that ownership/property in the goods is not to pass to the buyer until the goods have been paid for.

rights issue The offer by a listed company of new shares to existing equity shareholders on a pro rata basis on a renounceable basis which entails issuing renounceable letters of allotment. The new shares are offered at a discount to the market price and the rights can be assigned for consideration.

scheme of arrangement procedure The statutory procedure set out in Part 26 of the Companies Act 2006 which facilitates changes being made to the rights of creditors or shareholders without securing the unanimous approval of those affected by the changes.

secondary market The market in which to buy securities from existing security owners rather than from the company.

securities A general name for loan and debenture stock and shares of all types.

secured creditor A creditor who has a property interest in all or part of the property of the company to secure the debt.

secured debenture A debenture the holder of which has a property interest in all or part of the property of the company by way of a fixed or floating charge (or the benefit of which charge is held on his behalf (typically by a debenture trustee)).

shadow director Any person in accordance with whose directions or instructions the directors are accustomed to act, except where that person gives advice in a professional capacity (e.g. a solicitor or accountant).

share certificate The documentary evidence issued by a company and held by a shareholder to indicate the ownership of shares.

share premium See premium.

share premium account An account into which all payments made for shares over and above their nominal value are credited.

share warrant (to bearer) A document issued by the company entitling the bearer (holder) to the number of shares in a company stated in the warrant. Such shares are transferable merely by delivery, i.e. without the need for an instrument of transfer. Share warrants can be issued by any limited company provided the Articles allow them to be issued.

Societas Europaea (SE) A corporate vehicle designed for corporate groups which operate in more than one European Union member state.

Societas Privata Europaea (SPE) A form of European Private Company (SPE) proposed by the European Commission to assist both large corporate groups wishing to reduce the costs of administering their groups of subsidiaries in Europe and SMEs seeking to operate in more than one Member State.

sole trader An individual who is in business on his own account i.e. he is not in partnership nor does he trade through a corporate body.

special notice The notice required from the proposing shareholders to the company for certain ordinary resolutions to remove a director or remove, appoint or reappoint an auditor.

special resolution Used for significant decisions. Requires a 75% majority and must be described as a special resolution in any notice, which should set out the exact text of the resolution.

squeeze out In the context of a takeover, the right of the offeror, under the Companies Act 2006, s. 979 to acquire outstanding shares on a compulsory basis where it has acquired (or unconditionally contracted to acquire) not less than 90% (i) in value of, and (ii) of the voting rights carried by, the shares to which the takeover offer relates.

stakebuilding Purchase of individual blocks of shares by a member or concert party, often as a prelude to a takeover bid.

stakeholders Groups with an interest in the company, such as employees, shareholders, customers, directors and the local communities in which it operates.

stamp duty Tax payable, amongst others, by the purchaser on the transfer of shares or stock.

statutory accounts The individual or group accounts which are required to be filed with the Registrar of Companies. These may be full accounts or, where permitted, abbreviated accounts.

statutory declaration of solvency A statement made by the board which confirms that the company is solvent and will be able to meet all liabilities which arise within 12 months from the commencement of a voluntary winding up.

stock Securities representing a loan to the company by investors who receive interest, usually at a fixed rate. These are not a class of share.

stock transfer form Instrument of transfer; the form completed by the transferor of shares to transfer the shares to the transferee.

subsidiary company A company which is controlled by another company, known as its holding company.

summary financial statement A shortened form of the annual report and accounts of the company which may be circulated to shareholders instead of the full report. All companies have the choice of issuing summary financial statements.

Table A A set of default Articles for the management of a company limited by shares which, for companies registered under the Companies Act 2006, has been superseded by two sets of Model Articles: the Model Articles for Private Companies Limited by Shares and the Model Articles for Public Companies.

takeover The process whereby one company acquires a controlling interest in another company.

trading certificate The certificate issued by the Registrar of Companies a public company is required to obtain before it can lawfully trade or borrow.

trading company A company defined in s. 360C of the Companies Act 2006 as a company any shares of which carry rights to vote at general meetings, and are admitted to trading on a regulated market in an EEA state.

transfer The process where the ownership of share passes from one person to another as a result of sale or gift.

tort A civil wrong such as negligence, defamation, trespass or passing off.

transmission The legal process where the ownership of a share passes from one person to another (e.g. following the death or bankruptcy of a member). This is not the same as a transfer.

UK Corporate Governance Code The code on corporate governance published by the FRC most recently updated and renamed in June 2010. Previously called the Combined Code on Corporate Governance.

UK Listing Authority or UKLA The FCA when it acts as the competent authority under Part VI of FSMA 2000, i.e. the UK's securities regulator.

ultra vires The expression used to refer to a transaction entered into by a company that is beyond its legal capacity (historically, outside the scope of its objects clause). In this strict sense, *ultra vires* has been abolished in relation to non-charitable registered companies. Sometimes used to refer to a transaction beyond the powers of the directors, but this use of the term is best avoided.

uncalled capital The amount of a company's issued share capital that remains to be paid by its members.

underwriter A person who agrees to purchase shares offered to the public if they are not applied for by the public.

underwriting An agreement usually made between the company and a merchant bank to purchase shares in an issue if they are not fully taken up by the public. Underwriting removes the risk that the company will not receive its full subscription monies.

unincorporated association An organisation typically formed or run to further social, environmental or cultural objectives for the benefit of its members, the local community or the public generally, including sports or other social clubs and cooperatives, often charities, not being incorporated or a sole trader or a partnership.

unregistered transfer Transfers which have not yet been registered, and where the name of the transferee has not yet been listed in the register of members.

voluntary winding up The winding up of a company commenced by a special resolution of its members.

winding up The liquidation of a company.

winding up order A court order to liquidate a company.

written resolution In law, a resolution of a private company proposed and passed in writing in accordance with Chapter 2 of Part 13 of the Companies Act 2006. Public companies can not pass written resolutions. Not to be confused with the non-legal use of the term to describe a resolution of directors of a company passed unanimously outside a board meeting where the Articles of Association of the company permit such.

wrongful trading A director of a company that has gone into insolvent liquidation who allowed the company to continue to trade when he knew or ought to have concluded that there was no reasonable prospect that the company would avoid going into insolvent liquidation has wrongfully traded and may be ordered by the court to make a contribution to the company's assets.

Directory

Further reading

General Reference

Boyle, Anthony, *Gore-Browne on Companies* (Jordans). A two-volume, loose-leaf work.

Butterworths' Company Law Handbook (Lexis- Nexis). Annual editions. The relevant texts of the most important statutes, statutory instruments and European legislation, as well as certain FCA regulation.

Butterworths' Corporate Law Service (Lexis Nexis). Multi-volume, loose-leaf/CD-ROM work, which embraces all aspects of company law. It contains numerous forms, precedents, procedural tables, model accounts and checklists.

Morse, Geoffrey K., *Palmer's Company Law* (Sweet & Maxwell). The most comprehensive and respected book on UK company law.

Walmsley, Keith, *The ICSA Companies Act 2006 Handbook*, 2nd edition (ICSA Publishing 2009). Complete text of the Act with commentary and indexes.

Company Law Student Text Books

French, D., Mayson, S. and Ryan, C., *Mayson, French and Ryan on Company Law* (Oxford University Press) updated annually.

Gower & Davies *Principles of Modern Company Law* (Sweet & Maxwell) 9th edition (Sweet & Maxwell 2012).

Company Law Student Cases and Materials Books

Sealy, L. and Worthington, S., *Sealy's Cases and Materials in Company Law*, 10th edition (Oxford University Press 2013).

French, D., *Blackstone's Statutes on Company Law 2012–2013*, 16th edition (Oxford University Press).

Hicks, A. and Goo, S., *Cases & Materials on Company Law*, 7th edition (Oxford University Press 2011).

Shepherd, C., *Company Law: 150 Leading Cases*, 3rd edition (Old Bailey Press 2004).

Company Incorporation and Constitution

Bruce, Martha, *A Practical Guide to the Memorandum and Articles of Association*, 2nd edition (ICSA Publishing 2009).

Reece, Thomas and Ryan, *The Law and Practice of Shareholders' Agreements* 3rd edition and CD (Lexis Nexis). Comprehensive coverage of the law and drafting agreements.

Directors

Dattani, Rita, *The ICSA Directors' Handbook* (ICSA Publishing, 2009).

Loose, Peter, Griffiths, Michael and Impey, David, *The Company Director, the Powers, Duties and Liabilities*, 11th edition (Jordans, 2011).

Bruce, Martha, *Rights and Duties of Directors*, 13th edition (Bloomsbury Professional 2013).

Davis-White, M. and Walters, A., *Directors' Disqualification and Insolvency Restrictions*, 3rd ed (Sweet & Maxwell 2009).

Shareholders

Hollington, Robin, *Shareholders' Rights*, 7th edition (Sweet & Maxwell 2013 regularly updated).

Meetings

Hamer, Andrew, *The Law and Practice of Company Meetings*, (ICSA Publishing, 2013). A practical guide to running company meetings, which addresses the law and practice in both public and private companies.

Impey, David, *The Modern Law of Meetings*, 3rd edition (Jordans, 2013).

Shearman, Ian, *Shackleton on the Law and Practice of Meetings*, 12th edition (Sweet & Maxwell, 2012).

Restructuring and Winding Up

Beale, Simon, *Insolvency and Restructuring Manual* 2nd ed. (Bloomsbury Professional 2013)
Guide to the principles and procedures involved corporate insolvency and restructuring.
Goode, R., *Principles of Corporate Insolvency Law*, 4th edition (Sweet & Maxwell 2011)

Magazines and Newsletters

Governance & Compliance. The monthly magazine of the ICSA covering news and features on developments in all areas of interest to company secretaries www.govcompmag.com

Inhouse Lawyer (Legalease Ltd) Monthly magazine for Heads of Legal Departments, company secretaries and senior directors, covering changes and developments in company and business law www.inhouselawyer.co.uk

List! (FCA) free quarterly newsletter on developments and policy from the FCA

PLC (PLC Publications) A monthly magazine focusing on technical legal issues for in-house lawyers and company secretaries.

The Register (Companies House). A free, quarterly magazine on Companies House and other company law developments.

Web Resources

Charity Commission
www.charity-commission.gov.uk
The Charities Regulator for England and Wales

The CIC Regulator
www.cicregulator.gov.uk
Independent regulator for Community Interest Companies

Companies House
(see Registrar of Companies)

The Department for Business, Innovation & Skills
www.bis.gov.uk

Financial Reporting Council
www.frc.org.uk
for full text of the UK Corporate Governance Code and the Stewardship Code

Financial Conduct Authority
www.fsa.gov.uk
Independent body responsible for regulating financial services firms, markets and exchanges in the UK. The Listing Rules, Prospectus Rules and Disclosure and Transparency Rules are available from the FCA. See also the UK Listing Authority.

The Insolvency Service
www.insolvency.gov.uk

Institute of Chartered Secretaries and Administrators
www.icsa.org.uk.
The ICSA Policy Unit produces a range of Best Practice Guides and Guidance Notes covering aspects of company law and regulation.

The Panel on Takeovers and Mergers
www.thetakeoverpanel.org.uk

The Registrar of Companies for England & Wales, Companies House
www.companieshouse.gov.uk
Government department responsible for maintaining the data on all limited companies required by the Companies Act 2006 and related legislation, and making it publicly available. Companies House publishes a wide range of helpful guidance, all available from the website

UK Listing Authority
www.fsa.gov.uk
The regulator of securities and markets in the UK. The UKLA maintains the Official List of securities and through the current Listing Regime, maintains and enforces standards.

Index

Actual authority
  meaning 112
Administration 323–8
  administrators, role and powers 327
  appointment by order of court 325
  commencement 324–5
  effect 325–6
    contracts, on 326
    directors, on 326
    employees, on 326
    insolvency proceedings, on 325–6
    legal process 325–6
    property, on 326
  ending 327–8
    conversion to creditors' voluntary winding up 328
    dissolution of company 328
    public interest winding up 328
  out of court appointments 324
  purpose 323
  termination where object achieved 327–8
Admission of securities to AIM 122
Admission of securities to LSE Main Market 123
Admission to Official List 125–6
Admission to trading on LSE Main Market 126
Agency
  consequences of incorporation, and 71–3
AIM
  admission of securities to 122
Allotment of shares 149
  authority of directors 150
  exercise of authority 150
Annual financial report 57
Annual general meeting 282–3
Annual reports and accounts 55–6
  group accounts 56
  individual company accounts 56
  narrative reporting 56
Annual returns 55
Articles of association 84–6
  amending 92–7
    accrued rights, removal of 94
    Allen principle, application of 95–7
    bona fide for benefit of company as a whole 94–5
    contractual provisions 93–4
    court-developed restrictions 94–7
    introducing article that could not have been included on incorporation 94
    provisions in Articles 93
    provisions in company contracts 93
    provisions in shareholders' agreements 94
    reform of *Allen* principle 97
    squeeze-out cases 96–7
    statutory provisions 92–3
  ascertaining 84
  content 84–6
  contracts with terms derived from 98
  drafting 84
  enforcement 87–92
    company, by 88
    internal irregularity 91–2
    member suing to enforce outsider rights 89–91
    members, by 88–92
  implied actual authority and ostensible authority contrasted 115–6
  limits on content 85–6
  Model 84
  range of issues typically covered by 84–5
  statutory contract, as 87–92
Asset shielding 26
Audit exemption 222
Audit requirement 222
Auditor 222–6
  appointment 223
  audit requirement 222
  duties 224
  liability 225–6
    company, to 225
    criminal 226
    third parties, to 226
  removal 223–4
  resignation 223–4
  rights 224
  website publication of audit concerns 224
Authority of individuals to bind company 111–6
  actual authority 112
  ostensible authority 114–5

Bearer shares 160–61
Board decisions 293–4
  chairman's casting vote 294
  conflicts of interest 294
  public companies 293–4
  UK Corporate Governance Code 294

Board meetings 292
Board of directors 207–8
　authorisation 208
　authority to bind company 106–11
　　common law position 110–11
　　Companies Act 2006 107
　　dealing in good faith 109
　　persons 'dealing with the company' 108–9
　　persons entitled to rely on s. 40 107
　　situations outside s. 40 109–10
　delegation 208
　governing body, as 207–8
　powers 207
Book debts
　charges over 193–5
　fixed charges over 194–5
　meaning 193
Building societies 31–2
Business names
　companies, used by 52

Capacity of company 81–3
Capital maintenance 164–85
　cakes and ale case law 180–81
　common law principles 184
　doctrine of 168–9
　financial assistance for purchase of own shares 181–4
　fundamental legal principles 168
　gratuitous payments to non-shareholders 180
　political donations 181
　shareholder last principle on winding up 180
Case law 8–9
Certificate of incorporation 44–5
Charges
　book debts, over 193–5
Charitable incorporation organisations 30
Chartered companies 19
City Code on Takeovers and Mergers 9–10
Class meetings 284
Closely-held companies 11–12
Community interest companies 30
Companies limited by guarantee 20
Companies limited by shares 20
Company as distinct legal person 59–79
Company formation companies 41
Company investigations 275
Company law 3
　meaning 3–8
　model company 11
Company meetings 281–4
　corporate representatives 290
　electronic communications 290–91
　proxy 281, 290
　quorum 281
　shareholder engagement 290–91
　UK Stewardship Code 291
Company names 48–52
　goodwill, and 50–51
　objection to 50–51
　passing-off 50
　procedure to change 51
　rights to refuse to register 48–9
　Secretary of State's rights to direct change 49
　trading disclosures 51–2
Company numbers 46–8
Company registers and records 54–5
Company restructuring 299–306
　Insolvency Act 1986, s110 299–301
　　availability 299–300
　　creditor protection 300–301
　　dissenting share holder protection 300
　　procedure 300
　　usage 299–300
Company seals 104
Company secretary 219–22
　appointment 219–20
　authority to bind company 221
　officer of company, as 221–2
　qualifications 219–20
　register 219
　requirement for 219
　responsibilities 220–21
　role 220–21
Company voluntary arrangements 320–22
Constitution of company 80–101
　impact of 2006 Act 82
　meaning 80
　pre-Companies Act 2006 81
Contracts made by company 105
Contracts made on behalf of companies 106
Contracts that bind company 104–6
Core company law 3–4
　limits 4
Corporate governance 4, 6–8
　approach to 7–8
　large companies 6
　ownership and control, separation of 7
　scope of impact of business operations 6–7
　small companies 6
Corporate groups 21
Corporate law 3
Corporate rescue 320–31
Corporation
　meaning 59–60
　registered company as 59
Corporation aggregate 60
Corporation sole 60
Court-ordered meetings 284
Credit unions 31
Creditors 10
　share capital, and 164–8
Creditors, interests of
　directors' duties, and 231–2

Cross-Border Merger Regulations
  PLC mergers and divisions 304–6

Debenture stock 187
Debentures 186–7
  bare 186
  bearer 187
  convertible 187
  meaning 186
  naked 186
  non-convertible 187
  permanent 187
  redeemable 187
  registered 187
  secured 186
  trust deed, use of 187
  types 186–7
Deeds 102–3
  looking behind 103
  requirements for company to be bound by 102–3
  use of 102
Department for Business, Innovation and Skills 12
Directors 208–18
  appointment 211
  de facto 209
  de jure 209
  definition 208–11
    disqualification 213–4
    employees, as 215
    executive 209–10
    independent contractors, as 215
    long-term director service contracts shareholder approval 217
      long-term incentive plans shareholder approval 217
        managing 211
        nominee 211
        non-executive 209–10
        number of 212
    payment for performing role 215
    payment on termination of office 216–8
      non-director services provided as independent contractor 216
      service contracts 216–7
      statutory protection 217
    public disclosure of remuneration 217–8
      companies with officially listed securities 218
      quoted companies 218
      small companies 217
      unquoted companies 217
  removal 212–3
  remuneration 214–5
  public disclosures 217–8
    UK Corporate Governance Code Principles 218
  retirement 212–3
  service contracts
    shareholder inspection 217
  shadow 209
  types 208–11
  who can be 212
Directors' duties 228–54
  act within powers 232–4
  benefits from third parties 244–5
  categorisation 229
  company, owed to 230–31
  conflict of interest 239–45
    authorisation 241–2
    conditions for effective authorisation 242
    corporate opportunities 242–4
    directors ceasing to hold office 242–4
    duty to avoid 240–41
    meaning 242
    private company authorisation 241
    public company authorisation 241
  contracting with companies 245–50
    credit transactions 249
    loans 249
    long-term service contracts 249
    payment for loss of office 249
    quasi-loans 249
    shareholder approval 247–250
    statutory declaration of interest 245–7
    substantial property transactions 248–9
  control of conflict of interest 228–9
  control of corporate governance behaviour 229–30
  corporate governance 232–9
  corporate management 233
  creditors, interests of 231–2
  enlightened shareholder value 231
  exclusion of liability 253
  exercise independent judgement 235–7
    nominee directors 236
  exercise reasonable care, skill and diligence 237–9
  indemnification 253
  insurance 253
  key specific corporate governance duties 239
  legal 228–30
  legislative reform 230
  promote success of company 234–5
  relief from liability 252–3
    court-granted 253
  remedies 250–52
    account of profits 251
    breach of duty to exercise reasonable care, skill and diligence 250
    breach of equity-based duties 250–51
    equitable compensation 251
    failure to obtain shareholder approval 252

rescission of contracts made in breach of duty 251
    removal from office 252
Disqualification of directors 213–4
Dissolution 338–9
Distributions 173–80 see also Dividends
    definition 173–4
    disguised 174
    kind, in 177–9
    net asset test 177
    profits available for purpose 175–6
    realised losses 177
    realised profits 177
    regulation 173–80
    relevant accounts 176
    restrictions 175–7
        common law 175
        statutory 175
    transfer of asset at above book value 178
    transfer of asset at below book value 178
    transfer of asset at book value 178
    unlawful, remedies for 179–80
        common law 179–80
        directors, against 179
        equitable 179–80
        shareholder, against 179
        s. 847 statutory remedy 179
Dividends 173–80 see also Distributions
    interim 173
    restrictions 175–7
Duomatic principle 288

EEIG 13, 32
Enlightened shareholder value
    directors' duties, and 231
EU
    influence 12–13
European Association 34
European Cooperative Society 33–4
European Foundation 34
European Mutual Society 34
European organisation legal structures 32–4
Extortionate credit transactions 346

Facade theory 74–6
Fiduciary duties 11
Financial assistance for purchase of company's own shares 181–4
    civil remedies for breach 184
    criminal sanctions for contravention 184
    exceptions to prohibition 183
    incidental part carve-out 183
    limits of prohibition 183
    principle purpose carve-out 183
    typical examples 182
    what is prohibited 182
Financial Conduct Authority 14
First registered companies 10
Fixed charge 188–91
    book debts, over 194–5
    floating charge distinguished 188, 199
    meaning 188–91
    rights of holder 189
    stages of enforcement 189, 190
Floating charge
    crystallisation 192–3
    different classes of assets, against 192
    fixed charge distinguished 188, 199
    invalid 344–6
    meaning 191
    role of 191
    single class of assets, against 192
Formal agreements 104
Foss v Harbottle, rule in 255–8
    business judgment rule 256
    limits to proper claimant principle 256–8
    majority rule 256
    majority shareholders as wrongdoers 258
Fraudulent trading 78, 350
Friendly societies 31

General meetings 282–4
    special notice 283
    special resolution 283
    written resolutions 283–4
Goodwill
    company name, and 50–51

Half-yearly financial reports 57
Historical development of company law 10–12
Holding companies 21

Incorporated
    meaning 10
Incorporated business organisations 19–28
Incorporation
    consequences 61–62
    limits on implication of 68–78
Industrial and provident societies 31
Initial public offerings 123
Inside information disclosure 57
Insider dealing 130–32, 129
    criminal offences 130
    criminal penalties 132
    defences 131–2
    inside information 130–31
    insider 130
    made public 131
    price-sensitive information 132
Insolvency law 5
    sources 333
Insolvent company names
    prohibition on re-use 339
Issue of shares
    completing 151
    exercise of authority 150
    separate legal personality, and 64

Interim management statements 57
Invalid floating charges 344–6

Just and equitable winding up petitions 272–4
   alternative order 273–4
   foundation of jurisdiction 272–3
   unfair prejudice claims, and 273–4
   who may apply 272
Justice theory 76

Legal persons
   types 60
Legal structures of business organisations 16–35
Legislation 8
Limited companies 20
Limited liability 64–6
   arguments for and against 10–11
   justifications 66
   limited companies 65
   shareholder payments to company that is being wound up 65–6
   shareholder payments to company that is trading 65
   unlimited companies 65
Limited liability partnerships 27–8
Limited partnerships 18
Liquidator 334, 5
   challenging pre-liquidation transactions 341
   disclaiming onerous property 341
   effect of appointment 334
   fraudulent trading 350
   misfeasance proceedings 349
   personal contributions 348–50
   preferences 343–4
      consequences 344
      desire 343–4
      factual 343
      relevant time 343–4
   property not available to 336–7
      property or assets held on trust 336–7
      property or assets subject to fixed charges 336
      retention of title 336
   role 334–5
   swelling company's assets 348–50
   wrongful trading 349–50
Listed companies 23
Listed securities 23–4
Listing particulars 128
Listing Regime 14–15
Listing Rules 15
Loan capital 186–200
LSE Main Market
   admission of securities to 123
   admission to trading on 126

Managing director 211
Market abuse 129–32
   civil regime 134
   criminal liability 130–34
   defences 135
   penalties 135
   safe harbours 135
Market manipulation 129, 133–4
   criminal offences 133
   criminal penalties 134
   defences 133
Medium-sized companies 24–5
Meetings see also Board meetings; Company meetings
   record 285
Member
   becoming 138
Members 10
Memorandum of Association
   new-style 83
   old style 81
Minority shareholder protection 255–77
   company investigations 275
   just and equitable winding up petitions 272–4 see also Just and equitable winding up petitions
   personal and representative actions 262–4
   reflective loss 263–4
   statutory derivative claims 258–61 see also statutory derivative claims
   unfairly prejudicial conduct petitions 265–72 see also Unfairly prejudicial conduct petitions
Misfeasance proceedings 349
Model Articles for private companies limited by shares 353–67
   decision making by shareholders 363–6
   directors 355–9
   distributions 359–63
   interpretation 355
   limitation of liability 355
   shares 359–63
Model Articles for public companies 368–94
   administrative arrangements 392–3
   communications 392
   decision-making by members 377–81
   directors 372–7
   directors' indemnity and insurance 393–4
   distributions 381–92
   interpretation 370–71
   limitation of liability 370–71
   shares 381–92
Mutual organisations 30–32

Narrative reporting 56
Nature and structure of company 1–15
Negotiable instruments 187

Objects of company 81–3
Ostensible authority
  meaning 114–15
Overseas companies 20–21

Partnerships 17–19
Partly-paid shares 161–2
  calls 161–2
  forfeiture 162
  liens 161–2
  surrender 162
Passing-off 50
Periodic disclosure
  Financial Services and Markets Act 2000, under 57
Piercing corporate veil 73–6
  court-developed limits 73–6
  façade theory 74–6
  justice theory 76
  single economic entity theory 73–4
Political donations 181
Pre-emption rights 153–6
  contravention, consequences 156
  limits on application 155–6
  rationale for 153–5
Pre-incorporation contrasts 38–41
  adoption 40
  company becoming party to 41
  enforcement 40
  meaning 38–9
  ratification 40
  subject to any agreement to the contrary 39
Priority of charges 197–9
  fixed and floating charges 197–8
  two floating charges 198
  two general floating charges 199
Private companies 22
Promoters 36–8
  fiduciary duty 37–8
Prospectus 121–7
  admission of securities to AIM 122
  admission of securities to LSE Main Market 123
  approval 125
  civil liability 126–7
    failure to provide key information 126–7
    general law 127
    misleading statements 126–7
    non-issue 126
    untrue statements 126–7
  company information requirements 124–5
  content 123–5
  criminal liability 126
    exemptions 122
    general duty of disclosure 123
    initial public offerings 123
    liability for 126–7
  securities information requirements 125

  specific content 123–4
  statutory requirement 121–2
  summary 124–5
Public companies 22
Purchase and redemption of company's own shares 171–3
  acquisition out of capital 172–3
  acquisition out of proceeds of new issue 171
  acquisition using distributable profits 171–2
  private companies 172–3
  public companies 171–2

Quoted companies 23

Realised losses
  meaning 177
Realised profits
  meaning 177
Register of members 138
Registered companies 19–20
  asset shielding 26
  internal dispute resolution 26
  key legal characteristics 25–7
  transferable shares 26
Registering UK company 41–4
  application 42
  requirements 43
  submitting application to register 43–4
  where to register 41
Registrar of companies 10
Registration of charges 195–7
  certificate of registration 196
  documents to be delivered 196
  land, over 197
  late 196
  Registrar of Companies, with 195–7
Re-registration of UK company 52–4
  private to public 52–3
  public to private 53–4
Relevant accounts
  meaning 176
Resolutions 285–90
  Duomatic principle 288
  informal unanimous consent 288
  judicial constraint on exercise of voting rights by shareholder 289–90
  poll vote 286
  proportion of votes needed to pass 285–6
  quoted companies and poll vote 287
  records 285
  vote on show of hands 286
  voting methods 286
  written vote 287–8

Salomon v A. Salomon & Co Ltd 62–4
  Court of Appeal decision 63
  first instance decision 63

House of Lords decision 63–4
Schemes of arrangement 301–06
   availability 301–02
   Cross-Border Merger Regulations, and 305–06
   Part 26 procedure 302–04
   section 900 reconstructions and amalgamations 304–05
   usage 301–02
Section 900 reconstructions and amalgamations 304–05
Secured creditors 188–200
Securities regulation 5–6
   public company 5
Self-regulation 9–10
Separate legal personality
   consequences 61–2
   corporate groups, and 66–8
   fraudulent trading 78
   insurance, and 64
   limits on implication of 68–78
      agency 71–3
      contractual arrangements 71
      piercing corporate veil 69
      self-help action 69, 71–3
      statutory provisions 69–71
      statutory provisions supplementing available remedies 76–8
         Companies Act 2006, s. 767 (3) 77
         Company Directors Disqualification Act 1986, s. 15   77
      wrongful trading 78
Share capital 146–8
   alteration 149
   called-up 148
   creditors, and 164–8
   importance of 165
   importance to creditors 168
   increasing 149
      reasons for 149
   language of 147–8
   minimum requirements 169
      private companies 169
      public companies 169
   nominal value 147–8
   premium 147–8
   public company reduction 170–71
      court confirmation 171
   public disclosure of increase 151
   relevance over life of company 167–8
   statements 147
   statutory prohibition on reduction 169–71
      private company 169–70
      right of shareholders and creditors to object 170
      solvency statement 170
Share certificates 160
Share warrants 160–61
Shareholders
   becoming 137
   closely-held companies, in 204
   default powers 206
   division of powers in Articles 205
   governing organ of company, as 203–07
   listed companies, in 204
   statutory powers 206
      Companies Act 2006 206
      Insolvency Act 2006 206
Shareholders' agreements 98–100
   enforceability, effect 100
   enforcing 99–100
   parties to 99
Shares
   bonus, issue of 153
   capitalisation 153
   class names 140
   class rights 140–46
      ascertaining 140–41
      concept 141–2
      variation 143–6
   classes 139–40
   equity 140
   founders' 140
   issue price 151
   legal nature of 139
   non-equity 140
   payment for 152
   preference 140
   premium, issue at 152
   redeemable 140
   residual ordinary 139
   transfer 157–60
      certificated shares 157
      dematerialised shares 157–60
      stamp duty 157
      stock transfer form 157, 158
      uncertified shares 157–60
   transferable 26
   transmission 160
   types 139–40
Simple contracts 104
Single economic entity theory 73–4
Small companies 24–5
Small company moratorium 322–3
Small private companies
   benefits of incorporation 26–7
Social enterprise private legal structures 28–32
Societas Europaea 13, 33
Societas Privata Europaea 13, 33
Sole traders 16–17
Sources of company law 8–10
Statutory companies 19
Statutory derivative claims 258–61
   application for permission to continue 259–61
   costs 261
   discontinuance 261

grounds 259
parties 259
permission to continue 261
procedure 259–61
Subsidiary companies 21–2

Table A 84
Takeovers 307–19
  acquisitions, and 308–09
  basic bid process 311–12
  break fees 315
  change of control 308
  City Code 307–08
    general principles 310
    nature 310
    purpose 310
    scope of application 309
  competition law 313
  concert parties acquiring stake in target 314
  creating false market in offerors' shares 314
  defensive action by target company board 314–15
  Disclosure and Transparency Rules 313
  disposals, and 308–09
  EU Takeover Directive 307–08
  FCA Listing Rule 313
  insider dealing in shares of both parties 314
  mandatory offers on acquisition of controlling stake 312–13
  mergers, and 308–09
  minority shareholder treatment 312–13
  non-solicitation agreements 315
  Panel 315–17
    Committees 316–17
    composition 315–16
    funding 315–16
    review of decisions 317
    role 316
    statutory empowerment 316
  Part 26 scheme of arrangement 309–10
  Prospectus Rules 313
  restructuring, and 308
  scope of application of City Code 309
  sell-out rights 313
  system for regulating 315–17
  Takeover Appeal Board 316–17
Traded companies 23
Trading certificate 46
  application for 47

Trading disclosures
  company name, and 51–2
Transactions at an undervalue 341–3
Twentieth-century developments 12

Ultra vires doctrine 81–2
Underwriting 128
  commission 128–9
Unfairly prejudicial conduct petitions 265–72
  basis of share valuation 271–2
  behaviour complained of 266
  buy-out orders 270–71
  company's affairs 266
  costs 270–72
  fair valuation of shares 271
  interests-based equitable approach 268–9
  interests of members 266–70
  petitioners 265
  remedies 270–72
  respondent 265
  rights and interests 267
  timing of share valuation 271
  typical lawful conduct 269–70
  unfairly prejudicial conduct 266
Unincorporated associations 28–9
  contracts 29
  criminal liability 29
  property ownership 29
  tort liability 29
Unincorporated business organisations 16–19
Unlimited companies 20
UK Corporate Governance Code
  accountability 402–404
  effectiveness 399–402
  leadership 397–9
  main principles 396–7
  remuneration 405
  text 395–406

Winding up 333
  commencement 334
  compulsory 333–4
  connected persons 347–8
  effects 334
  insolvent 334
  order of distribution of assets 337–8
  transactions at an undervalue 341–3
  voluntary 333
Wrongful trading 78, 349–50